NEWCOMER'S HANDBOOK®
FOR MOVING TO AND LIVING IN

Boston

*Including Cambridge,
Brookline, and Somerville*

3rd Edition

FIRST BOOKS®

6750 SW Franklin
Portland, OR 97223
503-968-6777
www.firstbooks.com

© Copyright 2004 by First Books®. All rights reserved.

3rd edition

Newcomer's Handbook® and First Books® are registered trademarks of First Books.

Reproduction of the contents of this book in any form whatsoever is not permissible without written permission from the publisher, First Books, 6750 SW Franklin Street, Suite A, Portland, OR 97223-2542, 503-968-6777.

First Books® is not legally responsible for any change in the value of any enterprises by reason of their inclusion or exclusion from this work. Contents are based on information believed to be accurate at the time of publication.

First Books® has not accepted payment from any firms or organizations for inclusion in this book.

Author: Heather Gordon
Contributors: Marietta Hitzemann and Ed Golden
Series Editor: Bernadette Duperron
Publisher: Jeremy Solomon
Design and composition: Erin Johnson/Erin Johnson Design
Maps provided by Jim Miller/fennana design
Transit map courtesy of the Massachusetts Bay Transit Authority. Used with permission.

ISBN 0-912301-54-6
ISSN 1547-9749

Printed in the USA on recycled paper.

Published by First Books®, 6750 SW Franklin Street, Portland, OR 97223-2542, 503-968-6777, www.firstbooks.com.

What readers are saying about Newcomer's Handbooks:

I recently got a copy of your Newcomer's Handbook for Chicago, *and wanted to let you know how invaluable it was for my move. I must have consulted it a dozen times a day preparing for my move. It helped me find my way around town, find a place to live, and so many other things. Thanks.*

—Mike L.
Chicago, Illinois

*Excellent reading (*Newcomer's Handbook for San Francisco and the Bay Area*) … balanced and trustworthy. One of the very best guides if you are considering moving/relocation. Way above the usual tourist crap.*

—Gunnar E.
Stockholm, Sweden

I was very impressed with the latest edition of the Newcomer's Handbook for Los Angeles. *It is well organized, concise and up-to-date. I would recommend this book to anyone considering a move to Los Angeles.*

—Jannette L.
Attorney Recruiting Administrator for a large Los Angeles law firm

I recently moved to Atlanta from San Francisco, and LOVE the Newcomer's Handbook for Atlanta. *It has been an invaluable resource – it's helped me find everything from a neighborhood in which to live to the local hardware store. I look something up in it everyday, and know I will continue to use it to find things long after I'm no longer a newcomer. And if I ever decide to move again, your book will be the first thing I buy for my next destination.*

—Courtney R.
Atlanta, Georgia

In looking to move to the Boston area, a potential employer in that area gave me a copy of the Newcomer's Handbook for Boston. *It's a great book that's very comprehensive, outlining good and bad points about each neighborhood in the Boston area. Very helpful in helping me decide where to move.*

—no name given (online submit form)

The Newcomer's Handbook for Moving to London *is amazing. I'm a student and tranferred to a college in London, so I needed to know about where I was living. The book had information on all the important areas, I knew where to go for everything I needed. I recommend the Newcomer's Handbooks to everyone, especially students! I am going to Los Angeles for a term, so I am definitely buying the Los Angeles edition.*

—Neka Brown
London, England

TABLE OF CONTENTS

1	**Introduction**
15	**Street Address Locator**
21	**Neighborhoods**

Maps, boundaries, profiles, and neighborhood resources

Suffolk County/Boston
- **22** Map of Suffolk County
- **24** Map of downtown Boston neighborhoods
  - 27 Allston-Brighton
  - 31 Back Bay
  - 35 Beacon Hill/West End
  - 39 Charlestown
  - 42 Dorchester
  - 45 Downtown (Chinatown, Leather District, Financial District/Downtown Crossing)
  - 48 East Boston
  - 51 Fenway/Mission Hill
  - 57 Jamaica Plain
  - 61 NorthEnd/Waterfront
  - 64 Roslindale
  - 67 South Boston
  - 70 South End/Bay Village
  - 75 West Roxbury
  - 77 Also in Suffolk County: Revere, Chelsea, Winthrop

- **78** **Surrounding Communities**
- **78** **Middlesex County:**
- **80** **Map of Middlesex County**
  - 78 Arlington
  - 83 Belmont
  - 85 Cambridge
  - 96 Malden
  - 98 Medford
  - 101 Newton
  - 108 Somerville
  - 112 Waltham
  - 116 Watertown

CONTENTS

118 *Norfolk County:*
120 *Map of Norfolk County*
    118   Brookline
    125   Dedham
    128   Milton
    130   Needham
    133   Quincy

137 *Greater Boston Area*
138 *Map of Greater Boston Area*
    137   Bristol County
    139   Essex County
    142   Middlesex County
    145   Norfolk County
    147   Plymouth County

149 **Finding a Place to Live**
Suggestions on renting or buying a home in Boston, including tips on finding an apartment or sublet, rental and real estate agents, leases, security deposits, tenant resources, renter's/homeowner's insurance

181 **Moving and Storage**
Truck rentals, movers, consumer complaints, road restrictions, storage, moving with kids, taxes

191 **Money Matters**
Bank accounts and services, consumer complaints, credit cards, taxes, starting or moving a business

199 **Getting Settled**
Utilities, garbage and recycling, driver's licenses and state IDs, automobile registration, parking, voter registration, social security cards, passports, obtaining a library card, television stations, cable TV service, newspapers and magazines, finding a healthcare provider, pets, safety and crime

237 **Helpful Services**
Domestic services, including dry cleaning delivery, house cleaning, and pest control; mail and shipping services; automobile repair; consumer protection; services for the disabled; gay and lesbian life

253   **Childcare and Education**
Referral services for childcare, daycare, babysitting, nannies; public and private school resources

269   **Shopping for the Home**
Shopping districts, department stores, malls, household shopping, secondhand shopping, food shopping

289   **Cultural Life**
How to take advantage of the city's cultural opportunities, including: tickets, music, nightclubs, theaters, film, museums, literary life, colleges and universities

323   **Sports and Recreation**
Professional and college sports; spectator events; participant sports and activities; health clubs

355   **Greenspace and Beaches**
City, state, and national parks; forests; wildlife sanctuaries; beaches

371   **Weather and Climate**
Local weather, air pollution, insects, allergens

377   **Places of Worship**
Area churches, mosques, temples, and other spiritual centers

393   **Volunteering**
Getting involved once you've gotten settled

403   **Transportation**
Getting around by car, taxi, T, commuter rail, bus, bike, ferry, train; airports and airlines

419   **Temporary Lodgings**
Hotels, hostels, short-term leases, B&Bs, YMCAs and YWCAs, summer-only

425   **Quick Getaways**
Nearby destinations for day or weekend trips throughout New England

433   **A Boston Year**
Annual greater Boston area events

CONTENTS

441	A Boston Reading List
447	Useful Telephone Numbers and Web Sites
465	Index
483	About the Author
484	Reader Response Form
485	Order Form
486	MBTA T Map
487	MBTA Commuter Rail Map
488	Boston Zip Codes and Area Codes Map

INTRODUCTION

IN THE 1850S, OLIVER WENDELL HOLMES REFERRED TO BOSTON AS the "Hub of the Solar System," a title proud Bostonians swiftly changed to the "Hub of the Universe." Since then, Boston has earned many other nicknames, including the "Athens of America" and "Beantown." Whatever the moniker, Boston is one of the most desirable, albeit expensive, places to live in the country. A recent nationwide analysis of housing markets and overall cost of living by Runzheimer International placed Boston among the top 10 most expensive cities in the US. In 2002, the same firm surveyed nationwide apartment rental costs and placed Boston, with its annual rental cost of almost $16,000 in the top three, only behind San Jose and San Francisco. High costs aside, Boston is a nice place to call home. Less intimidating than New York City, less gray than Seattle, Boston proper is a small city with decent public transportation, easy access to the Atlantic Ocean and three mountain ranges (White, Green, and Berkshire), dozens of colleges and universities, museums, professional and college sports teams, music and theater, and a slew of historical sites. Live here and you can gorge on fried clams, visit Paul Revere's house, rollerblade for miles through the heart of the city along the Charles River, catch free Boston Pops concerts and free Friday night, family-friendly movies at the Hatch Memorial Shell, or spend days testing coffee at coffee shops and book stores in Harvard Square.

Of course, life in Boston isn't without fault: the city's stores, restaurants, bars, and theaters, while good, are not quite as plentiful as what you'll find in bigger cities; much of Boston's nightlife and many of its neighborhoods are geared toward the college crowd; summer weather brings hordes of tourists to some neighborhoods, particularly the North End, Back Bay, and Beacon Hill; winters are cold; street patterns seem designed to take drivers to the brink of madness; and Bostonians are "fast-paced" (read: impatient), and may not appear to be very welcoming. Just have patience, there *are* good places to live and socialize for the post-college crowd; the tourist season *does* subside each winter, which, while cold is often filled with sunny days; and once you've settled in you're bound to make friends. You may even find that getting around isn't quite as difficult as it seemed initially. It just takes time.

Back to the weather, Boston is a four-season town. Summers are warm, usually around 80° to 90° Fahrenheit, and often blanketed by the "three H's" (hazy, hot, and humid). Autumn, typically beginning in late September and lasting into November, is crisp and beautiful with legendary foliage. Winter is cold and often well below freezing, although typically not below zero. The amount of snow in Boston fluctuates from year to year: sometimes it seems Boston is buried every week by a Nor'easter (strong areas of low pressure moving in from the Atlantic Ocean and bringing ferocious winter storms), and other times a whole winter can pass with barely a dusting. Spring is often a quick flutter of cool wet weather and blossoming flowers sandwiched between late winter frosts and early summer heat. Fortunately, while sometimes the occasional recipient of a blizzard or hurricane, Boston is not especially prone to the natural disasters that plague other regions of the country.

> POLITICALLY, THE COMMONWEALTH OF MASSACHUSETTS IS FIRMLY LIBERAL, ALTHOUGH LAWMAKERS ON BEACON HILL HAVE MANAGED TO RETAIN SOME ODD VESTIGES OF BOSTON'S CONSERVATIVE PAST.

Politically, the Commonwealth of Massachusetts is firmly liberal, although lawmakers on Beacon Hill have managed to retain some odd vestiges of Boston's conservative past. For example, despite the large population, including a substantial number of students who are prone to keeping late hours, bars and clubs stay open no later than 2 a.m., and the subway stops running around 12:30 a.m. every night (although the Massachusetts Bay Transit Authority recently instituted later night bus service along the T routes). In addition, Boston is still subject to the "blue laws" prohibiting the sale of alcohol on Sundays and restricting alcohol sales to liquor stores only. That generally means that no beer, wine, or other spirits are available in any grocery stores, gas stations, or convenience stores; however, one location of every grocery chain is entitled to sell wine and beer, but not on Sundays.

Today, the biggest thing in Boston is the Big Dig. The city has undertaken an enormous construction project to rid itself of the antiquated Central Artery, the main route in and out of the city that was no longer able to handle the ever-increasing volume of traffic. A bigger, better roadway replacement has been built underground, and at press time, northbound and southbound traffic were using the new tunnel. Efforts are now focused on demolition of the existing elevated Central Artery, and land restoration, including the development of open space and some commercial and residential space. Big Dig completion is expected in 2004. Until then locals continue to endure the noise, dust, detours, and traffic delays. For project updates, visit www.bigdig.com.

Even upon completion of the Big Dig, you will probably find driving Boston's streets to be time-consuming and frustrating. Since much of the city originally was built for 17th and 18th century traffic (read: pedestrians and horse drawn carriages), many streets are winding, indirect, narrow and only permit one-way traffic. Giving or receiving directions is difficult, and finding parking is expensive and exasperating as spots are scarce. Depending on where you choose to live, newcomers should consider whether a car is necessary. Boston's efficient public transportation system makes life without a vehicle convenient and hassle-free in much of the city. Alternately, a car-sharing company, Zipcar, caters to those who don't want the aggravation or responsibility of owning a vehicle. Boston residents using the service can rent cars affordably for short periods of time and do things like run errands or go to the beach. (See **Transportation** for more details).

This book covers more than just Boston proper. According to the 2000 Census, the City of Boston contains 589,000 people, the greater Boston area (including Boston) adds up to almost 3.5 million people. Newly profiled Boston neighborhoods added to this latest edition of the *Newcomer's Handbook® for Moving to and Living in Boston* are the Fenway/Mission Hill, South Boston, Downtown, and Bay Village (included with the South End); new or greatly expanded community profiles include Cambridge, Malden, Dedham, Needham, and Milton, as well as many smaller profiles of cities and towns in the greater Boston area. In addition, the **Finding a Place to Live** chapter has been updated to include a section on landlord responsibilities and tenants rights, as well as an expanded section on buying a house. Also new, chapters on **Moving and Storage**, **Volunteering**, **Places of Worship**, and **Quick Getaways**, a **Childcare and Education** chapter for parents with school-aged children, **A Boston Reading List** to help you familiarize yourself with local authors and books about Boston, a chapter on **Weather and Climate**, and a chapter on **Helpful Services**, which surveys resources and services for people with disabilities, has a gay and lesbian life section. As a new resident, answers to many questions, from property and excise taxes to press releases from the mayor to fun things to do with the kids can be found at www.cityofboston.gov.

As usual, we welcome reader suggestions and comments on the tear-out page at the back of the book. We hope that the information presented on the following pages will help you establish a Boston residence smoothly and speedily. We also hope that once you select your neighborhood and settle in, the book will help you get on with the pleasure part: enjoyment of the city's many treasures, sites, and resources. Welcome to the "Hub of the Universe!"

HISTORY

According to the Massachusetts Office of Travel and Tourism, nearly 27 million visitors come to the state each year, many of whom are drawn by the historical wealth of the region. Massachusetts' history includes the Plimouth Plantation, the Salem Witch Trials, and the Boston Tea Party. Since being founded nearly four centuries ago, Boston has been the launch site of influential politicians, authors, musicians, and tragedies and triumphs that have shaped the world.

Until the arrival of the first group of Pilgrims on the Mayflower, this region was home to many different Native American tribes. Locally, the most common tribes were the Massachusetts, Wampanoags, Pokanokets, Nausets, Pamets, Narragansetts, Agawams, Pennacooks, and Pawtuckets. Obviously, the state takes its name from the Massachusett tribe, which translated means "people of the great hills," a reference to the Blue Hills south of Boston. Many towns and cities here have been named to either commemorate the settlers' British roots or those of the local Native Americans. Thus, many places in the region reflect either towns in England where the European settlers originally lived, the Native American words for places, or the native tribes that inhabited them.

European explorers including Captain John Smith in 1614, Giovanni Verrazano in 1524, and John Cabot in 1497, knew of the Massachusetts Bay area well before it was actually colonized. And there is speculation that Leif Ericson's Viking colony of Vinland was actually situated in Cambridge along the Charles River. Generally, though, it is accepted that 1620 is the date of the first European settlement in Massachusetts. It is the well known story of the Pilgrims who settled on a south shore of Massachusetts in a colony they called Plymouth. Today, Plymouth has many exhibits and relics of its Pilgrim past, including a replica of their ship and a living museum of the plantation.

Over the decade following 1620, more settlers came from England, including those who founded Salem and Charlestown. In 1630, Governor John Winthrop of the Massachusetts Bay Company led a group of between 700 and 800 Puritans who sailed eleven ships over from England. Initially Winthrop and his Puritans put into port at Salem, but there were already too many people in that settlement to make room for all of them. Some stayed, but the rest headed south to Charlestown, where again, resources were limited. And so they headed across the

INTRODUCTION

Charles River. On the Shawmut Peninsula at the foot of what is now Beacon Hill, there lived an Anglican pastor-cum-hermit by the name of William Blaxton. This pastor, originally a minister to a group of settlers who had since returned to England, had stayed behind to live a quiet life with his books. Winthrop purchased the peninsula from Blaxton for £30, and he and a remaining 150 Puritans finally started the colony that was to become Boston. For his part, Blaxton moved south to Rhode Island where he eventually abandoned his antisocial ways and preached religious freedom to his fellow dissenters.

These early Puritan settlers greeted a much different landscape than exists today. Governor Winthrop first called this settlement "Trimountaine" for the three hills that he could see on the narrow peninsula from his vantage point of Charlestown. Before their arrival, the local Native Americans called this peninsula "Mushauwomuk," meaning "where there is a big river." English settlers later changed the name to Boston in reference to the town in England from where many of this group hailed. Today, the name Trimountaine survives (shortened to Tremont) as a street name. Two of the three hills are gone, the third (Beacon Hill) is dramatically shorter, and the original, thin Shawmut peninsula has been filled-in and bears almost no resemblance to its pre-Puritan topography.

Religious beliefs and practices were a pressing concern of the early Puritan colonists who set up shop along the Massachusetts Bay. Although they fled their home country in search of freedom from religious persecution, they had little tolerance for non-Puritans. As a result, hostilities arose between the Puritans and the Native Americans and the settlers of other religious traditions. Anyone not Puritan, i.e. Quakers, Presbyterians, Baptists, and Catholics to name a few, was branded a heretic and was forbidden from Puritan Massachusetts. Many took refuge in nearby Rhode Island. Indeed, within their first century here, this religious-themed exclusivity and paranoia reached a fevered pitch in 1692, when Salem's notorious trials resulted in 19 people being hanged as witches.

Boston emerged as a key port in the Triangle Trade route during the colonial period. Sugar cane harvested in the West Indies came to Boston

> THESE EARLY PURITAN SETTLERS GREETED A MUCH DIFFERENT LANDSCAPE THAN EXISTS TODAY. GOVERNOR WINTHROP FIRST CALLED THIS SETTLEMENT "TRIMOUNTAINE" FOR THE THREE HILLS THAT HE COULD SEE ON THE NARROW PENINSULA FROM HIS VANTAGE POINT OF CHARLESTOWN.

where it was turned into rum, which was then shipped to West Africa and traded for slaves, who were sent to the West Indies to harvest sugar cane and so on. Merchant families grew wealthy and their financial means began to elevate them to the status of the local aristocracy. Later, they would be christened the "Boston Brahmins" by Oliver Wendell Holmes and immortalized in a John Collins Bossidy poem that pays homage to Boston as "the home of the bean and the cod, where the Lowells talk to Cabots, and the Cabots talk only to God." As Boston's popularity and prosperity grew, so did the taxes levied upon it by the British. American colonists were angered by this and protested, and the ensuing clamping down of imperial rule from England eventually escalated into the Revolutionary War. First came the "Boston Massacre" in 1770, when a mob of rabble-rousing civilians began taunting a redcoat guard posted alone in front of the Customs House by throwing snowballs at him. The conflict grew until a small British squad fired shots into the crowd, killing five colonials. The Boston Massacre became fodder for the patriotic movement, which smoldered along until the "Boston Tea Party," when the British Empire gave the East Indian Tea Company a monopoly to sell tea in the colonies and then taxed that tea. As an act of protest, sixty Bostonians, some disguised, marched down to Griffin's Wharf, secretly boarded three British ships, and then dumped 342 chests of tea into Boston Harbor.

By 1775, the British Empire had had it with its rebellious American colonies, especially Massachusetts. April 18th, 1775 saw the start of the Revolutionary War when "sons of liberty" Paul Revere and William Dawes, later joined by Samuel Prescott, were sent to alert the colonials that the British were finally mounting the expected attack. Two lanterns, fashioned by Revere himself, were hung in the Old North Church (then known as Christ Church) as a signal that the British were approaching by water, not land. Their patriotic acts were commemorated in Henry Wadsworth Longfellow's poem "Paul Revere's Ride," which erroneously gives the impression that Revere was the star of this show. In reality, he was caught relatively early on in his ride, but his name provided the best rhyme for the purposes of the poem. Regardless of which patriot gave the warning, the

INTRODUCTION

colonial militia heard the call to arms and on the morning of April 19, nearly 500 colonials, who referred to themselves as Minutemen, clashed with the British in Lexington and Concord. By the end of this crucial day, 300 British soldiers lay dead or wounded, in comparison to only 100 colonials.

Two months later, on June 17, 1775, the Battle of Bunker Hill was fought (a bit of a misnomer, it actually transpired on Breed's Hill). Though dramatically outnumbered and low on ammunition, the ragtag colonial militia managed to inflict heavy damages upon the better trained and outfitted British. They held the line for two of three charges, and British casualties eventually doubled that of the colonials'. In the end, the British won the day, but it was a tremendous confidence booster to the colonists whose performance gave their fellow patriots hope that they had a chance against the mightiest power in the world. Years later, their brave stand was commemorated with the Bunker Hill Monument, a 221-foot tall obelisk, which still stands in Charlestown. Modern Bostonians celebrate their battle every June on Bunker Hill Day with a parade in the neighborhood around the monument.

General George Washington took charge of the colonial troops in Boston the following month and stayed here until he won the city back from England in March of 1776. His final visit here in 1789 inspired the renaming of downtown's major thoroughfare, and that of the intersecting streets (the names of streets crossing Washington are different on one side and the other. For instance, Winter Street on one side of Washington becomes Summer Street on the other side).

Many tourists interested in the sites made famous in colonial and revolutionary Boston walk the Freedom Trail, a 2.5 mile alternately red painted and red brick path that runs through the city. It connects Bunker Hill and the USS Constitution in Charlestown with Paul Revere's house, Copp's Hill Burying Ground, and the Old North Church in the North End, and continues on to Faneuil Hall. It then goes into downtown Boston, passing by the Old South Meeting House, the Old State House, and the King's Chapel and Burying Ground, where some of Boston's early settlers, including John Winthrop, are buried. The trail ends in Beacon Hill at the Boston Common.

After the colonies won their independence, Massachusetts began the work of rebuilding itself, much of it having been decimated during the war. Once again, merchants rose to prominence, diversifying their reach into the whaling and shipbuilding industries. Beginning in the late 1700s, immigrants from all over Europe came to Boston, many to work as laborers in the factories and warehouses. By 1822, Boston's numbers had swelled enough (over 43,000 residents clocked by the census of 1820) to warrant a change from the "Town of Boston" to the "City of Boston." Tiny Shawmut Peninsula, home of the original settlement, was no longer able to contain its burgeoning population and city founders were forced to find a solution.

First, they leveled the steep hills of Boston and extended the shorelines of the Charles River and Boston Harbor, increasing the livable space within the existing peninsula. Then, in the mid-1800s, the city commenced a string of landfill projects which created new real estate, first constructing the South End, then other neighborhoods like the Back Bay, Chinatown, and the Fenway. In 1883, noted landscape architect Frederick Law Olmstead moved his offices to the adjoining community of Brookline. Shortly thereafter, he began the design and construction of the beloved Emerald Necklace, an interconnected chain of parks (including three he didn't design) that stretch across seven miles of the city. The year 1887 saw the country's first subway system open in Boston. Streetcars connected nearby environs with Boston, earning them the moniker "streetcar suburbs" and causing them to experience booms of their own.

In the 19th century, moneyed Bostonians sought to build a refined city, and their focus became the creation of cultural institutions on par with those of their European counterparts. Libraries and museums went up, and within the first decade of the 1800s Boston began attracting and turning out notable literati. Over the century, Massachusetts produced writers whose works play an integral role in the world's literary cannon, including Ralph Waldo Emerson, Henry Wadsworth Longfellow, Nathaniel Hawthorne, Edgar Allen Poe, Herman Melville, Louisa May Alcott, Emily Dickinson, and Henry David Thoreau.

Alongside the physical and cultural transitions of the 19th century, Boston's population underwent a metamorphosis as well. During the late 1700s, a slave named Phillis Wheatley became the first African-American on the continent to publish poetry. She began publishing her poems at the young age of fourteen, having only learned English a few years before. Wheatley was emancipated in 1773, followed by the emancipation of all Boston slaves in 1783. By the 1800s, Boston's prominent African-American community was the largest in the nation. Most of the city's black citizenry lived on the northern slope of Beacon Hill and the West End where they erected the African Meeting House in 1806 and the Abiel Smith School in 1835. Despite federal laws to the contrary, local authorities generally considered a fugitive slave who'd escaped to Boston to be free. When Congress passed the Fugitive Slave Act in 1850, which entitled Federal Marshals to capture and arrest escaped slaves anywhere within the country, black and white Bostonians banded together to prevent them from doing so on their turf. If anything, the law served to catalyze Boston's community into rallying for Abolition. Vocal opponents of slavery such as Frederick Douglass furthered the movement by establishing the New England Anti-Slavery Society, and many locals smuggled runaway slaves in safe houses on the Underground Railroad. One of the most famous of these homes belonged to and was run by Harriet and

Lewis Hayden, and still stands at 66 Phillips Street. It was during the Civil War when the white Bostonian Robert Gould Shaw led his all-black 54th Regiment of the Massachusetts Volunteer Infantry—the first African-American regiment in the North—into battle. Sixty two soldiers of 54th Massachusetts, including Shaw, died during the assault on Fort Wagner in Charleston, South Carolina. Those wanting to know more can walk the 1.6 mile Black Heritage Trail, which traverses the north slope of Beacon Hill. It includes many of the historic sites mentioned here, including a memorial to Shaw and his men, who were depicted in the Academy Award-winning film *Glory*.

Another particularly influential group in nineteenth century Boston was the Irish Catholics, who began migrating here throughout the first third of the 1800s and then in droves between 1845 and 1852, during the Irish Potato Famine. As is often the case, many citizens were prejudiced against the new group of immigrants, but after the Civil War, negative public sentiment against the Irish diminished as their skills were needed to help rebuild the city. Original Irish enclaves include Charlestown, South Boston, and Dorchester, where many remain today. As the twentieth century began, the Irish Catholics created what was been described as a "political machine," attaining a toe-hold on Boston politics that has proven unshakable even into the present time. In 1906, the grandfather of JFK, John "Honey Fitz" Fitzgerald, became Boston's first Boston-born Irish Catholic mayor. Less than 10 years later, the corrupt, yet beloved "Boss" James Curley took office. His career in Boston politics, during which time he held a number of influential offices including governor of Massachusetts, spanned until 1949 despite the fact that he spent portions of his terms in prison! In 1946, the Fitzgerald family returned to office in Massachusetts when future president John Fitzgerald Kennedy, who was born in Brookline, assumed Curley's vacant seat in the House of Representatives, followed by his election to the US Senate in 1952.

During the early- to mid-1900s, Boston experienced a major economic and cultural decline. Businesses and families moved out of the city for the cheaper, cleaner suburbs, and Boston fell into a serious state of disrepair. Many attribute the problems to the inability of the city's two most influen-

> ANOTHER PARTICULARLY INFLUENTIAL GROUP IN NINETEENTH CENTURY BOSTON WAS THE IRISH CATHOLICS, WHO BEGAN MIGRATING HERE THROUGHOUT THE FIRST THIRD OF THE 1800s AND THEN IN DROVES BETWEEN 1845 AND 1852, DURING THE IRISH POTATO FAMINE.

tial groups—the conservative, wealthy, Protestant old guard lawmakers and the Irish Catholic politicians—to cooperate. Adding to the decline was 40 years of censorship. In 1904, Boston appointed an official whose function was to censor or ban all morally indecent art for the good of the public. This city censor oversaw and banned questionable books, plays, and films, anything that might "corrupt" upstanding Bostonians, lending credence to and making famous the phrase "Banned in Boston." During this period of "cultural communism," Boston saw its cultural status within the nation suffer as artists mimicked the Quakers' flight to Rhode Island of the 1600s. This time, many headed south to nearby New York.

It was also during the mid-point of the 20th century, particularly after WWII, when many of the city's mansions and old Victorian residences were partitioned into apartment buildings or sold off to local colleges. John B. Hynes, who served as interim mayor while Curley was doing a stint in jail, became Boston's official mayor in 1949, signaling a change for the better. Mayor Hynes set about the task of revitalizing the crumbling city, launching the still active Boston Redevelopment Authority (BRA) in 1957. The goal: to form a "New Boston" by targeting Boston's problem areas for urban renewal. Although in many ways the much rejuvenated status of modern Boston is attributable to Hynes's vision, one of the first of these projects—the razing of the West End—was, in retrospect, a huge mistake. Although the intentions were nothing but good—to clear away a foundering area and make it more appealing so as to reinvigorate the city center—it didn't work. Bay Staters were bitter about the destroyed West End. This thriving and integrated immigrant neighborhood was so quickly demolished that many residents were displaced without provisions and the area was so thoroughly leveled that virtually no vestiges of it survive. Today, portions of the Mass General Hospital campus stand in the space. In the wake of this project, historic societies cropped up throughout the city specifically to prevent such bulldozing of other districts. Later projects saw seedy Scollay Square's bars, jazz clubs, and adult entertainment venues razed to make way for City Hall Plaza and Government Center, followed by the gigantic Prudential Center's offices, apartments, and shops that went up in the Back Bay.

> MAYOR HYNES SET ABOUT THE TASK OF REVITALIZING THE CRUMBLING CITY, LAUNCHING THE STILL ACTIVE BOSTON REDEVELOPMENT AUTHORITY (BRA) IN 1957. THE GOAL: TO FORM A "NEW BOSTON" BY TARGETING BOSTON'S PROBLEM AREAS FOR URBAN RENEWAL.

INTRODUCTION

Boston's mid-nineteenth century African-American population centered around Roxbury and the South End, which housed the city's jazz scene of the 1950s. It was during this era that Dr. Martin Luther King, Jr. attended theology school at BU and preached on the weekends at Roxbury's Twelfth Baptist Church. During the 1950's and '60's, as the civil rights movement grew, the issue of segregation was targeted. Because the Boston School Committee had made no effort to desegregate its schools, the NAACP filed a lawsuit in 1972. In June of 1974, Federal Judge Arthur Garrity, Jr. ordered an immediate integration of Boston's public schools by a system in which black students were bused to public schools in white neighborhoods and vice versa. It is an understatement to say the busing program was not well met by many residents of affected neighborhoods; during its early years it set off a great deal of racial conflict and regrettable violence within the city. Today, in addition to remaining the epicenter of Boston's African-American community, Roxbury is notable as the childhood home of the former contemporary of Malcolm X and modern leader of the Nation of Islam, Louis Farrakhan.

During this first decade of the 21st century, Boston has once again come into its own. Much of the downtown area has been revived and property is at such a premium that Boston's outlying and previously less-favored neighborhoods continue to gentrify, providing desirable accommodations. Before the dotcom crash of the late 1990s, Massachusetts was considered a "mini silicon-valley." High-tech professionals moved here *en masse* and many graduating students of area universities stayed to take advantage of the economic opportunity. At the turn of the century, the housing vacancy rate was less than one percent. In the wake of the more recent economic downturn, many of the unemployed dotcommers moved on, creating a more reasonable residential marketplace. While vacancy rates shift with the economy, it is never an inexpensive proposition to rent or buy a home in Boston.

Further out from the city, Bostonians partake of the best that New England has to offer. Some summer on Cape Cod, Newport, RI, or Lake Winnipesaukee, NH. Bed and breakfasts in rural Vermont are frequented by many Bostonians, and in the winter, skiing in the Green and White Mountains beckons. Fresh lobster, and outlet shopping are big draws in Maine. Closer to home, the possibilities are seemingly endless. See **Cultural Life** and **Quick Getaways** for a rundown on area events and nearby vacation destinations.

WHAT TO BRING

- **Walking shoes**; this is a walkable city, for the most part. With all the traffic and the expensive taxis, tourists and locals alike often chose to

hoof it from place to place. The architecture is varied, and cozy neighborhood squares are inviting and much easier to access without having to park the car.
- **A map**; a good idea anywhere, but essential in Boston! For those used to the ease of a city or town where the streets are laid out in a sensible and easily navigable grid, Boston will be quite a surprise. Boston's somewhat hilly topography combined with its centuries-old streets that meander or turn into one-ways, make getting around difficult. Get a map that covers the greater Boston area, not just downtown Boston.
- **Exact change for the T**; the local transit system is called the MBTA, or simply the "T." If you don't ride the subway or buses often enough to warrant a (very affordable) monthly pass, you will probably need a mixture of T tokens and exact change to pay as you go. Although you can purchase T tokens at many stations, at others, such as many of the above ground Green Line trolley surface stops, there are no such provisions and you must pay when you get on the train or bus with exact change or with a token.
- **Patience and optimism**; there's no doubt about it, Boston is quirky. The street patterns will confuse you at first, and if you drive, be prepared for the honking of impatient residents. Also, many Bostonians have lived here their whole lives and therefore already have defined social circles, which can be challenging to break into. Don't be too discouraged when you encounter these obstacles, they will pass. Boston is a vibrant, rich city and if you give it time you will find your own rewarding place in it.

LOCAL LINGO

Certainly you've heard lots about the unmistakable Boston accent, and it's probably all true. In what can be described as part Kennedy and part speech impediment, Bostonians do things like drop their "r's" ("Clahk" Kent is "Supahman's" alta ego), and then recycle them by sticking them on the ends of other words (if your name is Linda, get used to being called "Linder"). Stretching out some vowels (aunt is "awnt," not "ant") and squishing others ("room" is more like "rum") is common. You'll figure this all out pretty quickly. What you may not have heard as much about are the less obvious Massachusetts slang terms. Compiled here is a small list of essential local lingo and pronunciations. (Many abbreviations listed here will be used throughout the book.)
- **Across the River**: Cambridge, on the other side of the Charles River from Boston
- **BC**: Boston College

INTRODUCTION

- **Beacon Hill**: although this usually refers to a neighborhood in Boston, sometimes it is extended to mean the local government, as the state house is located here.
- **Big Dig**: the enormous project to put the majority of the traffic flowing on major highways in and out of the city underground, eliminating the Central Artery.
- **Blue Laws**: conservative legislation enacted in Puritan New England settlements regarding behavior, so called for the blue paper upon which they were printed. Some of these laws are still on the books, and today the term "blue laws" usually refers to the strict rules regarding the sale of alcohol.
- **Book**: a verb meaning to hurry away
- **Brahmin**: from the earlier centuries of Boston's elite class: Anglo-Saxon Protestant upper-class families: Appleton, Bacon, Boylston, Cabot, Codman, Coolidge, Cunningham, Forbes, Hunnewell, Lodge, Lowell, Parkman, Russell, and Shaw.
- **BU**: Boston University
- **The Cape**: Cape Cod. Not to be confused with Cape Ann, that is on the North Shore, and isn't referred to as "the Cape."
- **The Central Artery**: previously the main route in and out of Boston, the big, several-decked, traffic-clogged thoroughfare is in the process of being demolished.
- **The Charles**: the Charles River
- **The Combat Zone**: former red-light district in the Chinatown area. It is mostly phased out now, although there are a couple of seedy stores and establishments still remaining.
- **Comm Ave.**: Commonwealth Avenue
- **Concord**: town to the west of Boston that figured prominently in the Revolutionary War, pronounced like "conquered" as in what you do when you defeat someone, not "con-CORD" as in the type of airplane or grape
- **Dot Ave.**: Dorchester Avenue
- **Dedham**: suburb west of Boston, pronounced "DEAD-um"
- **Eastie**: East Boston
- **Framingham**: city west of Boston, pronounced "FRAY-ming-ham"
- **Frappe**: a milkshake with ice cream, pronounced "frap," not "frapp-ie"
- **The General**: Massachusetts General Hospital, also referred to as MGH
- **Gloucester**: town on the north shore, pronounced "GLOSS-ter"
- **Haverhill**: town on the border of New Hampshire, pronounced "HAY-vrill"
- **Jimmies**: chocolate sprinkles on ice cream
- **JP**: Jamaica Plain

- **Mass Ave.**: Massachusetts Avenue
- **Natick**: town west of Boston, pronounced "NAY-tick"
- **Needham**: suburb west of Boston, pronounced "NEED-um"
- **Nor'Easter**: fearsome winter storm, often responsible for heavy snows or even blizzards. Technically, a Nor'Easter is a strong area of low pressure that moves in off the Atlantic and brings heavy snow or rain (if it picks up enough moisture on its way in), oversized waves, and gusty northeasterly winds, hence the name.
- **Packie**: package store, i.e. liquor store
- **Peabody**: a town on the north shore of Boston, pronounced "PEE'-b'dee"
- **The Pike**: the Massachusetts Turnpike, which runs east-west across the state
- **Pissa**: as in "pisser," meaning excellent
- **The Pru**: the Prudential Tower
- **P-town**: abbreviation for Provincetown, a gay community on the tip of Cape Cod
- **Quincy**: city just south of Boston, pronounced "KWIN-zee"
- **Reading**: town north of Boston, pronounced "RED-ing"
- **Rotary**: traffic circle; not common in other states, locals love them here—particularly for how frustrating they are for newcomers
- **Rozzie**: Roslindale
- **Scrod**: white fish catch of the day, usually cod or haddock, pronounced "skrawd"
- **Southie**: South Boston, not the South End
- **The T**: The subway, short for MBTA
- **Tonic**: soda pop; soft drinks are also called "soda," but *never* "pop!"
- **Triple-decker**: a three-floor, three-family house originating from the 1800s, popular in this region due to the need to pack lower class immigrant workers into cheap housing. Within the city of Boston, one quarter of the one- to three-family housing stock was listed as a triple-decker at the turn of the millennium.
- **Waltham**: city northwest of Boston, pronounced "WALL-tham," not "Wall-thum" or "Walt-ham"
- **Woburn**: suburb north of Boston, pronounced "WOO-burn"
- **Winchester**: suburb north of Boston, pronounced "WIN-cheh-stir"
- **Worcester**: city about one hour west of Boston, pronounced "WIRS'-tur," not "War-ses-tur," "Worsh-stir," or anything else.

STREET ADDRESS LOCATOR

YOU WILL GET LOST IN BOSTON ... OFTEN. KEEP IN MIND HOWEVER, that during these times of seemingly aimless wandering on side streets, one ways, and confusing traffic circles (rotaries), you may happen upon unexpected treats—quaint squares with inviting bookstores and cozy cafes, or lovely tucked away parks. Never feel embarrassed about being lost here; even lifelong Bostonians occasionally have trouble finding their way.

So how are Boston's streets organized? Local legend holds that the streets of Boston were carved out of old cow trails, and while, outside of a few streets around Boston Common, that's not actually true, it certainly feels like it given the illogical street patterns running through the city. In fact, the original Shawmut peninsula upon which Boston was settled was so small and hilly that residents walked most everywhere and thus created the winding footpaths that circled around salt marshes and tidal flats. It was these foot, not cow, paths that laid down Boston's original, and nowadays confusing, street patterns in much of downtown, including the Financial District, North End, and Beacon Hill. It wasn't until the 1800s, when Boston began an epic effort to increase its real estate with several landfill projects, that some rhyme and reason came to city street planning. Thus, neighborhoods that developed later, such as the Back Bay, the South End, South Boston, and East Boston, were laid out in logical grids and are easier to navigate.

The good news is that, although many of the street patterns throughout the city and surrounding areas are convoluted, Boston is so compact you'll quickly learn to recognize major landmarks and roadways. The best advice on getting around Boston is to buy a good map, one that details downtown Boston as well as surrounding communities and outlying areas. (You can go to www.firstbooks.com, publisher of this *Newcomer's*

Handbook®, for the best Boston area maps.) When scouting an address, keep in mind that Boston is small and you may inadvertently leave the city limits without realizing it. Furthermore, most Boston area towns and cities have streets with the same names and which aren't necessarily connected, so when looking for an address, make sure you are certain of its city location. Common street names in Boston and surrounding communities include Broadway, Cambridge, Harvard, and Washington. When asking for directions, you should know that when people tell you something is "on massave," what they mean is it's "on Mass Ave.," short for Massachusetts Avenue. Similarly, something "on commave" is on Commonwealth Avenue. Learning the names and locations of the significant squares in and around the city is a good idea because directions are often given in relation to the nearest square. (FYI, frequently squares are triangular.) Also become familiar with the old New England traffic institution called the rotary, which you might know as a roundabout or traffic circle. The most important thing to remember about rotaries is that the person on the rotary has the right of way, *not* the person coming on to it.

The following tips should prove useful as you begin your discovery of Boston's labyrinthine streets.

- **Washington Street**, named for George Washington after his visit to Boston in 1789, is unique in that all streets change names at their intersection with it: Court Street turns into State Street, Winter Street turns into Summer Street, LaGrange Street turns into Beech Street, East Brookline Street turns into West Brookline Street, etc. The exceptions to this rule are Mass Ave., Columbus Avenue, and Melnea Cass Boulevard.
- **Some streets change names at town borders**; other streets change names for no apparent reason, such as the Fenway, which becomes Riverway, Jamaicaway, and Arborway as you head south. Major streets that *keep* the same name as they run from community to community are Mass Ave., Comm Ave., Beacon Street, Boylston Street, Washington Street, and Pleasant Street, although the numbering changes from town to town—good to keep in mind if you are searching for a particular address. Other streets disappear and then reappear—Boylston Street, for example.

Grided parts of Boston include:
- The **Back Bay**, designed by city planners in the French style to resemble the Champs-Elysees, was laid out in an easy-to-memorize grid. The major boulevards that run in a roughly east/west direction are: Beacon Street, Marlborough Avenue, Comm Ave., Newbury Street and Boylston Street. Comm Ave. is the only one of these streets with two-way traffic. The smaller cross streets, which run roughly north/south, are named after British royals and run alphabetically in alternating one-

way directions: Arlington Street, Berkeley Street, Clarendon Street, Dartmouth Street, Exeter Street, Fairfield Street, Gloucester Street, and Hereford Street. After Hereford, the Back Bay ends at Mass Ave., which has two-way traffic.

- In **South Boston**, the streets are also laid out in a grid fashion, although they're not as clear cut as those of the Back Bay, since Southie's landmass is shaped somewhat like the letter "v." In general, streets running north/south are lettered, and run alphabetically (M Street, N Street, O Street), and east/west running streets are numbered, and arranged consecutively. Numbered streets are further modified by either east or west, depending on where they fall in relation to Broadway.
- **East Boston** is also fairly grid-like, although there's no easy mnemonic device by which you can remember how the streets here lie. Some of East Boston's thoroughfares are Saratoga, Bennington, and Meridian.

Main thoroughfares in Boston:
- **Beacon Street** begins at Tremont Street downtown and runs in an east/west direction parallel with the Charles River through the Back Bay and Kenmore Square. It continues in a straight line heading southwest through Brookline until Cleveland Circle in Brighton, where it curves around the Chestnut Hill Reservoir and then winds slightly through Newton, terminating at Washington Street/Route 16. Note: do not confuse Beacon Street with North Beacon Street, an entirely separate roadway in northern Brighton, between Cambridge Street and the Mass Pike, which then crosses into Watertown where its name changes to just Beacon Street.
- **Boylston Street** begins downtown at Washington Street and runs east/west through the Back Bay, parallel to the Charles River and ending at the Fens. Boylston picks up again on the other side of the Fens and continues straight through until it ends at Brookline Avenue. Boylston Street begins again further south in Brookline at the border of Olmstead Park, which is where Route 9 (formerly Huntington Avenue) becomes Boylston Street.
- **Columbus Avenue** begins in the Back Bay, picking up Route 28, and heading southwest through the South End, curving south in Roxbury and terminating at the northern border of Franklin Park.
- **Comm Ave**. begins at the Public Gardens and runs east/west, parallel with the Charles River, through the Back Bay and Kenmore Square, passing BU, until it intersects with Brighton Avenue in Allston-Brighton. Then Comm Ave. meanders through Allston-Brighton and continues into Chestnut Hill, Newton, and runs past Boston College (BC).
- **Dorchester Avenue** (**Dot Ave.**) begins at Congress Street on the Downtown Waterfront and heads south over Fort Point Channel

through the western boundary of South Boston and into Dorchester, terminating at Adams Street just north of the Neponset River.
- **Mass Ave.** begins at the intersection with Columbia Road in Dorchester and runs northwest through the South End, the Fenway, and the Back Bay until it crosses over the Charles River into Cambridge. In Cambridge it passes through MIT and Central Square, hooks north in Harvard Square, continues through Porter Square and on into Arlington and then Lexington.
- The **Mass Pike (Massachusetts Turnpike)/I-90** is a major toll road that runs from Boston to the state's western border. When the Big Dig is complete, the Pike will be extended past I-93, all the way to Logan Airport in East Boston.
- **Storrow Drive** is a small, several-lane roadway that runs along the banks of the Charles River. It begins at the Central Artery, just north of Mass General Hospital and just east of the Museum of Science, and follows the river past Beacon Hill, the Back Bay, and BU until it joins up with Soldiers Field Road through Allston-Brighton.
- **Summer Street** begins at Downtown Crossing and runs southeast over the Fort Point Channel by the South Boston wharves and then over the Reserved Channel into the rest of Southie and ending at Dorchester Bay.
- **Tremont Street** begins at Government Center and heads southwest past Boston Common and New England Medical Center into the South End and Roxbury, ending at the intersection with Columbus Avenue.
- **Washington Street**: begins at Downtown Crossing and runs southwest through Chinatown, the South End, Roxbury, JP, Roslindale, West Roxbury, and into Hyde Park.

Main thoroughfares in Cambridge
- **Mass Ave.** runs southeast to northwest, bisecting Cambridge all the way from Boston to Arlington, passing through MIT, Central Square, Harvard Square, and Porter Square.
- **Memorial Drive**, Cambridge's equivalent of Storrow Drive, it runs on the Cambridge side of the Charles River. Although it is several lanes wide, it is very windy and narrow at points, so be careful.
- **Broadway** and **Cambridge streets** run east/west from East Cambridge and ending at Harvard Square. Cambridge Street goes right through Inman Square.
- **Fresh Pond Parkway/Alewife Brook Parkway** run north/south on the western edge of Cambridge, past Fresh Pond on the south end up to Arlington in the north. Also called **Routes 2**, **3**, and **16**.
- **Main Street** begins by the Charles River at the end of the Longfellow Bridge and runs through Kendall Square, terminating at its intersection

with Mass Ave. in Central Square.

Main thoroughfares in Brookline
- **Beacon Street** cuts east/west through the most densely populated section of Brookline, from Kenmore Square to Cleveland Circle, where it heads into Newton.
- **Boylston Street** runs east/west, roughly parallel to Beacon Street, but further south, from the Fenway area of Boston to Newton. Passes by the Brookline Reservoir, Brookline Village, and Brookline Hills. Also called **Route 9**.
- **Harvard Street** heads north/south from Brookline Village at Boylston Street through Coolidge Corner at the intersection of Beacon Street and north into Allston.
- **Washington Street** runs southeast to northwest from Boylston Street through Washington Square and into Brighton.
- **Hammond Pond Parkway** runs north/south through southwestern Brookline into Newton. On the southwest side of the Putterham Meadows Golf Course it meets up with Newton Street.

Main thoroughfares in Somerville
- **Somerville Avenue** runs southeast/northwest through the southern portion of Somerville.
- **Beacon Street** is a southeast/northwest thoroughfare along the border with Cambridge. Turns into Hampshire Street when it crosses the border.
- **Holland Street**, **Elm Street**, **and College Avenue** all intersect in Davis Square.
- **Broadway** runs east/west through the northern portion of Somerville, from the McGrath Highway into Arlington. Passes by Tufts University.

For more information on the local highways (I-93, Route 1, Route 90/Mass Pike, and Route 20), see the **Transportation** chapter.

NEIGHBORHOODS

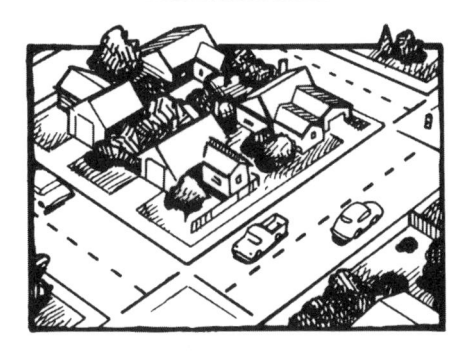

Boston, a city of ethnically, economically, and socially diverse neighborhoods, is a mosaic of distinctive communities. The Italians are in the North End, the Irish in South Boston, the gay community fills the South End, and the "upper crust" are in Beacon Hill. On first glance, not a whole lot of ethnic diversity may be apparent, but Boston is much more diverse than is initially obvious: according to the 2000 Census, half of the city's residents are ethnic minorities, which include a large African-American population, and many of Asian and Hispanic descent. In addition, with more than 40 colleges and universities in the metro area, the population on the whole is certainly young; during the school year in particular, Boston is unquestionably a college town. From the move ins on September 1, to the move-outs in May and June, students form an influential sub-group within the city, and many of the living, dining, and social options here are targeted to those in school or those who have just graduated. If you're further along in life, finding dining and entertainment options more suitable may take a little more effort, but it is possible.

Over the years, Boston has successfully annexed many of the surrounding areas such as Charlestown and Roslindale. What this translates to for today's city residents is the option to report an address as being in either "Roslindale" or "Boston." To complicate matters further, there are many surrounding areas that are very much part of Boston's cityscape, but which eluded annexation, such as Cambridge and Brookline, and are therefore not Boston addresses. So, when a local says she lives in Boston or in "the city," she could mean a surrounding area like Cambridge, one of the annexed areas like Charlestown, or somewhere in Boston proper like the North End. Newcomers should keep in mind that non-Boston proper neighborhoods are very much part of the metropolitan area and all are linked to public transit. And, as many surrounding communities are more affordable, it's a good idea to consider places like Brookline, Cambridge, or Somerville for living options.

In terms of personal safety, crime in Boston, as it is in any major US city, is a fact of life. The good news is that it is less prevalent in Boston than in

22

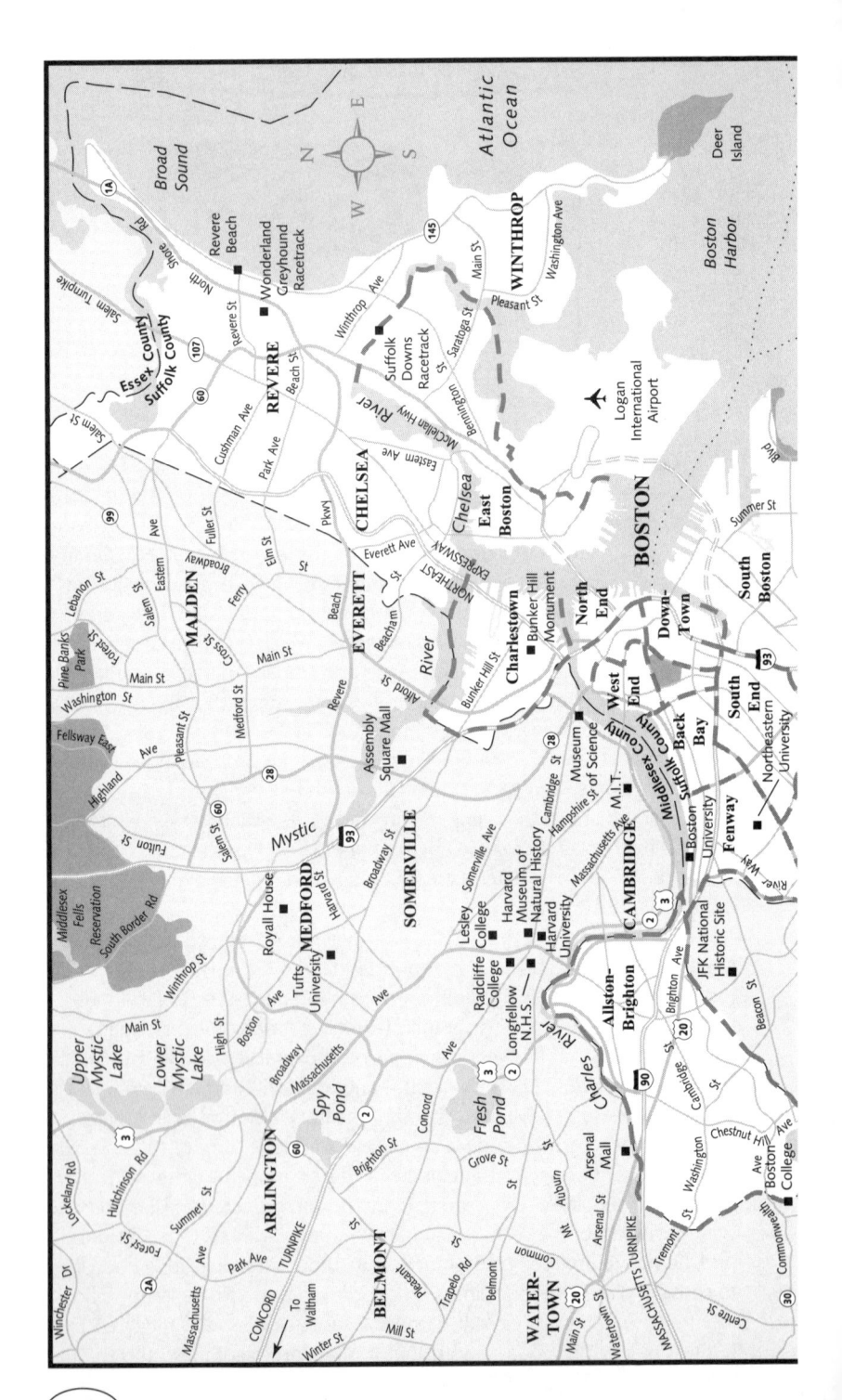

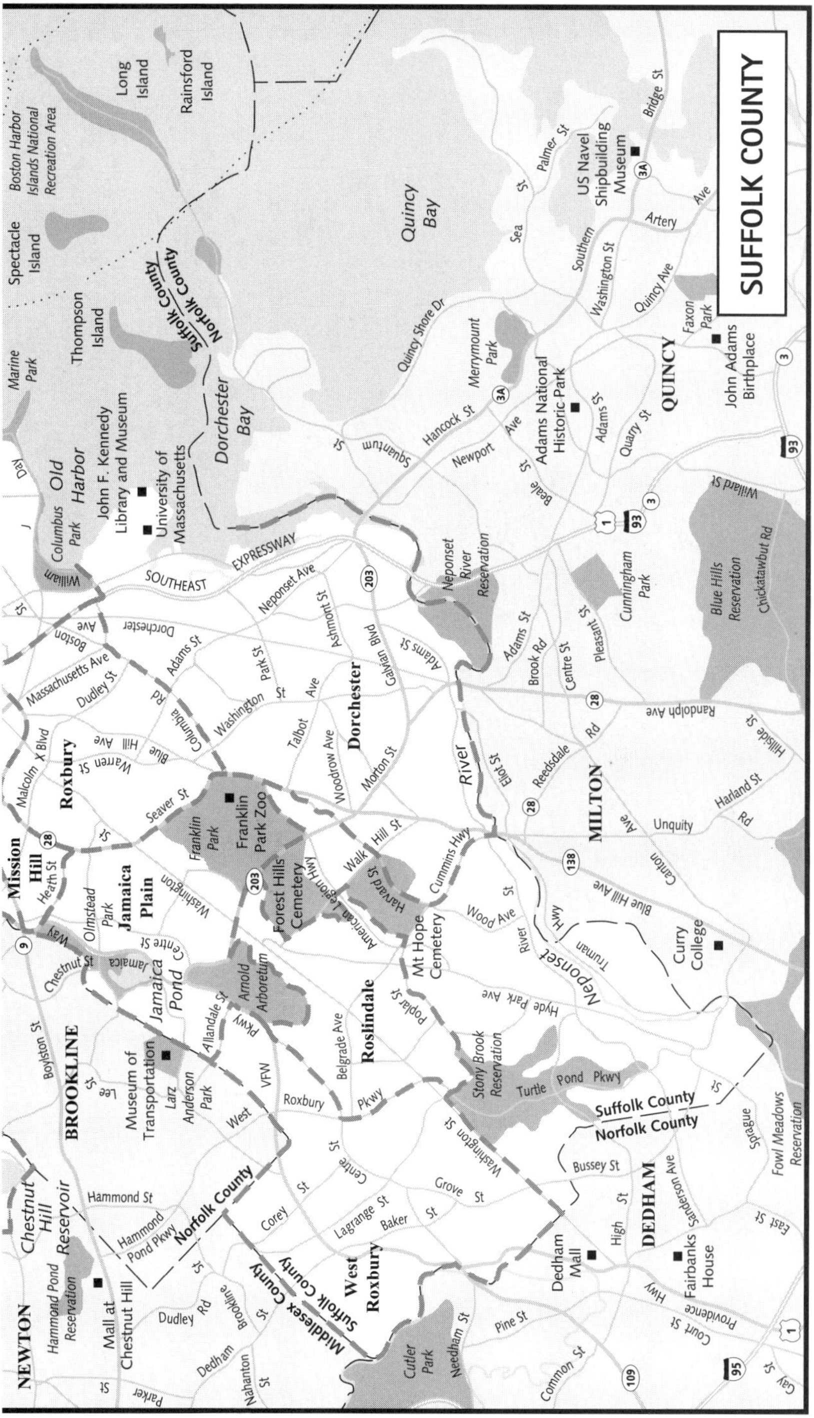

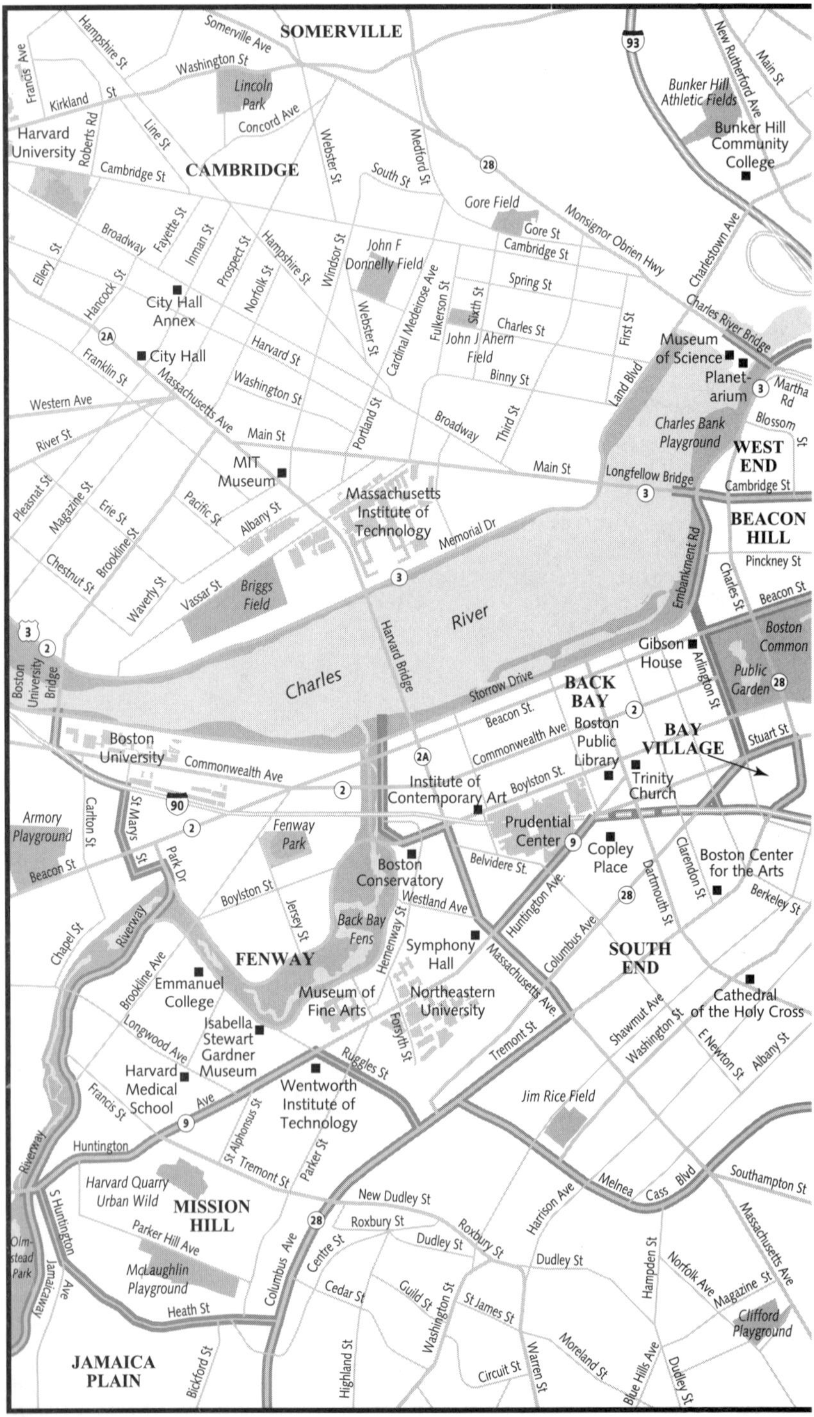
SOMERVILLE
CAMBRIDGE
Harvard University
Lincoln Park
City Hall Annex
City Hall
MIT Museum
Massachusetts Institute of Technology
Briggs Field
John F Donnelly Field
Gore Field
John J Ahern Field
Bunker Hill Athletic Fields
Bunker Hill Community College
Museum of Science
Planetarium
Charles Bank Playground
WEST END
BEACON HILL
Boston Common
Public Garden
Gibson House
BACK BAY
BAY VILLAGE
Boston Public Library
Trinity Church
Charles River
Boston University
Boston University Bridge
Harvard Bridge
Longfellow Bridge
Charles River Bridge
Institute of Contemporary Art
Prudential Center
Copley Place
Boston Center for the Arts
Armory Playground
Fenway Park
Boston Conservatory
Back Bay Fens
FENWAY
Symphony Hall
Emmanuel College
Museum of Fine Arts
Northeastern University
SOUTH END
Cathedral of the Holy Cross
Isabella Stewart Gardner Museum
Harvard Medical School
Wentworth Institute of Technology
Jim Rice Field
Harvard Quarry Urban Wild
MISSION HILL
McLaughlin Playground
Olmstead Park
Clifford Playground
JAMAICA PLAIN
Somerville Ave
Washington St
Hampshire St
Francis Ave
Kirkland St
Roberts Rd
Line St
Concord Ave
Cambridge St
Webster St
Medford St
South St
Monsignor Obrien Hwy
New Rutherford Ave
Main St
Charlestown Ave
Broadway
Fayette St
Inman St
Prospect St
Norfolk St
Windsor St
Cardinal Medeirose Ave
Fulkerson St
Sixth St
Spring St
Charles St
Binny St
Gore St
First St
Land Blvd
Third St
Portland St
Ellery St
Hancock St
Franklin St
Massachusetts Ave
Harvard St
Western Ave
River St
Pleasnat St
Magazine St
Erie St
Pacific St
Albany St
Chestnut St
Brookline St
Waverly St
Vassar St
Memorial Dr
Martha Rd
Blossom St
Embankment Rd
Pinckney St
Beacon St
Arlington St
Storrow Drive
Commonwealth Ave
Boylston St.
Stuart St
Carlton St
St Marys St
Park Dr
Belvidere St.
Huntington Ave.
Dartmouth St
Clarendon St
Berkeley St
Westland Ave
Jersey St
Boylston St
Hemenway St
Chapel St
Riverway
Brookline Ave
Columbus Ave
Longwood Ave
Forsyth St
Tremont St
Shawmut Ave
Washington St.
E Newton St
Ruggles St
Francis St
Huntington Ave
St Alphonsus St
Parker St
Melnea Cass Blvd
Southampton St
Harrison Ave
New Dudley St
Roxbury St
Dudley St
S Huntington Ave
Jamaicaway
Parker Hill Ave
Heath St
Centre St
Cedar St
Guild St
St James St
Hampden St
Norfolk Ave
Highland St
Circuit St
Warren St
Moreland St
Blue Hills Ave
Dudley St
Bickford St
93
28
2A
3
2
90
9

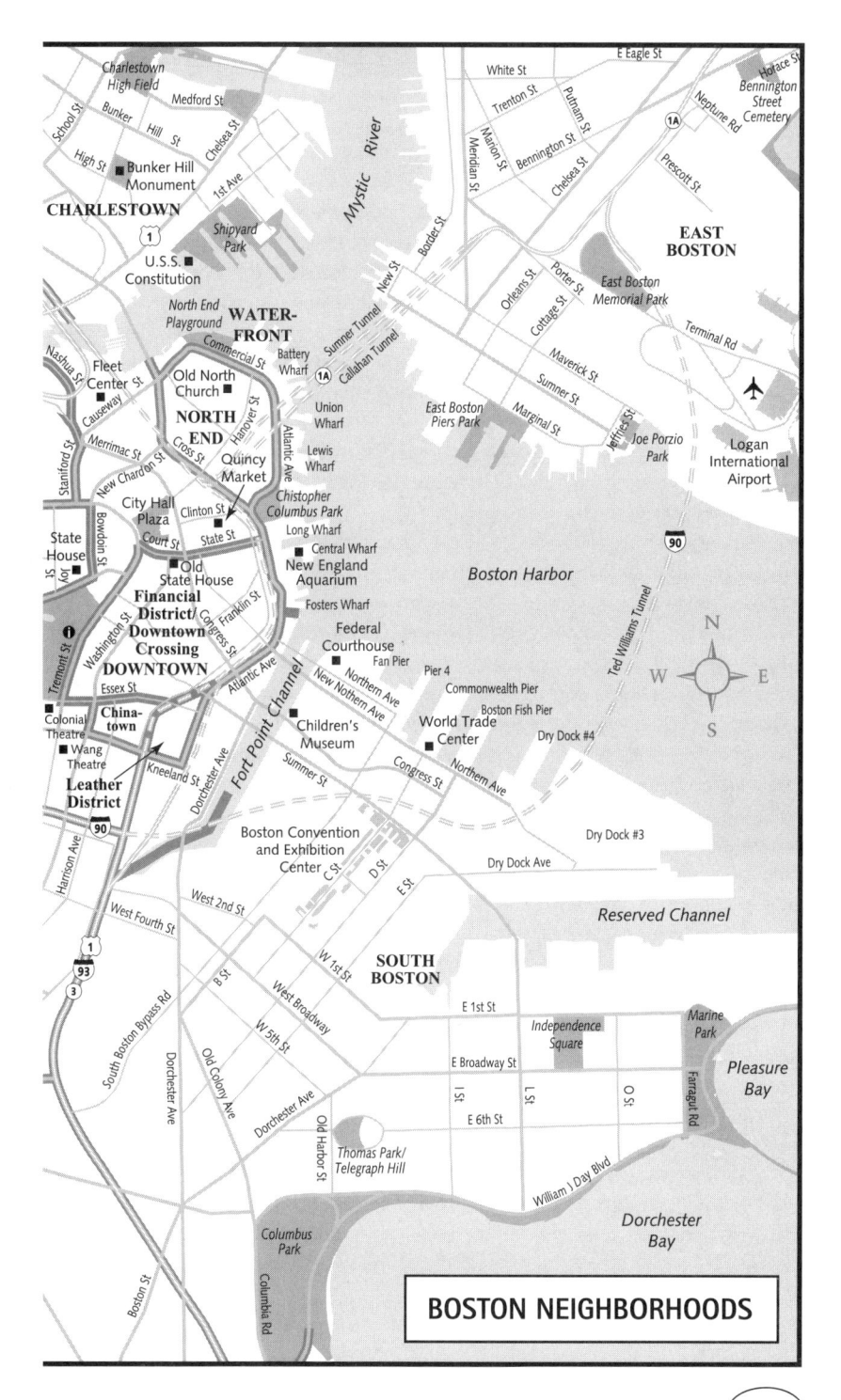

BOSTON NEIGHBORHOODS

many other cities. Recent reports by the state's Executive Office of Public Safety listed the biggest problems in Boston as aggravated assault and vehicle theft, for which Boston ranked 14th and 16th in the nation. (For more on crime rates, you can visit www.disastercenter.com or the FBI's Uniform Crime Reports at www.fbi.gov/ucr/00cius.htm.) Keep in mind that everyone's comfort level varies and what is good for some may not work for others. Those arriving here from another big city should feel at ease in most Boston neighborhoods. Newcomers from smaller cities or rural areas will want to pay close attention to how comfortable they are when visiting prospective neighborhoods. The communities profiled in this book should appeal to most newcomers in terms of amenities and safety issues. However, regardless of where you live, you should always be aware of your surroundings and take safety precautions. For more, see the **Crime and Safety** section of the **Getting Settled** chapter.

Parking in much of Boston and the surrounding communities is often difficult to find and winter only exacerbates the situation. Once someone has shoveled out "his" spot, he will often mark it with a trashcan or chair. If it's a wintry day and you are circling for parking, no matter how desperate you are, it's probably best to leave such spaces alone. For more details about street parking, parking permits, and ease of parking, see the neighborhood profiles (below), as well as the **Parking** section in **Getting Settled**.

County demarcations are mostly a thing of the past in the Bay State. If you see them mentioned at all, it is usually in terms of weather advisories or political campaigns. However, for ease of navigating this book, we have broken out the region by county and then listed the neighborhoods alphabetically therein. Boston itself, along with Chelsea, Revere, and Winthrop are in Suffolk County. To the north and west, in Middlesex County lie the profiled communities of Arlington, Belmont, Cambridge, Malden, Medford, Newton, Somerville, Waltham, and Watertown. To the west and south, we profiled the Norfolk County communities of Brookline, Dedham, Milton, Needham, and Quincy.

In this third edition of the *Newcomer's Handbook® for Moving to and Living in Boston*, in addition to the newly included profiles of some Boston neighborhoods, such as the Fenway and South Boston, you will also find more detailed descriptions of the aforementioned significant surrounding communities that, while not technically part of Boston, really do make up what is considered Boston. Neighborhood or community profiles include statistical information and descriptions of housing, area amenities, etc. After each profile is a list of resources: post offices, library branches, police stations, parks, and the like.

Also included are brief summaries of some of the more popular suburbs surrounding Boston, where many people choose to live and then commute into the city to work. These suburbs and satellite cities in the greater Boston area have been arranged by county and then alphabetically. Under the **Greater Boston Area** heading, you will find a few lines describing the character, housing, and contact information for communities on the North and South shores and the metro-west region in Norfolk, Middlesex, Essex, Plymouth, and Bristol counties.

SUFFOLK COUNTY

ALLSTON-BRIGHTON

Boundaries: **North**: Charles River; **East**: Fenway; **West**: City of Newton; **South**: Brookline

ALLSTON VILLAGE
PACKARD'S CORNER
BRIGHTON CENTER
OAK SQUARE
NORTH BEACON/MARKET
CLEVELAND CIRCLE
ABERDEEN

Allston-Brighton may not be the prettiest place in the city, but what it lacks in aesthetics it makes up in affordability and convenience. It's for these reasons that Allston-Brighton is popular with students (undergraduate and graduate), recent graduates, young families, and immigrants. Wedged between BC to the west, BU to the East, and Harvard to the north, it's big, safe, and has a T line running right through it.

While technically separate neighborhoods, Allston and Brighton evolved together and do not seem separate; the boundaries between them are so fuzzy that rarely do you hear or see one listed without the other. Even the parking signs read "Allston-Brighton resident permit only." In terms of actual boundaries, most agree that the section connecting Allston-Brighton to the rest of Boston along the Charles River (the Boston University area) is Allston, and the side further south and west, closer to Newton and Brookline is Brighton. Established in 1635 with colonial land grants, Allston-Brighton originally was part of the city of Cambridge. In 1807, the Allston-Brighton neighborhood (then called Little Cambridge) found itself disconnected from Harvard Square due to a damaged bridge, and when government officials did not move to repair it, Allston-Brighton seceded from Cambridge and became its own entity. Eventually Allston and Brighton were home to stockyards, slaughterhouses, and meatpacking, an industry made possible by the Charles River and the railroad. In 1874 Allston and Brighton were annexed by Boston, and once the Back Bay was filled in and the streetcars extended here, houses were added. Many of the Victorians built during this time are still standing.

Today, Allston-Brighton is part industrial and part residential, made up of a diverse populace. Those of Irish, Italian, Greek, Jewish, Asian, African-American, Russian, and Hispanic descent can all be found in this part of Boston. Homes and their surrounding grounds vary in size and style, from the tried and true triple-decker, to Victorian bow-fronts, to 1960s-style block apartment complexes. Location, general lack of upkeep, and simple architecture all contribute to keeping housing prices low, particularly when compared to the more sought after parts of town. While living quarters here tend to be much bigger than what is available downtown, and you might even get a parking spot, quaint just isn't a word that comes to mind in Allston-Brighton. On the other hand, this neighborhood has everything you'll need for services: hardware, sporting goods, antique, carpet and furniture stores; as well as a variety of high-quality and affordable ethnic restaurants, pubs and taverns, and all the nightlife a young Bostonian could ever want. The prime shopping areas are along Comm Ave., Brighton Avenue/Beacon Street, Harvard Street, Cambridge Street, and Washington Street. And when those aren't enough for you, you can hop on the Green Line B Train, which makes frequent stops all the way down Comm Ave. from Boston College to downtown. With so many stops on this line, the train ride into the city center can be tedious, but it is nonetheless convenient, and apartments close to the Green Line stations are a good find.

Because parts of both Boston University's and Harvard's campuses actually lie within the bounds of **Allston**, it is more heavily devoted to and populated by students than Brighton. Named for Packard's Sales Stable and Riding School present here in the late 1800s and early 1900s, **Packard's Corner**, where Comm Ave. intersects with Brighton Avenue, is at the western end of BU's campus. This area wasn't much developed until around 1910, when the streetcars arrived and spurred construction. Much of the housing stock here dates from this same period: mostly three- to five-story brick masonry apartments representative of the Georgian, classical, Renaissance, and Federal Revival styles. BU's presence is apparent in both the official university property that extends along Comm Ave., and in the unofficial, but obviously student-geared businesses in the area.

For the past decade or so, Harvard has been buying parts of north Allston in preparation of future expansion. Harvard's Business School is already located in Allston, just across the JFK Bridge from Cambridge, and surprisingly the university owns more land here than it does in Cambridge. Despite this, Harvard's identity is centered in Cambridge, so the debates as to what parts of the school will be transferred to Allston are bound to go on for a long time before any real development begins. In the meantime, students from Harvard and BU living in Allston lend this neighborhood a busy and funky beat. This vibe is especially noticeable between BU and the **Allston Village** area around Harvard Avenue, between Comm and Brighton avenues, which boasts the majority of Allston's shops, bars, and local services. If you don't mind nightlife, then this is the place to be. If you want it a little quieter, think more seriously about Brighton.

While undergraduates and grads live in Brighton, it is peppered with a heavier mix of young families and young professionals. The length of Comm Ave. is lined with apartment complexes and the Green Line runs along it. **Brighton Center**, where Market Street intersects with Washington Street, is home to a large established Irish population as well as many orthodox Jews, which, if the renovated storefronts, new construction, and new businesses are any indication, appears to be gentrifying quickly. **Oak Square**, at the intersection of Faneuil and Washington streets in the northwest corner of Brighton by the Newton border is predominantly residential with mostly single- and two-family homes. Although it is not near any T lines, a library and the fire station are here, there are buses, and it is close to the Mass Pike. Just north of Oak Square, the **North Beacon/Market** area offers a good selection of condominium complexes, and south, in **Cleveland Circle** where Beacon Street (not North Beacon) intersects Chestnut Hill Avenue at the terminus of the C train, a lot of BC students have taken up residence. Cleveland Circle was developed mostly between 1870 and 1950, and architecture here reflects the Queen Anne, shingle, and classical revival styles for single-family homes, and classical and Georgian revival (as well as your basic 1950s and '60s block buildings) for apartment complexes. Assets in this subneighborhood include being within walking distance of the B, C, and D train lines, not to mention the (Chestnut Hill) Reservoir, a large freshwater body of water with a nice park surrounding it. **Aberdeen** is the territory around Comm Ave., between Washington Street to the east, Brookline to the south, and Cleveland Circle on the west. This hilly region was heavily developed between 1890 and 1940, and although Comm Ave. has plenty of apartment buildings, most of Aberdeen has larger, single and multiple-family homes (with lawns). With its proximity to the B line along Comm Ave., Aberdeen does have some access to the T, and there is the C line along Beacon Street, just over the Brookline border.

If you live in Aberdeen or Cleveland Circle, you're probably set in terms of public transportation. In the rest of Brighton, further off Beacon Street or Comm Ave. (i.e. Oak Square, Brighton Center, North Beacon/Market), having a car is handy. Be advised: the winter parking wars in Brighton are as fierce as anywhere in the city. Resident sticker-only parking is required in the densely populated areas of Aberdeen and Cleveland Circle.

Web Sites: www.cityofboston.gov, www.allstonvillage.com, www.allstonvillage.com/AVMS, www.brightonmainstreets.org, www.oaksquare.com
Area Code: 617
Zip Codes: 02134, 02135
Post Offices: Allston Station, 47 Harvard Avenue, 617-789-3769; Brighton Retail, 409 Washington Street, 617-254-5929; www.usps.com
Police: District D-14, 301 Washington Street, 617-343-4260; www.cityofboston.gov/police
Emergency Hospital: St. Elizabeth's Medical Center of Boston, 736 Cambridge Street, 617-789-3000, www.semc.org; Kindred Hospital Boston, 1515 Comm Ave., 617-254-1100, www.kindredhealthcare.com/hospitals/boston
Libraries: Brighton Branch, 40 Academy Hill Road, Brighton, 617-782-6032; Faneuil Street Branch, 419 Faneuil Street, Brighton, 617-782-6705, www.bpl.org
Parks & Open Space: Charles River Reservation (along the northern border); Chestnut Hill Reservoir (at Comm Ave., Beacon Street, and Chestnut Hill Avenue); Chandler Pond/St. John's Seminary (at Kenrick Street and Lake Street); Soldiers Field/Harvard Athletic Fields (Soldier's Field Road north of Western Avenue and Harvard Street); Ringer Playground (between Gordon and Allston streets); Rogers Park (between Lake and Foster streets); McKinney Playground (roughly bound by Leicester, Faneuil, and Goodenough streets and Ryan Road); Hobart Park (at Hobart and Brooks streets)
Public Schools: Boston Public Schools, 26 Court Street, 617-635-9000, www.bostonpublicschools.org
Community Publication: *Allston-Brighton TAB*, www.townonline.com/allston/, 617-254-7530
Community Resources: Jackson/Mann Community Center, 500 Cambridge Street, 617-635-5153; Community Rowing, 1400 Soldiers Field Road, 617-782-9091; Harvard University, Business School, Soldiers Field, 617-495-1000, www.harvard.edu; Boston University, 121 Bay State Road, 617-353-2000, www.bu.edu; Allston/Brighton APAC, 143 Harvard Avenue, 617-783-1485, www.bostonabcd.org/people/abapac; Bryman Institute, 1505 Comm Ave., 888-741-4271, http://bryman-institute.com; Maven Institute, 1845 Comm Ave., 617-779-9975, www.maveninstitute.org; Allston-Brighton YMCA, www.tiac.net/users/abymca; Brighton Board of Trade, www.brightonbot.com; Brighton Allston Historical Society, www.bahistory.org/bahfirst; Hobart Park Neighborhood Association, www.hobartpark.org; Allston Brighton Community Development Corporation, www.allstonbrightoncdc.org; Allston-Brighton Healthy Boston Coalition, www.abhealthyboston.org

Public Transportation: *Trains*: Green Line B trolleys run between BC and downtown with many surface stops along Comm Ave; Green Line C trolleys run down Beacon Street through Brookline, from Cleveland Circle to downtown; Green Line D trolleys are accessible to those in the Cleveland Circle area from the Reservoir stop and go downtown.
Buses: for MBTA route and schedule information contact the MBTA Traveler's Information Center: 617-222-3200, 800-392-6100, or go to www.mbta.com.

BACK BAY

Boundaries: **North**: the Charles River; **East**: Arlington Street and the Public Garden; **South**: (roughly) the Mass Turnpike/Huntington Avenue/Columbus Avenue; **West**: Mass Ave./Charlesgate East

Sitting on the front stoop of your $10 million Comm Ave. ivy-covered Beaux-Art brownstone mansion looking around at the other brownstones across the mall on a quiet spring morning it's easy to believe, save for the cars, this area hasn't changed in 200 years. Boy, how wrong you'd be. Almost two centuries ago what is now the Back Bay consisted of swampy mudflats that were created in 1819 by the damming of the Charles River. So nasty and foul-smelling, this area was declared "nothing less than a cesspool" by the Boston City Council. In 1849, the health department demanded the land be filled, and thus was born the Back Bay neighborhood, one of Boston's several land-fill projects that ultimately reshaped the face of the city. From 1857 to 1882, mostly Irish laborers filled more than 450 acres in the Back Bay basin with earth and gravel brought in from Needham. The outcome: yet another splendid neighborhood for Boston's lucky affluent. What a difference 25 years can make.

A carefully planned community of Victorian architecture, the Back Bay was designed by architect Arthur Gilman, who laid out its streets according to Baron Haussmann's Parisan boulevard model. However, the Back Bay diverges from and perhaps improves upon this tradition in that his streets hold to a strict grid pattern. No pretty-but-perplexing pathways arisen from footpaths here, but rather stick-straight northeast to southwest running avenues (Beacon, Marlborough, Commonwealth, Newbury, Boylston, St. James, and Stuart), crossed by smaller residential streets arranged in alphabetical order (from Arlington to Hereford) and named to honor British earls, dukes, and lords. This sensible and easily-navigable scheme is indeed a true rarity in this town.

Comm Ave. runs up the center of the Back Bay, which, unlike most other streets here, has two-way traffic; a grassy, tree-lined, statue-filled mall runs along the middle, separating traffic. In the winter, the mall comes alive with twinkling holiday lights. Residents, particularly dog owners, stroll amidst the varied monuments honoring such figures as Alexander Hamilton and Leif Ericson.

The Back Bay is as an architecture buff's dream come true, home to too many significant structures to give their full due here. Let it suffice to say that most of the buildings survive from the Victorian era, inspired by various European styles of the time, particularly French and Italian. Coexisting with the quiet brownstones are such Boston greats as the Ritz-Carlton Hotel, a remnant from the roaring 1920s, the Trinity Church, a granite and sandstone Romanesque giant in the middle of the Copley Square, the Prudential or "Pru," which is the Back Bay's first skyscraper built in 1965, and the Boston Public Library, a relic of the Italianate Renaissance style. And lest we forget, I.M. Pei's dignified 790-foot-high mirrored John Hancock Tower, Boston's tallest building, wedged in next to the Trinity Church. Colored lights from the Hancock beam out the weather forecast from its crowning beacon. The following poem helps Bostonians remember how to interpret its signals:

Steady blue, clear view.
Flashing blue, clouds are due.
Steady red, rain ahead.
Flashing red, snow instead.

(If you notice flashing red from the Hancock Tower in the summer and are perplexed, never fear: it's not the end of the world, but close—the Red Sox game has been cancelled.)

While Comm Ave. and Marlborough and Beacon streets are predominantly residential, Newbury and Boylston streets are commercial centers. Boylston Street has more offices to complement its selection of stores, restaurants, and bars, and Newbury Street is referred to as Boston's "Rodeo Drive," offering upscale shopping to hordes of people. Perhaps more visible here than Boston's moneyed residents is the concentration of the wealthy and often flashy international tourists and college students who glide in and out of posh boutiques, private art galleries, and cafés. The closer to the Public Garden, the more upscale the shops; thus towards the Arlington end of both Newbury and Boylston streets, you can browse at stores like Hermès and Brooks Brothers, whereas as you near the Mass Ave. end, the choices are a little more down-to-earth, including Allston Beat, Newbury Comics, and Trident Booksellers & Café. Should these shopping options not be enough, the Copley Plaza and the Prudential Center are two indoor malls right in the heart of the city, and house the typical Gap/Banana Republic mall fare as well as Lord & Taylor, Macy's, and Saks (the Neiman-Marcus building stands independently, but is in the vicinity), plus a Westin and Marriott, multiple food options, and a Loews movie theater, all connected by a skywalk.

When the Back Bay was first developed, many of Boston's wealthy moved here from Beacon Hill and from the South End to their new mansions. It remains a coveted and pricey neighborhood. If you are lucky enough to be in the Back Bay price bracket, it poses a variety of living options, including either transformed or preserved mansions on quiet and shady Marlborough and Comm Ave., apartments above the trendy stores of Newbury, or modern condos found in the Pru or in high-rises on Beacon, which afford views of the city or the Charles River, respectively.

Some things to consider if you're apartment/house-hunting here: the quality of available housing and available parking. First, the Back Bay was no less affected than any of Boston's other neighborhoods during the city's decline that started after WWII and ended, by some accounts, in the 1980s. During these years, many of the magnificent mansions were purchased and converted into apartments, school dorms, and even frat houses for some of Boston's colleges. As a result, you may come across some apartments that, while toting a high Back Bay price, are of low, "student-ghetto" quality. Parking in the Back Bay is difficult and resident sticker restrictions apply. Residents might find it easier to park in the parking garages beneath Boston Common, the Copley, or the Pru, rather than fighting for a spot with the hordes who come for a day of shopping or a night at the clubs. Some of the high-rises and townhouses feature parking spots, and there are some back alley garages, an option well worth the money. Also, mice and rats have been an issue here in recent years.

By car and public transport, you can easily access the rest of downtown, Storrow Drive, Brookline, Allston-Brighton, and Cambridge. In addition to its shopping and dining delights, the Back Bay has all the standard amenities, including a Star Market in the Pru and a new Trader Joe's on Boylston for the value-conscious grocery gourmet. Many Back Bay residents enjoy their proximity to the Public Garden, Boston Common, the Charles River and Esplanade, the lawn in Copley Square, the Comm Ave. Mall, and The Fens. In addition to all the galleries on Newbury, art lovers can walk to the Institute of Contemporary Art, Berklee Performance Center, and the Boston Symphony Orchestra. Basically, no matter your tastes, if you want to live smack dab in the middle of the action, the Back Bay is a good choice.

Web Sites: www.cityofboston.gov, www.urbanphoto.org/boston/backbay
Area Code: 617
Zip Codes: 02115, 02116, 02117, 02199
Post Offices: Astor Station, 207 Mass Ave., 617-247-2429; Back Bay Annex Station, 390 Stuart Street, 617-236-7800; Prudential Center Post

Office, 800 Boylston Street, 617-267-4164; Kenmore Station, 11 Deerfield Street, 617-437-1113; www.usps.com

Police: District D-4, 650 Harrison Avenue, 617-343-4250, www.cityofboston.gov/police

Emergency Hospitals: Mass General Hospital, 55 Fruit Street, 617-726-2000, www.mgh.harvard.edu; Boston University Medical Campus/Boston Medical Center, 88 East Newton Street and 771 Albany Street, 617-638-5000, www.bumc.bu.edu

Libraries: Central Library, Copley Square, 700 Boylston Street, 617-536-5400, www.bpl.org; Goethe Institute, 170 Beacon Street, 617-262-6050; French Library, 53 Marlborough Street, 617-912-0400

Parks & Open Space: Clarendon Street Tot lot (on corner of Clarendon and Comm); Comm Ave. Mall; Boston Common (between Beacon, Park, Tremont, Boyston, and Charles streets); Public Garden (between Beacon, Arlington, Boylston, and Charles streets); Esplanade (along Storrow Drive and the Charles between Arlington and Fairfield streets); Charles River Reservation (along the entire northern border of the city); Charlesgate (between Storrow Drive, the Fens, Mass Ave. and Kenmore Square); Copley Square (at Dartmouth and Boylston streets)

Public Schools: Boston Public Schools, 26 Court Street, 617-635-9000, www.bostonpublicschools.org

Community Publication: *Back Bay Courant,* 617-267-2700

Community Resources: Community Boating, 21 David Mugar Way, 617-523-1038, www.community-boating.org; Hatch Memorial Shell; Back Bay Guide (guide to the offerings of Newbury Street and the Back Bay), www.backbayguide.com; Back Bay Chorale, 617-730-7430, www.backbaychorale.org; Blackstone Community Center, 50 West Brookline Street, 617-635-5162; Gibson House Museum, 137 Beacon Street, 617-267-6338; Institute of Contemporary Art (ICA), 955 Boylston Street, 617-266-5152, www.icaboston.org; BosTix Booth (half-price ticket outlet), Copley Square at the corner of Boylston and Dartmouth; Hynes Convention Center, 900 Boylston Street, 617-954-2000; Prudential Center, 800 Boylston Street, 800-746-7778, www.prudentialcenter.com; Copley Place, 100 Huntington Avenue, 617-369-5000, www.shopcopleyplace.com; Lyric Stage, 140 Clarendon Street, 617-437-7172; Boston Architectural Center, 320 Newbury Street, 617-262-5000, www.the-bac.edu/ce; Back Bay NAG (Neighborhood Action Group), www.backbaynag.org; Boston's Back Bay Association (for businesses), www.bostonbackbay.com; Neighborhood Association of the Back Bay (NABB), www.nabbonline.com

Public Transportation: *Trains*: Green Line at Arlington, Copley, Hynes/ICA, and Prudential (all trains go to Arlington and Copley; all trains but the E train goes to Hynes/ICA, only the E train goes to Prudential); Orange Line and Commuter Rail at Back Bay Station

Buses: for MBTA route and schedule information contact the MBTA Traveler's Information Center: 617-222-3200, 800-392-6100, or go to www.mbta.com.

BEACON HILL/WEST END

Boundaries: *Beacon Hill*: **North**: Cambridge Street; **East**: Bowdoin Street; **South**: Beacon Street; **West**: Storrow Drive; *West End*: **North**: Nashua Street; **East**: Staniford Street; **South**: Cambridge Street; **West**: the Charles River

SOUTH SLOPE
NORTH SLOPE
FLAT OF THE HILL
LOUISBURG SQUARE
WEST END

Formerly home to such notables as Louisa May Alcott, Nathaniel Hawthorne, Daniel Webster, John Hancock, and Henry James, there is perhaps no area of the city that's more quintessentially Boston than Beacon Hill. This neighborhood has the dubious distinction of being the only one of Boston's three original hills to remain, although at the end of the 18th century its top 60 feet were removed for the building of North Station. Initially referred to as Sentry Hill for the guards who stood watch, its name eventually changed to reflect the 65-foot tall beacon pole complete with a flame pot that was positioned on its crest in 1634, to be lighted in the event of an enemy attack. So well preserved is this neighborhood, with its gorgeous brick row houses, gaslights, redbrick sidewalks, and even the occasional cobblestone street, that one is virtually transported back to America's earlier days. Horses and carriages come to mind in this neighborhood of opulence. Architectural styles in Beacon Hill include Federal, Greek, Victorian, mixed in with early 20th century colonial revivals and tenements. Thanks to the birth of the Beacon Hill Historic District in 1955 and the strict architectural restraints it imposes upon residents, Beacon Hill's distinct historical architecture will be preserved.

An area that measures barely one square mile, Beacon Hill consists of a **South Slope**, a **North Slope**, and the **Flat of the Hill**. The South Slope is what most imagine when they think of Beacon Hill; developed for Boston's wealthiest families in the early 19th century with carefully laid-out streets, townhouses, window boxes, ornate doorways, pear trees, and hidden courtyards. It rises up from Charles Street, the neighborhood's main commercial thoroughfare and home to many upscale restaurants and stores, particularly antique and home furnishing shops. Stretching out from Charles Street to Storrow Drive is the Flat of the Hill, a landfill that was originally part of the Charles River. Some larger homes in this area look as though they would make apt settings for an Edith Wharton novel. Toward the top of the hill between Pinkney and Mount Vernon streets lies the *pièce de resistance* of Beacon Hill, nay of Boston, **Louisburg Square** (pronounced Lewisburg)—a privately-owned grassy park surrounded by a cobblestone way and townhouses. On the other side with its more colorful history descends the North Slope. Over the years, this section has been home to Bostonians of simpler means, including freed slaves and immigrants from Eastern and Southern Europe. Accordingly, significant sites along the Black Heritage Trail are found here. Although slightly less fancy than the South Slope, this side of the hill still fetches otherworldly prices for its brick walk-ups and tenement style buildings.

Much of Beacon Hill has always been Boston's premiere seat of wealth, power, and prestige. It is home to the Bulfinch-designed State House on Beacon Street, with its imposing structure and golden dome. In years past area residents represented a stronghold of Boston's most elite social aristocracy, collectively entitled the "Brahmins" by Dr. Oliver Wendell Holmes in 1860. In recent years, money has spoken louder than pedigree, and most of the Brahmin caste has moved off the hill in search of greener and more suburban pastures, replaced by successful newcomers.

What you will get for your money in Beacon Hill is decidedly less (space-wise) than what you'll be able to find elsewhere in an already pricey town. The amount you might pay for a decent-sized apartment outside of Beacon Hill may only be enough for a cramped, Manhattan-esque closet in this neighborhood—albeit a safe, well-located closet with a gorgeous exterior. When house hunting here, be aware that building interiors can vary from lovely, redone, and worth every penny homes to shoddily built money pits whose exterior majesty hides major, original design flaws or just centuries of wear and tear. While many residences have been updated to support modern conveniences, if the abundance of laundromats throughout the district is any indication, many buildings have not been fully modernized. The neighborhood itself, however, has moved into the current century in terms of amenities, if not aesthetics. Drug stores, a Stop & Shop, ethnic and upscale restaurants, bars, a new deluxe Loews movie theater, and other services of use are within walking distance. Beacon Hill is Boston's hub, with the Theater District, Chinatown, the Back Bay, North Station, City Hall Plaza, the Boston Common, the Public Gardens, and the Esplanade only minutes away by foot. Yet, despite being surrounded by the most bustling areas of Boston, the seat of local government, a tourist destination, and having quick access to major roadways, Beacon Hill is startlingly residential, quiet, and homogeneous. Each Mother's Day, Charles and Mt. Vernon streets are closed off for the "Make Way for Ducklings" parade, a procession of children dressed like ducklings retracing the route detailed in the much loved locally-set children's story of the same name. Depending on where you live on the hill, getting to public transportation might require a slight walk. But that is clearly preferable to searching for on-street parking, which is as bad as it gets and done by resident permit (see **Getting Settled** for more information about residential parking permits). Many homes here are without garages, putting Beacon Hill as one of the few places in the US where you can find millionaires scraping their windshields on cold winter mornings. A public parking garage underneath the Boston Common supplements the few street spots for residents.

The North Slope of Beacon Hill runs down to include parts of Boston's **West End**. This former neighborhood was razed during the massive urban renewal that Boston experienced in the late 1950s and early '60s under mayor John B. Hynes. Like so many of Boston's neighborhoods, for years this area was home to the newly arrived: in the late 1800s the Irish edged out the African-Americans, and they themselves gave way to a mixture of Italians, Jews, Greeks, Armenians, and Syrians. It was 1958 when the city, wanting to create a business center here, razed the West End, displacing many of its residents. At the last minute a few historic buildings were preserved, such as the first Harrison Gray Otis House and the Vilna Shul, but much of the rest was wiped out. Although the West End still officially exists, most Bostonians would give you a puzzled look if you asked for it by that name. The area, flanked by the Government Center and Cambridge Street as it runs to the Charles, is mostly devoted to the Massachusetts General Hospital and Mass Eye & Ear Infirmary. A few high- and low-rise apartment buildings do exist along Storrow Drive, notably the Charles River Park, developed by Jerome Rappaport to entice a higher class of resident back into the city from the suburbs with its infamous, if tempting "If you lived here, you'd be home by now" billboards. In terms of culture and local amenities, however, the West End as a residential enclave is no longer.

Web Sites: www.cityofboston.gov, www.beaconhillonline.com, www.urbanphoto.org/boston/beaconhill
Area Code: 617
Zip Codes: *Beacon Hill*: 02108, 02114; *West End*: 02114
Post Offices: Charles Street Station, 136 Charles Street, 617-723-7434; JFK Station, 25 New Chardon Street, 617-523-6566; State House Station, (in the State House at) 24 Beacon Street, Room 2, 617-742-0012; www.usps.com

Police: District A-1, 40 New Sudbury Street, 617-343-4240, www.cityofboston.gov/police

Emergency Hospital: Mass General Hospital, 55 Fruit Street, 617-726-2000, www.mgh.harvard.edu

Libraries: West End Branch, 151 Cambridge Street, 617-523-3957; Kirstein Business Branch, 20 City Hall Avenue, 617-523-0860; www.bpl.org; Boston Athenaeum (private membership for proprietors and shareholders), 10 1/2 Beacon Street, 617-227-0270, www.bostonathenaeum.org/home; Congregational Library, 14 Beacon Street, 617-523-0470

Parks & Open Space: Boston Common (between Beacon, Park, Tremont, Boyston, and Charles streets); Public Garden (between Beacon, Arlington, Boylston, and Charles streets); Esplanade (along Storrow Drive and the Charles); Charles River Reservation (along the entire northern border of the city); Charlesgate (between Storrow Drive, the Fens, Mass Ave., and Kenmore Square); Louisberg Square (between Pinkney and Mt. Vernon streets at Willow Street)

Public Schools: Boston Public Schools, 26 Court Street, 617-635-9000, www.bostonpublicschools.org

Community Publication: *The Beacon Hill Times*, 617-523-9490, www.beaconhilltimes.com

Community Resources: Community Boating, 21 David Mugar Way, 617-523-1038, www.community-boating.org; Hatch Memorial Shell; Museum of Science (includes Hayden Planetarium and Mugar Omni Theater), Science Park, 617-723-2500, www.mos.org; Museum of Afro American History, 46 Joy Street, 617-725-0022, www.afroammuseum.org; Suffolk University, 8 Ashburton Place, 617-573-8000, www.suffolk.edu; City Hall Plaza, Congress Street; State House, 24 Beacon Street, 617-727-3676; Black Heritage Trail; The Beacon Hill Business Association, www.beaconhillonline.com/bhba; the Beacon Hill Civic Association, www.bhcivic.org/home; Beacon Hill DOG, www.beaconhilldog.com

Historical Sites in this area are too numerous to list, but a few of import are: First Harrison Gray Otis House, 141 Cambridge Street, 617-227-3956; African Meeting House, 46 Joy Street and 8 Smith Court, 617-742-5415; Old Historic Vilna Synagogue, 14 Phillips Street; Charles Nichols House Museum, 55 Mount Vernon Street, 617-227-6993; Granary Burying Ground, Tremont and Bromfield streets; King's Chapel and Burying Ground, 58 Tremont Street, 617-227-2155; Park Street Church, 1 Park Street, 617-523-3383.

Public Transportation: *Beacon Hill*: **Trains**: Red Line at Charles/MGH; Red and Green lines at Park Street (with an underground walk through to the Orange Line at Downtown Crossing);

Green and Blue lines at Government Center; Blue Line at Bowdoin; **West End**: *Trains*: Red Line at Charles/MGH; Blue Line at Bowdoin; Green Line, Orange Line and Commuter Rail at North Station; Green Line at Science Park
Buses: #43 (Ruggles Station-Park and Tremont Steets); #55 (Jersey and Queensberry Streets-Copley Square or Park and Tremont Streets via Ipswich Street); for MBTA route and schedule information contact the MBTA Traveler's Information Center: 617-222-3200, 800-392-6100, or go to www.mbta.com.

CHARLESTOWN

Boundaries: **North**: the Mystic River; **East**: Boston Harbor; **South**: Boston Harbor and the Charles River; **West**: roughly, I-93

MONUMENT SQUARE
CITY SQUARE
THOMPSON SQUARE
WINTHROP SQUARE/TRAINING FIELD
SCHRAFFTS TOWER
SULLIVAN SQUARE
CHARLESTOWN NAVY YARD

Located just across the Charles River north of downtown Boston is Charlestown. First settlers to the area were a group of Puritans in the 1620s. By 1847 the town of Charlestown was annexed by Boston.

Perhaps Charlestown's most famous resident was John Harvard, who lived here just over a year before dying of tuberculosis in 1638. He left half of his estate to the new College at Newtowne, which was subsequently named after him. But Charlestown itself is best known for the battle of Bunker Hill. In 1775, one of the first battles of the Revolutionary War was waged here on Breed's Hill (not Bunker Hill). After the war, construction began on the Bunker Hill Monument, which commemorates the colonials' brave stand.

Because the British burned the eastern section of the town to the ground in 1775, the oldest surviving buildings in Charlestown date back to the 1780s. The Warren Tavern on Pleasant Street, built in 1780, and named after one of the patriots who died at Bunker Hill, is the oldest tavern in New England. Paul Revere held Masonic meetings here and George Washington visited it when he was in town. Every April 17th, Paul Revere's famous ride is recreated in Charlestown (his role is played by one of his ancestors), and every June, residents are treated to a Bunker Hill Day parade.

Today, Charlestown's population remains divided between the substantial and close-knit Irish-American population referred to as "townies" that dates back to the 1800s, and a newcomer population of young professionals and their families who are looking for a safe urban setting and spacious housing options. There is also a burgeoning Latino population growing around the Bunker Hill housing development, which is adding to Charlestown's diversity. Newcomers may feel most comfortable residing in the areas closest to the Bunker Hill Monument, namely Monument Square, City Square, and Thompson Square. These enclaves run together in a very small space and are quite homogenous. **Monument Square** is, as you might expect, the area directly surrounding the Bunker Hill Monument. As you head down the western slope of the hill you will come to **Thompson Square** and **City Square**, the northern and southern ends, respectively, of Main and Warren streets. These one-way streets run parallel to each other in opposite directions and form the main routes through the heart of Charlestown. Here you will find Charlestown's largest cluster of small businesses and restaurants. On the more southerly side of the hill is **Winthrop Square** or **Training Field**, a plot of green set aside in 1632 for the local militia to practice drills and now surrounded by rather desirable housing. Heading down the other side of the hill, is Bunker Hill Street. It's in this direction where you will find the less attractive areas of northwestern Charlestown, including the **Schraffts Tower** and **Sullivan Square**, a traffic circle where much of Charlestown's public transportation converges. Futher south along New Rutherford Avenue lies Bunker Hill Community College.

A national historic district, Charlestown has many homes dating from the eighteenth and nineteenth centuries representing the Federal, Greek Revival, and Queen Anne styles. Its look is similar to that of Beacon Hill, with masonry and wooden clapboard row houses and gas-lit cobblestone sidewalks, but it costs much less to live here. Apartments and homes are nice and many have been redone. Not to mention the fact that they are significantly larger than their downtown counterparts, and parking here, although done by resident permit in the "downtown" portion, is substantially less aggravating. If more modern housing is your bag, then head southeast of Route 1 over to the **Navy Yard** for a luxury condo in one of the gray slate buildings on Charlestown's portion of the waterfront. Established in 1800, the Charlestown Navy Yard saw the building and launching of thousands of warships before its closure in 1974 and subsequent redevelopment as living space. The Freedom Trail cuts through the Navy Yard, taking tourists to the USS Constitution, its museum, and the Charlestown Visitor's Center. But the Navy Yard is also a working port with water shuttles to Boston, the Courageous Sailing School, and restaurants and bars such as the Tavern on the Water, whose two floors and balcony positively bust at the seams in the summer. In the Navy Yard, a pretty penny will buy you a dreamlike view of Boston and the water. Large, upscale housing complexes, such as Constitution Quarters, offer luxury units with modern conveniences, including high-speed internet access, fitness rooms, concierge service, and garage parking. Beware of parking near the Navy Yard, though, especially on 1st Avenue which runs parallel to Route 1, as petty car breaks can be a nuisance.

For some, a downside of Charlestown is that although it is pretty, safe, clean, and residential, it can also feel a little isolated. Charlestown may afford divine views of Boston, but you are looking at the city from a distance and are distinctly not in it. Instead, it has more of a friendly little village feel with only a few restaurants and bars. There is a full size Foodmaster, and now Todd English (Boston's biggest restauranteur) has established two restaurants here: a Figs and an Olives. The Orange Line provides T access to downtown, but its infrequency is legendary and getting to it requires a bit of a walk to the Sullivan Square or Community College stops, neither of which are especially close to the major residential areas. Then again, in nice weather you can actually just walk from the heart of Charlestown over the Charlestown Bridge and be in the North End in about 15 minutes, and driving into the city, its surrounding areas, or into the suburbs via I-93 or Route 1 is a cinch.

Web Sites: www.cityofboston.gov, http://charlestown.ma.us, www.urbanphoto.org/boston/charlestown
Area Code: 617
Zip Code: 02129
Post Office: Charlestown Station, 23 Austin Street, 617-241-5322; www.usps.com
Police: District A-5, 40 New Sudbury Street, 617-343-4240; www.cityofboston.gov/police
Emergency Hospital: Mass General Hospital, 55 Fruit Street, 617-726-2000; www.mgh.harvard.edu
Library: Charlestown Branch, 179 Main Street, 617-242-1248, www.bpl.org
Parks & Open Space: Monument Square (between Pleasant, Tremont, Lexington, and High streets); Charlestown Naval Shipyard Park (between Route 1 and Boston Harbor); City Square (by the Charlestown Bridge and Route 1-93 at the Boston Harbor); John Harvard Mall (between Harvard, Henley, and Main streets); Training Field/Winthrop Square (between Winthrop and High streets); Barry Playground (at Medford Street and Chelsea Street on the Little Mystic Channel)
Public Schools: Boston Public Schools, 26 Court Street, 617-635-9000, www.bostonpublicschools.org
Community Publication: *Charlestown Patriot*, 617-241-9511

Community Resources: Charlestown Community Center, 255 Medford Street, 617-635-5169; Golden Age Center, 382 Main Street, 617-635-5175; Kent Community Center, 50 Bunker Hill Street, 617-635-5177; Bunker Hill Burying Ground; Bunker Hill Monument, Monument Square, 617-242-5641, www.nps.gov/bost/Bunker_Hill; Bunker Hill Community College, 250 New Rutherford Avenue, 617-228-2000, www.bhcc.mass.edu; USS Constitution, Charlestown Navy Yard, 617-242-5671, www.ussconstitutionmuseum.org; Navy Yard Visitor Center and Bunker Hill Pavilion, Outside Gate 1, Constitution Road, 617-241-7575, www.nps.gov/bost/Navy_Yard

Public Transportation: *Trains*: Orange Line at Community College and Sullivan Square

Buses: for MBTA route and schedule information contact the MBTA Traveler's Information Center: 617-222-3200, 800-392-6100, or go to www.mbta.com.

Boats: Navy Yard (Pier 4)-Long Wharf; Charlestown Navy Yard-North Station (Lovejoy Wharf); www.mbta.com

DORCHESTER

Boundaries: **North**: Columbia Road; **South**: Neponset River and Cummins Highway; **West**: Harvard Street and Franklin Park; **East**: Dorchester Bay and Boston Harbor

COLUMBIA POINT/JFK/UMASS
EDWARD EVERETT SQUARE
MEETING HOUSE HILL
SAVIN HILL
FIELDS CORNER
CODMAN SQUARE

FOUR CORNERS
DUDLEY
SHAWMUT
ASHMONT
ADAMS VILLAGE
NEPONSET

In terms of population and size, Dorchester is Boston's largest neighborhood. Long reputed as one of Boston's dodgier areas, Dorchester is enjoying a renaissance of sorts. Finally! Not that it is without its rough patches, but by and large Dorchester is quite livable and worth thinking about if you'd like to live in Boston but are of modest means. The cost of housing here is markedly below the city's average: you can rent a three- or four-bedroom apartment for the same price of a one-bedroom in the more glamorous addresses of downtown Boston, Brookline, or Cambridge.

The story of Dorchester goes back to 1630 when a group of Puritans landed at what is now **Columbia Point**, where the Kennedy Library and UMASS-Boston are located. Dorchester was annexed by Boston in 1869.

Some of the region's oldest historical sites are here, including the city's oldest standing house, the 1648 Blake House on Columbia Road located near **Edward Everett Square**, and the Dorchester North Burying Ground, which dates back to 1633. On Parish Street, on top of **Meeting House Hill**, is the Mather School, the nation's oldest elementary school, which was founded in 1639.

Today, Dorchester Avenue, also known as "Dot Ave.," is the main drag and is home to Irish pubs, bakeries, Southeast Asian markets, and West Indian grocers selling fragrant curries and spices. Downtown Boston is accessible in a matter of minutes via either the Red Line or car, which you won't mind having in Dorchester since it is not too difficult to find parking. (Then again, the main route into the city, I-93, is pretty much the last place you'll want to be during rush hour.) There are some parks and open spaces and some waterfront access as well. The most significant outdoor area is along Dorchester's eastern border, where you will find Franklin Park (the final link in Olmstead's Emerald Necklace—more about that in the **Greenspace** chapter) and the revamped Franklin Park Zoo.

Dorchester has a racially diverse population and includes well-established Vietnamese and Haitian communities. The Vietnamese population is centered between the **Savin Hill** and **Fields Corner** sub-regions of Dorchester. Residents run the gamut socio-economically, from a significant number living below the poverty line, to working class, to upwardly mobile professionals. Given the cultural and economic diversity and the only recent move toward gentrification here, housing is affordable.

With such a vast range in population demographics, it should come as no surprise that Dorchester is really a big area comprised of many smaller sub-neighborhoods, many of which are generally safe, but some are still transforming. Recently Boston revived the Operation Ceasefire program here in attempt to reduce inner-city violence by breaking up street gangs. Specifically, the program targets Dorchester's Washington Street corridor, which runs through Dorchester Center and includes the **Codman Square** and **Four Corners** neighborhoods. The **Dudley** area of north Dorchester and Roxbury along Dudley Street is one of Boston's most economically depressed neighborhoods.

Despite these rougher areas, some of Boston's most beautiful Victorian homes are in Dorchester, mingling with a proliferation of wooden triple-deckers that were popular in the early 1900s. There are too many sub-neighborhoods with their own nuances to list, and it will be a personal choice as to which area is most suitable, but as a general rule, newcomers may be more comfortable in the areas with train service, including (from north to south roughly around Dorchester Avenue) the **JFK/UMASS**, Savin Hill, Fields Corner, **Shawmut**, and **Ashmont** neighborhoods. Primarily residential in nature, the JFK/UMASS area sees a lot of students and tourists.

The UMASS T stop also provides access to Morrissey Boulevard, a highly commercial and not-so-pedestrian-friendly strip. Other sub-regions in southern Dorchester worth considering include **Adams Village** around the intersection of Adams Street and Gallivan Boulevard, and **Neponset**, in southeast Dorchester by the Neponset River Reservation.

Web Sites: www.cityofboston.gov, www.bostonmainstreets.com, www.ashmonthill.org
Area Code: 617
Zip Codes: 02121, 02122, 02124, 02125
Post Offices: Codman Square Center, 554 Washington Street, 617-929-4144; Dorchester Station (Fields Corner), 218 Adams Street, 617-288-0834; Grove Hall Station, 647 Warren Street, 617-445-2253; Uphams Corner Post Station, 551 Columbia Road, 617-287-9626; www.usps.com
Police: District C-11, 40 Gibson Road, 617-343-4330, www.cityofboston.gov/police and http://c11bpd.com
Emergency Hospital: Carney Hospital, 2100 Dorchester Avenue, 617-296-4000, www.carneyhospital.org
Libraries: Lower Mills Branch, 27 Richmond Street, 617-298-7841; Uphams Corner, 500 Columbia Road, 617-265-0139; Codman Square Branch, 690 Washington Street, 617-436-8214; Adams Street Branch, 690 Adams Street, 617-436-6900; Fields Corner Branch, 1520 Dorchester Avenue, 617-436-2155; www.bpl.org
Parks & Open Space: Tenean Beach (at Tenean and Conley streets, just east of I-93 on Dorchester Bay); Columbia Point (at UMASS-Boston on Dorchester Bay); Savin Hill/Malibu Beach (at Savin Hill Avenue and Southview Street, east of I-93 on Dorchester Bay); Dorchester Park (between Dorchester Avenue and Adams Street at Carney Hospital); Franklin Park, Franklin Park Golf Course, and Franklin Park Zoo, www.zoonewengland.com (bound by Seaver Street, Blue Hill Avenue, and the American Legion Highway); Neponset River Reservation (at Butler and Ventura streets, past the rail line on the north banks of the Neponset River); Ronan Park (between Quincy Street and Mt. Ida Road at Robinson Street)
Public Schools: Boston Public Schools, 26 Court Street, 617-635-9000, www.bostonpublicschools.org
Community Publications: *Boston Irish Reporter*, 617-436-5275, www.bostonirish.com; *Dorchester Community News*, 617-282-3543; *The Dorchester Reporter*, 617-436-5275, www.dotnews.com; *Boston Haitian Reporter*, 617-436-5275, www.bostonhaitian.com
Community Resources: UMASS Boston, 100 Morrissey Boulevard, 617-287-5000, www.umb.edu; JFK Library & Museum, Columbia Point, 877-616-4599, www.cs.umb.edu/jfklibrary; Bayside Expo Center,

200 Mt. Vernon Street, 617-474-6000, www.baysideexpo.com; Cleveland Community Center, 11 Charles Street, 617-635-5141; Holland Community Center, 85 Olney Street, 617-635-5144; Marshall Community Center, 35 Westville Street, 617-635-5148; Murphy Community Center, 1 Worrell Street, 617-635-5150; Perkins Community Center, 155 Talbot Avenue, 617-635-5146; Louis D. Brown Peace Institute, 1452 Dorchester Avenue, 617-825-1917, www.institute4peace.org; Bird Street Community Center, 500 Columbia Road, 617-282-6110, www.birdstreet.org; Jones Hill Neighborhood Association, www.joneshill.com; Columbia-Savin Hill Civic Association, www.columbiasavinhillcivic.org; Meeting House Hill Civic Association, www.columbiasavinhillcivic.org/MHHCA; Melville Park Association, www.melvillepark.org; Dorchester Historical Society, http://dorchester.historic.org

Public Transportation: *Trains*: Red Line and Commuter Rail at JFK/UMASS; Red line at Savin Hill, Fields Corner, Shawmut and Ashmont

Buses: for MBTA route and schedule information contact the MBTA Traveler's Information Center: 617-222-3200, 800-392-6100, or go to www.mbta.com.

DOWNTOWN BOSTON

Boundaries: *Financial District/Downtown Crossing*: **North**: State Street; **East**: Atlantic Avenue; **South**: Essex Street; **West**: Tremont Street; *Chinatown*: **North**: Essex Street; **East**: I-93; **South**: Kneeland Street; **West**: Washington Street; *Leather District*: **North**: I-93; **East**: Atlantic Avenue; **South**: Kneeland Street

CHINATOWN
LEATHER DISTRICT
FINANCIAL DISTRICT/DOWNTOWN CROSSING

A few places you may not have considered include those in the downtown area, such as Chinatown, the Leather District, and the Financial District/Downtown Crossing. Depending on your needs, they may be worth more than a passing thought.

As is true of much of Boston, **Chinatown**, and its sub-neighborhood the lesser-known **Leather District**, are landfill areas dating from the 1800s. In the 1840s, immigrants from around the world poured in here—Chinese, Irish, Italian, Jewish, Syrian, etc.—and eventually it was the Chinese who stayed and claimed what is now Chinatown. Toward the latter part of the 19th century, disenfranchised Chinese laborers, many of whom had worked temporarily on the transcontinental railroad or as strikebreakers at a shoe factory in Lawrence, MA, settled in this area of Boston and gained employment laying phone lines for the nearby central office of Bell Telephone Company. Further immigration was greatly limited by the Chinese Exclusion Act of 1882, but Boston's slowly growing Asian population gained steam when some of those stringent immigration laws were repealed during the 1940s.

Although considered small in comparison to other Chinatowns nationwide, Boston's Chinatown does have an active community and a long history of standing up to city-wide projects that threatened its survival, such as the development of the Central Artery, Mass Pike, and the New England Medical Center. Residents here were also crucial to the success of cleaning up the (now mostly defunct) "combat zone," a collection of porn shops, strip clubs, and other tawdry businesses. Today, Chinatown concerns itself with the business of welcoming not only tourists, but of immigrants from all over Asia, including Japan, Vietnam, Korea, and Thailand, and helping them adapt to life here.

Like the North End, Chinatown is full of ground level storefronts and restaurants, topped by densely-packed apartment space above. Although potential luxury developments in the neighborhood are being discussed, for now many of the buildings are large and industrial in appearance. Parking is a nightmare here where restaurants have the uncommon distinction of really burning the midnight oil; not only do Bostonians go to Chinatown for the most authentic Asian cuisine at 7 p.m., but they also flock in at 2 a.m., since it is one of the few areas in the city where restaurants are open late. Interstate 93 and the Mass Pike are easily accessible, as is the rest of downtown Boston, especially the common and the Theater District, by car, foot, T, or bus.

Just east of Chinatown, across Atlantic Avenue from South Station is the tiny, but up and coming **Leather District**. After a good portion of Boston was wiped out by the Great Fire of 1872, the leather industry established itself in this corner, and remained here until the 1940s and '50s when the Central Artery construction threw the neighborhood into chaos. In more recent years, artists have been moving into the somewhat revitalized Leather District, using the nineteenth century brick warehouses as galleries, studios, and loft space. Restaurants have cropped up to handle the residents, and with South Station, Boston's bus and train terminus, just across the street, as well as I-93, Route 1, and the Mass Pike, it's a convenient place to live. The neighborhood is being touted as the next Greenwich Village, and although some lofts are priced for struggling artists, others are more expensive, attracting professionals who work in the nearby financial district.

The **Financial District/Downtown Crossing**, and areas in between, are just what you would expect: non-residential and devoted mostly to office workers and tourists. As its name implies, the Financial District is home to a lot of the city's suits scuttling in and out of the tall buildings that hover around Post Office Square. During weekdays and weeknights, the many bars and restaurants are bustling with the lunch and post-work crowds, but on weekends the area is almost deserted. Downtown Crossing is an adjoining open air shopping area centering around the intersection of Washington Street and Winter and Summer streets, with some pedestrian-only streets, vendor carts, and chain and department stores including Macy's and Filene's. The Freedom Trail cuts through here; sites include the Old State House and the Old South Meeting House. Though these areas of Boston are almost entirely commercial, some luxury developments have been built. For example, the Devonshire in the Financial District and a few upscale buildings on Tremont Street along the common provide homes for those who can afford them. Obviously, there's no real neighborhood sense here, but some find the views, the doormen, and the luxury accommodations satisfying enough to call it home. Parking is a challenge, but if you can afford to live in the new Ritz-Carlton apartments on Tremont, then you can probably handle the additional cost for a private space.

Web Sites: www.cityofboston.gov, www.urbanphoto.org/boston/china town, www.bostonez.org/about/chinatown, www.bostonmainstreets. com/chinatown, www.bostonez.org/about/downtown

Area Code: 617

Zip Codes: 02101-02111, 02208-02210

Post Offices: Lafayette Station, 7 Avenue de Lafayette, 617-423-7822; John W. McCormack Station, 90 Devonshire Street, 617-720-3800; Fort Point Station, 25 Dorchester Avenue, 617-654-5302; www.usps.com

Police: District A-1, 40 New Sudbury Street, 617-343-4240; www.cityof-boston.com/police

Emergency Hospitals: New England Medical Center, 750 Washington Street, 617-636-5000, www.nemc.org/home; Mass General Hospital, 55 Fruit Street, 617-726-2000, www.mgh.harvard.edu

Libraries: Chinese Culture Center, 65 Harrison Avenue, 617-482-3292. There are no branches of the Boston Public Library in this area; your closest and best bet is the central library at 700 Boylston Street, 617-536-5400, www.bpl.org

Parks & Open Space: Boston Common (between Beacon, Park, Tremont, Boyston, and Charles streets); Public Garden (between Beacon, Arlington, Boylston, and Charles streets)

Public Schools: Boston Public Schools, 26 Court Street, 617-635-9000, www.bostonpublicschools.org

Community Publications: *Banker and Tradesman*, 617-428-5100, www.bankerandtradesman.com; *Boston Business Journal*, 617-330-1000, www.boston.bizjournals.com; *Boston Chinese News*, 617-338-1170; *The*

Jewish Advocate, 617-367-9100, www.thejewishadvocate.com; *Sing Tao Newspaper*, 617-426-9642; *World Journal-Chinese Daily News*, 617-423-3347, www.worldjournal.com

Community Resources: Quincy/Boston Chinatown Neighborhood Community Center, 885 Washington Street, 617-635-5129; Emerson College, 120 Boylston Street, 617-824-8500, www.emerson.edu; Downtown Crossing (shopping area), intersection of Washington Street with Winter and Summer Streets; Suffolk University, 8 Ashburton Place, 617-573-8000, www.suffolk.edu; Custom House; Old State House/Bostonian Society and Museum, 206 Washington Street, 617-720-3290; Old Corner Bookstore, 1 School Street; Old South Meeting House, 310 Washington Street, 617-482-6439; King's Chapel and Burying Ground, 64 Beacon Street, 617-227-2155; Orpheum Theatre, 1 Hamilton Place, 617-679-0810; Granary Burying Ground, Tremont and Bromfield streets; Park Street Church, 1 Park Street, 617-523-3383; Asian American Civic Association, 200 Tremont Street, 617-426-9492; Dreams of Freedom (Museum), 1 Milk Street, 617-338-6022, www.dreamsoffreedom.org; Boston Chinatown Neighborhood Center, www.bcnc.net

Public Transportation: *Trains*: Orange Line at Chinatown, State and Downtown Crossing; Blue Line at Government Center and State; Red Line at South Station, Park Street and Downtown Crossing; Green Line at Boylston, Government Center and Park Street

Buses: for MBTA route and schedule information contact the MBTA Traveler's Information Center: 617-222-3200, 800-392-6100, or go to www.mbta.com.

EAST BOSTON

Boundaries: **North**: Suffolk Downs and the Chelsea River; **East**: Logan Airport, Bells Isle Inlet, Boston Harbor; **West**: Boston Harbor; **South**: Boston Harbor and Logan Airport

EAGLE HILL
JEFFRIES POINT
BROPHY PARK
MAVERICK SQUARE
ORIENT HEIGHTS

Like much of the rest of Boston, East Boston, or "Eastie" as it's referred to by residents, is built on landfill. Once upon a time, East Boston, which paradoxically in no place touches Boston proper and is only connected to the city by tunnels, was actually five separate islands in Boston Harbor. Who knew? For the first two centuries after Boston was settled, Noddle's Island, Hog (or Breed's) Island, Governor's Island, Apple Island, and Bird Island were primarily under private ownership and used for farming, grazing, and military fortifications. In 1833, General William H. Sumner, owner of Noddle's island, got caught up in the landfill craze that swept Boston and formed the East Boston Company. Sumner and his company filled in the marshes between Noddle's Island and Hog Island to form the major commercial and residential portion of East Boston. In 1923, the company disbanded. Construction of Logan International Airport began when the waters surrounding the three remaining islands were filled in.

East Boston's ample waterfront has greatly influenced its character over the years. Initially promoted as a resort community, the large Victorian homes built for vacationers changed hands and character when East Boston became a shipbuilding center. In came the people to work in the shipyards. Eastie was also transformed into an immigrant processing center second only in this region of the country to New York's Ellis Island. Between the Civil War and WWI, Eastie welcomed waves of Canadians, Irish, Italians, and Russian and Eastern European Jews to its industrial areas along the waterfront for work. Single family homes were converted into multi-family units, and brick apartment buildings and triple-decker tenements were built. To this day, Eastie maintains a strong Italian-American heritage, intermixed with new waves of immigrants who have been arriving since the 1960s: South Americans, Central Americans, Haitians, Southeast Asians, and Eastern Europeans. The variety of shops and restaurants that line the narrow streets are evidence of Eastie's diverse population.

Today, Eastie is a densely populated district that lacks the aesthetic charm of other downtown neighborhoods. The proliferation of the functional triple-deckers and homes with multi-colored stone fronts that survive from Eastie's shipbuilding years makes it feel more like Queens than Boston. Though laid out in a grid pattern, the streets converge at angles in squares that are traffic nightmares. Despite its less than polished environs, Eastie is a safe, family-oriented neighborhood, home to many long-time residents. Women with babies in strollers and other children tagging along are plentiful, and there still exist strong Italian and Hispanic Catholic communities. Amidst the triple-deckers, some large Victorian homes in predominantly Greek and colonial revival styles have survived. These are particularly evident in **Eagle Hill**, the section at the northwest tip of Eastie, accessible from Meridian Street; **Jeffries Point**, at the southwest end of the residential area along Sumner Street; and **Brophy Park** (formerly Belmont Square) along Sumner Street between **Maverick Square** on Eastie's southwest end and Jeffries Point. Brownstones can be found on Webster Street, and the **Orient Heights** section in northeast Eastie has single-family homes with lawns clustered on its hill. Piers Park on Marginal Street offers a vivid view of Boston.

Those who live in Eastie are greatly affected by the presence of Logan International Airport and Suffolk Downs. One third of East Boston is taken up by Logan, one of the country's busiest airports. While noise pollution is a concern to residents living near Logan, the Massachusetts Port Authority has overseen a project to reduce the effects in area homes in East Boston, Winthrop, Revere, and South Boston. Call the Massachusetts Port Authority for details at 617-561-1636. For those who like to play the ponies, Suffolk Downs is in East Boston.

Eastie residents definitely benefit from its natural resources in addition to its commercial ones. Parks and beaches along the waterfront are up for further redevelopment, and the Boston Natural Areas Fund and the Trust for Public Land have gotten a grant to create a "greenway" path connecting Piers Park, Constitution Beach, and the Belle Isle Marsh, a large wetland area that offers a glimpse of what East Boston looked like 200 years ago. Parking in East Boston is not bad, and getting to and from the city is a cinch: the Sumner, Callahan, and Ted Williams tunnels carry traffic between East Boston and downtown; Route 1A cuts through its center; and Eastie has five T stops and several bus and ferry routes.

Web Sites: www.cityofboston.gov, www.eastboston.com, www.eastbostonmainstreets.com
Area Code: 617
Zip Code: 02128, 02228
Post Offices: East Boston Station, 50 Meridian Street, 617-561-3900; Air Mail Center and Airport Facility Mail Station, 139 Harborside Drive, 617-567-1611, www.usps.com
Police: District A-7, 69 Paris Street, 617-343-4220, www.cityofboston.gov/police
Emergency Hospitals: East Boston Neighborhood Health Center, 10 Grove Street, 617-569-5800; offers urgent care service.
Libraries: East Boston Branch, 276 Meridian Street, 617-569-0271; Orient Heights Branch, 18 Barnes Avenue, 617-567-2516, www.bpl.org
Parks & Open Space: Belle Isle Marsh Reservation, www.mass.gov/dcr; Constitution/Orient Heights Beach (south of Bennington and Saratoga streets on the Atlantic); Piers Park (along Marginal Street and Boston Inner Harbor); Paris Street Pool, 113 Paris Street, 617-635-5122
Public Schools: Boston Public Schools, 26 Court Street, 617-635-9000, www.bostonpublicschools.org
Community Publications: *East Boston Sun Transcript*, 781-485-0588, www.eastbostonindependent.com; *Brazilian Newspaper*, 617-561-0063
Community Resources: Suffolk Downs, 111 Waldemar Avenue, East Boston, 617-567-3900, www.suffolkdowns.com; Harborside Community Center, 312 Border Street, 617-635-5114; Orient Heights

Community Center, 86 Boardman Street, 617-635-5120; Paris Street Community Center, 112 Paris Street, 617-635-5125; Piers Park Sailing Center, 95 Marginal Street, 617-561-6677, www.piersparksailing.org; Jeffries Yacht Club, 565 Sumner Street, 617-567-9656; East Boston Activity Center, 237 Marion Street, 617-567-3116; Jeffries Point Neighborhood Center, 425 Sumner Street, 617-569-6045; East Boston's Italian American Cultural Association, www.italiaunita.org; East Boston Artists Group, www.eastbostonartistsgroup.org; Neighborhood of Affordable Housing, www.noahcdc.org; East Boston Foundation, www.eastbostonfoundation.org

Public Transportation: *Trains*: Blue Line stops at Maverick, Airport, Wood Island, Orient Heights, and Suffolk Downs

Buses: #112 (Wellington-Wood Island via Central Avenue, Mystic Mall and Admiral's Hill); #114/116/117 (Wonderland-Maverick via Revere Street), #120 (Orient Heights-Maverick via Bennington Street, Jeffries Point, Waldemar Loop); #121 (Wood Island-Maverick via Lexington Street); for MBTA route and schedule information contact the MBTA Traveler's Information Center: 617-222-3200, 800-392-6100, or go to www.mbta.com.

Ferries: Logan Airport-Long Wharf-Quincy Shipyard (Harbor Express); Logan Airport-Rowes Wharf/Boston Harbor Hotel (Massport); www.mbta.com

FENWAY/MISSION HILL

Boundaries: *Fenway*: **North**: Storrow Drive/Charles River; **East**: Charlesgate East and Mass Ave.; **South**: Tremont and Ruggles streets; **West**: BU Bridge, St. Mary Street and the Riverway; *Mission Hill*: **North**: Huntington Avenue; **East**: Ruggles Street; **South**: Heath Street; **West**: the Riverway and Jamaicaway

EAST FENWAY
WEST FENWAY
KENMORE SQUARE
AUDUBON CIRCLE
LONGWOOD
MISSION HILL

Home to many of Boston's educational institutions, as well culture and sporting venues, residentially the Fenway is often overlooked, particularly by newcomers. It is, in fact, similar to the South End in terms of population and socio-economics, but without all the flash it rarely gets due press.

Thirty-three thousand call the Fenway home, and it is about one and a quarter square miles in size, radiating outwards from the Back Bay Fens, the first of Frederick Law Olmstead's parks. A latecomer to Boston's landfill and development projects, the Fens came about at the end of the nineteenth century. Until the 1870s it was yet another plot of stinky marshland. It was drained and Olmstead was commissioned to design the Fens, part of a seven-mile system of connected green space. The Fens consists of a reedy park around the man-made Muddy River, the Victory Gardens (public gardening plots made in 1942 from landfill taken when the Kenmore T stop was being constructed), the James P. Kelleher Rose Garden, and the Roberto Clemente Field (with baseball and basketball lots).

Throughout the Fenway you will find a population of varying ethnic backgrounds, incomes, professions, and lifestyles. This neighborhood is minority-friendly, with significant gay and immigrant populations. Nearly half of its residents are students who attend one of the several major colleges located here. Despite a significant number of families, however, the Fenway has no public elementary or middle schools within its bounds. As a result, young children are dispersed to schools throughout the rest of downtown.

With this mix of people comes a range of living options. Newly-built and affordable housing developments (that is, complexes where at least one quarter of the units are affordable by lower income households who earn less than 80% of the median income for the area) stand shoulder to shoulder with luxury units. Although there is some newer construction here, such as the industrial looking Church Park building, most of the housing reflects turn-of-the-century styles. You'll see a little more stone work mixed in with the brick bowfronts here, giving the feel of New York's Upper West Side. Rents are mid to high range for the city, that is to say slightly less than Beacon Hill, but more than Brookline or Jamaica Plain. A look at the upkeep of the outside of a building can usually give you a clue as to whether it houses students or professionals, and the conditions of the apartments therein.

According to the active Fenway Community Development Corporation, the Fenway actually consists of five sub-neighborhoods: East Fenway, West Fenway, Kenmore Square, Longwood, and Audubon Circle. Roughly covering the area between the Fens, Mass Ave. and Tremont Street, **East Fenway** encompasses the big hitters of Boston's cultural and educational offerings. Herein lies Northeastern University, Berklee College of Music, the Boston Conservatory of Music, the New England Conservatory of Music, Horticultural Hall, the Massachusetts Historical Society, and the BU Theatre. As such, East Fenway is crawling with academics, musicians, and sundry artsy types, making their way to classes or concert halls. Visitors come from around the city, country, and globe to marvel at the gargantuan stone headquarters of the Christian Science

Church, to take in world-class exhibitions at the Museum of Fine Arts, and to enjoy the perfect acoustics at Symphony Hall. Tiny tree-lined streets such as St. Botolph, which runs just behind the Christian Science Center, are quaint and unexpectedly quiet.

West Fenway stretches from the Park Drive side of the Fens northwards, and includes Lansdowne Street, a strip of loud and glitzy clubs and bars that abut the illustrious and green home of the Red Sox, Fenway Park. At present, a heated debate brews around whether Fenway Park, the nation's oldest baseball stadium, should be torn down and replaced with a larger, more profitable stadium or preserved as is. A particularly contentious area is nearby Boylston Street, which may become the site of a new park for the Red Sox. Currently a very unattractive and pedestrian-unfriendly throughway, community planners are eyeing it instead as a space to be rebuilt/revamped, creating new housing, schools, businesses, and better streets.

Kenmore Square is the area that surrounds the Kenmore Square T stop, where Brookline and Commonwealth avenues and Beacon Street all come together at Charlesgate. Stretching west down Comm Ave. to Allston-Brighton, the Boston University campus makes up most of the Kenmore area. Although many local shops are giving way to national chains such as The Gap and Pizzeria Uno's, some are managing to survive, albeit it in a more subdued manner. For example, the beloved Deli-Haus on Comm Ave. formerly one of Boston's few late-night eateries, has traded in its duct-taped booths and blaring music for more civilized décor, a much smaller menu, and earlier hours. Housing in Kenmore Square tends to be shoddy student-variety digs, and unless you are a student yourself, you'll probably want to look elsewhere in the Fenway for neighbors who more accustomed to the nine to five schedule.

The BU population thins out somewhat toward **Audubon Circle**, which roughly covers the area between Beacon Street and Brookline Avenue, between Kenmore Square and Brookline. Although mostly residential, Audubon Circle has seen the conversion of the old Sears Building at the intersection of Brookline Avenue and Park Drive into the Landmark Center. The complex now holds a giant art store, Bed, Bath, & Beyond, and the Fenway 13, a large movie theater with stadium seating and plenty of parking. A few privately owned restaurants and bars line Brookline Avenue between the Landmark Center and Kenmore Square.

Continuing southwest down Brookline Avenue across the Fenway will bring you to **Longwood**, or the **Longwood Medical Area**, so named for the cluster of hospitals here. In addition to Beth Israel Deaconess, Children's Hospital, Dana-Farber, Brigham & Women's, and the Joslin Diabetes Center, Longwood also completes the rest of the Fenway's educational and cultural offerings with Wheelock College, Emmanuel College, Simmons College,

Mass College of Art, Mass College of Pharmacy, and Wentworth Institute of Technology. Longwood is also home to the extravagant Isabella Stuart Gardner Museum. An unconventional woman of the Victorian era who is rumored to have marched down Tremont Street with a lion, Isabella Stuart Gardner (nicknamed "Mrs. Jack") used her inheritance to construct a palatial home. A museum since 1925, it is a three-story Venetian palazzo where she lived and kept her extensive art collection. In 1990, the estate had the misfortune to be subjected to the world's largest art theft when thieves made off with works by Vermeer, Degas, and Rembrandt.

All in all, the Fenway makes for a positive living experience. The most frequently heard complaint is, of course, the parking or lack thereof, which is mostly on street, regulated by resident sticker, and impacted by the large student population. Parking is even worse for those living close to Fenway Park. Most important if you live here: take note of the Sox game schedule so you can avoid the throngs of often drunken fans.

Although the Fenway is well served by the T, it's not as close to the major Massachusetts highways (routes 1 and 93) as some other areas. Drivers can access either Storrow Drive at Charlesgate or BU, or the Mass Ave. entrance to the Pike. However, if you're headed for Jamaica Plain, Brookline, Allston-Brighton or Cambridge (via the BU Bridge), the Fenway is well situated. It is also a safe neighborhood, with the exception of the Fens at night—by day a lovely park for the community to enjoy, at night the Fens can be trouble and should be avoided.

The area called **Mission Hill**, which covers the three-quarter mile area just south of Longwood, bordering JP and Brookline, is in the process of redefinition. In terms of placement, some official city groups put Mission Hill in with the Longwood area, others group it with Roxbury, and still others consider Mission Hill an entity unto itself. In terms of neighborhood characteristics, simply put, Mission Hill is a community in progress: not quite up-and-coming, but slowly taking its fledgling steps toward that status. During Revolutionary War times, Mission Hill was made up of farms and large estates, followed by the establishment of breweries and a mass of German and Irish immigrants who worked in them. Long called Parker Hill after a man named John Parker who'd built his home at its peak, the name eventually changed to Mission Hill for the mission that German Redemptorist priests established in 1869. In 1876, they built the Mission Church, a twin-spired Romanesque basilica. Today the breweries are gone, but the cathedral remains. A national historic landmark, it is also a functioning church with services in Spanish and English. Parker Hill Avenue climbs up from Huntington to the actual hill, which is densely covered in homes. Much of the housing in Mission Hill dates from the late 1800s: Queen Anne homes coexist with triple-deckers, brick rowhouses, and some low-cost housing projects from the last century. In parts of Mission Hill, housing is notably dingy, but some buildings, such as those along the Riverway, are quite attractive and your dollar here will buy a lot more space than it would downtown.

For the better part of the twentieth century, Mission Hill has struggled with a reputation for crime and failed residential development projects. But post-2000, crime is down and Mission Hill is being revived, due in part to the efforts of organizations such as Mission Hill Main Streets and Empowerment Zone, an organization dedicated to generating sustained community revitalization. Also, the city has invested $15 million to make Huntington Avenue more pedestrian-friendly and commercially viable. Residents here include students and medical staff from the neighboring Longwood medical area. Many, including families, young professionals, and those needing low-income housing, are drawn to Mission Hill for its reasonable rents and convenient services. With the E train running down Huntington Avenue, Mission Hill residents can get to downtown in 10 to 20 minutes.

Despite recent efforts, safety is still an issue here. Reports of housebreaks, drug dealing, and other crimes are common. Is Mission Hill safer than it was ten years ago? Most assuredly. Should you leave your doors unlocked at night? No. Those used to an edgier urban environment should have no problem feeling at home here.

Web Sites: www.cityofboston.gov, www.urbanphoto.org/boston/fenway, www.missionhillmainstreets.org

Area Code: 617

Zip Codes: 02115, 02215, 02120

Post Offices: Astor Station, 207 Mass Ave., 617-247-2429; Kenmore Station, 11 Deerfield Street, 617-437-1113; Mission Hill Station, 1575 Tremont Street, 617-566-2040; www.usps.com

Police: *Fenway*: District D-4, 650 Harrison Avenue, 617-343-4250; *Mission Hill*: District B-2, 135 East Dudley Street, 617-343-4270; www.cityofboston.gov/police

Emergency Hospitals: Beth Israel Deaconess Hospital, 330 Brookline Avenue, 617-667-7000, www.bidmc.harvard.edu; Brigham & Women's Hospital, 75 Francis Street, 617-732-5500, www.brighamandwomens.org; Children's Hospital, 300 Longwood Avenue, 617-355-6000, www.childrenshospital.org

Libraries: Central Library, Copley Square, 700 Boylston Street, 617-536-5400; Parker Hill Branch, 1497 Tremont Street, 617-427-3820; www.bpl.org

Parks & Open Spaces: Back Bay Fens (roughly between Park Drive, The Fenway, Brookline Avenue, and the Fens); Charles River Reservation (along the northern border of the city); Charlesgate (between Storrow Drive, the Fens, Mass Ave., and Kenmore Square); Evans Way Park (between Evans Way, Tetlow Street, and The Fenway); Forsyth Park (between Forsyth Way, Hemenway Street, and The Fenway); Lee Playground-Clemente Field (South Basin of the Fens); Victory Gardens (North Basin of the Fens); Kelleher Rose Garden (South Basin of the Fens); Riverway (roughly between Brookline Avenue, Route 9, Chapel Street, and The Riverway); Southwest Corridor Park (covers 4.2 miles from Copley Place at Dartmouth Street to Roxbury)

Public Schools: Boston Public Schools, 26 Court Street, 617-635-9000, www.bostonpublicschools.org

Community Publications: *The Fenway News,* 617-266-8790; *Mission Hill Gazette,* 617-524-2626, www.jamaicaplaingazette.com/missionhill.htm; *Daily Free Press,* 617-732-0505, www.dailyfreepress.com

Community Resources: Art Institute of Boston, 700 Beacon Street, 617-585-6600, www.aiboston.edu; Northeastern University, 360 Huntington Avenue, 617-373-2000, www.neu.edu; Berklee College of Music, 1140 Boylston Street, 617-266-1400, www.berklee.edu; Boston Conservatory, 8 The Fenway, 617-536-6340, www.bostonconservatory.edu; New England Conservatory of Music, 290 Huntington Avenue, 617-585-1100, www.newenglandconservatory.edu; School of the MFA, 230 The Fenway, 617-369-3699, www.smfa.edu; Symphony Hall, 301 Mass Ave., 617-266-1492, www.bso.org; Isabella Stuart Gardner Museum, 2 Palace Road, 617-566-1401, www.gardnermuseum.org; Fenway Park, 4 Yawkey Way, 617-482-4SOX, www.redsox.com; Massachusetts Horticultural Society, 300 Mass Ave. (Horticultural Hall), 617-933-4900, www.masshort.org; Massachusetts Historical Society, 1154 Boylston Street, 617-536-1608, www.masshist.org; Museum of Fine Arts, 465 Huntington Avenue, 617-267-9300, www.mfa.org; Wheelock College, 200 The Riverway, 617-879-2000, www.wheelock.edu; Emmanuel College, 400 The Fenway, 617-735-9700, www.emmanuel.edu; Simmons College, 300 The Fenway, 617-521-2000, www.simmons.edu; Mass College of Art, 621 Huntington Avenue, 617-879-7000, www.massart.ed; Wentworth Institute of Technology, 550 Huntington Avenue, 617-989-4590, www.wit.edu; New England School of Photography, 537 Comm Ave., 617-437-1868, www.nesop.com; BU Theatre/Huntington Theatre Company, 264 Huntington Avenue; Tobin/Mission Hill Community Center, 1481 Tremont Street and 68 Annunciation Road, 617-635-5216; Mission Hill Neighborhood Housing Services, 1530 Tremont Street, 617-442-5449; Mission Hill Artists Collective, www.geocities.com/mhacollective; Fenway Action Coalition, 617-499-4842, www.fenwayaction.org; Save Fenway Park, 617-367-3771, www.savefenwaypark.com; Colleges of the Fenway, 475 Longwood Avenue, 617-632-2729, www.colleges-fenway.org; Fenway Community Development Corporation, www.fenwaycdc.org; Fenway

Cultural District, www.fenwayculture.org; Empowerment Zone, www.bostonez.org/about/missionhill

Public Transportation: *Trains*: Green Line B, C & D trains to Hynes/ICA and Kenmore Square; B train stops at Blanford Street, BU East, BU Central, BU West; D train stops at Fenway and Longwood; E train stops at Prudential, Symphony, Northeastern, MFA, Longwood Medical Area, Brigham Circle, Fenwood Road, Mission Park, Riverway, Back of the Hill, and Heath Street; Orange Line at Ruggles

Buses: for MBTA route and schedule information contact the MBTA Traveler's Information Center: 617-222-3200, 800-392-6100, or go to www.mbta.com.

JAMAICA PLAIN

Boundaries: **North**: Heath Street; **East**: Columbus Avenue and Franklin Park; **South**: VFW Parkway and Arnold Arboretum; **West**: Jamaica Pond and Brookline (Riverway and Chestnut Street areas)

ELIOT SQUARE
HYDE SQUARE
SUMNER HILL
FOREST HILLS

Welcome to Jamaica Plain! At one time a summer-resort area for Boston's Colonial- and Federal-era rich and famous, "JP," as the locals call it, has become one of Boston's most ethnically, politically, and socio-economically diverse neighborhoods. Scenic Jamaica Plain, once called the "Eden of America," has four community centers, strong neighborhood associations, and lots of open space.

Different accounts exist as to how Jamaica Plain acquired its name, but sources at its historical society believe the area is named after a Native American woman named Jamaica who lived in the area. Settled in 1639 as a farming community, during the 1800s, JP was transformed to accommodate the area's burgeoning industry, including breweries like those in neighboring Mission Hill. Along with German and Irish immigrant workers, Boston's elite came and set up summer homes along Jamaica Pond, lending a resort quality to the area. By 1874, Jamaica Plain, along with West Roxbury and Roslindale, was annexed by Boston.

In addition to the establishment of Boston's privileged on Jamaica Pond's shores, JP benefited greatly from Boston's parks and green space planning of the late 1800s. A major portion of Olmstead's park system is either in or adjacent to JP, including Olmstead Park, Jamaica Pond, the

Arnold Arboretum, and Franklin Park. The posthumously named Olmstead Park consists of 180 acres of parkland with pedestrian and bike paths that connect the manmade Muddy River and Leverett Pond to the north with the naturally occurring Jamaica Pond to the south. This glacial kettle hole, which also happens to be the largest body of water within Boston's city limits, is so pristine it serves as the city's back-up reservoir. It's a popular outdoor recreation area where locals come to canoe, fish, jog, and sunbathe. The Arnold Arboretum came into being after 1842 when Benjamin Bussey left 250 acres of land to Harvard. The arboretum has over 15,000 trees and shrubs, and on the third Sunday of every May (Lilac Sunday) over 20,000 visitors come to see the many blossoms. Franklin Park, which Olmstead believed to be some of his best work, lies to the south and west of JP, and features a woodland preserve, golf course, and zoo. Not part of the Olmstead system, but still green and inviting, is the Forest Hills Cemetery just south of Franklin Park.

Today Jamaica Plain is a neighborhood of left-leaning politics and artists and artisans, many of whom sell their wares in front of the Arts Center on Centre Street, with community gardens, and multi-cultural community festivals. With brightly painted murals scattered about, the nation's oldest community theater group, and an art gallery (The Gallery @ Green Street) at the Green Street T stop, the arts are a positively integral part of the JP experience. In terms of day to day life, you will probably find this neighborhood more like the Harvard and Central Square areas of Cambridge than any other area of Boston. Once home to e.e. cummings, Eugene O'Neill, and Anne Sexton, today JP has a large number of artists, writers, musicians, and graduate students from Harvard Medical School, Northeastern University, and Boston University. There is a thriving gay and lesbian population (especially lesbian) and, in addition to its considerable African-American populace, JP is home to Boston's largest Hispanic community.

Housing is relatively affordable in Jamaica Plain, but prices are rising, and apartment options are mostly either triple-deckers or large single-family homes that were broken up into separate units to accommodate several families. Condominiums and single-family homes are reasonably priced as well. Whatever you are seeking, housing stock in JP is substantially roomier than that in downtown Boston. And you're more likely to get other perks such as a lawn, garden, deck, and easy parking. Many of the homes and public structures in JP survive from as early as the 18th century, and the intermingling of 200 years' worth of architecture contribute to the area's eclectic and colorful appearance. Triple-deckers, 1960s style apartment complexes, live-in artists' studios, and shiny new cookie-cutter condos mix with large Federal, Gothic Revival, Queen Anne, Italianate, Greek Revival, Georgian, stick style, Second Empire, shingle style, and classic revival houses and mansions. Also here are rowhouses along Centre Street, some public housing, and one luxury high rise, Jamaicaway Towers, on Perkins Street.

JP's commercial spine is in the **Eliot Square** area along Centre Street and South Street and has an interesting selection of one-of-a-kind shops and small businesses. Jamaica Plain boasts an array of neighborhood pubs, like the laid-back James' Gate, an Irish pub with a full menu and a cozy fireplace, ethnic restaurants, cafes, boutiques, and any other services you might need. And let's not forget the combination dance club/bar/bowling alley/eatery, the Milky Way Lounge and Lanes. For those who like to cook at home, JP's specialty food markets include the Harvest Co-op on South Street and City Feed and Supply on Boylston Street, a large Hispanic supermarket, Hi Lo in **Hyde Square**, and a large Stop & Shop on Centre Street.

Like the South End, JP is generally safe, but not without some criminal activity. Small crimes and housebreaks sometimes occur, and women especially should take care to not walk alone at night. As a general rule, newcomers may feel more comfortable in the west of JP along the Brookline border, particularly the pond-side area, and in the western section of central Jamaica Plain, the area between the Arboretum and South Street, and **Sumner Hill** or **Forest Hills**.

Although JP does feel somewhat distant from downtown, it's not as far as you might think and its relaxed, green, and friendly atmosphere more than makes up for the distance. For those with pets, JP is probably a good option to consider both due to the space (both in the homes, and green space outside) and the higher likelihood of finding a landlord who allows pets. There are a number of public transportation options that can get you downtown relatively quickly, including buses and the Orange and Green lines of the T. At present, the trolleys are still not running along the crowded Centre Street, but this may change in the near future. If you have a car, parking in JP is not too difficult; only sometimes is it regulated by resident sticker, although winter parking can be difficult along the more densely populated streets.

Web Sites: www.cityofboston.gov, www.boston-online.com/jp, www.jamaicaplain.com; www.planetjp.org, www.bostonmainstreets.com/CentreSouth, www.bostonmainstreets.com/hj
Area Code: 617
Zip Code: 02130
Post Office: Jamaica Plain Station, 655 Centre Street, 617-524-3620, www.usps.com
Police: District E-18, 1249 Hyde Park Avenue, 617-343-5600; District E-13, 3347 Washington Street, 617-343-5630, www.cityofboston.gov/police
Emergency Hospitals: Faulkner Hospital, 1152 Centre Street, 617-983-7000, www.faulknerhospital.org; Beth Israel Deaconess Medical Center,

330 Brookline Avenue, 617-667-7000, www.bidmc.harvard.edu; Brigham and Women's Hospital, 75 Francis Street, 617-732-5500, www.brighamandwomens.org; Children's Hospital, 300 Longwood Avenue, 617-355-6000, www.childrenshospital.org; Lemuel Shattuck Hospital, 170 Morton Street, 617-522-8110, www.state.ma.us/dph/hosp/lsh

Libraries: Connolly Branch, 433 Centre Street, 617-522-1960; Jamaica Plain Branch, 12 Sedgwick Street, 617-524-2053; www.bpl.org

Parks & Open Space: Arborway (between Jamaica Pond and the Arnold Arboretum); Arnold Arboretum, www.arboretum.harvard.edu; English High Athletic Fields (Washington Street by McBride Street); Forest Hills Cemetery (at Franklin Park's southwest border with Morton Street); Franklin Park Golf Course, www.sterlinggolf.com/franklin; Franklin Park Zoo, www.zoonewengland.com; Franklin Park (east of Arnold Arboretum); Jamaica Pond/Jamaica Park (between the Arborway and Olmstead Park); Olmstead Park (bound roughly by the Jamaicaway, Pond Avenue, Perkins Street, and Route 9); Riverway (roughly between Brookline Avenue, Route 9, Chapel Street, and The Riverway-street); Southwest Corridor Park (covers 4.2 miles from Copley Place at Dartmouth Street to Roxbury)

Public Schools: Boston Public Schools, 26 Court Street, 617-635-9000, www.bostonpublicschools.org

Community Publications: *JP Gazette*, 617-524-2626, www.jamaicaplaingazette.com

Community Resources: Agassiz Community Center, 20 Child Street, 617-635-5191; Curtis Hall Community Center, 20 South Street, 617-635-5193; English High Community Center, 144 McBride Street, 617-635-5244; Hennigan Community Center, 200 Heath Street, 617-635-5198; Eliot School of Fine and Applied Arts, 24 Eliot Street, 617-524-3313, www.eliotschool.org; Footlight Club, www.footlight.org; The Gallery @ Green Street, www.jameshull.com; Sam Adams Brewery, 30 Germania Street, 617-522-9080, www.samadams.com; Arborway Coalition, www.arborway.net/coalition; Emerald Necklace Conservancy, 2 Brookline Place, Brookline, 617-232-5374, www.emeraldnecklace.org; Arborway Committee, 617-222-3085, www.arborway.net/Irv/; JP Neighborhood Council, http://groups.yahoo.com/group/JPNC-Network; JP Historical Society, 617-524-5992; JP Community Center, www.alri.org/ltc/jpalp; JP Neighborhood Development Corporation, www.jpndc.org

Public Transportation: *Trains*: Green Line E train stops at Riverway, Back of the Hill, and Heath Street; Orange Line at Stony Brook, Green Street and Forest Hills

Buses: for MBTA route and schedule information contact the MBTA Traveler's Information Center: 617-222-3200, 800-392-6100, or go to www.mbta.com.

NORTH END/WATERFRONT

Boundaries: *North End*: **North**: Commercial Street; **East**: Commercial Street and Atlantic Avenue; **South**: Cross Street; **West**: Cross Street and North Washington Street; ***Waterfront***: **North and East**: Boston Harbor; **South**: Fosters Wharf; **West**: Commercial Street and Atlantic Avenue

NORTH END WATERFRONT
DOWNTOWN WATERFRONT

Boston's answer to Little Italy, the **North End** is a little bit New York City, a little bit Florence, and a little bit *The Godfather* all rolled into one. It is both home to some of Boston's most noteworthy landmarks and is the epicenter of Boston's ethnic Italian community. Once the city's least desirable neighborhood, during the 19th century the North End saw its population change repeatedly with each new wave of immigrants. It welcomed in succession, African-Americans, Irish, Jews, and Portuguese before the Italians finally arrived in the 1890s. A desirable area, the North End is experiencing another wave of immigration of sorts, with young professionals seeking to make their homes in this tight-knit, urban community. Despite this recent trend, the North End is mostly made up of families of Italian descent, some long-timers and others more recently arrived.

Today, the Freedom Trail, a 2.5 mile-long red paint/brick path linking many of Boston's historical sights, cuts straight through the North End, bringing with it swarms of tourists in search of vestiges of America's past. Paul Revere's house, the Old North Church, and the Copp's Hill Burying Ground are all to be found within the North End. Old and young, residents and tourists fill the neighborhood's latticework of narrow and winding streets all day and well into the night. Many spend time at one of the neighborhood's forty plus restaurants and cafes, nearly all of which specialize in Italian cuisine. Locals can often be heard speaking Italian to one another, and during several weekends in July and August the community sponsors ornate parades down North End streets in honor of the feast days of various saints.

With Boston's recent population boom and concurrent housing crisis, rents in the North End are high, but slightly more reasonable than those in the Back Bay or Beacon Hill neighborhoods. Apartments can run the gamut from old, dark labyrinths to nicely refurbished units. Those who can afford to live in the city are drawn to the North End by its lively character, central location, and reputation as one of Boston's safest neighborhoods. Those wanting to buy a home will find prices in the North End to be much more affordable than they are in the Back Bay or Beacon Hill.

North enders are within walking distance of the Fleet Center, Faneuil Hall's shops, restaurants and bars; the Aquarium, Downtown Crossing, Government Center, Haymarket (a year round Friday/Saturday open air produce and fish market), Charlestown, and three of the four MBTA lines, as well as the commuter rail.

The North End's main strip is the densely-populated Hanover Street, with its three- and four-story brick walk-ups, many of which have ground level storefronts and restaurants. During the warmer months, wonderful smells from hundreds of Italian kitchens combine with the friendly and animated conversations in the street, creating a warm and inviting atmosphere. There are no large stores here—there's no room for them—so grocery shopping is done as it is in Europe, in little butcher shops, produce shops, and bakeries that primarily run along Salem Street. (Those with cars can drive to the Stop & Shop in the Government Center or Foodmaster in Charlestown.) Street parking in the North End is unpleasant to say the least, but done with resident sticker. The situation grows even more desperate in the winter, when residents will defend parking spaces they've struggled to shovel out. There are parking provisions for visitors, but those spots are extremely hard to come by; regular visitors often head straight for one of several parking lots and garages in the area.

A word of caution: if it is peace and quiet you are looking for, the North End may not be for you. Many may find the constant hustle and bustle comforting, but with people constantly talking, singing or even yelling in the streets, trucks rumbling through even into the wee hours of the morning, and the occasional sirens of ambulances and fire engines, the North End is a little noisy. The side streets not directly surrounding Hanover Street are less clamorous.

Like many parts of the city, Boston's **Waterfront** neighborhood is being transformed by current city developments. While various city neighborhoods, including Charlestown, Southie, Eastie, and Dorchester, greet the Atlantic, when one hears reference to "the waterfront," it usually means this region along the harbor running from the North End to downtown. Commercial Street and Atlantic Avenue are the boundaries between the North End and the Waterfront. Starting at the Charlestown Bridge, the Waterfront is a mixed-use area with businesses, restaurants, and upscale condos and converted warehouses situated along wharves. Specifically, Constitution, Battery, Lincoln, Union, Sargent's, Lewis, and the North Commercial and South Commercial wharves, make up the **North End**

Waterfront. In addition to the stunning views across the harbor of the USS Constitution, Charlestown, and the incoming and outgoing planes at Logan Airport, the Waterfront is additionally blessed by two parks. The North End Playground, at the northern end next to the Cost Guard Pier, includes tennis and bocce courts, baseball fields, and an outdoor swimming pool and skating rink. At the southern end, at the intersection between the North End and Downtown waterfronts lies Christopher Columbus Park, a patch of green along the water with a fountain and a wisteria and vine arbor.

The wharves: Long, Central, India, Rowes, and Foster, pick up where the North End Waterfront leaves off to continue imperceptibly into the **Downtown Waterfront**. Very much in transition with the Big Dig and the resultant rerouting of traffic through its streets, once the dust settles the Downtown Waterfront will be a great place to call home, particularly if you are working in the nearby Financial District. Even with the continual construction and concurrent noise and air pollution, the Waterfront has managed to consistently attract a social crowd of tourists, diners, and drinkers. With its gorgeous views, proximity to the Financial District, and happening restaurants, this area is popular with Boston's after-work crowd, especially in the summer. On the first warm night of the season and until the last one, the Waterfront bubbles with a happy crowd.

Less residential and more tourist oriented than other Boston enclaves, the Downtown Waterfront is home to a few of the city's more impressive hotels and restaurants. Here, amidst all the water traffic—tour boats, whale watches, water taxis, etc.—you will find the New England Aquarium, the Boston Harbor Hotel, and the Marriott Long Wharf. And lest we forget the Custom House, it stands 16-stories tall, dominating the cityscape with its unforgettable clock tower and housing, of all things, a Marriott.

Web Sites: www.cityofboston.gov, www.northendboston.com, www.northendweb.com
Area Code: 617
Zip Codes: 02113, 02109, 02110
Post Offices: Hanover Street Station, 217 Hanover Street, 617-723-6397; McCormack Station, Post Office Square, 90 Devonshire Street, 617-720-3050; JFK Station, 25 New Chardon Street, 617-523-6566; Lafayette Station, 7 Avenue de Lafayette, 617-423-7822
Police: District A-1, 40 New Sudbury Street, 617-343-4240, www.cityofboston.gov/police
Emergency Hospital: Mass General Hospital, 55 Fruit Street, 617-726-2000, www.mgh.harvard.edu
Library: North End Branch, 25 Parmenter Street, 617-227-8135, www.bpl.org

Parks & Open Space: North End Playground (at Commercial and Foster streets); Christopher Columbus Park (at Atlantic Avenue and Richmond Street); Paul Revere Mall (between Hanover and Unity streets at Tileston Street)

Public Schools: Boston Public Schools, 26 Court Street, 617-635-9000, www.bostonpublicschools.org

Community Resources: Saint Leonard's Community Center, 44 Prince Street, 617-523-0350; Faneuil Hall, 15 State Street; New England Holocaust Memorial, Carmen Park at Congress and Union streets; Haymarket (open on Fridays and Saturdays); Paul Revere and Pierce/Hitchborn House, 19 North Square, 617-523-2338, www.paulreverehouse.org; Old North Church, 193 Salem Street, 617-523-6676; Copp's Hill Burial Ground, Charter Street at Snowhill Street; New England Aquarium, Central Wharf, 617-973-5200, www.neaq.org; Fleet Center, 1 Fleet Center Place, 617-624-1050, www.fleetcenter.com; North End Business Alliance, www.northendboston.com/neba

Public Transportation: *North End*: *Trains*: Orange and Green lines at Haymarket; Green and Blue Lines at Government Center; Green Line and commuter rail at North Station; *Waterfront*: *Trains*: Blue Line at Aquarium

Buses: for MBTA route and schedule information contact the MBTA Traveler's Information Center: 617-222-3200, 800-392-6100, TTY 617-222-5246 or go to www.mbta.com.

Boats: note: you must differentiate the public transportation listed here from the tour boats (cruises, whale watches, harbor tours) and privately owned water taxis that stop on many points along the harbor: Rowes Wharf-Hewitt's Cove, Hingham (MBTA); Rowes Wharf-Logan Airport (Massport); Long Wharf-Charlestown (MBTA); Long Wharf-Pemberton Point, Hull (MBTA); Long Wharf-Quincy Ship Yard-Logan Airport (Harbor Express); www.mbta.com

ROSLINDALE

Boundaries: **North**: VFW Parkway and Arnold Arboretum; **East**: Forest Hills Cemetery and Mt. Hope Cemetery; **South**: Stony Brook Reservation; **West**: West Roxbury Parkway and Centre Street

CENTRE STREET
ROSLINDALE SQUARE/ROSLINDALE VILLAGE

Although Roslindale is not serviced by the subway (buses and commuter trains run here) and parts have a *very* suburban feel, it is a part of Boston. Like

JP, Roslindale, referred to affectionately as "Rozzie" (or "Roslinopoulos" for its substantial Greek population) was annexed by Boston in 1874. This area was rural until the late 1880s when streetcars were extended to Roslindale Square. Roslindale is a classic streetcar suburb and many of its homes date from one of its two building booms: the first in the 1890s and the second in the 1920s and '30s. Public churches, schools and institutional buildings built during these times are all still extant and have been the focus of the Roslindale Village Main Street program, a project sponsored by the National Trust for Historic Preservation. Amongst the utilitarian triple-deckers and low-rises added in the 20th century are some impressive examples of Gothic Revival and Empire Baroque architecture, including an enormous "summer house" on Metropolitan Avenue built by William Fox of 20th Century Fox before he lost all his money (and the house) during the Great Depression.

Roslindale is a moderate density residential area: over 75% of its housing stock consists of one to four unit buildings, usually with backyards. A good deal of housing, particularly along Washington Street, which runs the length of the neighborhood, is of the triple-decker variety with stacked balconies. An example of function over form, these homes can pack in three families but are distinctly plain, and many, especially those closer to Jamaica Plain, could use some upkeep. Then again, the **Centre Street** side of the neighborhood, closer to West Roxbury, is lined with some lovely homes. Housing options here are similar to what you might find in JP—lots of room for a good price.

Residents love Roslindale most for its quiet feel, cultural diversity, and ample green space. To the south, the Stony Brook Reservation is a 500-acre forest in the middle of the city, next to which is the George Wright Golf Course. To the north and east, Roslindale is bordered by the Arnold Arboretum and Mt. Hope Cemetery, respectively. **Roslindale Square** or **Roslindale Village** (either is correct) is the heart of the community and Washington Street serves as its commercial spine. The area between Roslindale Village (and its commuter rail stop) and the Arnold Arboretum is by far the most active part of Roslindale's real estate market.

Since there is no direct route from Roslindale into Boston, if you live here and work downtown, your commute will be plagued by back roads, traffic lights, and stop-and-go traffic. Also, public transit here isn't great. Ergo, most residents find it difficult to live in Roslindale without a car. One plus: Roslindale does not suffer the winter parking wars that most of Boston endures during the cold months, mostly because many homes have driveways.

With outstanding Greek bakeries, some decent restaurants and diners, an indoor community pool, and all of the necessary daily services—hardware stores, video stores, laundry mats—Roslindale lacks only nightlife. A plus for many.

Web Sites: www.cityofboston.gov, http://ftp.std.com/NE/roslindale, www.roslindale.net
Area Code: 617
Zip Code: 02131
Post Office: Roslindale Station, 16 Cummins Highway, 617-323-0791, www.usps.com
Police: District E-5, 1708 Centre Street, West Roxbury, 617-343-4560, www.cityofboston.gov/police
Emergency Hospital: VA Hospital, 1400 VFW Parkway, 617-323-7700, www.boston.med.va.gov; Faulkner Hospital, 1153 Centre Street, JP, 617-983-7000, www.faulknerhospital.org
Library: Roslindale Branch, 4238 Washington Street, 617-323-2343, www.bpl.org
Parks & Open Space: Arnold Arboretum (roughly bound by Centre, Morton, Walter, and South street), www.arboretum.harvard.edu; Fallon Field (between South, Walter, and Walworth streets); Franklin Park Golf Course, www.sterlinggolf.com/franklin; Franklin Park Zoo, www.zoo newengland.com, and Franklin Park (east of Arnold Arboretum); George Wright Golf Course (at West and Hautevale streets); Healy Playground (Firth Road and Washington Street); Hillside Street Play Area (roughly at Poplar Street and Delano Park); Metropolitan Avenue Urban Wild (Delano Park and East Metropolitan Avenue); West Roxbury Parkway (around the West Roxbury Parkway road, starting at the intersection of Anawan Avenue and Beech Street and heading south to the Stony Brook Reservation); Stony Brook Reservation, www.mass.gov/dcr
Public Schools: Boston Public Schools, 26 Court Street, 617-635-9000, www.bostonpublicschools.org
Community Publications: *West Roxbury and Roslindale Transcript*, 617-327-2608
Community Resources: Archdale Community Center, 125 Brookway Road, 617-635-5256; Flaherty Pool, 160 Florence Street, 617-635-5181; Roslindale Community Center (with pool), 6 Cummins Highway, 617-635-5185
Public Transportation: *Trains*: Needham Line Commuter Rail at Roslindale Village
Buses: for MBTA route and schedule information contact the MBTA Traveler's Information Center: 617-222-3200, 800-392-6100, TTY 617-222-5246 or go to www.mbta.com.

SOUTH BOSTON

Boundaries: **North**: Boston Harbor; **East**: Boston Harbor, Pleasure Bay and Castle Island; **West**: Fort Point Channel and I-93 (Southeast Expressway); **South**: Dorchester Bay and Columbus Park

SOUTH BOSTON WATERFRONT/SEAPORT DISTRICT
FORT POINT CHANNEL
LOWER SOUTH BOSTON
CITY POINT

South Boston or "Southie," as it is affectionately called, is safe and affordable, relatively close to downtown, has decent parking, is full of beaches, pubs, restaurants and stores, and has lots of Irish! In 1804 the peninsula of South Boston was annexed to Boston. The city of Boston built a bridge, connecting South Boston to downtown, and laid out the community on a grid, naming the streets by letters and numbers—a hallmark that denotes a Southie address to this day. As the 1800s rolled on, industry grew in the area and in came the immigrant laborers, most notably the Irish who stayed and made South Boston their home. Today Southie is much the same, having a substantial Irish enclave, and continuing as a first stop for many newly arrived immigrants. Although, as is the case with the North End neighborhood, many locals would prefer to have the neighborhood remain entrenched in its solid ethnic heritage and customs, Southie is becoming increasingly popular with young professionals of non-Irish descent.

Essentially, South Boston can be divided in half: between the **South Boston Waterfront**, also known as the **Seaport District** (both names are bandied about for this developing neighborhood), and then the rest of South Boston—what most people mean when they say "Southie." The South Boston Waterfront/Seaport District covers the northern portion of South Boston and lies just across the channel from downtown Boston and South Station, bordered by Boston Harbor to the north and Fort Point Channel to the west. The city plans to develop a mixed-use area of the South Boston Waterfront/Seaport District. Currently there are a few places of interest here for tourists, but the bulk of the Seaport District/South Boston Waterfront is industrial. Designs call for more offices, condos, apartments, stores, parks, a convention center and maybe even a stadium. At present, the Museum Wharf between the Congress Street and Northern Avenue Bridges is a tourist hot spot with the Children's Museum and the Boston Tea Party Ship and Museum. To the north along the harbor you will find the new US Federal Courthouse on Fan Pier, the World Trade Center on Commonwealth Pier, and the Harborlights Pavillion on Wharf 8. Fish

Pier is where much of the local catch comes in each day. Many restaurants in the area capitalize on their waterfront location, bringing in locals and tourists alike to their selections of fresh fish, shellfish, and beer. None are so popular as Anthony's Pier 4 or Jimmy's Harborside (on Northern Avenue by Fish Pier). The sub-section of the South Boston Waterfront/Seaport District that abuts the channel is sometimes referred to as **Fort Point Channel**, which is similar to the Leather District with which it is virtually contiguous. Those who move here often use the warehouses for both work and living space; it's particularly popular with artists.

The rest of South Boston is less glitzy than the Waterfront area. Here is the bastion of Boston's traditional Irish, and accordingly, home of the city's annual St. Patrick's Day Parade. Like East Boston, Southie is full of triple-deckers and rowhouses, but somehow the buildings seem to have weathered the years better here than in Eastie. The main strip, Broadway, is host to a healthy mix of commercial and residential activity. West Broadway covers "**Lower Southie**," closer to downtown Boston where the homes are packed more tightly together and parts appear very industrial. If you travel east on Broadway (until it becomes East Broadway), you will encounter more contemporary construction, including condos and apartment complexes from the 1960s, mixed in with Victorian bowfronts and clapboard homes. Once you reach the **City Point** neighborhood by Pleasure Bay, the homes, most built in the last 100 years, are spacious and have lawns. Film buffs may enjoy knowing that the L Street Tavern here was the local bar in the film *Good Will Hunting*.

Southie is a practical place to live. One-bedroom apartments are reasonably priced, and all the services you need are nearby, including, of course, authentic Irish pubs. While it cannot rival JP with all its green space, Southie has cornered the market on beaches: four to be exact. Good for walks and safe for swimming, the oceanfront at City Point and Southie's south shore attract local residents as well as those from elsewhere in the city. Every New Year's Day the "L Street Brownies" depart from the Curley Recreational Facility or "L Street Bathhouse" to one of these beaches for their yearly polar bear dip. Of note on Castle Island, at the northern tip of Pleasure Bay, is Fort Independence. Built in 1779 at the command of George Washington, this five-bastioned granite fortification in the shape of a pentagon provided the inspiration for Edgar Allan Poe's *The Cask of Amontillado*. It is open to the public, and there are guided tours every weekend during the summer. And, lest you think Olmstead left this section of Boston entirely untouched, you will be relieved to learn that he is responsible for the Strandway, the strip of green from Castle Island to Columbus Park.

South Boston's proximity to downtown as well as its affordability has made it very appealing for some professional types who like the easy commute to work and an easier time finding parking. For those who prefer public transportation, Southie is accessible, but a little complicated. The Red Line only services Lower Southie with the Andrew and Broadway stops. But buses do cover the rest of the Southie expanse and run all the way down to City Point.

Web Sites: www.cityofboston.gov, www.southbostononline.com, www.adaptenv.org/seaport, www.bostonmainstreets.com/south
Area Code: 617
Zip Codes: 02210, 02127
Post Offices: South Boston Station, 444 East 3rd Street, 617-269-9948; Fort Point Station, 25 Dorchester Avenue, 617-654-5302; www.usps.com
Police: District C-6, 101 West Broadway, 617-343-4730, www.cityofboston.gov/police
Emergency Hospitals: Mass General Hospital, 55 Fruit Street, 617-726-2000, www.mgh.harvard.edu; New England Medical Center, 750 Washington Street, 617-636-5000, www.nemc.org
Libraries: South Boston Branch, 646 East Broadway, 617-268-0180; Washington Village Branch, 1226 Columbia Road, 617-269-7239; www.bpl.org
Parks & Open Space: Carson Beach (off of William J. Day Boulevard and Columbus Park); Castle Island-Fort Independence (at the northern tip of William J. Day Boulevard at East Lane); City Point Beach (Columbia Road and the harbor, just south of Pleasure Bay); Columbus Park (east of Columbia Road, north of the border with Dorchester on Old Harbor); Independence Square (bound by 1st, 2nd, M, N, and Acadia streets and Brodway); L Street Beach (at Columbia Road and L Street on the harbor); M Street Beach (M Street and William J. Day Boulevard at the harbor); Marine Park (William J. Day Boulevard and Broadway on Pleasure Bay); Thomas Park/Telegraph Hill (between Telegraph, East Sixth, Old Harbor and G streets)
Public Schools: Boston Public Schools, 26 Court Street, 617-635-9000, www.bostonpublicschools.org
Community Publications: *The Irish Emigrant*, 617-268-8322; *South Boston Tribune*, 617-268-3440, www.southbostoninfo.com
Community Resources: Condon Community Center, 200 D Street, 617-635-5100; Curley Community Center, 1663 Columbia Road, 617-635-5104; PAL/Walsh McDonough Gym Community Center, 535 East Broadway, 617-635-5640; Tynan Community Center, 650 East 4th Street, 617-635-5110; Boston Children's Museum, 300 Congress Street, 617-426-8855, www.bostonkids.org; Boston Tea Party Ship and Museum, Congress Street Bridge, 617-338-1773, www.bostonteapartyship.com; World Trade Center, 1 Seaport Lane, 800-367-9822, www.wtcb.com; St. Patrick's Day Parade; Seaport Alliance for a

Neighborhood Design, 617-423-4299, www.bostonseaport.com; South Boston Neighborhood House, 521 East Seventh Street, www.sbnh.org

Public Transportation: *Trains*: Red Line and Commuter Rail at South Station; Red Line at Broadway and Andrew

Buses: for MBTA route and schedule information contact the MBTA Traveler's Information Center: 617-222-3200, 800-392-6100, TTY 617-222-5246 or go to www.mbta.com.

SOUTH END/BAY VILLAGE

Boundaries: *South End* (roughly): **North**: I-90 (Mass Turnpike); **East and Southeast**: Albany Street/I-93 (Fitzgerald Expressway); **South**: Melnea Cass Boulevard; **West and Southwest**: Huntington Avenue/Mass Ave./Southwest Corridor; *Bay Village*: **North**: Stuart Street; **East**: Charles Street South; **South**: Cortes Street and Marginal Road; **West**: Berkeley Street

SOUTH END
BAY VILLAGE

A note to newcomers: when a Bostonian says "Southie," it is a reference to South Boston (see above), *not* the South End. Home to an ethnically diverse population and center of Boston's gay community, the South End is located between the Back Bay to the north, the Fenway to the west, Roxbury and I-93 to the south, and Bay Village, Chinatown and the Theater District to the east. It is also the largest neighborhood of intact Victorian rowhouses in the US, according to the National Register of Historic Places. Like the Back Bay, the **South End** is the product of yet another of Boston's landfill projects initiated to create land to cope with Boston's continuing expansion in the 1800s. In 1834 the city began filling in the mudflats around Boston Neck (used at the time as an execution ground). Developed as a neighborhood suitable for Boston's elite, the South End was designed with homes clustered around small parks in the style of redbrick Georgian bowfronts with grand stoops and latticework railings, balconies, and window boxes. Within a generation, however, the South End was no longer the chic spot for the wealthy. Residents, many of them of the rich mercantile class, moved from the South End to the more recently developed Back Bay with its grand boulevards and French style architecture. Thus began the story of South End's immigrant history. Over the next hundred or so years, Irish, Jews, Italians, Chinese, Greeks, Syrians, Lebanese, Hispanics, and African-Americans came, many attracted by the low rent lodging houses into which the mansions had been converted. By the 1950s, an active African-American community gave birth to Boston's jazz scene. One remnant, Wally's Café, a hole-in-the-wall jazz club near the Mass Ave. T stop, has survived since 1947 and still earns rave reviews from Boston's music aficionados.

These days the trendy and artsy South End is back in favor as one of Boston's most sought-after addresses, on par with the North End and just slightly less coveted than Beacon Hill or the Back Bay. Not your stereotypical Boston neighborhood, the South End is a visible amalgam of the phases it has experienced, managing to gentrify while maintaining the imprints of many who have come before. In a city that continues to be ethnically and socio-economically divided, the South End is a melting pot of residents. You'll find multigenerational families, artists, students, and professionals, not to mention the gay population, particularly gay men, that has pretty much made the South End its "official" home. On the busy Tremont Street, rainbow flags dominate, signaling the many gay-friendly stores, restaurants, bars, and services.

Many sub-regions actually comprise the South End, often evolving around the squares and parks they surround. At last count, 18 neighborhood associations claimed mini-sections. Newcomers should note that some of these sub-regions are distinctly safer than others; in particular, muggings and car breaks are not uncommon, and prostitution and drug dealing is still a problem in the southernmost parts between Washington and Albany streets. Tremont Street serves as South End's rough divider between the safer (north of Tremont, towards the Back Bay) and seedier sides (south of Tremont, towards Roxbury). What this also means is that the real estate south of Tremont is slightly more affordable than that on the north side of Tremont. The sub-neighborhoods north of Tremont Street include St. Botolph, Cosmopolitan, Claremont, Ellis, Pilot Block, and Rutland Square. **St. Botolph** corresponds to the upscale area of neatly manicured rowhouses just behind Copley and the Pru, around St. Botolph's Street between Mass Ave. and the Mass Pike. **Cosmopolitan** includes the blocks heading east from the Back Bay Station between Carleton and West Newton streets and Columbus Avenue. **Claremont** covers the square section from Claremont Street to Tremont Street, from West Newton Street to Gainsborough Street, with the exception of **Rutland Square**, which is its own sub-neighborhood. Claremont, Cosmopolitan, and Rutland Square are all more expensive and desirable parts of the South End, although Claremont becomes slightly dodgier as you pass Mass Ave. heading west. **Ellis** is the fashionable area between the Mass Pike to the east and West Canton Street to the west, bound by busy Columbus Avenue and Tremont Street on the north and south, respectively. This sub-region includes several of the hip South End commercial establishments, some of its most picturesque streets such as the irresistible Appleton Street, and the substantial Boston Center for the Arts. Between Ellis and Claremont, is **Pilot Block**, which encompasses more of the commercial attractions on these main streets.

Sub-sections south of Tremont include Castle Square, Eight Streets, Union Park, Old Dover, Bradford, Inquilinos Boricuas En Acción/Villa Victoria, Rutland Street, West Concord Street, Hurley Block, Chester Square, Worcester Square, and Franklin-Blackstone. From the Pike to East Berkeley Street between Tremont Street and Shawmut Avenue is **Castle Square**, a relatively industrial region around the Herald building on the South End's border with Chinatown. East Berkeley Street to Waltham Street, from Tremont Street to Shawmut Avenue is the residential **Eight Streets**. Just west is **Union Park**, a rectangular sub-region from Tremont Street south to Harrison Avenue, around the oval-shaped park of the same name. The section of Union Park directly around the park itself is reasonably sought-after, but a block further Washington Street looks stripped after an elevated transit system was torn down in the 1980s and nothing was rebuilt in its place. In an effort to revive the southern portion of the South End, and Washington Street in particular, the Boston Redevelopment Authority has ideas for projects ranging from affordable to luxury housing in this area. In addition, the T has instituted the new Silver Line, an articulated bus system that runs along the Washington Street corridor. From Shawmut Avenue to the Pike, between Waltham Street and the South End's southern boundary with I-93, is a fairly large, quiet, residential neighborhood called **Old Dover**, although the portion directly around Bradford Street between Shawmut Avenue and Washington Street is actually called **Bradford**. Next to Union Park is **Inquilinos Boricuas En Acción/Villa Victoria**. Bound roughly by Upton, West Newton and Tremont streets and Shawmut Avenue, **Villa Victoria** has a large Puerto Rican population. The Catholic Cathedral of the Holy Cross is on Washington Street and is New England's largest cathedral. Continuing in a southwesterly direction from Villa Victoria are three sub-neighborhoods only a street long: **Rutland Street**, **West Concord Street**, and **Hurley Block**. **Chester Square**, at the southwestern edge of South End by Roxbury, from West Springfield to Lenox streets, and Tremont to Washington, surrounds Chester Park. Just south of Chester Square at the southwesternmost tip of the South End is **Worcester Square**, bound by Lenox, Washington, Albany, Concord, and East Brookline streets and Harrison Avenue. It encompasses both Worcester Park and the campus of the Boston University Medical Center, which illuminates Harrison Avenue. The final sub-region in the South End is **Franklin-Blackstone**, so named for the adjacent Franklin and Blackstone squares that crop in either direction from Washington Street. Franklin-Blackstone cuts into Worcester Square, bordering on the medical campus. Despite all of the hospital-related activity and green space, Worcester Square, Chester Square, and Franklin-Blackstone are sub-neighborhoods with an edgier reputation.

Overall, the character of the South End varies from block to block, with some streets looking posh and gorgeous and others reminiscent of cramped and down-trodden late 19th century rowhouses. However, thanks to the active South End Historical Society, in general the quality of the interior of the homes throughout the South End is good. A South End apartment or home means a majestic stoop, with ornate cast iron railings. Unfortunately, many of the single-family Victorian brownstones were separated into apartments. Some are spacious, however, with exposed brick walls, hardwood floors, and roof decks. It's not unheard of to find an apartment with working fireplace and original architectural detailing.

T service to the South End isn't as comprehensive as it is for other neighborhoods, and you may have a bit of a hike to the Back Bay/South End or Mass Ave. T stop. Bus service does supplement the T and the new Silver Line has been added. Car owners are blessed with easy access to the Mass Pike and I-93. Parking in the South End is a hassle and usually requires a resident permit, although it's not quite as difficult as in the Back Bay, Beacon Hill, or the North End.

The South End is home to plenty of green space, thanks to its English-inspired design. One park, Peters Park, is dog-friendly. The Southwest Corridor, a four mile pedestrian and bike path with public tennis and basketball courts, a children's playground, and public gardening plots, stretches from the Mass Ave. T stop all the way to Roxbury. Specialty boutiques, trendy eateries, and bars, many on Tremont Street, attract people from all over the city. In addition to having all the conveniences of city living—dry cleaners, hardware stores, drug stores, corner markets—Copley Square is just as accessible to the South End as it is to the Back Bay. The symphony area is a hop, skip and a jump to the corner of Huntington and Mass Ave. South Enders in search of artistic entertainment need not stray as far as that, since many artists live and work here and exhibit for the public every September during the South End Open Studios weekend. Many of these studios are in the Boston Center for the Arts (BCA), located between Tremont, Clarendon, and Berkeley streets and Warren Avenue.

Just north of the South End, stuffed between the Back Bay and the Theater District, lies **Bay Village**, a neighborhood so tiny, quiet, and unassuming that most Bostonians would swear there is no such place. Almost entirely residential, Bay Village covers an expanse of just six blocks, with only about 700 residents. Bay Village has two notable claims to fame. First, it is the birthplace of Edgar Allan Poe, and second, Boston's worst disaster happened here. On November 28, 1942, fire engulfed a popular nightclub called the Coconut Grove. With a jammed revolving door, four locked doors, and two doors that opened inward, 492 of the club's patrons were trapped inside and perished. As a result, country-wide regulations were passed requiring all doors in public buildings to open outwards.

Today Bay Village looks like a mix of all of Boston's grander neighborhoods thrown together—a combination of sturdy colonials with grand

Victorians. Red brick buildings with painted shutters and some wrought iron work are common here. Mostly the neighborhood is solidly residential, upscale, tucked away, and cozy, but the boundary with the Theater District around the vicinity of Charles Street South and Stuart Street, feels a little more exposed and edgy. The tiny Bay Village is privy to the nearby amenities of the South End, Back Bay, and Chinatown.

Web Sites: www.cityofboston.gov, www.southend.org, www.bostonez.org/about/southend, www.bayvillage.net, www.southend.org/associations

Area Code: 617

Zip Code: 02118, 02111

Post Offices: Cathedral Station, 59 West Dedham Street, 617-266-0989; Back Bay Annex Station, 390 Stuart Street, 617-236-7800; Astor Station, 207 Mass Ave., 617-247-2429; Prudential Center Post Office, 800 Boylston Street, 617-267-4164, www.usps.com

Police: District D-4, 650 Harrison Avenue, 617-343-4250, www.cityofboston.gov/police

Emergency Hospitals: BU Medical Center (formerly Boston City Hospital), 88 East Newton Street and 840 Harrison Avenue, 617-638-5000, www.bumc.bu.edu; New England Medical Center, 755 Washington Street, 617-636-5566, www.nemc.org

Libraries: South End Branch, 685 Tremont Street, 617-536-8241; Central Library, Copley Square, 700 Boylston Street, 617-536-5400; www.bpl.org

Parks & Open Space: Blackstone Square (between Shawmut Avenue and Washington, West Newton and West Brookline streets); Chester Park (Mass Ave. between Tremont Street and Shawmut Avenue); Franklin Square (between West Newton, West Brookline, Washington and St. George streets); Peters Park (at Washington and Wilkes streets); Southwest Corridor Park (covers 4.2 miles from Copley Place at Dartmouth Street to Roxbury); Union Park (Union Park Street between Tremont Street and Shawmut Avenue); Worcester Square (Worcester Street between Washington Street and Harrison Avenue)

Public Schools: Boston Public Schools, 26 Court Street, 617-635-9000, www.bostonpublicschools.org

Community Publications: *Bay Windows* and *South End News*, 617-266-6670, www.baywindows.com

Community Resources: Blackstone Community Center, 50 West Brookline Street, 617-635-5162; Boston Center for the Arts (BCA), 539 Tremont Street, 617-426-5000, www.bcaonline.org; Boston Center for Adult Education: Studio 122, 122 Arlington Street, 617-267-4430, www.bcae.org; Benjamin Franklin Institute of Technology, 41 Berkeley

Street, 617-423-4630, www.bfit.edu; South End Historical Society, 532 Mass Ave., 617-536-4445, www.southendhistoricalsociety.org; Inquilinos Boricuas En Acción, 617-927-1707, www.iba-etc.org

Public Transportation: *South End*: **Trains**: Orange Line at Back Bay/South End or Mass Ave.

Buses: #1 (Harvard/Holyoke Gate-Dudley Square via Mass Ave. and BU Medical Center); #8 (Harbor Point/UMASS-Kenmore Station via South End Medical Area and Dudley Station; #9 (City Point-Copley Square via Broadway Station); #10 (City Point-Copley Square via Andrew Station and Boston Medical Area); #39 (Forest Hills-Back Bay Station via Huntington Avenue); #43 (Ruggles Station-Park and Tremont Streets); #47 (Central Square, Cambridge–Broadway Station via South End Medical Center, Dudley Station and Longwood Medical Area); Silver Line Bus (Dudley Square-Downtown Boston via Washington Street); for MBTA route and schedule information contact the MBTA Traveler's Information Center: 617-222-3200, 800-392-6100, TTY 617-222-5246 or go to www.mbta.com.

Bay Village: **Trains**: Green Line at Arlington; Orange Line at New England Medical Center

Buses: #9 (City Point–Copley Square via Broaday Station); #39 (Forest Hills–Back Bay Station via Huntington Ave.); #43 (Ruggles Station via Park and Tremont Streets); #55 (Jersey and Queensberry–Copley Square or Tremont and Park Streets via Ipswich Street); for MBTA route and schedule information contact the MBTA Traveler's Information Center: 617-222-3200, 800-392-6100, TTY 617-222-5246 or go to www.mbta.com.

WEST ROXBURY

Boundaries: **North**: Allandale Street; **East**: West Roxbury Parkway and Centre Street; **South** and **West**: Suffolk County Line

West Roxbury and Roslindale were once part of Roxbury. Initially the area was sparsely settled by farming families; later wealthy Boston families built their summer estates here. In 1851, West Roxbury seceded from Roxbury, bringing Jamaica Plain and Roslindale along with it. In 1874, West Roxbury was officially annexed to Boston.

The oldest private grammar school in the country, the Roxbury Latin School established in 1645, is located here. Also in West Roxbury is Brook Farm, the utopian experimental community created in the 1840s by Bronson Alcott (Louisa May's father) and his following of transcendentalists. Today West Roxbury is Boston's most suburban-feeling neighborhood with a predominantly white population, median age 41 years (median age in Boston is 31.1 according to the 2000 Census), of middle- to upper-middle class means. The homes here are nice, the city services efficient, and the streets mostly crime free. An unsung Irish Catholic enclave here may well outnumber those in either Southie or Charlestown. More like Brookline than Boston, West Roxbury is more expensive than Jamaica Plain and Roslindale but less expensive than Newton and Brookline. West Roxburyans by and large live in single-family homes covering the gamut of architectural styles from the 1800s and 1900s: Queen Annes, Tudors, Gothic Revivals, etc., with big backyards and ample parking. It also has some 1960s style apartment complexes and cute condo developments interspersed throughout. Washington Street is where you'll find restaurant chains and gas stations, and Centre Street offers a quaint mix of new storefronts as well as a Roche Bros. Supermarket.

As in Roslindale, getting to downtown Boston from West Roxbury is not easy; residents must make use of the bus or the commuter rail (West Roxbury has three stops, as opposed to Roslindale's one), or else drive into the city through circuitous routes like the VFW Parkway or city roads like Centre and Washington streets.

Web Sites: www.cityofboston.gov, www.westroxbury.com, www.bostonmainstreets.com/WestRoxbury
Area Code: 617
Zip Code: 02132
Post Office: West Roxbury Station, 1970 Centre Street, 617-325-4043, www.usps.com
Police: District E-5, 1708 Centre Street, 343-4560, www.cityofboston.gov/police
Emergency Hospitals: Faulkner Hospital, 1153 Centre Street, JP, 617-983-7000, www.faulknerhospital.org; VA Hospital, 1400 VFW Parkway, 617-323-7700, www.boston.med.va.gov
Library: West Roxbury Branch, 1961 Centre Street, 617-325-3147, www.bpl.org
Parks & Open Space: Bellvue Hill Reservation (at Bellevue Hill Road, the West Roxbury Parkway, and Washington and LaGrange streets); Billings Field (between Quinn Way, Sturges Road, and LaGrange and Bellevue streets); Westerly Burying Ground (between LaGrange and Centre streets and Chapin Avenue); West Roxbury Parkway (around the West Roxbury Parkway road, starting at the intersection of Anawan Avenue and Beech Street and heading south to the Stony Brook Reservation); Stony Brook Reservation, www.mass.gov/dcr
Public Schools: Boston Public Schools, 26 Court Street, 617-635-9000, www.bostonpublicschools.org

Community Publication: *West Roxbury and Roslindale Transcript*, 617-327-2608

Community Resources: West Roxbury YMCA, www.ymcaboston.org; Draper Pool, 5275 Washington Street, 617-635-5021; Ohrenberger Community Center, 175 West Boundary Road, 617-635-5183; Roche Community Center, 1716 Centre Street, 617-635-5066; West Roxbury Community Center, 1205 VFW Parkway, 617-635-5066

Public Transportation: ***Trains***: Needham Line of Commuter Rail at West Roxbury, Highland and Bellevue

Buses: #35 (Dedham Mall/Stimston Street-Forest Hills via Belgrade Avenue and Centre Street); #36 (Charles River Loop or VA Hospital-Forest Hills via Belgrade Avenue and Centre Street); #37 (Baker and Vermont Streets-Forest Hills via Belgrade Avenue and Centre Street); #38 (Wren Street-Forest Hills via Centre and South Streets); #51 (Cleveland Circle-Forest Hlls via Hancock Village); for MBTA route and schedule information contact the MBTA Traveler's Information Center: 617-222-3200, 800-392-6100, TTY 617-222-5246 or go to www.mbta.com.

ALSO IN SUFFOLK COUNTY

The three other cities to share Suffolk County with Boston:

- **Chelsea**; small, multicultural working class industrial inner suburb three miles north of Boston bordered by the Mystic River and the Chelsea River. Features good views of downtown Boston and quick access to the city and the airport via Route 1. No T stops here, but it does have the commuter rail and bus service. City homepage: www.ci.chelsea.ma.us; municipal offices: 617-889-8200.
- **Revere**; a large, working-class community just five miles north of Boston. Has easy access to the airport and city via the Blue Line (Beachmont, Revere Beach, and Wonderland stops), and by vehicle on routes 1 and 1A. Has the country's oldest public beach (Revere Beach), as well as a Showcase Cinemas movie theater, the Wonderland greyhound race tracks, and shares Suffolk Downs with East Boston. City homepage: www.revere.org; community page: www.revere.com; municipal offices: 781-286-8100.
- **Winthrop**; working- to middle-class neighborhood on a peninsula jutting into the Atlantic just northeast of East Boston and southeast of Revere. Somewhat more isolated than the other surrounding neighborhoods as no major highways serve Winthrop; you must access it via Route 1A in Revere or East Boston. No T or commuter rail service, only bus. Many beaches and beachfront property as well as close access to the airport, although noise from the planes can be a problem here. Municipal offices: 617-846-1742.

SURROUNDING COMMUNITIES

Over Boston's nearly four centuries of existence, the city has annexed many neighboring communities. However, while cities such as Chicago, New Orleans, and even London took over neighboring areas as they grew, in Boston, a significant number of metropolitan communities managed to resist annexation. Thus, Brookline, Somerville, Medford, Cambridge, and Watertown, while integral to the fabric of the Boston metropolitan area, maintain their political individuality. As a newcomer, you probably won't notice when you're crossing from one town to another. As a result, when locals refer to living, working, or going out in "Boston" or "the city," the statement warrants qualification: they may just as easily be referring to Cambridge as they are the Back Bay.

Where Boston and some of the surrounding communities differ is cost of living. A neighboring town such as Arlington or Waltham may be substantially more affordable and just as feasible a living option, especially since many are served by the T. The following communities are arranged by counties—Middlesex then Norfolk—and the cities within are arranged alphabetically. All cities and towns that share a border with Boston are profiled.

MIDDLESEX COUNTY

ARLINGTON

Boundaries: **North**: Winchester and Medford; **East**: Cambridge and Somerville; **South**: Belmont and Cambridge; **West**: Lexington

EAST ARLINGTON
ARLINGTON CENTER
ARLINGTON HEIGHTS

Arlington, located on the western perimeter of metro Boston and covering only five and a half square miles, is a nice residential area with a dense population of over 40,000. Not long ago it was profiled in *Boston Magazine* as one of Boston's safest neighborhoods. Arlington is popular with those who don't want to live in downtown, but still want easy access to the city or Cambridge.

Originally part of Cambridge, Arlington was first known as Menotomy then West Cambridge, finally becoming Arlington in 1867. Many historically and architecturally significant homes survive in Arlington, which has seven historic districts. Along Battle Road are colonial houses with Revolutionary

War connections. Arlington also features a variety of 19th century housing, including Victorians along Mass Ave. and Pleasant Street, and workers' cottages along Mill Brook. As with many of Boston's outlying communities, Arlington underwent a building boom in the late 1800s, spurred when public transportation was extended out from Boston's center.

From east to west, Arlington's three regions are known as **East Arlington**, **Arlington Center**, and **Arlington Heights**, which borders Lexington. Arlington is less expensive than Belmont and Lexington, and it is home to many renters who enjoy the safe, residential reputation. Newcomers seeking nightlife should note that there are only four existing liquor licenses belonging to restaurants that seat 100 people. Although there are some small restaurants (all of which are smoke-free) and shops in Arlington, especially in Arlington Center, there are no real corner bars and cafes. Community resources here include the theater group, Arlington Friends of the Drama, the Arlington Philharmonic Society, and a second-run movie house, the Capitol Theatre at 204 Mass Ave. For nightlife, residents generally head down Mass Ave. to Cambridge. There are three malls in the immediate area: Meadow-Glen Mall in Medford, Fresh Pond Mall in Cambridge and Arsenal Mall in Watertown (see **Shopping for the Home**).

With seven elementary schools, Arlington is an attractive choice for young families. The town also features a swimming area at Arlington Reservoir on the town border with Lexington between Mass Ave. and Route 2A; Menotomy Rocks Park is located just northwest of the intersection of routes 2 and 60, and the Minuteman Bikeway goes right through town. Just northeast of the intersection of routes 2 and 50 and south of Mass Ave. is the lovely kettlehole, Spy Pond.

Public transportation is available in or near Arlington: the Red Line terminus at the Alewife T Station is on the border of Arlington and Cambridge; the commuter rail stops in neighboring Belmont; and buses run throughout town. For those with cars, Arlington is close to I-93. Overnight on-street parking is not allowed, so make sure your new place includes a parking spot. For guests, the police department should be notified to avoid being ticketed.

Web Sites: www.arlington-mass.com, www.town.arlington.ma.us
Area Code: 781
Zip Codes: 02474-02476
Post Offices: Arlington Branch, 10 Court Street, 781-648-5376; Arlington Heights Branch, 1347 Mass Ave., 781-643-3888; East Arlington Branch, 240 Mass Ave., 781-643-4482; www.usps.com
Police: Community Safety Building, 112 Mystic Street, 781-316-3900, www.town.arlington.ma.us/pd/indexapd.htm
Emergency Hospitals: The Cambridge Hospital, 1493 Cambridge Street, 617-665-1000, www.challiance.org; Mt. Auburn Hospital, 330 Mt.

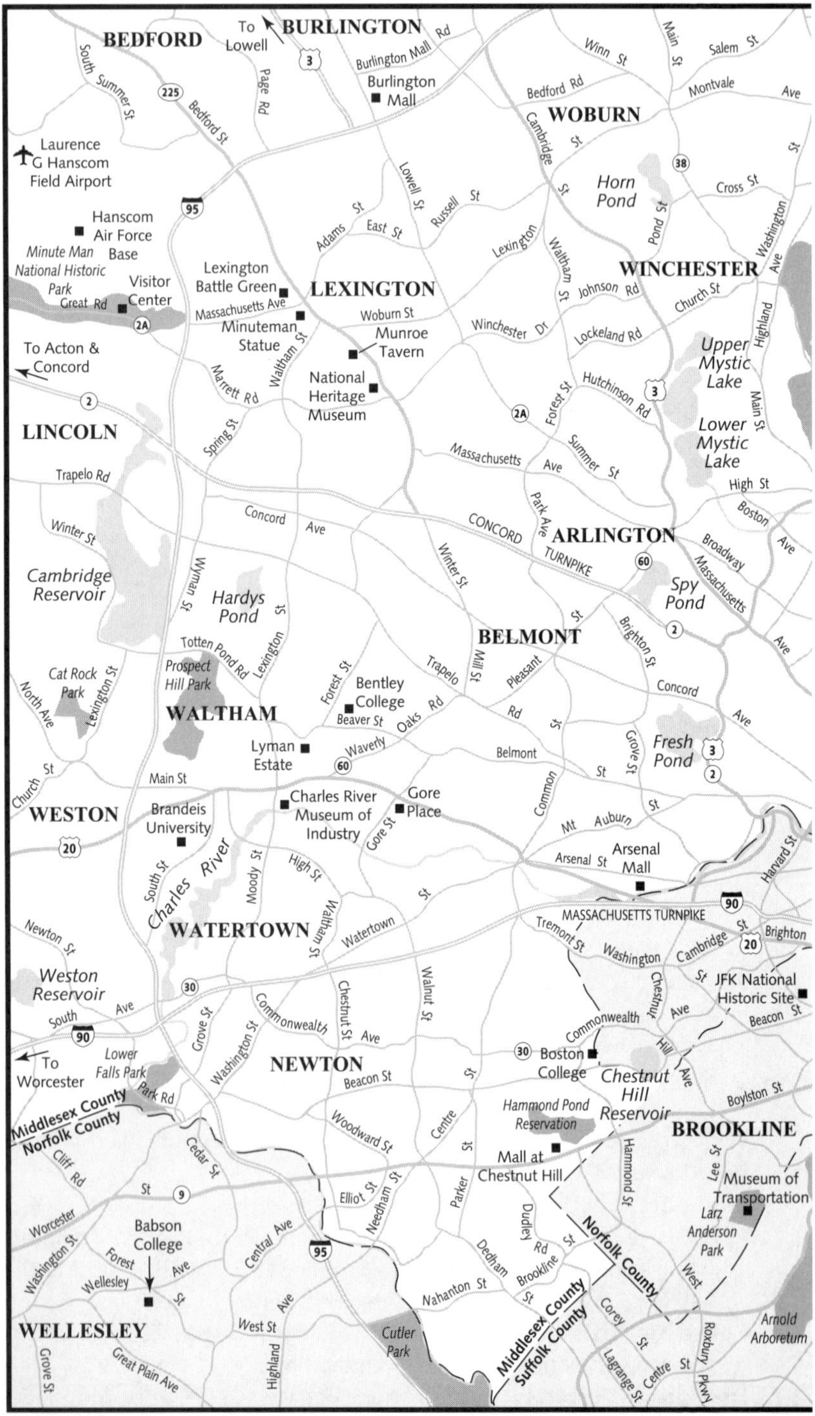

BEDFORD
To Lowell
BURLINGTON
South Summer St
225
Bedford St
Page Rd
3
Burlington Mall Rd
Burlington Mall
Winn St
Main St
Salem St
Bedford Rd
Montvale Ave
WOBURN
Cambridge St
Laurence G Hanscom Field Airport
95
Lowell St
Russell St
38
Horn Pond
Pond St
Cross St
Washington Ave
Hanscom Air Force Base
Minute Man National Historic Park
Adams St
East St
Lexington
Waltham St
Lexington Battle Green
LEXINGTON
WINCHESTER
Visitor Center
Great Rd
2A
Massachusetts Ave
Minuteman Statue
Woburn St
Munroe Tavern
Johnson Rd
Church St
Winchester Dr
Lockeland Rd
Highland
Upper Mystic Lake
To Acton & Concord
Marrett Rd
National Heritage Museum
Hutchinson Rd
Forest St
2
LINCOLN
Spring St
Main St
Lower Mystic Lake
Massachusetts Ave
Summer St
Trapelo Rd
High St
Concord Ave
Park Ave
Boston Ave
CONCORD TURNPIKE
ARLINGTON
Winter St
Broadway
Massachusetts Ave
60
Spy Pond
Cambridge Reservoir
Wyman St
Hardys Pond
Lexington St
St
Brighton St
BELMONT
Totten Pond Rd
Prospect Hill Park
Mill St
Pleasant St
Cat Rock Park
Lexington St
Trapelo Rd
Concord Ave
North Ave
Forest St
Bentley College
WALTHAM
Beaver St
Oaks Rd
Fresh Pond
Grove St
Lyman Estate
Waverly
Belmont St
Church St
Main St
Charles River Museum of Industry
Gore Place
Common
Mt Auburn St
WESTON
Brandeis University
Gore St
20
Arsenal St
Arsenal Mall
Harvard St
Charles River
Moody St
High St
South St
Waltham St
MASSACHUSETTS TURNPIKE
90
Brighton
Newton St
WATERTOWN
Watertown St
Tremont St
Washington St
Cambridge St
Chestnut Hill Ave
Weston Reservoir
30
Chestnut St
Walnut St
JFK National Historic Site
South Ave
Commonwealth Ave
Beacon St
Grove St
Washington St
Commonwealth
To Worcester
Lower Falls Park
NEWTON
Boston College
Chestnut Hill Reservoir
Park Rd
Beacon St
Boylston St
Middlesex County
Norfolk County
Woodward St
Centre St
Hammond Pond Reservation
Hammond St
BROOKLINE
Cedar St
Cliff Rd
Mall at Chestnut Hill
Lee St
Museum of Transportation
9
Elliot St
Needham St
Parker St
Larz Anderson Park
Worcester
Babson College
Central Ave
Dudley Rd
Norfolk County
Washington St
Forest Ave
Dedham
Brookline St
West
Wellesley St
Nahanton St
Middlesex County
Suffolk County
Corey St
Arnold Arboretum
WELLESLEY
West St
Highland Ave
Cutler Park
Roxbury Pkwy
Grove St
Great Plain Ave
Lagrange St
Centre St

MIDDLESEX COUNTY

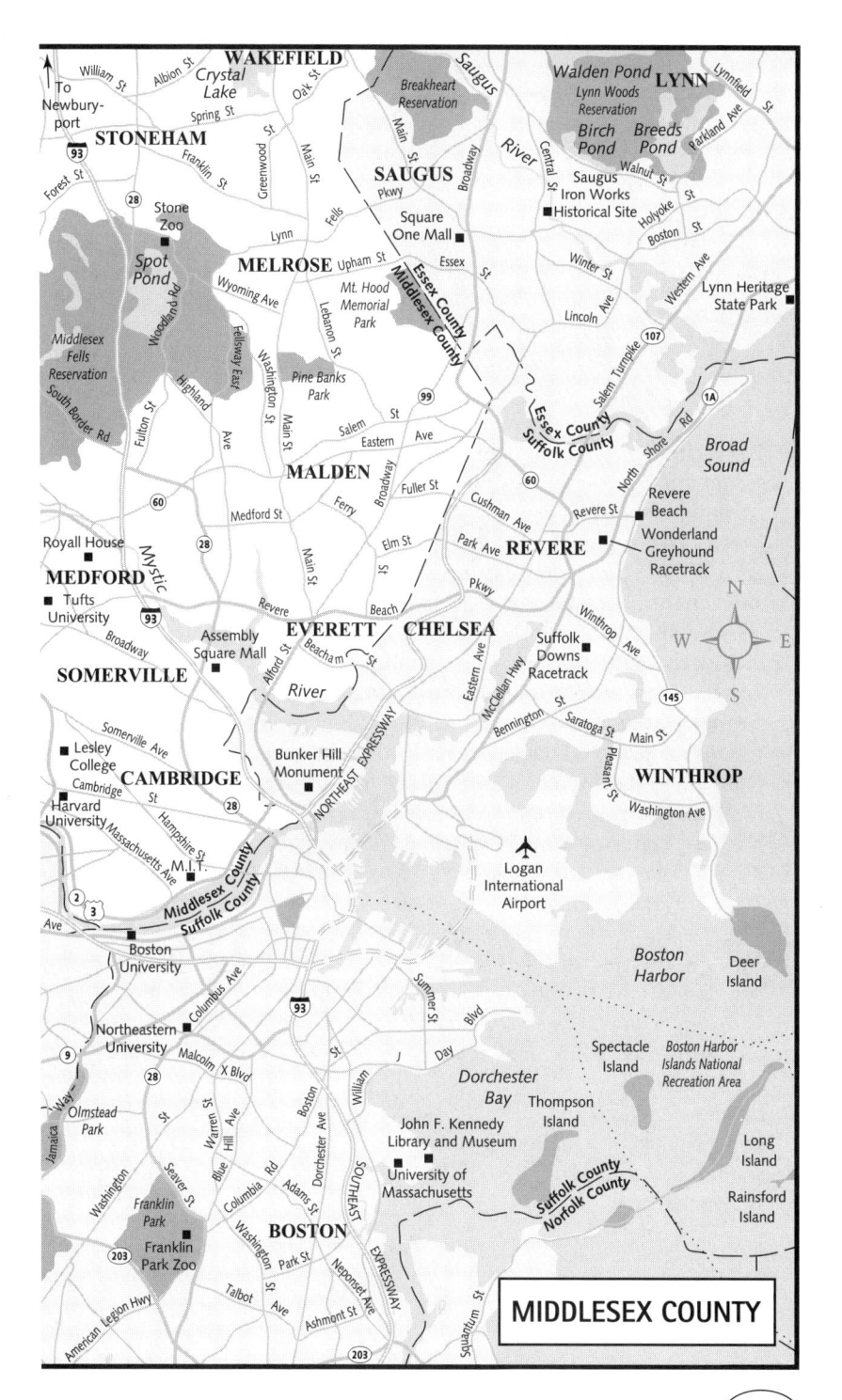

Auburn Street, Cambridge, 617-492-3500, www.mountauburn.caregroup.org; Somerville Hospital, 230 Highland Avenue, Somerville, 617-591-4500, www.challiance.org

Libraries: Robbins Library, 700 Mass Ave., 781-316-3200; Fox Branch, 175 Mass Ave., 781-316-3198; www.robbinslibrary.org

Parks & Open Space: Alewife Brook Reservation, www.mass.gov/dcr; Hill's Pond and Menotomy Rocks Park (near the border with Belmont at Spring Street and Menotomy Rocks Road); Minuteman Bikeway; Spy Pond and Field (northeast of the intersection of routes 60 and 2); Arlington Heights Playground (at the border with Lexington, north of Mass Ave.); Arlington Reservoir (on the border with Lexington, south of Lowell Street); Turkey Hill Reservation (northern Arlington, near Dodge Street and Carl Road); Upper and Lower Mystic Lake (northeast Arlington border, between Route 3 and the Mystic Valley Parkway); Mystic River (south of the Mystic Lakes along the Mystic Valley Parkway); Robbins Farm Park, www.robbinsfarmpark.org

Public Schools: Arlington Public Schools, 869 Mass Ave., 781-316-3501, www.arlington.k12.ma.us

Community Publication: *The Arlington Advocate*, 781-643-7900, www.townonline.com/arlington/news.html

Community Resources: Arlington Chamber of Commerce, www.arlingtoncc.org; Whittemore-Robbins House, 670 R Mass Ave., 781-316-3260; Old Schwamb Mill, 17 Mill Lane, 781-643-0640; George A. Smith Museum/Jason Russel House, 7 Jason Street, 781-648-4300; Dallin Art Museum/Jefferson Cutter House, 631 Mass Ave., 781-641-0747; Capitol Theater, 204 Mass Ave., 781-648-4340; Regent/Bombay Theater (Indian films), 7 Medford Street, 781-646-4849; Arlington Historical Society, www.arlingtonhistorical.org; Arlington Center for the Arts, www.acarts.org; Arlington Friends of the Drama, www.afdtheatre.org; Menotomy Minute Men, www.menotomy.org; Philharmonic Society of Arlington, www.psarlington.org

Public Transportation: *Trains*: Red Line at Alewife; Commuter Rail at West Medford or Belmont Center

Buses: nos. 62/76, 67, 78, 79, 80, 84, 87, and 350/351; for MBTA route and schedule information contact the MBTA Traveler's Information Center: 617-222-3200, 800-392-6100, TTY 617-222-5146 or go to www.mbta.com.

BELMONT

Boundaries: **North**: Arlington/Route 2; **East**: Cambridge (at Fresh Pond); **South**: Watertown (along Belmont Street); **West**: Waltham and Lexington

BELMONT CENTER
WAVERLY
CUSHING SQUARE
PAYSON HILL
PRESIDENTIAL

Belmont was first settled in 1630 and was incorporated as a town in 1859. Originally inhabited by the Native American Pequosette tribe, what is now Belmont was sold to Sir Richard Saltonstall and about 40 families that left the Massachusetts Bay Colony and came here to farm. Vestiges of the earliest inhabitants remain: Washington Street over Payson Hill to Fresh Pond, and Common, School, and Grove streets follow the original paths of Native American trails.

The railway, which reached Belmont in the mid-1800s, was responsible for changing this neighborhood from an agricultural town to a Boston suburb. By the mid-1900s, Belmont's commercial cores had emerged: **Belmont Center** with a Victorian town hall and depot, **Waverly** (almost in Waltham) with its Victorian firehouse, and **Cushing Square** which features retail blocks. Further expansion occurred with the streetcar-based building boom in the early 1900s, resulting in multiple-family housing in the lowlands (southern area) and single-family estates on the high ground. Belmont is a good bet if you are looking for an old home: two surviving first period houses have been preserved on Washington Street, Victorians can be found in Belmont Center and Waverly, **Payson Hill** offers examples of revival styles, and the **Presidential** area (a neighborhood with streets named after presidents) has many well-kept colonials.

Today Belmont is a well-to-do sleepy suburb, where residents appreciate its quiet, low-key reputation. There are some shops and services, but a trip to Cambridge or Boston is necessary for nightlife and fine dining. The town's public school system is excellent, with well-financed music and athletic departments.

Although Belmont doesn't have as many rental properties as Arlington or Watertown, some can be found along the Watertown border. Many Harvard affiliates opt to live here, as it is more affordable than Cambridge.

Web Site: www.town.belmont.ma.us
Area Code: 617

Zip Codes: 02478–02479

Post Offices: Belmont Branch, 405 Concord Avenue, 617-484-4201; Waverly Branch, 492 Trapelo Road, 617-484-4724; www.usps.com

Police: Belmont Police, 460 Concord Avenue, 617-484-1212, www.belmontpd.org; Belmont Public Safety, 617-484-3473

Emergency Hospitals: The Cambridge Hospital, 1493 Cambridge Street, Cambridge, 617-665-1000; www.challiance.org; Mt. Auburn Hospital, 330 Mt. Auburn Street, Cambridge, 617-492-3500, www.mountauburn.caregroup.org

Libraries: Belmont Public Library, 336 Concord Avenue, 617-489-2000; Benton Branch, 75 Oakley, 617-489-2000 ext. 125; Waverly Branch, 445 Trapelo Road, 617-489-2000 ext. 126; www.belmont.lib.ma.us

Parks & Open Space: Beaver Brook Reservation, www.mass.gov/dcr; Pequosette Park; Belmont Country Club (off Winter Street, south of Route 2); Habitat Education Center and Wildlife Sanctuary, 10 Juniper Road, www.massaudubon.org/Nature_Connection/Sanctuaries/Habitat; Clay Pit Pond (north of Concord Avenue); Mill Pond (on the Waltham border at Regent Street); Duck Pond (at the Waltham border, south of Mill Pond); Little Pond (between Route 2 and Concord Street by the Cambridge border)

Public Schools: Belmont Public Schools, 644 Pleasant Street, 617-484-2642, www.belmont.k12.ma.us

Community Publications: *Belmont Citizen-Herald*, 617-484-2633, www.townonline.com/belmont/news.html

Community Resources: Watertown-Belmont Chamber of Commerce, www.wbcc.org; Arlington-Belmont Chorale, www.psarlington.org/chorale.htm; Powers Music School, 380 Concord Avenue, 617-484-4696, www.powersmusic.org; Belmont Studio Cinema, 376 Trapelo Road, 617-484-1706, www.studiocinema.com

Public Transportation: *Trains*: Commuter Rail at Belmont Center and Waverly; Red Line at Alewife

Buses: nos. 73, 74/75, and 78; for MBTA route and schedule information contact the MBTA Traveler's Information Center: 617-222-3200, 800-392-6100, TTY 617-222-5146 or go to www.mbta.com.

CAMBRIDGE

Boundaries: **North**: Arlington and Somerville; **East**: Boston Harbor; **South**: the Charles River; **West**: Watertown and Belmont

EAST CAMBRIDGE (includes Lechmere and Science Park)
MIT (includes Kendall Square)
WELLINGTON-HARRINGTON (includes Inman Square)
AREA 4
CAMBRIDGEPORT
MID-CAMBRIDGE (includes Harvard Square and Central Square)
RIVERSIDE
AGASSIZ
PEABODY/NEIGHBORHOOD 9
WEST CAMBRIDGE/NEIGHBORHOOD 10
NORTH CAMBRIDGE (includes Porter Square)
CAMBRIDGE HIGHLANDS (includes Fresh Pond)
STRAWBERRY HILL

As pivotally and permanently conjoined are Boston and Cambridge, the latter has its own distinct flavor. Cambridge is, first and foremost, an academic capital. Its attractive, low-key streets with quaint buildings, pretty green areas, and bookstores galore can obscure that important fact. The left leaning "People's Republic of Cambridge," as it's jokingly called, is Boston's veritable fraternal twin—inextricably linked, but unmistakably different. The one-time capital of the Massachusetts Bay Colony, Cambridge has 101,000 residents in its 6.25 square miles. Those numbers swell to 400,000 during the day as people flood in to work, study, visit, eat, and drink.

The city was founded as Newtowne in 1630, when John Winthrop and his band of Puritans settled just south of what is now Harvard University, near the Charles River. In 1636, Harvard was established with a grant of £400 from the Massachusetts General Court as a school to train young ministers, and not, as is commonly thought, by John Harvard. Assistant Pastor John Harvard entered the picture two years later when he died, bequeathing half his money and his entire library to the new school. It was in light of this act of generosity that Harvard was renamed—after its primary funder, not founder. When the school received Harvard's donation and subsequently named itself in his honor, the general court of Newtowne then renamed their town Cambridge, after the university in England, which many of them had attended.

For its first 150 years, Cambridge developed as a settlement fairly separate from Boston, establishing itself as a farming and college community.

By the time of the Revolutionary War, most Cantabrigians were descendents of the first Puritan settlers, with the exception of a few British loyalists (Tories) whose homes clustered along Tory Row, now Brattle Street. At the advent of the Revolutionary War, the rebelling colonial government confiscated many of these estates, and General George Washington set up headquarters in one of them for nine months. The same house is now known as the Longfellow National Historic Site because Henry Wadsworth Longfellow lived there in the 1840s. General Washington also ordered the erection of several forts along the river, one of which, Fort Washington, remains today at 101 Waverly Street.

Just as the natural barrier of the Charles River protected the patriots from invasion during the war, it also prevented easy access between Boston and Cambridge. The first bridge built across the Charles River was the Great Bridge, erected in 1662. Until then, the only way to get to Boston—short of taking a ferry from Charlestown, a long endeavor in itself—was to travel a time-consuming and indirect eight mile route, starting with crossing the river via ferry at JFK Street, and following a path (now North Harvard Street) through Brookline and Roxbury into Boston. Over the years, eight bridges have been built, spanning the Charles at various points along the length of Cambridge. Their presence profoundly impacted the city's development, opening it up as a Boston community. In spite of the accessibility, Cantabrigians are known to balk at "crossing the river," preferring to keep close to home.

Today, people representing many nations and lifestyles live in Cambridge. It is home to professors, scientists, students, artists, industrial workers, immigrants, "techies" and other young professionals. Its international flavor comes from the thousands of foreign students and professors who live here during the school year as well as a strong immigrant community that includes many small business and restaurant owners. Not only are there people from every walk of life, but of every financial status as well. Many residents are of modest economic means, some living in area public housing. However, of all large cities in the nation, Census 2000 named Cambridge as having the largest concentration of homes (nearly 12% or one in eight) worth over $1 million, followed by San Francisco. As with housing prices, rents in Cambridge are relatively high, but some areas are more reasonable than others. Most homes date from pre-WWII, although triple-deckers, high-rises, chic urban apartments with exposed brick, pricey colonials, and contemporary single-family homes can also be found.

A major perk in Cambridge is how easy it is to live here without a car. The Red Line runs the length of the city with stops in the major squares (Kendall, Central, Harvard, and Porter), and the Green Line stops at Lechmere and Science Park. Areas not covered by the T are served by bus. If you do have a car, parking can be a problem, but generally not as bad as in Boston. Major throughways are Mass Ave., Route 2 to Route 128, Route 16, and I-93. As for green space in Cambridge, while not expansive, there is Cambridge Common on the western end of Harvard Square, the entire shore of the Charles, and Fresh Pond by the border with Arlington, not to mention pocket parks and lawns.

Like many university towns, Cambridge caters to academics, offering late night eateries, coffee shops, second-hand bookshops, and health food stores galore, as well as a thriving nightlife. Short of a few busy streets, including Mass Ave., the main commercial corridor that runs the length of Cambridge from Boston all the way to Arlington, Cambridge has plenty of sleepy, tree-lined side streets.

Cambridge can be broken up into 13 official areas: East Cambridge, MIT, Wellington-Harrington, Area Four, Cambridgeport, Mid-Cambridge, Riverside, Agassiz, Peabody, West Cambridge, North Cambridge, Cambridge Highlands, and Strawberry Hill, all of which have additional sub-neighborhoods. It's useful to know the sub-neighborhood names when reviewing real estate and rental listings.

EAST CAMBRIDGE (LECHMERE AND SCIENCE PARK)

East Cambridge (with sub-neighborhoods Lechemere and Science Park) is the area between the Charles River on the east, the B&A railroad tracks to the west, and bounded by Main Street and Broadway to the south and Somerville to the north. In 1809 the Canal Bridge was built, opening eastern Cambridge for development. Just a hop away from downtown Boston, furniture and glass factories opened here, establishing the community as a working-class community of Irish, followed by Polish, Portuguese, and Italian immigrants. Today, East Cambridge continues to be an ethnically diverse area (although the number of manufacturing jobs has declined), with some of the most affordable rents in Cambridge. It's conveniently located for easy access to Somerville, Charlestown, North Station, Beacon Hill, and Route 1 or I-93. In East Cambridge is the courthouse and prison, as well as upscale developments like the Cambridgeside Galleria Mall in the **Lechmere** neighborhood, near the Lechmere T stop (terminus for the Green Line), and **Science Park**. Although the Museum of Science, set back from the Canal Bridge and overlooking the Charles, is technically on the Boston side of the boundary, it clearly feels more a part of Cambridge and the surrounding neighborhood. The museum and its neighborhood are accessible by the Science Park T stop.

MIT (KENDALL SQUARE)

Just south of East Cambridge, bounded by Main Street, Broadway, and the railroad on the north and sprawled along the Charles River, is the **MIT** neighborhood. Encompassing the Massachusetts Institute of Technology and

Kendall Square, this region of Cambridge was defined in 1916 when MIT moved out of Boston. Today, this world-renowned technical institute commands 142 acres of land along the Charles River. The Harvard Bridge, also known as the Mass Ave. Bridge, runs through the center of campus and connects a heavily traveled, stoplight-laden section of Mass Ave. to Boston's Back Bay. Memorial Drive, Cambridge's less crowded alternative to Storrow Drive, curves between the green space along the river and the campus buildings. It's a great alternative to consider during rush hour if Storrow is packed.

Beginning at the northern tip of MIT's campus is **Kendall Square**, where Broadway and Main Street branch off just west of the Longfellow (a.k.a. "Salt and Pepper") Bridge. Home to the MIT Press Book Sale Annex, the Volpe Transportation Center, businesses, offices, and a Marriot Hotel, Kendall all but shuts down at dusk when the nine-to-fivers head home. Just a few blocks away, 1 Kendall Square offers a little pocket of dining and entertainment options that stay open until midnight or so. Included here: the wonderful independent film theater, Landmark Cinemas, Flatop Johnny's pool hall, the local Cambridge Brewing Company, and several popular resaurants. With the exception of a public housing complex on Main Street, there is very little housing throughout Kendall. Most residents are students living in university housing. Faculty and staff are more apt to live elsewhere in Cambridge. The MIT population is, according to local police, generally well-behaved. Unlike many university towns, it seems most students here are too busy studying to wreak much havoc, short of a mischevious annual prank. The area is served by the Kendall/MIT T stop on Main Street—the first stop of the Red Line on the Cambridge side of the river.

WELLINGTON-HARRINGTON (INMAN SQUARE)
West of East Cambridge, north of Kendall Square, and south of Somerville is **Wellington-Harrington**, an area about half the size of East Cambridge, which extends to and includes **Inman Square**, where Cambridge and Hampshire streets intersect. Inman/Harrington is densely populated, with housing that ranges from single- to three-family homes and apartment complexes. Home to European immigrants in the 1800s and through the mid-part of the last century, today the trend of welcoming incoming foreigners continues. The mixed-use Cambridge Street is the main thoroughfare, connecting the Cambridgeside Galleria and Lechmere part of East Cambridge with Inman Square and then eventually Harvard Square. Because Inman Square is not served by a T stop, it feels like an out of the way treasure, accessed mostly by bus or car. It is at least 20 minutes on foot from Central or Harvard squares. Without T access, Inman has resisted gentrification, resulting in a stronghold of small one-of-a-kind businesses, including the oh-so-rewarding S&S Deli, Ryles Jazz Club, a women's bookstore called New Words, the 1364 Coffee Shop, the B-Side Lounge,

and more international restaurants than you can shake a stick at. Inman also borders Somerville and is only a few blocks south of Union Square.

AREA 4
Bounded by Prospect Street to the west, Hampshire Street to the north, the B&A tracks to the east, and Mass Ave. to the south, between MIT and Central Square lies **Area 4**. Comprised mostly of two- and three-family homes, with some large apartment complexes and two public housing developments, a large percentage of its occupants are families. Area 4 is home to *El Mundo*, Massachusetts' oldest Spanish newspaper, and has many specialty food markets and international restaurants. Sennet Park hosts free concerts and street fairs. Small-businesses, including those that can only be seen in a place like Cambridge, such as the Miracle of Science bar (an MIT/techie hangout, which posts the menu in the form of a periodic table and serves the bill in beakers), populate the Mass Ave. and Main Street intersection. Residents enjoy easy access to Central Square and its T stop, located on its western edge, or the quick, clear shot to Boston via either the Longfellow or the Harvard bridges. Criminal activity is more common here than in other parts of Cambridge.

CAMBRIDGEPORT
Settlement of **Cambridgeport** began in earnest with the building of the Longfellow Bridge (then called the West Boston Bridge) in 1793. Notable residents at the time included Margaret Fuller, the first woman to use the Harvard library, and William Henry Garrison, an abolitionist. It was also here during the Revolutionary War that George Washington had Fort Washington built to protect his troops during the siege on Boston.

Cambridgeport spreads south from Central Square to the Charles River between MIT to the east and River Street to the west. Popular with immigrants from the 1800s until the 1980s when most industry moved elsewhere, in recent years Cambridgeport has experienced a huge resettlement. Buildings previously used for industrial purposes were revamped or demolished altogether, and now the area is predominantly residential, made up of single- to multi-family homes and large apartment complexes. Its population is a mix of artists, working class, young professionals, university faculty, and even some seasoned executives. Although Cambridgeport may have developed as a result of the Longfellow Bridge, residents now also have the BU Bridge and River Street Bridge right in their laps, making for easy access to Allston. The neighborhood enjoys its proximity to the Charles, and there is reason to believe that with the river clean up, Magazine Beach will become popular once again. For now, Cambridgeport is best known for some large stores, gas stations, and hotels, including a Hyatt along Memorial Drive. There are a few small stores here and there toward Central Square, and truthfully, it can be a challenge to define where Central Square ends and Cambridgeport begins.

MID-CAMBRIDGE (HARVARD SQUARE AND CENTRAL SQUARE)

Bound by three of Cambridge's five major squares: Central Square on the east, Inman Square on the northeast, and Harvard Square on the west, between Mass Ave. and the Somerville border, is **Mid-Cambridge**, the geographical and institutional heart of the city. Both Central Square and the main portion of the Harvard campus in Harvard Square are part of Mid-Cambridge, which also lays claim to Cambridge Hospital, city hall, the main branch of the Cambridge Public Library, and Cambridge Rindge and Latin School. A great deal of the same multi-family homes and large apartment complexes that can be seen throughout the city can be found in Mid-Cambridge, supporting the largest population in all of Cambridge.

Central Square is a busy place, what with the T stop, an active bus station, busy taxi ranks, and droves of students. It is also home to Cambridge's municipal business, located on Riverside's eastern edge and Cambridgeport's northern, where Western Avenue and River and Magazine streets converge upon Mass Ave. Here you will find city hall, the police station, the main post office (the latter two technically are in Riverside), the YMCA and YWCA, a homeless shelter, the Dance Complex building, and a number of restaurants, cafes, and bars offering a diverse menu of music, poetry and food. The number businesses, pedestrian traffic, and stop lights make Central Square one of the biggest traffic juggernauts along Mass Ave. Renowned for its international cuisine, Central Square celebrates its diversity by hosting the World's Fair every summer, displaying a conflagration of food and art from around the world. Nightlife here offers a little something for everyone: Irish pubs like the Plough and Stars and The Field, the Soviet-themed People's Republik, the Cantab Lounge for jazz and blues lovers, and the Middle East for middle eastern food *and* music. Since the late 1990s, Central Square has seen stores such as Starbucks and the Gap move in, along with skyrocketing rental prices. Still, Central Square maintains a good deal of its beloved secondhand stores, particularly on its fringes. And it remains the center of Cambridge's progressive political scene.

West on Mass Ave. is **Harvard Square**, the *pièce de resistance* of Cambridge. Served by the third Cambridge T stop on the Red Line, the area is the second Cambridge square located on Mass Ave., and covers ground in Mid-Cambridge, West Cambridge, Riverside, and Peabody/Neighborhood 9. The heart of Harvard's campus, Harvard Yard, and a good chunk of Harvard Square falls within Mid-Cambridge's bounds. Known for bookstores, street musicians, and university culture, Harvard

Square is home to an amazing array of sights, sounds, shops, newspapers, events, restaurants, and history. The Square teems with masses of tourists, locals, shoppers, performers, diners, university faculty, and students, all taking in the many sights and sounds within the brick walls and iron gates of the ivy-clad school. As one can imagine, people-watching is a favorite Harvard Square activity. Coffee is abundant. Book and music stores proliferate, as do poetry readings, lectures, and earnest political discussions. Also here are jazz, folk, and rock music performances in area nightclubs; and bars, movie houses, a repertory theater, and a wide array of museums. The city licenses over 300 street performers, which makes for inexpensive entertainment on summer evenings. Many famous performers (including Bob Dylan, Tracy Chapman, and Guster) began their careers here. People are often crowded outside the Harvard COOP, around "the pit"—the main entrance to the Harvard T stop—or by the entrance to the bus stop to watch and listen to the free entertainment.

The idea of moving to such a colorful enclave may be appealing but the reality of finding a place to live here can be difficult—and expensive. If you are a student or a faculty member, the Harvard Housing Services office, www.hpre.harvard.edu/RRE/index.html, is a good place to start. Parking for residents is also a challenge.

RIVERSIDE
Riverside is the section of Cambridge south of Mass Ave. along the Charles between River Street and JFK Street—or easier, the area behind Central Square between Cambridgeport and Harvard Square. Like Cambridgeport, Riverside, one time home to W.E.B. DuBois, is a transitional area between the Harvard-influenced western part of Cambridge and the lower-budget, industrial section to the east. A number of Harvard's dorms take up Riverside's western edge along the Charles, but the neighborhood loses its ivy influence as you head east. The dorms make the overall median age for the neighborhood young. There are sizable African-American and Asian populations here, creating a solid sense of community despite the influx of seasonal inhabitants. It is predominantly middle-class and residential. The three final bridges spanning the Charles in Cambridge are in Riverside, connecting Cambridge to Allston. The Western Avenue Bridge, at the southern tip of Harvard's Campus, provides a fairly straight shot to the Mass Pike. The Anderson Bridge, near the middle of Harvard territory, links the university to its north campus in Allston. And the John Weeks Foot Bridge near Cowperthwaite Street provides pedestrian access to the other side. On summer Sundays, Memorial Drive should be avoided, as parts of it in Riverside and West Cambridge are closed off for pedestrians and bike riders only.

AGASSIZ

Agassiz (pronounced AG-uh-see) encompasses Mass Ave. north of its intersection with Cambridge Street and all parts east up to the Somerville border. Roughly, it is the area between Harvard and Porter squares. Lesley College as well as Harvard's Law and Divinity schools account for the southern portion of this triangular neighborhood. Agassiz is historically significant as African-American headmistress Maria Baldwin lived here at the turn of the last century. After holding home-study classes for African-American students at Harvard (including W.E.B. DuBois) in 1889, Cambridge-native Baldwin was named headmaster of the Agassiz school. Dense, residential, and full of students and professors from Cambridge's schools as well as young professionals, Agassiz is a comfortable place to live. It includes brick-lined sidewalks and, due to the mixture of apartment buildings and multi- and single-family homes, isn't overwhelmingly upscale. The neighborhood is quiet and is within walking distance of Harvard Square, Porter Square, and Davis Square in Somerville. Parking along this stretch of Mass Ave. is easier than up the street in the center of Harvard Square. Commercial and retail offerings along Mass Ave. as well as the portion of Beacon Street in Somerville that runs parallel to Agassiz are more than adequate and include several boutiques, restaurants, and bars. Porter Square, at the northernmost point of Agassiz is at the conjunction of several neighborhoods. For this reason, there is conflicting information as to which neighborhood it belongs. (Official word from the City of Cambridge states that it is part of North Cambridge, so it will be discussed below.)

PEABODY/NEIGHBORHOOD 9 (AVON HILL)

Peabody, a.k.a. **Neighborhood 9**, is shaped rather like an ice cream cone—Mass Ave. on the east and Garden and Concord streets on the west stem out from the bottom of the cone to where they intersect, and the rounded top is formed by the boundary marked by the B&M railroad tracks. Here you will find the Radcliffe campus and the Longy School of Music, as well as access to the Cambridge Common and Danehy Park. Peabody/Neighborhood 9 is separated into two distinct areas, with Upland Road serving as the divider. Just south of Upland, is **Avon Hill**, one of the more desirable neighborhoods in Cambridge. In the shadow of Porter Square, it has a mixture of grand older homes (some single, some multi-family) and brick apartment complexes. To the north of Upland, housing options tend to be more diverse and readily available, and include large apartment buildings, a public housing development called Lincoln Way, and a mixture of single and multi-family homes of varying styles, including the triple-decker. Heading away from Harvard and Radcliffe, chances of getting parking (driveways!) increase greatly.

WEST CAMBRIDGE/NEIGHBORHOOD 10
Located south of Peabody/Neighborhood 9, bounded by JFK Street in Harvard Square on the east and Fresh Pond on the west, is the biggest neighborhood in the Cambridge, **West Cambridge**, which contains a good portion of Harvard Square. Brattle Street, called Tory Row during the Revolutionary War, still holds some of the lavish homes of that time. Those in the market for some of the oldest real estate in the country or just a beautiful mansion, need look no further. The large and stately, homes, most on large lots, makes this some of the most desirable and expensive real estate in Cambridge. Aside from the aforementioned gorgeous historic housing, West Cambridge has the most green space of any neighborhood in the city, even if much of it is for the deceased: the Mt. Auburn Cemetery, the Cambridge Cemetery, and the Old Burying Ground are all here. On its western edge, residents enjoy proximity to Fresh Pond, Kinglsey Park, Mt. Auburn Hospital, and Buckingham Brown and Nichols School. Not to mention easy access to Memorial Drive and Route 16. Note: West Cambridge, like Riverside, is apt to be affected by the summertime Sunday morning closures of Memorial Drive for pedestrian/bike use only. Residents on the east side can use the Harvard T stop; residents on the northwest side might be close enough to walk to the Alewife T stop; residents toward the southwest have no T stop.

NORTH CAMBRIDGE (PORTER SQUARE)
Everything north of the railroad tracks, west of and including Porter Square to the borders of Arlington, Belmont, and Somerville count as **North Cambridge**. In the mid-1800s, Irish immigrants moved here, many of whom worked in North Cambridge's claypits and brickyards. They were followed by a wave of French Canadians around the turn of the 20th century. Largely a working class neighborhood until the late 1990s, North Cambridge is now gaining popularity with a host of young professionals and students who were forced to look to outlying areas such as Porter Square (and Davis Square in Somerville) during Boston's turn-of-the-millennium housing crunch. Homes here vary from triple-deckers to a public housing development to the large Fresh Pond Apartments highrise complex. North Cantabrigians have access to two Red Line T stops: Porter Square, which also has the commuter rail, and Alewife, which is the Red Line terminus with an enormous parking lot for commuters. There is easy access to Mass Ave. and Route 16 and a good amount of green space, including the Clarendon Avenue Playground, Linear Park, Rindge Field, Gergin Playground, and the O'Callaghan Little League field.

   Porter Square, in North Cambridge, is the third Cambridge square on Mass Ave. and the fourth Cambridge T stop on the Red Line. Home to the Porter Square Shopping Mall, the Porter Exchange Mall (housed in the old Sears Building) and the Porter Arcade which inhabits an old auto dealership, this neighborhood is not to be overlooked, especially for those going to school or working along the Red Line. Although substantially further from downtown Boston, Porter Square is safer and slower paced than Central Square, and the distance from the city makes it more affordable. In Porter Square itself are restaurants, bars, health clubs, cute boutiques, chain stores, and some specialty Japanese shops, like the Sasuga Japanese Bookstore (www.sasugabooks.com) on the corner of Upland and Mass Ave., and an Asian food court in the Exchange building. Either way down Mass Ave., toward Arlington or toward Agassiz/Peabody further into Cambridge, are even more commercial options. Within walking distance from Porter Square are Harvard and Davis squares, and downtown Boston is only about 15 minutes away via T.

CAMBRIDGE HIGHLANDS (FRESH POND)

Cambridge Highlands is the tiny area accounting for the northern portion of **Fresh Pond** bordered by the B&M railroad tracks (on the east, the tracks coincide with the Fresh Pond Parkway) and the Belmont border. There are less than 300 households in Cambridge Highlands, which coexist with some warehouses, the Fresh Pond (strip) Mall, Fresh Pond Cinema, and assorted restaurants and stores that line Fresh Pond Parkway. In addition to the short distances to commercial amenities, residents enjoy a low crime rate and easy access to the Alewife T stop and routes 2, 13, and 16. Also in Cambridge Highlands is Cambridge's main water supply—Fresh Pond, which provides an expanse of greenspace, good for walking and jogging, and is especially popular with dog-owners.

STRAWBERRY HILL

Bound by the pond to the north, Aberdeen Avenue to the east, and the Watertown and Belmont town lines to the south and west, **Strawberry Hill** is yet another quiet little nook at the far end of Cambridge. With about four times the population of Cambridge Highlands, it too boasts a low crime rate. Here you will find mostly large, single-family homes on small lots, but there are some apartments, including a large complex at 700 Huron Avenue. Strawberry Hill and Cambridge Highlands are about as far from downtown Cambridge and downtown Boston as can be while still in Cambridge. Although Strawberry Hill isn't very near the Red Line, the Fresh Pond Parkway to Memorial Drive or Brattle Street are easy routes to Boston or the rest of Cambridge.

Web Sites: www.cambridgema.gov, www.urbanphoto.org/boston/harvard, www.urbanphoto.org/boston/central, www.harvardsquare.com/
Area Code: 617

Zip Codes: 02138–02142

Post Offices: Cambridge Main Post Office, 770 Mass Ave., 617-876-0550; East Cambridge Station, 303 Cambridge Street, 617-876-8558; Harvard Square Station, 125 Mt. Auburn Street, 617-876-3883; Inman Square Station, 1311 Cambridge Street, 617-864-4344; Kendall Square Station, 250 Main Street, 617-876-5155; MIT, 84 Mass Ave., 617-494-5511; Porter Square Retail Unit, 1953 Mass Ave., 617-876-5599; www.usps.com

Police: Cambridge Police, 5 Western Avenue, 617-349-3301, www.cambridgepolice.org; Harvard University Police, 1033 Mass Ave., 6th Floor, 617-495-1212, www.hupd.harvard.edu; MIT Police, 120 Mass Ave., 617-253-1212, http://web.mit.edu/cp/www/

Emergency Hospitals: The Cambridge Hospital, 1493 Cambridge Street, 617-665-1000, www.challiance.org; Mt. Auburn Hospital, 330 Mt. Auburn Street, 617-492-3500, www.mountauburncaregroup.org

Library: Main Branch (Mid-Cambridge), 449 Broadway, 617-349-4040, www.cambridgema.gov/~CPL

Parks & Open Space: Alewife Brook Reservation, www.mass.gov/dcr; Mount Auburn Cemetery (on the western border with Watertown, between Route 16 and the Charles); Tip O'Neill Golf Course (at Fresh Pond, Grove Street and Concord Avenue); Fresh Pond (west of Fresh Pond Parkway and Concord Avenue); Cambridge Cemetery (next to the Mt. Auburn Cemetery, between Coolidge Avenue and the Charles River); Charles River; Magazine Beach (at Magazine Street between the Charles and Memorial Drive); Cambridge Common (west part of Harvard Square, between Mass Ave. and Concord Avenue); Russell Field (in North Cambridge, off the Alewife Brook Parkway and Rindge Avenue); Donnelly Field (in East Cambridge at Cambridge Street and Berkshire Street)

Public Schools: Cambridge Public Schools, 159 Thorndike Street, 617-349-6400, www.cpsd.us; Cambridge Rindge and Latin School, 617-349-6630, www.cps.ci.cambridge.ma.us/crls

Community Publications: *Cambridge Chronicle*, 617-577-7419, www.townonline.com/cambridge/news.html; *El Mundo*, 617-522-5060

Community Resources: Chamber of Commerce, www.cambridgechamber.org; Harvard University, University Hall, 617-495-1000, www.harvard.edu; MIT, 77 Mass Ave., 617-253-1000, www.mit.edu; Lesley University, 29 Everett Street, 800-999-1959, www.lesley.edu; Longy School of Music, 1 Follen Street, 617-876-0956, www.longy.edu; Cambridge Center for Adult Education, 42 Brattle Street, 617-547-6789, www.ccae.org; Cambridge College, 1000 Mass Ave., www.cambridge.edu; Longfellow National Historic Site, 105 Brattle Street, 617-876-4491, www.nps.gov/long; Fresh Pond Mall, 185 Alewife Brook Parkway, 617-491-4431; Brattle Theatre, 40 Brattle Street, 617-876-6837, www.brattlefilm.org; Harvard Film Archive, 24 Quincy

Street, 617-495-4700; Fogg Art Museum, 32 Quincy Street, www.artmuseums.harvard.edu/fogg; Sackler Museum, 32 Quincy Street, www.artmuseums.harvard.edu/sackler; Busch-Reisinger Museum, 32 Quincy Street, 617-495-2317, www.artmuseums.harvard.edu/busch; Harvard Museum of Natural History, 26 Oxford Street, 617-495-3045, www.hmnh.harvard.edu; Peabody Museum of Archaeology and Ethnology, 11 Divinity Avenue, 617-496-1027, www.peabody.harvard.edu; Museum of Science, Science Park, 617-723-2500, www.mos.org; Hooper-Lee-Nichols House, 159 Brattle Street, 617-547-4252; MIT List Visual Arts Center, 20 Ames Street, 617-253-4680, http://web.mit.edu/lvac; MIT Museum, 265 Mass Ave., 617-253-4444, http://web.mit.edu/museum; American Repertory Theatre, 64 Brattle Street, 617-547-8300, www.amrep.org; Jose Mateo Ballet Theatre, 400 Harvard Street, 617-354-7467, www.ballettheatre.org; Brazilian Cultural Center of New England, 310 Webster Avenue, 617-547-5343; Hasty Pudding Theatre, 12 Holyoke Street, 617-495-5205, www.hastypudding.org; Improv Boston, 1253 Cambridge Street, 617-576-1253, www.improvboston.com; Market Theater, 89-91 Winthrop Street, 617-576-0808, www.markettheater.org; Cambridgeside Galleria, 100 Cambridgeside Place, 617-621-8666, www.shopcambridgeside.com; Cambridge Multicultural Arts Center, 41 Second Street, 617-577-1400, www.cmacusa.org; Buckingham Browne & Nichols School, 80 Gerrys Landing Road, 617-547-6100, www.bbn-school.org
- **Public Transportation**: *Trains*: Red Line stops at Kendall/MIT, Central Square, Harvard Square, Porter Square, Alewife; Green Line D and E train stops at Lechmere
- *Buses*: nos. 1, 47, 62/76, 64, 66-70, 70A, 71-73, 74/75, 77, 77A, 78-80, 83, 84-88, 91, 96, 350/351, CT1, and CT2; for MBTA route and schedule information contact the MBTA Traveler's Information Center: 617-222-3200, 800-392-6100, TTY 617-222-5146 or go to www.mbta.com.

MALDEN

Boundaries: **East**: Revere; **South**: Everett; **West**: Medford; **North**: Stoneham and Melrose

Malden, about five square miles in size, lies five miles north of Boston. First settled in 1629 and then referred to as Mystic Side, the town was incorporated in 1649 and as a city in 1882. In the last century, its desirability has fluctuated somewhat—from a solidly middle-class suburb during the baby boom years of the 1940s, '50s, and '60s, to a more working-class area in a bit of economic decline during the 1970s, '80s and '90s. During its heyday,

Malden was especially popular with Italian and Jewish families who moved here from the city in search of bigger homes and bigger lawns. When baby boomers came of age, however, those who could afford to leave went to the even greener suburbs of the North Shore. Today Malden is on the upswing, with young professionals, families, and newly arrived immigrants moving in. Many of those who cannot or perhaps do not want to pay the high rents in the city come here, enjoying Malden's proximity and easy access to the city without the higher cost of living. Malden is an economically and racially diverse community; the Chinese and Vietnamese presence is especially visible in the many Asian establishments, particularly restaurants.

Maldonians, as residents are called, live mostly in one-, two- or three-family triple deckers and Victorians. Although there are a few apartment complexes, such as the Granada Highlands (popular with the elderly community), Malden is noted for its large Victorian homes with lawns, turrets, porches, ambling stairways, and driveways. But there is more of an urban outskirt-feel here than that of a green leafy suburb. Ten percent of Malden's housing stock is subsized low- to moderate-income, which is more than can be found in some of Boston's other suburban communities.

Malden lacks the number of historical or cultural sites that dominate much of the greater Boston area. It has no major universities or theaters, nor is it a "destination," per se. But as far as housing goes, compared to Boston, Malden may offer better value for your dollar. It also offers quick access to downtown, with two Orange Line T stops, and routes 1 or 28 that will get you to town in 10 to 15 minutes. New restaurants, storefronts, and bars, from the Ryan Family Amusement Center (bowling alley) on Main Street to the Applebee's on Middlesex Street have opened up in recent years catering to the recent influx of residents. However, those wanting an exciting night out head to Boston.

Web Site: www.ci.malden.ma.us
Area Code: 781
Zip Code: 02148
Post Offices: Malden Branch, 109 Mountain Avenue, 781-322-4685; www.usps.com
Police: Malden Police Department, 200 Pleasant Street, 781-397-7171
Emergency Hospitals: Lawrence Memorial Hospital, 170 Governers Avenue, Medford, 781-306-6000, www.hallmarkhealth.org; Melrose-Wakefield Hospital, 585 Lebanon Street, Melrose, 781-979-3000, www.hallmarkhealth.org; Whidden Memorial Hospital, 103 Garland Street, Everett, 617-389-6270, www.challiance.org
Libraries: Main Library, 36 Salem Street, 781-324-0218; Linden Branch Library, 141 Oliver Street, 781-397-7067; http://mbln.lib.ma.us/malden/index.htm

Parks & Open Space: Malden River; Fellsmere Pond and Park (western Malden, off of the Fellwasy, north of Pleasant Street); Bell Rock Park (off of Main and Wigglesworth Street); Devir Park (border with Medford); Middlesex Fells Reservation, www.mass.gov/dcr (at the northwestern border with Stoneham); Pine Banks Park (at the Melrose border just north of the Forest Dale Cemetery); Roosevelt Park (between Eastern Avenue and Salem Street); Forest Dale Cemetery (in north Malden at Forest Street); Holy Cross Cemetery (in southeast Malden)

Public Schools: Malden Public Schools, 200 Pleasant Street, 781-397-7204, wwww.malden.mec.edu

Community Publications: *Malden Evening News*, 781-321-8000; *Malden Observer*, 781-322-6957, www.townonline.com/malden/news.html

Community Resources: Old Parsonage (Judson House); Davenport Memorial Home, 70 Salem Street, 781-324-0150; Stop & Shop, 60 Broadway, 781-321-2367

Public Transportation: *Trains*: Orange Line and Commuter Rail at Malden Center

Buses: nos. 97, 99, 101, 104/109, 105, 106, 108, 130-132, 136/137, 411, 427, and 430; for MBTA route and schedule information contact the MBTA Traveler's Information Center: 617-222-3200, 800-392-6100, TTY 617-222-5146 or go to www.mbta.com.

MEDFORD

Boundaries: **East**: Everett and the Malden River; **South**: Mystic River and Somerville; **West**: Mystic Valley Parkway and Upper and Lower Mystic Lake; **Northwest**: Stoneham and Middlesex Fells Reservation

SOUTH MEDFORD
WEST MEDFORD
WELLINGTON
FULTON HEIGHTS
LAWRENCE ESTATES
MEDFORD HILLSIDE
MEDFORD SQUARE

Located five miles northwest of Boston off Interstate 93, Medford is home to Tufts University, an honor it shares with nearby Somerville. The presence of Tufts means that students, faculty, and staff make up a large contingent of Medford's almost 56,000 residents. In pre-colonial times, Medford was home to the Pawtucket Indians. A monument honoring Sagamore John—a Pawtucket—and his fellow tribesmen, stands in Sagamore Park in West

Medford. During much of the 17th century the area was a subsistence-farming plantation owned by Matthew Craddock, a London-born merchant, shipbuilder, governor, and founder of the town. The area became Medford, "the ford by the meadow," first as a town in 1695 and as a city in 1892.

Medford's early commerce was of a mercantile nature; as a seaport situated on the tidewaters of the Mystic River which runs into the Atlantic Ocean, the town was well located for trading. A man named Thatcher Magoun utilized the riverside location to commence a clipper shipbuilding industry. The seaport also enabled Medford to participate in the Triangle Trade Route, for its part distilling molasses into its then famous "Medford Rum." Ships left Medford loaded with rum and headed for West Africa where the alcohol was traded for slaves, then headed to the West Indies where slaves were sold and molasses purchased, and then back to New England where the molasses was distilled into rum. By the 1800s, the brick making industry also took hold in Medford, and immigrants, particularly Irish, moved in to work the local brickyards and the Medford granite quarry. Magoun's shipyard was booming in 1855, at which time it is said to have employed 1,100 people. Later in the century, with the decline of shipbuilding, the city's businesses expanded into textiles, shoe-making machinery, chemicals, and manufacturing.

In 1852, Charles Tufts, a brickmaker and descendant of one of the first settlers of neighboring Malden, gave 20 acres of land atop a hill straddling the Somerville and Medford line to the Unitarian Church on the condition that it be used for a college. The school got its charter from the state of Massachusetts that same year and became Tufts University, named after its first benefactor. Subsequent land gifts boosted Tufts' property size up to 100 acres.

Beyond the areas around Tufts, which have an understandably collegiate feel, Medford is a working- and middle-class enclave adjacent to Boston, and serves as a haven for those who want urban living, decent city access, and more affordable (than Boston) housing prices. Housing styles run the gamut, and include Federal, Greek Revival, and Victorian homes, as well as the ever-present triple-deckers, although most residences are packed close together and sit on small lots. Some historic homes are here, including the Isaac Royall estate, which holds the dubious title of being the only surviving building in the north with its attached slave quarters intact. There are older two- and three-family homes in **South Medford** or newer (20th century) construction in **West Medford** off High Street. Other areas, such as **Wellington** (near the Orange Line T stop in southeast Medford), **Fulton Heights**, **Lawrence Estates**, and **Medford Hillside** (in west Medford, just north of Tufts) also tend toward 20th century architecture, offering bungalows, cottages, ranches, colonials, and Cape Cods.

Medford's shopping amenities are basic, tending more toward grocery, variety, and liquor stores than luxury boutiques. Unlike many of the tree-lined residential areas, the shopping districts of Salem Street, Main Street, Riverside Avenue, and High Street in **Medford Square** and **West Medford** are fairly urban. For greater shopping pursuits, head to the Meadow Glen Mall along the Mystic River on Route 16. With 60 stores, including an Old Navy, Marshall's, Foot Locker, Bath & Bodyworks, and Waldenbooks you should be covered. Medford residents who like to get outside are in luck: the Middlesex Fells Reservation (better known simply as the Fells) is 2,000 acres of meadows, wetlands, forests, and ponds, located along most of Medford's northern border. People come here, as well as to the Mystic River Reserves to enjoy expanses of flora and fauna and to fish, hike, bike, and jog.

The trip to Boston is relatively easy by car via I-93 and Route 28, both of which run through Medford. Also easily accessed are routes 95/128, 2, and 495. For those without a car, living in Medford will be more of a challenge, as T access is sparse—with only the peripheral Orange Line stop at Wellington and a commuter rail stop at West Medford. Buses are available.

Web Site: www.medford.org
Area Code: 781
Zip Codes: 02155, 02153, 02156
Post Offices: Medford Branch, 20 Forest Street, 781-396-2444; Tufts University Branch, 470 Boston Avenue, 617-625-5755; West Medford Branch, 485 High Street, 781-483-3090; www.usps.com
Police: Medford Police, 100 Main Street, 781-391-6404; www.medford.org/fGoverment.htm
Emergency Hospitals: Lawrence Memorial Hospital, 170 Governors Avenue, 781-306-6000, www.hallmarkhealth.org; Tufts University Health Service, 124 Professors Row, 617-627-3350, http://ase.tufts.edu/healthservices
Library: Medford Public Library, 111 High Street, 781-395-7950; www.medfordlibrary.org
Parks & Open Space: Tufts Park (Medford Street and Morton Avenue); Columbus Park (Albion and Exeter streets); Carr Park (Winslow Avenue and Fulton Street); Harris Park (between Fellsway and Bradbury avenues and 3rd and 2nd streets); Barry Park (Gourley Road and Summer Street); Brooks Park (Century Street and Playstead Road in northwest Medford); Oak Grove Cemetery and Brooks Pond (Grove and Main streets); Hickey Park (Fellsway West and Park Street); Wrights Pond/City Park (north of Elm Street and Fellsway West); Middlesex Fells Reservation, www.mass.gov/dcr; Mystic River Reserve (along the Mystic River)

Public Schools: Medford Public Schools, 489 Winthrop Street, 781-393-2387, www.medford.k12.ma.us

Community Publications: *Medford Transcript,* 781-396-1982, www.townonline.com/medford/index.html

Community Resources: Medford Chamber of Commerce, www.medfordchamberma.com; North Medford Club, www.northmedfordclub.org; Friends of the Middlesex Fells Reservation, www.fells.org; Tufts University, Medford, 617-628-5000, www.tufts.edu; Isaac Royall House, 15 George Street, 781-396-9032; Tufts (Cradock) House, 350 Riverside Avenue; Grandfather's House, 114 South Street; New England Storm (Women's Professional Football), Hormel Stadium, 781-395-TEAM, www.newenglandstorm.com; Chevalier Memorial Auditorium and Gene Mack Gymnasium, 617-628-4665; Meadow Glenn Mall, 3850 Mystic Valley Parkway, 781-395-6710, www.meadowglen.com; Black Lab Craft and Fine Art Event, www.sharpeshot.com; West Medford Open Studios, 77 Monument Street, 781-483-3605

Public Transportation: *Trains*: Orange Line at Wellington; Commuter rail at West Medford

Buses: nos. 80, 90, 94-97, 99-101, 106, 108, 110, 112, 134, 325, 326, and 352; for MBTA route and schedule information contact the MBTA Traveler's Information Center: 617-222-3200, 800-392-6100, TTY 617-222-5246 or go to www.mbta.com.

NEWTON

Boundaries: **North**, **West**, and **South**: bordered by the Charles River; **East**: Middlesex County line, Brighton, Brookline, West Roxbury

NEWTON CORNER	NEWTON HIGHLANDS
NEWTON UPPER FALLS	FOUR CORNERS
NEWTON LOWER FALLS	WABAN
NONANTUM	NEWTONVILLE
NEWTON CENTRE	AUBURNDALE
THOMPSONVILLE	WEST NEWTON
CHESTNUT HILL	OAK HILL

Newton is Boston suburbia at its finest, comprising between 11 and 14 villages: Auburndale, Chestnut Hill, Four Corners, Lower Falls, Newton Centre, Newton Corner, Newton Higlands, Newtonville, Nonantum, Oak Hill, Thompsonville, Upper Falls, Waban, and West Newton. (There is some discrepancy at the city level as to whether to distinguish Four Corners, Newton Corner, Thompsonville, and Oak Hill as neighborhoods on their own or as part of the other villages. Official city and state publications include all, some, or none of them when detailing Newton.) The villages cover over 18 square miles of some of the most a desirable land in the greater Boston area.

Referred to as the "Garden City," Newton was originally part of the Cambridge land grant of 1630, incorporating as a separate town in 1688. By 1873, Newton had become a city, complete with a Mayor, Board of Aldermen, and Common Council. Also dating back to the 1630s, the **Newton Corner** area near the Newton-Brighton line was the original settlement. Sometimes just called "Newton," this neighborhood boasts Newton's own historic museum, Jackson Homestead. Sparsely populated in its earliest years, it served as a stagecoach stopping point. More came here to live in the 1830s and '40s when the Boston & Worcester Railroad brought commuter tracks here.

By the early 1700s, people were being drawn to the powerful glacial waterfalls and rapids along the Charles River, constructing the industrial villages of Newton Upper Falls and Newton Lower Falls. **Newton Upper Falls**, in southern Newton across the Charles River from Needham, is where a sawmill was established in 1688, followed by a grist mill (1710), a woolen mill (1715), snuff and wire mills (late 1700s), and finally a cotton mill in 1823. Much of this area is now a historic district. The closest T access is the Green Line D train/Eliot stop, at Route 9 and Woodward Street. **Newton Lower Falls**, across the Charles, got its start in 1704 when John Hubbard and Caleb Church dammed the river to create an ironworks. By the 1800s, paper mills began cropping up in Lower Falls—by 1816, there were nine mills spread out over two dams. Sadly, the urban renewal of the 1970s destroyed much of this neighborhood's historic architecture, but a few remnants of the original mill village, including a Georgian mansion and some late 19th century Victorian architecture, survive on Washington Street. Although it may not be within walking distance for many Lower Falls residents, there is access to the Woodland T stop on the Green Line D train at Washington Street northeast of Beacon Street, near the Newton-Wellesley Hospital.

Nonantum, named after the local Algonquins, was also a site for waterpower generation. Considered Newton's own mini version of Little Italy, this tight Italian community celebrates various saints' days, and the streets substitute red, green, and white stripes for traditional yellow lane markers. One of the most affordable neighborhoods in greater Boston, Nonantum welcomes all newcomers. There is no T access, but residents can head a bit south for the Newtonville commuter rail stop.

Newton Centre is the area around Centre Street between Beacon Street and Comm Ave. Until the mid-1800s, this area was sparsely settled. In the 1850s, the Charles River Railroad came through, and in the 1870s it was upgraded to include commuter service to Boston, which turned

Newton Centre into an affluent suburb. Hence, much of the architecture in this part of town is representative of late 19th century suburban styles. Residents of this village also have T access: the Newton Centre Green Line D train stop is on Union Street between Herrick Street and Langley Road.

The Village of **Thompsonville**, just south of Newton Centre and east of Chestnut Hill, is mentioned in some city documents, but left out of many others and is not included in the historical annals of the city. According to the City of Newton, Thompsonville is the area roughly bound by Beacon and Boylston streets to the north and south, respectively, and the Hammond Pond Parkway and Parker street to the east and west. However, the village's community group, the Bowen Thompsonville Neighborhood Association, asserts that Thompsonville's boundaries are slightly further north and thus overlap with Newton Centre. Regardless, one of the area's larger theological schools, the Andover Newton Theological Seminary, falls within Thompsonville's boundaries. Villagers use the Newton Centre T stop.

Railroad extensions through Newton that connected it with Boston were responsible for the development of many of the other villages, including Chestnut Hill (1850s), Newton Highlands (1870s) and Waban (1880s). **Chestnut Hill**, at Newton's eastern border with Brighton and Brookline, was once owned almost entirely by the Hammond Family, who settled there in 1665. The Charles River Railroad and Beacon Street were extended to this part of town in the early 1850s, piercing Chestnut Hill's isolation by connecting it to Boston and Brookline. By the late 1800s, settlement here began in earnest. Area housing features Georgian, Colonial Revival, and shingle homes, in particular. It is also in Chestnut Hill where Boston College is located. Residents have access to the Chestnut Hill T stop on the Green Line D train, and those near the BC campus have access to the BC stop on the Green Line B train.

The area just north of Route 9, where it intersects with Woodward and Walnut streets, belongs to the village of **Newton Highlands**. Much of this area once belonged to John Haynes, the governor of the Massachusetts Bay Colony in 1635. Newton Highlands was predominantly agricultural until the mid- to late–1800s, when the railroad-related population booms in neighboring Newton Corner and West Newton caused real estate developers to look toward the highlands. The Charles River Railroad cut through the area in 1850, but didn't present a commuter option until the 1870s. Before then, trains were used to haul dirt for the Back Bay landfill project. Today's commuters have access to two Green Line stops: Newton Highlands at Lincoln and Walnut streets near the village shopping district, and Eliot near Route 9 and Woodward Street. Many homes in the area date back to the 1870s. Examples of Victorian architecture abound, along with examples of mansard, Italianate, and colonial revival styles.

South of Newton Highlands (and sometimes considered part of it) is **Four Corners**, situated around the intersection of Walnut and Beacon streets and including the Newton Cemetery.

West of Newton Highlands and along the Charles, across from Newton's border with Wellesley, is the village of **Waban**. Until 1855, the area comprised four farms. During that year, Beacon Street was extended westward to the junction of Woodward and Washington streets—the intersection of the four farms. In 1886, the Charles River Railroad commuter service to Boston came through, and more development followed. Today, the private Braeburn Country Club takes up a good portion of Waban's land. Modern commuters still enjoy the proximity to train lines: the Green Line D Waban stop is on Beacon Street in Waban Square, and the Woodland stop is on Washington Street.

Newtonville is the area around the intersection of the Mass Pike and Walnut Street. Previously a broad, well-watered plain used for agriculture, the daily commuter trains along the Boston & Albany railroad that came through in the latter half of the 19th century helped create the environs seen today. Housing developments began on small plots near the railroad line in the 1840s, but the area didn't become popular until Newton built its first high school in 1859. By the Civil War, Newtonville had arrived. As with other Newton villages that developed during the 19th century, Victorian architecture abounds, and you can find Greek and colonial revivals, and friendly tree-lined parks. While Newtonville residents have no T stop, there is bus service and a commuter rail stop between Harvard and Walnut streets by the Mass Pike. Of course, this village is also convenient for commuters who wish to take the Pike into Boston.

At Newton's westernmost tip, just north of Newton Lower Falls, along the Charles River and boundary with Weston, lies **Auburndale**. Until the 1830s, this village was a remote tract of farmland, marsh, and rolling wooded hills; even in 1831 Auburndale had only seven families. That all changed, however, by 1837 when the Boston & Worcester Railroad extended to this area. By the 1860s, Auburndale was a bona fide village with residents who enjoyed easy access to the Charles and the Stony Brook Reservoir. Like neighboring Newton Lower Falls, Auburndale was adversely affected by the construction of Route 128 and the Mass Pike. However, unlike Newton Lower Falls, Auburndale was able to hold onto some of its older housing stock. Look for homes from the 18th, 19th, and 20th centuries here, including farmhouses and colonial revivals. Auburndale retains its original roots as a commuter stop; today's commuters have easy access to the Pike, the Auburndale commuter rail stop (on Lexington Street at the Pike), and two Green Line T stops—Woodland (at Washington and Beacon streets) and Riverside (the D train terminus on Grove Street off Route 128).

Finally, just northeast of Auburndale is the village of **West Newton**, the final railway village located between the Mass Pike and Newton's northern border with Waltham. Like Auburndale, West Newton was once a thinly settled agricultural area full of forests and swamps. West Newton originally made the map in 1764, when it became the religious center for northwestern Newton with the building of the West Parish (Congregational) Church. When the Boston & Worcester line was set up as a commuter rail line in 1834, the area began its life as a suburb. By 1850, new, year-round homes were going up on West Newton Hill, and Irish immigrants and other local workers were moving into modest cottages along the River Street flats. Today, West Newton residents enjoy easy access to the Pike, and there is some remaining nineteenth century construction, including simple Greek Revivals and Italianate homes with long front porches and bay windows. West Newton residents have no T access but, like Newtonville, they do have bus service, a commuter rail stop, which is on Route 16, and easy access to the Mass Pike.

Oak Hill was created specifically as a neighborhood of affordable, modern homes for WWII veterans. In Newton's southernmost territory, this village is roughly bound by Mt. Ida College to the north, West Roxbury to the south, Dedham Street to the east, and the Charles River on the west. Formerly a sand and gravel pit, the City of Newton financed the construction of Oak Hill. At the time, only veterans who were Newton residents before the war were allowed to move here. The village features a series of cul-de-sacs and the houses themselves are small, modern cottages cut from six basic designs; each has a living room, dining area, kitchen, three bedrooms, bath, and utility room, but no basement. The original owners had their choice of clapboard, cedar shingle, or asbestos shingle siding, and hip or gable roofs, as well as garages, porches, and breezeways as the extras. When built, most of the homes faced public walkways, away from the street, but over the years, many have been remodeled so the front doors now face the street. Additionally, many residents have added second floors. Northern Oak Hill was not part of the original housing development, and hence the architecture is slightly different. Expect split-levels here. Streets throughout the original Oak Hill development are named after Newton residents who died during WWII. Oak Hill has no T or commuter rail access, but it does have bus service. The Charles River Country Club (private) is also here.

Today Newton's villages include enormous homes on sprawling greenery to more tightly packed, citified areas, like Route 9 and Newton Corner. Even so, during peak rush hours, this city is much quieter than Boston. Newton is one of Boston's priciest environs, a solidly residential enclave with good public schools, lovely parks, and easy access to Boston. The variety of housing is incredible. You'll find Victorians, colonials, Dutch

Colonials, Brick Colonials, Tudors, 19th century cottages, Craftsman Bungalows, and picturesque Revivals.

It's probably easier to buy a house in Newton than to find an apartment, although it's such a sought after address, there is competition on the home buying front. Those who rent will find Newton a much better deal than downtown. Most renters here are students at one of Newton's several small colleges, particularly BC, but young professionals can be found in places like Newton Corner. Its appeal is obvious: renters can live in a multi-room apartment, if not a house, for the same amount one would pay for a shoebox in Boston. Newton does have its commercial amenities—restaurants, shops, bars, grocery stores, movie theatres, and two malls (across the street from one another), and there are many Green Line and commuter rail T stops and bus routes throughout—though there is not much offered in the way of entertainment or night-life.

As a general rule of thumb, the more affordable homes are in West Newton, Newton Corner, Auburndale and Nonantum; pricier neighborhoods include Chestnut Hill, Newton Centre, Waban and Newton Highlands. Newton Corner and Chestnut Hill also offer high-rise apartments.

There is a substantial Asian population in Newton, and it shares the title as the seat of Boston's Jewish community with neighboring Brookline. You'll find many active synagogues in Chestnut Hill, Newton Lower Falls, Oak Hill, Newton Centre and Newton Corner, as well as a great number of churches. Newton Centre also houses the Andover Newton Theological Seminary, and Catholic churches can be found in Waban and in Nonantum.

Most Newton neighborhoods have all the necessary services and usually a good restaurant or pub to boot, but since the villages evolved independently, there is no real center of town. Most head to Boston for a night out.

As for T access, Newton is so big that many residents do not have a stop within walking distance. Other villages have only bus access. Exceptions are around BC, where students can get on the B train, and in the center of the shopping districts of some villages. Newton is a great place to live for car owners. Parking is aplenty by Boston standards, and most of Boston is accessible in about 15 minutes via the Mass Pike. Newton also has easy access to routes 9, 1, and I-95/128.

Web Sites: www.ci.newton.ma.us, www.newtoncitizens.com
Area Code: 617
Zip Codes: Chestnut Hill, 02467; Newton, 02458; Newtonville, 02460; West Newton, 02465; Newton Centre, 02459; Newton Lower Falls, 02462; Newton Highlands, 02467; Newton Upper Falls, 02464; Waban, 02468; Auburndale, 02466
Post Offices: Boston College Branch, 136 Comm Ave., Room 204C (McElroy Building), 617-552-3522; Chestnut Hill Branch, 12 Middlesex

Road, 617-566-0941; Newtonville Branch, 897 Washington Street, 617-244-2355; West Newton Branch, 525 Waltham Street, 617-244-2502; Newton Center, 716 North Beacon Street, 617-558-1399; Newton Lower Falls Branch, 2344 Washington Street, Suite 1, 617-527-4391; Newton Upper Falls, 81 Oak Street, 617-527-7774; Newton Highlands Branch, 63 Lincoln Street, 617-527-3033; Waban Branch, 83 Wyman Street, 617-527-3673; Auburndale Branch, 2122 Comm Ave., 617-527-1970; Nonantum Branch, 326 Watertown Street, 617-244-2379; www.usps.com

Police: Newton Police Headquarters, 1321 Washington Street, 617-552-7240; www.ci.newton.ma.us/Police

Emergency Hospital: Newton-Wellesley Hospital, 2014 Washington Street, 617-243-6000, www.nwh.org

Libraries: Newton Free Library Main Branch, 330 Homer Street, Newton Centre, 617-796-1360; Auburndale Branch, 375 Auburn Street, 617-552-7158; Newton Corner Branch, 126 Vernon Street, 617-552-7157; Nonantum Branch, 144 Bridge Street, 617-552-7163; Waban Branch, 1608 Beacon Street, 617-552-7166, www.ci.newton.ma.us/Library

Parks & Open Space: Bullough Pond (at the intersection of Comm Ave. and Walnut Street); Burr Park (Arlington, Waverly, and Park streets); Charles River Country Club (Nohanton and Dedham streets); Chestnut Hill Country Club (border with Brighton, between Comm Ave. and Kenrick Street); Chestnut Hill Reservoir (at the eastern border with Brookline and Brighton); Crystal Lake Park (between Centre, Beacon, and Walnut streets); Edmands Park (west of BC, at Blake and Mill streets); Hamilton Playground; Hammond Pond Reservation, www.mass.gov/dcr; Newton Centre Park (between Beacon Street and Comm Ave. at Centre Street); Oak Hill Playground (off of Wheeler Road); Hemlock Gorge, Friends of Hemlock Gorge, www.channel1.com/users/hemlock

Public Schools: Newton Public Schools, 100 Walnut Street, 617-559-6100, www.newtonpublicschools.com

Community Publications: *Newton TAB,* www.townonline.com/newton/news.html, 617-969-0340

Community Resources: Andover-Newton Theological Seminary, 210 Herrick Road, 800-964-ANTS, www.ants.edu; Boston College, 140 Comm Ave., 617-552-8000, www.bc.edu; Hebrew College, 160 Herrick Road, 617-559-8600, www.hebrewcollege.edu; Lasell College, 1844 Comm Ave., 617-243-2000, www.lasell.edu; Mt. Ida College, 777 Dedham Street, 617-928-4500, www.mountida.edu; Jackson Homestead, 527 Washington Street, 617-552-7238; New Art Center, 61 Washington Park, 617-964-3424, www.newartcenter.org; Newton Choral Society, 617-527-SING; New Repertory Theatre, 54 Lincoln

Street (inside Newton Highlands Congregational Church), 617-332-1646, www.newrep.org; Newton Country Players, 1601 Beacon Street, 617-244-9538; Turtle Lane Playhouse, 283 Melrose Street, 617-244-0169, www.turtle-lane.com; The Mall at Chestnut Hill, 199 Boylston Street (Route 9), 617-965-3037, http://themallatchestnuthill.com/; Atrium Mall, Route 9, 617-527-1400, www.shopsimon.com; New Philharmonia Orchestra, 617-527-9717, www.newphilharmonia.org; Newton Symphony Orchestra, www.newtonsymphony.org; Newton Community Chorus, 617-373-4725, www.newtonarts.com

Public Transportation: *Trains*: Green Line D train at Chestnut Hill, Newton Centre, Newton Highlands, Eliot, Waban, Woodland, and Riverside; Commuter Rail at Auburndale, West Newton, and Newtonville

Buses: nos. 52, 57, 59, 60, 500-502, 504, 505, 553, 554, 556, and 558; for MBTA route and schedule information contact the MBTA Traveler's Information Center: 617-222-3200, 800-392-6100, TTY 617-222-5146 or go to www.mbta.com.

SOMERVILLE

Boundaries: **North**: Medford and the Mystic River; **East**: Charlestown; **South** and **southwest**: Cambridge; **West**: Arlington

DAVIS SQUARE	POWDERHOUSE CIRCLE
TEN HILLS	BALL SQUARE
PROSPECT HILL	TEELE SQUARE
UNION SQUARE	TUFTS UNIVERSITY
MAGOUN SQUARE	WEST SOMERVILLE
WINTER HILL	SPRING HILL

In 1997, *Utne Reader* placed Somerville, particularly the neighborhood of **Davis Square**, among the top 15 "hippest places to live" in the US and Canada. This reputation holds true today. Conveniently located west of Charlestown and north of Cambridge, Somerville is a compact city that continues to be popular with the mod squad. With its relatively affordable housing (by Boston standards), and scads of individually owned coffee shops, bars, and eateries, not to mention Tufts University, it's easy to understand its popularity with the younger crowd. Also here, artists, long time Irish- and Italian-American residents, newly arrived immigrants, and young professionals. Overall, Somerville apartments are old, large, and inexpensive although they increase in price closer to Davis Square.

Somerville was included in the Charlestown land grant of 1630, but became an independent town in 1842 and incorporated as a city in 1872.

John Winthrop, the first governor of the Massachusetts Bay Colony, made his home in Somerville during the 1600s. He lived in a neighborhood along Somerville's northern border with the Mystic River that today is called **Ten Hills**. The neighborhood features homes of old and new construction, as well as some light industrial land and parkland along the Mystic.

Originally Somerville was a grazing area for colonial dairy farms, and then served as an important military location for the Revolutionary Army. **Prospect Hill**, in the city center between Highland and Somerville avenues, was the site of military fortifications, some remnants of which still exist in Prospect Hill Park. Today the neighborhood boasts wide, tree-lined streets, older homes, many parks, and views of Boston. Other historical notes: the first American flag was raised here in January of 1776, and Major General Charles Lee used a house on Sycamore Street as his headquarters during the Revolutionary War.

By the early 19th century, Somerville was located right along the transportation corridor linking Boston to the northwest, thus positioning the town perfectly as an industrial center along the Mystic River. Although Somerville also had dairy, agriculture, pottery, and slate industries at the time, it was the brickyards that became its major source of commerce. During the mid-1800s, Irish immigrants came by the droves to labor in the brickyards, each year producing over one million bricks by hand, and even more after the development of a patent press. By 1842, Highland Avenue had become Somerville's civic center, while **Union Square**, in southeastern Somerville, became its center of commerce. Bow Street in Union Square still features many well-preserved period commercial buildings.

Boston's extension of the trolley tracks in the late 19th century paved the way for the expansion. Almost 50% of Somerville's current housing stock was built between 1890 and 1910. As a result, much of the architecture is devoted to sturdy triple-deckers and multiple-family housing, intended originally for those who came to work in the local brickyards, iron mills, tube works, and meat packing plants. The abundance of multiple-family housing in Somerville is responsible for its impressively high-density population: according to the 2000 Census, Somerville has almost 77,500 people living in just over four square miles. Peak occupancy here was during WWII, when over 105,000 people lived here! Triple-deckers have roomy interiors, and renters can get a positively spacious multi-room apartment, with a lawn and possibly a parking space, for what one would spend for a "closet" in downtown Boston. For something more historic and aesthetically pleasing, early 20th century brick apartment houses and tenements can be found, especially on Highland Avenue and around Union Square. There are a few historic districts, including Spring Hill, Mt. Vernon, and Westwood Road. Summer Street is made up predominantly of colonial revivals, with well-preserved Victorian churches. The retail areas of Davis Square feature the architecturally important Somerville Theatre (see **Davis Square** below), great coffee shops, an art-deco bank, and the Rosebud Diner.

Union Square, close to Cambridge's Inman Square, is located in a triangular area where Prospect Street, Webster Avenue, Somerville Avenue, and Washington Street all intersect. In addition to municipal buildings surviving from Somerville's earliest days, this area has many small businesses and ethnic restaurants, including a Portuguese restaurant and bakery and several Indian eateries. For those without wheels getting around will be an issue; there are no T stops within walking distance.

Davis Square, located where College Avenue and Highland Street intersect with Holland, is the only Somerville square stop on the subway line. Rents are higher here than elsewhere in Somerville. It is a bustling place, with interesting stores, coffee shops, restaurants, and bars that draw a distinctly young crowd, and a notable gay presence. (In this instance, young does not necessarily mean college-aged.) In terms of artistic presence, Davis Square hosts Somerville Open Studios (an annual arts festival each spring) and houses the Somerville Theatre, which in addition to mainstream second-run movies, shows international shorts, art films, and hosts the international animation festival each year. Community theatre and comedy shows are at the Boston Baked Theatre, 255 Elm Street.

Magoun Square, just off Medford Street, between Winter Hill and Powderhouse Circle, is an old-fashioned commercial area, with storefronts looking as they might have appeared in the 1950s and '60s. **Winter Hill**, just north of Highland Avenue in central Somerville, is a predominantly residential neighborhood with several parks and somewhat affordable homes. In northern Somerville, **Powderhouse Circle**, between Highland and Boston avenues, Elm Street, and Tufts University, is where you'll find gracious homes on large lots with views of the Tufts athletic fields. **Ball Square** is just past Trum Field on Broadway and is home to many small bakeries. **Teele Square**, which overlaps with **Tufts University**, is also on Broadway near Powderhouse Boulevard and borders Route 16 near Arlington. Davis Square's nightlife spills out toward Teele Square, but Teele is more residential. Both Ball and Teele squares are located in the heart of the Tufts' territory, and subsequently their triple-deckers are positively teeming with coeds. Stores in these areas cater to the college set.

Somerville's picturesque neighborhoods include West Somerville and Spring Hill. Due west of Davis Square along the Arlington border, **West Somerville** has some older Victorian homes and a suburban, residential feel. East of Cambridge's Porter Square between Highland and Somerville avenues is **Spring Hill**, another residential neighborhood with lots of lawns, gardens, and hills—and views of Boston and Cambridge.

Parking in Somerville can be tight, but it's certainly easier than in Boston. On-street parking is done by resident permit (obtainable for a whopping $1/year). The Tufts University area is very crowded and parking can be difficult.

All in all, Somerville has a lot to offer: a pub on most every corner, great pizza places, a large suburban-style mall at Assembly Square (near Wellington Fellsway Bridge to Medford), and easy access to routes 1, 2, 16, 28, 38, 90, 128 and I-93 and I-95. The original Bertucci's at 197 Elm Street, an absolutely heavenly ice cream shop, Denise's Ice Cream in Davis Square, and an impressive university are all here. While Somerville isn't as well endowed with green space as other Boston communities, houses often have big backyards and many people have gardens, so you may not even miss the parks.

Web Sites: www.ci.somerville.ma.us, www.the-ville.com, www.somervillenet.org, www.urbanphoto.org/boston/davis
Area Code: 617
Zip Codes: West Somerville, 02144; Tufts, 02153; Winter Hill, 02145; Union Square, 02143
Post Offices: Somerville Branch, 237 Washington Street, 617-666-2332; West Somerville Branch, 58 Day Street, 617-666-2255; Winter Hill Branch, 320 Broadway, 617-666-5225; Tufts University Branch, 490 Boston Avenue, 617-625-5755; www.usps.com
Police: Somerville Police, 220 Washington Street, 617-625-1600
Emergency Hospitals: Somerville Hospital, 230 Highland Avenue, 617-591-4500, www.challiance.org
Libraries: Central Branch, 79 Highland Avenue, 617-623-5000; West Branch, 40 College Avenue; East Branch, 115 Broadway; www.somervillepubliclibrary.org
Parks & Open Space: Alewife Brook Reservation, www.mass.gov/dcr; Conway Park (Somerville Avenue and Bleachery Court); Foss Park (Route 28 and Broadway); Lincoln Park (Washington and Perry streets); Mystic River Reservation, www.mass.gov/dcr; Trum Field and Playground (in north Somerville at Broadway and Cedar Street)
Public Schools: Somerville Public Schools, 181 Washington Street, 617-625-6600, www.ci.somerville.ma.us
Community Publications: *Somerville Journal,* www.townonline.com/somerville/news.html, 617-625-6300
Community Resources: Chamber of Congress, www.somervillema.org; Somerville Arts Council, www.somervilleartscouncil.org; Tufts University, 617-628-5000, www.tufts.edu; Loews Assembly Square, 35 Middlesex Avenue, 617-628-7000; Somerville Theatre, 55 Davis Square, 617-625-5700; Nexus Theater Center, 255 Elm Street, 617-623-0627, www.nexustheater.org; Theatre Cooperative, 277

Broadway, 617-625-1300; Washington Street Art Center, www.kickball.com/wsac
Public Transportation: *Trains*: Red Line at Davis Square
Buses: nos. 80, 83, 85-92, 94, 101, and CT2; for MBTA route and schedule information contact the MBTA Traveler's Information Center: 617-222-3200, 800-392-6100, TTY 617-222-5146 or go to www.mbta.com.

WALTHAM

Boundaries: **North**: Lexington; **East**: Belmont and Watertown; **Southeast**: Newton; **Southwest**: Weston; **West**: Lincoln

SOUTHEAST WALTHAM (including The Island)
WALTHAM CENTER (including The Highlands, The Bleachery, The Chemistry, and Warrendale)
WEST END (including Brandeis University, Angleside, Robert's, Banks Square, Cedarwood)
TECHNOLOGY HIGHWAY
NORTH WALTHAM (Lakeview, Piety Corner, The Lanes, Bentley College)

Waltham, named after Waltham, England, covers over 13 square miles in the westernmost part of metro Boston, inside Route 128. Bisected in the south by the Charles River, Waltham's proximity to Boston, good housing values, and commercial and entertainment venues has made it a popular place to live. Residents include wealthy sports stars on Boston's professional athletic teams, young professionals who work on Technology Highway (a section of Route 128 where many high-tech companies are headquartered), as well as young families and college students and faculty of Brandeis University and Bentley College, which are both located within its bounds.

Originally a part of Watertown, Waltham became an independent town in 1738. Main Street (now also Route 20) was the post road from Boston and has served as the civic and commercial center of Waltham since the early 18th century. The northern section of Waltham got its start as an agricultural area, while industry, particularly watchmaking, developed along the Charles River in the south. In 1854, Aaron Dennison opened the Waltham Watch Company there. It flourished for over 100 years, and today Waltham is nostalgically known as "Watch City." Two rural federal period estates survive and are open for tours: Gore Place, just south of Main Street in southeastern Waltham by the Watertown line and The Vale (also known as the Lyman Estate) in central Waltham just north of Lyman Pond.

Although there are many sub neighborhoods throughout the city (and corresponding neighborhood associations), most people think of Waltham in terms of north, southeast, west, and central. **Southeast Waltham** is a working-class area with many young families. From Beaver Street south to the town line you'll find affordable multiple family housing. The westernmost portion of Southeast Waltham adjacent to Auburndale in Newton and across the Charles from Angleside is called the **Island**. It's a residential neighborhood of mixed housing, from multi-family structures to small cottages to large Victorians situated around Cram's Cove and Purgatory Cove, inlets of the river. To get here, you must go through a light industrial area that separates the Island from the rest of the residences of Southeast Waltham, either via Rumford or Woerd avenues. Residents have easy access to green space in Auburndale, including Norumbega Park.

Waltham Center, roughly the area where Main and Moody streets intersect just north of the Charles River, has surviving 19th century factory complexes as well as brick Victorian and neo-classic civic and business buildings. This is the veritable city center, full of all the commercial offerings the local student set and young professionals could need. The northern section of Waltham Center houses a large population of mostly young professionals. Many live in expensive condo complexes and exclusive rentals in sub-neighborhoods like the **Highlands**, which is the area just east of Prospect Hill Park. Southern Waltham Center is becoming more popular. The part of Waltham Center between Grove Street and the River is called the **Bleachery**, after the former Waltham Bleachery and Die Works. The area around Pine Street and the river is called the **Chemistry**, after the Newton Chemical Company that used to be here. The Bleachery and the Chemistry are good examples of former factory areas along the riverbank that have been changed to support more modern uses, such as running and walking paths. Both neighborhoods feel virtually contiguous with the center of town. The area to the east of Waltham Center between the center and the Watertown border is **Warrendale**.

The middle and southwestern portion of the city is called the **West End**, taken up mostly by **Brandeis University**. In 1948, Brandeis, the only nonsectarian Jewish college in the US, moved onto its 235 acre campus in southwest Waltham. Brandeis centers around South Street, with a Victorian cemetery as its neighbor, and overlaps with **Angleside**, the sub-neighborhood to the south at the city's southern tip, and **Robert's**, from South Street west to the river. Also in the vicinity: **Banks Square**, where Main Street and Weston Road intersect forms the rough boundary between the West End and Waltham Center; and north of the Brandeis campus is the **Cedarwood** neighborhood. Angleside, Banks Square, Robert's, and

Cedarwood all offer convenient housing for Brandeis students, faculty, and staff, and are all within walking distance of the university.

Route 128/95 runs north/south through Waltham's western boundary with Weston. It is this stretch of freeway that is sometimes referred to as **"Technology Highway"** for all the high-tech businesses here. In fact, outside of Boston proper, Waltham has the most office space in the greater Boston area.

North Waltham is the most affluent section of the city, with large estates, and expensive homes and apartment complexes. Also here, the self-contained campus of the business school, **Bentley College**. Considering the long distance from Boston's T line (outside of driving, Waltham-ites can only reach Boston via bus or commuter rail), apartment complexes are on the pricey side—a two-bedroom here approaches Boston prices. However, some complexes offer residents private shuttle service to the Alewife T Station in Arlington, and many feel the swimming pools and tennis courts are worth the price. Also popular, the onetime resort area of **Lakeview**, located around Hardy Pond between Lake Street and the Lexington border. **Piety Corner** and the **Lanes**, north and south of the intersection of Totten Pond Road and Lexington Street respectively, have condominium complexes and exclusive rentals. These portions of Waltham are made up mainly of single, young professionals.

While Boston is a 15 minute drive (without traffic) on the Pike, Waltham residents need not go far beyond their front door for day to day services ranging from chain stores, restaurants, and grocers to one-of-a-kind eateries, farm stands, and quaint neighborhood markets. Moody Street is undergoing a gentrification of its own, with trendy new restaurants and bars cropping up to cater to the crowds. Places like the Watch City Brewing Company and Iguana Cantina are always full, and Campania, an Italian restaurant, actually draws diners in from the city, as does the Embassy Cinema, the independent movie theater on Pine Street.

Although Waltham has a fair amount of open space, most of it is private—part of Bentley, Brandeis, and private estates. However, there are some public spaces: Waltham City Hall is set on a common; Lyman Pond has an athletic field and park; Prospect Hill Park is sizeable and even has a ski area; and Beaver Brook Reservation is located on the Belmont border. Overall, Waltham, with its low crime rate, local services, easy highway access, and minimal parking problems, is an appealing place to live.

Web Sites: www.city.waltham.ma.us, www.waltham-community.org, www.discoverwaltham.com
Area Code: 781
Zip Code: 02154

Post Offices: Waltham Branch, 776 Main Street, 781-893-9752; North Waltham Branch, 854 Lexington Street, 781-893-9520; South Waltham Branch, 38 Spruce Street, 781-893-9841; www.usps.com
Police: Waltham Police, 155 Lexington Street, 781-314-3600; www.city.waltham.ma.us
Emergency Hospital: Deaconess-Waltham Hospital, Hope Avenue, 781-647-6000, www.waltham.caregroup.org
Libraries: Main Library, 735 Main Street, 781-314-3425, www.waltham.lib.ma.us
Parks & Open Space: Beaver Brook Reservation, www.mass.gov/dcr; Prospect Hill Park and ski area (Totten Pond and Prospect Hill roads); Riverwalk Park (south Waltham, along the Charles); Charles River; Stony Brook Basin (at the border with Weston by I-95); Hardy Pond (north Waltham, south of Trapelo Road off of Hibiscus Avenue); Lyman Pond (southeast of Geaver and Lyman streets); Cambridge Reservoir (northwest Waltham, along Route 95 and Totten Pond Road)
Public Schools: Waltham Public Schools, 617 Lexington Street, 781-314-5440, www.city.waltham.ma.us
Community Publications: *Daily News Tribune*, www.dailynewstribune.com, 781-647-7898; *West Weekly*, 508-820-4200
Community Resources: Chamber of Commerce, www.walthamchamber.com; Bentley College, 175 Forest Street, 781-891-2000, www.bentley.edu; Brandeis University, 415 South Street, 781-736-2000, www.brandeis.edu; Waltham Museum, 196 Charles Street (rear building), 781-893-8017, www.walthammuseum.com; Charles River Museum of Industry, 154 Moody Street, 781-893-5410, www.crmi.org; Gore Place, 52 Gore Street, 781-894-2798, http://ne-arts.net/goreplace; Rose Art Museum, 415 South Street, 781-736-3434, www.brandeis.edu/rose/; Paine Estate, 100 Robert Treat Paine Drive, 781-314-3290, www.waltham-community.org/Paine; Lyman Estate, 185 Lyman Street, 781-891-7095, www.waltham-community.org/Lyman; Waltham Historical Society, 190 Moody Street, 781-891-5815; American Jewish Historical Society, 2 Thornton Road (Brandeis Campus), 781-891-8110, www.ajhs.org; Hovey Players, 9 Spring Street, 781-893-9171; Reagle Players, 617 Lexington Street, 781-891-5600; Spingold Theater Center, 415 South Street (Brandeis campus), 781-736-3400
Public Transportation: *Trains*: Commuter Rail at Brandeis/Roberts, Waltham and Waverly
Buses: nos. 70, 70A, 505, 553, 554, 556, and 558; for MBTA route and schedule information contact the MBTA Traveler's Information Center: 617-222-3200, 800-392-6100, TTY 617-222-5146 or go to www.mbta.com.

WATERTOWN

Boundaries: **North**: Belmont; **East**: Cambridge; **South**: the Charles River; **West**: Waltham

COOLIDGE SQUARE
WATERTOWN SQUARE
ARSENAL
MT. AUBURN STREET
OAKLEY COUNTRY CLUB

Watertown, established in 1630, ceded much of its land to the surrounding communities of Waltham, Weston, Lincoln, Cambridge, and Belmont. Today the town covers only 4.1 square miles. Except for one small portion set off from Newton on the south side of the Charles, Watertown is located on the north shore of the Charles River.

A fairly unassuming place, Watertown's history includes being the temporary seat of government during the Revolutionary War; it was home to patriot Paul Revere and where he printed Massachusetts' first paper currency; and is where the Old Bemis Mills were located (weavers of the canvas sails for the USS Constitution). Today Watertown is a residential community with a mix of young singles and couples, many of whom chose Watertown for the Cambridge-type location without the Cambridge prices; and with one of the largest Armenian populations outside of Armenia itself, Watertown has earned itself the moniker "Little Armenia." Armenian markets are abundant (particularly around **Coolidge Square**), as well as restaurants, an Armenian Cultural Center, and a museum.

Watertown varies from moderately urban to downright suburban, with big houses on big lawns, easy street parking or better yet, driveways, and quiet streets. Many of Boston's young professionals are buying houses here while they're still affordable, enjoying close proximity to the city and major transportation routes, and convenient shopping at nearby big box stores like Best Buy, Target, and Home Depot.

Watertown Square, with its location along the river, developed along with the mills as the town's economic center. By the mid-19th century, Watertown Square's presence was further enhanced when it was linked directly to Boston with the arrival of the railroads and then streetcars. Today, the Square retains Victorian and neo-classic retail blocks.

During the federal period, the **Arsenal** Street corridor was home to the US arsenal. Parts of it now comprise the recently revamped Arsenal Mall and its selection of chain stores. Along the residential **Mt. Auburn Street**, you can find interesting diners and a number of greengrocers and

Armenian markets. In addition, the area around the **Oakley Country Club**, which borders Belmont, has become a desirable place to live. It features brick, stone, clapboard, and stucco colonials, and Victorians with wrap-around porches.

Watertown is greener than many sections of Somerville and Cambridge, bordered by the Mt. Auburn Cemetery on the east and the running paths and parks and recreation facilities along the Charles River. There are playgrounds, tot lots, and an ice skating rink. Housing prices are more affordable here than in Arlington and the selection is mostly multi-family, with some apartment complexes and single family houses.

Watertown Square doesn't offer a lot of nightlife, although it does have a few chic restaurants and smart shops. There are pubs in Orchard Park and on the Waltham and Cambridge borders, but many residents head to Cambridge or Boston for their evening entertainment. In terms of transportation, the motto is: have car, will travel. Residents have easy access to the Massachusetts Turnpike, Memorial Drive, and I-95. There are no subway stations in Watertown, but there are express buses to downtown Boston, as well as regular bus service to the Red Line and Cambridge.

Web Site: www.watertown-ma.com
Area Code: 617
Zip Code: 02471 - 02472
Post Offices: Watertown Finance Branch, 126 Main Street, 617-924-1215; East Watertown Branch, 589 Mt. Auburn Street, 617-924-1407; New Town Branch, 123-125 Galen Street, 617-926-2606; www.usps.com
Police: Watertown Police, 34 Cross Street, 617-972-6500; www.watertownpd.org
Emergency Hospital: Mt. Auburn Hospital, 330 Mt. Auburn Street, Cambridge, 617-492-3500, www.mountauburn.caregroup.org
Libraries: Main Library, 123 Main Street, 617-972-6431; East Branch Library, 481 Mt. Auburn Street, 617-972-6441; North Branch Library, 265 Orchard Street, 617-972-6442; www.watertownlib.org
Parks & Open Space: Charles River; Beacon Park (between Beacon and Arsenal streets); Mt. Auburn Cemetery (at the border with Cambridge between Arlington and Mt. Auburn streets); Sawine Pound (between Coolidge Avenue and Arlington Street); Oakley Country Club (off Belmont and Common streets)
Public Schools Watertown Public Schools, 30 Common Street, 617-926-7700, www.watertown.k12.ma.us
Community Publications: *Watertown TAB & Press*, www.townonline.com/watertown/news.html
Community Resources: Watertown-Belmont Chamber of Commerce, http://wbcc.org/; Perkins School for the Blind, 175 North Beacon

Street, 617-924-3434, www.perkins.pvt.k12.ma.us; Arsenal Mall, 485 Arsenal Street, 617-923-4700, www.shopsimon.com; Armenian Library and Museum of America, 65 Main Street, 617-926-2562, http://armenianheritage.com

Public Transportation: *Buses*: nos. 52, 57, 70, 70A, 71, 502, and 504; for MBTA route and schedule information contact the MBTA Traveler's Information Center: 617-222-3200, 800-392-6100, TTY 617-222-5146 or go to www.mbta.com.

NORFOLK COUNTY

BROOKLINE

Boundaries: **North**: Comm Ave. (Boston) **East**: St. Mary's Street, the Riverway, the Jamaicaway, St. Paul's Avenue; **South**: Jamaica Plain, West Roxbury, and Newton; **West**: Allston-Brighton and Newton

FISHER HILL	**ST. MARY/LOWER BEACON STREET**
BROOKLINE VILLAGE	**JFK CROSSING**
LONGWOOD	**WASHINGTON SQUARE**
COOLIDGE CORNER	**CHESTNUT HILL**
ASPINWALL HILL	**PUTTERHAM CIRCLE**
BROOKLINE HILLS	**WESTBROOK VILLAGE**

Technically a separate town of 6.6 square miles and 57,000 residents in the center of western Boston, Brookline is very much part of the city. Surrounded by Boston on all sides except the southwest, Brookline offers the perfect compromise between urban and suburban: it is beautiful and safe, with lots of green space, plentiful amenities, and a good mix of high-density areas and quiet neighborhoods. Residential areas include sprawling houses and/or mansions on spacious lawns, as well as ample, large, and somewhat more affordable apartments and condos than are available in downtown Boston. The schools in Brookline are high-quality, and T and bus access is plentiful.

If you have heard that Brookline is the center of Boston's Jewish community, you have heard right. Brookline became home to many Jews that immigrated to America during the 1800s and 1900s from Germany and Eastern Europe, including Orthodox and Hassidic Jews, a small Sephardic community, and more recently there has been an influx from Russia. Brookline's thriving Jewish populace is evident in the many temples around town, especially the large Revival style synagogues on **Fisher Hill** (just northeast of the intersection of Chestnut Hill Avenue and Route 9). Harvard

Street is lined with kosher delis, bakeries, and bagel shops, and features a few Israeli import and Judaica shops. And where else could you find two kosher Chinese restaurants and a kosher Korean restaurant? This is not to say that everyone in Brookline is Jewish. Other, more recent arrivals include Asians mostly of Chinese and Japanese descent. Brookline is a convenient location for many college students, including those attending classes at any of the colleges in the Fenway, as well as those who go to Pine Manor, Newbury, or Boston colleges, all near Cleveland Circle and Chestnut Hill. Safer and slightly more affordable than Boston and with a top-notch public school system and quick commute to Boston, Brookline is particularly appealing to young professionals with families. Like Newton, it is indeed a great place to raise a family, and with so many cultural and civic amenities, it is obvious why many choose to settle here for good. Renters can get more space for their dollar here than in downtown Boston, and even the sections along Beacon Street tend to be quieter and greener.

Originally called the "Muddy River Hamlet," this area was farmland in the 1630s. By 1705 it became an independent town. Perhaps what is most unique about Brookline is that it successfully resisted annexation by Boston, unlike all other surrounding communities. Brookline's economy remained solidly agricultural until the early 1800s, when substantial residential development began. As in Jamaica Plain, Brookline's character segued from agrarian to residential when wealthy Bostonians (many of them merchants) built summer homes here. Famous residents have included Zabdiel Boylston (who introduced the smallpox vaccine to the US), Frederick Law Olmstead, John and Robert Kennedy, as well as current resident, former Massachusetts governor and presidential candidate Michael Dukakis.

With Boston's mid-19th century streetcar expansion came another building boom for Brookline that included the making of **Brookline Village**, a development of picturesque subdivisions, as well as the **Longwood** area, a collection of early Gothic style stone houses and churches. **Coolidge Corner**, a welcoming collection of brick and faced stone apartments along Beacon Street and Comm Ave., developed during the early 20th century; and higher density blocks were built on **Aspinwall Hill**. More modern and utilitarian triple-deckers can be found around the intersection of Cypress and Boylston streets, adjacent to the Brookline Hills T stop and Brookline High School.

Bisecting Brookline is Route 9 (a.k.a. Boylston Street), a thoroughfare that connects Boston to its western suburbs. Those areas of Brookline that fall to the north of Route 9, that is, the side closer to Boston, have a distinctly urban feel. Apartments, stores, and restaurants line the busy but pedestrian-friendly Beacon Street corridor from stem to stern of its Brookline stretch between Boston and Newton. Running along here is the Green Line C train, connecting Cleveland Circle (Brighton) to downtown. The D train of the

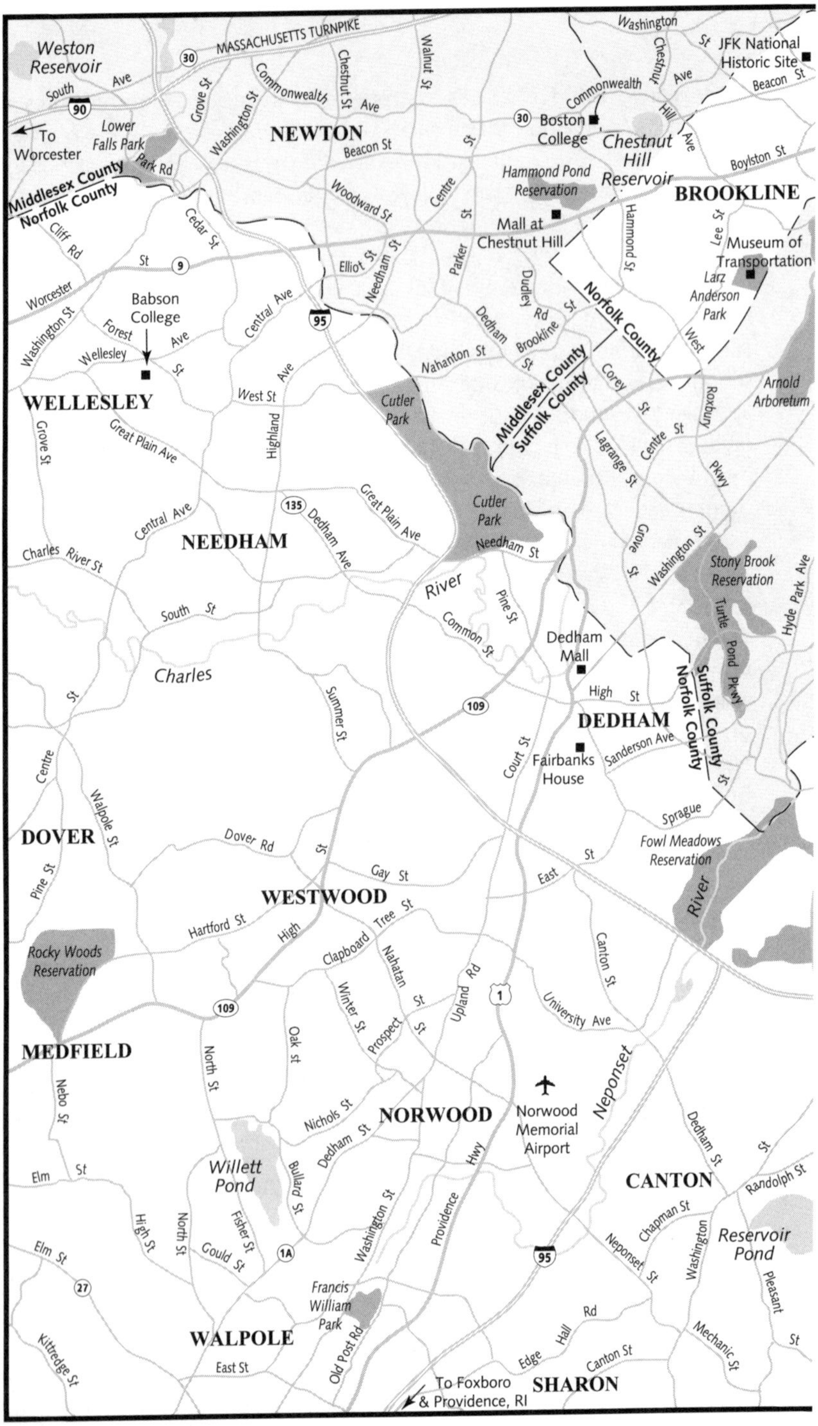
Weston Reservoir
MASSACHUSETTS TURNPIKE
South Ave
To Worcester
Lower Falls Park
Park Rd
Middlesex County
Norfolk County
Grove St
Washington St
Commonwealth Ave
Chestnut St
Walnut St
NEWTON
Beacon St
Woodward St
Centre St
Boston College
Commonwealth
Washington
Chestnut Hill Ave
JFK National Historic Site
Beacon St
Chestnut Hill Reservoir
Boylston St
Hammond Pond Reservation
Mall at Chestnut Hill
BROOKLINE
Hammond St
Lee St
Museum of Transportation
Larz Anderson Park
Cedar St
Cliff Rd
Worcester St
Washington St
Babson College
Forest Ave
Wellesley St
Central Ave
Elliot St
Needham St
Parker St
Dudley Rd
Dedham St
Brookline St
Norfolk County
Nahanton St
Middlesex County
Suffolk County
Corey St
West Roxbury Pkwy
Arnold Arboretum
WELLESLEY
West St
Highland Ave
Cutler Park
Great Plain Ave
Grove St
Lagrange St
Centre St
Great Plain Ave
Dedham Ave
Central Ave
NEEDHAM
Charles River St
Needham St
Grove St
Washington St
Stony Brook Reservation
Hyde Park Ave
Turtle Pond Pkwy
River
Pine St
Common St
South St
Charles
Dedham Mall
High St
St
Summer St
Suffolk County
Norfolk County
DEDHAM
Sanderson Ave
Fairbanks House
Court St
Centre
Walpole St
Sprague St
DOVER
Dover Rd
St
Fowl Meadows Reservation
Gay St
East St
River
Pine St
WESTWOOD
Hartford St
Tree St
High
Clapboard
Nahatan St
Canton St
Rocky Woods Reservation
Winter St
Upland Rd
University Ave
Prospect St
MEDFIELD
North St
Oak st
Neponset
Norwood Memorial Airport
Nebo St
Nichols St
NORWOOD
Dedham St
Hwy
Dedham St
Elm St
Willett Pond
Bullard St
CANTON
Randolph St
Chapman St
Reservoir Pond
High St
North St
Fisher St
Washington St
Providence
Neponset St
Washington
Elm St
Gould St
Pleasant St
Francis William Park
Rd
Hall
Mechanic St
Edge
Canton St
Kittredge St
WALPOLE
East St
Old Post Rd
To Foxboro & Providence, RI
SHARON

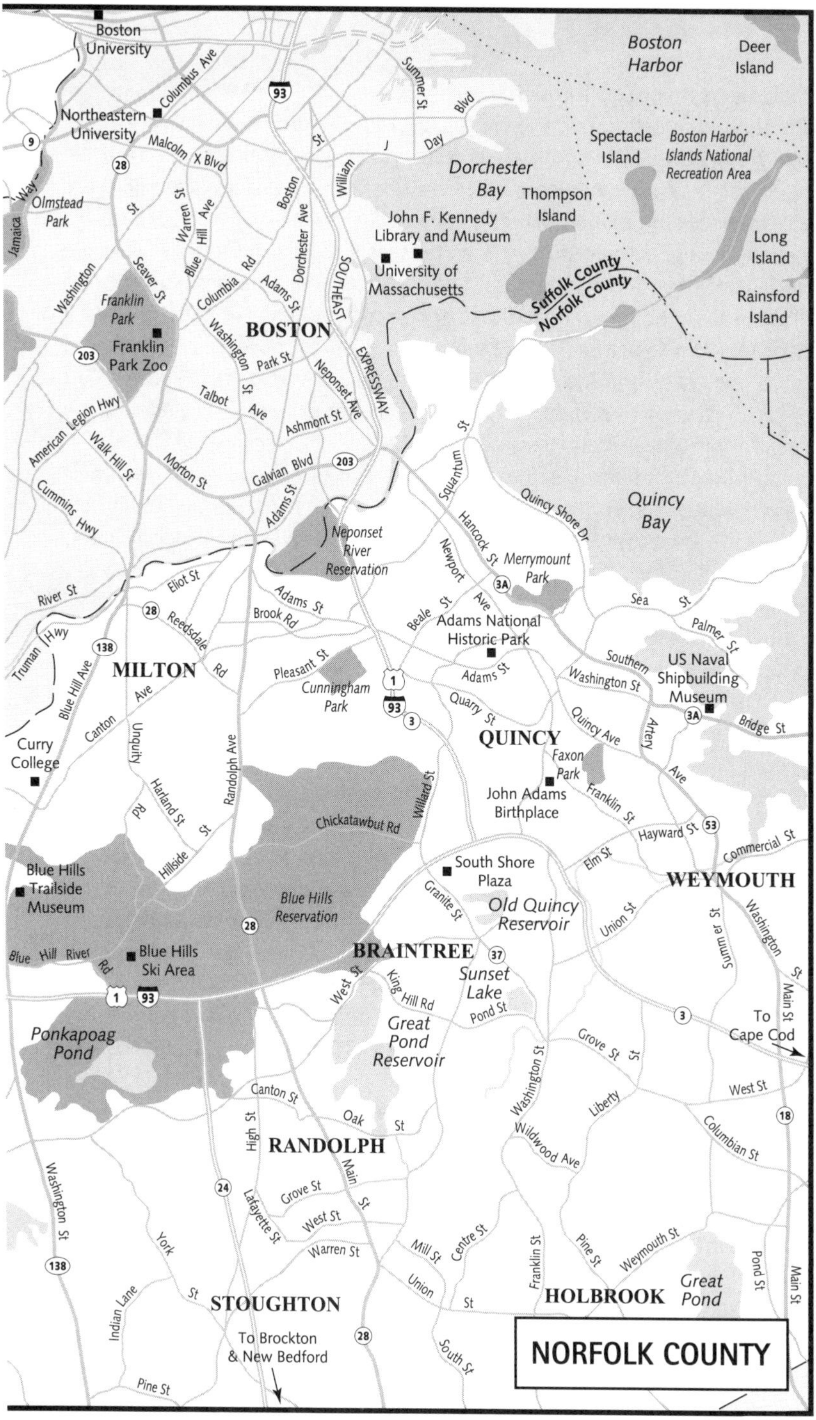
NORFOLK COUNTY
Boston University
Northeastern University
Columbus Ave
93
9
28
Malcolm X Blvd
Olmstead Park
Jamaica Way
Washington St
Warren St
Blue Hill Ave
Boston St
Dorchester Ave
Summer St
Day Blvd
William J
Boston Harbor
Deer Island
Spectacle Island
Boston Harbor Islands National Recreation Area
Dorchester Bay
Thompson Island
Long Island
Rainsford Island
John F. Kennedy Library and Museum
University of Massachusetts
SOUTHEAST EXPRESSWAY
Suffolk County
Norfolk County
Seaver St
Franklin Park
Franklin Park Zoo
Columbia Rd
Adams St
BOSTON
203
Park St
Neponset Ave
Talbot Ave
Ashmont St
American Legion Hwy
Walk Hill St
Morton St
Galvian Blvd
Cummins Hwy
Squantum St
Quincy Shore Dr
Quincy Bay
Hancock St
Newport Ave
Neponset River Reservation
Merrymount Park
3A
River St
Eliot St
Adams St
Brook Rd
Reedsdale Rd
Beale St
Adams National Historic Park
Sea St
Palmer St
Truman Hwy
138
MILTON
Blue Hill Ave
Pleasant St
Cunningham Park
1
Quarry St
Southern Artery
Washington St
US Naval Shipbuilding Museum
Bridge St
Canton Ave
Unquity Rd
Curry College
QUINCY
Quincy Ave
Faxon Park
John Adams Birthplace
Franklin St
Harland St
Randolph Ave
Willard St
Chickatawbut Rd
Hillside St
Hayward St
53
Commercial St
Elm St
South Shore Plaza
WEYMOUTH
Blue Hills Trailside Museum
Blue Hills Reservation
Granite St
Old Quincy Reservoir
Union St
Summer St
Washington St
Blue Hill River Rd
Blue Hills Ski Area
BRAINTREE
37
Sunset Lake
West St
King Hill Rd
Pond St
Main St
To Cape Cod
Ponkapoag Pond
Great Pond Reservoir
Grove St
Canton St
Oak St
Washington St
Liberty St
West St
18
High St
RANDOLPH
Wildwood Ave
Columbian St
Washington St
24
Grove St
Lafayette St
West St
York St
Warren St
Mill St
Centre St
Franklin St
Pine St
Weymouth St
Pond St
Main St
Union St
Indian Lane
STOUGHTON
HOLBROOK
Great Pond
To Brockton & New Bedford
South St
Pine St

Green Line meanders through the area south of Beacon Street and north of Route 9, connecting commercial areas—**Longwood**, **Brookline Village** and **Brookline Hills**—with rapid access to the city. Although many of the streets that cross Beacon and Boylston streets quickly disseminate into more suburban-feeling neighborhoods, south of Route 9 is where true suburbia lies. In one of Boston's most well-to-do areas, this part of Brookline is where you're apt to find enormous, gorgeous, and expensive homes. The housing stock is fairly uniform throughout northern Brookline—mostly pre WWII apartments and brownstone row houses similar to those in the Fenway, a few newer high- and low-rise developments, as well as some houses on small to medium-sized lots. Apartments are more prevalent closer to the major thoroughfares and commercial hubs.

Although Brookline is mainly residential, it does have major commercial centers, several of which are tied to some of its most popular neighborhoods. These commercial centers include St. Mary/Lower Beacon Street, Coolidge Corner, JFK Crossing, Brookline Village, Washington Square, Longwood, and Chestnut Hill. **St. Mary/Lower Beacon Street**, so named for Beacon's cross street, has many small, independent businesses and restaurants, and even a few guesthouses.

Further down Beacon Street, the next major neighborhood/commercial center is **Coolidge Corner**, where Beacon and Harvard streets intersect. Coolidge Corner is Brookline's core shopping and dining district, made up of a mix of chain and non-chain stores, ethnic restaurants, bookstores, clothing shops, coffee shops, and toy stores. Also here, the Coolidge Corner movie theater, which offers a variety of second-run, art, international, independent, and specialty films, as well as book readings, which are done in cooperation with the independently owned Brookline Booksmith across the street. With such a selection of local amenities, it is not surprising that rents in and around Coolidge Corner are higher than the rest of Brookline. You'd expect parking here to be difficult, but there seems to be just enough metered parking on this stretch of Harvard and Beacon streets to keep the issue to a minimum.

The area of Harvard Street north of Coolidge Corner, roughly between Beals Street and the Brighton border, is **JFK Crossing**—so named because both John F. Kennedy, and Robert F. Kennedy were born at 83 Beals Street. Aside from this piece of history, JFK Crossing is most well-noted for its established Jewish community and conglomeration of kosher eateries, food stores, book shops, and Judaica stores. Four hand-painted outdoor murals on Harvard Street depict the neighborhood's history of transition from an agricultural community to a city, the Kennedy family, and the Jewish immigration. JFK Crossing is fairly close to Comm Ave. in Boston, for which reason residents will find it a closer walk to the B train than to the C train.

South from Coolidge Corner on Harvard Street is **Brookline Village**, at the intersection of Boylston and Harvard streets and extending up Washington Street. Brookline Village is the civic center of Brookline, home to the fire department, police station, and municipal court. Accessible by the D Line, this neighborhood is quaint, perhaps best described as "villagey," with its clusters of interesting stores and boutiques, eateries, antique shops, children's stores, and a puppet theater called the Puppet Showplace. Most businesses are independently owned, although there are a couple of larger chains, including Bertucci's in Brookline Place. It has both a posh side—the antique shops and some of the restaurants are pricey—and a hipper side, with thrift stores, an old-fashioned barbershop, and a diner. Traffic around this intersection can get congested and parking is sometimes hard to come by.

Further down Beacon Street from Boston at the intersection of Washington Street is **Washington Square**. This commercial/residential neighborhood is smaller and less glamorous than Coolidge Corner or Brookline Village, but offers all the basics, including dry cleaners, dentists, law offices, as well as a few restaurants, an ice cream parlor, a few coffee shops, Asian and Russian grocers, and even a cat hospital. While the housing stock has remained fairly unchanged through the years, the neighborhood's commercial face is undergoing some restoration.

Between the D train stops of Brookline Village and Fenway is the Longwood stop, serving the **Longwood** area of Brookline. Longwood in Brookline is synonymous with Longwood in the Fenway in Boston—they are two halves of the same whole, named for the medical area that straddles the border of Boston and Brookline. Technically, the boundary is the Riverway—everything east is Boston, and everything west is Brookline. Generally speaking, the medical buildings and many of the commercial buildings are on the Boston side, and most of the residences are in Brookline, which are home to many medical students and hospital staff. Perhaps the most distinctive housing option in this area is Longwood Towers, originally built as a hotel in 1924 it's been converted into luxury residences, offering long- and short-term rentals.

The **Chestnut Hill** area of Brookline, an extension of the Chestnut Hill Village of Newton, covers the area at the western edge of Brookline between the Hammond Pond Parkway and Hammond Street, just south of and including Route 9. Route 9 is heavily built-up, offering easy access to some swanky restaurants, such as Legal Seafoods and Figs, as well as smaller shops and services, a large movie theater, and a Star Market. In terms of residential options, this is an up-market area; most of the housing stock is single-family, and ranges from well-manicured estates to upscale condominiums. Chestnut Hill, accessible by the Chestnut Hill stop on the D train, also includes the Country Club, the Putterham Meadows Golf Course, and the Longview Cricket Club.

On the eastern edge of Chestnut Hill is Pine Manor College and on the northern edge is Newbury College. Just to the south is **Putterham Circle**, which, in terms of housing and commerce, is similar to Chestnut Hill. The **Westbrook Village** area in the southwest corner of Brookline is where you will find typical Brookline homes (read expensive), and not a lot of rental properties.

Unfortunately, there is no overnight on-street parking in Brookline, not even for guests. If you have a car, you'll have to pay for a parking space, either at your building or at one of the several town lots, which of course, have waiting lists. For more information on parking in Brookline, see the **Getting Settled** chapter.

Web Site: www.town.brookline.ma.us
Area Code: 617
Zip Codes: 02445-02447
Post Offices: Brookline Branch, 1295 Beacon Street, 617-738-1649; Brookline Village Branch, 207 Washington Street, 617-566-1557; www.usps.com
Police: HQ, 350 Washington Street, 617-730-2222; www.brooklinepolice.com
Emergency Hospitals: Beth Israel Deaconess Hospital, 330 Brookline Avenue, 617-667-7000, www.bidmc.harvard.edu; Brigham & Women's Hospital, 75 Francis Street, 617-732-5500, www.brighamandwomens.org; Children's Hospital, 300 Longwood Avenue, 617-355-6000, www.childrenshospital.org
Libraries: Main Library (Town Hall Branch), 361 Washington Street, 617-730-2375; Coolidge Corner Branch, 31 Pleasant Street, 617-730-2380; Putterham Branch, 959 West Roxbury Parkway, Chestnut Hill, 617-730-2385; www.town.brookline.ma.us/Library
Parks & Open Space: Larz Anderson Park (southwest Brookline at the border with JP, off Goddard Avenue); Brookline Reservoir (middle of Brookline at Route 9 and Lee Street); Chestnut Hill Reservoir (at the border with Brighton in Cleveland Circle); Jamaicaway (between Route 9 and Perkins Street); Olmstead Park (at Perkins Street and the Jamaicaway along the border with JP); Riverway (between Route 9 and Park Street along the border of JP); Putterham Meadows Golf Course (southwest Brookline, at Hammond and Newton streets); Dane Park (at Hammond Street and Woodland Road); Allandale Farm, 259 Allandale Road, www.allandalefarm.com; The Country Club; www.townofbrooklinemass.com/Conservation/Parks.html

Public Schools Brookline Public Schools, 5th Floor, Town Hall, 333 Washington Street, 617-730-2400, www.brookline.mec.edu

Community Resources: Longyear Museum, 1125 Boylston Street, Chestnut Hill, 800-277-8943, www.townofbrooklinemass.com; Kennedy Historic Site, 83 Beals Street, 617-566-7937; Olmstead Historic Site, 99 Warren Street, 617-566-1689, www.townofbrookline mass.com; Brookline Adult and Community Education Program, 115 Greenough Street (Brookline High School), 617-730-2700, www.brooklineadulted.org; Coolidge Corner Theater, 290 Harvard Street, 617-734-2500, www.coolidge.org; Pine Manor College, 400 Heath Street, 617-731-7000, www.pmc.edu; Newbury College, 129 Fisher Avenue, 617-730-7076, www.newbury.edu; Puppet Showplace Theatre, 32 Station Street, 617-731-6400, www.puppetshowplace.org

Community Publications: *Brookline TAB*, www.townonline.com/brookline/news.html; *Boston Russian Bulletin*, www.russianmass.com

Public Transportation: ***Trains***: Green Line C trolley makes surface stops along Beacon Street from downtown to Cleveland Circle at St. Mary's Street, Hawes Street, Kent Street, St. Paul Street, Coolidge Corner, Winchester Street/Summit Avenue, Brandon Hall, Fairbanks Street, Washington Square, Tappan Street, Dean Road and Englewood Avenue; Green Line D trolley at Longwood, Brookline Village, Brookline Hills, Beaconsfield, and Reservoir

Buses: nos. 51, 60, 65, 66, and 86; for MBTA route and schedule information contact the MBTA Traveler's Information Center: 617-222-3200, 800-392-6100, TTY 617-222-5146 or go to www.mbta.com.

DEDHAM

Boundaries: **North**: Charles River, Needham, and West Roxbury; **East**: Readville (Boston); **South**: Fowl Meadows Reservation, Islington, and Westwood; **West**: Westwood and Needham

ASHCROFT
ENDICOTT
OAKDALE
EAST DEDHAM

To the southwest of Boston at the border of West Roxbury and Readville lies Dedham, population 24,000. Like Malden, Dedham is an example of a solid working-class town adjacent to the city and with good highway access. Founded in 1636, Dedham has been around almost as long as

Boston, but has fewer historical points of interest. The town does have one relic however, North America's oldest wooden-frame house, the Fairbanks House built in 1737, is near the center of town.

Initially an agricultural town, Dedham's character was forever changed with the digging of Mother Brook in 1637. Mother Brook connected the Charles River with the Neponset River, thus paving the way for industry, particularly mills. For over 200 years, the Neponset River's waterpower fed Dedham's mills (wool, cotton, grain, etc.), and supplied the power necessary to run the factories. Immigrants from Ireland and Germany in particular came to work and settle in Dedham. Toward the end of the 19th century, many local industries closed shop; by the end of WWI, the remaining textile plants closed as well.

Today, Dedham's affordability and safety make it a popular choice for many. Unfortunately, most of the architecture from its colonial days has not survived; the majority of the housing stock was built in the 20th century. Most Dedham residents live in sturdy, single-family homes and duplexes, although the dedicated home seeker may be able to find a historic gem. Dedham has a rather uniform feel with little architectural variation between neighborhoods, though the west side of town is more thinly settled and feels more rural, and the eastern half is fairly dense and more commercial. Houses are on good-sized lots, and are shaded by mature trees.

In **Ashcroft**, on the eastern border with Readville, you'll see a lot of small and relatively new single-family homes with siding. The **Endicott**, to the west of Ashcroft around the intersection of East Street and Sprague Street, and **Oakdale** (just north of that) neighborhoods are a little more upscale than Ashcroft and the rest of Dedham. At the town's northeast border with Boston and running over to Mother Brook is **East Dedham**, which houses affordable duplexes and inexpensively built homes. About 20% of Dedham's residents are renters, and a good deal of its apartment stock is in East Dedham.

Commercial offerings include two movie theaters and the Dedham Mall on the Providence Highway. Dedham residents are quite proud of their historical municipal center that is made up of buildings in well-preserved architectural styles, including a granite Greek Revival courthouse and a Romanesque Revival public library. If you'd like to get outdoors, Dedham has several small ponds and waterways, including a segment of the Charles. Also nearby: the Fowl Meadow Reservation, the Stony Brook Reservation, and the large Blue Hills Reservation.

Like Malden, Dedham has great highway access for those who want to commute into the city for work. As Dedham borders Boston on its southwest side, it is relatively far from Boston's center, and to get there entails a trip through West Roxbury or Jamaica Plain—not too difficult, but not overly convenient. However, Dedham is perfectly poised to pick up routes 128 and 95 to head north and south to the shores of Massachusetts. The Dedham portion of I-95 is also very close to its junction with I-93, another major route into Boston. Public transportation, sadly, is not so hot. The options are bus or commuter rail into the city. The Franklin line of the commuter rail has two stops in Dedham: Endicott (on Washington Avenue off East Street) and Dedham Corporate (East Street off Route 128).

Web Site: www.town.dedham.ma.us
Area Code: 781
Zip Codes: 02026, 02027
Post Offices: Dedham Main Office, 611 High Street, 781-326-4768; East Dedham Station, 280 Bussey Street, 781-326-4910; www.usps.com
Police: Dedham Police, 600 High Street, 781-326-8460, www.dedhampolice.org
Emergency Hospitals: Deaconess-Glover Hospital, 148 Chestnut Street (Needham), 781-453-3000, www.glover.caregroup.org; Milton Hospital, 92 Highland Street, Milton, 617-696-4600, www.miltonhospital.org
Libraries: Dedham Public Library, 43 Church Street, 781-751-9280; Endicott Branch, 257 Mt. Vernon Street, 781-326-5339; www.dedhamlibrary.org
Parks & Open Space: Charles River (north Dedham); Weld Pond (west Dedham by I-95 and High Street); Wigwam Pond (east of VFW Parkway at West Jersey Street); Motley Pond (at the end of the Charles northwest of the intersection of Common and Bridge streets); Fowl Meadow Reservation (along southeast Dedham's border with Canton at I-95); Cutler Park, www.mass.gov/dcr; Stony Brook Reservation, www.mass.gov/dcr
Public Schools: Dedham Public Schools, 30 Whiting Avenue, 781-326-5622, www.dedham.k12.ma.us
Community Resources: Dedham Historical Society (Museum and Library), 612 High Street, 781-326-1385, www.dedhamhistorical.org; Dedham Mall, 300 Providence Highway, 781-329-1210; Fairbanks House, 511 East Street, 781-326-1170, www.fairbankshouse.org; Noble & Greenough School, 10 Campus Drive, 781-326-3700, www.nobles.edu; Dedham Community Theater, 580 High Street, 781-326-1463
Community Publications: *Daily News Transcript*, www.dailynewstranscript.com
Public Transportation: *Trains*: commuter rail at Endicott and Dedham Corporate Center
Buses: nos. 33, 34, 34E, 35, and 52; for MBTA route and schedule information contact the MBTA Traveler's Information Center: 617-222-3200, 800-392-6100, TTY 617-222-5146 or go to www.mbta.com.

MILTON

Boundaries: **North**: Neponset River and Boston; **East**: Quincy; **South**: Blue Hills Reservation and Canton; **West**: Boston and Fowl Meadows Reservation

MILTON VILLAGE
MILTON CENTER
EAST MILTON

Just south of Dorchester across the Neponset River and bordering Hyde Park is the well-heeled town of Milton, which can be summed up in one word: gorgeous. That is, if you find large, well-preserved colonial homes on roomy, green lots in a sylvan setting, with in-town amenities, and easy highway, forest, and city access appealing. Thirteen square miles in size, this community of about 26,000 people is made up mostly of homeowners. If it's urban living you're looking for, then Milton is probably not your best choice. But if you want what could be considered the prototypical *Better Homes & Gardens* sort of white picket fence American suburb, look no further.

The birthplace of former president George Bush, Milton was used by the British as a trading post as early as the 1620s, and was incorporated as a town in 1662. Like Dedham, starting in the last quarter of the seventeenth century, Milton was the site of many mills, which harnessed the Neponset River's ample water supply. The town also was home to what is thought to be the oldest piano factory in the US, established in 1800 by Benjamin Crahoe. It was the extension of the streetcar lines to Milton from Boston in the late 1800s that transformed the town into the affluent streetcar suburb that you see today.

As Milton developed, large estates were built alongside farms, and although much of the original acreage was broken up and subsequently developed with smaller homes, this area is still unmistakably affluent. For a pretty penny you can have your pick of a colonial, a 19th century country home, a New England farmhouse, a large Georgian estate, or a worker's cottage nicely offset from the street with a lawn.

Milton is sandwiched between the Blue Hills Reservation to the south and the Neponset River and Boston's Dorchester neighborhood to the north and thus tends to be more heavily settled the closer you are to Boston, particularly near Milton Village, Milton Center, and East Milton. **Milton Village**, located at the northeast border with Dorchester near where Adams Street and Central Avenue cross the river, and **Milton Center**, right in the center of town, are both made up of a cluster of streets, along which are colonial and Victorian homes, and a few commercial offerings, including Kate's at Milton Hill restaurant, Personalized Fitness Gym, and Fleet and Citizens banks. Residents often head over the river into Dorchester for more shopping and services. To the east of Milton Center are Milton Hospital, Milton Academy, and Fontbonne Academy campuses, and past these, toward Quincy, is **East Milton**. Resembling parts of Cambridge and Arlington, East Milton is toned down, although still very nice. It is slightly busier, with shops and some Victorian apartment blocks, and modest homes. The western and southern portions of Milton are more thinly settled and nicely shaded with sturdy maples and oaks. Here you will find the campus of Curry College, an independent liberal arts school, as well as the Blue Hills Reservation, a 7,000-acre park that offers horseback riding, hiking, skiing, and more. Also in Milton is the Neponset River Reservation, which has playgrounds, bird watching, fishing, and much more.

Commuting to Boston from Milton is best done by car. Interstate 93 (the Southeast Expressway) cuts right through East Milton; it circles the town to the south through the Blue Hills Reservation, where it meets I-95 and Route 128. If you don't feel like fighting the often wretched traffic on I-93, you can also just head through Hyde Park, Mattapan, and Dorchester via Hyde Park, Dorchester, or Blue Hills avenues. As for public transportation, aside from a couple of MBTA South Shore bus routes (nos. 215, 217, 240, and 245), the Red Line of the T is an option, sort of. It's really a trolley that costs extra and connects to the Cambridge/Dorchester Red Line at Ashmont. You can board the trolley at Milton Station (Adams and Eliot streets), Central Avenue Station (Central Avenue off Eliot Street), Valley Road Station (Valley Road off Eliot Street), or Capen Street Station (Capen Street off Eliot Street).

Web Sites: www.townofmilton.org, www.key-biz.com/ssn/Milton
Area Code: 617
Zip Code: 02186
Post Offices: Milton Branch, 499 Adams Street, 617-698-8139; Milton Village Branch, 50 Adams Street, 617-698-8109; www.usps.com
Police: Milton Police, 40 Highland Street, 617-698-3800, www.milton-pd.com
Emergency Hospital: Milton Hospital, 92 Highland Street, 617-696-4600, www.miltonhospital.org
Libraries: Milton Central Library, 476 Canton Avenue, 617-698-5757; East Milton Branch, 334 Edgehill Road, 617-698-1733; www.miltonlibrary.org
Parks & Open Space: Wollaston Golf Club (Randolph Avenue, Woodside Drive, and Marshall and Longmeadow roads); Town Forest (south part of Milton at Unquity Road and Harland Street); Blue Hills Reservation and Trailside Museum, 1904 Canton Avenue, 617-333-0690,

www.mass.gov/dcr; Fowl Meadows Reservation (southwest border of Milton with Dedham and Canton, at Milton Street and Brush Hill Road); Neponset River Reservation (northeast border of town with the Neponset River by I-93), www.mass.gov/dcr

Public Schools: Milton Public Schools, 1372 Brush Hill Road, 617-696-4809, www.miltonps.org

Community Resources: Milton Academy, 170 Centre Street, 617-898-1798, www.milton.edu; Curry College, 1071 Blue Hills Avenue, 617-333-0500, www.curry.edu; Fontbonne Academy, 930 Brook Road, 617-696-3241, www.mec.edu; Captain Forbes House Museum, 215 Adams Street, 617-696-1815, www.key-biz.com/ssn/Milton; Blue Hill Meteorological Observatory, 617-696-0389, www.bluehill.org; Suffolk Resolves House/Milton Historical Society, 1370 Canton Avenue, 617-333-9700; The Milton Players, 183 Pleasant Street, 617-698-7469, www.miltonplayers.org

Community Publications: *Milton Record-Transcript*, 617-698-6563; *Milton Times*, www.miltontimes.com

Public Transportation: *Trains*: Mattapan/Red Line (trolley connector) at Milton, Central Avenue, Valley Road and Capen Street

Buses: nos. 215, 217, 240, and 245; for MBTA route and schedule information contact the MBTA Traveler's Information Center: 617-222-3200, 800-392-6100, TTY 617-222-5146 or go to www.mbta.com.

NEEDHAM

Boundaries: **North**: Wellesley and Newton; **East**: West Roxbury and Newton; **South**: Dover, Dedham and Westwood; **West**: Wellesley

NEEDHAM HEIGHTS
NEEDHAM CENTER
CHARLES RIVER VILLAGE

West of Boston and south of Newton lies Needham—over 12-square miles of rolling middle- to upper-middle class suburbia. Originally part of Dedham, settlers to this area hailed from East Anglia in England. Thus, when Needham officially separated from Dedham and became a village in 1711, it was named Needham, after the familiar town of Needham Market in Suffolk (East Anglia), England.

Needham got its start as an agricultural community and managed to stay that way into the 1800s. Surrounded as it is on the north and the south by the Charles River, 18th century settlers built grist and saw mills along the banks. In the 19th century, with the arrival of the railroad, Boston's wealthy came to build summer homes. At the same time, dirt from Needham was transported by railroad to be used as fill to construct Boston's elite Back Bay neighborhood.

Needham's biggest transformation came in 1931 with the building of Route 128, which cuts through the eastern edge of town. This route not only directly linked Needham to Boston, it also helped create the town's commercial center. Like Waltham to the north, Needham's strip of Route 128 is part of a major industrial and commercial center, and many significant Boston area businesses can be found here, including the Community Newspaper Company (now owned by the *Boston Herald*), which runs most of the greater Boston area's newspapers and Channel 5, Boston's ABC affiliate.

Many of Needham's 27,500 residents live in clusters near the Route 128 corridor—mostly in a triangle created between the intersections of Route 128 on the east and north, Central Avenue to the west and north, and South Street to the south. Homes are close together; most lots are well-kept and are small to mid-sized. To call this area a prototypical example of American suburbia is not an exaggeration. Most homes in town were built in the 20th century, with some Victorians and a few remaining 18th century summer homes interspersed. Houses tend to be modest, nothing flashy, with a lot of brick and/or wood construction; nearly everyone has a two-car garage; porches are common, and you'll see a good deal of flags, hanging plants, and shrubbery. While only 20% of Needham's residents are renters, it's definitely cheaper to rent here than in the city, and may be a particularly good option for those working along Route 128.

Although there's not a large amount of variation between them, the two major neighborhoods in Needham's northeast corner are Needham Heights and Needham Center. Both have their own commuter rail stop. **Needham Heights** is the area around and just east of the intersection of West Street and Highland Avenue. The commercial strip in this area has some attractive store fronts, including a Canelli's Market, Boston Video Rental, and a CVS pharmacy. Continue south along Highland Avenue where it meets up with Great Plain Avenue, Dedham Avenue, and Chestnut Street, to get to **Needham Center**, where you will find Needham Town Hall (1471 Highland Avenue), the main post office (1150 Great Plain Avenue), and Deaconess-Glover Hospital. Some newer condo developments can be found near the Memorial Field, just east of Highland Avenue.

Western and southern Needham is more rural and is where you will find lovely rolling hills, forestland, and Needham's pricier real estate. As you head out of town on Dedham Avenue homes, both old and new, are bigger; South Street becomes curvy and wooded, lined with large new homes on roomy lots that are set back from the street. **Charles River Village** is in Needham's southeast corner, inside the intersection of Central Avenue and Charles River Street. Housing here is more modest compared to South Street, but there are some older treasures to be found.

Driving to downtown Boston via either the Mass Pike or Route 9 through Newton takes about 20 minutes, and there are four commuter rail stations, so public transit is possible.

Web Sites: www.town.needham.ma.us, www.needhamonline.com
Area Code: 781
Zip Codes: 02492, 02494
Post Offices: Needham Branch, 1150 Great Plain Avenue, 781-449-0707; Needham Heights Station, 844 Highland Avenue, 781-444-0355; www.usps.com
Police: Needham Police, 99 School Street, 781-455-7570
Emergency Hospital: Deaconess-Glover Hospital, 148 Chestnut Street, 781-453-3000, www.glover.caregroup.org
Library: Needham Free Public Library, 1139 Highland Avenue, 781-455-7559, www.town.needham.ma.us/Library/
Parks & Open Space: Ridge Hill Reservation; Charles River; Cutter Park; Needham Golf Course
Public Schools: Needham Public Schools, 1330 Highland Avenue, 781-455-0400, www.needham.k12.ma.us
Community Resources: Needham Children's Museum, 781-455-8114, www.afunplacetolearn.org; Needham Community Theatre, 781-444-4740, www.needhamonline.com; Roche Bros., 377 Chestnut Street, 781-444-0411; Sudbury Farms, 1177 Highland Avenue, 781-449-9180; Babson College (Needham campus), 231 Forest Street, Babson Park, 781-235-1200, www.babson.edu
Community Publications: *Needham Times*, www.townonline.com/needham/news.html
Public Transportation: *Trains*: commuter rail at Hersey, Needham Junction, Needham Center, Needham Heights
Buses: no. 59 (Needham Junction-Watertown Square via Newtonville); for MBTA route and schedule information contact the MBTA Traveler's Information Center: 617-222-3200, 800-392-6100, TTY 617-222-5146 or go to www.mbta.com.

QUINCY

Boundaries: **North**: Dorchester and Quincy bays and the Neponset River; **South**: Braintree and the Blue Hills Reservation; **West**: Blue Hills Reservation and Milton; **East**: Quincy Bay

NORTH QUINCY	ADAMS SHORE
QUINCY POINT	HOUGH'S NECK
PRESIDENTS HILL	ATLANTIC
WEST QUINCY	GERMANTOWN
WOLLASTON	MERRYMOUNT
WOLLASTON HILL	MONTCLAIR
SQUANTUM	QUINCY CENTER
MARINA BAY	SOUTH QUINCY

Quincy, pronounced "Quin-zee," is so named and so pronounced because the original Quincy family that settled here at Mount Wollaston pronounced their name with a "z" rather than a "c" sound. Family members included Colonel John Quincy, the city's namesake and the grandfather of President John Adams. Also known as the "City of Presidents," Quincy has the distinction as birthplace and home to the second and sixth presidents of the United States, the aforementioned John Adams and his son, John Quincy Adams, as well as John Hancock.

Originally part of Braintree (just to the south), Quincy became an independent town in 1792 and a city in 1888. In addition to having been an agricultural community and home to many famous early American colonists and political figures, Quincy saw early industry in shipbuilding and granite quarrying, which coincided with a wave of European immigration.

Almost 17 square miles in size, Quincy lies nine miles south of Boston, separated from it by the Neponset River. As it is situated between the Blue Hills and Quincy Bay, this city offers easy access to a great deal of Massachusetts' natural environs, in particular beaches to the east and hilly forestland to the west, while still offering residents ample shopping and dining options and relatively quick access to Boston via car or public transit. While most choose to live in Quincy and commute to Boston for work, there is enough commerce here to sustain some office buildings, in addition to the usual town amenities. Quincy is a mix of suburban residential areas, local shopping developments, and seaside beaches along its ample waterfront. While the city was once considered an Italian- and Irish-American enclave, today's demographics reveal an increasing number of African-Americans and even more Asian-Americans among its 88,000 residents. Whether you're looking for a modern apartment in a big complex or a single family home in a grand old colonial, Quincy probably has something for you. Since the city was settled as early as Boston itself, a great deal of its homes reflect its status as one of America's oldest communities. Because of the time/distance factor in terms of getting to downtown Boston (you either have to fight the thick Southeast Expressway traffic or take a 30-minute T ride), housing is less expensive here than in Boston and other inner ring communities such as Cambridge and Somerville.

Quincy's bona fide municipal center of town, at the intersections of Hancock and Washington streets, **Quincy Center** is historic and charming, with an authentic Tudor structure and an art-deco Fleet Bank. **North Quincy**, between Hancock Street and Quincy Bay, is fairly middle-class, with busy shops, a few chain stores, and many brick homes. Because of a horse racing track that operated in this area during the 1800s, it wasn't until the early 1900s when North Quincy was laid out with dense, single-family lots. Near the marina and **Quincy Point** you can find triple-decker homes that were built around the turn of the 20th century.

The more upscale neighborhoods throughout Quincy include **Presidents Hill** at Furnace Brook Parkway and Adams Street, Governor's Road in West Quincy, and Wollaston Hill, Squantum, and trendy Marina Bay. If you're looking for an old colonial or Victorian, check in **Wollaston** and **Wollaston Hill**, just north of the Furnace Brook Golf Course in central Quincy. Wollaston, named for Captain Wollaston who first settled Quincy in 1625, is one of the older parts of Quincy, and is popular for its easy access to public transit. Like much of the city, Wollaston presents a dense grid of residential streets, and has a good array of commercial offerings, including the Wollaston Theatre on Beale Street. Closer to the T stop you can find some apartments. Southwest of the golf course is **West Quincy**, where you'll find some truly impressive homes on lovely lots with positively enormous trees. Along with **South Quincy**, which is near the border with Braintree, West Quincy got its start with the quarrying industry and was initially home to many of the immigrant workers who came to work and then never left. The waterfront areas of Quincy, including **Squantum** (the finger of land jutting into the Bay in north Quincy), **Adams Shore**, and **Hough's Neck** (on the peninsula east of Quincy Center), provide beautiful views of Boston Harbor and the Boston skyline. These neighborhoods are reminiscent of Cape Cod, with their laid-back, beachfront feel, cottage homes, and shops. Squantum, once home to Native Americans of the same name, got its start as a summer vacation area for Bostonians. Over the last century, the summer cottages were converted into year-round homes, and Squantum was connected to the mainland by a causeway. Further south, Adams Shore shares a peninsula with Germantown and Hough's Neck, jutting out into Quincy Bay just east of Quincy Center. Similar to Squantum,

Adams Shore went from summer resort to a year-round community with desirable beachfront property. As the Harbor, and thus Quincy Bay, gets cleaner, these neighborhoods become even more sought after. Further out on this peninsula is Hough's Neck, which was developed a little later than other areas of the city. This neighborhood remained agricultural until the 1800s before it became a summer destination for fishing and beaching. Today the cottages are year-round residences for "Neckers," as locals call themselves. This part of the peninsula, known as "God's Country," is home to many close-knit extended families, but it is still popular with newcomers who appreciate the ocean views and aren't put off from trying to carve out a new niche in this well-established neighborhood. Include **Marina Bay**, with its condos, restaurants, and a boardwalk along the harbor, in this bunch as well. Marina Bay also has a "New Urbanist" development called Chapman's Reach—a collection of modern homes set up with porches and well-manicured lawns designed to foster a stronger sense of community. Area amenities include nearby pubs and the marina.

Germantown, on the peninsula between Adams Shore and Hough's Neck, is one of Quincy's more affordable neighborhoods. It is also one of the oldest—settled in the 1640s. Originally called Shed's Neck, this neighborhood became Germantown when German immigrants came in droves to seek work at nearby Fore River Shipyard. In recent years, Germantown has seen the building of single family homes, and 900 public housing units. Still on the mainland, between Quincy Center and Adams Shore, is the neighborhood of **Merrymount**, with most housing built during the early 20th century.

Quincy is transforming from a Boston bedroom community to a corporate office park destination in and of itself. The completion of the Big Dig as well as improvements to the T should help with Quincy's continued establishment as a shopping and workplace destination. Quincy has good public transit, including four major Red Line stations with large parking areas, as well as several bus routes to and from Boston. Via car, Route 3A connects to I-93 for easy Boston access, at least in theory. Frustratingly, traffic on I-93 south of the city is often abysmal; getting through this stretch of highway, and not just during rush hour, is often arduous. Alternate methods of travel, such as commuter ferry to Long Wharf in Boston or taking the T, should be considered.

And finally, although the Fore River Shipyard closed in 1986, there is a renewed effort to revive shipbuilding in the Fore River area. Military enthusiasts can get a glimpse of one of the great warships, the USS Salem, a decommissioned heavy cruiser now anchored at the US Naval Shipbuilding Museum, near the Fore River Bridge. Other historical sites include the Adams' birthplaces, as well as their burial plots in the United First Parish Church.

Web Sites: www.quincyonline.com, http://ci.quincy.ma.us, http://key-biz.com/ssn/Quincy, www.quincymass.com
Area Code: 617
Zip Codes: 02169-02171
Post Offices: Quincy Branch, 47 Washington Street, 617-773-6641; North Quincy Branch, 454 Hancock Street, 617-328-1716; Wollaston Branch, 5 Beach Street, 617-472-1263; www.usps.com
Police: Police Headquarters, 1 Sea Street, 617-479-1212, http://ci.quincy.ma.us
Emergency Hospital: Quincy Medical Center, 114 Whitwell Street, 617-773-6100
Libraries: Thomas Crane Public (Main) Library, 40 Washington Street, 617-376-1301; Adams Shore Branch, 519 Sea Street, 617-376-1325; North Quincy Branch, 381 Hancock Street, 617-376-1320; Wollaston Branch, 41 Beale Street, 617-376-1330; http://ci.quincy.ma.us/tcpl
Parks & Open Space: Nickerson Beach (Squantum); Adams National Historic Park, www.nps.gov/adam (Adams Street in Quincy Center); Wollaston Beach (off Quincy Shore Drive, north of Merrymount Park); Merrymount Park (between Quincy Shore Drive and I-93); Faxon Park (Quincy Avenue and Faxon Park Road); Mount Wollaston Cemetery (I-93 and Sea Street); Quincy Shore Reservation, www.mass.gov/dcr
Public Schools: Quincy Public Schools, 70 Coddington Street, 617-984-8700, www.quincypublicschools.com
Community Resources: Colonel Josiah Quincy House, Muirhead Road, 617-227-3956; Granite Railway Quarry, Ricciuti Drive, 617-698-1802; Nantucket Lightship, Marina Bay, 617-727-5250; Quincy Homestead, Butler Road, 617-727-5250; US Naval Shipbuilding Museum, 739 Washington Street, 617-479-7900, www.uss-salem.org; Quincy College, 34 Coddington Street, 800-698-1700, www.quincycollege.edu; Wollaston Theatre, 14 Beale Street, 617-773-4600; United First Parish Church, 1306 Hancock Street, 617-773-1290, www.ufpc.org
Community Publication: *Patriot Ledger*, http://ledger.southofboston.com
Transportation: *Trains*: Red Line at North Quincy, Wollaston, Quincy Center, and Quincy Adams; commuter rail at Quincy Center
Buses: nos. 210-212, 214-217, 220-222, 225, 230, 236, 238, 245, and 276; for MBTA route and schedule information contact the MBTA Traveler's Information Center: 617-222-3200, 800-392-6100, TTY 617-222-5146 or go to www.mbta.com.
Boats: Quincy Shipyard-Logan Airport-Long Wharf (Harbor Express)

GREATER BOSTON AREA

Many people live in the surrounding suburbs, referred to collectively as the greater Boston area. Here are just a few communities worth looking into, particularly if you don't need to commute into Boston every day. As is the case in the cities and towns outside major cities, housing in the greater Boston area tends to be more spacious and on bigger lots, and the communities offer either a suburban or small town lifestyle. For towns not profiled below, you can get information on the web at www.state.ma.us/cc.

BRISTOL COUNTY

- **Attleborough** (population 42,000) is a manufacturing city with a small-town, almost country atmosphere. As it is 32 miles southwest of Boston, this town is actually closer to Providence. Small to mid-sized homes, mostly of 19th and 20th century construction are here—including post-WWII builds and some modern condos. Residents shop in strip malls downtown, and enjoy the Capron Park Zoo and the Industrial Museum. Easily accessible via Route 1 and I-95, and there is a commuter rail stop at Attleboro station. Town web site: www.ci.attleboro.ma.us; municipal offices: 508-223-2222
- **Mansfield** is an unpretentious and unassuming suburb of 22,500, located 26 miles south of Boston at the intersection of I-95 and I-495. It is residential, save for the Tweeter Center, a major outdoor music venue. The commuter rail stop is at Mansfield station. Town web site: www.mansfieldma.com; municipal offices: 508-261-7370
- **New Bedford** (population 99,000) sits on the southern tip of Massachusetts near Rhode Island and Cape Cod, 54 miles south of Boston. Formerly a major whaling center (said to have inspired Herman Melville's *Moby Dick*), it is now an appealing oceanfront city with a vibrant community that is proud of its working waterfront, museums, theaters, shopping, dining, beaches, and festivals. There is a substantial Portuguese population. New Bedford is accessible via routes 6 and 140, and I-195. Commuter rail access to Boston has been proposed. Town web site: www.ci.new-bedford.ma.us; municipal offices: 508-979-1400
- **Taunton** is a quiet community of 56,000. A former mill town on the Taunton River, it has a friendly rural feel. The Weir neighborhood is the exception, with its higher density environs and rougher edges. In addition to several commercial areas, including a Federalist-looking town center, an industrial park, and the Silver City Galleria mall and movie theater, Tauton is known for its green areas, which include parklands, swamps, and Lake Sabbatia. Housing stock is mostly from the 19th and

GREATER BOSTON

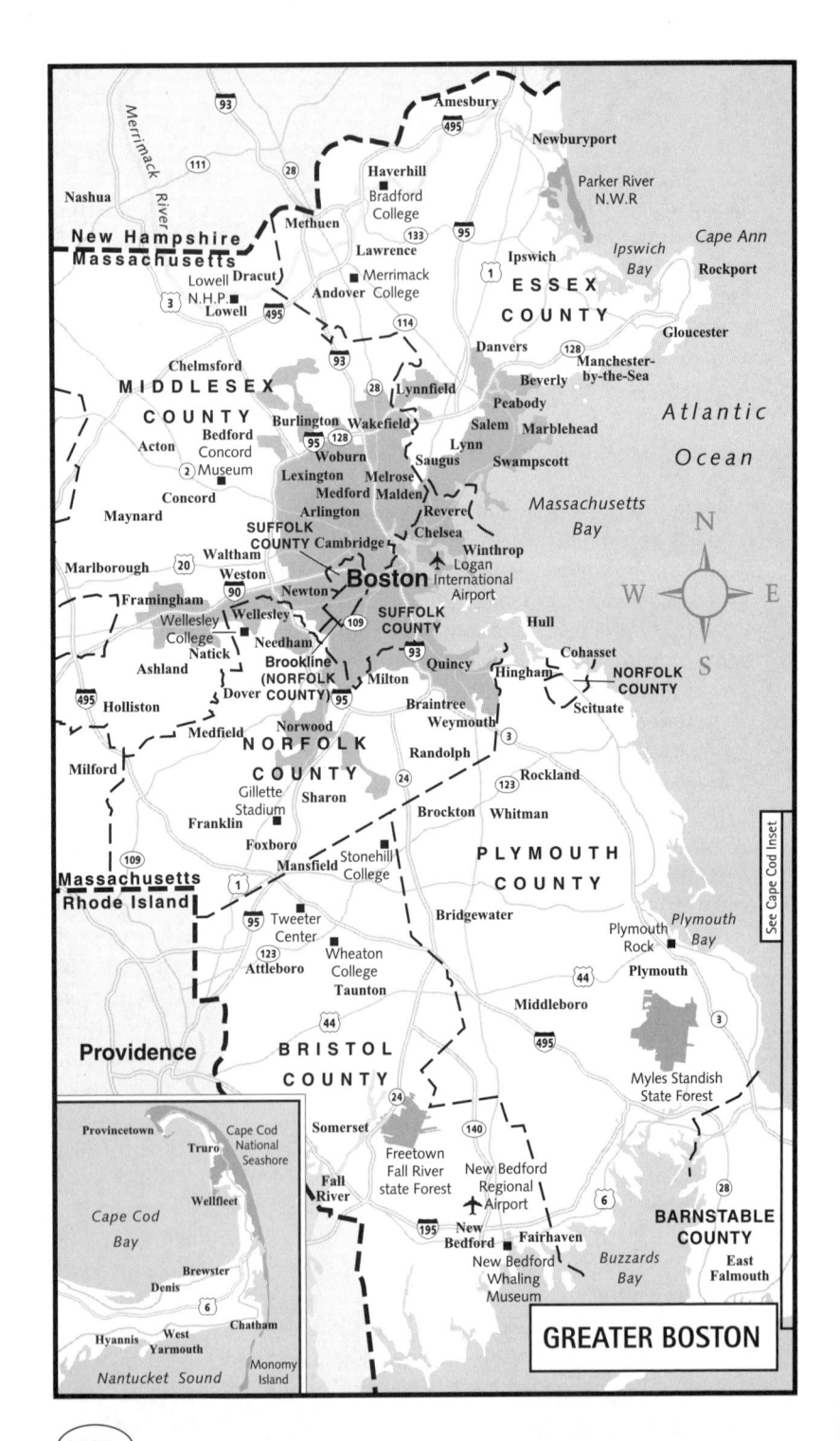

20th centuries; there are some condos, and 40% of available housing is rentals. Taunton is located 33 miles south of Boston, close to Providence, and accessible via I-495, but with no commuter rail stop. Town web site: www.ci.taunton.ma.us; municipal offices: 508-821-1000

ESSEX COUNTY

- **Andover** is an affluent suburb of just over 31,000 residents, located 22 miles north of Boston. Winding roads pass through heavily wooded areas, which are interspersed with large homes (some old and traditional, some more modern in design) on expansive lots. There are a few industrial parks occupied by such large companies as Raytheon, Gillette, and AT&T. Also in Andover is Phillips Andover Academy, one of the most prestigious private high schools in the country. Highway access includes I-495 and I-93; commuter rail stops are at Andover Center and Ballardvale. Town web site: www.town.andover.ma.us; municipal offices: 978-623-8200
- **Beverly** was settled even before Boston. This mid-sized seaport community lies just 18 miles north of Boston. Once a major industrial center (particularly noted for shoemaking), Beverly now prides itself on being 85% residential, with a lot to offer in the way of commercial and social options. The North Shore Music Theatre is here, and the downtown area around Cabot Street is densely built up with stores, restaurants, and even a small movie house. Local industry includes high-tech and biotech businesses. Endicott College, North Shore Community College, and Montserrat College of Art are here. Life here is not too urban, not too rural. The downtown and waterfront areas, where you'll find some rentals, are heavily settled with not much in the way of green space or beaches, although the harbor does offer some respite. Northern Beverly and Beverly Farms offer greener environs and large homes and mansions. Head to Boston and surrounding towns via routes 1A and 128. Commuter rail stops are at Beverly Farms, Prides Crossing, Montserrat, North Beverly, and Beverly Depot. Town web site: www.ci.beverly.ma.us; municipal offices: 978-921-6000
- **Gloucester** (population 30,000) is a major fishing port located 31 miles northeast of Boston. Homes for area fishermen—many of them of Italian and Portuguese descent—are modest, and contrast sharply with the tremendous estates that can be found along the coast. In addition, Gloucester has several office parks and an art scene that produced the likes of painters Winslow Homer and Edward Hopper and currently is host to playwright Israel Horowitz at the Gloucester Theatre Company. The tourists, drawn by the beaches and artists, swell the town's numbers by almost one third in the summer. Access to the rest of the region

is available via Route 128; commuter rail stops are at Gloucester and West Gloucester. For a sneak preview of this community, see the movie *The Perfect Storm*. Town web site: www.ci.gloucester.ma.us; municipal offices: 978-281-9720
- Bisected by the Merrimack River, **Lawrence** is a densely populated, industrialized urban area located near Lowell, 26 miles north of Boston. Priding itself on its history and continuing status as a multicultural gateway-city for newcomers to the US, Lawrence refers to itself as "Immigrant City." Many of Lawrence's 72,000 residents are of Hispanic descent, although recent population influxes include newcomers from Laos and Cambodia. Over one-third of local industry is in manufacturing and over two-thirds of the available housing stock is rentals. Lawrence is accessible via I-93 and I-495, and has a commuter rail stop at Lawrence station. Town web site: www.ci.lawrence.ma.us; municipal offices: 978-794-5803
- Nine miles north of Boston is **Lynn**, a city of 89,000. Historically known for shoemaking, Lynn continues as an urban manufacturing community. In addition to its very built-up business areas—strip malls and car dealerships galore on the Lynnway—Lynn has the campus of North Shore Community College, isolated green space in the Lynn Woods Reservation, and some of the greater Boston area's most affordable waterfront property along the Atlantic. Routes 1, 1A, and 128 are accessible from the ends of town, and there are bus routes and a commuter rail stop at Lynn Station. Town web sites: www.lynnma.net, www.ci.lynn.ma.us; municipal offices: 781-598-4000
- Only four and a half square miles in size, **Marblehead** is a scenic waterfront town of 20,000 on Boston's North Shore. Originally a seafaring community dating back to the mid-1600s, many historic colonial houses survive, complete with plaques commemorating the sailors and sea captains who built them. Marblehead Neck in particular is crowded with quaint historic homes on postage stamp-sized lots, with unbeatable views of the harbor. Although the town is technically not far from Boston (only 18 miles northeast), it isn't situated near the major highways, therefore daily commutes to the city are cumbersome. Local services are available and include upscale clothing and knick-knack shops and seafood restaurants. Neighboring Salem and Swampscott are also easily accessible. It is also home to one of the more sizeable Jewish communities on the North Shore. Marblehead is accessible via routes 1A, 114, and 129; bus routes go into the city, but no commuter rail stops are in town. Town web site: www.marblehead.org; municipal offices: 781-631-0528
- Serving as the state capital before Boston and one of Massachusetts' smallest cities, **Newburyport** is situated in the northeastern-most corner of the state at the junction of the Merrimack River with the Atlantic

Ocean. Residents (approx. 17,000) enjoy the town's quaint charm with the gaslights and boardwalk along the harbor, wildlife sanctuaries, museums, theaters, restaurants, and coastal sites, including harbor cruises and whale watching. Despite being older than Boston, Newburyport's historic architecture, particularly in and surrounding downtown, tends more toward grand Federalist style homes and buildings built for wealthy whaling and clipper ship merchants. One third of the housing stock is rentals, and many residents use the commuter rail stop at Newburyport station or the easy access to Route 1 or I-95 to commute to Boston. Town web site: www.cityofnewburyport.com; municipal offices: 978-465-4413

- Thirty-seven miles north of Boston, on the tip of Cape Ann, **Rockport** is an old and charming seafaring community. Eight thousand people call it home, including a small artists' colony. There are plenty of gray, weathered wood homes (as is typical both here on Cape Ann and south on Cape Cod) nestled together. Rockport is made up of tiny art studios, museums, theaters, shops, restaurants, and inns, with a large coastal area that offers both rocky and sandy beaches, lobster pots, and pleasure boats. Residents range from young professionals who commute to Boston, to resident artists and retirees. Note: Rockport is a dry town; residents must buy alcohol in neighboring Gloucester, but are permitted to bring their own drinks to restaurants. The commuter rail stops here at Rockport Station. Town web site: www.rockportusa.com

- **Salem**, 16 miles north of Boston and on the ocean, is the historic home of Nathaniel Hawthorne and infamous for the witch trials of 1692. Today's Salem is a city of over 40,000, complete with a community college and witch-themed tourist attractions, including museums, mystics, wharves, and gift shops. Although Salem has many surviving colonial and Federalist buildings (especially evident in a downtown area replete with brick and cobblestone structures and streets), many homes and condos are modern, and a full half of its residents are renters. Salem is a diverse community with almost 20% of its population comprising minorities. It is accessible via Route 1A and a commuter rail stop at Salem station. Town web site: www.salemweb.com; municipal offices: 978-745-9595

- **Swampscott** is a seaside bedroom community of only three-square miles with almost 14,500 residents. Thirteen miles north of Boston on the Atlantic, Swampscott was once home to Mary Baker Eddy, the founder of the Christian Science church, and the summer retreat of President Calvin Coolidge. It is now home to a sizeable Jewish community. This is a quiet, wealthy town with large, stunning homes on good-sized lots along the coast. There are five beaches and some commerce along the waterfront, although the major commercial amenities are restricted to an inland area called Vinnin Square. Swampscott is somewhat out of the way in terms of major highways. Access is via Route 1A and a commuter rail stop at Swampscott station. Town web site: www.town.swampscott.ma.us; municipal offices: 781-596-8856

MIDDLESEX COUNTY

- **Acton** is a town of nearly 18,000 residents, next to Concord and 25 miles northwest of Boston. Acton's surroundings range from rural stretches resplendent with historic homes and the quintessential town green to mini-malls. Commuting from Acton to Boston can take from 45 minutes to an hour, by either car or commuter rail (which stops in South Acton). Acton is a quaint, traditional community with local museums and a community theater, good services, and a solid educational system with some of the highest MCAS scores in the state (ranked 4th by the state among all communities in 2003). Area population has grown 10% in recent years. Town web site: www.town.acton.ma.us; municipal offices: 978-264-9615
- **Bedford**, home of "the oldest complete flag in the United States," sits 15 miles northwest of Boston and has good highway access to Route 128 and I-495. Population 13,000, this community prides itself on its colonial and Revolutionary War history, and its outdoor recreational opportunities, such as bike and footpaths. There is a mixture of business and industry complementing the local Middlesex Community College and Hanscom Air Base. Town web site: www.town.bedford.ma.us; municipal offices: 781-275-0083
- **Burlington** is a community of about 23,000, lying 13 miles northwest of Boston. A major resource in the Massachusetts business economy, Burlington has much in the way of industrial space and office parks, and is home to many major local, national, and international corporations. Also here are several hotels and the well known Burlington Mall. Although there are no Burlington stops on the commuter rail, buses run between Burlington and Boston, and many major highways (routes 3, 3A, 62, 128, and I-495) run either through or close to town. Town web site: www.burlington.org; municipal offices: 781-270-1600
- **Concord**, a wealthy, historic suburb of roughly 17,000, is located 18 miles northwest of Boston. Famous for Revolutionary War battles (reenacted annually on Patriot's Day), as well as famous literary figures—the Alcotts, Emerson, Thoreau, Hawthorne—Concord draws a lot of tourists. Residents like their beautiful and somewhat staid New England town, with its well-preserved relics, colonial and Victorian homes, wooded green spaces (including Walden Pond and the meeting of the Sudbury, Assabet, and Concord rivers), a non-commercialized town center, and a select private high school—Concord Academy. West

Concord, a tad dressed down in comparison, is complete with a still functioning Victorian Gothic style prison. Access to Boston and around the region is easy via routes 2, 128, and I-495, and commuter rail stops at Concord Station and West Concord. Town web sites: www.concord net.org, www.concordma.com

- **Framingham**, 19 miles west of Boston and with over 65,000 residents in its 25 square miles, is a bustling city in its own right. It offers a wide variety of housing, including apartments, Victorians, and ranch style homes. Neighborhoods run the gamut too, and include the Village of Saxonville, as well as industrial parks and shopping malls. Framingham is mixed socio-economically and culturally, with a large Hispanic population. Not just a bedroom community by any means, this town is a working and shopping destination in and of itself. For getting in and out of Framingham, major local routes include the Mass Pike and Route 9; commuter rail stop at Framingham; and local buses around the area. Town web site: www.framinghamma.org; municipal offices: 508-620-4811
- Linked to Concord through their shared Revolutionary War experiences, **Lexington** is slightly closer to Boston than Concord, and also slightly more affordable. This suburb is eleven miles northwest of Boston with about 30,000 residents. Here you can live in a colonial home dating to before the Battle of Lexington, a small Cape Cod, or a more modern option. Amenities include green space (conservation lands, Minuteman Bikeway), the town center with galleries and restaurants, and close proximity to Boston. It is known for its school system, so solid that, according to the *Boston Globe*, 93% of residents send their children to public schools here. No commuter rail stops, though; you'll need to drive, bike, or take the local bus to the Alewife T station. Town web site: http://ci.lexington.ma.us; municipal offices: 781-862-0500
- **Lowell** is a large, densely populated (105,000), industrial city 25 miles north of Boston on the Merrimack River. A former mill town and birthplace of Jack Kerouac, the mills have been converted to office space, and tourist sites complement trolley and canal boat tours. There are cultural festivals, including Riverfest and the Lowell Folk Festival, a self-sustaining playhouse called the Merrimack Repertory Theater, concert halls, and two colleges—UMASS-Lowell and Middlesex Community College. Housing stock includes Victorians, colonials, Capes, ranches, and triple-deckers suitable for one to three families, and apartments and condos. Lowell is accessible via Route 3 and I-495, and has a commuter rail stop at Lowell station. Town web site: http://web.ci.lowell.ma.us; municipal offices: 978-970-4000
- **Maynard**, a small town (a little over five mostly-rural square miles) of 10,500, sits 22 miles northwest of Boston on the Assabet River. While

Maynard is without a commuter rail stop and no major local highways, it has nonetheless managed to put itself on the map as a commercial area. It is popular with high-tech and internet companies, most notably housing Monster.com's headquarters. A converted mill complex in the downtown area serves as business space. Outside of downtown, Maynard is fairly wooded and green, and residents live in single- and multi-family housing. Town web site: http://web.maynard.ma.us; municipal offices: 978-897-1000

- **Melrose** (population 27,000) is a small satellite city of Boston. Conveniently located just seven miles north of Boston off of Route 1, and with good public transit, Melrose is a good location for anyone who needs to commute into the city or to other parts of the North Shore. The town has benefited from Boston's continuing urban sprawl, and gentrification has brought unique storefronts and restaurants to the Victorian downtown area. Housing ranges from Victorians to 20th century colonials, and a good selection of rentals, including some apartment complexes. Green space can be found on the perimeter of town at the Middlesex Fells Reservation and the Mt. Hood golf course. Commuter rail service is available at Melrose Highlands, Cedar Park, and Wyoming Hill, and Malden's Oak Grove T station is just over the town line. Town web site: www.cityofmelrose.org; municipal offices: 781-979-4500
- **Natick** is a busy town of almost 32,000 residents, located 18 miles southwest of Boston. It is a middle- to upper-middle class suburb—similar to Burlington and Framingham—complete with malls, local industry, surrounding rural areas, green spaces, and old New England colonial areas. Housing is reflective of Natick's 350-year history: colonials, Victorians, post-war, and some apartments and condos. City access is via the Mass Pike, routes 9 and 16 and there are commuter rail stops at Natick and West Natick stations. Town web site: www.infotech-maine.com/natcikma; municipal offices: 508-647-6400
- **Wakefield** is a commuter suburb of 25,000, located 10 miles north of Boston, at the hub of Route 128/I-95 and I-93. Its location offers quick access into Boston via the highway, and commuter rail stops at Wakefield and Greenwood. Although Wakefield is primarily residential, there is a central business district and some office and industrial park space in town. Lake Quannapowitt is the center of many community outdoor activities. Modern homes coexist with a variety of older historic ones: colonials, Georgians, Greek Revivals, Gothic Revivals, Italianates, and Queen Annes, among others. Town web site: www.wakefieldma.org; municipal offices: 781-246-6390
- Twelve miles west of Boston, **Weston** (population 11,500), consistently ties with Dover as the wealthiest place in the state. Mansion-like

homes sit on secluded and expansive lots in this rural and seemingly-out-of-the-way community. There are a good deal of outdoor recreation opportunities including golfing, horseback riding, cross country skiing, and plenty of forest trails for hiking. Weston is also home to Regis College, a Catholic liberal arts school for women. Access Boston and the local region via the Mass Pike and Route 128; commuter rail stops are at Silver Hill, Hastings, and Kendall Green. Town web site: www.weston.org; municipal offices: 781-893-7320

- A suburban industrial city of 37,000, 10 miles north of Boston, **Woburn** has a long history as a manufacturing community, which has morphed into a business belt along Route 128. Its industrial nature does rob Woburn of some residential attractiveness of smaller neighboring communities, but what it lacks in quaintness it gains in function and ease. Large office spaces, stores, restaurants, and a movie theater, crop out from the highway. Woburn is contiguous to Burlington, and they feel similar. Renters here are able to find large, modern units providing many amenities. Commuter rail stops are at Mishawum and Anderson/Woburn. Town web site: www.ultranet.com/~woblib/cityinfo; municipal offices: 781-932-4400

NORFOLK COUNTY

- **Braintree** is a residential suburb of nearly 34,000, just 12 miles south of Boston. At the crux of I-93 and Route 3, with a Red Line T stop and a commuter rail stop, one of the obvious benefits of living in Braintree is its easy access to both Boston and Cape Cod. Many residents live and work here, rather than commute to Boston. There are industrial parks, office and commercial space, and amenities include good private and public schools, the South Shore Plaza (a shopping mall), and the General Cinemas movie theater on Grandview Road. Green space is prevalent throughout town and on its northwestern border with the Blue Hills Reservation. Most homes here are mid-sized, single-family units built post-WWII, and sit on smallish lots, with a few condos and apartment complexes mixed in. Town web site: www.key-biz.com/ssn/Braintree; municipal offices: 781-848-1870
- **Cohasset** is a sylvan, seaside suburb of just over 7,000 residents, located on the South Shore. Named after the Conohasset tribe, the original inhabitants of this area, the name means "long rocky place." Life here is quintessential New England, with its lush greenery, boat-filled harbor and waterfront, and the colonial town common. Residents live in big homes, including colonials, and Victorians, all sitting nicely on large, well-kept, wooded lots. An active community, vibrant arts scene, four shopping areas, and the South Shore Music Circus all make Cohasset a

desirable location. However, the town is a bit far flung for those needing to commute to the city. Twenty miles southeast of Boston, there is no commuter rail access (as yet), and it is set away from routes 3A and 228. Town web site: www.key-biz.com/ssn/Cohasset; municipal offices: 781-383-4100

- **Dover**, 16 miles southwest of Boston, contends with Weston for the title of wealthiest suburb. Big homes, large lots, and hefty price tags in one of the most posh regions of the country. Originally an agricultural community, Dover saw some industry with the mills after the damming of the Charles in the late 18th century and became the site for some staggeringly large country estates by the late 19th and early 20th centuries. Dover is small—only 5,500 residents share the bucolic settings of horse farms and green spaces. There are no major highways or commuter rail stops, although Dover is relatively close to Route 128/I-95. Town web site: http://doverma.org; municipal offices: 508-785-0032
- **Foxboro**, home of the New England Patriots and a community of 16,000, sits 24 miles south of Boston. Despite the new CMGI Field and accompanying heavy traffic and general mayhem during football games and events, Foxboro is a pleasant, small town with some forested areas and the noteworthy Orpheum Theater. Bound by Route 1 and interstates 95 and 495, Foxboro has excellent road access, but commuter rail access only during events at the stadium. Town web site: www.town.foxborough.ma.us; municipal offices: 508-543-1200
- **Norwood** is a town of 28,500, about 14 miles south of Boston. This is a standard suburb, with small to medium-sized 20th century homes and a dignified urban downtown complete with civic amenities and several churches, as well as one synagogue. Boston is easily accessible via routes 1, 1A, and 128/I-95, and there are three commuter rail stops at Norwood Depot, Norwood Central, and Windsor Gardens. Town web site: www.ci.norwood.ma.us; municipal offices: 781-762-1240
- **Sharon** is a woodsy suburb of 17,000, located 19 miles south of Boston. Sharon's 23 square miles offer outdoor recreational opportunities, including a berry farm, Massapoag Lake, the Borderland State Park, and an Audubon Society wildlife sanctuary. Indoor pursuits include a movie theater and the Kendall Whaling Museum. Sharon has a reputation for being religiously and ethnically diverse, and the town has both a substantial Jewish presence and is home to the Islamic Center of New England. Many homes are modern and tend to be small to mid-sized on heavily-wooded lots, although there are some more opulent options. Town web site: www.townofsharon.net; municipal offices: 781-784-1515
- **Wellesley** (population 26,000) is a lovely and exclusive suburb. A small and picturesque community with a "Tree City, USA," designation, it is

- home to Wellesley, Babson, and Massachusetts Bay Community College. Famous past and current residents include three Nobel Prize winners, poets Anne Sexton and Sylvia Plath, and Alexander Graham Bell. Wellesley is situated just 13 miles west of Boston, has easy highway access to routes 9, 16, 128/I-95, and is close to the Mass Pike. Commuter rail stops are at Wellesley Square, Wellesley Hills, and Wellesley Farms. Town web site: www.ci.wellesley.ma.us; municipal offices: 781-431-1019
- The hilly, coastal, middle-class town of **Weymouth** (population 54,000) sits just 12 miles southeast of Boston. More urban than neighboring South Shore communities, Weymouth is well situated on Route 3 as a suburb, and has a commuter rail stop at South Weymouth (and more possibly in the works). Weymouth has substantial commercial offerings, plus the waterfront, a pond, and a beach. Some older colonial homes, as well as pre-WWII construction are available. One-third of Weymouth residents rent, and you'll find a variety of apartment buildings and townhouses. Town web site: www.weymouth.ma.us; municipal offices: 781-335-2000

PLYMOUTH COUNTY

- **Brockton**, an industrial city made up of over 94,000 people, is just over 21-square-miles in size, and lies 20 miles south of Boston. Between the Civil War and WWII, Brockton was a major shoe producer, more recently Brockton gained fame for its boxers Rocky Marciano and Marvelous Marvin Hagler. Today, Brockton comprises a major urban area that can be rough in spots. There are plenty of triple-decker homes, and all basic amenities, including grocers, restaurants, and city office space. Residents also enjoy the city's Fuller Museum of Art. Nearly 45% of Brockton residents are renters, and the minority population here is substantial. Route 24 is the major route, and there are commuter rail stops at Montello, Brockton, and Campello. Town web site: www.brockton.net; municipal offices: 508-580-7123
- Located 15 miles southeast of Boston, **Hingham** is a friendly, affluent, seaside community, similar in nature to Weymouth, Cohasset, and Scituate. The harbor is filled with boats, a country club, a small movie theater, and expensive waterfront properties with views of Boston and the Atlantic. Primarily residential, this community of almost 20,000 is very proud of its colonial roots. The town has preserved its early buildings, has six designated historic districts, and many Cape Cod, Federalist, and colonial homes. Downtown living is tight, but further out the lots are big and wooded, and the town has some affordable housing. Like neighboring Cohasset, Hingham is set back from the

major highways, but is accessible via Route 3A. A commuter rail line servicing these communities has been proposed, however Hingham has water shuttle service to Rowes Wharf in Boston. Town web sites: www.hingham-ma.com and www.key-biz.com/ssn/Hingham; municipal offices: 781-741-1400

- **Hull** is a popular commuter suburb of Boston. It's made up of 11,000 residents packed onto a narrow strip of land (only three square miles in size) that juts out into the Atlantic. Housing styles are varied, and most homes are small to medium-sized on cramped lots. There is not much in the way of green space, but virtually all homes here could be described as waterfront or water-view. One quarter of the housing market is rentals. Hull is set even further back from major highways than other South Shore communities off Route 228. There is no commuter rail, but it does have a water shuttle to Long Wharf in Boston. Town web site: www.town.hull.ma.us; municipal offices: 781-925-2262
- **Plymouth** is a pleasant, big (over 96 square miles), and safe town of nearly 52,000. A little more suburban and with pilgrims instead of witches, this town has a similar feel to Salem. This is the Plymouth of *Mayflower* fame and has several historic landmarks, museums, restaurants, hotels, shopping, and pilgrim-themed services that cater to tourists. Plymouth's seaside downtown is busy. Among the sites, a working harbor, beaches, and an Ocean Spray cranberry bog. Houses consists of colonials, Cape Cods, and more recent postwar construction. Thirty-seven miles southeast of Boston, Plymouth is very close to Cape Cod and accessible to both via Route 3; a commuter rail stop is at Cordage/Plymouth station. Town web sites: www.townofplymouth.org and www.key-biz.com/ssn/Plymouth; municipal offices: 508-747-1620
- The residential suburb of **Scituate** (pronounced SIT-chew-it) is home to 18,000. It is situated 23 miles south of Boston among the South Shore cluster of waterfront communities: Cohasset, Hingham, Weymouth, and Hull. Its inviting beaches, windy cliffs and lighthouses, and a working harbor mix with recently built modern homes and traditional New England styles. Like the neighboring oceanfront communities, Scituate is not immediately accessible to the major highways and it does not have commuter rail service. Town web site: www.town.scituate.ma.us; municipal offices: 781-545-8700

FINDING A PLACE TO LIVE

UNFORTUNATELY, IN TERMS OF COST OF LIVING, BOSTON GIVES you much less bang for your buck than just about anywhere else in the country. The April 2002 real estate edition of *Boston Magazine* reported that Massachusetts came in 48th of the 50 states in terms of home affordability. In late 2002, the *Boston Globe* reported that a drop in home construction in the greater Boston area had spurred a 50% rise in home prices since 1998 and, according to Runzheimer International, apartment rental costs, which averaged an annual $15,833 in Boston, ranked third most costly in the country, preceded only by San Jose and San Francisco. In addition, according to the *Globe*, rentals even in traditionally lower-cost inner ring communities such as Malden and Medford, have increased up to 40% since 1995. Despite scary statistics, other analyses point out that, while Boston's cost of living tops the charts, incomes tend to be higher, making the expense more manageable. Also, in June 2002, the *Globe* reported that, of the country's largest metropolitan areas, Boston fell right in the middle in regard to its housing burden (the proportion of households spending 35% or more of their gross income on home ownership). And Runzheimer International reported that Boston's income tax burden was also in the middle when compared to other large metropolitan areas.

With such facts and figures in mind, you still need to find a place to live. Armed with the proper information, you will be able to find the right apartment or home to rent or buy in the city or its environs. If cost is an issue, it's just as important to know where not to go looking as it is to know where to look. Central location, good public transportation routes, and nearby historical sites may all add on to the price tag of an apartment or house.

A good clearinghouse of information for prospective homeowners and renters is the **Massachusetts Housing Consumer Education Centers**. Call them at 800-224-5124 or check www.masshousinginfo.org.

APARTMENTS

For the first time in almost a decade, Boston has good news for apartment hunters. During the mid- to late-1990s, Boston's rental market was full, and prospective renters were faced with a vacancy rate of less than one percent, more recently, however, things are looking up. By 2002, the vacancy rate had risen to five percent, and rental rates had leveled off, if not fallen slightly. To entice renters, landlords and property agencies sometimes offer incentives to prospective tenants, like no security deposit or a break on the first month's rent. While this is good news for renters, the best apartments don't stay on the market for long, and despite the softer market, by most standards, living in Boston is still quite expensive. Whether or not you experience sticker-shock at the price of apartments will depend on where you're moving from; newcomers from the Midwest or the South will probably find prices high, while those from New York City or San Francisco will not. As far as **rent control** goes, in 1994 Massachusetts voters declined rent control, and in 2002, Boston's city council vetoed Mayor Thomas Menino's proposal to introduce a form of rent control to area landlords. He called it "rent stabilization," which would have allowed landlords in Brookline, Cambridge, and Boston to increase rents at will, but given tenants the right to challenge rent raises they found unfair. It is reasonable to assume that the rent control issue will be revisited.

APARTMENT HUNTING

When going about finding an apartment, first determine how much you can or are willing to spend each month on rent. The standard formula holds that rent should be no more than one-third of your salary. The more centrally located and/or historic and scenic neighborhoods, such as Beacon Hill and the Back Bay, are among the most expensive. Housing opportunities located further out from the city center but still on the T, such as Allston-Brighton, Jamaica Plain, and Charlestown, have more mid-range price tags. For the best Boston bargains, head to communities with only bus or commuter rail service but lots of good parking, such as Roslindale or West Roxbury. And don't forget the suburbs, where prices may be cheaper still.

Next, you'll need to figure out your space needs. A small, dark studio with a kitchen doubling as a hallway that is centrally located in one of Boston's prime neighborhoods may be worth it if your office is within walking distance or if you are rarely home. If you plan on working from your apartment, convenient location to Boston's center probably will not be as much of an issue, and instead you'll want extra space for a home office. A roommate situation may become more appealing as you search for an affordable rental in, say, Beacon Hill. An airy, light-filled, two-bedroom apartment may be a lot more appealing than a dark, cramped studio and often will not cost much more than a one-bedroom rental. Keep in mind that, while you may have been able to afford a one-bedroom in your previous living situation, a one-bedroom unit here may be out of your price range. (If a roommate sounds like a good idea, check the resources below under **Newspaper Classifieds** and **Online Resources—Renting**.)

Other considerations as you look for an apartment include the following:
- Do you prefer living in a quiet residential area, or is a more densely populated urban area preferable?
- Will you be happy surrounded by college students?
- Do you have a car and need a parking space, which may cost extra, or will you rely on public transit?
- Since summers are hot, a major concern when you look for an apartment or home will be climate control. Obviously, central air is your best option, followed window air conditioning units, or, if nothing else, electric fans. Even if you plan on being at work most of the day, think about how easy it will be to sleep—a sometimes difficult and uncomfortable task when it is a muggy 90 degrees in your apartment and you have no cross ventilation.
- A large dog probably will not be okay in a small apartment, and if you do have a dog, a place close to a large park will be a must. Those with pets should be sure to mention it right away when calling about places, and you can expect the apartment search to be more challenging.
- If you are already employed, be sure to consider where your job is and find a neighborhood convenient to your place of employment. Living close to the T line is ideal if your job is close to the line as well; but even a direct bus route will work, and a place not on the T line will cost less. Bus or commuter rail routes that entail transfers will get old quickly.

While Boston has its share of high-rises, rentals of two- and three-family dwellings, often in the form of triple-deckers built during the 1800s to make room for the influx of immigrants, are abundant. They provide housing for three families—one per floor, and while not the most elegant of styles, tend to provide fairly spacious apartments.

As a general rule: the further out you are from downtown Boston, the more living space you'll get for your money, although there are exceptions. Apartments in the city's most coveted neighborhoods, such as Beacon Hill and the Back Bay, built between the colonial and Victorian eras, tend to be cramped. The South End and the North End, with housing stock dating back to similar time periods, tend to offer a little more space and are of a higher quality. Quarters in the so-called "student slums" are often as one might expect; many of them from old Victorians that have been chopped into efficiencies and one-bedroom apartments. Cambridge has a little of everything, from triple-deckers, to brownstones, to Victorians, to modern buildings. A typical triple-decker in Brighton, Jamaica Plain, or Somerville has three bedrooms and a foyer. Many have front and back porches, as well.

If you prefer character to modern convenience and efficiency, keep in mind that it may cost you. That gorgeous, spacious apartment in a Queen Anne triple-decker will be a lot more expensive to heat than a two-bedroom unit in a downtown high-rise. If the apartment has gas or electric heat, you can call the utility company to find out the unit's average monthly bill; however, many buildings are still heated with oil, in which case you'll have to ask your potential landlord and/or neighbors about heating costs during the winter months.

Many think that most Boston apartments become available in the late spring when the city's students graduate or leave for the summer. That is a mistake. Most fixed-term leases in Boston are for a year and turn over in August/September. While the early summer months are a good time to find a sublet, the best time to hunt for an apartment is mid- to late-summer.

Area police departments can supply you with safety information about a specific area. Call the community officer in your precinct (see the **Neighborhood Profiles** for these numbers) with questions about a prospective neighborhood and for information about local crime watch organizations.

Even though the rental market in the greater Boston area is a little less daunting than it has been in recent years, it's still a challenge. You'll want to employ all methods at your disposal to find a good rental. The most popular and often simplest way to locate a place is by scanning the major newspapers for rental listings. You will notice that most landlords in Boston list their units through rental agents. This is good and bad. On the upside, one ad in the *Globe* can put you in touch with a rental agent able to show you numerous properties. On the downside, if this agent does succeed in finding your apartment, you'll have to pay him a fee. Unfortunately, renter's fees (usually equal to one half to one month's rent) are the standard here, and you'll be hard pressed to find an agent who doesn't charge.

However, there are other tactics you can employ that may help you find an apartment without using a rental agent. For example, if you're affiliated with a local college or university, check with their housing office. Also try pavement pounding: go to the neighborhoods that are appealing to you and check for posted phone numbers of landlords and management companies. You can also look for vacancy postings, but they're less common here than in other cities. Don't forget the handwritten roommate postings on café bulletin boards, on kiosks, and at T stops. Boston also has a number of free apartment magazines advertising vacant rentals, as well as web sites geared toward apartment searching (see below).

NEWSPAPER CLASSIFIEDS

The first thing most people do when looking for an apartment in the greater Boston area is to search the classifieds, either online or in print form. If nothing else, a quick scan will give you an idea as to the price ranges in the various neighborhoods in and around the city. As we mentioned previously, a good deal of these ads are placed through rental agents and it's not always clear who you will be reaching—the landlord or agent—when you call.

- **Boston Globe**, 617-929-2000, www.boston.com; especially the Sunday edition, may be the most popular periodical for apartment listings in Boston and the greater Boston area. Listings are posted online daily.
- **Boston Herald**, 617-426-3000, www.bostonherald.com; extensive apartment listings, especially on Saturday.
- **Boston Phoenix**, 617-536-5390, www.bostonphoenix.com; alternative weekly, comes out on Thursday. Includes greater Boston area rentals, and ads for sublets and shares. Find it free in newspaper boxes.
- **Boston Metro**, www.metropoint.com; free newspaper that comes out Monday-Friday: includes daily classifieds advertising apartments and roommate listings, as well as a special real estate section on Fridays. Find it in newspaper boxes around the city.
- **Improper Bostonian**, 617-859-1400; www.improper.com; a free biweekly magazine that comes out on Wednesdays and primarily serves as a current events/entertainment/culture guide. It has a small section with a few rental and roommate listings, and real estate advertisements. Free in newspaper boxes and in stores.
- The **TAB**; in addition to the general **Boston TAB**, many of Boston's neighborhoods and much of eastern Massachusetts publishes individual weekly newspapers that include apartment listings. Check www.townonline.com to find specific information on the **Somerville Journal**, the **Cambridge Chronicle**, the **Allston-Brighton TAB**, the **Brookline TAB**, the **Newton TAB**, the **Watertown TAB & Press**, the **West Roxbury Transcript**, and others.
- Neighborhood papers include the **Jamaica Plain Gazette**, 617-524-2626, www.jamaicaplaingazette.com and the **South End News**, 617-266-6670. Information about additional community publications is available after each individual neighborhood profile.

OTHER RENTAL PUBLICATIONS

In addition to the general local periodicals, there also are a number of rental and/or housing publications. These are often free, and are available in newspaper boxes, grocery stores, cafes, and storefronts throughout the city. They supply information regarding area real estate, rentals, and sometimes roommates. Many of their listings come from rental companies and will possibly result in your paying a fee. Here are a few:

- **Boston Homes**; although this weekly publication is geared towards the Boston real estate market (specifically the Back Bay, Beacon Hill, Charlestown, downtown, the Fenway, JP, South Boston, the South End, the North End, and the Waterfront). It also offers a listing of apartments for rent and rental agents. Pick it up in newspaper boxes around the city. Call 888-828-1515, or visit www.homefind.com.
- **Just Rentals**; free rental guide to properties in the greater Boston area. Pick it up in newspaper boxes in the city. Call 800-242-1335, or visit www.bostonforrent.com.
- **Suburban Real Estate News**; free weekly newspaper that lists properties for sale in the greater Boston area, including Worcester, Cape Cod, and Maine. Find it in newspaper boxes in the city. Call 800-221-2078, or visit www.suburbanpublishing.com.

ONLINE RESOURCES—RENTING

Boston is well covered in terms of online sites for those seeking rentals. Most are affiliated with a local college or university, a newspaper, or a rental agency; some cost, some don't. Many sites post apartment listings only; others help match roommates, and/or supply moving-related information or links to other moving-related sites. Here are a few:

- **Apartment Access**, www.apartmentaccess.com; listings for large metropolitan areas in the US, including Boston. Skim their listings of apartments to see if it appeals to you, then pay a flat rate of $40 to use the service. Since the landlords can list their units at no cost, your subscription buys you access to updated listings of apartments that you can lease without a realtor fee.
- **Apartment Ratings**, www.aptratings.com; not an apartment listing service but rather a nation-wide rating service. Residents of the greater Boston area post assessments of where they live for the benefit of those in search of an apartment.
- **A Boston Loft**, www.abostonloft.com; free listings of lofts for rent and for sale in Boston, Cambridge, and Somerville.

- **Boston Apartments/Boston Realty**, www.bostonapartments.com, free daily listings of properties to rent (fee and no fee) and to buy.
- **Boston.com/Real Estate**, http://realestate.boston.com; a guide to everything housing related in the greater Boston area, including rentals, sales, and moving tips
- **Craig's List**, http://boston.craigslist.org, the Boston component of this popular web site serving many cities across the US posts listings for fee and no-fee apartment rentals, roommates, and sublets.
- **Easy Rent**, www.easyrent.com, for a flat rate of either $39 for seven days, $79 for one month, or $99 for two months, you can search apartments in the greater Boston area. This web site is also connected to a roommate-matching service: www.easyroommate.com.
- **First Boston Apartments**, www.1st-boston-apartments.com, fill out a form and they'll contact you with rental listings in Boston. Free to renters.
- **Homebuilder.com**, www.homebuilder.com, comprehensive web site where you can find apartments, homes (both sales and rentals), and roommates in Massachusetts and the rest of New England. Free to renters.
- **Homestore**, www.homestore.com, a comprehensive portal for the potential buyer or renter, with house and apartment listings in the greater Boston area and information on moving and mortgages. Free to renters.
- **Just Rentals**, www.justrentals.com, online rental listings for the greater Boston area. Free to renters.
- **Massachusetts Housing Finance Agency** (**MHFA**), www.mhfa.com; offers information about renting and buying from the state's affordable housing (e.g., Section 8 housing).
- **Matching Roommates**, www.matchingroommates.com, pay a flat rate of $75 to this roommate referral company, which will screen and match you with other applicants.
- **MIT European Club,** http://euroclub.mit.edu/; extensive and popular posting of apartment/roommate want ads.
- **RoommateService.com**, http://city.roommateservice.com/ma_boston; find a roommate or a room. Free services include basic listings, searches, and links to moving-related sites; for a low flat-rate you can use advanced search and posting options.

SHORT TERM/SUBLETS

If you prefer to take your time finding just the right home, you might benefit from a **short-term sublet**. Most of the leases in Boston last one year, and many of them run from September 1 to August 31. Because a large number of Boston's renters are students, many of whom find themselves with several months left on their leases during the summer months, it's easiest to find a sublet in the spring.

If you are interested in finding a temporary housing arrangement, you should research many of the same avenues used by apartment seekers (above). In particular, local papers like the *Phoenix* and the *TAB*, and the roommate matching web sites listed above are great resources for sublet listings. In addition, check for notices posted on college kiosks and neighborhood notice boards (at laundromats, cafes, T stops, etc.). Short-term rental opportunities might include a weekly or monthly rental situation. See the **Temporary Lodgings** chapter near the end of this guide for ideas.

RENTAL AGENTS

In Boston, most apartments available for lease are brokered through a rental agent, especially during low-vacancy markets. Unfortunately, it's the tenant who pays the finder's fee. While there is no set amount, a rental agent's commission generally runs one half to one month's rent.

Rental offices in and around Boston are plentiful. Agents place most apartment classifieds found in the major news dailies and the free weekly shoppers. When you respond to these ads, more often than not you'll find a rental agent on the other end of the phone with several properties that match your requests. Many seekers choose to go directly to a rental office in their neighborhood of interest. Agents will have some paper work for you to fill out to help them determine your apartment specifications. Be clear about what you want: price range, amenities, preferred neighborhoods, etc. Good brokers won't waste your time taking you to apartments that don't meet your needs. As most agents have the majority of their properties located in one or two neighborhoods, you'll quickly determine which agents will work best for you. Do not feel committed to just one agent. Call on as many rental agencies as you like, and view as many properties as you can, until you find the broker and apartment that suits you best. Usually, you arrange to meet the broker at an appointed location and time, and then he either walks or drives you around to other properties in the neighborhood.

Here are a **few rental agents** (many also handle real estate sales as well):

- **Anzalone Realty**, 100 Prince Street, 617-367-1300, www.boston apartments.com/anzalone (North End/Waterfront)
- **Boston Realty Works**, 252 Newbury Street, 617-236-2062, www.bosrealty.com (Back Bay/Beacon Hill)
- **Bremis Realty**, 1177 Broadway, Somerville, 617-623-2500, www.bremis.com (Somerville)
- **Brownstone Real Estate**, 225 Newbury Street, 617-262-4250, www.brownstone-real-estate.com (Back Bay/Beacon Hill)
- **Cabot & Company**, 213 Newbury Street, 617-262-6200, www.boston apartments.com/cabot (Back Bay/Beacon Hill)

- **Century 21 Adams**, 486 Common Street, 617-489-6900, www.c21 adams.com (Belmont)
- **Century 21 Advance Realty**, 284 Salem Street, 781-395-2121 or 888-261-7203, www.c21advance.com (Medford)
- **Century 21 Annex Realty**, 49 Beale Street, 617-472-4330 or 800-345-4614, www.century21.com (Quincy)
- **Century 21 Carole White Associates**, 1766 Centre Street, 617-323-4670 or 800-290-5281, www.century21.com (West Roxbury)
- **Century 21 Elizabeth Roberts Realty**, 920 Providence Highway, 781-329-9700, www.century21.com (Dedham)
- **Century 21 West Realty**, 161 Mt. Auburn Street, 617-926-5280 or 800-244-5280, www.century21.com (Watertown)
- **Chobee Hoy Associates**, 18 Harvard Street, 617-739-0067, www.chobeehoy.com (Brookline)
- **City-Wide Real Estate**, 344 Harvard Street, 617-738-8080, www.citywideusa.com (Brookline)
- **Coldwell Banker**, 171 Huron Avenue, 617-864-8566 (Cambridge); 321 Columbus Avenue, 617-266-8000 (South End); 635 Mass Ave., 781-643-6228 (Arlington); 702 Main Street, 781-893-0808 (Waltham); 858 Walnut Street, 617-965-7171 (Newton); www.coldwellbanker.com
- **East Coast Realty**, 103 Hemenway Street, 617-536-2900, www.all-boston-realty.com (Fenway)
- **First Choice Realty**, 1310 Comm Ave., 617-734-8200, www.firstchoiceboston.com (Allston-Brighton)
- **Gibson Real Estate**, 142 Main Street, 617-242-3073, www.gibsonre.com (Charlestown)
- **Gibson Domain Domain Real Estate**, 227 Newbury Street, 617-375-6900, (Back Bay/Beacon Hill); 553 East Broadway, 617-268-2011, (South Boston); 556 Tremont Street, 617-426-6900, (South End); www.gibsondomaindomain.com
- **Greater Boston Properties**, 696 Tremont Street, 617-536-4900, www.gbproperties.com (South End)
- **Greater Boston Realty Group**, 404 South Huntington Avenue, 617-522-2120 (JP)
- **Justin Reynolds Associates**, 5 Banks Street, 781-899-2003 (Waltham)
- **JVT Realty, 931 Mass Ave.**, 781-643-1004, www. bostonapartments.com/jvt (Arlington)
- **Newton Centre Associates**, 50 Union Street, Suite 200, 617-965-3300, www.bostonrealty.com/nca (Newton)
- **Olde Forge Realty**, 12 Clarendon Street, 617-227-6600, www.oldeforgerealty.com (South End)

- **Otis & Ahearn**, 81 Newbury Street, 617-267-3500, (Back Bay/Beacon Hill); 85 Atlantic Avenue, 617-227-6070, (North End/Waterfront); 90 Main Street, 617-242-7393, (Charlestown); www.otisahearn.com
- **Pleasant Realty**, 713 Centre Street, 617-522-4600 (JP)
- **Preservation Properties**, 439 Newtonville Avenue, 617-527-3700, www.preservationproperties.com (Newton)
- **Real Estate 109**, 459 Common Street, 617-489-5110, http://realestate109.com (Belmont)
- **Realty Resource Associates**, 1340 Comm Ave., 617-730-5300, www.realtyresource.net (Allston-Brighton)
- **Resnick Real Estate Group**, 214 Harvard Street, 617-730-9800, www.resnickgroup.com (Allston-Brighton)
- **Resource Capital Group**, 843 Mass Ave., 617-491-8315, www.resourcecapitalgroup.com (Cambridge)
- **Skyline Realty**, 10 Magazine Street, 617-547-8700, www.skylinerealty.com (Cambridge)
- **Werman Real Estate**, 617-497-7888, www.aptgods.com (Cambridge)

CHECKING IT OUT

Unless you're just looking for a temporary sublet to get you through the next couple of months, newcomers should be confident about a place before signing a lease. Yes, it's a tight market, but not so tight that you should feel pressure to commit to an apartment that is not right for you.

When checking out prospective apartments, in addition to aesthetics and price, keep in mind some of the following:

- Outside the living areas, is there enough space, including closets and storage? Sometimes additional storage space is available elsewhere in the building, like a basement or a locker. In the kitchen, check that there are enough drawers, shelves, and cabinets. Some Boston apartments are so compact that they have little to no cupboard space, and no kitchen drawers! While in the kitchen, check that the stove works. Boston landlords are not required to supply a refrigerator with rental units, so check if the apartment is equipped with one.
- If you're living with roommates, are there enough provisions, particularly bathrooms, for everyone? Most older Boston apartments do not have more than one bathroom, though some apartments make it easier on multiple tenants by having the toilet and shower in one room, and the sink in another. Run the faucets and the showerhead, and flush the toilets to check the water pressure. Ask how big the water tank is and if it serves more than one unit.

- Are you comfortable in this neighborhood? Is it too loud, particularly on weekend nights, or conversely, does it feel too isolated? Also consider building security and safety devices.
- Is there a second exit in case of fire? Old buildings have fire escapes that have been "grand-fathered" into building inspection approval, but newer buildings must have two exits to meet code. Are there smoke or heat detectors, which alert you to a change in air or temperature in case of a fire, carbon monoxide detectors, fire extinguishers, and fire alarms?
- Are you close to the T, bus, or commuter rail? Your daily commute to work or school will play a huge role in how happy you are in your new place. If you will be bringing a car, consider parking and distance to a thoroughfare or highway.
- Does the building allow pets? Good to know if you have a pet, even better if you are allergic to pets.
- Is there laundry in the building or hook-ups for washers/dryers in the unit? If there are no facilities on site, check to see how close the neighborhood laundromat is.
- Do you see any signs of insects or vermin? Even nice buildings can have rat and mice troubles, and apartments over restaurants are particularly prone to cockroaches. Ask what the landlord does in terms of vermin prevention, and keep in mind that sometimes, despite a landlord's best efforts, pests might come back from time to time.
- What monthly utility bills are covered in the lease, and what are bills are you required to pay? In Massachusetts, landlords must pay for water, and many pay for heat. Consider asking for the past year's fuel bills—both heat and electric, to get an idea how much more monthly expenditures you will be faced with.
- For units that do not come with air-conditioning, either central air or a window-unit, consider if this will be a problem. Summers here are hot and humid—very uncomfortable, though less so if you are in a garden (basement) unit.
- How is the technology in the building? Is it wired for cable? DSL? And on a more basic note, are there enough electrical outlets?
- Who do you contact in case of an emergency; how far away are they; and can you call at all hours?

If you'd like to do some more pre-apartment hunting research, check Ed Sacks' *Savvy Renter's Kit*, which contains a thorough renter's checklist.

STAKING A CLAIM

As mentioned previously, Boston's rental market has been fast-paced and competitive for years. While slower now, chances are that there are several other people angling for the same place you're viewing. If the apartment you are considering fits your basic specs and is in the neighborhood where you want to live, don't dawdle—*take it!*

The process usually requires filling out an application wherein you'll need to supply information about your job, bank account, credit and personal references, and previous landlord(s). It's best to bring these documents with you when viewing prospective apartments. If you have bad credit, consider having your lease cosigned by a parent, or other person who can vouch for your financial stability. In such a case, be sure your cosigner has his/her banking information and social security number. Most importantly, don't forget to bring your checkbook so can put down a deposit.

If you do get the apartment, you will have to pay the agent's fee, and in addition, expect to pay your new landlord the first and last month's rent, security deposit (equal to the first month's rent), and a fee for purchasing and installing a key and lock. This means, for example, a one-bedroom apartment at $1,200 per month will require between $600 and $1,200 for an agent's fee, $2,400 for first and last month's rent, and a $1,200 security deposit, plus the key cost, for a total of between $7,200 and $7,800.

LANDLORDS AND TENANTS

LEASES

There are two types of rental situations in Massachusetts: fixed-term and tenant-at-will. A fixed-term lease, an agreement to rent a unit for a specified amount of time, typically one year, is the most common. During this period, a landlord can neither raise your rent, nor evict you, unless you violate specific lease clauses. At the end of the agreed-upon term, you can opt to renew or leave. If you need to leave before the end of the term, you will possibly need to pay out the remainder of the lease or find an acceptable sub-letter to take over your lease. A tenant-at-will scenario, called a month-to-month agreement in other parts of the country, is where you pay rent at intervals, usually monthly. The upside to this arrangement is that it is easy to move out. The downside is that your landlord can raise your rent or evict you at any time, providing he gives you 30 days notice.

Always read a lease carefully. Many landlords use forms weighted in their favor. You can negotiate with your landlord, however, striking unacceptable clauses and adding others, if the landlord agrees to the changes. Do this before you sign, and be sure to have the landlord initial the changes. Typical issues include sublet restrictions and pet clauses. Some leases contain illegal clauses, but they are not enforceable, even if you don't catch them before signing. For example, a lease requiring the tenant to pay for water and sewage cannot be enforced. Also, some landlords will stipu-

late in a lease that if your rent is late, they will charge a penalty fee. This is legal, but only if the rent is over 30 days late. Landlords creating a penalty for rent that is less than 30 days past due are not in compliance with the law. Valid leases in Massachusetts include the following:
- The amount of monthly rent
- The date on which your tenancy begins and ends
- The amount of your security deposit and your rights concerning it (see below).
- The names, addresses, and phone numbers of your landlord and any other person responsible for maintaining the property
- The tenant authorized to receive notices and court papers

Make sure you get all promises not included on the lease in writing and that all blank spaces are filled out. Finally, make sure you can prove the state of your apartment when you moved in. The best thing is to insist on a walk-through with your landlord, creating an inspection checklist that you then both sign. This could save you in case the landlord makes unjustifiable deductions from your security deposit to cover repairs upon your exit.

SECURITY DEPOSITS

In Massachusetts, a security deposit must be placed in an interest-bearing escrow account in a Massachusetts bank. Within 30 days a landlord is required to give you a receipt for this deposit, indicating the bank's name and address, amount of deposit, and account number. Should he not do so, you are permitted to have your security deposit returned to you. Also, according to *The Tenant's Commandments,* published by the Massachusetts Executive Office of Consumer Affairs, which you can get by calling 617-727-7780 or at www.tenant.net/Other_Areas/Massachusetts/mrights.txt, "interest is payable to you each year on the anniversary date of your tenancy." Each year your landlord must tell you how much interest your deposit has accrued, and either give you said interest or deduct it from your next month's rent. Security deposits must be returned within 30 days after the tenancy ends. Landlords may deduct any reasonable cost of repairs for damage caused by the tenant, but normal wear and tear expenses are *not* deductible. If your landlord does not return your deposit within 30 days, you can sue for up to three times the amount of the deposit plus court costs and attorney fees.

Be aware that some landlords tack on bogus costs such as "rental fees," "pet fees," "fees for credit checks," or "holding deposits." These prepayments are illegal. If you choose to pay them rather than lose the apartment, you can consider subtracting the charges from your future rent payments, however, doing so might set up a rancorous landlord/tenant relationship, which no one wants. It is best to rent from a fair landlord who isn't going to try to gouge you with illegal fees.

LANDLORD/TENANT RIGHTS AND RESPONSIBILITIES

As a tenant, it's a good idea to know your rights and responsibilities, as well as the landlord's rights and responsibilities.
- The State of Massachusetts requires that landlords **provide safe buildings**: doors to the building, the main entryway, and individual units must lock, as must all opening exterior windows. Landlords are responsible for maintaining all smoke detectors in the building, but not fire extinguishers or carbon monoxide detectors. Some buildings also still have lead paint in their units, but it's against the law for children under six to live in them. If you have small children and are interested in a unit that has lead paint, a landlord cannot refuse to rent it to you, instead he has to have the paint removed. (See the **Child Safety** section in the **Childcare and Education** chapter for more information about the lead poisoning prevention program in Massachusetts.)
- As mentioned earlier, refrigerators do not always come with a unit, however, if a landlord provides one he must continue to do so. Other **kitchen appliances**, including sinks, dishwashers (if included in the unit), and stoves must be in good working condition.
- A landlord must keep the general living environment **clean and free of vermin**. If your building has three or more units, the landlord is responsible for the disposal of garbage, and he must make sure the common areas are free from refuse.
- Massachusetts tenants do not pay for **water**, and a landlord is required to have enough hot water (between 110° to 130°) for normal tenant use. Tenants generally pay for fuel to heat their water unless otherwise noted in the lease. As far as heating the unit, from September 16 to June 14, units must be heated to a minimum of 68° during the day and 64° at night. A landlord pays for heating fuel, unless otherwise specified in the lease.
- In the winter, the landlord is responsible for **snow and ice removal**, including clearing all exits and fire escapes.
- Lease provisions allowing a landlord **legal access to a unit** include entrance to inspect (e.g., for insurance purposes), to make repairs, and to show the unit for rental or purchase, provided the tenant has been given notice and has given permission. As a tenant, you are obliged to allow your landlord "reasonable access," but unless the lease states otherwise, the landlord isn't even entitled to a key. All other entrance clauses that may appear on a lease are not legal. In emergency circumstances (i.e., fire, flood) a landlord may enter a unit without warning. He may also enter without warning if you appear to have

abandoned your unit, so it's a good idea to alert your landlord if you are going away for an extended period of time.
- It is **illegal for a landlord to refuse to rent to you** based on your race, religion, gender, sexual orientation, age, marital status, military status, or disability. Nor may you be discriminated against based on whether you have children or your source of income. A landlord may require proof that you have enough income to make the rent, but he cannot discriminate regarding the source of those funds. In Massachusetts, there are some instances in which a landlord may refuse to rent to a person with children: if the landlord is leasing out his own unit for less than a year; if it's a two-family house and the landlord lives in the other unit; or if it's a three-family (or less) house, and one of the other tenants is elderly/infirm to the point that having children in the building would create undue hardship.

Massachusetts provides some **legal protection for tenants**. Boston, Worcester, and Springfield provide mediation services for landlords and tenants through their court systems. The following are some organizations and municipal departments that can offer you more information about your rights and may be able to help if you have a dispute with your landlord.
- **Action for Boston Community Development**, 178 Tremont Street, Boston 02111, 617-357-6000, www.bostonabcd.org
- **Boston College Legal Assistance Bureau**, www.neighborhoodlaw.org
- **Boston Fair Housing Commission**, City Hall, Room 966, Boston 02201, 617-635-4408, www.cityofboston.gov/civilrights
- **Boston Inspectional Services**, 1010 Mass Ave., 5th Floor, Boston 02118, 617-635-5300
- **(Boston) Mayor's Office of Consumer Affairs and Licensing**, 1 City Hall Plaza, Room 817, Boston 02201, 617-635-3834, www.cityofboston.gov/consumeraffairs
- **Cambridge Economic Opportunity Committee, Inc.**, 11 Inman Street, Cambridge 02139, 617-868-2900
- **Cambridge Eviction Free Zone**, 55 Norfolk Street, Cambridge 02139, 617-354-1300
- **Cambridge Inspectional Services Department**, 831 Mass Ave., Cambridge 02139, 617-349-6100, www.ci.cambridge.ma.us
- **Community Action Agency of Somerville**, 66-70 Union Square #104, Somerville 02143, 617-623-7370
- **Community Legal Services and Counseling Center**, 1 West Street, Cambridge 02139, 617-661-1010, www.neighborhoodlaw.org/community
- **Greater Boston Legal Services**, 197 Friend Street, Boston 02114, 617-371-1234 or 800-323-3205, www.gbls.org

- **Harvard Legal Aid Bureau**, 1511 Mass Ave., Cambridge 02138, 617-495-4408
- **Massachusetts Attorney General's Office face-to-face Mediation Program**, 200 Portland Street, 4th Floor, Boston 02111, 617-727-2200, www.ago.state.ma.us; other services are available through the **Consumer Protection Division**.
- **Massachusetts Bar Association Lawyer Referral Service**, 20 West Street, Boston 02111, 617-654-0400, www.massbar.org/lawhelp/need_lawyer
- **Massachusetts Commission Against Discrimination**, (for problems of housing discrimination) 1 Ashburton Place, 6th floor, Boston 02108, 617-994-6000, TTY 617-994-6196, www.state.ma.us/mcad
- **Massachusetts Department of Housing & Community Development's Housing Services Program**, 1 Congress Street, Boston 02114, 617-727-7765, www.state.ma.us/dhcd
- **Massachusetts Tenants' Organization**, 14 Beacon Street, Boston 02108, 617-367-6260
- **Somerville Board of Health**, 50 Evergreen Avenue, Somerville, 617-625-6600, www.ci.somerville.ma.us
- **Tenant Advocacy Project**, Harvard Law School, Austin Hall, Room 009, 1515 Mass Ave., Cambridge 02138, 617-495-4394, www.law.harvard.edu/academics/clinical
- **Volunteer Lawyers Project**, 29 Temple Place, Boston 02108, 617-423-0648, www.vlpnet.org

Boston tenants with **emergency landlord problems**—no heat or threatened lockout—can call the Mayor's 24/7 hotline for intervention: 617-635-4500.

RENT AND EVICTION CONTROL

Put to voters in 1994 in a statewide ballot was the issue of **rent control**. The outcome prohibited rent control in Massachusetts, effective December 1996, meaning that landlords can legally increase rent as much as they want at the end of your lease. Generally, landlords have not abused this privilege, and most increases stay in the standard $50/month range.

In an effort to assist those heavily affected by the rent control decision, the **Rental Housing Resource Center** (formerly the Boston Rent Equity Board), Boston City Hall, 1 City Hall Plaza, Room 709, Boston 02201; 617-635-4200; www.cityofboston.gov/rentalhousing, provides mediation between landlords and tenants, legal advice for both landlords and tenants, and assistance in housing placement for elderly, handicapped, or low-income residents.

Eviction can occur only under certain circumstances—rules differ according to whether the tenant is in a fixed-term lease or is a tenant-at-will. If you are a tenant-at-will, a landlord can decide to end your tenancy whenever he wants, as long as you are given 30-days' notice, and there is reason to evict.

Massachusetts landlords are forbidden from using eviction as a means of retaliating against their tenants. For instance, complaining to the landlord or a government agency about housing conditions, or joining a tenants' union is not grounds for eviction. Should your landlord try to evict you, raise your rent, or otherwise change the terms of your lease within six months after you've taken any of the aforementioned actions, his behavior will legally be assumed to be retaliation.

ADDITIONAL RESOURCES—TENANTS

- **Massachusetts Office of Consumer Affairs and Business Regulation**, 10 Park Plaza, Suite 5170, Boston, MA 02116, 617-973-8787 or 888-283-3757, www.state.ma.us/consumer; provides a list of applicable links for tenant/landlord rights and issues in the state. This office also puts out *The Tenant's Commandments*, a pamphlet that describes tenants' rights; available from their office or online at www.tenant.net/Other_Areas/massachusetts/mrights. They also have links to information about tenant and landlord rights and responsibilities, moving in Massachusetts, and the state sanitary code.
- **The Massachusetts Attorney General's Offices**: 1 Ashburton Place, Boston, 02108; 200 Portland Street, Boston, 02114, 617-727-2200, www.ago.state.ma.us; publishes a tenant guide: *The Attorney General's Guide to Tenants' Rights*.
- **Tenant.net**, www.tenant.net/Other_Areas/Massachusetts
- **Boston Apartments**, www.bostonapartments.com/rentips; offers links to several pertinent web sites posting information for Massachusetts renters.
- ***Legal Tactics***: ***Self-Defense for Tenants in Massachusetts***, produced by the Massachusetts Law Reform Institute, 99 Chauncy Street, 5th Floor, Boston 02111; 617-357-0700, www.mlri.org. Cost is $15.

RENTER'S/HOMEOWNER'S INSURANCE

Even though Boston isn't known for severe weather or natural disasters, bad things do happen here to good apartments and houses. For these reasons, renter's or homeowner's insurance is a good idea. Renter's insurance is usually quite affordable, and depending on the policy, it can protect you in the event of a number of catastrophes, including theft, fire, and water damage, and sometimes personal liability.

You can start researching policies through the **Massachusetts Division of Insurance**, 1 South Station in Boston, 617-521-7794, www.state.ma.us/doi. They offer information on renter's and homeowner's insurance and can provide specifics about insurance rates by community. They will also supply a list of insurance agencies in the state. **Insure.com**, and **Quicken**, www.insweb.com, also offer comparison shopping, instant quotes, and additional insurance information.

To order your order your CLUE (Comprehensive Loss Underwriting Exchange) report, write to **ChoicePoint Asset**, P.O. Box 105108, Atlanta, GA 30348-5108, or go to www.choicetrust.com. This national database of consumers' automobile and homeowner's insurance claims is used by insurers when determining rates or denying coverage. Contact ChoicePoint if you find any errors in your report.

A few of the major insurers in the greater Boston area include:
- **Allmerica**, www.allmerica.com
- **Arbella**, www.arbella.com
- **Liberty Mutual**, www.libertymutual.com
- **MetLife**, www.metlife.com
- **Royal & Sun Alliance**, www.royalsunalliance.com

Renter's insurance is available through an insurance agent or you can apply directly to **FAIR (Fair Access to Insurance Requirements)** Plan. In Massachusetts, this program is administered by the Massachusetts Property Insurance Underwriting Association, located at 2 Center Plaza in Boston across from City Hall Plaza: 617-723-3800, 800-392-6108, www.mpiua.com.

HOUSE/CONDO HUNTING

As is the case with renting, going about buying a home in the greater Boston area may be a bit daunting. And, unless you're from California or New York, you'll likely experience some sticker shock at the prices of homes.

Many newcomers arrive with the intention of buying a house, but decide to rent, at least at first. If you don't think you will be in the area longer than a couple years, renting may also be your best option. But, if you can afford to, and you are positive about your location preference, buying real estate tends to be a good long-term investment. Monthly mortgage payments may not be that much more than monthly rent, plus you're building equity. There are also tax breaks to consider when purchasing a home.

Housing styles in Massachusetts vary widely. Buyers have a range of choices, the most prevalent being Cape Cods, ranches, colonials, Gothic Revivals, Greek Revivals, Tudor Revivals, and Victorians. Many homes in the greater Boston area are old enough to be on the National Register of Historic

Places. When you drive or walk around town, you'll notice homes boasting small plaques showing the name and date of the family who built them.

Aside from rental units, most housing options in Boston's city center are condos and co-ops, which often are in multiple-story colonial and Victorian buildings, although there are a few luxury units in more modern high-rise type structures, particularly in downtown. There are some single family residences (a.k.a., mansions), particularly in Beacon Hill, the Back Bay, and the South End; some are brick Victorian rowhouses, which escaped being chopped up and parceled out into apartments during the mid-1900s (a fate suffered by many).

In neighborhoods like Allston-Brighton, JP, and West Roxbury, you'll encounter a mix of housing options, including units for sale (condos or co-ops) in old brownstones and in big, practical 1960s construction; as well as houses, both triple-deckers and more classic styles. Similarly, the communities directly surrounding Boston (Cambridge, Somerville, Brookline, etc.) also have a mix. As you head further out from the city, you'll find stereotypical suburbia: bigger homes with lawns and driveways. These communities have more houses and fewer condos, co-ops, or rental options.

DECIDING WHETHER, WHAT, AND WHERE TO BUY

If you are **considering buying a home**:
- Consider how long you plan to live in your potential home. On average, it takes three to four years for your home's value to appreciate enough to cover the purchasing and selling costs. If you plan on leaving after only two years, it may be in your best financial interest to rent.
- Consider your space needs. Are you planning on having children in the near future or are your children about to leave? Will four flights of stairs for a swank townhouse work for a retired couple?
- What kind of house do you want: a single-family house, a unit in a co-op or condominium, or a unit in a three-plex? Do you want old or new? A vintage Victorian can be an absolute gem of a house when all the renovations are complete, but this may be no easy task. Families with children in particular should take care with any housing renovations, as disturbing long-hidden lead paint is hazardous.
- Investigate the neighborhood. This is particularly important if you have children. Consider nearby parkland, the quality of the schools, property values, heavy traffic, crime rates, and planned future construction in the community. Even if all of these factors aren't crucial to you personally, they can affect the appreciation of your home and thus the value of your investment.
- When looking at housing in a particular community, pay attention to how quickly houses sell and if there are often large gaps between list price

and sale prices. Buying a place in an "up and coming" area can be a good investment, but keep in mind, not all "up and coming" areas come up. Pay attention to high-density streets (a lot of apartments), heavy traffic, poor public transportation, and an absence of neighborhood services.
- Generally, it's good to know that two-bedroom condos sell more easily than one-bedroom condos, two-bedroom/one-bath homes are less desirable than three-bedroom homes, and the nicest house on the block is not as easy to sell as the more middle-of-the-road house just two doors down.

CONDOMINIUMS (CONDOS) AND COOPERATIVES (CO-OPS)

Co-ops and condos are similar housing arrangements. Both tend to offer environments that are more social than what you'd experience in a detached single-family home, if for no other reason than the need to make decisions about upkeep and use of the communal parts of the property. Maintenance fees are common in both, and in addition to paying your assessment, from time to time you may be required to give more for unexpected repairs or capital improvements. Prospective buyers should take as much time to examine the condo's or co-op's financial reports as to view the available unit. Also look at recent capital improvements and have the grounds inspected to forewarn you of any upcoming repair needs—outside decks, recreation area, landscaping, roof, windows, etc.

In a **condo**, you purchase an individual unit, but the land and common areas are jointly owned by the condo association, of which you would be a part. When you live in a **cooperative** (**co-op**), you actually own a share of the corporation that owns the building, as opposed to the unit itself. In this situation each shareholding entity (i.e., tenant) has a unit reserved for his use. In the past, co-ops were more favorable to selling to those with substantial economic means, and tended not to allow financing, although that is not necessarily the case any longer. Condos, on the other hand, did and do permit standard mortgage financing. Times have changed, and although some co-ops maintain the cash-only policy, others have revised their bylaws to allow in "desirable" buyers with high enough incomes but inadequate savings. Another thing to keep in mind when considering a co-op is that co-op units can take longer to sell due to the rigorous screening process of applicants and higher down payments, which is not good if you find yourself needing to sell quickly. When buying a unit in a co-op, be prepared to disclose your financial information to the board. A well-run co-op will be careful to make sure incoming tenants are financially dependable, they may also scrutinize your personal life. On your end, you should be sure to get a prospectus, minutes of the last meeting of the board, and a financial statement from the co-op (or condo for that matter) and go over them with your broker and your lawyer. If your purchase is rejected, expect no explanation. Be aware that co-op size may affect your ability to get a mortgage; in co-ops with less than 12 units, lenders may be more likely to reject a mortgage application because the relatively small number of shareholders in such buildings raises the collective risk of default. Also, keep in mind that co-op maintenance fees (the cost of upkeep for everything outside the walls of your apartment) can be steep, and only some of the maintenance fee (the portion of the fee that is allocated for property tax payments) is tax deductible.

Purchasing a condo is similar to purchasing a single-family home, the difference being you will have to contend with (annual or monthly) condo fees that cover the expenses of taking care of communal areas and shared amenities, such as garage, laundry room, and pool. Again, obtain a copy of condo association records to determine not only how often association fees have gone up, but also by how much.

For more information about housing associations, visit the **Community Associations Institute** at www.caionline.org or the **American Homeowners Resource Center** at www.ahrc.com. Both are national organizations that offer information and tips on how to live in a community association.

FINDING A PLACE TO BUY

Tried and true methods of finding a place to buy include driving around a neighborhood looking for "for sale" signs, working with a real estate agent, and perusing the newspapers. The Sunday *Boston Globe* and the Saturday edition of the *Boston Herald* are the primary source of real estate ads for the region; both papers have extensive real estate sections, with listing of condos and houses and their respective agencies (see above under **Newspaper Classifieds**).

Once you start viewing homes, several things will help make the process easier. First, make a list of your "must haves," and then make a list of "wants." Take a copy of them with you, and mark on the list which homes have which amenities. Brokers recommend that you seriously consider no more than three houses at a time. Of course, it will probably take a lot of outings before you find your top three. To help keep your memory fresh, keep a written log for each house, including the date you saw it, with which broker, and then make notes on the listing sheet. If the agent/owner allows it, consider taking some digital photos or Polaroids. You also can get a map of the neighborhood(s) in which you're looking and mark spots of the homes you've seen.

WORKING WITH A REAL ESTATE BROKER

Although you do not have to work with a real estate broker when buying a home, having one can be very helpful. More people than not choose to retain their services, either on the buying or selling end. In Massachusetts, real estate brokers are licensed and are legally bound to put their clients' interests first, maintain confidentiality about information provided, comply with clients' wishes, keep clients apprised of any useful information, and account for any money involved.

Because buying and selling homes is a realtor's daily business, he will be a great resource during your journey toward home ownership. Real estate brokers are qualified to advise you on how much you can afford to spend; how to find alternative financing or recommend a lender; what personal data you'll need when going for your loan approval; the property values, taxes, utilities costs, services, zoning ordinances in certain neighborhoods; and where to find a good inspector. Additionally, a realtor can save you a lot of time and effort by showing you houses that are in your price range and in your preferred neighborhoods. Often a realtor will have access to homes that, while on the market, are not visibly advertised.

The first thing you should know when picking a real estate broker is that there is a difference between a seller's agent and a buyer's agent. A **seller's agent** represents the person trying to sell a house; a **buyer's agent** represents the person trying to buy the house. In Massachusetts, one person can legally be a broker for both sides of a real estate deal, called a "dual agent," if both the buyer and seller are aware of this and have given informed consent. But, since the seller is trying to get the highest price and the buyer is trying to pay the lowest price, and the seller is usually the one to pay the realtor's commission, the likelihood is that the realtor will work harder, however unwittingly, for the seller. Therefore, you should think seriously about getting yourself a good buyer's agent, whose sole responsibility is to represent you.

Even real estate professionals recommend you shop around a little before settling on a real estate broker to represent you. Important qualities in an agent are how well he knows the market and how well he finds and manages listings. Chemistry/compatibility are important too.

Good ways to find an agent are to visit open houses in your neighborhood of choice and meet with the representing agent, or to ask for recommendations from friends and co-workers. Some things to think about when you're deciding on an agent include the following:
- Is he licensed and in good standing? What credentials does he have?
- Does he belong to a Multiple Listing Services or other online buyer's research service?
- How does he plan to help you get what you want in a home?

If you find a buyer's broker, have him sign a written buyer's brokerage agreement to be your "Buyer's Agent." You will promise to work only with this agent for a specified amount of time (usually three months) and not buy from anyone else. The commission will still come from the seller, but your agent must present the offer. Also, it pays to be discreet when disclosing information to any realtor. Unless you've gotten him to sign on as a buyer's agent, you should presume that anything you say to a realtor will go straight to the seller, and that might not always be ideal.

The **Board of Registration of Real Estate** answers real estate-related questions, at www.state.ma.us/reg/boards/re. If you're looking for a real estate agent, you might want to check with the **Massachusetts Association of Realtors**, www.marealtor.com, or the **Greater Boston Real Estate Board** (**GBREB**), 617-423-8700, www.gbreb.com. In addition to providing names of real estate agents, they also have a number of property listings and advice on obtaining financing. GBREB's site also offers downloadable software to help prospective homeowners figure out how they can fit a mortgage into their budget. Most of the rental brokers listed above also handle sales.

ONLINE RESOURCES—HOUSE HUNTING

Web sites for would-be homeowners include the following (also see **Additional Resources** below):
- **ABoston Lofts**, www.abostonloft.com; free listings of lofts for rent and sale in Boston, Cambridge and Somerville.
- **Abele Owner's Network**, www.owners.com
- **Boston Apartments/Boston Realty**, www.bostonapartments.com; free daily listings of properties to rent (fee and no fee) and to buy, as well as of management companies, in Massachusetts and New Hampshire.
- **Boston Condos**, www.bostoncondos.com; free listings of condos for sale throughout the greater Boston area, including full agent contact information and sometimes photos.
- **Boston.com/Real Estate**, http://realestate.boston.com; the *Globe's* online guide to everything real estate in the greater Boston area: rentals, sales, moving, tips, etc.
- **BostonRealEstate.com**, www.bostonrealestate.com
- **Condo Mart**, www.condomart.com
- **FISBO Registry for Homebuyers**, www.fisbos.com
- **Homebuilder.com**, www.homebuilder.com; comprehensive site where you can find apartments, homes, and roommates; sales and rentals.
- **HomeGain**, www.homegain.com
- **Homes.com**, www.homes.com
- **Homestore**, www.homestore.com

- **MSN House and Home**, http://houseandhome.msn.com
- **The National Association of Realtors**, www.realtor.com
- **Real Estate Book**, http://realestate.cityserach.com
- **ZipRealty**, www.ziprealty.com, a national real estate site.

If you want to do some investigation of homes **for sale by owner**, try:
- **For Sale By Owner**: http://www.4salebyowner.com
- **IsoldMyHouse.com**: www.isoldmyhouse.com
- **For Sale By Owner Network**: www.fsbonetwork.com
- **HomesByOwner.com**: www.homesbyowner.com

THE BUYING PROCESS

The first thing you need to consider when buying a house is how much you can spend. Start with your gross monthly income, then tally up your monthly debt load: credit cards, car loans, personal debt, child support, alimony, etc. For revolving debt (like credit card debt), use your minimum monthly payment for the calculation. For the purposes of this calculation, ignore any debts you expect to have paid off entirely within six months' time. As a rule, your monthly housing costs shouldn't exceed 28% of your total monthly income, and your debt load shouldn't exceed 36% of it. That said, these days lenders might tailor the 28/36 ratio depending on your situation (assets, liability, job, credit history).

When calculating your budget, don't forget to factor in closing costs, which include insurance, appraisals, attorney's fees, transfer taxes, and loan fees. Fees normally range from three to seven percent of the purchase price. Likewise, when figuring out your budget, be sure to factor in the additional monthly outgoes of homeowner's insurance, property taxes (tax deductible), utilities, condo fees, improvements, and maintenance.

Lenders suggest that you "pre-qualify" or, better still, get "pre-approved" for a loan. **Pre-qualification** is, in essence, an educated guess as to what you'll be able to afford for a loan. With **pre-approval**, your financial claims are verified, thus, your ability to pay the stated amount is guaranteed by the lender. To be pre-approved, your loan officer will review your financial situation (by running a credit check, going over your proof of employment, savings, etc.) and then you will be given a letter documenting that the bank is willing to loan you a particular amount based on your proven financial situation. Pre-approval is a bit more labor-intensive for you and the lender, but putting in the effort shows you are a serious buyer and may give you a competitive edge over other prospective buyers. Also, in the end, you'll know for sure what you can and cannot afford for a house, and sellers and real estate agents will take you more seriously if you show up with a pre-approval letter in hand.

If you are planning to get pre-qualified or pre-approved for your loan, go to your lender prepared with documentation of your financial history, and contact the three major credit bureaus listed below to make sure your credit history is accurate. You will need to provide your name, address, previous address, and Social Security number with your request. Contact each company for specific instructions, or visit www.icreditreport.com for online access to all three. You can obtain a free report if you've been denied credit within the last 30 days. A credit report will show your credit activity for the past seven years, including your highest balance, current balance, and promptness or tardiness of payments. After seven years, the slate is wiped clean for any credit transgressions, except in the case of bankruptcy, which will appear on your record for 10 years. Fortunately, lenders are more concerned with your most recent track record than how you behaved seven years ago. It's best to try to pay all your bills in full and on time for at least a year before you apply for a loan. Even if you pay your bills on time, having too much credit can be a problem. Generally, you can get away with a couple of "blemishes" on your record and still get low rates. And even if your credit report isn't stellar, you most likely can still get a loan, though your rates (interest and fees) may be higher. Also, saving up a lot of money can counteract credit flaws to make you a more appealing financial risk to a lender.

The major credit bureaus are:

- **Experian** (formerly TRW), P.O. Box 2104, Allen, TX 75002-2104, 888-397-3742
- **TransUnion Corporation**, P.O. Box 390, Springfield, PA 19064-0390, 800-916-8800
- **Equifax**, P.O. Box 105873, Atlanta, GA 30348, 800-685-1111

It's best to get a copy of your credit report from each bureau, as each report may be different. If you discover any inaccuracies, you should contact the service immediately and request that it be corrected. By law they must respond to your request within 30 days. If you are insecure about your credit record, call Fannie Mae's non-profit credit counseling service at 800-732-6643 before you apply for a mortgage. Be aware that too many credit record inquiries can lower your credit status.

Most buyers need a **mortgage** to pay for a house. A typical house mortgage is for either 15 or 30 years and consists of four parts, commonly referred to as "PITI" (principal, interest, taxes, and insurance). The **principal** is the flat sum of money that you borrowed from the lender to pay for the property. The larger the down payment, the less you will need to borrow to meet the total purchase price of your home. The lender charges **interest**, a percentage of the principal, as repayment for the use of the money that you've borrowed. It is how lenders make their money. (Points, each one equal to 1% of the amount you borrow for your mortgage, might also contribute to the interest.) Your community charges you **taxes** based on a percentage of your property value; you'll continue paying these even after your mortgage is paid off. The final component of PITI is home **insurance** against calamities such as fire, theft, and natural disasters. It is a requisite to buying a house. In many cases, people deposit funds to cover insurance and taxes into an escrow or trust account.

There are many loan programs around. Search the internet, newspapers, and books, and speak with financial planners, real estate agents, and mortgage brokers to find out what's available. Direct lenders (banks) and mortgage brokers are the most common places to go for a loan. A **direct lender** is an institution with a finite number of in-house loans, whose terms and conditions are controlled by the lender. A **mortgage broker**, on the other hand, is a middleman who shops around to various lenders and loan programs to find what's best for your needs. Because brokers are free to check for the best interest rates, it's often worth paying their fee. Most major lenders and brokers have their own web sites. For a list of local banks, look in the **Money Matters** chapter.

When educating yourself about mortgages, be sure to take the time to research institutions' loan costs and restrictions: interest rates, broker fees, points, prepayment penalties, loan term, application fees, credit report fees, and cost of appraisals. The Bank Rate Monitor, www.bankrate.com, offers pages of information on mortgages and interest rates at over 2000 banks. It may pay to shop around.

Down payments vary. Lenders are offering some new programs that require as little as five percent down. An example of these programs is Fannie Mae's three/two loan program, which gives a first-time buyer 95% of the price of a home. The buyer is required to supply three percent of the down payment; the other two percent can be a gift from family, a government program, or a non-profit agency. Other programs require no down payment at all. If you go for anything less than 20% as a down payment, however, your lender will want the loan to be qualified by an outside party (i.e. the Veterans Administration, Federal Housing Authority, or a private mortgage insurer to protect them against any mortgage defaults). Note: for all loans made after July 29, 1999, once your balance gets to 78% of the purchase price, you no longer have to pay for private mortgage insurance. Also, if you are a first-time buyer, which is defined as someone who hasn't owned property within the past three years, you may qualify for state-backed programs that feature lower down payment requirements and below-market interest rates. A popular first-time buyer mortgage program in Massachusetts is MassAdvantage, run by **MassHousing**; read up on it at www.masshousing.com.

Although some believe that Massachusetts' officially defined **affordable housing** (below market rate) is not as available as it should be, even in the suburbs, the state does have housing assistance programs. The biggest portal for this information is through the **Massachusetts Department of Housing and Community Development**, www.state.ma.us/dhcd. Also check with the **Citizens Housing and Planning Association** (**CHAPA**), 617-742-0820, www.chapa.org, a nonprofit devoted to the issues of affordable housing and community development in Massachusetts. The **Boston Redevelopment Authority**, www.cityofboston.gov/bra, is a decades-old organization devoted to development projects, including affordable housing in Boston. The local branch of the **Department of Housing and Urban Development** (**HUD**), www.hud.gov/local, may also be of use.

When filling out the **final paperwork for your loan approval**, keep in mind that intentionally offering incorrect information on a loan application is a federal offense. Within three business days of applying for your loan, your lender must give you a "good faith estimate" of how much your closing costs will be. Once you are approved, you can make an offer on the house (even if you are not formally approved, but are pre-qualified, you can make an offer, but it will have to be contingent on funding). If you want your offer to be seriously considered, particularly in a tight market, be sure to offer a fair market price, include a bank statement on the source of your down payment, your pre-approval letter, and even a note to the seller about why/how much you want the house. If cost is an issue, try to do your house hunting during the off-season (November to January), when competition will not be as intense. Note: in Massachusetts, it is customary for the buyer to make a good faith deposit of five- to ten-percent of the total purchase price at the time of the offer. The deposit is usually held in escrow until the seller accepts the offer, at which time the funds are transferred.

Once you have made the offer, the house will need to be appraised, and the title will need to be sent to the lender for a **title search**.

Offers, which should be submitted in writing to the seller, may mention the following:
- Address and legal description of the property
- Price you will pay for the home
- Terms (how you will pay)
- Seller's promise to provide clear title
- Target date for closing (when the property is actually transferred to you, and the funds are transferred to the seller)
- Down payment accompanying the offer—how much and in what form
- Plan for prorating utilities, taxes, etc., between buyer and seller
- Provisions: who will pay what extra costs (e.g., insurance, survey)
- Type of deed
- Contingencies

Common contingencies include a buyer's getting financing or selling a current residence, and receiving a satisfactory inspection report of the property. In Massachusetts, for residences built before 1978, buyers are entitled to a housing inspection within 10 days of the offer's acceptance; if the house fails inspection (i.e., is not up to what the state deems as satisfactory structural, mechanical, and environmental building code standards), the seller must fix the defects or you may back out of your offer. Offers on newer homes traditionally include the 10-day inspection period as well, although state law does not automatically give buyers a right to a home inspection, so the sellers have to approve that contingency in the offer. (See more about inspections below.) Another common contingency you might consider putting into your offer is "on terms to be approved by the buyer's attorney." This clause gives the buyer the freedom to have the purchase agreement reviewed by your lawyer before it becomes binding.

Many people hold the misconception that the closing is the most important part of the buying process. In fact, it is the offer that is most crucial. The closing is just signing the paperwork that finalizes what you agreed to in your offer. If the seller agrees to your offer, it becomes a binding sales contract, a **purchase and sale (P&S) agreement**. If you default on this contract, you can lose your deposit money. If the seller defaults, you can sue him to force the sale to which he agreed in writing.

That said, after you make an offer, the buyer will accept it, reject it, or make a counter offer; at which point you may accept, reject, or change the counter offer, and so on. When both parties agree, it becomes a binding purchase agreement. Some negotiable items in an offer include many of the transaction costs and who pays them, including brokers' commission, inspection costs, escrow or attorneys' fees, title search, owner's title insurance, transfer taxes, and recording fees. You can also negotiate on which items in the house you might want to purchase. While in theory anything attached to or installed in a home constitutes part of the house, in practice it doesn't always work this way. Thus, it's best to work out in the contract whether or not you'll be getting the washer and dryer or the living room drapes.

As mentioned above, **inspections** are crucial, particularly for older homes. The standard home inspection costs under $400, although it depends on the neighborhood and size of house. According to the Commonwealth of Massachusetts, such inspections entail "a visual examination of the physical structure and major interior systems" of a residence. Inspectors will assess the quality of "the readily accessible exposed portions of the structure of the home, including the roof, the attic, walls, ceilings, floors, windows, doors, basement, and foundation, as well as the heating/air conditioning systems, interior plumbing and electrical systems, for potential problems." An **environmental inspection**, which isn't always part of the standard deal, is worth considering, particularly because in Massachusetts it is legal to sell a residence with onsite environmental hazards. Typical environmental hazards you'll want to check for are unsafe drinking water, radon, pests, airborne asbestos, lead (present in the paint of three quarter's of the country's housing stock), urea formaldehyde foam insulation (UFFI), and oil spillage. As of 2001, housing inspectors in Massachusetts must pass an examination and meet state standards to become licensed; however, do not confuse a license with home inspector "certifications," which are designations from trade societies or companies, and while not bad, are not part of the state's licensing requirement. You can find an inspector by looking in the Yellow Pages under "Home Inspection Service" or "Building Inspection Service, or get a recommendation from a friend, your broker or realtor, or call the **American Society of Home Inspectors** at 800-743-ASHI, or the **Division of Professional Licensure**, 617-727-4459, www.state.ma.us/reg/boards/hi. When it comes time for the inspection, ask if you can go along so you can be sure the inspector is thorough, and then discuss what he finds. If you're in doubt about an appraisal or safety inspection, get a second opinion.

Assuming the inspection goes well and/or all issues are resolved to your satisfaction, it is time for closing. At the **closing**, also known as "settlement" or "escrow," costs, such as transfer taxes, closing costs, legal fees, and adjustments are paid. It is a brief process in which the title to the property is transferred from seller to buyer; the seller gets his payment and you get the keys, and the closing agent officially records your loan. If you balk at anything at this point and refuse to sign and complete the process, you'll probably end up in court.

As for the insurance portion of home ownership, you will need title insurance, homeowner's insurance, and possibly flood insurance; and you may want a home warranty. **Title insurance** is purchased at the time of closing and is a one-time fee. It protects you in case the title to the property somehow turns out to be invalid. Types of title insurance include lenders' policies, which protect the buyer for up to the mortgage value of the property, and owners' policies, which protect the mortgage amount as well as the down payment value. Most lenders generally require title insurance up to the amount of the loan. Lenders require **homeowner's insurance**, which covers your home and belongings against disasters such as fire, storm damage, and break-ins. Homeowner's insurance is separate from **flood insurance**, which is issued by the federal government and may be a requirement in high-risk areas. Finally, buyers might want to consider **home warranties**—one-year service agreements that you buy from a third party (not the seller, builder, or lessor) to cover problems that crop up in the day-to-day business of having a home, including appliances. as opposed to pre-existing defects or conditions. Depending on the policy, you either call the warranty agency when something goes wrong and they send one of their people to come out to do the repairs, or else you may be allowed to select your own repair person with their prior approval. If you'd like additional insurance information, go to www.state.ma.us/doi/Consumer/CSS_homeowners.html.

ONLINE RESOURCES—MORTGAGES

In addition to the information included in the text of this chapter, the following sites might help you on your quest to finance a home:
- **Bankrate.com**, www.bankrate.com; everything about mortgages and lending.
- **Countrywide Financial**, www.countrywide.com; nationwide mortgage rates, credit evaluations, etc.
- **Dirs.com**, www.dirs.com; links and information on mortgages and home equity loans.
- **Fannie Mae**, www.fanniemae.com; loans for real estate purchases; dedicated to helping American's achieve the dream of homeownership.
- **Freddie Mac**, www.freddiemac.com; provides information on low-cost loans, a home inspection kit, and tips to help avoid unfair lending practices.
- **Interest.com**, www.interest.com; shop for mortgages and rates.
- **Massachusetts Housing Finance Agency (MHFA)**, www.mhfa.com; information about renting and buying from the state's affordable housing bank.
- **Massachusetts Mortgage Clearing House**, www.mmch.com
- **The Mortgage Professor**, www.mtgprofessor.com; demystifies and clarifies the confusing and often expensive world of mortgage brokers, helpfully written by an emeritus Wharton professor who answers questions(!), useful calculators.
- **Owners.com**, www.owners.com; all things mortgage and home sale related.
- **Quicken Home**, www.quickenloans.com

ADDITIONAL RESOURCES—BUYING A HOME

Finally, aside from the selection of books you can pick up at your local bookstore or at an online book seller, consider the following resources and publications:
- *100 Questions Every First Time Homebuyer Should Ask: With Answers from Top Brokers from Around the Country*, 2nd edition (Times Books) by Ilyce R.Glink
- *The 106 Common Mistakes Homebuyers Make (And How to Avoid Them)*, 3rd edition (Wiley) by Gary W. Eldred

- **City of Boston Assessing Department**, www.ci.boston.ma.us/assessing; the City of Boston's web site offers a service with an easy to fill out form so that you can find out the official value of a property.
- **City of Boston Taxpayer Referral and Assistance Center (TRAC)**, www.ci.boston.ma.us/trac; the City of Boston also offers some information about tax breaks for homeowners on this portion of its web site.
- The **Commonwealth of Massachusetts** provides information for potential Baystate homebuyers through its web site, www.state.ma.us/consumer.
- **Community Associations Institute**, www.caine.org; informational web site of the New England chapter of the alliance of condo, co-op, and homeowner associations.
- *The Co-Op Bible: Everything You Need to Know About Co-Ops and Condos: Getting In, Staying In, Surviving, Thriving* (Griffin Trade Paperback) by Sylvia Shapiro
- *Opening the Door to a Home of Your Own*: a pamphlet by Fannie Mae for first time homebuyers. Call 800-834-3377 for a copy.
- **Score Card**; if you're particularly concerned about environmental toxins at your new property, check out www.scorecard.org, a site sponsored by the Environmental Defense Fund.
- *Your New House: the Alert Consumer's Guide to Buying and Building a Quality New Home*; (Windsor Peak Press) by Alan and Denise Fields

MOVING AND STORAGE

BEFORE YOU CAN START YOUR NEW LIFE IN BOSTON, YOU AND your worldly possessions have to get here. How difficult that will be, depends on how much stuff you've accumulated, how much money you're willing or able to spend on the move, and where you're coming from.

In Boston, most fixed-term leases are for one year and turn over in August/September, which makes moving during those two months a time of chaos in many neighborhoods, particularly those near colleges or universities.

TRUCK RENTALS

The first question you need to answer: am I going to move myself or will I have someone else do it for me? If you're used to doing everything yourself, you can rent a vehicle and head for the open road. Look in the Yellow Pages under "Truck Rental" and call around and compare; also ask about any specials. Below we list four national truck rental firms and their toll-free numbers and web sites. For the best information you should call a local office. Note: most truck rental companies now offer "one-way" rentals (don't forget to ask whether they have a drop-off/return location in or near your destination) as well as packing accessories and storage facilities. Of course, extras are not free and if you're cost conscious you may want to scavenge boxes in advance of your move and make sure you have a place to store your belongings upon arrival.

If you're planning on moving during the peak moving months (May through September), call well in advance of when you think you'll need the vehicle—a month at least. It is not unheard of for truck rental companies to "have no record" of your truck reservation, leaving you high and dry on your scheduled moving day. To avoid this inconvenience, it's a good idea to double or triple check on your truck reservation the week before your moving date. Or, make a back-up reservation, assuming you can cancel it without incurring any expense.

Once you're on the road, keep in mind that your rental truck may be a tempting target for thieves. If you must park it overnight or for an extended period (more than a couple of hours), try to find a safe place, preferably somewhere well-lit and easily observable by you.

- **Budget**, 800-467-9337, www.budget.com
- **Penske**, 888-996-5415, www.pensketruckrental.com
- **Ryder**, 800-467-9337, www.ryder.com
- **Uhaul**, 800-468-4285, www.uhaul.com

Not sure if you want to drive the truck yourself? Commercial freight carriers, such as **ABF**, 800-355-1696, www.upack.com, offer an in-between service: they deliver a 28-foot trailer to your home, you pack and load as much of it as you need, and they drive the vehicle to your destination (usually with some commercial freight filling up the empty space). Keep in mind though, if you have to share truck space with another customer you may arrive far in advance of your boxes—or bed. Try to estimate your needs beforehand and ask for a date when you can expect your boxes to arrive. You can get an online estimate from some shippers, so you can compare rates. If you aren't moving an entire house and can't estimate how much truck space you will need, keep in mind this general guideline: two to three furnished rooms equal a 15 foot truck. Four to five rooms, a 20-foot truck. Keep in mind, depending on the neighborhood you are moving to, a 28-foot trailer may not be a good option, as in some parts of Boston it will be impossible to park and unload. See below under **Road Restrictions** for information on street occupancy permits.

MOVERS

INTERSTATE MOVES

First, the good news: moving can be affordable and problem-free. The bad news: if you're hiring a mover, the chances of it being so are much less. Probably the best way to find a mover is through a **personal recommendation**. Absent a friend or relative who can point you to a trusted moving company, you can turn to what surveys show is the most popular method of finding a mover: the **Yellow Pages**. Then there's the **internet**; just type in "movers" on a search engine and you'll be directed to hundreds of more or less helpful moving-related sites.

In the past, **Consumer Reports**, www.consumerreports.org, has published useful information on moving. You might ask a local realtor, who may be able to steer you towards a good mover. Members of the **AAA** can call their local office and receive discounted rates and service through their Consumer Relocation Service.

But beware! Since 1995, when the Interstate Commerce Commission was eliminated, the interstate moving business has degenerated into a wild and virtually unregulated industry with thousands of unhappy, ripped-off customers annually. (There are so many reports of unscrupulous carriers that we no longer list movers in this book.) Since states do not have the authority to regulate interstate movers and since the federal government won't, you are pretty much on your own when it comes to finding an honest, hassle-free interstate mover. That's why we can't emphasize enough the importance of carefully researching and choosing who will move you.

To aid you in your search for an honest and hassle-free **interstate** mover, we offer a few general recommendations.

First get the names of a half-dozen movers and check to make sure they are licensed by the **US Department of Transportation's Federal Motor Carrier Safety Administration** (**FMCSA**). With the movers' Motor Carrier (MC) numbers in hand, call 888-368-7238 or 202-358-7000 (offers the option of speaking to an agent) or go online to http://fhwali.volpe.dot.gov, to see if the carrier is licensed and insured. If the companies you're considering are federally licensed, your next step should be to check with the **Better Business Bureau**, www.bbb.org, in the state where the moving company is licensed as well as with that state's **consumer protection board** or **attorney general**. Also check FMCSA's **Household Goods Consumer Complaint** web site, www.1-888.dot.saft.com, where they maintain complaints that have been filed against interstate movers. Assuming there is no negative information, you can move on to the next step: asking for references. Particularly important are references from customers who did moves similar to yours. If a moving company is unable or unwilling to provide references or tells you they can't because their customers are all in the Federal Witness Protection Program, eliminate them from your list. Unscrupulous movers have even been known to give phony references who will falsely sing the mover's praises—so talk to more than one reference and ask questions. If something feels fishy, it probably is. One way to learn more about a prospective mover: ask them if they have a local office (they should) and then walk in and check it out.

Once you have at least three movers you feel reasonably comfortable with, it's time to ask for price quotes (always free). Best is a binding "not-to-exceed" quote, of course in writing. This will require an on-site visual inspection of what you are shipping. If you have *any* doubts about a prospective mover, drop them from your list before you invite a stranger into your home to catalog your belongings.

Recent regulations by FMCSA require movers to supply five documents to consumers before executing a contract. These include a pamphlet called "Your Rights and Responsibilities When You Move," a written estimate of charges, details of the mover's arbitration program, specifics about how the mover handles customer complaints and inquiries, and the mover's tariff containing rates, rules, regulations, and classifications. For more about FMCSA's role in the handling of household goods you can go to their consumer page at www.fmcsa.dot.gov/factsfigs/moving.htm.

ADDITIONAL RECOMMENDATIONS:

- If someone recommends a mover to you, get names (the salesperson or estimator, the drivers, the loaders). To paraphrase the NRA, moving companies don't move people, people do.
- Remember that price, while important, isn't everything, especially when you're entrusting all of your worldly possessions to strangers.
- Ask about the other end—subcontracting increases the chances that something could go wrong.
- In general, ask questions, and if you're concerned about something, ask for an explanation in writing. If you change your mind about a mover after you've signed on the dotted line, write them a letter explaining that you've changed your mind and that you won't be using their services. Better safe than sorry.
- Ask about insurance, the "basic" 60 cents per pound industry standard coverage is not enough. If you have homeowner's or renter's insurance, check to see if it will cover your belongings during transit. If not, ask your insurer if you can add that coverage for your move. Otherwise, consider purchasing "full replacement" or "full value" coverage from the carrier for the estimated value of your shipment. Though it's the most expensive type of coverage offered, it's probably worth it. Trucks get into accidents, they catch fire, they get stolen—if such insurance seems pricey to you, ask about a $250 or $500 deductible. This can reduce your cost substantially while still giving you much better protection in case of a catastrophic loss.
- Before a move takes place, ask your mover to give you a copy of "Your Rights and Responsibilities When You Move," which provides detailed information about your rights and what you can expect from your moving company. Ask for it as soon as you decide on a mover.
- Whatever you do, *do not* mislead a salesperson/estimator about how much and what you are moving. And make sure you tell a prospective mover about how far they'll have to transport your stuff to and from the truck as well as any stairs, driveways, obstacles or difficult vegetation, long paths or sidewalks, etc. The clearer you are with your mover, the better he or she will be able to serve you.

MOVING AND STORAGE

- Think about packing. If you plan to pack yourself, you can save some money, but if something is damaged because of your packing, you may not be able to file a claim for it. On the other hand, if you hire the mover to do the packing, they may not treat your belongings as well as you will. They will certainly do it faster, that's for sure. Depending on the size of your move and whether or not you are packing yourself, you may need a lot of boxes, tape and packing material. Mover boxes, while not cheap, are usually sturdy and the right size. Sometimes a mover will give a customer free used boxes. It doesn't hurt to ask. Also, *don't* wait to pack until the last minute. If you're doing the packing, give yourself at least a week to do the job, two or more is better.
- You should transport all irreplaceable items such as jewelry, photographs or key work documents. Do not put them in the moving van! For less precious items that you do not want to put in the moving truck, consider sending them via the US Postal Service or by UPS.
- Ask your mover what is not permitted in the truck: usually anything flammable or combustible, as well as certain types of valuables.
- Although movers will put numbered labels on your possessions, you should make a numbered list of every box and item that is going in the truck. Detail box contents and photograph anything of particular value. Once the truck arrives on the other end, you can check off every piece and know for sure what did (or did not) make it. In case of claims, this list can be invaluable. Even after the move, keep the list; it can be surprisingly useful.
- Before moving pets, attach a tag to your pet's collar with your new address and phone number in case your furry friend accidentally wanders off in the confusion of moving. Of course, never plan on moving a pet inside a moving van.
- Movers are required to issue you a "bill of lading"; do not hire a mover who does not use them.
- Consider keeping a log of every expense you incur for your move, i.e., phone calls, trips to Boston, etc. In many instances, the IRS allows you to claim these types of expenses on your income taxes. (See **Taxes** below.)
- Be aware that during the busy season (May through September), demand can exceed supply and moving may be more difficult and more expensive than during the rest of the year. If you must relocate during the peak moving months, call and book service well in advance of when you plan on moving. A month at least. If you can reserve service way in advance, say four to six months early, you may be able to lock in a lower winter rate for your summer move.
- Listen to what the movers say; they are professionals and can give you expert advice about packing and preparing. Also, be ready for the truck

on both ends—don't make them wait. Not only will it irritate your movers, but it may cost you. Understand, too, that things can happen on the road that are beyond a carrier's control (weather, accidents, etc.) and your belongings may not get to you at the time or on the day promised.
- Treat your movers well, especially the ones loading your stuff on and off the truck. Offer to buy them lunch, and tip them if they do a good job.
- Be prepared to pay the full moving bill upon delivery. Cash or bank/cashier's check may be required. Some carriers will take VISA and MasterCard but it is a good idea to get it in writing that you will be permitted to pay with a credit card since the delivering driver may not be aware of this and may demand cash. Unless you routinely keep thousands of dollars of greenbacks on you, you could have a problem getting your stuff off the truck.

INTRASTATE MOVES

Intrastate moves (moves within Massachusetts) are regulated by the **Transportation Division of the Massachusetts Department of Telecommunications and Energy**. Intrastate movers must apply for authority to transport passengers or property for hire, through chapters 159A and B of Massachusetts law. You can contact the department for more information at 800-392-6066, or visit their web site at www.state.ma.us/dpu.

Those **moving within the greater Boston area** with minimal belongings (renters, singles, etc.) probably won't need a huge truck to complete the task. If you (and all of your friends) are not interested in loading and unloading a rented truck, you may want to consider hiring a local mover. **Local movers** generally charge by the hour, not by the size and weight of your shipment. When shopping around for a local mover you will be given a "not to exceed price" for your move, which is based on how much stuff you have and the ease or difficulty of getting you out of your old place and into your new—how many stairs, how far to the truck, etc. Other contributing cost factors include how many men will be needed to move your belongings, the size of the van, the distance traveled to your new place, etc. This "not to exceed" price should be in written form, and cover all services. If your move goes faster than the salesperson estimated, you should be charged less.

CONSUMER COMPLAINTS—MOVERS

To file a complaint about an **interstate** mover, contact FMCSA's **Household Goods Consumer Complaint** web site at www.1-888.dot.saft.com or call 888-368-7238. Also, be sure to register your complaint with the state attorney general's office and the Better Business Bureau of the state where the mover is located.

For problems with an **intrastate** move that you are unable to resolve directly, you can talk to the **Transportation Division of the Massachusetts Department of Telecommunications and Energy**. Call them at 800-392-6066 or visit their web site at www.state.ma.us/dpu. The **Massachusetts Office of Consumer Affairs and Business Regulation's** web site is www.state.ma.us/consumer, and you can call them at 888-283-3757 or 617-973-8787. If satisfaction still eludes you, begin a letter writing campaign: to the state Attorney General, your congressional representative, the newspaper, the sky's the limit. Of course, if the dispute is worth it, you can hire a lawyer and seek redress the all-American way.

ROAD RESTRICTIONS

Because many of Boston's streets are old and narrow, you won't necessarily be able to just roll in with a big moving truck without some pre-arrangements. In particular, those who are moving into an older building that does not have a loading zone will have to get a **Street Occupancy Permit** to park a moving van on the street. First, you must be bonded with the City of Boston Public Works Department. To do this, go to Room 714 of City Hall. Then, to apply for the Street Occupancy Permit, go over to the Boston Transportation Department office in Room 721. You will need to tell them why you need the permit, for how long you need it, how vehicular and pedestrian access will be allowed, and a copy of your bond. You'll pay a small fee; the exact amount will depend on how many signs you will need and how much space you'll be taking up.

After you get the permit, it is your responsibility to notify the neighbors and businesses that will be affected by your parked moving van by posting signs in the area at least 48 hours in advance, noting the time and date of the restricted access. For more information, go to the city's web site at www.cityofboston.gov/transportation/streetoccupancy or call the **Boston Transportation Department** at 617-635-4675.

STORAGE

If your new pad is too small for all of your belongings, or if you need a temporary place to store your stuff while you find a new home, self-storage may be the answer. Most units are clean, secure, insured, and inexpensive, and you can rent anything from a locker to your own mini-warehouse. You may need to bring your own padlock and be prepared to pay first and last month's rent up front. Many will offer special deals to entice you, such as the second month free. Probably the easiest way to find storage is to look in the Yellow Pages under "Storage—Self Service" or "Movers & Full Service Storage." Online, go to a search engine and type in "Storage—Household,

Commercial." Your mover may also offer storage and while this may be easier than moving it into storage yourself, it may also be more expensive.

A recent wrinkle in the self-storage business is "containerized storage." This means the storage company will drop off a (large) storage bin at your house, you fill it up, and they return with a truck and cart it off to their storage facility.

Keep in mind that like everything else, demand for storage surges in the prime moving months (May through September), so try not to wait until the last minute to rent storage. Also, if you don't care about convenience, your cheapest storage options may be out in the boonies. You just have to figure out how to get your stuff there and back. Things to keep in mind when considering a storage facility:
- When do I have access?
- Do my belongings need heat and/or AC? If so, ask if the facility is "climate controlled."
- What about security and insurance?
- Will I feel safe visiting the facility?
- Are there carts or hand trucks for moving in and out?
- What are the payment options?

Finally, a word of warning: unless you no longer want your stored belongings, pay your storage bill and pay it on time. Storage companies may auction the contents of delinquent customers' lockers.

STORAGE FACILITIES

Listing here does *not* imply endorsement by First Books. For more options check the Yellow Pages.
- **Public Storage**, has facilities throughout the Boston area. 800-447-8673, www.publicstorage.com
- **The Storage Depot**, Twin City Plaza, Cambridge, 617-864-5450, www.thestoragedepot.com
- **Storage USA**, 235 North Beacon Street, Brighton, 617-782-1177, www.sus.com

CHILDREN

Studies show that moving, especially frequent moving, can be hard on children. According to an American Medical Association study, children who move often are more likely to suffer from such problems as depression, worthlessness and aggression. Often their academic performance suffers as

well. Aside from not moving more than is necessary, there are a few things you can do to help your children through this stressful time:
- Talk about the move with your kids. Be honest but positive. Listen to their concerns. To the extent possible, involve them in the process.
- Make sure the child has his or her favorite possessions with them on the trip; *don't* pack "blanky" in the moving van.
- Make sure you have some social life planned on the other end. Your child may feel lonely in your new home and such activities can ease the transition.
- Keep in touch with family and loved ones as much as possible. Photos and phone calls are important ways of maintaining links to the important people you have left behind.
- If your children are school age, take the time to introduce them to their new school as soon as possible, preferably before they start the new school year. In this way, they can dispel any unfounded fears and apprehensions they have about the next school. And finally, try to involve yourself in their new school and in their academic life.

For children ages 6-11, **The Moving Book: A Kids' Survival Guide** by Gabriel Davis is a wonderful gift. For general guidance, read *Smart Moves: Your Guide through the Emotional Maze of Relocation* by Nadia Jensen, Audrey McCollum and Stuart Copans (Smith & Krauss). Visit firstbooks.com to order either publication.

TAXES

If your move is work-related, some or all of your moving expenses may be tax-deductible—so you may want to keep those receipts. Though eligibility varies, depending for example, on whether you have a job or are self-employed, generally, the cost of moving yourself, your family and your belongings is tax deductible, even if you don't itemize. The criteria: in order to take the deduction your move must be employment-related, your new job must be more than 50 miles away from your current residence, and you must be here for at least 39 weeks during the first 12 months after your arrival. If you take the deduction and then fail to meet the requirements, you will have to pay the IRS back, unless you were laid off through no fault of your own or transferred again by your employer. It's probably a good idea to consult a tax expert regarding IRS rules related to moving. However, if you're a confident soul, get a copy of IRS Form 3903 (www.irs.gov) and do it yourself!

RELOCATION AND MOVING INFORMATION

- **www.erc.org**, the Employee Relocation Council, a professional organization, offers members specialized reports on the relocation and moving industries.
- **www.firstbooks.com**, relocation resources and information on moving to Atlanta, Boston, Chicago, Los Angeles, Minneapolis-St. Paul, New York City, Seattle, Washington, D.C., as well as London, England.
- **www.homestore.com**, realty listings, moving tips, and more.
- *How to Move Handbook* by Clyde and Shari Steiner, an excellent resource.
- **www.usps.com**, relocation information from the United States Postal Service.

MONEY MATTERS

If POSSIBLE, WHEN MOVING TO BOSTON FROM OUT OF STATE, KEEP a checking account open. It can be difficult to rent an apartment without a bank account, and without a permanent address it may be harder to open a Boston account.

Once you've found your new Boston pad, you'll want to set up services with a local bank. Following is some information about money matters in the Boston area.

FINANCIAL INSTITUTIONS

BANKS

Most of the bigger banks in Boston have dozens of branches and hundreds of ATMs across the area, including Cape Cod. Smaller banks, too, will offer access to a wide network of ATMs, though they may charge you for this service.

For a complete list of local banks, you can visit the MassHome Directory of Banks at www.masshome.com/banks or the Massachusetts Division of Banks at www.state.ma.us/dob. Local and national banks include:

- **Fleet Bank**, 800-841-4000, www.fleet.com
- **Compass Bank**, 617-739-9500, www.compassbank.com
- **Boston Federal Savings Bank**, 800-688-2372, www.bfsb.com
- **Brookline Bank**, 877-668-2265, www.brooklinebank.com
- **Cambridge Savings Bank**, 888-418-5626, www.cambridgesavings.com
- **Cambridge Trust Company**, 617-441-1444, www.cambridgetrust.com
- **Century Bank**, 866-8-CENTURY, www.century-bank.com
- **Citizens Bank**, 800-922-9999, www.citizensbank.com
- **East Boston Savings Bank**, 800-657-EBSB, www.ebsb.com

- **Eastern Bank**, 800-EASTERN, www.easternbank.com
- **Peoples Federal Savings Bank**, 617-254-0707, www.pfsb.com
- **Sovereign Bank**, 877-SOVBANK, www.sovereignbank.com
- **The Cooperative Bank**, 617-325-2900, www.thecooperativebank.com
- **Watertown Savings Bank**, 800-207-2525, www.watertownsavings.com
- **Hyde Park Cooperative Bank**, 888-722-1191, www.hydeparkcoop.com

You may want to shop around, as fees, products, and quality of service vary. According to a 2000 Federal Reserve report, consumers who bank at large institutions with branches in more than one state are charged significantly higher fees than those banking at smaller banks with only in-state branches. Typically, these fees are added to consumer services such as non-interest checking accounts, stop-payment orders, overdrafts, and ATM use.

CREDIT UNIONS

According to the **National Credit Union Administration (NCUA)**, "A federal credit union is a nonprofit, cooperative financial institution owned and run by its members. "Organized to serve, democratically controlled credit unions provide their members with a safe place to save and borrow at reasonable rates. Members pool their funds to make loans to one-another. The volunteer board that runs each credit union is elected by the members.

According to *American Banker*'s annual survey, credit unions continually rank high in customer satisfaction. Because credit unions limit membership based on set criteria, you'll need to investigate a few for a match. Organizations such as employers, unions, professional associations, churches, and schools (alumni associations) typically provide membership.

Here are a few credit unions in the Boston area:
- **Alpha Credit Union**, for employees of various medical institutions in the Longwood area, 617-632-8164, www.bidmc.harvard.edu/alpha/
- **City of Boston Credit Union**, for Commonwealth of Massachusetts employees and their families, 888-366-2607, www.cityofbostoncu.org
- **Industrial Credit Union**, for anyone living or working in the greater Boston area, 617-742-1616, www.icu.org
- **Tremont Credit Union**, for many area employers and schools, 781-843-5626, www.tremontcu.org
- **University Credit Union**, for current and former employees of many local schools, medical institutions, and others, 888-828-9828, www.universitycu.org

For a complete list of local credit unions or information about them, you can visit the **MassHome Directory of Credit Unions** at www.masshome.com/crunions, the **Massachusetts Division of Banks**, www.state.ma.us/dob, the **National Association of Credit Union Service Organizations**, www.nacuso.org, or the **NCUA**, http://ncua.gov.

ONLINE BANKING

Today, it is rare when a bank does not offer online banking. Generally this includes simple balance and other account information, making transfers, paying bills, and even applying for loans from the comfort of your own home. Security should be a chief concern when accessing your private financial information over the internet. While banks should encrypt your personal information and password, the user should also take standard precautions as well. Don't share your password with anyone, and change it often; don't send confidential information through e-mail or over unsecured web space; and restrict your banking interactions to private computers—not a work computer with a shared network or at an internet café.

Online access services and fees may vary from bank to bank, so check with individual institutions for information. Sometimes access is directly through the bank's web site; sometimes you'll first need to download a program or use specialized banking software.

CHECKING AND SAVINGS ACCOUNTS

It's easy to open checking or savings accounts—all you need is identification, an address and, of course, money. Today, some banks will even open a new account over the phone. You will need a social security number, identification, and employment information.

For fee-free checking, you may need to maintain a certain monthly balance, and fee free accounts are not normally interest-bearing accounts. Some opt to connect checking with savings for overdraft protection. Other products and services to inquire about: debit cards, online or telephone banking, certificates of deposit, safe deposit boxes, hours, and fees.

CONSUMER COMPLAINTS—BANKING

Federal and state governments regulate bank policies on discrimination, credit, anti-redlining, truth-in-lending, etc. If you have a problem with your bank, you should first attempt to resolve the issue directly with the bank. Should you need to **file a formal complaint** against your financial institution, you can do so through the Board of Governors of the **Federal Reserve System, Division of Consumer and Community Affairs**. For specifics, call 202-452-3693 or go to www.federalreserve.gov/pubs/complaints/. You can also pursue the issue with the following agencies:

- Nationally chartered commercial banks go through the **US Comptroller of the Currency**, Customer Assistance Group, 1301 McKinney Street, Suite 3710, Houston, TX 77010; 800-613-6743; www.occ.treas.gov.
- **US Office of Thrift Supervision**, 1700 G Street NW, Washington, D.C. 20552, 202-906-6000, www.ots.treas.gov; for thrift institutions insured by the Savings Association Insurance Fund and/or federally chartered (i.e., members of the Federal Home Loan Bank System).
- For state chartered banks, contact: **Massachusetts Division of Banks and Loans**, Consumer Assistance Office, 1 South Station, Boston, MA 02210, 800-495-2265, www.state.ma.us/dob; **Mortgage Review Board**, Massachusetts Division of Banks, 1 South Station, Boston, MA 02210, 617-965-1500, www.state.ma.us/dob.
- State chartered banks that are members of the Federal Reserve System should contact: **Federal Reserve Bank of Boston**, Bank Examination Division, 600 Atlantic Avenue, Boston, MA 02106, 617-973-3000, www.bos.frb.org; **Federal Deposit Insurance Corporation** (**FDIC**), 15 Braintree Office Hill Park, Braintree, MA 02184, 781-794-5500, www.fdic.gov.
- Federally chartered credit unions and state chartered credit unions with federal insurance: **National Credit Union Administration**, 9 Washington Square, Washington Avenue Extension, Albany, NY 12205, 518-862-7400, www.ncua.gov.

CREDIT CARDS

A list of low-rate card issuers can be found on the internet at **CardWeb**, www.cardweb.com, 301-631-9100; **Consumer Action**, www.consumer-action.org; and **BankRate.com**, www.bankrate.com, 561-630-2400.

To request a credit card application you can contact one of the following:
- **American Express**, 800-THE-CARD, www.americanexpress.com
- **Diner's Club**, 800-2-DINERS, www.dinersclubnorthamerica.com
- **Discover Card**, 800-347-2683 (or apply at a Sears store), www.discovercard.com
- **VISA** and **MasterCard** can be obtained through banks and other financial service associations. Check first with your bank, and shop around for the lowest interest rate, annual fees, and frequent flyer miles deals.
- **Department store credit cards** are marketed at check-out counters. Often the store offers an incentive for you to fill out an application immediately—a discount off that day's purchases—and membership has continual benefits, such as coupons, advance sales notice, mail or phone orders, and free shipping.

CREDIT REPORTS

Those interested in seeing a personal credit report can go to www.icreditreport.com where you can obtain a copy of your credit report from the three main credit bureaus (Equifax, Experian, and TransUnion).

For more information see **The Buying Process** in the **Finding a Place to Live** chapter.

TAXES

In 1789, Benjamin Franklin said, "in this world nothing can be said to be certain, except death and taxes." High taxes in Massachusetts—sales tax, use tax, income tax (both federal and state), excise tax, and motor vehicle tax—as well as additional fees and tolls have earned the State of Massachusetts the nickname "Taxachusetts." It is for this reason that Bostonians sometimes head across the border to New Hampshire to make purchases—particularly of alcohol at the state liquor store. Some even live in New Hampshire and then commute to work in Massachusetts.

According to the Massachusetts Executive Office of Administration and Finance, 64% of the state's revenue comes from taxes. The rest comes from lottery revenues, federal reimbursements, rainy day reserves, and fines and fees (mostly from the Registry of Motor Vehicles). Taxes go to fund schools, transportation, roads, health and human services programs, public safety, environmental protection, health insurance for state employees, housing and community development, assistance to low income families, and economic and workforce development, among other things.

SALES AND USE TAXES

Sales tax in Massachusetts is five percent on all retail sales of tangible personal property, and on certain telecommunications services rented in the Commonwealth—mostly cell phone transmissions. Goods purchased out of state or out of country that will be used/consumed in Massachusetts require a "use tax" of five percent—this includes mail order items and automobiles. Report and pay use tax on your personal income tax returns—Form 1, Telefile, or Form 1-NR/PY.

Confused? It's not quite as bad as it seems. Many items are **exempt from sales and use tax**, including food, clothing, periodicals, stationery, health care items, small household items, admission to events, utilities, heating fuel to residences and small businesses, telephone services to residences, personal or professional services, and transportation charges. Luxury items, however, including clothing items over $175, and restaurant dining are taxed. Big ticket household items like appliances and furniture are also taxed, as are gas and cigarettes.

For more detailed information on Massachusetts sales and use tax, visit the **Commonwealth of Massachusetts Department of Revenue** at www.dor.state.ma.us or call 617-887-MDOR. They publish a booklet entitled *A Guide to Sales and Use Tax* that you may find helpful; it is accessible online.

PROPERTY TAX

Massachusetts residents and business owners pay **property taxes** on residences, and commercial and personal property. As a general rule, property taxes finance local government and city services, such as public schools, fire and police protection, roads, health programs, parks, city streets, sewer systems, garbage disposal and public libraries.

For more information on property tax in Massachusetts, contact the Massachusetts Division of Local Services' Property Tax Bureau at 617-626-2400 or www.dls.state.ma.us/ptb.htm.

MOTOR VEHICLE TAX

All Massachusetts residents who own a car must pay a **motor vehicle excise tax**. The Registry of Motor Vehicles charges $25 per thousand dollars of the value of your vehicle. This excise tax is due thirty days from the date the notice is mailed. Excise tax also applies to truck, motorcycles, and trailers. If you don't pay the excise tax, your registration and driver's license can be suspended.

For more information call the Registry of Motor Vehicles, 617-351-4500, or go to www.mass.gov/rmv or see the **Automobiles** section in the **Getting Settled** chapter.

FEDERAL INCOME TAX

Here are some resources for federal income tax information and forms:
- **Federal income tax forms** can be obtained by calling 800-829-FORM, or picking them up at public libraries and post offices.
- **IRS Tax Help Line,** 800-829-1040, www.irs.gov; for consumers with questions and/or in need of forms.
- **IRS Boston branch**, 25 New Sudbury Street, JFK Building, Room 775, Boston, MA 02203, 617-316-2850, www.irs.ustreas.gov.
- **Federal Teletax information line**, 800-829-4477

STATE INCOME TAX

Beyond state sales, use, and property taxes, residents must also pay income tax. Newcomers with questions on income taxes should contact the **Customer Service Bureau of the Massachusetts Department of Revenue** at 617-887-MDOR or 800-392-6089 or go online to www.dor.state.ma.us. Come April 15, this is the office to contact to find out which forms you'll need (especially if you haven't lived in Massachusetts for the whole tax year) or for other income tax questions. Forms are available through the Massachusetts Department of Revenue or at public libraries, post offices, and some banks. The Massachusetts Department of Revenue's Boston office is located at 51 Sleeper Street.

For additional income tax help, the **Boston Bar Association** has a **Volunteer Income Tax Program** that is generally held at the Boston Public Library's Copley Square branch. Check with the Bar Association for exact dates, times and location: 617-742-0615, www.bostonbar.org.

ELECTRONIC INCOME TAX FILING

These days, you can file both your federal and state taxes online: using the proper tax software, through an online service, or by going through an accredited agency. According to the IRS, online filing is faster, more accurate, and lower cost than doing it the old-fashioned way. To research the many tax filing software options, go to any search engine and type in "tax software." **Quicken TurboTax**, www.turbotax.com, is just one of many that are available.

The **IRS's e-file** site, www.irs.gov/efile, includes such features as convenient payment options or direct deposit for those expecting a return. This site will also direct you to IRS accepted software brands.

For some qualified individuals (singles or married couples below a certain income level), the IRS accepts electronic filing over the telephone. Call 800-829-1040 for more details.

To file your state taxes online, go to the **Massachusetts Department of Revenue's** web site, www.dor.state.ma.us; for Telefile, call 617-660-2001.

STARTING OR MOVING A BUSINESS

If you chose to open a new business or move your existing business to Boston, you may want to hire an attorney who is familiar with the process. To do some legwork on your own, the following resources will be helpful:

- **Massachusetts Bar Association**, 20 West Street, Boston 02111, 617-338-0500, www.massbar.org
- **Boston Bar Association**, 16 Beacon Street, Boston 02108, 617-742-0615, www.bostonbar.org
- **Internal Revenue Service**, 800-829-1040, where you need to go to get an employer tax ID number
- **Commonwealth of Massachusetts**, www.state.ma.us, has a portal with all sorts of information regarding opening a business, including links to the Department of Economic Development, the Secretary of the Commonwealth, the Division of Employment and Training, the Office of Consumer Affairs and Business Regulation, and the Massachusetts Department of Revenue.
- **US Small Business Administration Home Page**, 800-827-5722, www.sba.gov

GETTING SETTLED

NOW THAT YOU'VE FOUND THE HOME OF YOUR DREAMS, OR AT least a place to hang your hat, you'll need to get your utilities hooked up and your cable and internet service connected. If you have a car, you'll need to get it registered, apply for a new driver's license, and perhaps figure out your parking situation. Other items of business may include a library card, finding a physician, subscribing to a newspaper and, if you've brought Fido, getting a dog license and finding a vet.

If you'd like online information about the municipal services for the greater Boston area, city web sites are listed following the **Neighborhood** profiles. Also, the Commonwealth of Massachusetts has an excellent web site, www.mass.gov, possibly your first online stop for any unanswered questions you may have as you settle in.

UTILITIES

When it comes time to set up your utilities, the distribution companies and the areas they serve are listed below or you can check with your landlord, building manager, or real estate agent. Services vary from town to town and utility to utility. For example, electricity and gas are utilities moderated by the state, so each community generally has only one service provider. However, oil, which is used to heat most Massachusetts homes, comes from independent suppliers. Utilities in the state are overseen by the **Massachusetts Department of Telecommunications and Energy** (**DTE**), 617-305-3500, www.state.ma.us/dpu.

ELECTRICITY

Before March 1998, your local utility company handled every facet of your electrical service. Now electricity is generated by **competitive power suppliers** who set their own prices (i.e., prices are not regulated by the

DTE). The regulated electric utility, known as the **distribution company**, distributes power to your individual home or business. You'll pay separate charges for both.

Generally landlords don't turn off the electricity at the end of the prior lease, so you will usually just have to call your distribution company to have your name put on the account. Customer service representatives will ask you standard questions over the phone when you call to set up your account; no deposit is required. If electric service wasn't extended throughout the vacancy, it should only take a day or two for service to be turned on.

If you have questions about energy distribution in Massachusetts or would like a consumer's guide on the matter, you can call the **Department of Energy Resources** at 888-PLUG-IN-99. To report a complaint, call the **DTE** at 800-392-6066. For fraud or unfair practices, you can also call the **Office of the Attorney General** at 617-727-2200.

The following is a list of **distribution companies** for Boston area communities:

- **NSTAR Electric (formerly Boston Edison)**, 800-592-2000, www.nstaronline.com, for electric service in Boston (any section), Brookline, Cambridge, Dedham, Milton, Needham, Newton, Somerville, Watertown, and Waltham. Arlington still subscribes to NSTAR, but at press time was rallying for municipal services. Check out Arlington's web page, www.town.arlington.ma.us, for current details.
- **Massachusetts Electric**, 800-322-3223, www.masselectric.com, provides service to Quincy, Malden, Medford.
- Belmont's electric service is run through its municipal light department: **Belmont Municipal Light Department**, 40 Prince Street, Belmont, 617-484-2780, www.town.belmont.ma.us/Public_Documents/BelmontMA_Light/index

GAS

Next, you'll want to set up gas service for your stove and hot water heater. Like local electric service, gas in Massachusetts is also regulated by the DTE. There are ten investor-owned and four municipal gas utilities in the state. Call in advance to set up service, especially during the busy months of August and September, when it could take days to get an appointment to have your gas service connected. Connection may require a home visit, especially if service has been turned off before you move in, so you'll need to schedule a time when you or your landlord can be around to provide the gas company access to your apartment and your meter.

GETTING SETTLED

Here are the major Boston area **gas providers** and the communities they serve:

- **KeySpan Energy Delivery** (formerly **Boston Gas**), 800-732-3400, www.keyspanenergy.com; covers Arlington, Belmont, Boston, Brookline, Malden, Medford, Newton, Quincy, Waltham, and Watertown. You can call KeySpan from 8 a.m. to 7 p.m., Monday-Friday, and 9 a.m. to 3 p.m. on Saturdays. KeySpan generally will give you an appointment for a three- to four-hour window, and has evening hours to turn on service.
- **NSTAR Gas** (formerly **Commonwealth Gas**), 800-592-2000, www.nstaronline.com, provides gas service to residents of Cambridge, Dedham, and Needham. NSTAR's business hours are 8:30 a.m. to 5 p.m., Monday-Friday. They can't promise to be at your apartment at a specific time, but they will promise you an 8 a.m.-to-noon or noon-to-4 p.m. arrival. If you'd like, you can make an appointment for after 4 p.m. on weekdays or anytime on weekends for a $90/hour fee.

In **Milton** and **Somerville**, both NSTAR and Keyspan are providers. Call and ask which one serves your address.

To check on current gas rates, check out the state gas adjustment listed by season at www.state.ma.us/dpu/gas/cgac_page.htm. Gas utilities have energy savings plans. Contact your gas company for details.

OIL

According to the Energy Information Administration, oil is the primary home heating fuel in Massachusetts. Oil is not supplied by a utility so you can choose your own supplier. In an apartment situation, your landlord may already have a service agreement with an oil supplier who will also maintain the furnace burners and filters. If you need to find a supplier there are many listed in the Yellow Pages. Some only service certain areas, such as just the North Shore or South Shore. You might consider an oil cooperative; for a membership fee of $10 to $15, your oil will cost less per gallon than normal rates from non-co-op suppliers. The Boston area has two oil cooperatives:

- **Mass Energy Consumers Alliance** (formerly **Boston Oil Consumers Alliance**), 617-524-3950, 800-287-3950, www.massenergy.com, offers a renewable energy program in addition to the oil cooperative.
- **Ecological Innovations Oil Buying Network**, 617-349-6247, 800-649-7473

TELEPHONE

Like gas and electric utilities, the telecom industry in Massachusetts is regulated by the DTE, and covers local and long distance carriers, area codes, cellular phones, pagers, and some internet services.

AREA CODES

Due to the increase of phone, fax, and mobile numbers, many states across the nation are running through available exchanges. Consequently, new area codes continue to be added to handle the ever-increasing volume. In 1998, the number of area codes in Eastern Massachusetts was increased from two to four: 617, 508, 781, and 978. In 2001, those four area codes split again, for a total of eight. Basically, two area codes serve each region: 617/857 for Boston and some directly surrounding areas (Cambridge, Somerville, Brookline, Watertown, Milton, Quincy, Newton, Everett, Chelsea, Winthrop, and Belmont); 781/339 for the surrounding ring of communities, including Waltham, Needham, Dedham, Medford, Malden, Revere, and Arlington; 508/774 for southern Massachusetts, Cape Cod, Martha's Vineyard, Nantucket, and the south central portion of the state out to Worcester; and 978/351 for the northern and north central areas of the state. The entire western portion of Massachusetts is in the 413 area code. Eleven-digit dialing (one, plus the area code, plus the phone number) is always required, whether you are dialing your neighbor who has the same area code, or someone in Bar Harbor, Maine. To verify the area code for your community, go to www22.verizon.com/AreaCodes.

LOCAL PHONE SERVICE

Once upon a time, it was New England Telephone, then it was NYNEX, then Bell Atlantic, and now, the local phone service company is **Verizon**. You can call them well before you get here to have your local phone service set up. Verizon has several calling plans and offers such options as call waiting, caller ID, call intercept, voice mail, and more.

Setting up your phone service involves a small fee. Call Verizon at 800-870-9999 between 7:30 a.m. and 7 p.m. weekdays, or between 8 a.m. and 5 p.m. on Saturdays. Customer service representatives will set up your long distance service with the carrier of your choice when you call to set up local service. If you prefer, you can set up service online, just follow the instructions on their web site: www.verizon.com.

LONG DISTANCE

When you're researching long distance plans, as with all else, make sure to read the fine print. Carriers may advertise low per-minute rates, but if you have to pay a flat fee to get that rate and you don't use your long distance service very much, it might make sense to go for a plan with no flat fee and only slightly higher rates, or to use a prepaid phone card. Also, many are opting to skip traditional landlines altogether, instead relying on their cell phones.

If you want to compare long distance pricing, go to **SmartPrice** at www.smartprice.com or call 877-550-5317. You will be asked questions regarding your phone usage, your area code and the first three digits of your phone number. They will then provide a free instant analysis of the carriers available in your area. You can also contact **Telecommunications Research and Action Center (TRAC)**, a consumer organization that publishes charts comparing plans and prices at 202-263-2950, www.trac.org.

Major **long distance service providers** include:

- **AT&T**, 800-222-0300, www.att.com
- **GTC Telecom**, 800-486-4030, www.gtctelecom.com
- **IDT**, 800-889-9126, www.idt.net
- **MCI**, 800-444-3333, www.mci.com
- **Qwest Communications**, 800-899-7780, www.qwest.com
- **Sprint**, 800-877-4646, www.sprint.com
- **Verizon**, 800-870-9999, www.verizon.com
- **Working Assets**, 800-362-7127, www.workingforchange.com

If you have problems with your phone service, or if you find you have been "slammed" (your long-distance provider changed without your consent), read ahead to the **Utility Complaints** section of this chapter for advice. For more information on slamming, visit www.state.ma.us/dpu/telecom/MASlamming.htm.

CELLULAR PHONES

Cell phone calling plans include flat rate plans where you buy a certain number of minutes per/month and nationwide network plans where every number you dial within the US is a "local" call. As technology advances, options and calling plans will only get more consumer-friendly in this highly competitive market.

Boston is a major urban area, and thus cellular coverage in the city and its surrounding areas is good, although, depending on the suburb and the provider, cellular service that works in the city might be spotty (at best) even as close as 45 minutes outside of downtown. If you're heading to the mountains of Vermont or New Hampshire for the weekend, you may not be able to use your cell phone at all.

For guidance with choosing a cell phone or pager plan in the greater Boston area, you can visit the **Cellular Telecommunications and Internet Association** (**CTIA**), www.wow-com.com, a trade association for the telecommunications industry that offers information to insiders and consumers regarding market research, news, and consumer FAQs. You can also check with **TRAC** (see above). The Yellow Pages lists numerous cellular phone services, and *Consumer Reports* periodically reviews cellular providers and plans.

DIRECTORY ASSISTANCE

For local and national telephone directory assistance, dial 411. Most calling plans include a certain number of calls to 411 in your base fee, but if you run over that, the cost of using 411 varies according to your calling plan.

In today's web-oriented world, directory assistance does not have to cost money. Online assistance is available from **Verizon**, www.verizon.com, and numerous sites are dedicated to providing telephone listings and web sites at no charge.

INTERNET SERVICE PROVIDERS (ISPs)

Internet service varies, from traditional modems over phone lines available to anyone with a home phone, to cable modems and DSLs. Cable modem and DSL availability varies on whether service has been extended to your area or building. Also available in some areas are **bundled telecommunications**, digital cable, telephone, and internet services that are grouped into one plan. (See **Comcast** below under **Cable Television** for more information.) Depending on your ISP, you can expect service to run between $20-$40 per month. A good resource for information about local online options is **Boston Internet Special Interest Group**, www.signet.org/isig/, which focuses on internet issues, from ISPs to e-commerce, and offers helpful resources and links.

LOCAL INTERNET SERVICE PROVIDERS

- **Channel 1**, 617-864-0100, www.channel1.com.
- **Galaxy Internet Services**, 888-334-2529, www.gis.net
- **The World**, 617-739-0202, www.theworld.com

NATIONAL INTERNET SERVICE PROVIDERS

- **Comcast**, 800-COMCAST, www.comcast.com
- **America Online**, 888-265-8003, www.aol.com
- **Broadwing**, 888-714-1565, ww.broadwing.net
- **Compuserve**, 800-848-8199, www.compuserve.com
- **Earthlink**, 800-511-2041, www.earthlink.net
- **Juno**, 877-665-9995, www.juno.com
- **Microsoft**, 800-426-9400, www.msn.com
- **NetZero**, 877-665-9995, www.netzero.com
- **Prodigy**, 800-776-3449, http://myhome.prodigy.net
- **RCN**, 800-RING-RCN, www.rcn.com

WATER

WATER SERVICE

Most communities get their drinking water from reservoirs. Although there are several primary and back-up reservoirs around the state, most of Massachusetts' water supply originates in the **Quabbin Reservoir** in western Massachusetts.

If you're renting, your water bill will be taken care of by your landlord. Homeowners are responsible for their monthly water bill. Water service in Massachusetts is organized as electrical service is—with suppliers and distributors. Since 1984, the **Massachusetts Water Resources Authority (MWRA)** has been the public water and sewer wholesale service provider for the greater Boston area, brokering Quabbin Reservoir water to 2.5 million people, 5,500 large industrial users, and 61 metro Boston communities. MWRA provides water and sewer service to Arlington, Belmont, Boston, Brookline, Malden, Medford, Milton, Newton, Quincy, Somerville, Watertown, and Waltham. A "middleman" then distributes the water to your community, and this is who you should contact to set up your water service (read on).

Residents of Cambridge get their water from the MWRA only in special situations. Otherwise, their water comes from **Fresh Pond**, and their water utility service is provided by the municipally owned **Cambridge Water Department**, www.ci.cambridge.ma.us/~Water, 617-349-4770. Dedham residents have a similar back-up emergency arrangement with the MWRA, but otherwise their water comes from local wells, provided through the **Dedham-Westwood Water District**, www.dwwd.org, 781-329-7090. In **Needham**, residents should contact the **Department of Public Works' Water and Sewer Division**, 781-455-7547.

If you are moving to a community further out, call 617-788-1170 or go online to www.mwra.com to find out if your new home is served by the MWRA. You can also check with your local city hall.

Distributors may vary from community to community, but water is mostly distributed by each town's Department of Public Works. In Boston, it's the **Boston Water and Sewer Commission** (**BWSC**). Here's a contact list to get you started, including the MWRA:

- **MWRA**, 100 First Avenue, Charlestown Navy Yard, Boston 02129, 617-788-1170, www.mwra.com; FYI, the MWRA flouridates the water.
- **BWSC**, 980 Harrison Avenue, Boston 02119, 617-989-7000, www.bwsc.org; serves Boston proper.
- **Arlington DPW**, Highway/Water/Sewer Division, 780 Mass Avenue, 781-316-3108, www.town.arlington.ma.us/townhall.htm
- **Belmont Water Department**, 35 Woodland Street, 617-489-8280, www.town.belmont.ma.us/water.htm
- **Brookline DPW**, Water and Sewer Division, 4th Floor, Town Hall, 617-730-2156, www.townofbrooklinemass.com/Dpw
- **Malden Water and Sewer Department**, 781-397-7040, www.ci.malden.ma.us/government
- **Medford DPW**, Water and Sewer Division, 781-393-2420, www.medford.org/fGoverment.htm
- **Milton DPW**, Water and Sewer Division, 617-696-5731
- **Newton DPW**, Water and Sewer Utilities Division, 1000 Comm Ave., 617-796-1040, www.ci.newton.ma.us
- **Quincy DPW**, Water bill hotline, 617-376-1918, www.wjdal300.com/directory/drctdpw.htm
- **Somerville DPW**, Water Division, 1 Franey Road, 617-625-6600, www.ci.somerville.ma.us
- **Waltham DPW**, Water and Sewer Department, 781-314-3810 or 781-314-3820, www.city.waltham.ma.us/pubworks/waterdept.htm
- **Watertown DPW**, 617-972-6420

WATER QUALITY

The DEP rates Boston's water as "very safe." If you'd like more specifics about water quality in Massachusetts, you can go to the **National Water Quality Assessment Program** of the US Geological Survey: http://water.usgs.gov/owq/dwi/states/ma-ri.htm. Or contact the **Massachusetts DEP Drinking Water Department**, 617-556-1165, www.state.ma.us/dep; the **Massachusetts Department of Public Health**, 617-624-6000, www.state.ma.us/dph; the **EPA's Safe Drinking**

Water Hotline, 800-426-4791, www.epa.gov/safewater; the **EPA's Storet Water Quality System Hotline**, 800-424-9067 www.epa.gov/storet; or the **Water Quality Association** at 800-749-0234, www.wqa.org. The EPA also has a number of publications on water and water quality; go to www.epa.gov.ogwdw/pubs/index.html to download. The EPA also does a water quality survey in each state every two years. To view the most recent **EPA water quality assessment**, visit www.epa.gov/305b.

CONSUMER PROTECTION—UTILITY AND OIL COMPLAINTS

The Massachusetts Department of Telecommunications and Energy (DTE), formerly the Department of Public Utilities, is the consumer protection agency that regulates the quality of utility services (telecom, electric, transportation, cable, water, and gas). According to the DTE, its mission is to "ensure that the Commonwealth's customers are provided with safe, reliable service at a reasonable cost." Creating regulatory policies that help develop a competitive marketplace for these services is one way in which the DTE promotes its mission. If you have problems with your utility company, you should try to resolve it with the company first. If satisfaction eludes you, the DTE has a consumer division branch you can call. Alternately, you can also turn to the Consumer Protection Division of the Massachusetts Attorney General's Office or the Division of Energy Resources. Some water issues can be handled through the Massachusetts DEP.

- **Massachusetts DTE**, Consumer Division, 1 South Station, Boston 02110, 617-305-3531 or 800-392-6066, www.state.ma.us/dpu
- **Massachusetts Attorney General's Office**, Consumer Protection Division, 200 Portland Street, 4th Floor, Boston 02114, 617-727-2200 or 888-514-6277, www.ago.state.ma.us
- **Massachusetts Division of Energy Resources**, 70 Franklin Street, 7th Floor, Boston 02110, 617-727-0030, www.state.ma.us/doer
- **Massachusetts Department of Environmental Protection**, 1 Winter Street, Boston 02108, 617-292-5500, www.state.ma.us/dep

Additionally, if you look at your phone bill and think you've been **slammed** (your long distance provider or established services were changed without your approval) or **crammed** (calls you didn't make were added to your bill), and you can't get help from your local service provider or from the Attorney General's Office, you can file a complaint with the Federal Communication Commission's Consumer Center, 888-225-5322, www.fcc.gov; or the Federal Trade Commission, 202-382-4357, www.ftc.gov.

GARBAGE AND RECYCLING

If you're a renter, the most you're going to need to know about garbage is where and when to put it out, and how to handle your recycling—questions your landlord can answer. In Boston, homeowners should contact the **Sanitation Division of the DPW**, 1 City Hall Plaza, Room 714, Boston 02201, 617-635-4900, www.cityofboston.gov/publicworks/sanitation, to set up trash and recycling removal. Depending on where you live, refuse will be picked up between one and three times per week. You may have a dumpster or you may be required to put your trash out in well-tied garbage bags or in cans at appointed pickup times.

Recycling is free in Boston. For residents of buildings with six or more units, landlords or building management agencies are required to provide the large recycling receptacles (between 30 and 90 gallons). For buildings with less than six units, the city does curbside recycling. Contact the DPW to get the requisite blue boxes and then put out your recycling according to the following schedule: the same time as your garbage pickup if you only have one pickup day per week; on the first day if your trash is picked up twice weekly; and on the middle day if your garbage is picked up three times a week. There is also a drop-off center in Mission Hill at the Boston Building Materials Co-op at 100 Terrace Street. Put plastics, metals, and glass in the designated blue box; recycle paper, cardboard, and phone books in brown paper bags. For further recycling questions, you can call the **DPW's Recycling Hotline** at 617-635-4959 or go to www.bostononline.com/recycling.html.

Outside the City of Boston, contact the following resources for your sanitation and recycling services:
- **Arlington**: Arlington DPW, 780 Mass Ave., 781-316-3108, www.town.arlington.ma.us/townhall.htm
- **Belmont**: Belmont Highway Department, 40 Prince Street, 617-489-7171, http://town.belmont.ma.us/highway/trash.htm
- **Brookline**: Brookline DPW, Sanitation Division, 4th Floor, Town Hall, 617-730-2156, www.townofbrooklinemass.com/dpw
- **Cambridge**: Cambridge DPW, 147 Hampshire Street, 617-349-4800, www.cambridge.ma.gov
- **Dedham**: Dedham DPW, Solid Waste Services, 55 River Street, 781-326-5770, www.town.dedham.ma.us/recycle
- **Malden**: Malden DPW, 781-397-7160, www.ci.malden.ma.us/government
- **Medford**: Medford DPW, www.medford.org/fGoverment.htm, Highway Division: 781-393-2417; recycling: 781-393-2419

GETTING SETTLED

- **Milton**: Milton DPW, Solid Waste Division, 617-696-5732
- **Needham**: Needham DPW, RTS, 1421 Central Avenue, 781-455-7568, www.town.needham.ma.us/DPW
- **Newton**: Newton DPW, 1000 Comm Ave., 617-796-2000, www.ci.newton.ma.us
- **Quincy**: Quincy DPW, 617-770-BINS, www.wjdal300.com
- **Somerville**: Somerville DPW, 1 Franey Road, 617-625-6600 ext. 5100, www.ci.somerville.ma.us
- **Waltham**: Waltham DPW, Street and Forestry Division, 781-314-3855 or 781-314-3850, www.city.waltham.ma.us/pubworks/street.html
- **Watertown**: Watertown DPW, 617-972-6420 or Watertown Recycling, 617-972-6413

BROADCAST AND PRINT MEDIA

TELEVISION

Boston television viewers can pick up broadcasts from New Hampshire and Rhode Island as well as Boston, so you'll find a lot of network repetition as you channel surf.

BOSTON
Channel 2, WGBH-TV, PBS
Channel 4, WBZ-TV, CBS
Channel 5, WCVB-TV, ABC
Channel 7, WHDH-TV, NBC
Channel 25, WFXT-TV, FOX
Channel 27, WUNI-TV, UNIVISION (Spanish)
Channel 38, WSBK-TV, UPN
Channel 44, WGBX-TV, PBS
Channel 56, WB56-TV, The WB
Channel 68, WBPX-TV, PAX

EXTENDED REGION
Channel 6, WLNE-TV (ABC out of Rhode Island)
Channel 9, WMUR-TV (ABC out of New Hampshire)
Channel 10, WJAR-TV (NBC out of Providence/New Bedford)
Channel 11, WENH-TV (PBS out of New Hampshire)
Channel 12, WPRI-TV (FOX out of Providence)
Channel 50, WNDS-TV (independent out of Derry, NH)
Channel 60, WGOT-TV (independent out of Merrimack, NH)

CABLE TELEVISION

Cable television (basic cable only) is regulated in Massachusetts through the **Department of Telecommunications and Energy**, 1 South Station, Boston, 617-305-3580, www.state.ma.us/dpu. Expanded, premium, and pay-per-view services are unregulated. At press time there were ten cable carriers throughout the commonwealth, although most communities have service from only one, and **Comcast** was the only company providing **bundled telecommunications**: digital cable, internet, and phone. In Boston, the **Office of Cable Communications** is at 43 Hawkins Street, Boston 02114, 617-635-3112, www.cityofboston.gov/cable.

Check with the following list for the cable carrier in your town or city. If your community isn't mentioned, contact your city officials to find out who your cable carrier is, or visit www.state.ma.us/dpu/catv for a complete list of all cable systems in Massachusetts, who they serve, and how to contact them.

- **Adelphia Cable**, 877-227-9658, www.adelphia.net, serves Cape Ann, Martha's Vineyard, the Berkshires, Amesbury, Plymouth, and other northern areas.
- **Comcast**, 800-COMCAST, 617-562-4200, www.comcast.com, serves Boston, Brookline, Arlington, Cambridge, Dedham, Malden, Medford, Milton, Needham, Newton, Quincy, Somerville, Waltham, Watertown, and a great deal of the state. In Boston, call 617-787-6616. In Brookline, call 617-731-4160.
- **Charter Communications**, 800-634-1008, www.chartercom.com, covers the Worcester area and some more rural areas of the state.
- **RCN**, 800-746-4726, www.rcn.com, shares a lot of territory with AT&T, serving Boston, Arlington, Brookline, Burlington, Dedham, Framingham, Lexington, Natick, Needham, Newton, Somerville, Wakefield, Waltham, Watertown, and Woburn.
- **Time Warner**, 888-633-4266, www.timewarnercable.com, covers Chelsea, Everett, Lynn, Malden, Medford, Melrose, Salem, Somerville, Stoneham, Swampscott, Wakefield, and Winthrop.

RADIO STATIONS

Here's a rundown of a few of the major players in the local radio market. Depending on where you are, you'll get signals from New Hampshire, Cape Cod, Rhode Island, or Worcester, or from other smaller stations throughout the region. Some smaller stations or college stations, such as those from Tufts and Wellesley, share a frequency.

ALTERNATIVE AND CLASSIC ROCK
- WFNX, 101.7 FM
- WZLX, 100.7 FM
- WBOS, 92.9 FM

CLASSICAL
- WBOQ, 104.9 FM
- WCRB, 102.5 FM

COUNTRY
- WKLB, 99.5 FM

ETHNIC
- WAMG, 1150 AM (Spanish)
- WNTN, 1550 AM (Greek, Haitian, Irish, Indian, Arabic)
- WUNR, 1600 AM (Yiddish, Spanish, Greek)

FAMILY
- WMKI, 1260 AM (Radio Disney)

FOLK
- WUMB, 91.9 FM

HARD ROCK
- WAAF, 101.3 FM
- WBCN, 104.1 FM

OLDIES
- WODS, 103.3 FM
- WXKS, 1430 AM (Standards)
- WROR, 105.7 FM ('60s, '70s, and '80s)

POP
- WBMX (MIX985), 98.5 FM

(Pop, continued)
- WEGQ (STAR937), 93.7 FM
- WXKS (KISS 108), 107.9 FM

PUBLIC RADIO
- ALLSTON-BRIGHTON FREE RADIO, 1670 AM
- WBUR, 90.9 FM (NPR)
- WGBH, 89.7 FM (NPR, Garrison Keillor, Business, Talk, Jazz, Blues, Classical, World Music)

RELIGIOUS
- WEZE, 590 AM (Christian)
- WJLT, (JLIGHT), 650 AM (Christian)

SOFT ROCK/EASY LISTENING
- WMJX, (MAGIC 106.7), 106.7 FM
- WPLM, (EASY 99.1), 99.1 FM
- WXRV, (THE RIVER), 92.5 FM

TALK RADIO
- WBIX, 1060 AM (Business)
- WBNW, 1120 AM (Business/Financial)
- WBZ, 1030 AM (News)
- WEEI, 850 AM (Sports)
- WESX, 1230 AM (News)
- WJDA, 1300 AM (News/Ethnic)
- WRKO, 680 AM (News)
- WTKK, 96.9 FM
- WWZN, 1510 AM (Sports)

UNIVERSITY STATIONS
- WBRS, 100.1 FM (Brandeis)
- WERS, 88.9 FM (Emerson)
- WHRB, 95.3 FM (Harvard)
- WMBR, 88.1 FM (MIT)
- WMFO, 91.5 FM (Tufts)
- WRBB, 104.9 FM (Northeastern)
- WZBC, 90.3 FM (BC)
- WZLY, 91.5 FM (Wellesley)

URBAN
- WBOT, 97.7 FM
- WJMN (JAM'N-94.5), 94.5 FM

NEWSPAPERS AND MAGAZINES

The two major dailies in the Boston news market are **The Boston Globe**, www.boston.com/globe, 617-929-2000, and **The Boston Herald**, www.bostonherald.com, 617-426-3000. **Boston Magazine**, www.bostonmagazine.com, 617-262-9700, offers an elegant account of life in the metropolitan area, including events, news, and places to live, work, study, shop, eat, and play. Pick it up on newsstands, or sign up for a yearly subscription for $10.

GETTING SETTLED

Several other papers/magazines that cover a variety of issues, such as jobs, money, real estate, sports events, arts events, attractions, concerts, restaurants, bars, and seasonal events, are free:

- The **Improper**, www.improper.com, 617-859-1400, is an independent fortnightly "what's happening" style magazine. Good source for current-events information. Look for it every other Wednesday in stores and vending boxes throughout the Boston area, or subscribe for $15 per year.
- The **Metro**, www.metro.lu, 617-357-5706, is a newcomer to the Boston market, a free daily that you'll find in newspaper boxes and often handed out near T stations.
- The **Phoenix**, www.bostonphoenix.com, 617-536-5390, is known for its edgy, hip, alternative feel. The paper bills itself as "New England's largest arts and entertainment weekly," but you will find a lot of news, editorial content, and other useful information. It comes out on Thursdays, and you can find it in vending boxes and in stores.
- **Stuff@night**, www.bostonphoenix.com/boston/stuff@night, 617-536-5390, is the uber-cool biweekly guide to Boston's nighttime entertainment options. Look in vending boxes and stores around the city on Wedsnesdays.
- **The Weekly Dig**, http://weeklydig.com/, 617-426-8942, focuses on current events, movies, music, etc., comes out on Wednesdays.

Most neighborhoods or communities have their own papers. Some are free, some charge, and many of them are run by the Community Newspaper Company, now owned by the *Herald*. Hence, a great deal of them can be found online through the same web site: www.townonline.com. Below are a few of the local papers serving the metro Boston towns, communities, or interests.

- **Allston-Brighton TAB**, 617-254-7530, www.townonline.com/allston
- **Arlington Advocate**, 781-643-7900, www.townoline.com/arlington
- **Atlantic Journal of Transportation**, 617-328-0005, www.ajot.com; weekly
- **Bay State Banner**, 617-261-4600, www.baystatebanner.com; weekly newspaper for the African-American community.
- **Bay Windows**, 617-266-6670, www.baywindows.com; weekly newspaper for the gay and lesbian community
- **Beacon Hill Times**, 617-523-9490, www.beaconhilltimes.com/times_toc.mv
- **Belmont Citizen-Herald**, 617-484-2633, www.townonline.com/belmont
- **Boston Business Journal**, 703-973-1000, www.boston.bizjournals.com/boston
- **Boston Haitian Reporter**, 617-436-1222, www.bostonhaitian.com

- **Boston Irish Reporter**, 617-436-1222, www.bostonirish.com
- **Brookline TAB**, 617-566-3585, www.townonline.com/brookline
- **Cambridge Candle**, 617-491-2520, www.cambridgecandle.com; alternative community paper
- **Cambridge Chronicle**, 617-577-7149, www.townonline.com/cambridge
- **Christian Science Monitor**, 617-375-4000, www.csmonitor.com; daily
- **Dorchester Reporter**, 617-436-1222, www.dotnews.com
- **Jamaica Plain Gazette**, 617-524-3921, www.jamaicaplaingazette.com
- **Jewish Advocate**, 617-367-9100, www.thejewishadvocate.com
- **Malden Observer**, 781-322-6957, www.townonline.com/malden
- **Newton TAB**, 617-969-3640, www.townonline.com/newton
- **Quincy Patriot Ledger**, 617-786-7000, www.patriotledger.com
- **Somerville Journal**, 617-625-6300, www.townonline.com/somerville
- **South Boston Tribune**, 617-268-3440, www.southbostoninfo.com
- **South End News**, 617-266-6670
- **Watertown TAB & Press**, 617-926-8897, www.townonline.com/watertown
- **West Roxbury Transcript**, 617-327-2608, www.townonline.com/westroxbury

AUTOMOBILES

DRIVER'S LICENSES AND STATE IDS

In an automotive sense, life here is a little more New York than LA: public transportation is good, parking is a hassle, and insurance is expensive, the end result being that many choose to live here without a car. For those coming with an automobile, you will want to contact the **Massachusetts Registry of Motor Vehicles** (**RMV**), 617-351-4500 or 800-858-3926, www.mass.gov/rmv, about information for owning and operating an automobile or motorcycle in Massachusetts. (Parking permit requirements will vary depending upon your city.) The RMV's comprehensive web site can answer virtually all your vehicular questions and it offers transactions online.

DRIVER'S LICENSE

Massachusetts residents are legally required to have a valid Massachusetts license to drive here, which means you should convert your out-of-state license right away. Of course, many (particularly students who only live here during part of the year) don't bother changing their license until their out-of-state one is about to expire ... or until they get caught.

Whether you're converting an old license, getting your first one, replacing a lost license, or just getting a state ID, you'll do it through the RMV. Go to www.mass.gov/rmv for a complete list of the types of documentation you should bring when registering your vehicle and for a list of fees.

The **Boston RMV**, located at 630 Washington Street in Chinatown, is the main full-service office. Hours are 8:30 a.m. to 5 p.m. Monday-Wednesday and Fridays; extended hours are on Thursday: 8:30 a.m. to 7 p.m. Additional full service branches are in Quincy and Watertown. Limited service branches are in Watertown and Roslindale; a License Express is in the Cambridgeside Galleria, 100 Cambridgeside Place, open Monday to Friday, 10 a.m. to 7 p.m. License Express offices (often located in malls) can take care of quick and simple licensing needs, such as license or registration renewals, name or address changes, and plate returns. There are many full and limited service RMV offices and License Express offices throughout the state. Check www.mass.gov/rmv/branches or call 800-858-3926 for a complete list and contact information.

Massachusetts licenses are valid for up to five years and expire on the birthday of the license holder. You can **renew** your license anytime during the year preceding the expiration date. The state may refuse to renew your license if you have outstanding parking or abandoned vehicle tickets, unpaid excise tax or violations at tollways, or outstanding warrants and child support obligations.

In Massachusetts, everyone under 18 years of age is subject to the **Junior Operator License Law**, a graduated license law that requires young drivers pass a number of phases before getting full driving privileges. Check with the RMV for complete details.

To convert your out-of-state license to a Massachusetts driver's license, you'll have to pay for all application, testing, and license fees. If your out-of-state license is current or has been expired for less than a year, you will not have to take a written or road test to convert your license. A standard Class D license will cost you $90. Go to an RMV or License Express equipped with either your Social Security card or current passport, and three additional pieces of ID (check online at www.mass.gov/rmv for acceptable forms of identification). Also bring: payment, which can be a checkbook, money order, or credit card; your current out-of-state photo license; and proof of Massachusetts' residency (such as a local utility bill in your name).

The requirements for **converting a foreign license** to a Massachusetts driver's license will depend upon which country issued your license. To convert a current Canadian, Mexican, or US Territory license, you will have to obtain a certified driving record no more than a month old from the country in which you're licensed, as well as pass an eye exam. Requirements for lapsed Canadian, Mexican, or US Territory licenses are the same as for out-of-state ones. Newcomers hailing from any other country must take the full licensing exam from scratch and may require a sponsor; International Driving Permits cannot be converted.

If you're planning on driving a **motorcycle**, you'll have special requirements to complete for your licensing. Check with the RMV for specifics.

STATE IDS

Massachusetts ID cards look like driver's licenses and are available to state residents, 16 years old or older, who do not have a driver's license. Bring your social security card or valid passport, and other documents proving your date of birth, signature, state residency, and parental consent (for minors) to a full service RMV. IDs cost $15 and never expire, although you may wish to upgrade to a liquor ID card when you turn 21. **Massachusetts Liquor ID cards** also look like drivers' licenses but cost $25 and expire every five years.

According to Runzheimer International, Boston is one of the most expensive cities in the nation in which to own a car. Vehicles need to be registered, titled, insured, and to pass inspection. As with licenses, the RMV web site is very helpful for answering questions about automobile registration.

AUTOMOBILE REGISTRATION, TITLING, INSPECTION, AND INSURANCE

TITLES

In Massachusetts, you must have the title to your automobile, which proves ownership and documents the vehicle's history. The state's **Title Law** requires that all vehicles and trailers be titled within 10 days of purchase. Exemptions include dealer cars, cars owned by the government, and cars owned by non-residents. A car will get a "clear title" if it is new or has not been in an accident. If you have a car that was totaled it gets a "salvage title." A "memorandum" title means that the car was brought in from out of state with a lien on it, and the lienholder is in possession of the out-of-state title. Check www.mass.gov/rmv/titles for complete details. Expect to pay $50 to title your car plus any applicable sales tax.

REGISTRATION

If you are **bringing your car from another state**, by law you are required to register your car immediately; there is no grace period. If the car

GETTING SETTLED

has been registered elsewhere for more than six months the car is exempt from Massachusetts state sales tax. To convert your out-of-state registration, go to a full service RMV and complete form MVU-29 (the Affidavit in Support for Exemption from Sales or Use Tax for Motor Vehicle Purchased Outside of Massachusetts.) You can download it online from the Massachusetts RMV site. Then, set up an insurance policy with a Massachusetts insurance agent, and have him or her stamp and sign the Application for Registration and Title (form RMV-1). Verify that all the information is correct, sign it, and bring it to a full service RMV, along with your out-of-state title, out-of-state registration, and completed MVU-29 form. Fees are the same as for newly purchased vehicles, minus the five-percent sales tax. If your car was registered elsewhere for less than six months, skip the MVU-20 step, head to the insurance agent, and proceed as before, bearing in mind that you'll have to pay the sales tax at the RMV when you register. (See the **Money Matters** chapter for more information about state and use tax.)

To register a new vehicle in Massachusetts, you must first insure it with a Massachusetts insurance agent. Regardless of whether you purchase the car here or in another state, have your dealer fill out a RMV-1 form. Then set up an insurance policy with an agent licensed in Massachusetts; he or she must also stamp and sign off on the RMV-1. Verify that all the information is correct before you put your own signature on it, and then bring the form and a Certificate of Origin, which you get from the dealer and acts in place of a title, to a full-service RMV. For a standard (non-commercial) vehicle, you'll pay $25 for the registration plus a $50 title fee and five-percent sales tax. If you're buying a **used car from a dealership**, the procedure is the same, except you will take your completed paperwork, along with either the previous owner's title (if the vehicle is titled) or the bill of sale and proof of last registration (if non-titled) to a full service RMV. The fees are the same as for new cars purchased from a dealer. For instructions on **vehicles purchased from a non-dealer, or acquired from family or friends**, visit the RMV site at www.mass.gov/rmv/regs. Note: all new passenger vehicles sold and registered in Massachusetts are subject to the **Low Emission Vehicle Program**. Specifically, new vehicles with less than 7,500 miles on them must meet cleaner California emission standards, i.e. have factory-installed California-certified advanced emission control systems.

Upon completing the registration transaction for all types of vehicles, the RMV will give you the registration certificate, new license plates, and the year of expiration decal, which goes on the rear plate. The RMV will process your new title and mail it to you (or to the lienholder if you have a loan); it should arrive in six to eight weeks.

SAFETY AND EMISSIONS INSPECTIONS

Once your vehicle is registered with the RMV, you have **one week** (seven calendar days, not seven business days) to take you vehicle in for an **annual safety inspection**. Safety inspections cost $29. Go to http://vehicletest.state.ma.us/testinginfo.html for a complete list of stations. Inspectors will check your registration and plates; windshield; windshield wipers; headlights, taillights, break lights, turn signals, hazards, and any other lights; horn; exhaust system; tires; body panels/fuel tank; emergency brake; service brake; seat belts; and ball joints, steering, and suspension. They won't check airbags or anti-lock braking systems (although regular brakes must work), but a crack in any of your lights or windows could fail you, as will neon lights (they're illegal) and after-market glass tinting above 35%. Check with the RMV for state regulations. It will also have to pass an **emissions test**, unless the model is pre-1983 or it's brand new, in which case it is exempt for the first two years. Regardless of the last two caveats, if (visible) smoke pours out of your exhaust pipe during the safety inspection, the car won't pass.

When you pass the safety and emissions tests, the inspector will put a color-coded Certificate of Inspection sticker on the lower right hand corner of your windshield bearing the inspection date. It is valid for one year, and is to be taken seriously. The citation for non-compliance is $50, and failure to complete the inspection can result in a suspended registration. You have until the last day of whatever month your inspection certificate runs out to get it re-inspected each year.

AUTOMOBILE INSURANCE AND ACCIDENTS

Automobile insurance is required in Massachusetts. Coverage must include bodily injury to others, personal injury protection, bodily injury caused by an uninsured auto, and damage to someone else's property. Minimum **compulsory coverage** includes:
- **Bodily injury to others** at $20,000 per person, (maximum $40,000 per accident) for damages to anyone hurt or killed by your car in Massachusetts.
- **Personal injury protection** offers $8,000 for medical expenses; replacement services; and 75% of lost wages for you, passengers, and pedestrians regardless of who is at fault for an accident.
- **Bodily injury caused by an uninsured auto** covers a minimum of $20,000 per person and $40,000 per accident.
- **Damage to someone else's property** covers up to $5,000 for property damage in an accident.

You can opt for more coverage. Look in the Yellow Pages for a complete listing of insurance carriers. Massachusetts offers the **Safe Driver Insurance Plan** (**SDIP**), a program that aims to encourage safe driving by rewarding low risk drivers (those with cleaner driving records) with lower insurance rates. Essentially, the SDIP employs a point system to tally how risky a driver you are, factoring such things as at-fault accidents and traffic tickets to adjust your insurance premium accordingly.

If you do get into an accident, don't leave the scene. Always call the police to make a report, no matter how minimal the accident might seem.

The following may be useful as you try to track down an insurer:

- **Massachusetts Office of Consumer Affairs and Business Regulation**, Insurance Information, www.state.ma.us/consumer/Info/insur.htm
- **Citizen Information Service**, auto insurance discount information, www.state.ma.us/sec/cis
- **Massachusetts Division of Insurance**, 617-521-7777, www.state.ma.us/doi
- **Automobile Insurers Bureau for Massachusetts**, www.aib.org
- **Commonwealth Automobile Reinsurers**, www.commauto.com
- **Massachusetts RMV**, www.mass.gov/rmv
- **Better Business Bureau**, www.bbb.org/pubpages/autopub.asp
- **ChoicePoint Asset**, P.O. Box 105108, Atlanta, GA 30348-5108, www.choicetrust.com; order your CLUE (Comprehensive Loss Underwriting Exchange) report. This national database of consumers' automobile and homeowner's insurance claims is used by insurers when determining rates or denying coverage. Contact ChoicePoint if you find any errors.

AUTOMOBILE SAFETY

Most Bostonians will own up to their reputation as being some of the most impatient drivers anywhere. As the City of Boston's web site posts, "Boston drivers have created quite a name for themselves—and for good reason. If you choose to join the mayhem and drive a car on the streets of Boston, good luck and be careful." Boston drivers tend to be aggressive, and many a traffic back up is caused by an unwillingness to allow merges. As one lifelong Bostonian says, "We're almost as bad as New Yorkers, except we leave our windows rolled up when we flip you the bird." Basically it's big city driving here, and if you drive on the offense, you'll probably fit right in.

Driving under the influence of drugs or alcohol is illegal in Massachusetts. The legal blood alcohol limit is .08. If you are pulled over for driving under the influence, you will likely be arrested, have your car towed, and given a breathalyzer test. (Refusing a breathalyzer in

Massachusetts will result in an automatic license suspension for between four months and two years.) If you fail the breathalyzer, you'll go to jail and your license will be suspended for between three and 15 months. For more details go to www.massghsb.com/detpages/safety221.html.

Massachusetts is a **seatbelt** state. All occupants of a vehicle—be it a car, truck or van—including children in safety seats, must be properly buckled in. To enforce this rule, Massachusetts instigated its "Click it or Ticket" campaign to promote increased safety belt use. All children under the age of five or older ones up to 40 pounds are legally required to be in a safety seat. For older children, seat belts must be used (child safety seats for all children up to 80 pounds are encouraged but not required.) A police officer can pull you over if he or she sees there is a child riding in the car without proper restraint. To learn more about Massachusetts' rules for driving with kids, visit the Governor's Highway Safety Bureau page on child passenger safety at www.massghsb.com/detpages/safety12.html. Also check the National Highway Transportation Safety Administration's web site, www.nhtsa.dot.gov, for tips on what you should be looking for in a safety seat.

Boston is subject to all sorts of variations in weather, the most dangerous of which is the wintertime snow, sleet, freezing rain, and ice. Black ice—basically invisible ice—is particularly treacherous. It's a good idea to have your car tuned up and have your tire treads checked before the snow flies. For more tips on driving here during the winter you can go to www.boston-online.com/windrive.

For up-to-the-minute **traffic alerts**, which are crucial considering the daily traffic jams in Boston, many use SmarTraveler: 617-374-1234 or go to www.smartraveler.com. If you're in your car, you can try WBZ news radio at 1030 AM.

CONSUMER PROTECTION—AUTOMOBILES

When you buy a car in Massachusetts, it's good to know about state lemon laws, which include the New and Leased Car Lemon Law, Used Vehicle Warranty Law, and Lemon Aid Law. These are intended to protect buyers from the misfortune of buying a car that is a dud. Legally, vehicle companies, after being given a fair crack at fixing the damage, have to replace their product. In Massachusetts, the **New and Leased Car Lemon Law** protects consumers who have bought or leased a new vehicle, motorcycle, van, or truck from a new-car dealer for personal or family purposes. It's good for up to one year or 15,000 miles, whichever comes first. State law defines a lemon as "a new or leased motor vehicle that has a defect which substantially impairs the use, market value, or safety of the vehicle, and which has not been repaired after a reasonable number of attempts," i.e., three times for the same problem or 15 business days out of service for any combination of problems. Then, you must give the manufacturer a formal seven-business days "final repair attempt" to fix the problem. Because the law doesn't have an exact requirement as to what constitutes a "substantial" defect, it can be tricky to provide proof. Be sure to keep a record of all repair attempts, number of days in the shop, and any comments from the mechanics who worked on your vehicle. If your car is indeed a lemon, you are entitled to either a refund or a replacement vehicle. The Massachusetts Office of Consumer Affairs and Business Regulation provides more information at www.state.ma.us/consumer/Pubs/lemon.htm. Additionally, the **Used Vehicle Warranty Law** protects used car buyers; it covers pre-owned cars, vans, trucks, and demonstration vehicles sold by a Massachusetts dealer or private party. Vehicles purchased from dealers must cost at least $700. The amount of coverage on a dealer-sold vehicle depends on the mileage on the odometer at the time of sale, and the warranty only covers defects that substantially impair the vehicle's use or safety. You can view full details online on the Massachusetts Office of Consumer Affairs and Business Regulation's web site at www.state.ma.us/consumer/Pubs/usedcar.htm. If you are suspicious that a used car you are considering buying might be stolen, run the vehicle identification number through **Carfax**, 888-422-7329 or www.carfax.com. For **vehicle recall** information go to www.car.com, the database of recalls issued by the National Highway Traffic Safety Administration. Last but not least, the aptly named **Lemon Aid Law** covers you if the new or used car or motorcycle, whether bought from a dealer or private individual, that has been purchased for family or personal use, fails inspection within seven days of the sale date and the estimated costs of repairs exceed ten percent of the purchase price. Go to www.state.ma.us/consumer/Pubs/lemonaid.htm for specifics.

PARKING

Finding parking along Boston's old and narrow streets is difficult and particularly bad in the historic districts such as downtown, the Back Bay, Beacon Hill, the North End, and Charlestown. Parking spaces are limited during the spring, summer, and fall and are almost nonexistent in the winter when piles of snow cover many choice spots. As the City of Boston's snow policy is one of snow repositioning rather than snow removal, parking wars are common. When city trucks come through to clear a path, they simply plow the center of the streets, which pushes masses of snow off to the sides of the street, burying any parked cars along the way. Residents who have to shovel their cars out when it's time to drive to work the next day often become very protective of "their" spot. So, be advised: if you value your car's paint job or tires, think twice before removing a trash can, box, or orange cone marking a shoveled parking space Also, if the street sign says no parking during a **snow emergency**, take heed. All cars on the street *will be towed* in the event of a winter storm.

BOSTON

RESIDENT PARKING STICKERS

Many areas in Boston require residents' cars to have parking stickers for legal on-street parking. The stickers are free, and the process to get them isn't terrible. Bring your vehicle's registration documents and proof of residency to Boston City Hall (Room 224, the Office of the Parking Clerk), which is open Monday-Friday, 8:15 a.m. to 5 p.m., with extended hours on Thursday. Be sure to pay any parking tickets *before* you get there because you won't get a sticker if you have any left unresolved. Proof of residence can be a recent utility bill, bank statement, water/sewer bill, or credit card bill. Just be sure it has your name and address on it. You'll fill out a form and walk away with a sticker to put on your car window, making it legal to park in your neighborhood in the specially-marked resident spots. Parking permits must be renewed on a yearly basis. You should receive notification from the Transportation Department, and you can renew the permit by mail or online. For more information call **Resident Permits at the Office of the Parking Clerk** (Boston Transportation Department), 617-635-4682, or go to the City of Boston's web site, www.cityofboston.gov/transportation. You can download application and renewal forms and fill them out before visiting the parking clerk.

PARKING TICKETS AND TOWING

Boston's parking enforcement officials are so zealous that some Boston residents include a parking ticket fund in their monthly budgets. Tickets start at $15 and can go as high as $120, depending on the offense. If you get too many unpaid parking tickets (five or more), or if you park in certain restricted spots, say handicapped spaces or ones with warning signs, your car might very well get towed (see below). If a ticket is unpaid after 21 days, the cost of the ticket rises.

To pay a parking ticket, mail your payment using the neon-orange envelope provided by the city, or do it online at www.cityofboston.gov/parking. If you want to appeal the ticket, head to the Office of the Parking Clerk at City Hall, or send a letter stating your intent. For more information, visit www.cityofboston.gov/transportation/appeal. If your car has been booted, you'll need to pay $56 for the boot removal *and* all outstanding parking violations. Methods of payment include cash, money order, cashier's check, credit card (MasterCard or VISA), or debit card; no personal or business checks. Once payment is received at either Boston City Hall (they have payment windows on the second floor; hours are Monday-Friday, 9 a.m. to 5 p.m.) or the BTD tow lot (600 Frontage Road, 617-635-3900; hours are Monday-Friday, 5:30 p.m. to 9:30 p.m. and Saturdays, 9 a.m. to noon), your car should be released from its tether within an hour and a half.

To find out if your car has been towed by the city for parking tickets or any other reason (such as a snow emergency) call **Public Information/Ticket Information** at the Office of the Parking Clerk, 617-635-4410. If it has been towed, you will be responsible for all outstanding tickets, a towing fee of $12, and a storage fee of $15 per day. For directions to the tow lot, go to www.cityofboston.gov/transportation/towdirections.

Sometimes automobiles are towed by private companies, which complicates matters. When you call the city, they might not have a record of the towing. So before you panic and file a stolen car report, check the area where you parked for signs posting the name and number of a towing company.

If you find it is not convenient to make the trip to the tow lot, you can pay someone else to retrieve your towed car from the city lot. **Freedom Ticket and Boot Removal Services**, 617-236-1200, will take care of your paperwork and set your wheels free for $25 plus eight percent of whatever you owe.

COMMUTER PARKING

Parking in Boston and its surrounding communities is miserable, so unless your office offers a parking space, commuting into the city by car should be a last option. Boston's public transit is good and includes the T, commuter rail, commuter boats, and buses. Many outside of Boston drive each day to an MBTA commuter lot or T station and head to downtown on a bus, commuter rail, or T train. Lots vary in price, but are usually just a few dollars for the day. Depending on size, location, and popularity with commuters, lots may fill up quickly. For example, the Alewife station lot has almost 2,600 spaces, but smaller stations lots, like the one at Oak Grove, have fewer than 1,000 slots and can be full before the morning rush hour is over. To check current parking rates at the MBTA lot nearest you, visit www.mbta.com. As an incentive to get commuters to use public transportation, you can receive a discount on auto insurance if you use monthly T (subway or bus) passes. Turn 11 out of 12 of them into your insurance company annually as proof, and you'll get 10% off collision and property damage insurance, up to $75.

If public transportation is not an option, there are parking ramps and garages around the city.

PARKING—BEYOND BOSTON PROPER

Outside of Boston, check with your local police or traffic department for specifics on parking citations, overnight on-street parking guidelines, snow restrictions, visitor permits, and towing details:

- **Arlington**: Traffic Department, 781-316-3943; Police Department, 781-643-1212
- **Belmont**: Parking Clerk, 617-489-8252, http://town.belmont.ma.us/parking; Police, 617-484-1215 ext. 105 (for questions about towing).
- **Brookline**: Transportation Department, Town Hall, 333 Washington Street, 4th Floor, 617-730-2177, www.town.brookline.ma.us; Police Department, Traffic and Parking Clerk, 617-730-2230, www.brooklinepolice.com/tickets (to pay citations online).
- **Cambridge**: Traffic, Parking, and Transportation Department, 238 Broadway, 617-349-4700, www.ci.cambridge.ma.us/~Traffic; citations, call 617-491-7277; towing, 617-349-3300
- **Dedham**: Parking Clerk, 781-326-2141; Police Department, 781-326-8460
- **Malden**: Traffic Commission, 200 Pleasant Street, 781-397-7173; Police Department, 781-397-7171
- **Medford**: Office of the Parking Clerk, Room 110, Medford City Hall, 85 George P. Hassett Drive, 781-393-2440, www.medford.org/fGoverment.htm; Police Department, 781-391-6404
- **Milton**: Parking Clerk, 617-696-5604; Police Department, 40 Highland Street, 617-698-3800, www.miltonpd.com
- **Needham**: Parking Clerk, 781-455-7532; Police Department, 781-455-7570; Town Hall Treasurer's Office, 1471 Highland Avenue (to pay parking citations)
- **Newton**: Parking Department, 617-796-1344, www.ci.newton.ma.us; Police Department, Traffic Division, 25 Chestnut Street, West Newton, 617-552-7245 (parking stickers); 617-552-7240 (towing)
- **Quincy**: Parking Clerk, 617-376-1060; 617-376-1905 (with questions about towing)
- **Somerville**: Somerville Office of Traffic and Parking, 133 Holland Street, 617-625-6600, www.ci.somerville.ma.us; if your car has been towed in Somerville, call Pat's Towing Service directly at 617-776-5810; for information about snow emergencies, call Somerville DPW at 617-625-0300.
- **Waltham**: Parking Clerk, City Hall, 781-893-4040; Traffic Commission, Waltham Government Center, 119 School Street, 781-314-3400, www.city.waltham.ma.us/Transportation (for a list of public lots)
- **Watertown**: Traffic Office of the Watertown Police, 617-972-6547, www.watertownpd.org/faq.html#ParkingRegs

STOLEN AUTOMOBILES

When you move to the Boston area, it is recommended you consider protecting your car from theft. Many Boston car owners invest in some sort of anti-theft device. These range from simple steering wheel locks to electron-

GETTING SETTLED

ic alarms to systems that shut off your engine if a secret code isn't punched in after the engine has been started.

If your car is missing, first make sure you know which town you parked in (boundaries can be blurry for newcomers) before you call to find out if it has been towed. Once you're sure it hasn't been towed, you must go to the police precinct that has jurisdiction over the area from which the car was stolen and fill out a report (see the **Neighborhood Profiles** for precinct addresses and phone numbers). You will need your vehicle ID number, the title, and the license plate number. If you have photocopied your title, registration, and proof of insurance, and placed them in your wallet, your task will be much easier.

VOTER REGISTRATION

In addition to being able to register to vote the old-fashioned way at your local election office or city or town hall, you can also do it when you get your driver's license or by mail. Massachusetts residents who are US citizens at least 18 years of age on or before election day are eligible to vote. If you'd like a mail-in registration form, call 617-727-2828 or 800-462-VOTE to have one sent to you, or go online to www.state.ma.us/sec/ele/studix. If you'd prefer do it in person, head to your city or town hall, or go to a Massachusetts RMV branch office or License Express. To vote in an upcoming election, you must be registered 20 days in advance. You will need proof of residence, which can be a lease, utility bill, or driver's license. For a comprehensive link to all things voting related in the Commonwealth, go to the Citizens' Information Service at www.state.ma.us/sec/ele/eleidx.htm.

Following is a listing of **voter registration information**:

- **Boston**, Boston Election Commission, 617-635-4635; Election Department, City Hall Plaza, Room 241, 1 City Hall Square (Government Center)
- **Arlington**, Town Hall, 730 Mass Ave., 781-316-3071
- **Belmont**, Town Hall, 455 Concord Avenue, 617-489-8203
- **Brookline**, Town Clerk's Office, Town Hall, 333 Washington Street, 617-730-2010
- **Cambridge**, City Hall, 795 Mass Ave., 617-349-4260
- **Dedham**, Town Hall, 26 Bryant Street, 781-326-1638
- **Malden**, City Hall, 200 Pleasant Street, Room 323, 781-397-7116
- **Medford**, Election Commission, City Hall, 85 George P. Hassett Drive, 781-393-2424
- **Milton**, Town Hall, 525 Canton Avenue, 617-696-5414
- **Needham**, Town Hall, 1471 Highland Avenue, 781-455-7510
- **Newton**, Elections Commission Department, City Hall, 1000 Comm Ave., 617-796-1200

- **Quincy**, Elections Commission, City Hall, 1305 Hancock Street, 617-376-1131
- **Somerville**, Election Department, City Hall, 93 Highland Avenue (corner of Highland and School), 617-625-6600
- **Waltham**, City Clerk's Office, City Hall, 610 Main Street, 781-893-4040
- **Watertown**, Town Clerk's Office, Town Hall, 149 Main Street, 617-972-6486

Political parties with offices in the area include:
- **Massachusetts Democratic Party**, 617-472-0637, www.massdems.org
- **Massachusetts Republicans**, 781-224-7461, www.massgop.com
- **Libertarian Party**, 800-JOIN-LPM, www.lpma.org
- **Green Party**, 978-688-2068, www.massgreens.org.

To reach the **Massachusetts League of Women Voters**, call 617-723-1471. For questions or to report ethical issues (voter fraud, illegal contributions, etc.), contact the **State Ethics Commission**, 617-727-0060 or www.state.ma.us/ethics.

SOCIAL SECURITY

All information for new and replacement Social Security Cards can be found on the Social Security Administration's (SSA) web site, www.ssa.com. You can download the application form (Form SS-5), and then either mail it or take it to the nearest Social Security office with the proper supporting documentation. You don't need an appointment and it doesn't cost anything.

The main Social Security office in Boston is at 10 Causeway Street, Room 148 in the Tip O'Neill Building by North Station. However, there are other offices in the greater Boston area that might be more convenient; find one by entering your zip code on the SSA web site. If you don't want to go online, you can call 800-772-1213 and get all the same information and forms.

PASSPORTS

If you want to get a passport or renew an old one, there are several options. Passports are available from passport agencies and other passport acceptance facilities, such as libraries, post offices, courts, and county and municipal offices.

Depending on your needs, you may apply either in person or through the mail. You must apply for your passport in person if: you are applying for a passport for the first time; your previous passport was lost or damaged;

your previous passport was issued over 15 years ago and has expired or was issued before you were 16; your name is different than it was on your last passport and you don't have any legal proof of the change; or you are between the ages of 14 and 17 years old. Otherwise, you may apply through the mail. Either way, you should allow about six weeks for processing.

Passport application forms are available at the US Department of State's Bureau of Counselor Affairs web site, www.travel.state.gov/download_applications, from passport acceptance facilities (see below) or at the Boston Passport Agency. When you apply for your passport, you'll need to fill out the application form (DS-11), and bring proof of US citizenship, proof of identity, two passport photos, money, and a social security number. Acceptable documents proving your citizenship include a previous passport, certified birth certificate, consular report of birth abroad, naturalization certificate, or certificate of citizenship. Acceptable documents proving your identity include a previous passport; naturalization certificate; certificate of citizenship; or a current and valid ID (driver's license, state ID, military ID). Passport photos, two identical 2" x 2" photos, either black and white or color, are easily gotten at many photo shops or AAA offices.

A new passport costs $85 for those over 16 years of age and $70 for those under 16; renewals are $55. Passport agencies accept VISA, MasterCard, American Express, or Discover cards, checks, money orders, or bank drafts. Passport acceptance facilities accept payment in the forms of check, money order, bank draft, and sometimes the exact amount in bills or credit cards.

You should start the process of getting your passport several months before a planned trip. However, if you have a more urgent situation, the State Department offers expedited processing for an extra $60. Whether you do it through the mail (in which event, they strongly suggest using dual-way overnight shipping) or in person, it should only take two weeks for your passport to be processed. Since Boston is one of the few cities in the US that has its own passport agency (it's the main passport issuing agency for all of New England, with the exception of Connecticut and upstate New York), you may visit it directly. If your trip will occur in less than two weeks, you should definitely go there. For life or death emergencies, call the NPIC first. The **Boston Passport Agency** is located in the Tip O'Neill Federal Building, 10 Causeway, Room 247. You may only use the Boston Passport Agency by scheduling an appointment (no walk-ins), and only if you are traveling within the next two weeks. Bring your tickets or itinerary showing your short-notice trip schedule along with the standard passport-related documents. Hours of operation are Monday-Friday, 9 a.m. to 4 p.m. The nearest T stop is North Station. Call 617-878-0900 for automated information 24/7, or visit their homepage at www.travel.state.gov/ppt_bn.

Within downtown Boston, you can get your passport at one of four official **passport acceptance facilities** (all operate weekdays only): the Back Bay Post Office, 390 Stuart Street, Boston, 617-236-7800, 10 a.m. to 3 p.m.; the City of Boston Treasury Department, 1 City Hall Square (in City Hall, Government Center), 617-635-4488, 9:30 a.m. to 3 p.m.; the JFK Branch Post Office, 25 New Chardon Street, 617-523-6566, 8 a.m. to 4 p.m.; and the USPS Passport Acceptance at the McCormack Branch Post Office, 90 Devonshire Street, 617-720-5514, 7:30 a.m. to 4 p.m. Passport acceptance facilities also operate in Cambridge, East Boston, Roxbury, West Roxbury, Brookline, Dorchester, Hyde Park, Mattapan, Malden, Medford, Watertown, Newton, Quincy. To find the passport acceptance facility most convenient for you, visit http://iafdb.travel.state.gov and enter your home or work address.

LIBRARY CARDS

Boston's main library at Copley Square was the first large city library in the US opened to the general public. Today, most of the greater Boston area libraries are networked, so if you have a library card in one city or town you will be able to check out books from other libraries or even at neighboring colleges. Public library memberships are free.

The **Boston Public Library** has branches in every neighborhood in Boston, and shares borrowing privileges with the communities of Chelsea and Malden through the **Metro Boston Library Network**. If you are a member of this network, you can use any of the Boston neighborhood branches, the libraries in the Boston public school system, the State Transportation Library, and the public libraries in Chelsea and Malden. The **Minuteman Library Network** links many major communities surrounding Boston and to the west, including Cambridge, Somerville, Wellesley, Arlington, Concord, Weston, Needham, Dedham, Medford, Brookline, Watertown, Waltham, Newton, Belmont, a few colleges, and more. To see the complete listing of linked communities and libraries, visit www.mln.lib.ma.us. Further out from the city are the **North of Boston Library Exchange**, www.noblenet.org, which links several north shore communities such as Peabody, Lynnfield, Beverly, Swampscott, Salem, Gloucester, and Marblehead; the **Merrimack Valley Library Consortium**, www.mvlc.org, which links the libraries further north, closer to the New Hampshire border like Burlington, Andover, Newburyport, Lawrence, and Haverhill; and the **Old Colony Library Network**, www.ocln.org, which links south shore communities like Hingham, Hull, Milton, Plymouth, Sharon, and Cohasset.

You will find exact library locations listed in the **Neighborhood Profiles** in this book, check there for the library closest to you. If you live further out from the city, you can check with the **Massachusetts Library Information Network**, www.mlin.org, 617-267-9400 or 800-952-7403, or visit the **Old Colony Library Network** web site, which lists links to the major library network systems throughout the state: www.ocln.org/ocln_libraries.html.

Boston's main library is at 700 Boylston Street, 617-536-5400, www.bpl.org. To get a library card, the Boston library system requires proof of Massachusetts residence and some sort of ID with your signature on it (it doesn't have to be a photo ID). Most cities require one proof of residence in the form of a driver's license, check book, bill, etc., which show both your name and an address in that town. Others require two forms of identification showing your name and local address, usually one of which is a photo ID. Call your local library or check their web site for membership requirements. (See **Literary Life** in the **Cultural Life** chapter for more on area libraries.)

FINDING A HEALTH CARE PROVIDER

Finding a new doctor is certainly not one of the most enjoyable parts of moving to a new city. However, finding yourself in a health emergency without an established relationship with a physician can be unpleasant. Boston has some of the most well-renowned medical institutions in the world. People come from all over to see specialists at Mass General or the Dana Farber Cancer Institute, and many hospitals are affiliated with medical schools: the Boston Medical Center recently merged with BU, and Harvard is connected to Boston's Longwood medical campus (Dana Farber, Children's Hospital, Beth Israel/Deaconess, Brigham and Women's, the Joslin Diabetes Center). So where to begin? Many find a health care professional, be it a dentist, general internist, or psychologist, by asking a friend or associate for a recommendation. Those with health insurance or coverage through an HMO or PPO may have a smaller pool of doctors, dentists, etc., from which to choose. For more on Massachusetts HMOs, go to the Department of Insurance web site, www.state.ma.us/doi. Those without insurance do not necessarily have to go without some kind of coverage. The **Massachusetts League of Community Health Centers** (**CHS**), 100 Boylston Street, Boston, 617-426-2225, massleague.org, can put you in touch with a community health center in your neighborhood. Community Health Centers provide comprehensive healthcare, such as primary care, OB/GYN, dermatology, and elder care, to the under-served (i.e., low-income, underinsured, high-risk patients). Ten percent of Bay State residents go to CHCs; there's a community health center in the North End, for example, that's staffed with Mass General doctors and is utilized by many in the neighborhood. Massachusetts Department of Health's **Division of**

Maternal, Child, and Family Health provides family planning services, including STD testing, birth control, pap smears, and pregnancy testing, to low-income, uninsured Massachusetts residents and all residents under the age of 20. Contact them for information or the family planning program site closest to you at 617-624-6018 or www.state.ma.us/dph.

In the event that you find yourself or a loved one in the position of needing emergency, inpatient psychiatric care, Boston is also the home to **McLean Hospital**, one of the most prestigious psychiatric hospitals in the world. Located on a hilly campus outside of the city at 115 Mill Street in Belmont, 617-855-2000, www.mcleanhospital.org, it is affiliated with Harvard University and Mass General. Another mental health resource is the **Massachusetts Department of Mental Health**, 25 Staniford Street, Boston, 617-626-8000, www.state.ma.us/dmh.

Medical resources include the following:

- **American Board of Medical Specialties Certification Verification**, 866-ASK-ABMS, www.abms.org; check to see if your specialist is certified by the national board.
- **Massachusetts Board of Registration in Medicine**, www.docboard.org/ma; get the full skinny on your physician's profile, including where he went to school, where he did his residency, and malpractice claims.
- **Division of Professional Licensure**, 617-727-3074, www.state.ma.us/reg; where you can verify licenses to practice medicine, including dentistry therapy, nursing, speech therapy, physical therapy, podiatry, nutrition, as well as any recent disciplinary actions.
- **Massachusetts Dental Society**, 508-480-9797, www.massdental.org/public/findadentist; find a dentist who is a member of this professional association.
- **Massachusetts Department of Public Health**, 250 Washington Street, Boston, 617-624-6000, www.state.ma.us/dph; a good basic starting point for all health issues in the state.
- **HealthGrades**, www.healthgrades.com, 303-716-0041; purchase a complete report on your physician or facility for $10.
- Should you run into problems with your health care provider, start with the DPH's **Office of Patient Protection**. Call 800-436-7757 or visit www.state.ma.us/dph/opp.

PETS

Unfortunately, like many big cities, Boston isn't especially dog-friendly. It's difficult to find a rental apartment where you can have a dog, and there are few parks where dogs are welcome or that offer off-leash dog runs. That said, Boston Animal Control claims there are approximately 65,000 dogs in the city. That's 10% of the city's human population! It will require a little extra effort to find a suitable place to live that includes a nearby green space. (See below for a listing of off-leash areas.) As anywhere, cat lovers are apt to have more luck finding an apartment.

A helpful guide to living in Boston with a dog is *The Dog Lovers Companion to Boston* by Joanna Downey and Christian J. Lau. You can also check www.dogfriendly.com, which is a national listing of pet-friendly places, or www.doggeek.com, which offers tips on choosing, obtaining, and caring for a dog, as well as local information.

ADOPTING A PET

If you want a pet, you can't beat adopting from a local shelter. Pets come spayed or neutered, many have been housebroken, and the cost is reasonable. The main headquarters of the **Massachusetts Society for the Prevention of Cruelty to Animals (MSPCA)**, 617-522-7400, www.mspca.org/boston, is in Jamaica Plain at 350 South Huntington Avenue. They have adoption hours for dogs, cats, rabbits, birds, and other more exotic animals from Tuesday to Saturday. They are also the best resource for animal information, including education, tips on renting an apartment if you have a pet, and vet recommendations. Affiliated shelters are located throughout the state on the north and south shores, western Massachusetts, Cape Cod, Nantucket, and Martha's Vineyard. For more information, contact MSPCA. Area private, **no-kill shelters** include: **Quincy Animal Shelter**, 56 Broad Street, Quincy, 617-376-1349, www.quincyanimalshelter.org; **Melrose Humane Society**, 781-662-3224, http://clydesightproductions.com/MHS; and **Scituate Animal Shelter**, 781-545-8703, www.neonedge.com/shelter.

Additional pet resources include:
- **Alliance for Animals Cat Adoption Center** in Arlington at 1241 Mass Ave., 781-648-6822, www.afa.arlington.ma.us/shelter.html; specializes in cats.
- **Alliance for Animals,** Metro Action Clinic, 232 Silver Street, South Boston, 617-268-7800, www.afa.arlington.ma.us; a non-profit humane organization dedicated to solving the problem of pet overpopulation.
- **Animal Rescue League of Boston**, 10 Chandler Street, 617-426-9170, www.arlboston.org; has an adoption center open daily; affiliated adoption centers are in Dedham, East Brewster (Cape Cod), and Pembroke.
- **Boston Animal Control** (including for dog licenses), 617-635-5348, www.cityofboston.gov/animalcontrol
- **Bostonpets.net**, www.bostonpets.net
- **City of Boston Animal Shelter and Adoption Center**, 26 Mahler Road in Roslindale, 617-635-1800, www.cityofboston.gov/animalcontrol

- **Dogpark.com**, www.dogpark.com, has links to registered breeders and rescue organizations, www.dogpark.com/dassoc.html.
- **Massachusetts Ferret Friends**, 781-224-1098, www.maferrets.org
- **Massachusetts House Rabbit Society**, 781-665-9962, www.mahouserabbit.org
- **Petfinder**, www.petfinder.com; search pets at shelters around the city and country.

PET LAWS AND SERVICES

Check with **Boston Animal Control**, 1 City Hall Plaza, Room 811, Boston, 617-635-5348, www.ci.boston.ma.us/animalcontrol, for information about dog licenses, animal and rabies control, adoptions, advice, pet abuse prevention, and more. If you have **lost your pet**, contact the shelter at 617-635-1800 (they hold an animal for between seven and 10 days).

Massachusetts requires dog owners to have their dogs licensed annually; non-compliance may result in a $50 fine. To obtain your **dog license** go to Boston Animal Control, bring proof of rabies inoculation. The fee for spayed or neutered dogs is less than unfixed animals—$6 vs. $17.

Dogs are required to be leashed in public areas at all times. In the state campgrounds where pets are permitted, dogs must be leashed, supervised, and wearing proof of their rabies vaccination. *No matter where you are, you must clean up after your dog.*

VETERINARIANS AND PET EMERGENCY SERVICE

Boston boasts one of the country's top animal hospitals, the **MSPCA Angell Memorial Animal Hospital**, 350 South Huntington Avenue, Jamaica Plain, 617-522-7282, www.angell.org. Come here for 24-hour emergency services or contact them for a referral for appropriate veterinary services for your pet.

Veterinarians abound throughout the city and the suburbs; see the Yellow Pages for information. Doggeek.com also posts a list of vets throughout the state at www.doggeek.com/vets/massachusetts. Generally, the best source for information on veterinarians is through referral, so talk with new neighbors, go for a walk in the park, or call the **MSPCA**. You can also check out a veterinarian's record with the **Division of Professional Licensure**, 617-727-3074, www.state.ma.us/reg. Here are a few to get you started:

- **Boston Cat Hospital** in Kenmore Square, 665 Beacon Street, 617-266-7877, www.bostoncathospital.com, specializes in felines.
- **Fresh Pond Animal Hospital**, 15 Flanders Road, Belmont, 617-484-1555, www.fpah.com

GETTING SETTLED

- **Boston Veterinary Associates**, www.bostonvet.com, have clinics in Southie, 659 East Broadway, 617-269-0610; Eastie, 984 Saratoga Street, 617-567-0101; and Revere, 317 Broadway, 617-289-8110.
- **Brookline Animal Hospital**, 678 Brookline Avenue, Brookline, 617-277-2030, www.brooklineanimalhospital.com
- **Parkway Veterinary Hospital**, 1202 VFW Parkway, West Roxbury, 617-469-8400, www.parkwayvethospital.com

OFF-LEASH AREAS AND DOG-FRIENDLY PARKS

- **Arnold Arboretum** in JP; (leashed), expansive park
- **Back Bay Fens**, in the Fenway (leashed)
- **Belle Isle Reservation**, for dogs in Eastie
- **Boston Common**; *the* common is now home to a pilot off-leash program, but beware—the common isn't fenced, and cars are fast on bordering Charles, Beacon, Boylston, and Park streets.
- **Carson Beach** in Southie (leashed)
- **Charlesgate Dog Run** in the Back Bay; small, fenced dog park on the corner of Mass Ave. and Beacon Street
- **Comm Ave. Mall**, where all the Back Bay residents walk their dogs
- **Dorchester Park**, Tenean Beach off Morrissey Boulevard in Dorchester
- **Fort Independence**, in Southie
- **Highland Park** in Roxbury
- **Kingsley Park** in Cambridge at Huron and Fresh Pond Parkway
- **Larz Anderson Park** in Brookline; strictly on-leash
- **Minuteman Dog Park** in the Back Bay at the corner of Mass Ave. and Storrow Drive
- **Washington Street Park** in the South End, intersection of Washington and Berkeley streets

FURTHER AFIELD

- **Acton Arboretum** in Acton; open during daylight hours
- **Bear Cove Park** in Weymouth; open during daylight hours
- **Blue Hills Reservation** is a huge state park in Milton (leashed)
- **Borderland Park**, south of the city in Easton (leashed)
- **Breakheart Reservation**, Lynn Fells Parkway in Lynn
- **Callahan State Park** on Millwood Road in Framingham
- **D.W. Fields Park**, south of the city in Brockton (leashed)
- **Foss Farm in Carlisle** on Bedford Road/Route 225; open during daylight hours
- **Groton Place and Sabine Woods**, south side of Route 225 in Groton

- **Greak Brook Farm** in Carlisle, on North Road; open during daylight hours
- **Middlesex Fells Reservation** offers 2,000 dog-friendly acres of forest in Stoneham, Medford, Malden, Melrose, and Winchester.
- **Newburyport Beach**, on the North Shore in Newburyport
- **Stodders Neck**, Route 3A in Hingham, offers a doggy-friendly, 3/4-mile looped trail along the water

SAFETY AND CRIME

Like all large American cities, Boston has its share of crime. If you find yourself the victim of a crime, you should first call the police, and then check with the **Massachusetts Office for Victim Assistance (MOVA)**, 1 Ashburton Place, Suite 1101, Boston, 617-727-5200, www.state.ma.us/mova, which offers a variety resources and support services.

According to studies cited by the Massachusetts Executive Office of Public Safety, the state ranked noticeably below the national average for the entire last decade of the 20th century in all crime categories except violent crimes and aggravated assault. Violent crimes finally dipped below the national average in the year 2000, but continued to be above the national average for aggravated assault—14th highest among all the states. The other troubling crime statistic here is vehicle theft; according to the Disaster Center (www.disastercenter.com) Massachusetts ranked 16th in the nation in 2000. If you are interested in seeing more detailed crime statistics, you can visit the **US Department of Justice's Bureau of Justice Statistics** web site, www.ojp.usdoj.gov/bjs. For more safety resources in the state of Massachusetts, go to www.state.ma.us and click on the "Safety" option on the "Resident" page.

The state's Public Safety Office received a federal grant to help curtail auto theft through Vehicle Identification Number (VIN) etching and night decals. Etching your VIN into the windows is cheap, quick, may reduce your auto insurance rate by 15%, and makes your car far less appealing to thieves who would have to replace the windows. "Watch Your Car" night decals are good for residents who do not normally drive during the wee hours of the morning; cars out and about between 1 a.m. and 5 a.m. that have a night decal should alert police that something may be amiss.

Those with concerns about domestic abuse should first contact the **Massachusetts Department of Transitional Assistance**, which runs a **Domestic Violence Unit**, www.state.ma.us/dta/assist/violence. Their mission is to help battered women and children live self-sufficient, violence-free lives. They have safety assessment specialists who can put you in touch with appropriate resources and agencies. MOVA also has a similar list of resources on their web site (see above).

The Massachusetts Department of Public Health (DPH) takes care of the state's **Sexual Assault Prevention and Survivor Services** office, and provides a list of rape crisis centers. They are located at 250 Washington Street, Boston. Go to www.state.ma.us/dph/sapss for more information. To contact the main **Boston Area Rape Crisis Center**, 99 Bishop Allen Drive, Cambridge, call 617-492-RAPE or visit www.barcc.org. If you need information from the state's **Sex Offender Registry Board** about victim services, resources, safety tips, etc., go to their web site at www.state.ma.us/sorb, or call them at 978-740-6400 or 800-93MEGAN.

In terms of what you can do to protect your home and be safe in your community, Massachusetts has been running the **Safe Neighborhood Initiative** (SNI), put together by the State Attorney General, the Boston Police Department, the City of Boston, and other offices, in 1993. SNI is a forum where community residents voice their concerns and advise their local police, neighborhood prosecutors, and city government about the crime and safety issues that confront them. The goal of the SNI program is to present coordinated law enforcement, revitalize neighborhoods, and prevent crime by intervening and treating high-risk offenders. If you'd like more information about SNI, or would like to initiate an SNI in your neighborhood, visit www.ago.state.ma.us and click on "Criminal Enforcement" or call 617-727-2200. Additionally, the **Massachusetts Neighborhood Crime Watch Commission**, 1 Congress Street, 10th Floor, Boston, 888-80-WATCH, www.state.ma.us/dhcd/components/crimewatch, has been around since 1992, and supervises all the neighborhood crime watches. Contact the commission if you'd like to be part of a neighborhood, waterfront, park, campus, mall, or transit watch system or a member of community crime busters.

There are a few common sense things about living in any city that newcomers should keep in mind to keep safe:
- Trust your intuition when something doesn't feel right.
- When outside, keep your eyes and ears open; always remain alert and aware of your surroundings.
- Never let a stranger get in your car, and don't get in a car with a stranger. Studies show that once you are in a vehicle with a would-be criminal, your chances of survival decrease dramatically.
- Don't move into a neighborhood where you don't feel comfortable. Before you take an apartment, walk around the neighborhood at different times of the day to see what the area is like.
- Protect your apartment or home from potential intruders. For example, in a ground floor or garden apartment, you should probably have sturdy bars on your windows. Check your door for a deadbolt. If it doesn't have one, request that your landlord install one for you. Always err on the side of caution when assessing your risk.

- On public transportation, try to sit with other people. On a bus, sit up front near the driver.
- Items like pepper spray and mace aren't legal in Massachusetts, no matter how small the canister. However, you can carry them with a concealed weapons permit, which you must get from the police. For information on carrying mace or pepper spray, visit www.cityofboston.gov/police/mace.asp.
- Strap purses and bags across your chest so they're not so easy to steal.
- Don't leave bags on the passenger seat of your car when you're driving; they're easy for someone to reach in and grab. Lock your car when you park it, and put any items in the trunk so as not to tempt thieves. Also, visible auto theft deterrent items, such as a steering wheel lock, make a car less tempting.
- Resist the temptation to travel alone or at night through an unfamiliar neighborhood.
- Report crime by calling 911. For non-emergency police questions, call 617-343-4200; they can tell you the location of your nearest District or Area police headquarters.

HELPFUL SERVICES

SETTING UP YOUR HOME MAY REQUIRE HIRING OUT FOR A FEW services. Some of the services you'll find in this chapter should make your life easier, like house cleaning and pest control. Other sections, such as **Services for People with Disabilities** and **Gay and Lesbian Life**, detail services relevant to specific communities.

DOMESTIC SERVICES

Sometimes a little help goes a long way, particularly around the house. Some of the following services are luxuries and some of them are must-haves, but regardless, they should make adjusting to life in your new home easier.

DIAPER SERVICES

Diaper services, while on the decline, do still exist in the area:
- **Baby's Laundry and Diaper Service**, 135 Boston Street, Salem, 978-744-4162
- **Changing Habits Diaper Service**, 800-286-6622, www.thediaperlady.net
- **Dede's Dide's Diaper Service**, Hillcrest Avenue, Peabody, 978-532-5901

DRY CLEANING DELIVERY

Dry cleaners aren't too difficult to find, however, if you prefer a pick-up and delivery service the list is smaller. Here are a few:
- **BostonDryClean.com**, 617-338-9191, www.bostondryclean.com

- **Cleaner by Nature**, environmentally-conscience cleaners with locations in Ashland, Boston, Belmont, Brookline, and Framingham. Check the Yellow Pages for the nearest location.
- **Charlesbank Cleaners**: 269 Western Avenue, Allston, 617-547-7868; 17 Myrtle Street, Beacon Hill, 617-523-6860; 151 Putnam Avenue, Cambridge, 617-547-7866; 318 Walnut Street, Newton, 617-527-6700
- **Ecoluxe**; two locations in Brookline: 1018 Beacon Street, 617-232-2658; 1 Harvard Street, 617-566-4407; environmentally-friendly cleaner that delivers to Newton, Wellesley, Cambridge, Weston, and parts of Boston.
- **Joseph's Dry Cleaners**, 24 Norwood Street, Everett, 617-387-9225
- **The Missing Sock**, 1846-A Comm Ave., Brighton, 617-566-4777
- **Pressed 4 Time**, serving Newton, Waltham, Belmont, Lexington, Watertown, Weston, and Wellesley, 781-899-1788
- **Sarni Cleaners of Greater Boston**, 617-389-7511; locations throughout Boston.
- **Stavros Cleaners**, 1292 Beacon Street, Brookline, 617-277-1215
- **Zoots Dry Cleaning** locations around the metro area including Cambridge, Quincy, and Newton. Check the Yellow Pages.

HOUSE CLEANING SERVICES

In addition to regular house cleaning, most services also offer special one-day cleaning arrangements for moving days (either in or out) or for fire restoration. Look in the Yellow Pages under "House Cleaning Service" for a complete list, or ask around for a recommendation. For added security, make sure the company is bonded and insured.
- **Boston Cleaning**, Boston, 617-539-9099
- **Chapman Home Cleaning Services**, 158R Chestnut Hill Avenue, Brighton, 617-782-4979 or 800-378-0612, www.chapmancleaning.com
- **Cleo's Cleaners**, 617-561-9897
- **Connie's Cleaning Service**, Brookline, Medford, Cambridge, and Woburn, 781-306-0477, www.commercialcleanings.com
- **MaidPro**, Boston, 617-742-8080, www.maidpro.com
- **The Maids**, Brookline, 617-969-1525
- **Merry Maids**; locations throughout the metro area, including Waltham, Dorchester, West Roxbury, and Brighton. Call 800-891-1598, or go online to www.merrymaids.com for the nearest location.
- **Trust Cleaning Services**, throughout the greater Boston area, 877-547-4800, www.cleaningwell.com

PEST CONTROL

Depending on where you live, you might experience a variety of pest problems—from cockroaches in apartments above restaurants in the North End to rats and mice, particularly in the Back Bay, the Fenway, and Beacon Hill. Further out from the city, the critters can be bigger—raccoons in the chimney, skunks tearing up your yard and going after neighborhood pets, and bats in your attic. Ants, termites, and wasps can also be an issue.

For pest infestations, check the Yellow Pages under "Pest Control Services" or try one of these:

- **Atlantic Pest Control**, greater Boston area, 866-989-0731, www.ybusa.com
- **Bay State Wildlife Management**, 866-954-5433, www.baystatewildlife.com
- **Brothers Pest Control**, 781-329-4600 or 781-961-2600, www.brospest.baweb.com
- **City Wildlife Control**, 617-547-3553, 24-hour emergency service
- **Environmental Health Services**, 263 Washington Street, Dedham, 781-326-5646, www.pest-mgmt.com
- **John D. Lyon Co.**, 1770 Mass Ave., Cambridge, 617-926-6200
- **NW Pest Control**, 877-522-7123, www.nwpestcontrol.com; several locations around greater Boston
- **Pestex**, Newtonville, 800-371-8577
- **Poulos & Sons**, 877-533-7378
- **Security Pest Elimination**, 800-362-2687; several locations around greater Boston
- **Target Pest Co.**, 800-649-9602; Medford, Somerville, and Wakefield
- **Terminix**, Boston and Newton, 800-377-3787, www.terminix.com

MAIL DELIVERY AND SHIPPING

Boston's main postal hub is the **Fort Point Channel Station** at 25 Dorchester Avenue near South Station. They are open for customers Monday-Friday 6 a.m. to midnight, Saturday 8 a.m. to 7 p.m., and Sunday noon to 7 p.m. Contact them at 617-654-5302.

There are many smaller branch post offices throughout Boston, including Allston, the Back Bay, Beacon Hill, the North End, the South End, Southie, Dorchester, downtown, JP, and West Roxbury. For more information on your local postal annex, check the resources listed after the neighborhood profiles at the beginning of this book. You can also ask about postal rates, services, zip codes, or make consumer complaints by calling 800-ASK-USPS (800-275-8777), or go to www.usps.com.

JUNK MAIL

Junk mail will surely follow you to your new locale. In order to curtail this kind of unwanted mail we suggest you send a written note, including name and address, asking to be purged from the **Direct Marketing Association's** list (Direct Marketing Association's Mail Preference Service, Box 643, Carmel, NY 10512). Some catalogue companies will need to be contacted directly with a purge request. For **junk e-mail**, you may also go to their web site, www.dmaconsumers.org/opoutform, and request an opt-out service for your e-mail address. The service will accept three non-business e-mail addresses at a time. This should reduce the amount of e-mail you receive from national e-mail lists. Another option is to call the "opt-out" line at 888-567-8688, and request that the main credit bureaus not release your name and address to interested marketing companies. (**Curb phone solicitations** by going to the government's "do not call registry," www.donotcall.gov, and registering your phone number, or call 888-382-1222, TTY 866-290-4236.)

The Massachusetts Office of Consumer Affairs and Business Regulation offers a few more tips on decreasing your junk mail flow on their web site, www.state.ma.us/consumer/Pubs/stopjunk.htm. You can also check the *JunkBusters Guide to Reducing Junk Mail* at www.junkbusters.com.

MAIL RECEIVING SERVICES

If you're in between addresses but need a place to receive mail, you can rent a box at the post office. Most local branch post offices have boxes, but if they're full, you can call the main Fort Point Channel station to request a box, 617-654-5302, or try a private service. Here are a few:

- **Bette James & Associates**, 727 Mass Ave., Cambridge, 617-661-2622, www.bettejames.com
- **Delta Letter Drop**, 58 Batterymarch Street, Boston, 617-423-3543
- **HQ Global Workplaces**, has locations throughout Boston, Cambridge, and Waltham. Check the Yellow Pages or visit www.hq.com, for the nearest location.
- **UPS Stores** (formerly **Mail Boxes, Etc.**), offers mail box rentals and shipping services. Check the Yellow Pages or go to www.theupsstore.com for details.

SHIPPING SERVICES

- **Boston Craters & Freighters**, 254 Bodwell Street, Unit B, Avon, 800-866-278-3787, www.cratersandfreighters.com; for especially heavy or bulky items.

HELPFUL SERVICES

- **DHL Airborne Express**, 800-AIRBORNE (800-247-2676), www.airborne.com
- **DHL Worldwide Express**, 800-CALL-DHL (800-225-5345), www.dhl-usa.com
- **FedEx**, 800-GO-FEDEX (800-463-3339), www.fedex.com/us/
- **UPS**, 800-PICK-UPS (800-742-5877), www.ups.com
- **US Postal Service Express Mail**, 800-ASK-USPS (800-275-8777), www.usps.com

AUTOMOBILE REPAIR

Should your vehicle need to be towed, there are many towing companies listed in the Yellow Pages. However, many find it practical to join an auto club. The local branch of the American Automobile Association is **AAA Southern New England**, and the standard yearly membership fee of $45 covers roadside assistance, car jumps, towing, free traveler's cheques, personalized route maps, passport photos, discounts on travel services (like car rentals and train tickets), insurance services, and more. For membership details, contact them at www.aaa.com or 800-JOIN-AAA; for roadside assistance (members only) dial 800-AAA-HELP.

Many of us feel at a loss when it comes time to take the car to the shop. To find an auto mechanic, check with friends, acquaintances, or co-workers for a reputable shop, try the "finding a mechanic" link on the Car Talk web site (see below), or try your chances in the Yellow Pages. You can always check with the **Better Business Bureau**, 508-652-4800, www.bosbbb.org, to find out if any complaints have been filed against an auto repair shop. Dealers are usually reliable and often stock the parts necessary to fix your car, but can be more expensive than a small independent shop. When all else fails, try calling **Car Talk**, 888-CAR-TALK, the popular NPR radio show where the entertaining Click and Clack brothers (Boston locals) try to diagnose your car's problems from your descriptions over the phone and then offer advice. Tune in Saturdays at 11 a.m. for the live show or listen to repeats on Saturday and Sunday nights at 6 p.m. on 90.9 FM, WBUR, http://cartalk.cars.com.

For information about the Massachusetts Lemon Laws, refer to **Consumer Protection—Automobiles** in the **Getting Settled** chapter.

CONSUMER PROTECTION—RIP-OFF RECOURSE

If you find yourself in the unfortunate situation of having been swindled or ripped off, there may be something you can do about it. A number of private organizations in Massachusetts provide information about business practices and consumer issues, and some will assist you in resolving your complaints. No matter what, it's always a good idea to check up on any service before you enter into an agreement. But if you've discussed terms with the proprietor, read the fine print, and still find yourself with a cubic zirconia when you were promised a diamond, there are some places you can turn for help. First go to www.state.ma.us (click on "Consumer" under "Home and Health") or check with the following:

- **Better Business Bureau**, 235 West Central Street, Suite 1, Natick, 508-652-4800, www.bosbbb.org; offers general information of products and services, reliability reports and background information on local businesses and organizations, and consumer guidance.
- *Citizens' Guide to Massachusetts State Services*, 617-727-2834, is a state publication that provides information on state matters of business/economy, children, consumer, education, arts, employment, environment, energy, health, housing, community development, licenses/paperwork, law enforcement, recreation, transportation, utilities, and more.
- **Consumer Product Safety Commission**, 10 Causeway Street, Room 469, Boston, 617-565-7730, www.cpsc.gov
- **Division of Registration Investigation Unit**, 100 Cambridge Street, 15th Floor, Boston, 617-727-7406
- **Federal Trade Commission**, Northeast Region, FTC, 1 Bowling Green, New York, NY 10004; for consumer complaints dial 877-FTC-HELP or go to www.ftc.gov. Responsible for working against fraudulent, unfair business practices. They also publish the *Consumer's Resource Handbook* for tips on finding the right services. For a free copy, write to Consumer Information Center, Pueblo, CO 81009.
- **Federal Citizen Information Center**, 800-FED-INFO, www.firstgov.gov; information for consumers from the federal government. Call with questions about job or wage discrimination.
- **Massachusetts Attorney General's Office**, two offices: 1 Ashburton Pace, Boston, and 200 Portland Street, Boston; 617-727-2200; www.ago.state.ma.us; protects the public's interest in the areas of healthcare, environment, consumer issues, civil rights, the elderly, children, the workplace, charity, high-tech, and criminal enforcement. Has several hotlines: consumer hotline, 617-727-8400; elder hotline, 888-AG-ELDER; fair labor, 617-727-3465; utilities, 888-514-6277; insurance fraud tip-line, 617-727-2200.
- **Massachusetts Consumers' Coalition**, 831 Mass Ave., Cambridge 02139, 617-349-6152, www.massconsumers.org; publishes a guide called "Car Smart," which covers purchasing a vehicle and consumer rights; insurance, 888-830-6277.
- **Massachusetts Office of Consumer Affairs and Business Regulation**, 10 Park Plaza, Suite 5170, Boston, 617-973-8700,

www.state.ma.us/consumer; consumer hotline: 617-973-8787 or 888-283-3757; offers assistance with automobiles, banking, cable TV and telecommunications, credit and debt, energy and fuel, fitness, health and medical care, home buying and construction, identity theft, insurance, investing, jewelry, junk mail, licensing, consumer groups, privacy, shopping issues, small claims court, tenant and landlord relations, travel, and worker's comp.
- **MassPIRG (Massachusetts Public Interest Research Group)**, 29 Temple Place, Boston, 617-292-4800, www.masspirg.org; a non-profit advocacy and research organization committed to protecting consumers and the environment. Provides information and referral on a variety of consumer and environmental issues. Reports are available for $5 each.

MEDIA SPONSORED CALL FOR ACTION PROGRAMS

Sometimes it can't hurt to have the power of the press behind you. The following are local consumer advocacy programs operated by Boston area TV and radio stations:
- **Help Me Hank**, WHDH (Channel 7) local reporter uses the local news to fight consumer battles for viewers in need. Contact Help Me Hank at helpmehank@whdh.com.
- **WBZ Call for Action**, 1170 Soldiers Field Road, Allston, 617-787-7070, http://wbz1030.com, telephone information and referral for individuals with consumer problems. Sponsored by WBZ-AM 1030 radio.

LEGAL MEDIATION/REFERRAL PROGRAMS

If you need legal advice or referrals, try one of the following:
- **Massachusetts Bar Association**, 20 West Street, Boston, 617-338-0500, www.massbar.org; Tel-Law line: 617-542-9069, 24-hour information tape on legal issues.
- **National Consumer Law Center**, 77 Summer Street, 10th Floor, Boston, 617-542-8010, www.consumerlaw.org
- For the complete listing of **state information for the elderly**, go to www.state.ma.us and click on "Seniors" under "Home and Health." Or contact AgeInfo: 800-AGE-INFO (800-243-4636), www.800ageinfo.com.

SMALL CLAIMS COURTS

For legal disputes of less than $2,000 that you are unable or unwilling to settle through negotiation or mediation, you can always take it to small claims court. The **Massachusetts Office of Consumer Affairs and**

Business Regulation, 10 Park Plaza, Suite 5170, Boston, 617-973-8787, www.state.ma.us/consumer/Pubs/smclaim, offers information and guidance regarding the ins and outs of taking a case to small claims court.

The following is a list of local small claims courts in the Boston metro area:

BOSTON
- **East Boston District Court** (also covers **Winthrop**), 37 Meridien Street, 617-569-7550
- **Municipal Court of the City of Boston** (all of **Suffolk County**), Old Court House, 55 Pemberton Square, Boston, 617-725-8000
- **Municipal Court of Brighton District** (also covers **Allston**), 52 Academy Hill Road, Brighton, 617-782-6521
- **Municipal Court of Charlestown District**, 3 City Square, Charlestown, 617-242-5400
- **Municipal Court of Dorchester District** (also covers **Mattapan**), 510 Washington Street, Dorchester, 617-288-9500
- **Municipal Court of the West Roxbury District** (also covers **Hyde Park**, **JP**, **Readville**, and **Rozzie**), 445 Arborway, JP, 617-971-1200
- **Roxbury District Court**, 85 Warren Street, Roxbury, 617-427-7000
- **Trial Court of the Commonwealth-District Court Department South Boston Division**, 535 East Broadway, Southie, 617-268-9292

SUFFOLK COUNTY
- **District Court of Chelsea** (also covers **Revere**), Williams Street, Chelsea, 617-252-0960

NORFOLK COUNTY
- **Brookline Municipal Court**, 260 Washington Street, Brookline, 617-232-4660

MIDDLESEX COUNTY
- **District Court of Newton**, 1309 Washington Street, West Newton, 617-244-3600
- **District Court of Somerville** (also covers **Medford**), 175 Fellsway, Somerville, 617-666-8000
- **First District Court of Eastern Middlesex** (covers **Everett**, **Malden**, **Melrose**, **Wakefield**), 89 Summer Street, Malden, 617-322-7500
- **Second District Court of Eastern Middlesex** (covers **Waltham**, **Watertown**, **Weston**), 38 Linden Street, Waltham, 781-894-4500
- **Third District Court of Eastern Middlesex** (covers **Arlington**, **Belmont**, **Cambridge**), 40 Thorndike Street, Cambridge, 617-494-4315

SERVICES FOR PEOPLE WITH DISABILITIES

Since the passage of the federal Americans with Disabilities Act in 1990, Boston has made great strides to serve the needs of disabled residents and visitors. Curbs have been rebuilt for easy wheelchair accessibility, and most public buildings have special disabled-friendly entrances. There is a well-coordinated effort within the public and private sector that works to meet the needs of the disabled here. Perhaps most notably, Boston has a substantial blind population; its combined small size, walkability, and good T service make it particularly popular with such residents.

Following are services, organizations, and resources to help make life easier for new Bostonians with special needs.

GETTING AROUND

- **The RIDE** is an individual, wheelchair-accessible para-transit program operated by the **MBTA** and offered to all Massachusetts residents who can't use regular trains, subways, or buses. RIDE passes are sold in booklets: 8 tickets for $12, 16 tickets for $24, or 32 tickets for $48. You must apply to become a registered RIDE user, which you can do through the T's web site or by contacting The RIDE, 10 Park Plaza, Room 4730, Boston 02116, 617-222-5123, 800-533-6282, TTY 617-222-5415, www.mbta.com. Once you're a registered user, you can purchase RIDE tickets over the counter at the Orange Line Back Bay Station.
- **Bus Service**: bus lines with wheelchair access are marked on maps and schedules. There are about 50 routes that are 100% handicap-accessible, the remaining are about 80% handicap accessible. But even if a route isn't fully accessible, checking in with the Call Ahead program at 800-LIFT-BUS, TTY 617-222-5854, guarantees that the driver will be aware of a special needs case. For more information, call customer service/travel information 617-222-3200, TTY 617-222-5146, or go to www.mbta.com.
- **Subway and Commuter Rail**: about half of the MBTA's subway and commuter rail stations are handicap-accessible with elevators and car-level platforms. To see if the station you want to use is one of them, visit www.mbta.com. To check if elevators are in working order in MBTA accessible stations, call the **MBTA Elevator Update line** at 617-222-2828, TTY 617-222-5854.
- **Service animals** are allowed on MTBA systems at all times, provided they are wearing their work gear (harness, etc.) and are under control.
- **The MBTA's Senior Pass Program and Access Pass Program** offers reduced fare passes to persons 65 years old or older, or to those

with disabilities. Applications available at MBTA Back Bay Station, 145 Dartmouth Street, Boston 02116-5162, or call 617-222-5438, TTY 617-222-5854.
- **Disability Plates, Placards, and Disability Veteran Plates** are issued to Massachusetts residents on a temporary or permanent basis. An application, available through the Medical Affairs Branch of the Registry of Motor Vehicles, has to be filled out by a physician before it's submitted for approval at a full service RMV branch office or sent through the mail to P.O. Box 199100, Boston 02119, 617-351-9222. For more information on plate prices, eligibility requirements, etc., or to download applications, visit www.mass.gov/rmv, or call 617-351-4500, TTY 617-536-7534.
- **Taxis**: many Boston taxi companies have accessible cabs. **Veterans Taxi** specializes in accessible transportation. Check the Yellow Pages, or call 617-527-0300 for their downtown Boston location.
- **Water transit and local bus carriers**: for non-MBTA transit services around the region, such as ferry service and regional bus lines, visit www.commute.com/disabilities.html.

COMMUNICATION

Verizon offers a range of equipment for people in Massachusetts who are blind, deaf, hard of hearing, vision- or speech-impaired and mobility-impaired. Services include amplified phones, big-button or memory-button phones, TeleTYpewriters (TTY), and cordless and speakerphones. Massachusetts residents who are Verizon customers with state-certified cognitive, hearing, motion, speech, or vision impairments may qualify for free or reduced-rate equipment. Call the Verizon Center for Customers with Disabilities at 800-974-6006 or e-mail vccd@verizon.com for an application.

Massachusetts Relay is an operator service that connects TTY with voice service and vice versa. Voice service is 800-439-0183. TTY service is 800-439-2370.

HOUSING

- **Attorney General's Guide to Tenant's Rights**, www.state.ma.us/Pubs/tenants
- **Boston Center for Independent Living**, 95 Berkeley Street, Suite 206, Boston 02116, 617-338-6665, TTY 617-338-6662; www.bostoncil.org
- **Citizens' Housing and Planning Association**, 800-466-3111, 617-742-0820, www.chapa.org; keeps track of housing and vacancy information.

- **Housing Court Department**, Edward W. Brooke Courthouse, 24 New Chardon Street, Boston 02114, 617-788-8483, www.state.ma.us/courts; the hub of legal jurisdiction regarding housing discrepancies.
- **Mass Access**, 617-742-0820, 800-466-3111, http://massaccesshousingregistry.org; an accessible-housing registry.
- **Massachusetts Architectural Access Board**, 1 Ashburton Place, Room 1310, Boston 02108, 617-727-0660 or 800-828-7222 (voice and TTY), www.state.ma.us/aab; a regulatory agency in place to make sure public buildings are handicapped accessible.
- **Massachusetts Department of Housing and Community Development**, 1 Congress Street, 10th floor, Boston 02114, www.state.ma.us/dhcd; the center for state housing information, includes a program book for tenant rules in state-aided housing covering handicap housing.
- **Massachusetts Office on Disability**, 617-727-7440 or 800-322-2020 (voice and TTY), www.state.ma.us/mod/comfunds; offers information on disability access and home modification funding, as well as service systems, and disability laws regarding housing.
- **Massachusetts Rehabilitation Council's Home Modification Loan Program**, 617-204-3636, www.state.ma.us/mrc/agency/homemods; offers loans for home modifications.
- **Massachusetts Rehabilitation Commission Adult Supported Living Program**, 27-43 Wormwood Street, Boston 02210, 617-204-3628, TTY 617-204-3815, www.state.ma.us/mrc/il/supportedliving; independent living support for young adults with physical disabilities.
- **Special Needs Housing/Supported Living** is available through the **Massachusetts Department of Mental Health**, 617-626-8000, www.state.ma.us/dmh, and the **Massachusetts Department of Mental Retardation**, 617-727-5608, www.dmr.state.ma.us.

ADDITIONAL RESOURCES

Massachusetts provides a variety of public and private services for physically or mentally challenged residents. Following is a list of **governmental and private agencies**:
- **Association of Late Deafened Adults**, www.alda.org
- **Boston Center for Independent Living**, 95 Berkeley Street, Suite 206, Boston 02116, 617-338-6665, TTY 617-338-6662, www.bostoncil.org
- **Braille and Talking Book Library at the Perkins School for the Blind**, 175 North Beacon Street, Watertown, 617-972-7240, www.perkins.org

- **Cambridge Commission for Persons with Disabilities**, 51 Inman Street, Cambridge, 617-349-4692, TTY 617-492-0235, www.ci.cambridge.ma.us/~DHSP/ccpd
- **Governor's Commission on Mental Retardation**, 1 Ashburton Place, Room 805, Boston 02108, 617-727-0517, www.state.ma.us/gcmr
- **Disabled Persons Protection Commission**, 50 Ross Way, Quincy 02169, 617-727-6465, 800-426-9009 (voice/TTY hotline), www.state.ma.us/dppc; protects disabled individuals from caregiver abuse through public awareness, investigation, oversight, and prevention activities.
- **Guide Dog Users of Massachusetts**, 617-926-9198, www.gdui.org
- **Massachusetts Commission for the Blind**, 88 Kingston Street, Boston, 02111, 617-727-5550, TTY 800-392-6556, www.state.ma.us/mcb
- **Massachusetts Commission for the Deaf and Hard of Hearing**, 150 Mount Vernon Street, Boston 02125, 617-740-1600; TTY 617-740-1700, www.state.ma.us/mcdhh; handles requests for interpreters and computer-aided real time translation (CART) reporters.
- **Massachusetts Department of Mental Retardation**, 500 Harrison Avenue, Boston 02118, 617-727-5608, TTY 617-624-7783, www.dmr.st.ma.us
- **Massachusetts Department of Public Health, Division for Special Health Needs**, 250 Washington Street, 4th Floor, Boston 02108, 617-624-5070, TTY 617-624-5992, www.state.ma.us/dph
- **Massachusetts Developmental Disabilities Council**, 174 Portland Street, 5th Floor, Boston 02114, 617-727-6374, TTY 617-727-1885, www.state.ma.ux/mddc; establishes state priorities in regards to individuals with developmental disabilities.
- **Massachusetts Law Reform Institute**, 99 Chauncy Street, 5th Floor, Boston 02111, 617-357-0700, www.mlri.org
- **Massachusetts Office on Disability**, 1 Ashburton Place, Room 1305, Boston, 02108, 617-727-7440, www.state.ma.us/mod
- **Massachusetts Rehabilitation Commission**, 27 Wormwood Street, Suite 600, Boston 02210, 800-245-6543 (voice/TTY), www.state.ma.us/mrc; provides services to individuals with disabilities to live independently and go to work.
- **Mental Health Legal Advisors Committee**, 194 Washington Street, Boston 02108, 617-338-2345, www.state.ma.us/mhlac; protects legal rights through advocacy, legal advice, referrals, etc.
- **Museums** in the Boston area have an access coordinator for the disabled: **Museum of Fine Arts**, 617-267-9300, TTY 617-267-9703, or go to www.mfa.org; **Museum of Science**, 617-723-2500, TTY 617-589-0417 or go to www.mos.org.

- **New England ADA Technical Assistance Center**, 374 Congress Street, Suite 301, Boston, 02110, 800-949-4232 (voice/TTY)
- **On a Roll** is a radio program for the disabled community hosted by Greg Smith out of Ohio. Broadcast in Massachusetts on Sundays, from 6 p.m. to 8 p.m. on WDIS, 1170 AM out of Norfolk, WMSX 1410 AM out of Taunton, and WNSH 1570 AM out of Beverly. www.ican.com/channels/on_a_roll
- **Perkins School for the Blind**, 175 North Beacon Street, Watertown 02472, 617-924-3434, www.oerkins.org
- **VSA Arts Massachusetts**, 617-350-7713, TTY 617-350-6836, www.vsamass.org; a non-profit organization that helps make it possible for people with disabilities to participate in Boston's arts and culture scene.

GAY, LESBIAN, BISEXUAL, AND TRANSGENDER (GLBT) LIFE

In 2003, the Massachusetts Supreme Court ruled that same sex couples have the legal right to marry, enabling such couples to enjoy the benefits and protections previously awarded only to heterosexual married couples. While the legal and political debate continues, the ruling is still great for Massachusetts' GLBT community. In Boston, a substantial and active GLBT population centers around the South End, with a satellite population in Jamaica Plain. In the summer, everyone who is anyone heads to Provincetown on Cape Cod. There are many organizations, including sport and social groups, support groups, businesses, and publications that exist solely for Boston's GLBT community. Here are a few:

- **BGL Advertising**, www.bgladco.com; links to Boston-area GLBT resources, including health, social, religious, athletic, and entertainment groups and venues.
- **Bisexual Resource Center**, P.O. Box 1026, Boston 02117, 617-424-9595; www.biresource.org; huge collection of local bisexual resources, including pamphlets, news, pride products, and support groups. They sell the Bisexual Resource Guide for $12.95 over their website.
- **GLBT-friendly places of worship** at www.johnrpierce.com/bostonglc.html
- **GLBT-friendly AA meetings** at www.geocities.com/dallasuapace/aa
- **GayBoston**, www.gayboston.ws; Boston guide
- **Calamus Bookstore**, 92B South Street, Boston 02111, 617-338-1931, www.calamusbooks.com
- **Fever!/Boston Lesbian Resources**, www.djdee.com/fever
- **Gay and Lesbian Helpline**, 617-267-9001 or 888-340-GLBT; toll-free national hotline providing information and support for GLBT callers.

- **Greater Boston Business Council**, P.O. Box 1059, Boston 02117, 617-236-GBBC, www.gbbc.org; the council of the GLBT business community
- **MLGBA**, P.O. Box 9072, Boston 02114, www.mlgba.org
- **We Think the World of You Bookstore**, 540 Tremont Street, Boston, 617-574-5000; GLBT bookstore in the South End

GLBT NEWSPAPERS, NEWSLETTERS, AND OTHER PUBLICATIONS

For frequently updated current events, information, and club listings from the pulse of Boston's GLBT community, try these publications:
- **Bay Windows**, 631 Tremont Street, Boston 02118, 617-266-6670, www.baywindows.com; "New England's leading gay and lesbian newspaper." Published every Thursday.
- **Boston Girl Guide**, www.bostongirlguide.com; all-female magazine of poetry and visual art.
- **In Newsweekly**, 450 Harrison Avenue, Ste. 414, Boston 02118, 617-426-8246, www.innewsweekly.com; "New England's largest gay and lesbian news & entertainment weekly." Published every Thursday.
- **Pink Pages**, 800-338-6550, www.pinkweb.com; GLBT yellow pages for New England and beyond.

GLBT SUPPORT AND ACTIVIST GROUPS

Everyone can use a little help. Fortunately, if you need support with issues pertaining to your sexual orientation, there are area organizations and groups at the ready. Here are just a few:
- **Boston Gay and Lesbian Adolescent Social Services (GLASS) Center**, 39 Mass Ave., 3rd floor, Boston, 617-266-3349, www.bostonglass.org; drop-in center for GLBT teens, located in the Back Bay.
- **Citizens Against Homophobia**, 324 Shawmut Avenue, Boston 02118, 617-576-9866, www.actwin.com/cahp; group using mass media to fight homophobia.
- **Coming Out Group**, Fenway Community Health Center, 7 Haviland Street, 617-927-6202; bimonthly support group
- **Dignity/Boston**, P.O. Box 408, Boston 02117, 617-421-1915, www.dignityboston.org; GLBT Catholic support group
- **Freedom to Marry Coalition of Massachusetts**, 325 Huntington Avenue, Suite 8, Boston 02115, 617-249-0534, www.ftmmass.org
- **Gay and Lesbian Advocates and Defenders**, 294 Washington Street, Suite 301, Boston 02108, 617-426-1350, www.glad.org

HELPFUL SERVICES

- **Greater Boston PFLAG**, P.O. Box 541619, Waltham 02154, 866-GBPFLAG or 781-891-5966, www.gbpflag.org; local chapter of the national support group for Parents and Friends of Lesbians and Gays
- **The History Project**, 46 Pleasant Street, Cambridge 02139, 617-641-8069, www.historyproject.org; researches and documents Boston's GLBT history.
- **Keshet**, 58 Glen Road #3, JP 02130, 617-524-9227, www.boston-keshet.org; support group for the local Jewish GLBT community
- **Peer Listening Line**, 800-399-PEER; trained GLBT voluneers provide assistance.
- **Speak Out**, 29 Stanhope Street, Boston 02116, 617-450-9776, www.speakoutboston.org; GLBT speakers bureau

CHILDCARE AND EDUCATION

WHEN MOVING TO A NEW AREA, ONE OF THE MOST IMPORTANT tasks parents face is finding good childcare and/or schools. The results of this search can be a deciding factor in, among other things, choosing a community in which to purchase a home. Key factors to consider when looking for a daycare center or school are affordability, convenience, safety, and, most importantly, the quality of care and instruction.

Please note: *listing in this book is merely informational and is **not** an endorsement. When entrusting your child to strangers, always err on the side of safety and caution.*

DAYCARE

In a city where many two-income families have small children, locating quality childcare can be a competitive and expensive proposition. Expecting parents should include the daycare search as part of the prenatal activities, as it can take a year or more to get your child into your preferred facility. And be prepared: full-time care in a childcare center is expensive. According to Runzheimer International, in 2004 Boston topped the charts nationwide for monthly daycare expenses, with an average monthly cost of $977.

The **Massachusetts Office of Child Care Services (OCCS)**, 1 Ashburton Place, Room 1105, Boston, 617-626-2000, www.qualitychildcare.org, can assist with your childcare search. The OCCS exists to make sure Massachusetts' children are getting quality education and childcare and is responsible for licensing and training childcare providers, running background checks, setting policy, and investigating complaints. In addition to using their database of licensed childcare providers in your area, the OCCS also offers educational pamphlets on such topics as child literacy, emergency planning, environmental safety, and child guidance.

Other **referral agencies** include the following:
- **Massachusetts Child Care Resource and Referral Agency**, 800-345-0131
- **Child Care Choices of Boston**, 105 Chauncy Street, 2nd Floor, Boston, 617-542-5437, www.bostonabcd.org/cccb, provides many services, including referral to childcare resources in Boston, Brookline, Chelsea, Winthrop, and Revere.
- **Child Care Resource Center**, 130 Bishop Allen Drive, Cambridge 02139, 617-547-9861, www.ccrcinc.org; provides information and referral on daycare programs in Cambridge, Arlington, Belmont, Brookline, Newton, Somerville, and Watertown.
- The **City of Boston** provides a listing of childcare resources at www.cityofboston.gov/bra/child_care.
- The **City of Cambridge** also has a **Childcare and Family Support Division** in its Human Services Department. Call 617-349-6254 to speak with the childcare enrollment coordinator or visit www.ci.cambridge.ma.us/~DHSP/childcare.
- The **Brookline Community Partnership for Children**, Sperber Education Center, 88 Harvard Street, Brookline, 617-264-6404, www.townofbrooklinemass.com/bcpc; offers a guide to programs and services, including childcare and pre-school referrals.
- **Community Care for Kids**, 1509 Hancock Street, Quincy, 800-637-2011 or 617-471-6473, www.semaccrr.org/ccfk; operated by Quincy Community Action Programs, connects parents with childcare providers in 20 South Shore communities.

Additional resources include *The Boston Parent's Paper*, 670 Centre Street, JP, 617-522-1515, www.parenthoodweb.com, a free publication with childcare related listings and advertisements. Look for it in stores, cafes, and public libraries. The Community Newspaper Company publishes **Parents and Kids**, www.townonline.com/parentsandkids, an online guide for Boston area parents. And don't forget the **Yellow Pages**: check under "Child Care," "Nanny Service," and "Baby Sitting Service."

If you only need **occasional daycare**, try **Bright Horizons Family Solutions**, which offers full-time care as well as backup and vacation care. They have offices all over Boston and Cambridge, and you can contact them at 617-673-8000 or www.brighthorizons.com for more information. You can also get back-up care from **Parents in a Pinch**, 617-739-KIDS, www.parentsinapinch.com; a childcare provider will come to your house, day or night.

WHAT TO LOOK FOR IN DAYCARE

One of the first credentials you will want to consider is whether or not a daycare facility is licensed by the OCCS, which proves the provider meets state sanctioned health, safety, and educational levels. The OCCS license should be visibly posted at the provider's place of business. There are several types of licensed daycare in Massachusetts:

- **Group Childcare** provides center-based care for infants, toddlers, and preschoolers, and includes part-time nursery schools and kindergartens. Head Start programs, which provide free, part-time care for children between the ages three and five to low-income families or children with disabilities, also fall under this category.
- **School Age Childcare** programs are extended day or after-school programs that provide care for children outside of school hours and during vacations.
- **Family Childcare** licenses authorize care in the provider's home for up to six children, including those of the provider.
- **Large Family Childcare** allows for up to 10 children in a home cared for by a provider and one assistant.
- **Family Childcare Plus** licenses are similar to Family Childcare licenses. They allow for care for up to six children (infants, toddlers, and preschoolers) and two school aged children.

In-home childcare provided by a nanny or sitter, childcare provided by a relative in the relative's home, or care provided by private and public preschools or after-school programs *do not require* special childcare licensing.

When investigating prospective daycare centers, visit each center at least a couple times, preferably unannounced. Consider the following:
- Is the center conscientious about how it handles check-ins and check-outs?
- Examine the kitchen, play area, bathroom, and grounds for safety and cleanliness: is disinfectant used in the kitchen and bathroom; are toys age appropriate and in good condition; are there any potential hazards lying around?
- Check for indoor and outdoor play areas.
- Watch the children at the center: do they seem happy, well-behaved, and well-supervised? Do they respond well to the attendants? Observe the caregivers with the children.
- Review the daily schedule to make sure the kids have what you think is an appropriate balance of active time and quiet time, and age-appropriate activities.
- You should also determine qualifications of the employees and ask about the staff turnover rate. Also, ask for references—names and phone numbers of other parents whose children are enrolled who you can contact.

ONLINE RESOURCES—DAYCARE

There are many parents' organizations in the greater Boston area. Consulting them online is an easy way to hook into a network of peers with knowledge about local childcare agencies, regulations, and child related events.
- **Beantown Kids**, www.beantownkids.com/btk, is an online community for parents and kids in Boston and the surrounding suburbs where you can chat with other parents about places to go with your children and get information about classes and programs.
- **Babyzone** has a Boston portal, http://boston.babyzone.com, where you can find information about local events, resources, healthcare, daycare, and parenting classes.
- **GoCityKids** has a Boston portal, www.gocitykids.com, which provides links to local services, stores, childcare, after school activities, and more.
- **MaChildCare.com**, www.machildcare.com, bills itself as "the online resource for childcare information."
- **Parents' P.L.A.C.E. (Parents Learning About Children's Education)**, 1135 Tremont Street, Boston, 617-236-7210, www.pplace.org, is the Massachusetts statewide Parent Information and Resource Center (PIRC). Offers individual referrals, workshops, bulletins, and resource library.
- **Warmlines**, 218 Walnut Street, Newtonville, 617-244-INFO, www.warmlines.org, is a parenting organization in Newton that links local families.

NANNIES

While very convenient, often the most expensive daycare option is to hire a nanny. You can expect to pay more for an experienced nanny and you will find that most nannies are not US born. While a cultural exchange with a foreign-born nanny can be wonderful, be sure she is legally authorized to work in the US and speaks enough English to respond to you and your child. If you are hiring a nanny without the help of an agency (see below), you'll want to do a background check, which can be done online. Go to any search engine and type in "employment screening." A host of companies are available to research criminal records, driving records, and credit information for you. Check local parent magazines or newspaper classifieds for listings of available nannies.

Nanny services in Boston, which will handle employment screening, include the following:
- **American Nanny Company**, P.O. Box 765, Newtonville Branch, Boston, 617-244-5154 or 800-262-8771, www.americannannycompany.com
- **Beacon Hill Nannies, Inc.**, 825 Beacon Street, Suite 19, Newton, 617-630-1577 or 800-736-3880, www.beaconhillnannies.com

- **Boston Nanny Centre, Inc.**, 135 Selwyn Road, Newton, 617-527-0114 or 800-456-2669, www.boston-nanny.com
- **Minute Women, Inc.**, 238 Bedford Street, Suite 7, Lexington, 781-862-3300 or 978-269-9171, www.minutewomeninc.com/childcare.htm
- **Nannies Nook, Inc.**, P.O. Box 220, Accord, 781-749-8097 or 800-543-4397, www.nanniesnook.com

NANNY TAXES

For those hiring a nanny directly (not using a nanny agency) there are certain taxes you will be responsible for calculating, specifically social security and Medicare, and possibly unemployment. For help with such issues, check the Nanitax web site, www.4nannytaxes.com, or call 800-626-4829. Nanitax provides household payroll and employment tax preparation services. You can also check with The Nanny Tax Company, 800-747-9826, www.nannytaxprep.com, or the IRS's household employer page, www.irs.gov/individuals/household, which discusses taxes for household employees (topic 756).

You also might want to enlist the aid of **Eisenberg Associates**, 800-777-5765, www.eisenbergassociates.com, a group that provides health insurance and other fringe benefits for nannies.

AU PAIRS

The US Information Agency oversees and approves the organizations that offer au pair service. Young women (usually between 18 and 25) provide a year of in-home childcare and light housekeeping in exchange for airfare, room and board, and a small stipend ($110 to $120 per week). The program is certainly valuable for the cultural exchange that goes on between the host family and the (usually European) au pair. The downside of the program is that it lasts only one year and the au pairs don't have the life or work experience of a career nanny. Any of the following national agencies will connect you with a local coordinator who will match up your family with the right au pair.

- **Cultural Care Au Pair**, 800-333-6056, www.culturalcare.com
- **Au Pair in America**, 800-727-AIFS, www.aupairinamerica.com
- **Au Pair USA**, 800-287-2477, www.interexchange.org

BABY-SITTING

So, you are new to town and need a night out. What to do with the little ones? If you're lucky, maybe you have family members or an already established network of friends or neighbors to help you out—either to watch the kids for you or who will give you their coveted list of trusted sitters. If not, and there are no available high school or college students (check area college employment offices) in your neighborhood, you can check with **Sittercity**, www.sittercity.com, a group that unites parents and college sitters. Or call **Parents in a Pinch**, 617-739-KIDS, www.parentsinapinch.com, for a day, evening, or overnight sitter.

CHILD SAFETY

The Massachusetts **Attorney General's Children's Protection Project**, 1 Ashburton Place, Boston, 617-727-2200, www.ago.state.ma.us, works to ensure the safety, health, and welfare of children across the state. The Board of Health provides safety pamphlets, especially with regards to lead paint in older homes and apartments.

Local hospitals host emergency training classes for infant and child CPR. You can also get a helpful safety catalogue from **The Childproofer**, 800-374-2525, www.childproofer.com, and a cornucopia of other tips at SafeKids, **www.safekids.org**, and **Boston Babyzone**, http://boston.babyzone.com. If you would like to enlist the help of a "professional childproofer," try **Safe Solutions**, 6 Blanvon Road #2, JP, 617-522-5111, www.safesolutions incofne.com.

LEAD POISONING

According to the EPA, lead is one of the most pervasive toxic substances in the country today. Lead in paint, which children ingest by eating paint chips or by inhaling paint dust, can result in serious and permanent damage to the brain, kidneys, bones, nervous system, and red blood cells. In the 1990s, the Massachusetts Department of Public Health reported that over 90% of all the cases of childhood lead poisoning in the state were a result of exposure in the home. And because Boston is such an old city, at least by American standards, a lot of its housing has lead paint. As the report says, "the older the house, the more likely it is to contain lead paint, and the higher the lead concentration is likely to be." Specifically, houses built before 1978 (the year lead was taken out of residential paint) are the primary culprits of lead poisoning in children. With almost 50% of Massachusetts' total housing stock built before 1950, it ranks second in the nation for its volume of old housing.

To protect children from lead exposure, the **State of Massachusetts Lead Law** mandates that any house built before 1978 with occupants younger than six must have its lead paint hazards removed or covered, whether it's a rental unit (cleanup would be done at the landlord's expense) or a single-family home. To determine if your house has lead paint, have your home inspected by a licensed lead inspector. Once the deleading work is finished and the house has been re-inspected, an inspector will send a letter of compliance to the homeowner.

For more information about lead poisoning and prevention in Massachusetts, contact the **Childhood Lead Paint Poisoning Prevention Program**, 56 Roland Street, Suite 100, Boston, 617-284-8400 or 800-532-9571, www.state.ma.us/dph/clppp.

SCHOOLS

Our nation's educational system has been undergoing a great deal of reform in recent years, and Boston area schools are certainly no exception to the rule. In addition to the national No Child Left Behind Act, there are statewide initiatives being put into practice in an attempt to improve the quality of education for Massachusetts' children. The biggest challenge has been the introduction of the **MCAS**, or **Massachusetts Comprehensive Assessment System** test. The MCAS (pronounced "em-kas") are standardized aptitude tests for English, math, and science (as well as history and social science in high school) that are required of fourth-, eighth-, and tenth-grade students. Many find the MCAS tests challenging, which is in line with the Massachusetts Department of Education's (DOE) goal to make Massachusetts schools among the best in the country. To find out more about area schools and where they fall in regards to the National Assessment of Educational Progress, visit http://nces.ed.gov/nationsreportcard.

All children in the Massachusetts public school system must pass the MCAS in order to graduate, including those in charter schools, educational collaboratives, students receiving publicly funded special education in private schools, those with disabilities who have an established Individual Education Program (IEP) or Section 504 instructional accommodations, and those with limited proficiency in English (assuming the student has been in the states at least three years and are ineligible for the Spanish version). Home-schooled students, however, are exempt as they are not considered part of the public school program. At this writing, high schoolers are given the MCAS first in the tenth grade so that they have ample time and multiple opportunities to retake it and pass before graduation at the end of twelfth grade.

All this said, there are many groups that oppose the MCAS, fearing it will actually increase the dropout rate, as opposed to increasing the quality of public education. For more about the MCAS, including testing schedules, sample questions, resources, and test results, visit www.doe.mass.edu/mcas or www.boston.com/mcas. If your child will have to take the MCAS and you think extra tutoring is in order, you can turn to the services of **MCAS Academy**, 63 Pine Grove Avenue, Lynn, 877-SOS-MCAS, www.mcas

academy.org, a non-profit organization that provides workbooks, workshops, and counseling to help children pass the MCAS. You can find MCAS scores for a given town or region by checking the DOE's web site, www.doe.mass.edu/mcas/results.html. You can also research school and district profiles at http://profiles.doe.mass.edu. Contact the **MCAS Parent Information Hotline** at 866-MCAS220.

More follows about how to investigate prospective schools, the public school enrollment process, listings of public schools, and information about parochial and private schools.

CHOOSING A SCHOOL

Massachusetts requires that in September all children over age six must be enrolled in a school. When choosing a school there are many factors to consider. According to an article called "Grading a School: a Parent's Guide" published in *US News & World Report* in 1999, the best schools share the following traits: challenging core curriculum, high standards and expectations, qualified, well-trained teachers, family-school partnerships, mentors, and high attendance rates. You also want to look at teacher turnover rates; how many students take advance-placement exams and how they perform; other test scores, including MCAS (in Massachusetts), SAT, and ACT; college acceptance rates; graduate/dropout rates; and class sizes. You should be able to find at least some of this information at the Massachusetts Department of Education site, which posts "report cards" for its schools. When viewing school rankings, keep in mind that, while smaller schools tend to have lower dropout rates, higher attendance rates, and fewer discipline problems, larger schools tend to have more resources, including a bigger selection of courses and extracurricular activities. And safety records can be deceptive; if a school has a low number of suspensions, expulsions, etc., it *can* mean a quiet, safe school, but it can also mean a lax principal.

When looking for a school, your best research will be firsthand. Visit with the principal and discuss the school's mission, staff motivation, staff autonomy, and teacher accomplishments. Also talk to the teachers and interview fellow parents. Find out about available technology, including computers and internet access. When visiting the principal, tour the school, looking into classrooms, the library, and bathrooms.

SCHOOL RESOURCES

A good place to start for all public school related information is the **Massachusetts Department of Education**, 350 Main Street, Malden, 781-338-3000, www.doe.mass.edu. If you have a preschool-age child, you might want to visit the Early Learning Services Department, www.doe.

mass.edu/els, 781-338-6368, which, among other things, provides a list of early childhood resource centers. Also, most cities and towns within Massachusetts have a municipal web site with a link to education (check the neighborhood profiles in this book, or visit www.state.ma.us/cc). For more information on public schools in Boston, check with **Boston Public Schools**, 26 Court Street, Boston, 617-635-9000, or go to www.bostonpublicschools.org.

Besides the Boston School Department and the Boston School Committee, there are other ways to gain information about the school choices available. One of them is **School Match**, 800-992-5323, a private company that offers ratings (for a fee) of public schools through their web site, www.schoolmatch.com. **The School Report**, www.theschoolreport.com, provides the stats on the school district of your choice. **School Wise Press**, www.schoolwisepress.com, offers free school rankings, profiles, and news articles, and in-depth reports for a fee. Also, each Boston public school zone has a **Family Resource Center** to answer your questions: West Zone is 617-635-8040; East Zone is 617-635-8015; North Zone is 617-635-9010. Parents of high schoolers should call 617-635-8890.

BOSTON PUBLIC SCHOOLS

Boston is the birthplace of the nation's first public school system. Boston Latin School, renowned as one of the country's best public high schools, is also the country's first ever (general) public school, having opened in 1635 and graduated such celebrated Bostonians as John Hancock, Samuel Adams, Benjamin Franklin, Ralph Waldo Emerson, and Leonard Bernstein. The nation's oldest public elementary school is Mather, which opened in 1639.

About 63,000 kids (K-12) are enrolled in Boston's 131 public schools. Of these, about 20% are enrolled in some sort of special educational program, and about 15% are enrolled in some kind of English as a second language program. Classroom sizes range between 22 and 31 students. As of 2003, 84 of the schools had either a mandatory or voluntary uniform dress code. It is up to the individual school whether or not to require uniforms or to allow students to wear them voluntarily, or not have them at all, so check with the particular school in which your kids are registered.

Of the unique offerings available to students through Boston Public Schools, is the **Boston Arts Academy**, the city's first public high school for students showing strong interest in dance, music, theater, and visual arts (admissions are based on interview and portfolio). There is also the **Boston Latin School**, the **Boston Latin Academy**, and the **John D. O'Bryant School of Mathematics and Science**, which require a qualifying entrance exam. At the elementary school level, full-day kindergartens are available.

In addition to the traditional public schools, there are also a number of **charter schools**, publicly funded schools headed by boards of educators and parents instead of cities or towns. As of 2003 there were 14 charter schools in Boston. For information on the charter school program in Massachusetts and listings of charter schools throughout the state, contact the DOE at www.doe.mass.edu/charter.

SCHOOL APPLICATION (APPLYING FOR THE SCHOOL OF YOUR CHOICE) AND ENROLLMENT

Boston Public Schools' elementary and middle grades are divided into three zones: North, East, and West. The **North Zone** covers East Boston, the North End, downtown Boston, the Back Bay, the South End, Roxbury, Mission Hill, and Allston-Brighton; the **West Zone** covers other parts of Roxbury, as well as West Roxbury, JP, and Roslindale; and the **East Zone** covers the neighborhoods of South Boston, Dorchester, Hyde Park, and Mattapan (see following for contact information).

School enrollment in Boston is based on the "**school choice**" system, meaning you can enroll your child in the school system of neighboring communities within your given zone. It's a good option if you feel your immediate school district is lackluster. Whether or not you get the school of your choice depends on several variables, such as whether or not your child has a sibling in the school, proximity (i.e., whether or not your child is within walking distance), and then random lottery. See below for more details. Five schools are **open to students regardless of their zone** (admission is based on a lottery): Hernandez School (K-8) in Roxbury, M.L. King, Jr. Middle School in Dorchester, Mission Hill School (K-8) in Roxbury, Trinity Middle School in Roxbury, and Young Achievers Science & Mathematics School (K-8) in JP. All high schools are open to students citywide. For more information, call **Boston Public Schools**, 26 Court Street, 617-635-9000. Also, check the Massachusetts Department of Education web site at www.doe.mass.edu.

Newcomers to Boston Public Schools will want to get a copy of Boston Public's *Introductory Guide*. It should answer many of your questions about selecting a school and registration, including when, how, and where. All **students who are new to Boston Public Schools must first *apply* to enroll**; applications are available at **Family Resource Centers**: Campbell Resource Center, 1216 Dorchester Avenue, Dorchester, 617-635-8015 for the East Zone; Barron Building, 515 Hyde Park Avenue, Roslindale, 617-635-8040 for the West Zone; and Madison Park Complex, 55 Malcolm X Boulevard, Roxbury, 617-635-9010 for the North Zone. School applications are not available online—you must visit the school during the appropriate registration period; however, you can pre-register and get other school assignment information at www.bostonpublicschools.org. You also *must* *apply* if your child will be starting kindergarten, will be entering grade six or nine, is in grade one at an Early Education Center or Early Learning Center, will be transferring zones, or is in a special program (e.g., ESL, interdisciplinary learning). If your child is already enrolled at one of the schools, you can pick up the application at your school. Enrollment deadlines vary depending on what grade your child is in, but are usually in the winter.

To apply, bring the application form, two preprinted proofs of address, such as a bank statement, utility bill, or lease; your child's birth certificate or passport; and your child's immunization record. School applications require that you list your three top choices. Those already in the Boston Public School system will have a leg up on newcomers as far as receiving their first choice of schools because students not in transition grades (entering kindergarten, six, or nine) are automatically reassigned to their same school, and those with siblings already enrolled in a school are given priority. The earlier you apply, the better. Placements are based first on availability at your top choice school, if it is full, other factors come into play, including random selection, siblings already attending a school, and if the school is within your "walk zone."

After applying, you will receive a notice in the mail of your child's assignment. If your child doesn't get his first choice school he will be put on the waiting list for it. If he doesn't make it into the second choice school, then he will be on the waiting list for both of them.

IMMUNIZATIONS

By kindergarten, children should be up to date on their diphtheria, tetanus, pertussis, polio, mumps, measles, and hepatitis B vaccines. You must also show proof your child has been vaccinated against or has already had the chicken pox. By the seventh grade a measles, mumps, rubella (MMR) booster is required. Even students who come to Massachusetts for college must show proof of two MMR shots, a recent tetanus shot (within the last ten years), and the full three doses of hepatitis B vaccine. Public school students new to the system must also present evidence of a complete physical within the past year; without one, children will be banned from participating in any athletic activity. You can contact the **Boston Public Schools Health Service** at 617-635-6788 with any questions about vaccinations or waivers for religious or medical purposes.

GREATER BOSTON AREA PUBLIC SCHOOLS

BRISTOL COUNTY
- **Attleboro**: Attleboro Public Schools, Rathbun Willard Drive, 508-222-0012, www.attleboroschools.com

- **Mansfield**: Mansfield Public Schools, 2 Park Row, 508-261-7500, www.mansfieldschools.com
- **New Bedford**: New Bedford Schools, 508-997-4511, www.newbedford.k12.ma.us
- **Taunton**, Taunton Public Schools, 508-821-1100, www.ci.taunton.ma.us

ESSEX COUNTY
- **Andover**: Andover Public Schools, 36R Bartlet Street, 978-623-8500, www.aps1.net
- **Beverly**: Beverly Public Schools, 20 Colon Street, 978-921-6100, www.beverlyschools.org
- **Gloucester**: Gloucester Schools, 978-281-9800, www.gloucesterschools.com
- **Lawrence**: Lawrence Public Schools, 255 Essex Street, 978-975-5905, www.ci.lawrence.ma.us
- **Lynn**: Lynn Public Schools, 90 Commercial Street, 781-593-1680, www.lynnschools.org
- **Marblehead**: Marblehead Public Schools, 9 Widger Road, 781-369-3141, www.marblehead.com/schools
- **Newburyport**: Newburyport Public Schools, 70 Low Street, 978-465-4456, http://newburyport.k12.ma.us
- **Salem**: Salem Public Schools, 29 Highland Avenue, 978-740-1212, www.salem.mec.edu
- **Swampscott**: Swampscott Public Schools, 207 Forest Avenue, 781-596-8800, www.swampscott.k12.ma.us

Middlesex County:
- **Acton**: Acton Public Schools, 16 Charter Road, 978-264-4700, http://ab.mec.edu/
- **Arlington**: Arlington Public Schools, 869 Mass Ave., 781-316-3501, www.arlington.k12.ma.us
- **Bedford**: Bedford Public Schools, 11 Mudge Way, 781-275-7588, www.bedford.k12.ma.us
- **Belmont**: Belmont Public Schools, 644 Pleasant Street, 617-484-2642, www.belmont.k12.ma.us
- **Burlington**: Burlington Public Schools, 123 Cambridge Street, 781-270-1801, www.burlington.mec.edu
- **Cambridge**: Cambridge Public Schools, 159 Thorndike Street, 617-349-6400, www.cpsd.us
- **Concord**: Concord Public Schools, 120 Merriam Road, 978-318-1500, www.concordnet.org
- **Framingham**: Framingham Public Schools, 14 Vernon Street, 508-626-9117, www.framingham.k12.ma.us

CHILDCARE AND EDUCATION

- **Lexington**: Lexington Public Schools, 1557 Massachusetts Avenue, 781-861-2580, http://lps.lexington.ma.org
- **Lowell**: Lowell Public Schools, 155 Merrimack Street, 978-937-7604, www.lowell.k12.ma.us
- **Malden**: Malden Public Schools, 200 Pleasant Street, 781-397-7204, www.malden.mec.edu
- **Manard**: Maynard Public Schools, Coolidge School Building, 12 Bancroft Street, 978-897-2222
- **Medford**: Medford Public Schools, 489 Winthrop Street, 781-393-2387, www.medford.k12.ma.us
- **Melrose**: Melrose Public Schools, 781-979-2294, www.melrose schools.com
- **Natick**: Natick Public Schools, 13 East Central Street, 508-647-6500
- **Newton**: Newton Public Schools, 100 Walnut Street, 617-559-6100, www.newtonpublicschools.com
- **Somerville**: Somerville Public Schools, 181 Washington Street, 617-625-6600, www.ci.somerville.ma.us
- **Wakefield**: Wakefield Public Schools, 60 Farm Street, 781-246-6400
- **Waltham**: Waltham Public Schools, 617 Lexington Street, 781-314-5440, www.city.waltham.ma.us
- **Watertown**: Watertown Public Schools, 30 Common Street, 617-926-7700, www.watertown.k12.ma.us
- **Weston**: Weston Public Schools, 89 Wellesley Street, 781-899-0620, www.westonschools.org
- **Woburn**: Woburn Public Schools, 55 Locust Street, 781-937-8233, www.woburnpublicschools.com

Norfolk County
- **Braintree**: Braintree Public Schools, 781-380-0130, www.key-biz.com/ssn/braintree
- **Brookline**: Brookline Public Schools, 5th Floor, Town Hall, 333 Washington Street, 617-730-2400, www.brookline.mec.edu
- **Cohasset**: Cohasset Public Schools, 781-383-6111, www.key-biz.com/ssn/cohasset
- **Dedham**: Dedham Public Schools, 30 Whiting Avenue, 781-326-5622, www.dedham.k12.ma.us
- **Dover**: Dover-Sherborn Public Schools, www.doversherborn.org
- **Foxboro**: Foxboro Public Schools, 508-543-1660, www.foxborough.k12.ma.us
- **Milton**: Milton Public Schools, 1372 Brush Hill Road, 617-696-4809, www.miltonps.org
- **Needham**: Needham Public Schools, 1330 Highland Avenue, 781-455-0400, www.needham.k12.ma.us

- **Norwood**: Norwood Public Schools, 781-762-6804, www.norwood.k12.ma.us
- **Sharon**: Sharon Public Schools, 1 School Street, 781-784-1570, www.sharon.k12.ma.us
- **Quincy**: Quincy Public Schools, 70 Coddington Street, 617-984-8700, www.quincypublicschools.com
- **Wellesley**: Wellesley Public Schools, 40 Kingsbury Street, 781-446-6200, www.wellesley.mec.edu
- **Weymouth**: Weymouth Public Schools, 111 Middle Street, 781-335-1460, www.weymouth.ma.us

Plymouth County
- **Brockton**: Brockton Public Schools, 508-580-7000, www.brocktonpublicschools.com
- **Hingham**: Hingham Public Schools, 781-741-1500, www.key-biz.com/ssn/hingham
- **Hull**: Hull Public Schools, 781-925-0771, www.town.hull.ma.us/schools.html
- **Plymouth**: Plymouth Public Schools, 508-830-4300, www.key-biz.com/ssn/plymouth
- **Scituate**: Scituate Public Schools, 606 Chief Justice Cushing Hwy., 781-454-8759

Suffolk County
- **Chelsea**: Chelsea Public Schools, 500 Broadway, 617-889-8414, www.chelsea.mec.edu
- **Revere**: Revere Public Schools, www.revereps.mec.edu
- **Winthrop**: Withrop School District: 617-846-5500

PRIVATE/PAROCHIAL/RELIGIOUS SCHOOLS

About one quarter of school-aged children living within Boston's city limits do not attend a public school, opting instead for private or parochial schools, charter schools, suburban public schools (through the METCO program), or homeschooling.

There are a number of well-regarded private schools in the area, including the famous **Phillips Academy** in Andover, about 40 miles north of Boston, and **Milton Academy** in Milton, just south of Boston. To find out more, contact **The Association of Independent Schools in New England**, 600 Longwater Drive, Norwell, 781-982-8600, www.aisne.org, which has listed over 160 member schools throughout the six-state region, beginning with pre-schools.

MONTESSORI SCHOOLS

The Montessori educational movement, founded by Maria Montessori in the early 1900s, prizes the development of a child's individual initiative through self motivated exploration of prepared materials and games. For more information about the Montessori method or to find a listing of schools, visit www.montessori.org.

WALDORF SCHOOLS

Waldorf schools, developed by Austrian Rudolf Steiner in 1919, employ an idiosyncratic, arts-oriented approach to education that is based on Steiner's spiritual philosophy, Anthroposophy. For more information on Waldorf Schools, contact the **Association of Waldorf Schools of North America**, www.awsna.org, 916-961-0927.

PAROCHIAL SCHOOLS

Religious schools in Boston have a long history of providing quality education, so much so that they are even popular with non-religious parents. The **Boston Archdiocese**, www.rcab.org, operates an extensive parochial school system. Contact their **Department of Education** at 617-298-6555 for more information or call 800-SCHOOL-4 to obtain a directory of schools. In addition to Catholic schools, there are also Christian (non-Catholic), Jewish, and Islamic programs. Here are a few religious schools in the region:

- **Al-Noor Academy**, corner of Chubbuck and South streets, Mansfield, 617-770-4012, http://anahs.org/; Islamic high school.
- **Austin Prep**, 101 Willow Street, Reading, 781-944-4900, www.austin.mec.edu; co-ed (Augustinian) Catholic high school
- **BC High School**, 150 Morrissey Boulevard, Dorchester, 617-436-3900, www.bchigh.edu; Jesuit high school for boys
- **Cambridge Friends School**, 5 Cadbury Road, Cambridge, 617-354-3880, www.cambridgefriendsschool.org; co-ed, Quaker, pre-K-8.
- **Cohen Hillel Academy**, 6 Community Road, Marblehead, 781-639-2880; co-ed, Jewish, K-8
- **Fontbonne Academy**, 930 Brook Road, Milton, 617-696-3241, www.fontbonneacademy.org; Catholic, college prep (high school) for girls
- **Islamic Academy of New England**, 84 Chase Drive, Sharon, 781-784-0519, www.iane.org; K-8
- **Jewish Community Day School**, 225 Nevada Street, Newton, 617-965-5100, www.jcdsboston.org; coed, K-8

- **Malden Catholic High School**, 99 Crystal Street, Malden, 781-322-3098, www.maldencatholic.org; high school for boys
- **Rashi School**, 15 Walnut Park, Newton, 617-969-4444, www.rashi.org; reform Jewish day school; co-ed, K-8
- **Sacred Heart High School**, 399 Bishop's Highway, Kingston, 781-585-7511; Catholic, co-ed, grades 7-12
- **Savio Prep High School**, 145 Byron Street, East Boston, 617-567-2710, www.savioprep.org
- **St. John's Prep**, 72 Spring Street, Danvers, 978-774-1050, www.stjohnsprep.org; Catholic boys, high school for boys
- **St. Sebastian's School**, 1191 Greendale Avenue, Needham, 781-449-5200, www.stsebs.org; Catholic high school for boys
- **St. Stephen's Armenian Elementary School**, 47 Nichols Avenue, Watertown, 617-926-6979

HOMESCHOOLING RESOURCES

Massachusetts children are required to be in school from ages 6 to 16, be it a private, parochial, public, or home school. According to the ***Worldwide Guide to Homeschooling*** (Broadman & Holman, 2002) by Brian Ray, between 1.6 and two million children are homeschooled nationwide.

If you wish to homeschool your child, the state requires you provide 900 hours of elementary education and 990 hours of secondary education in the areas of reading, writing, English language and grammar, geography, arithmetic, drawing, music, history, the US Constitution, citizenship, health (including CPR), physical education, and good behavior. You must get approval from the local school committee or superintendent to operate a home school and must officially withdraw your child from the public school system. There are no specifically required standardized tests a homeschooled child must take, but the school committee or superintendent is authorized to make such tests a stipulation for granting you the authority to homeschool your child. Also, at press time, home schooled children were prohibited from taking the MCAs, although this rule may be subject to change.

For assistance with homeshooling, you can contact:
- **Home School Legal Defense Association**, 540-338-5600, www.hslda.org; among other things, explains laws regarding home schooling in each state and offers links to necessary forms. They also will send you a free introductory guide to home schooling called ***Home Schooling: Start Here.***
- **Homeschool.com**, www.homeschool.com; resources, guides, local links
- ***Homeschooling Today***, 281-492-6050, www.homeschooltoday.com; a major "trade" publication that will keep you informed of all the important trends, events, and contacts.

SHOPPING FOR THE HOME

TRUE SHOPAHOLICS AND FASHIONISTAS MAY BE UNDERWHELMED when shopping in Beantown. Unlike New York or Chicago, where you can find a great number of swank boutiques and specialty stores, Boston is more mainstream and homogenous. The majority of the stores are local and national chains; even the posh shopping strips like Newbury Street are crowded with Gaps and Banana Republics. There are some smaller, independent shops around, but they may take awhile to locate and tend to be expensive.

SHOPPING DISTRICTS

In Boston, **Downtown Crossing** is a pedestrian-only, outdoor cobblestone paved area that is home to a variety of department stores (Macy's and Filene's), discount shopping (H&M, Marshalls, the original Filene's Basement, DSW Shoe Warehouse), chain bookstores (Borders, Barnes & Noble), traditional mall chain stores (Express, Bath and Body Works), and lots of little vendor carts. If you drive here, head to the parking garage under the common and then walk down Winter Street or a parallel running street to get to the main shopping area.

Charles Street, the main drag of Beacon Hill, is one area where you actually will find a selection of one-of-a-kind and often pricey shops, including Wish (clothes), Maxie (shoes), Koo di Kir (homegoods), and a string of antique shops. Those driving here can check for a metered spot on Cambridge or Beacon streets or park under the common.

Don't forget **Faneuil Hall/Quincy Market**, which, like Downtown Crossing, is a cobblestone pedestrian shopping area, but with a more upscale feel. Although tourists abound here—the Freedom Trail cuts through it and many families stop to watch the street performers—locals also enjoy browsing the 70+ mid-sized shops like Victoria's Secret, Ann

Taylor, and Abercrombie & Fitch, as well as the smaller independent stores and the fleet of pushcarts. If you get hungry, head for one of the 40+ food vendors or 18 restaurants and pubs. There are several parking garages in the area, so parking isn't a problem—although it isn't cheap. To find out more, go to Faneuil Hall's web site: www.faneuilhallmarketplace.com.

Shops in Back Bay, clustered along Boylston and Newbury streets, are where you'll find tattooed and pierced undergrads rubbing shoulders with fur-wearing Euro princesses shopping for high fashion, footwear, housewares, music, and foodstuffs. Many stores on **Boylston** are surprisingly large, and include a Crate & Barrel, Anthropologie, Marshalls, and EMS, all of which are mixed in with restaurants and some upscale boutiques, including Hermès, Escada, and the chic Priscilla of Boston bridal store. But Boylston pales in comparison to **Newbury**, Boston's premiere shopping street, which is lined from stem to stern with little one-up, one-down street level shops of three- or four-floor Victorian brownstones, many of which have apartments in the upper floors. Virtually anything you desire shopping-wise can be found here: restaurants (chic and low-key), hair dressers, and a thorough mix of big-name stores including Gap, Banana Republic, Virgin Megastore, Rockport, Betsy Johnson, Urban Outfitters, French Connection, Armani Exchange, Louis, Firestone, and many smaller boutiques. Parking on Newbury is always difficult, but if you can't find a metered spot there are parking garages nearby for the Copley and Pru, two shopping areas just a couple streets over from Newbury. **Copley Place** and the **Shops at the Prudential Center** are two upscale malls connected by covered pedestrian tubes. In addition to a repeat of many of the stores you'll find just blocks away on Newbury, there are also big department stores, including Lord & Taylor, Saks, and Neiman Marcus. Head a few blocks southwest of Copley and the Pru, and you'll hit **Tremont Street** in the South End, where you'll find funky one-of-a-kind boutiques and eateries. Some of these independent stores are pricey, but certainly not all, and it is worth the walk over.

In Cambridge, Mass Ave., between Central and Porter squares, is packed with shops. Central Square is being revamped, so the stores there are in flux; a heavier concentration of shops are to be found in the Harvard Square area, host to ethnic restaurants, two Gaps, Jasmine Sola, Urban Outfitters, Crate & Barrel, Salvation Army, Berk's Shoes, and Wordsworth Books, among others. Don't miss the Garage in Harvard Square—with its interesting selection of one-of-a-kind shops tucked inside.

The **Harvard Street/Coolidge Corner** area of Brookline also offers a variety of outdoor shopping, with chain shops such as Radio Shack, Pier 1, T.J. Maxx, and Barnes & Noble, and a few smaller independent stores specializing in Judaica.

SHOPPING MALLS

When it's 12 degrees outside, the idea of strolling along the street to window shop in quaint little stores may not be as appealing as an **indoor mall**:
- **Arsenal Mall/Watertown Mall**: 485 Arsenal Street, Watertown, 617-923-4700, www.shopsimon.com; has over 65 stores in the old Civil War arsenal, including an Old Navy and a Target.
- **The Atrium**, 300 Boylston Street, Newton, 617-527-1400, www.atriummall.com; smaller, ultra-upscale mall with only 35 specialty shops.
- **Burlington Mall**, 75 Middlesex Turnpike, Burlington, 781-272-8667, www.shopsimon.com; large mall with a food court and over 155 stores, including Filene's, Lord & Taylor, Sears, and Macy's.
- **Cambridgeside Galleria**, 100 Cambridgeside Place, Cambridge, 617-621-8666, www.cambridgesidegalleria.com; big, urban, multi-level mall with a food court, restaurant, and a variety of stores, including Best Buy, Borders, J. Crew, Victoria's Secret, Filene's, Banana Republic, and Old Navy.
- **Copley Place**, 2 Copley Place, Boston, 617-369-5000, www.shopcopleyplace.com; 9.5 acre site where the beautiful people come to shop at such stores as Pink, Tiffany's, Bebe, French Connection, Gucci, Armani Exchange, Louis Vuitton, Christian Dior, Williams-Sonoma, Hugo Boss, and the Artful Hand. Connected by a skywalk to the Pru.
- **Fresh Pond Mall**, 185 Alewife Brook Parkway, Cambridge, 617-491-4431; strip mall of a few clustered stores and a movie theater.
- **Liberty Tree Mall**, 100 Independence Way (routes 114 and 128), Danvers, 978-777-0794, www.simon.com; previously overshadowed by the nearby North Shore mall, the Liberty Tree Mall has been revamped to include a food court, a 20-plex movie theater, and big stores, including Sports Authority, Old Navy, Kohl's, and Marshalls.
- **The Mall at Chestnut Hill**, 199 Boylston Street, Chestnut Hill, 617-965-3038, www.mallatchestnuthill.com; upscale sister-mall to The Atrium, with many stores, including Bloomingdale's, Kedzie Kids, the Gap, Banana Republic.
- **Meadow Glen Mall**, 3850 Mystic Valley Parkway, Medford, 781-395-6710, www.meadowglen.com; over 50 stores in an urban setting, including Old Navy, Kohl's, and Marshalls.
- **Natick Mall**, 1245 Worcester Street, Natick, 508-655-4800; www.natickmall.com; over 170 stores in this standard mall, including Sears, Lord & Taylor, Macy's, Filene's, and child-friendly amenities like PlaySpace and kiddie rides.
- **North Shore Mall**, routes 114 and 128 in Peabody, 978-531-3440; www.shopsimon.com; over 120 stores including a Filene's, Macy's, Lord & Taylor, JCPenney, and Sears.

- **Porter Exchange Mall**, 1815 Mass. Ave., Cambridge; small collection of mostly Japanese wares, as well as a Gap, a fitness store, Lesley University's bookstore, and jewelry stores.
- **Shops at the Prudential Center**, 800 Boylston Street, Boston, 800-SHOP-PRU, www.prudentialcenter.com; over 75 shops and restaurants, including Lord & Taylor, Saks, Levi's, The Body Shop, Ann Taylor, Barnes & Noble, J. Jill, Arden B, The Cheesecake Factory, California Pizza Kitchen, Legal Seafoods, and a large food court. Attached to Copley Place.
- **South Shore Plaza**, 250 Granite Street, Braintree, 781-843-8200, www.shopsimon.com; standard mall including Lord & Taylor, Macy's, Filene's, Sears, and 180 specialty shops.
- **Square One Mall**, Route 1 South, Saugus, 781-233-8787; www.shopsimon.com; standard mall, including Filene's, Filene's Basement, T.J. Maxx, the Disney Store, Brookstone, a food court, and restaurants.
- **Walpole Mall**, Walpole, 5080-668-3437; www.thewalpolemall.com; includes Barnes & Noble, Gap, Kohl's, and Old Navy.

OUTLET MALLS

There are no outlet malls near Boston, although you can drive a few hours up the coast to Kittery or Freeport in Maine. Freeport, in particular, is a great day trip if only for the L.L. Bean Outlet, which is open 24-hours, 7 days/week. The following are outlet stores in the greater Boston area:
- **Saucony Factory Outlet**, 1036 Cambridge Street (near Inman Square), Cambridge, 617-547-4397
- **New Balance**, 40 Life Street, Brighton, 877-623-7867
- **Crate & Barrel Outlet**, 460 Wildwood Avenue, Woburn, 781-938-8777
- **Talbots Outlet**, 209 Lincoln Street, Hingham, 781-749-8720

DEPARTMENT STORES

Department stores are often the best place to find everything you need under one roof.
- **Bloomingdale's**, Chestnut Hill Mall on Route 9, Chestnut Hill, 617-630-6000, www.bloomingdales.com; an upscale national department store chain that got its start in New York's Lower East Side in the 1860s. Personal shoppers and interior designers are available.
- **Filene's** is a well-established, local (New England) chain. Offers a wide selection of clothes, gifts, wedding registry, home items, make up, perfume, shoes, etc. Many locations in the greater Boston area, including Belmont Center, 75 Leonard Street, Belmont, 617-484-3800, and

Cambridgeside Galleria, 100 Cambridgeside Place, Cambridge, 617-621-3800. Check the White Pages for more locations or go to www.filenes.com.

- **Harvard/MIT Cooperative Society**, known as "the Coop" (as in chicken), has two main locations: Harvard Square, 1400 Mass. Ave., 617-499-2000, and Kendall Square, 3 Cambridge Center, 617-499-3200; www.thecoop.com. The Coop is a cooperative that students, faculty, alumni, and employees of Harvard, MIT, Wheelock, and the Massachusetts College of Pharmacy can join. Members earn a rebate annually that is based on what they've spent throughout the year. It sells everything from appliances to deodorant.
- **JCPenney**; chock full of all the usual department store stuff for your home and you. There are no locations within the city, but a few in the surrounding suburbs: North Shore Mall, routes 114 and 128, Peabody, 978-977-3050; Hanover Mall, 1775 Washington Street, Hanover, 781-826-2096; 121-177 Concord Street, Framingham, 508-820-7059; www3.jcpenney.com.
- **Kohl's**, Penney's main competitor is new to the area. The closest store to Boston is at 3850 Mystic Valley Parkway in Medford, 781-395-6001, www.kohlscorporation.com. Other locations in the suburbs: Woburn, Burlington, Danvers, Hingham, Walpole, Framingham, Chelmsford, North Andover, and Pembroke.
- **Macy's**, is a solid, mid-range store with a large variety of items for the home, gifts, clothing, makeup, perfume, shoes, wedding registry, etc. Metro Boston locations include Downtown Crossing, 450 Washington Street, Boston, 617-357-3000; South Shore Plaza, 250 Granite Street, Braintree, 781-848-1500; Burlington Mall, 1300 Middlesex Turnpike, Burlington, 781-272-6000; North Shore Mall, Route 128, Peabody, 978-531-9000; Natick Mall, 1245 Worcester Road, Natick, 508-650-6400; www.macys.com.
- **Lord & Taylor**, run by the same company that owns Filene's (the May Company), Lord & Taylor is a slightly smaller, more upscale chain than Filene's, with 85 stores across the country. Boston area locations: Prudential Center, 760 Boylston Street, Boston, 617-262-6000; South Shore Plaza, 250 Granite Street, Braintree, 781-848-1970; Burlington Mall, 1320 Burlington Mall Road, Burlington, 781-273-1461; Northshore Mall, 210 Andover Street, routes 114 and 128, Peabody, 978-977-7400; Natick Mall, 1245 Worcester Road, Natick, 508-651-0744; www.lordandtaylor.com.
- **Neiman-Marcus**, 5 Copley Place, Boston, 617-536-3660, www.neimanmarcus.com; this posh department store offers an elegant collection of home goods, clothing, shoes, beauty items, gifts, shoes, etc., from the best designers. Come here for Manolo Blahnik shoes, Prada bags, Dolce and Gabbana dresses, and more.

- **Saks Fifth Avenue**, located downtown at the Prudential Center, Boston, 617-262-8500; www.saksfifthavenue.com; another of the nation's finest department stores, Saks has a big selection of upscale goods.
- **Sears**, the original department store, this is *the* place for refrigerators, lawnmowers, toolkits, washers and dryers, etc. And don't forget the automotive centers. Greater Boston area locations: Cambridgeside Galleria, 100 Cambridgeside Place, 617-252-3500; Square One Mall, 1325 Broadway/Route 1, Saugus, 781-231-4595; Dedham Mall, 300 Providence Highway, Dedham, 781-320-5125; South Shore Plaza, 250 Granite Street, Braintree, 781-356-6000; www.sears.com.

DISCOUNT DEPARTMENT STORES

Everyone loves a good deal. Home to Filene's Basement, Boston bargain shoppers will not be disappointed. Quality and style of goods vary from store to store, and often reflect the surrounding community. Discount shops in the more upscale communities often carry the best designer names.

- **Filene's Basement**; the original discount store, it opened in 1909 in the basement of Filene's Department store in Downtown Crossing. Come here for amazing markdowns, but be prepared: the Basement (particularly the original one) is not for the meek. It's crowded and sometimes messy. The Basement carries mostly clothing and shoes, but the second level has housewares, linens, and home decorations. Greater Boston area locations: Downtown Crossing, 426 Washington Street, Boston, 617-348-7848; South Shore Plaza, 250 Granite Street, Braintree, 781-849-0031; 215-227 Needham Street, Newton, 617-332-1295; North Shore Mall, routes 114 and 128, Peabody, 978-532-3400; Square One Mall, Route 1 South, Saugus, 781-231-8153; Arsenal Mall, 485 Arsenal Street, Watertown, 617-926-4474; www.filenesbasement.com.
- **DSW Shoe Warehouse**, is a gigantic, bargain, multi-floor shoe emporium. Not the place to find Jimmy Choo's, but still quite a lot of really good stuff. Greater Boston area locations: Downtown Crossing, 385 Washington Street, Boston, 617-556-0052; Dedham Mall, 344 Providence Highway, Dedham, 781-329-6310; 1 Worcester Road, Framingham, 508-270-0091; www.dswshoe.com.
- **Macy's Basement**, 450 Washington Street, Boston, 617-357-3000; right across the street from Filene's Basement, the atmosphere here is much more subdued, but you can still find great bargains.
- **Macy's Furniture Gallery**, Shoppers World Mall, routes 9 and 30, Framingham, 508-650-6000; unsold merchandise is sent here where it is marked down even further. You can find electronic equipment, beds, and furniture.

- **Kmart**, even staid Bostonians can't resist the lure of the blue light specials: 400 Western Avenue, Brighton, 617-562-4492; 77 Middlesex Avenue, Somerville, 617-628-9500; 180 Main Street, Saugus, 781-231-0404; 350 Grossman Drive, Braintree, 781-843-5400, www.kmart.com.
- **Marshalls**; one of the most popular discount shopping chains in the nation, it offers designer clothes, shoes, and items for the home in a comfortable atmosphere. Many locations throughout the area: 500 Boylston Street, Boston, 617-262-6066; Downtown Crossing, 350 Washington Street, Boston, 617-338-6205; 8D Alistate Road, Dorchester, 617-442-5050; 3850 Mystic Valley Parkway, Medford, 781-391-1331; 1399 North Shore Road, Revere, 781-289-3217; 275 Needham Street, Newton Upper Falls, 617-964-4987; 455 Arsenal Street, Watertown, 617-923-1004; www.marshallsonline.com.
- **Target**, Bostonians are particularly jazzed about the newly arrived Target stores. You name it, it's here: clothes, games, CDs, books, housewares, food, toys, etc. Expect a bit of a drive. Greater Boston area locations: 180 Somerville Avenue, Somerville, 617-776-4036; 1 Mystic View Road, Everett, 617-420-0000; Arsenal Mall, 550 Arsenal Street, Watertown, 617-924-6574; 101 Commerce Way, Woburn, 781-904-0002; 400 Lynn Fells Parkway, Saugus, 781-307-0000; www.target.com.
- **T.J. Maxx** is another national bargain bastion, similar to Marshalls in terms of goods, size, and atmosphere. Locations include Downtown Crossing, 350 Washington Street, Boston, 617-695-2424; 525 Harvard Street, Brookline, 617-232-5420; 702 The Fellsway, Medford, 781-393-0027; 198 Alewife Parkway, Cambridge, 617-492-8500; 100 Granite Street, Quincy, 617-328-1763; 300 Providence Highway, Dedham, 781-461-9896; 846 Lexington Street, Waltham, 781-893-2968; www.tjmaxx.com.
- **Wal-Mart**, come here for electronics, clothes, sporting goods, music, video games, toys, books, jewelry, etc. The five closest locations to Boston are all in the suburbs: 780 Lynnway, Lynn, 781-592-4300; 301 Falls Boulevard, Quincy, 617-745-4390; 450 Highland Avenue, Salem, 978-825-1713; 740 Middle Street, Weymouth, 781-331-0063; 55 Avalon Village Way, Danvers, 978-777-6977; www.walmart.com.

HOUSEHOLD SHOPPING

APPLIANCES, ELECTRONICS, COMPUTERS, AND SOFTWARE

Bostonians needing to augment or repair their home entertainment centers, upgrade their computer systems, or create home offices will find local proprietors eager to assist, as well as the more "self-service oriented" national chains. Check the Yellow Pages under "Appliances," "Electric Appliances," "Electronic Equipment & Supplies," and "Computers & Equipment" for a complete listing, or try one of the following:

- **Best Buy**, locations throughout the city and the suburbs: Cambridgeside Galleria, 100 Cambridgeside Place, 617-577-8866; Landmark Center, 401 Park Drive, Suite 4, Boston, 617-424-7900; Arsenal Mall, 500 Arsenal Street, Watertown, 617-926-0142; www.bestbuy.com.
- **Cambridge Sound Works**, Cambridgeside Galleria, 100 Cambridgeside Place, 617-225-3900; 68 Highland Avenue, Needham, 781-449-6442; 150 California Street, Newton, 617-630-1976; www.hifi.com
- **CompUSA**, five locations within 30 miles of Boston: 205 Market Street, Brighton, 617-783-1900; 335 Washington Street, Woburn, 781-937-0600; 500 Grossman Drive, Braintree, 781-843-0676; Liberty Tree Mall, 100 Independence Way, Danvers, 978-777-4778; Commonwealth Center, 500 Cochituate Road, Framingham, 508-875-8300; www.compusa.com.
- **Circuit City**, 65 Mystic Avenue, Somerville, 617-623-3400; suburban locations in Danvers, Saugus, Dedham, Braintree, Natick, Burlington, and Hanover; www.circuitcity.com.
- **Mystic Appliance**, 135 Cambridge Street, Charlestown, 617-242-9679
- **Radio Shack**; locations throughout the city and suburbs, visit www.radioshack.com for details.

BEDS, BEDDING, AND BATH

Locals call Cambridge the futon capital of Massachusetts. For a complete list of stores, check the Yellow Pages under "Mattresses" and "Futons." In the meantime, here's a list to get you started:

- **Bed, Bath, & Beyond**, Landmark Center, 401 Park Drive, Boston, 617-536-1090 (take advantage of their rare, in-city parking lot); 7 Mystic View Road, Everett, 617-387-1976; suburban locations in Burlington, Danvers, Braintree, and Framingham; www.bedbathandbeyond.com.
- **Big John's Mattress Factory**, 121 First Street, Cambridge, 617-876-6344, www.bigjohnsmattress.com
- **Boston Futon**, 97 Mass Ave., Boston, 617-266-8970
- **Home Designs**, 1033 Mass Ave., Cambridge, 617-354-2525
- **Bedworks**, Central Square, Cambridge, 617-547-6000, www.bedworks.net
- **Futonair**, 830 Mass Ave., Cambridge, 617-864-6000
- **Jennifer Convertibles**, 1 Porter Square, Cambridge, 617-661-0200; 1524 VFW Parkway, West Roxbury, 617-325-4891; 376 Boylston Street, Boston, 617-375-9083; www.jenniferfurniture.com
- **Linens 'n Things**, Arsenal Mall, 615 Arsenal Street, Watertown, 617-924-8800; 260 Needham Street, Newton, 617-964-0051; locations

throughout the metro area, including Braintree, South Weymouth, Burlington, Danvers, Framingham; www.lnt.com.
- **Sleep-A-Rama**, 1007 Mass Ave., Cambridge, 617-354-6993; 136 Worcester Street, Natick, 508-653-4900; 97 Mass Ave., Boston, 617-266-8970; 14 Spring Street, Peabody, 978-532-8193; 386 Columbia Road, Hanover, 781-826-8335; www.sleeparamabostonfuton.com

FURNITURE

A small area of Cambridge between Harvard and Central squares where Mass Ave. and Mt. Auburn Street intersect is called the "furniture district." This is a good place to start, but if you don't find what you want, there are many other furniture stores located throughout the region, and you can always check the selection at your favorite department store.
- **Adesso**, 200 Boylston Street, Boston, 617-451-2212; www.adesso-boston.com
- **Bernie & Phyl's Furniture**, 1 East Street, Cambridge, 617-868-7999
- **City Schemes**, 1050 Mass. Ave., Cambridge, 617-497-0707; 22 Kent Street, Somerville, 617-776-7777; 395 Worcester Road, Route 9 West, Natick, 508-655-3434; 799 Broadway, Saugus; www.cityschemes.com
- **Cocoon**, 170 Tremont Street, Boston, 617-728-9898
- **Crate & Barrel**, 140 Faneuil Hall, Boston, 617-742-6025; 777 Boylston Street, Boston, 617-262-8700; 48 Brattle Street in Harvard Square, Cambridge, 617-876-6300; 1045 Mass Ave., Cambridge, 617-547-3994; The Mall at Chestnut Hill, 199 Boylston Street, Newton, 617-964-8400; suburban locations in Braintree, Woburn, Burlington, and Natick. www.crateandbarrel.com
- **Domain Home Fashions**, 7 Newbury Street, Boston, 617-266-5252; The Mall at Chestnut Hill, 199 Boylston Street, Chestnut Hill, 617-964-6666; Burlington Mall, Middlesex Turnpike, Burlington, 781-273-2288; Norwood Warehouse Store, 52 Morgan Drive, Norwood, 781-769-9130; www.domain-home.com
- **Eastern Butcher Block**, 281 Concord Avenue, Cambridge, 617-497-9100; suburban locations in Braintree, Danvers, and Framingham; www.butcherblock.com.
- **Ethan Allen**, 840 Willard Street, Quincy, 617-471-3331; 636 Broadway, Saugus, 781-233-5663; 34 Cambridge Street, Burlington, 781-273-2515; www.ethanallen.com
- **Eurasia Furniture**, 31 Harrison Avenue, Boston, 617-350-0128
- **Home Designs**, 1033 Mass Ave., Cambridge, 617-354-2525
- **Dean's Home Furniture**, 1450 Boston Providence Turnpike, Norwood, 781-769-3437; 454 Main Street, Malden, 781-397-1700
- **Jennifer Convertibles**, 1 Porter Square, Cambridge, 617-661-0200;

1524 VFW Parkway, West Roxbury, 617-325-4891; 376 Boylston Street, Boston, 617-375-9083; www.jenniferfurniture.com
- **Maverick Designs**, 1117 Comm Ave., Boston, 617-783-0274, www.bostonwood.com
- **The Oak Gallery**, 201 Mass Ave., Lexington, 781-861-1500; www.oakgallery.com
- **Pottery Barn**, 122 Newbury Street, Boston, 617-266-6553; Atrium Mall, 300 Boylston Street, Chestnut Hill, 617-964-4001; South Shore Plaza, 250 Granite Street, Braintree, 781-849-8510; Burlington Mall, 75 Middlesex Turnpike Burlington, 781-229-2993; North Shore Mall, routes 114 and 128, Peabody, 978-532-5179; www.potterybarn.com
- **Restoration Hardware**, 711 Boylston Street, Boston, 617-578-0088; Atrium Mall, 300 Boylston Street, Chestnut Hill, 617-641-6770; North Shore Mall, routes 114 and 128, Peabody, 978-532-1714; www.restorationhardware.com
- **Roche Bobois**, 585 Commercial Street, Boston, 617-742-9611, www.roche-bobois.com
- **Shoomine**, 8 Park Plaza, Boston, 617-227-2021
- **Sofa Kingdom**, 50 Terminal Street, Charlestown, 617-241-0120
- **Workbench**, 1050 Mass Ave., Cambridge, 617-876-9754; 142 Berkeley Street, Boston, 617-267-8955; suburban locations in Lexington, Peabody, and Natick; www.workbenchfurniture.com.

HOUSEWARES

If you love to browse, you'll enjoy discovering the many talented artists who sell their unique housewares in small shops throughout the area. However, if you're in a rush to outfit your kitchen fast, you may want to try a department or discount department store or check Bed, Bath, & Beyond, Linens 'n Things or one of the following establishments:

- **Bowl & Board**, small local chain with a decent variety of cool housewares and furniture: 1354 Beacon Street, Brookline, 617-566-4726; 1063 Mass Ave., Cambridge, 617-661-0350; www.bowlandboard.com.
- **China Fair**, 2100 Mass Ave., Cambridge, 617-864-3050; 70 Needham Street, Newton Highlands, 617-332-1250
- **Crate & Barrel**, (see listing above).
- **Hold Everything**, container store with upscale storage pieces of all sizes: 349-351 Newbury Street, Boston, 617-450-9846; 1000 Mass Ave., Cambridge, 617-354-9771.
- **HomeGoods**, 978 Boylston Street, Newton, 617-965-5055
- **Pier 1 Imports**, 15 Mystic View Road, Everett, 617-389-2445; 1 Porter Square, Cambridge, 617-491-7626; 1351 Beacon Street, Brookline, 617-232-9627; www.pier1.com

- **Placewares**, 796 Beacon Street, Newton Centre, 617-527-9170; 59 Leonard Street, Belmont Center, 617-489-3555; 68 Central Street, Wellesley, 781-237-2860; 13 Walden Street, Concord, 978-369-1590; www.placewares.com
- **Pottery Barn**, 122 Newbury Street, Boston, 617-266-6553; Atrium Mall, 300 Boylston Street, Chestnut Hill, 617-964-4001; South Shore Plaza, 250 Granite Street, Braintree, 781-849-8510; Burlington Mall, 75 Middlesex Turnpike Burlington, 781-229-2993; North Shore Mall, routes 114 and 128, Peabody, 978-532-5179; www.potterybarn.com
- **Robell's Housewares Department**, 2275 Washington Street, Dorchester, 617-445-1713
- **Williams-Sonoma**, Copley Place, 100 Huntington Avenue, Boston, 617-262-3080; Chestnut Hill Mall, 300 Boylston Street, Newton, 617-969-7090; South Shore Plaza, 250 Granite Street, Braintree, 781-365-0515; Burlington Mall, 75 Middlesex Turnpike, Burlington, 781-273-1114; North Shore Mall, routes 114 and 128, Peabody, 978-531-9623; Natick Mall, 1245 Worcester Street, Natick, 508-647-4007; www.williamssonoma.com

HARDWARE AND GARDEN CENTERS

You should be able to find a hardware store in your neighborhood no matter where you live. The mega chain **Home Depot** (www.homedepot.com) can be found locally at 75 Mystic Avenue, Somerville, 617-623-0001; 5 Allstate Road (South Bay), Boston, 617-442-6110; 1 Mystic View Road, Everett, 617-389-2323; and 1213 VFW Pkwy, West Roxbury, 617-327-5000. For your local **Ace Hardware** go to www.acehardware.com, and for **True Value affiliates** visit www.truevalue.com.

SECOND-HAND SHOPPING

Rack-rummaging at thrift stores and looking for treasures at flea markets are hobbies for many, and Boston definitely has some quality antique shops offering old New England wares.

ANTIQUE SHOPS AND DISTRICTS

Those newcomers who are up on their Limoges and Hummels should be pleased with the local antiquing scene. To get started, check the Yellow Pages under "Antiques" or go to www.antiquing.com or www.antiqueinfo.com for recommendations of shops in your area. Following are area antique districts or markets:
- **Antique Alley**, if you're in the mood for a day trip, this stretch of

Route 7 between Great Barrington and the Connecticut border (mostly in Sheffield) is loaded with antique dealers.
- **Beacon Hill**; this area is paradise for many, particularly the stretch along **Charles Street**, where antique shops dominate.
- **Brimfield, MA**, home of the Brimfield Antique Shops; this is the largest outdoor antique show in New England, held over a one-mile stretch of Route 20 during the warmer months. Visit www.brimfield.com for details.
- **Brookline Village**; this conglomeration of upscale antique dealers is packed in the tight space on Harvard Street near its intersection with Route 9.
- **Essex, MA** is referred to as "America's Antique Capital," for its 35+ antique shops. Don't forget to stop off at Woodman's for fried clams.
- **Haverhill Antique Market**, 90 Washington Street, Haverhill, 978-374-6644, www.marketantique.com/haverhil; come here for 65+ dealer spaces on three floors. Not open Mondays.
- **Provincetown Antique Market**, 131 Commercial Street, Provincetown, 508-487-1115, www.marketantique.com/province; P-town, at the tip of Cape Cod, has a big antique market on weekends, Memorial Day through November.

THRIFT AND VINTAGE SHOPS

Not only can you find some really cool, cheap stuff at thrift shops, but charities and hospital programs frequently benefit from the proceeds. What could be better than shopping for a cause? You might also want to check the weekly paper for listings of local flea markets, garage sales, and auctions.
- **American Family Thrift Store**, 1698 Comm Ave., Brighton, 617-232-9694
- **Amvets Thrift Store**, 80 Brighton Avenue, Allston, 617-562-0720, www.amvets.org
- **Beacon Hill Thrift Shop**, 15 Charles Street, Boston, 617-742-2323
- **Beth Israel-Deaconess Medical Center Thrift Shop**, 25 Harvard Street, Brookline, 617-566-7016
- **Christ Church Thrift Shop**, 17 Farwell Place, Cambridge, 617-492-3335
- **The Garment District**, 200 Broadway, Cambridge, 617-876-5230, www.garment-district.com
- **Goodwill Stores**, 520 Mass Ave., Cambridge; 230 Elm Street, Somerville; 708 Centre Street, Jamaica Plain; 315 West Broadway, South Boston; 1010 Harrison Avenue, Boston; 461 Salem Street, Medford; www.goodwillmass.org
- **Quincy Center Flea Market**, 1183 Hancock Street, Quincy, 617-786-9166

- **Revere Flea Market**, 565 Squire Road, Revere, 781-289-7100
- **Salvation Army Thrift Stores**, 483 Broadway, Somerville, 617-395-9783; 328 Mass Ave., Cambridge, 617-354-9159; www.salvationarmyusa.org.
- **Second Time Around Collections**, 167 Newbury Street, Boston, 617-247-3504; 8 Eliot Street, Cambridge, 617-491-7185
- **St. Gerard's Guild Thrift Shop**, 251 Washington Street #A, Somerville, 617-666-3754
- **Thrift Shop of Boston**, 17 Corinth Street, Roslindale, 617-325-5300
- **Urban Renewals**, 122 Brighton Avenue, Allston, 617-783-8387; well loved by the alternative crowd.

FOOD

Boston's large immigrant population means you can find all sorts of international delicacies, and of course, fresh seafood is everywhere. See below under **Ethnic Districts** for a full detailing of Boston's ethnic enclaves. For more about supermarkets, warehouse shopping, farmers' markets and community gardens, and specialty grocers, read on.

SUPERMARKETS

Major grocery store chains in metro Boston are **Star Market**, **Shaw's**, **Stop & Shop**, and **FoodMaster**. Star Market and Shaw's are now under the same ownership, so you can use the same discount card at either of them. Foodmaster offers fewer gourmet items and tends to be less expensive.
- **FoodMaster**, 105 Alewife Brook Parkway, Somerville, 617-660-1342; 45 Beacon Street, Somerville, 617-660-1322; 51 Austin Street, Charlestown, 617-660-1372
- **Shaw's**, 246 Border Street, East Boston, 617-567-4116; 275 Beacon Street, Somerville, 617-354-7023; 299 Broadway, Somerville, 617-776-7733; 1065 Comm Ave., Allston, 617-783-5878; www.shaws.com
- **Star Market**, numerous locations, check your White Pages for the nearest one.
- **Stop & Shop**, numerous locations, check the White Pages or go to www.stopandshop.com for the nearest location.

HOME DELIVERY

Until recently, Boston had numerous home delivery services. These days there is one major grocery delivery service in Boston, **Peapod**, www.peapod.com, which is run by Stop & Shop. It's an internet service, and when you place your order you chose the day you would like your groceries delivered and a two-hour delivery window. If you're unhappy with the quality of the produce, you can send it back. Tipping is optional, and satisfaction is guaranteed. Visit them online to arrange for service.

WAREHOUSE SHOPPING

What warehouse stores (a.k.a. shopping clubs) lack in glamour, they make up for in affordability. You have to join and get a membership card to shop at them, but if you have a big family and go through lots of toilet paper and milk, this may be a good option.
- **BJ's Wholesale Club**, 278 Middlesex Avenue, Medford, 781-396-0451, www.bjs.com
- **Costco**, 400 Commercial Circle, Dedham, 781-251-9975; 2 Mystic View Road, Everett, 617-544-4806; and 71 Second Avenue, Waltham, 781-622-3883; www.costco.com

SPECIALTY GROCERS

Bread & Circus and **Whole Foods Market** are upscale, supermarket-sized natural food chains. Similarly, **Roche Brothers Wild Harvests**, which are owned by Shaw's/Star and are usually in or next to a Shaw's or Star Market, offer natural food selections. **Trader Joe's** is another specialty chain, with a reputation for good prices. **Harvest Cooperative** is a community-owned co-op that buys products that support fair trade, sustainable agriculture, and supports local farmers and food producers.
- **Bread & Circus**, 15 Westland Avenue, Boston, 617-375-1010; 14 Washington Street, Brighton, 617-738-8187; 115 Prospect Street, Cambridge, 617-492-0070; 200 Alewife Brook Parkway, Cambridge, 617-491-0040; 916 Walnut Street, Newton, 617-969-1141; 647 Washington Street, Newtonville, 617-965-2070; www.breadandcircus.com
- **Trader Joe's**, 899 Boylston Street, Boston, 617-262-6505; 748 Memorial Drive, Cambridge, 617-491-8582; 1317 Beacon Street, Brookline, 617-278-9997; 958 Highland Avenue, Needham, 781-449-6993; 1121 Washington Street, Newton, 617-244-1620; www.traderjoes.com
- **The Harvest Co-op Markets**, 581 Mass Ave., Cambridge, 617-524-1664, www.harvestcoop.com
- **Roche Bros.**, 377 Chestnut Street, Needham, 781-444-0411; Granite Crossing, 101 Falls Boulevard, Quincy, 617-471-0500; 1800 Centre Street, West Roxbury, 617-469-0757; www.rochebros.com
- **Whole Foods Market**, 340 River Street, Cambridge, 617-876-6990, www.wholefoods.com

FARMERS' MARKETS

For those hooked on farm fresh produce and meats, often organic, you can supplement your patronage of food co-ops by hitting the local farmers' markets. According to the Massachusetts Department of Food and Agriculture (MDFA), there are over 90 farmers' markets throughout Massachusetts, and many of them in the metro Boston area. Most are open only during warmer months, but Boston's famous **Haymarket** is open year-round. For exact schedules either call your town hall, or contact the MDFA at 617-626-1700, www.state.ma.us/dfa. Haymarket is not a farmers' market in the truest sense, open on Fridays and Saturdays, the Haymarket is where wholesalers try to sell produce that they couldn't sell to area retailers or restaurateurs. Everyone should experience the Haymarket at least once, but keep your wits about you and carry lots of singles. The Haymarket is a good place to go if you have specific bulk items in mind, for example, a case of limes or lemons for a margarita party, or strawberries for making jam. One Bostonian who frequents the Haymarket has gotten to know the sellers, and thus knows who has good produce, who will give her a good deal, and who will take back the goods if she gets it home and finds out they're spoiled. Fresh fish is sometimes available.

COMMUNITY GARDENS

Why pay someone else for fresh greens when you can grow them yourself? But where is that possible if you live in a densely populated neighborhood like Beacon Hill or the South End? A community garden is the answer. Over 200 community gardens exist in the greater Boston area. Perhaps two of the most visible in Boston proper are the community plots in the **Fens** (500 plots in the Richard Parker Memorial Victory Gardens, including some for children and special needs gardeners) and those in the **Southwest Corridor**, of which there are 15. Among other tasks, the **Boston Natural Areas Network** protects and supervises the local community gardens. To find out more about where the community gardens are, or sign up for a place to exercise your green thumb, contact them at 617-542-7696, www.bostonnatural.org/garden_list.php.

RESTAURANTS

Boston's dining opportunities run the gamut from expensive, high-end cuisine to hole-in-the-wall gems, with plenty of national chains. Newcomers may be a little disappointed on the mid-range, independent restaurant front. For example, there are not many fusion restaurants around here, and the ones that do open seem to have a hard time staying in business. It seems Bostonians are not natural food adventurers. Give us Irish pub fare and we are happy. Nearly every place has surf and turf, but vegans might have a hard time finding something suitable outside of more progressive neighborhoods like Jamaica Plain. That said, Boston does have some good, original establishments tucked away here and there. Choices range from small Italian eateries to sushi bars, and from low-key, but amazingly good, fried seafood shacks on the water to exclusive dining rooms like Locke-Ober or the next creation by Todd English—easily the city's most famous restaurateur.

If you'd like a little guidance as you explore area eateries, try the *Improper Bostonian* and *Stuff@Night*, both of which have ads you can skim for hip places to dine, and the former has restaurant reviews in every issue. You can also look to the "Food" sections of the *Herald*, *Globe*, *Phoenix*, and *TABs*, or to web sites like www.boston.citysearch.com and www.wheretodine.com. Ethnic food enthusiasts can supplement their knowledge by picking up a copy of *Boston Neighborhoods: A Foodlover's Walking, Eating, and Shopping Guide to Ethnic Enclaves in and Around Boston* by Lynda Morgenroth and Carleen Moira Powell (Globe Pequot Press). General restaurant advice can be found in the ubiquitous annual *Zagat Survey of Boston Restaurants*, www.zagat.com, or for the North End, try *Rosalie's Guide to Restaurants in the North End of Boston* by Rosalie Tagg Masella (published by Vesper).

ETHNIC FOODS

You can find the standard Chinese, Mexican, Indian, Vietnamese, Italian, French, and Middle Eastern restaurants spread throughout greater Boston. However, because Boston's distinct ethnic and immigrant groups tend to stick together, going to specific areas in the city will offer a selection of restaurants, bakeries, and grocers of the same cultural ilk.

Of course, the most obvious neighborhood in this respect is **Chinatown**, where you will find a well-rounded selection of not just Chinese, but also **Thai**, **Vietnamese**, and **Korean**. Chinatown is packed with independently-owned restaurants, and you can also shop for specialty groceries. Many of the restaurants stay open later than most of the rest of the city, so not only is Chinatown a great place to head with the family for dinner on a Sunday night, but it's also good during the wee hours of Sunday morning after a night out on the town. Other areas you might want to go for Vietnamese food include **Malden** and **Dorchester**, where some of the more recent Asian immigrants have settled.

Although we're about as far as you can get from the Pacific Rim and still be in the continental US, Boston does have decent sushi options. The biggest concentration of sushi bars and **Japanese** restaurants is in **Coolidge Corner** in Brookline. If you want to shop for specialty Japanese ingredients, you will need to cross over the Charles and head to the Porter Exchange building in Porter Square, where there is a Japanese supermarket and several sushi restaurants.

Because it is home to a large Jewish population, **Brookline** is also *the* place to go for **Jewish** food, particularly Coolidge and JFK corners. Delis, kosher kitchens, falafel joints, and bagel bakeries dot Harvard Street between Beacon Street and Comm Ave. You can even get kosher Chinese food at a restaurant near Brookline Village. If you are in Cambridge and you crave a knish and some matzo ball soup, try the S&S Deli in Inman Square, but be prepared for a long line to get in for weekend brunch. You might also want to check out Brookline (especially **Washington Square**) for **Russian** food. Some of the city's newer Russian immigrants have set up shop there, and you'll find a couple of restaurants and a grocery. As for **Armenian** food, head over to **Watertown**, home to one of the largest Armenian populations in the US.

While **Italian** restaurants are plentiful throughout the state, nothing beats the **North End** when you're looking for food from the old country. Over 40 restaurants and cafes take up the first floors of a significant number of the buildings. Some are big enough to take up two floors; some are so tiny they don't even have 10 tables; and some, like Giacomo's, are so popular they always have a line out the door, even on the coldest winter nights. There are also a number of small Italian groceries, or salumerias, which specialize in imported items from Italy. Keep in mind, parking in the North End is not an easy task. For other Italian enclaves, you might want to check out **Eastie** (specifically Sabatino's), although the Italian population there continues to lessen.

For newcomers in dire need a good **German** wiener schnitzel, try Jacob Wirth's, an unassuming pub in the Theater District. And if you have a car, take the 15-minute drive up Route 1 North to Karl's Sausage Kitchen, a small, specialty German grocer and deli along a particularly gaudy stretch of highway in Saugus that draws pilgrims from all over the area.

If **Greek** is your preference, you might want to hop in the car and check out **Roslindale**. You will also be interested to know that many Greek families own and run the pizza places/sub shops (a.k.a. submarine sandwich, grinder, hoagie, foot long, etc.) around the region. This means that when you stop into your neighborhood sub shop for a chicken-parmesan sub, you'll likely encounter pretty framed pictures of the Greek islands and be able to order a kabob as well.

For various types of **Latin** cuisine, your best bet may be to head to **East Boston** or **Cambridge**, both of which have many immigrants from Central and South America. Cambridge has a number of **Brazilan** and

Portuguese residents, and you can find some awesome restaurants serving those types of food between **Inman Square** and **East Cambridge**, particularly along Cambridge Street.

Cambridge is a melting pot where you are able to find ethnic foods of all sorts. This is best evidenced by Cambridge's Central Square, which bills itself as having an array of ethnic cuisines. So if you are hankering for something exotic but don't know what, take a stroll around. Check out Cardullo's in **Harvard Square**, a foreign grocery that imports goods from all over the world. Go there to find your English digestive biscuits or Australian vegamite.

SEAFOOD

One food market New Englanders have cornered is seafood. The abundance here is so great, that back in the early days, there were laws restricting the amount of times per month a wife could serve her husband lobster! First, a quick primer on local seafood culture. 1) There is a lot of fish on the menu here, and you will undoubtedly encounter something called "scrod." Scrod is *not* a type of fish, but rather the local term for the white fish that is the catch of the day, usually cod or haddock. 2) There is even more shellfish; options include shrimp, clams, scallops, mussels, oysters, and lobster. Crab is served, but it is not a specialty item. 3) Locals like to serve and be served their shellfish breaded and fried. Boston's nickname may be Beantown, but fried clams, fried shrimp, and fried scallops (all served with tartar sauce) are truly the local dish. Clams come two ways: strips, which are just the necks, and then the whole clams, which include the bellies along with the necks (whole clams are more desirable). Note: when you order a clam roll (or other type of shellfish), you'll be getting a fried helping of that shellfish on a hot dog roll. One exception, lobster rolls are made up of lobster meat, but not fried. 4) The other local dish is clam chowder. Undoubtedly you've eaten it before, but it is better here. New England clam chowder is the white kind; the red kind is Manhattan clam chowder. 5) And finally, the *pièce de resistance* of local shellfish is lobster. Some feel that eating lobster equals a whole lot of effort for only a little meat, but regardless, it is comfortably ensconced at the top of the shellfish chain in desirability and price. It is commonly the most expensive item on any menu, and often it will be listed at "market price," which means the price varies daily. You can have lobster boiled, steamed, Newberg, in bisque, in pie, or in a casserole, and when you eat it, the locals at nearby tables will be very, *very* excited if you've never had it before—there's nothing that can get a Bostonian to chat like asking for help opening your lobster. If you'd like to make it at home, it is easy and cheaper than ordering it at a restaurant. Throughout the region, grocery and seafood stores sell live lobsters.

Most fish and shellfish in Boston restaurants and grocery stores are bought daily from the fish pier in South Boston. If you'd like to experience this yourself, you can check it out, or you can head to Haymarket on Fridays and Saturdays for a smaller version. Follow your nose to the few fish vendors and take your pick.

One type of restaurant unique to New England is the clam shack, which serves mostly lobster and fried shellfish along the coast near beaches and harbors. They may look dodgy, but they're generally very good. The king of all these clam shack type establishments is Kelly's. There are lots of more medium-range and upscale seafood options around, too. You'll probably be tempted to try the Union Oyster House right next to Faneuil Hall. The ambiance and décor are fabulous, and it claims to be America's oldest restaurant, although some locals consider it as a tourist trap. Other popular places are Legal Seafoods, Jimmy's, and Anthony's Pier 4, also on the South Boston wharves.

LIQUOR STORES

Because of the so-called "blue laws" that regulate the purchase of alcohol, it's likely going to be more complicated to buy a bottle of wine than what you are probably used to. In Massachusetts you can't buy alcohol in grocery stores, gas stations, or convenience stores. There is one exception to the rule: a clause does allow supermarket chains to designate one store in an area as a liquor store—but still not on Sundays. You can buy spirits at liquor stores, otherwise known as package stores, or "packies"—but not on Sundays. Another secret: when driving through New Hampshire, locals, especially those who want to buy in bulk or on Sundays, like to stop off at the New Hampshire State Liquor Store (on Route 93) and take advantage of their lower consumer taxes on wine and liquor (no beer here).

CULTURAL LIFE

ONCE DUBBED THE "ATHENS OF AMERICA" FOR ITS VARIETY OF cultural offerings, Boston continues to uphold this weighty moniker. Options include music, movies, theater, opera, comedy, museums, lectures, events for kids, and just about anything else you can think of to pass the time and broaden your horizons. Institutions such as the Boston Symphony Orchestra and the Museum of Fine Arts are some of the oldest and best-regarded in the nation, and Boston's pop-music machine—best known for producing Aerosmith, New Kids on the Block, and the Cars—continues to influence the airwaves. The annual Boston Music Awards is evidence of how serious the music industry is here.

There is a nice theater district, which in addition to getting most major touring shows, frequently serves as a warm-up for the newest Broadway hit, big star cast included. And, if you're willing to venture a little north of the city, world famous playwright Israel Horowitz is the artistic director and founder of the Gloucester Stage Company.

During the warmer months, events in Boston are often staged outside. Summers are spent with the Boston Pops and other musical artists—from small local orchestras to major international bands—performing for free along the Charles River at the Hatch Shell on the Esplanade. On Friday nights Bostonians arrive in droves with chairs, blankets, and snacks in hand to take advantage of the Free Friday Flicks series of family-appropriate movies that take place at sundown. There are free shows on the common as well, like Shakespeare's *Henry V* and Bizet's *Carmen*.

Local newspapers are the best source for upcoming events. The dailies (the *Globe*, www.boston.com, and the *Herald*, www.townonline.com) produce special entertainment guides each week; the *Globe*'s "Calendar" is in the Thursday paper and the *Herald*'s "Scene" arrives on Friday. Both papers offer extensive entertainment sections on Sundays as well. Additional free sources are: the *Phoenix*, a weekly paper devoted to getting out and about, and the *Improper Bostonian* and *Stuff@Night*.

TICKETS

Specifics on ticket information are included in the newspaper listings. Depending on the venue, you'll either get your tickets from the theater or box office or through a ticket agency (usually Ticketmaster). If you cannot live without seeing an upcoming concert and the event is sold out, never fear, there are plenty of ticket resellers. Look them up in the Yellow Pages under "Ticket Sales Entertainment and Sports." Otherwise, try one of these options:

- **Arts Boston**, 325 Columbus Avenue, Suite 11, Boston, 617-262-8632, www.boston.com/artsboston, is a non-profit umbrella group partially funded by the Massachusetts Cultural Council. They sell discount tickets via mail order, letting you know what's available with their newsletter *Arts/Mail*. Call to get on their mailing list.
- **Berklee Performance Center**, 136 Mass Ave., Boston, 617-747-2261, www.berkleebpc.com; check with them at 617-747-8890 for recorded concert listings. Phone order tickets are through Ticketmaster. Onsite sales are cash, Master Card, or VISA only. The ticket booth is open Monday-Saturday, 10 a.m. to 6 p.m.
- **BOSTIX** is run by Arts Boston out of a booth at Faneuil Hall Marketplace and another at Copley Square. In addition to selling full-price advance tickets, you can also find half-price, day-of-show tickets and other bargains. Open Tuesday-Saturday between 10 a.m. and 6 p.m., and Sundays 11 a.m. to 4 p.m.; closed Thanksgiving and Christmas. Cash only, 617-482-BTIX, www.boston.com/artsboston/Bostix.
- **Boston Symphony Orchestra** offers 24-hour concert information; call 617-266-2378, or go to www.bso.org.
- **Next Ticketing**, 617-423-6000, www.nextticketing.com
- **Ticketmaster** most likely will have what you need. You can order tickets by phone at 617-931-2000 or online at www.ticketmaster.com.

MUSIC

Imagine seeing the next up-and-coming Branford Marsalis, Melissa Ferrick, or Melissa Etheridge, all alums of the Berklee College of Music. To catch current students' performances, head to the Berklee Performance Center. In various coffeehouses and small clubs around town, you can listen to modern folk singers. You can even find some bluegrass or line dancing in this Yankee bastion if you look hard enough. If more timeless fare is what you are after, there is certainly no shortage of world class jazz, blues, opera, and classical music to be found here.

PROFESSIONAL—SYMPHONIC, CHORAL, OPERA, CHAMBER

- Founded just 30 years ago, the **Boston Baroque**, P.O. Box 380190, Cambridge 02238, 617-484-9200, www.bostonbaroque.org, is actually the first Baroque orchestra in all of North America, and has been nominated for several Grammys. Like the Boston Philharmonic, seasonal shows go up at New England Conservatory of Music's Jordan Hall and Harvard's Sanders Theater; however, you should contact the Boston Baroque's own box office to buy individual tickets or season subscriptions.
- **Boston Camerata**, 140 Clarendon Street, Suite 503, Boston, 617-262-2092, www.bostoncamerata.com; this 50-year-old ensemble presents European medieval, renaissance and early baroque vocal and instrumental concerts at various locations around the metro area. On occasion they also perform 18th and 19th century American folk music.
- **Boston Chamber Music Society**, 10 Concord Avenue, Cambridge, 617-349-0086, www.bostonchambermusic.org, is an ensemble of eight and has been performing chamber music to local audiences for over 20 years. Performances are held at NEC's Jordan Hall on Friday night and at Harvard's Sanders Theater on Sunday night. All shows start at 7:30 p.m. Buy a subscription or tickets to individual concerts and special events through their box office.
- Performing as a gay community-based chorus for over 20 years, the acclaimed **Boston Gay Men's Chorus**, P.O. Box 1390, Boston 02117, 617-424-8900, www.bgmc.org, presents 175 singers. They perform diverse musical works covering the gamut of genres—from classical, to popular, to showtunes. Subscription series and individual tickets are available to the shows at Jordan and Symphony halls, as well as Northeastern's Blackman Auditorium and various special engagements around the region.
- Since 1958, elementary and secondary school students from all six New England states have been singing with the highly-esteemed **Greater Boston Youth Symphony Orchestras** (**GBYSO**), 855 Comm Ave., Boston, 617-353-3348, www.gbyso.org. Today, GYBSO contains four separate orchestras: Senior, Repertory, Junior Repertory, and Preparatory String. Over the years, GYBSO has performed all over the world, including in Europe, Israel, South America, and the White House. Locally, GYBSO usually performs its season at Symphony Hall, the Tsai Performance Center, BU Concert Hall, Sanders Theater (Harvard), and the Gardner Museum. Call the venue to purchase individual tickets or contact GBYSO for a subscription.

- Boston's major opera company, **Boston Lyric Opera**, 617-542-4912, www.blo.org, has been around since 1976. The opera's offices are located at 45 Franklin Street, but all performances are at the regal **Shubert Theatre**, 265 Tremont Street, in the theater district. Shows by the company's talented casts present all the visual splendor and vocal acrobatics one would expect of any established, well-funded opera company. The curtain is at 7:30 for evening performances and at 3 p.m. for matinees. English translations are provided on screens to either side of the stage for every show.
- **Boston Modern Orchestra Project (BMOP)**, 9 Birch Street, Roslindale, 617-363-0396, www.bmop.org, is one of the few full-size professional orchestras in the country devoted to performing works from only the 20th and 21st centuries. Look for between five and seven show series per year. Performances are held at various venues throughout the city, including Jordan Hall, MIT, Harvard, and Massachusetts College of Art. BMOP has a free tickets program for Boston area schools.
- The **Boston Philharmonic**, 295 Huntington Avenue, Boston, 617-236-0999, www.bostonphil.org, is a traditional classical orchestra, putting up shows at NEC's Jordan Hall and Harvard's Sanders Theater (www.fas.harvard.edu/~memhall). It's smaller than the Boston Symphony Orchestra, but wonderful, with talented soloists and a repertoire that ranges from classical to modern works. Contact the theaters' box offices for tickets.
- **Boston Symphony Orchestra and the Boston Pops**; in 1881, music-lover and philanthropist Henry Lee Higginson helped create the Boston Symphony Orchestra (BSO); by the turn of the century it had moved to its current home, Symphony Hall, located at 301 Mass. Ave. Acoustically, Symphony Hall is considered one of the world's finest concert halls, designed with the help of a Harvard assistant professor of physics, Wallace Clement Sabine, who, after visiting other acoustically-lauded concert halls, including Vienna's Musikvereinssaal and Leipzig's Neues Gewandhaus, chose a narrow, rectangular shoebox-like shape for the hall. It takes the echoes in Symphony Hall 1.8 seconds to die down with a packed house. The Boston Pops, first known as Boston Promenade, then as Popular Concerts, began in 1885, evolving out of Higginson's desire to keep the BSO musicians occupied during the summer. With a winter season only, many musicians were forced to tour Europe in the summers to stay financially solvent—and sometimes they didn't return to Boston. Today, the Pops orchestra and the BSO no longer share musicians. Beloved BSO musical director and conductor, Seiji Ozawa, recently retired after a 29 year stint with the orchestra—the longest tenure of any conductor with a major orchestra in the US. Pops conductor Keith Lockhart is still going strong, however. Every summer,

the BSO travels to Tanglewood in Lenox, Massachusetts, where patrons come *en masse* for outdoor concerts in the Berkshires. From May through July, the Boston Pops takes over Symphony Hall, and chairs are replaced with small tables for a festive, nightclub-like atmosphere. Each July, Boston Pops presents a series of free concerts at the Hatch Shell on the Esplanade. For **Pops tickets** call 888-266-1200 or 617-266-1200, or visit www.bso.org. **BSO tickets** are available in a number of ways:

- **Mail**: send orders that include a check and an SASE to the Symphony Hall Box Office, Symphony Hall, 301 Mass Ave., Boston, 02115 before June 1. If you are buying Tanglewood tickets after June 1, then send your orders to Ticket Office, Tanglewood, 207 West Street, Lenox, MA 01240.
- **Online**: buy your tickets online at www.bso.org; there is $4 per ticket online purchase fee.
- **Phone**: charge ticket orders by phone through Symphony Charge at 617-266-1200 or 888-266-1200. There is a $4 handling fee for each ticket ordered by phone. In the front of the Yellow Pages there is a floor plan of Symphony Hall to help you better pick your seats. Disabled patrons can call 617-638-9431 for specialized information; TTY/TDD 617-638-9289. If you are ordering **tickets for Tanglewood**, you must call Ticketmaster at 617-931-2000 or purchase in person. The Symphony Hall box office is open from 10 a.m. to 6 p.m., Monday-Saturday and through intermission on concert nights, except during the summer Tanglewood season. If you'd like to buy Tanglewood tickets at Tanglewood, the box office is open from 10 a.m. to 6 p.m. on weekdays, Saturdays 9 a.m. through intermission, and Sundays 10 a.m. through intermission. A limited number of **rush tickets** are made available on the day of the show for concerts held on Friday afternoon and Tuesday and Thursday nights. These tickets are less expensive ($8 vs. the usual $25 to $85 range) and are sold one per person at the Mass. Ave. entrance beginning at 5 p.m. on Tuesdays and Thursdays, and 9 a.m. on Fridays (cash only). An inexpensive option is to attend one of the BSO's **open rehearsals** on certain Wednesday nights and Thursday mornings throughout the season; these are the final rehearsals before BSO concerts. Call the concert line, 617-266-2378, to find out dates and times. Seating is unreserved.
- **New England Conservatory of Music (NEC)**, 290 Huntington Avenue, 617-585-1100, www.newenglandconservatory.edu; has been in existence for over 120 years and schools many prize-winning musicians, some of whom do nation-wide concert tours even before graduation. Musicians can earn both undergraduate and graduate degrees here. The school hosts over 400 concerts by faculty, students and

guests at varying locations on campus and many are free. NEC's **Jordan Hall** (box office: 617-536-2412), is on the National Register of Historic Places and boasts an acoustically superior performance facility. It's a little newer than Symphony Hall—turn of the 20th century—and boasts a pitched balcony and the traditional ornate decorations of all of Boston's old concert and theatrical halls. Unlike Symphony Hall, there is no room for concessions during intermission. Over 100 free concerts are given at this hall each year by NEC students and faculty. The hall also hosts a number of performances by the Boston Philharmonic, Handel & Haydn Society (H&H), Boston Gay Men's Chorus, and Boston Baroque. Jordan Hall seats 1,000 and is located at the corner of Huntington Avenue and Gainsborough Street in Boston.

- **Handel & Haydn Society**, Horticultural Hall, 300 Mass Ave., Boston, 617-266-3605, www.handelandhaydn.org, is BSO's older brother by 66 years. H&H was founded in 1815 to improve the choral music performance in Boston, and is the oldest continuously performing arts organization in the US. It is closely associated with such historical personages as Julia Ward Howe, better known as the composer of the Battle Hymn of the Republic. Classical choral enthusiasts may subscribe to H&H's annual series, split between Jordan and Symphony halls, or attend any of the other concerts around Boston and Cambridge. Musical seasons cover classical masterworks for choral and period orchestra.

COMMUNITY—SYMPHONIC, CHORAL, OPERA, CHAMBER

If you're interested in singing for fun, your first stop should be the **Greater Boston Choral Consortium**, www.bostonsings.org. This association of choral organizations in the greater Boston area will help you find the chorus that most closely matches your interests and geographical location. Other community musical groups include:
- **Boston Bel Canto Opera**, 168 West Brookline, Boston, 617-424-0900, www.bbcopera.com; presents operatic masterworks with the North Shore Philharmonic Orchestra at Jordan Hall.
- **Newton Symphony Orchestra**, 61 Washington Park, Newton, 617-965-2555, www.newtonsymphony.org
- **Philharmonic Society of Arlington**, www.psarlington.org; includes the Arlington-Belmont Chorale, Arlington Philharmonic Orchestra, and the Arlington-Belmont Chamber Chorus.
- **Pro Arte Chamber Orchestra**, 99 Bishop Allen Drive, Cambridge, 617-661-7067, www.proarte.org; freelance musician-run cooperative orchestra bringing a progressive mix of classical and new chamber music to the stage.

DANCE—BALLET, JAZZ, MODERN, FOLK, RELIGIOUS

Boston is home to a small number of dance companies, from the prestigious Boston Ballet to Dance Umbrella, which, in addition to other performances, hosts Mark Morris' dance troupe for two months every year. In the summer, don't forget to check out **Jacob's Pillow**, www.jacobspillow.org, a dance festival in western Massachusetts. For more information on the local dance scene, taking classes, or joining a company, try the non-profit **Boston Dance Alliance**, www.bostondancealliance.org, 617-482-4588.

THE BOSTON BALLET

Founded nearly 30 years ago, this ballet company and its ballet school enjoy a reputation as one of the country's finest. The Boston Ballet performs both full-length classics and modern works, including an acclaimed production of Tchaikovsky's *The Nutcracker*. Devoted subscribers come to see the ballet's lovely, world-caliber shows every season at the impressive Wang Center for the Performing Arts, a hall known for its luxurious and ornate 1920s architecture. **For tickets** contact the following:
- **The Boston Ballet**, 617-695-6950, www.bostonballet.org
- **The Wang Center for the Performing Arts**, 270 Tremont Street, Boston, 617-482-9393, www.wangcenter.org
- **Ticketmaster**, 617-931-2000, www.ticketmaster.com

Additional dance troupes and studios include:
- Founded in 1992 by choreographer Anna Myer, **Anna Myer and Dancers**, 39 Prince Street #3, Cambridge, 617-547-9699, www.annamyerdancers.org, this company has received much critical acclaim in both Boston and New York. Shows display the choreographer's unique brand of dance, described as a mix of classical, modern, and post-modern influences. The company performs at various venues throughout the region, including the Tsai and Orpheum theaters.
- The **Boston Liturgical Dance Ensemble**, 617-552-6130, www.blde.org, presents Christian-inspired dance performances, including the spiritual exercises of St. Ignatius Loyola, mostly at Catholic-affiliated universities across the region.
- **Dance Collective of Boston**, 143 Cummins Highway, Boston, 781-861-0735, http://dancecollective.org, is a contemporary dance company that performs in unusual locations such as train stations and malls, as well as a number of area theaters.
- **Green Street Studios**, 185 Green Street (Central Square), Cambridge, 617-864-3191, www.greenstreetstudios.org, is a small

Cambridge-based center for movement and dance, which includes a concert series and some special events.
- While many go to the **Jeannette Neill Dance Studio**, 261 Friend Street, 5th Floor, Boston, 617-523-1355, www.jndance.com, for lessons, there are also performances, including twice-yearly repertory shows at the Tsai Center for Performing Arts.
- **Mandala Folk Dance Ensemble**, P.O. Box 390642, Cambridge 02139, 617-868-3641, http://users.rcn.com/mandala.ma.ultranet/, is a multicultural folk-dancing troupe, performing shows representative of a variety of cultures, from Croatian to Chinese. They perform at various venues around the area.
- **Prometheus Dance**, 536 Mass Ave., Cambridge, 617-576-5336, www.prometheusdance.org, is a contemporary dance ensemble of 10 people presenting a repertory of shows that take on social and psychological issues. They perform in various locations throughout New England, and often tour the world.
- **Snappy Dance Theater**, P.O. Box 400075, Cambridge, 617-718-2497, www.snappydance.com, is a small, relatively new dance company.

CONTEMPORARY MUSIC

With all the young people here, Boston's modern music scene is hopping. Musicians and audiences fill the innumerable clubs on a nightly basis. Generally, Boston's club scene is split into four key areas: Harvard Avenue in Allston/Brighton; the North Station and Faneuil Hall areas in downtown Boston; Kenmore Square/Landsdowne Street, and Central Square in Cambridge.

CONCERT FACILITIES

The following play host to the big shows:
- **Fleet Center**, 1 Fleet Center Place, Causeway Street (North Station), Boston, 617-624-1000, www.fleetcenter.com
- **Orpheum Theater**, 1 Hamilton Place, Boston, 617-679-0810; right across from the Park Street T stop.
- **Fleet Boston Pavilion at Harbor Lights**, www.fleetboston.com; while the pavilion is actually located along the harbor in South Boston, you can buy your tickets either at the Orpheum Theatre's box office, or through Ticketmaster at 617-931-2000.
- **Gillette Stadium**, 1 Patriot Place, Foxboro, event line: 508-543-3900; tickets: 800-543-1776, www.gillettestadium.com
- **North Shore Music Theatre**, 62 Dunham Road, Beverly, 978-232-7200, www.nsmt.org; musicals, celebrity concerts, and concerts for children.

- **Somerville Theatre**, 55 Davis Square, Somerville, 617-625-4088, www.somervilletheatreonline.com
- **Tsongas Arena**, 300 Arcand Drive, Lowell, 978-848-6938, www.paul tsongasarena.com; although it's out on the campus of UMASS-Lowell, it's a popular and relatively convenient general admission venue for many tours coming to Boston. Parking is easy.
- **Tweeter Center**, 885 South Main Street, Mansfield, 508-339-2333, www.tweetercenter.com/boston; outdoor summer concert venue about an hour south of Boston, formerly known as Great Woods.
- **Worcester Centrum**, 50 Foster Street, Worcester, 508-755-6800, www.centrumcentre.com

NIGHTCLUBS

The following clubs feature mostly local and New England-based acts. They also host national musicians who are touring smaller venues. Many of the places that have live music aren't too rigid about the styles of artists they book. That is to say, one night a folk singer may be playing and the next night it will be an '80s cover band. With that in mind, call the venue to find out about upcoming performers.

ALTERNATIVE, ROCK, PUNK, HIP-HOP
- **Abbey Lounge**, 3 Beacon Street (Inman Square), Somerville, 617-441-9631, www.schnockered.com/abbey; it's the ultimate dive.
- **Avalon**, 15 Landsdowne Street, Boston, 617-262-2424, http://avalon.billcrook.com; where all the best DJ's come, but highly favored with the young set. Sometimes better known performers do intimate shows here.
- **The Burren**, 246 Elm Street (Davis Square), Somerville, 617-776-6896, www.burren.com; Irish, 1980s, rock, etc.
- **Common Ground**, 83 Harvard Avenue, Allston, 617-783-2071
- **Choppin' Block Pub**, 724 Huntington Avenue (Mission Hill), Boston, 617-734-4177
- **Christopher's**, 1920 Mass Ave. (Porter Square), Cambridge, 617-876-9180
- **Club Passim**, 47 Palmer Street (Harvard Square), Cambridge, 617-492-7679, www.clubpassim.org
- **Green Dragon Tavern**, 11 Marshall Street (Faneuil Hall), Boston, 617-367-0055, ww.celticweb.com/greendragon
- **The Harp**, 85 Causeway Street (North Station), Boston, 617-742-1010
- **Harper's Ferry**, 158 Brighton Avenue, Allston, 617-254-7380, www.harpersferryboston.com; roots rock and blues.
- **The Irish Embassy Pub**, 234 Friend Street (North Station), Boston, 617-742-6618, www.celticweb.com/embassy

- **The Kells**, 161 Brighton Avenue, Brighton, 617-782-9082
- **Kendall Café**, 233 Cardinal Medeiros Avenue (Kendall Square), Cambridge, 617-661-0993, www.thekendall.com; great beer selection.
- **Kirkland Café**, 425 Washington Street, Somerville, 617-482-4920
- **The Linwood**, 69 Kilmarnock Street, Boston, 617-267-8644
- **The Lizard Lounge**, 1667 Mass Ave., Cambridge, 617-357-5825
- **The Middle East**, 472 Mass Ave. (Central Square), Cambridge, 617-864-EAST, www.mideastclub.com
- **Midway Café**, 3496 Washington Street, JP, 617-524-9038, www.midwaycafe.com
- **Milky Way Lounge and Lanes**, 403-405 Centre Street, JP, 617-524-3740, www.milkywayjp.com; Latin, karaoke, rock, alternative—really anything goes here.
- **The Paradise Rock Club**, 969 Comm Ave., Boston, 617-562-8800
- **The Rack**, 24 Clinton Street (Faneuil Hall), Boston, 617-725-1061, www.therackboston.com
- **The Sky Bar**, 518 Somerville Avenue, Somerville, 617-623-5223
- **Toad**, 1920 Mass Ave. (Porter Square), Cambridge, 617-497-4950
- **TT the Bear's**, 10 Brookline Street (Central Square), Cambridge, 617-492-BEAR, www.ttthebears.com

FOLK/COFFEEHOUSES
- **Club Passim**, 47 Palmer Street (Harvard Square), Cambridge, 617-492-7679, www.clubpassim.org
- **Nameless Coffeehouse**, 3 Church Street, Cambridge, 617-864-1630, www.namelesscoffeehouse.org

REGGAE, FUNK, WORLD BEAT, GOSPEL, BRAZILIAN, AND SPANISH
If reggae's your thing, you can check the local scene at www.BostonReggae.com, to find out who is playing, when, and where. The following clubs offer international music (live and recorded) and run the gamut from gritty to glamorous:
- **All Asia**, 334 Mass Ave., Cambridge, 617-497-1544, www.allasiacafe.com
- **An Tua Nua**, 835 Beacon Street, Boston, 617-262-2121
- **Bill's Bar**, 5.5 Landsdowne Street, Boston, 617-421-9678, www.billsbar.com; reggae on Sundays
- **Green Street Grill**, 280 Green Street (Central Square), Cambridge, 617-876-1655, www.greenstreetgrill.com; offers jazz, rock, blues, salsa, funk, and so on
- **Hennessy's**, 25 Union Street (Faneuil Hall), Boston, 617-742-2121, www.somerspubs.com/hennessyspage; Irish, reggae, karaoke, bluegrass, Caribbean, dance music

- **The Middle East**, 472 Mass. Ave. (Central Square), Cambridge, 617-864-EAST, www.mideastclub.com
- **Milky Way Lounge and Lanes**, 403-405 Centre Street, JP, 617-524-3740, www.milkywayjp.com
- **The Paradise Rock Club**, 969 Comm Ave., Boston, 617-562-8800
- **Plough and Stars**, 912 Mass Ave. (Central Square), Cambridge, 617-441-3455, www.ploughandstars.com
- **Rhythm & Spice**, 315 Mass Ave., Cambridge, 617-497-4308, www.rspice.com
- **River Street Café**, 477 River Street, Mattapan, 617-698-7041
- **Roxy**, 279 Tremont Street, Boston, 617-338-ROXY, www.roxyplex.com
- **Ryles Jazz Club**, 212 Hampshire (Inman Square), Cambridge, 617-876-9330, www.rylesjazz.com; "Boston's finest jazz." Latin and salsa, too
- **Sophia's**, 1270 Boylston Street, Boston, 617-351-7001; *the* place for Latin music and salsa, with four floors of live music, dancing, and fun.
- **The Western Front**, 343 Western Avenue, Cambridge, 617-492-7772, www.thewesternfrontclub.com; jazz, reggae, Latin, salsa

JAZZ, BLUES, R&B, CABARET

Boston jazz and blues fans tend to be very discriminating, so expect some highly knowledgeable and appreciative audiences at the following venues:

- **Berklee College of Music/Berklee Performance Center**, 136 Mass. Ave., box office, 617-747-2261, www.berkleebpc.com; this 1,200-seat performance hall hosts jazz concerts.
- **The Cantab**, 738 Mass Ave. (Central Square), Cambridge, 617-354-2685, www.cantablounge.com, is a popular spot for some of everything, from jazz to blues to Tuesday night bluegrass to dancing to poetry slams.
- **Choppin' Block Pub**, 724 Huntington Avenue (Mission Hill), Boston, 617-734-4177
- **Encore Lounge**, 275 Tremont Street, Boston, 617-338-7699, www.roxyplex.com/encore; cabaret
- **The Good Life**, 28 Kingston Street, 617-451-2622; live jazz Thursday, Friday, and Saturday night
- **Harper's Ferry**, 158 Brighton Avenue, Allston, 617-254-7380, www.harpersferryboston.com; roots rock and blues
- **Johnny D's**, 17 Holland Street (Davis Square), Somerville, 617-776-2004, www.johnnyds.com; live music seven nights/week, including jazz brunch, and Sunday blues.
- **Les Zygomates**, 129 South Street, Boston, 617-542-5108, www.winebar.com; wine bar and bistro with jazz.

- **Limbo**, 49 Temple Place, Boston, 617-338-0280, www.limbo boston.com; for jazz, soul, and gospel
- **Lucky's Lounge**, 355 Congress Street (Fort Point Channel), Boston, 617-547-0759, www.luckyslounge.com; pays particular homage to Sinatra.
- **Pa's Lounge**, 345 Somerville Avenue, Somerville, 617-776-1557; blues jam
- **Regattabar**, in the swank Charles Hotel, 1 Bennett Street (Harvard Square), Cambridge, 617-661-5000
- **Ryles Jazz Club**, 212 Hampshire (Inman Square), Cambridge, 617-876-9330, www.rylesjazz.com; "Boston's finest jazz." Latin and salsa, too.
- **Scullers Jazz Club**, Guest Quarters Suite Hotel, 400 Soldiers Field Road, 617-562-4111, www.scullersjazz.com
- **The Sugar Shack**, 1 Boylston Place, Boston, 617-351-7000
- **Wally's Cafe**, 427 Mass Ave., Boston, 617-424-1408, www.wallys cafe.com; one of Boston's least assuming but most respected jazz clubs. Live music 365 days/year.
- **Wonder Bar**, 186 Harvard Avenue, Allston, 617-351-2665, jazz every night

COUNTRY/BLUEGRASS

Here in the Yankee home of the bean and the cod, country music is a little harder to find. Begin your search with one of these:
- **The Cantab Lounge**, 738 Mass Ave. (Central Square), Cambridge, 617-354-2684; popular spot for some of everything, from jazz to blues to bluegrass to dancing to poetry slams.
- **Hannah's**, 499 Broadway, Somerville, 617-623-5302, www.hannah somerville.com
- **Hennessy's**, 25 Union Street (Faneuil Hall), Boston, 617-742-2121, www.somerspubs.com/hennessyspage

IRISH AND CELTIC

Boston's huge Irish population makes for plenty of popular Irish pubs and in them authentic Celtic music. Here are just a few:
- **The Black Rose**, 160 State Street (Faneuil Hall), Boston, 617-742-2286, www.irishconnection.com/blackrose
- **The Burren**, 246 Elm Street (Davis Square), Somerville, 617-776-6896, www.burren.com. Irish, 1980s, rock, etc.; was featured in the film *Next Stop Wonderland*.
- **Green Briar**, 304 Washington Street, Brighton, 617-789-4100, www.briargroup.com/greenbriar
- **Green Dragon Tavern**, 11 Marshall Street (Faneuil Hall), Boston, 617-367-0055, www.celticweb.com/greendragon

- **The Harp**, 85 Causeway Street (North Station), Boston, 617-742-1010
- **Hennessy's**, 25 Union Street (Faneuil Hall), Boston, 617-742-2121, www.somerspubs.com/hennessyspage; Irish, reggae, karaoke, bluegrass, Caribbean, dance music
- **The Kells**, 161 Brighton Avenue, Brighton, 617-782-9082
- **The Kinsale**, 2 Center Plaza (Government Center), Boston, 617-742-5577
- **The Kinvara Pub**, 34 Harvard Avenue, Allston, 617-783-9400
- **O'Leary's**, 1010 Beacon Street, Brookline, 617-734-0049, www.olearys-pub.com
- **Plough and Stars**, 912 Mass Ave. (Central Square), Cambridge, 617-441-3455, www.ploughandstars.com
- **Tir na nÓg**, 366A Somerville Avenue (Union Square), Somerville, 617-628-4300, www.thenog.com

DJS/SPINNING, LOUNGES, PIANO BARS

Boston is just starting to offer loungey places that are so favored for their swank yet sociable atmosphere. Establishments where you can listen to some good tunes at a volume where you can still chat with your friends and not feel pressured to dance follow:

- **Blue Cat Café**, 94 Mass Ave., Boston, 617-247-9922; DJ spins several nights/week
- **Caprice**, 275 Tremont Street, Boston, 617-292-0080, www.capricelounge.com; pricey lounge that appeals to the Euro set.
- **Ekco Lounge**, 41 Essex Street (Chinatown), Boston, 617-417-0186
- **Enormous Room**, 567 Mass Ave. (Central Square), Cambridge, 617-491-5550; like it says, just one big room, but with nice couches and good drinks.
- **Felt**, 533 Washington Street (Ladder District), Boston, 617-350-5555, www.feltboston.com; swank lounging and pool
- **Jake Ivory's**, 9 Lansdowne Street, Boston, 617-247-1222, www.jakeivorys.com; dueling piano bar. A little on the cheesy side, but still popular, especially for bachelorette parties.
- **The Modern**, 30-36 Lansdowne Street, Boston, 617-351-2581
- **RiverGods**, 125 River Street, Cambridge, 617-576-1881; good spinning, low key and slightly out of the way, between Central Square and Cambridgeport.
- **West Street Grille**, 15 West Street, Boston, 617-423-0300, www.weseatyou.com/restaurants/700/wgr; bar downstairs, lounge upstairs

DANCE CLUBS (POP, TECHNO)

Most Boston club proprietors and club goers take themselves *very* seriously. Long lines, steep cover charges, and dress codes are the norm; men are often turned away for dress that is less than chic. Here today and gone tomorrow is common. Check the Yellow Pages under "Night Clubs" for the current list of options.

THEATER

Boston's theater district officially covers a three- to four-block area near both Boston Common and Chinatown, but theaters flourish all over the greater Boston area. You can find everything from longstanding favorite shows like Shear Madness and The Blue Man Group to national touring productions, to shows doing a pre-Broadway test run, to locally-produced musicals, comedies, and dramas—not to mention the college and community theater productions.

Aside from checking the current events sections of the local papers, visit the **Theater Mirror** web site at www.theatermirror.com, which includes listings of current shows, theaters, and audition dates around the city. If you're more interested in performing, check with **StageSource**, 617-720-6066, www.stagesource.org, the local "alliance of theater artists and producers" in New England. Their book, *The Source*, is an invaluable resource that lists Boston area theater companies, upcoming auditions, head shot photographers, acting lessons, and more.

In the summers, you can take advantage of the summerstock productions and festivals put on in western Massachusetts, such as Shakespeare & Company, www.shakespeare.org; the Berkshire Theatre Festival, www.berkshiretheatre.org; and the mother of them all—the Williamstown Theater Festival, www.wtfestival.org.

PROFESSIONAL THEATER

Many of the following theaters and performance centers stage a wide range of events in addition to plays. Theater junkies should consider getting a subscription to a particular house. Not only is it good for the theater, but your year membership tends to come with perks like reduced prices on tickets for you and friends and flexibility in seating and attendance dates.

BOSTON
- **Berklee Performance Center**, 136 Mass Ave., Boston, 617-747-2261, www.berkleebpc.com
- **Boston Center for the Arts/Cyclorama**, 539 Tremont Street, Boston, 617-426-ARTS, www.bcaonline.org; quality and size of shows can vary, from average productions of Christopher Durang plays in the tiny black box space to large, entertaining musicals such as *Batboy*.

- **Boston Playwrights' Theatre**, 949 Comm Ave., Boston, 617-353-5443, www.bu.edu/bpt; committed to producing new plays in their small, but professional, space.
- **Boston Rock Opera**, www.rockopera.com
- **Boston Theatre Works**, 617-728-4321, www.bostontheatreworks.com; shows go up at the Tremont Theatre, 276 Tremont Street.
- **Charles Playhouse**, 74 Warrenton Street, Boston, 617-426-6912, www.broadwayinboston.com
- **Charlestown Working Theatre**, 442 Bunker Hill Street, Charlestown, 617-242-3285, www.charlestownworkingtheater.org
- **Colonial Theatre**, 106 Boylston Street, Boston, 617-426-9366, www.broadwayinboston.com
- **Copley Theatre**, 225 Clarendon Street, Boston, 617-266-7262; the unassuming space may look more like a school auditorium than a professional theater space, but they host larger, well-done shows. One of the best kept secrets of Boston theater.
- **Emerson Majestic Theatre**, 219 Tremont Street, Boston, 617-824-8000, www.maj.org
- **Hatch Memorial Shell**, Charles River Esplanade, Boston, 617-727-5114; free concerts and other performances from mid-June to mid-September
- **Huntington Theatre Company**, 264 Huntington Street, Boston, 617-266-0800, www.bu.edu/huntington; one of Boston's foremost theaters, the Huntington actually isn't in the theater district. Students should take advantage of the great rates for a season flexpass—it works out to about $25/ticket for six shows, any available seat you want, any night per show.
- **Lyric Stage Company**, 140 Clarendon Street, Boston, 617-437-7172, www.lyricstage.com; this is a more modern, albeit cramped, space on the second floor of the YMCA between the Back Bay and the South End, but it has a great atmosphere and produces some important, fine-tuned pieces.
- **Playwrights' Platform**, P.O. Box 35151, Boston 02135, www.playwrightsplatform.org; cooperative developmental theater for new plays, including biweekly readings and a summer festival. Sunday evening meetings at the Abbott Theatre, 9 Spring Street, Waltham.
- **Publick Theatre**, 1400 Soldiers Field Road, Brighton, 617-PUBLICK, www.publicktheatre.com; classic outdoor summer theater, spoken and signed, including main stage and Shakespeare productions.
- **Shubert Theatre**, 265 Tremont Street, Boston, 617-482-9393, www.wangcenter.org; stages some of the biggest productions that pass through Boston.

- **Strand Theatre**, 543 Columbia Road, Dorchester, 617-282-8000, www.strandtheatre.org
- **The Wang Center for the Performing Arts**, 270 Tremont Street, Boston, 617-482-9393, www.wangcenter.org; a splendid theater dating back to the 1800s, with gold leaf dripping from the mural-covered ceilings. Like the Shubert, it is also home to some of the biggest shows (dance and theater) in the city.
- **The Wheelock Family Theatre**, 180 The Riverway, Boston, 617-734-4760, www.wheelock.edu/wft
- **The Wilbur**, 246 Tremont Street, Boston, 617-423-4008, www.broadwayinboston.com

BOSTON METRO AREA

- **American Repertory Theatre** (**ART**), Loeb Drama Center, 64 Brattle Street, Cambridge, 617-547-8300, www.amrep.org
- **Cambridge Multicultural Arts Center**, 41 Second Street, Cambridge, 617-577-1400, www.cmacusa.org
- **Gloucester Stage Company**, 267 East Main Street, Gloucester, 978-281-4433, www.gloucesterstage.com, with director in-residence, Israel Horovitz. Summer only.
- **New Repertory Theatre**, 1155 Walnut Street, Newton Highlands, 617-332-7050, www.newrep.org; 20-year-old theater performing serious works in a unique and intimate space inside a church.
- **Orpheum Regional Performing Arts Center**, 1 School Street, Foxboro, 508-543-ARTS, www.orpheum.org; although a bit outside of the city, this theater manages to attract actors like Olympia Dukakis and Raquel Welch to its impressive productions. A season membership is definitely worth considering.
- **Sanders Theatre**, Harvard University's Memorial Hall, 45 Quincy Street, Cambridge, 617-496-4595, box office, 617-496-2222, www.fas.harvard.edu/~memhall/sanders
- **Stoneham Theatre**, 395 Main Street, Stoneham, 781-279-2200, www.stonehamtheatre.org
- **Theatre Cooperative**, Elizabeth Peabody House, 277 Broadway, Somerville, 617-625-1300, www.theatrecoop.org; offers high-caliber plays despite their small size and funding level. The theater is hard to find, but parking is easy.
- **TheatreZone**, 100 Captains Row #306, Chelsea, 617-887-2336, www.theaterzone.org; based out of Chelsea, but puts up progressive shows at the Actor's Workshop in the Theatre District in downtown Boston.
- **Turtle Lane Playhouse**, 283 Melrose Street, Newton, 617-244-0169, www.turtle-lane.com

- **Underground Railway Theater**, 41 Foster Street, Arlington, 781-643-6916, www.undergroundrailwaytheater.org; national touring and local performing company presenting a synthesis of theater, puppetry, and music presented in a range from adult cabarets to full-length plays.

In addition to the above professional productions, the large number of colleges and universities ensure a variety of interesting, cheap, progressive student productions. Emerson and BU, in particular, are known for the quality of their theater departments, and Harvard's Hasty Pudding Club puts on a new, student-written, all-male show (famous for their traditional bawdy humor and cross-dressing) every year, in addition to the highly publicized roast of Hollywood icons. Check with individual schools to see what shows are going up at any given time.

FILM

Just look in the paper to find today's listings of the biggest Hollywood blockbusters showing at the nearest 20-plex. Those in search of the harder to find flicks, including art, revival, foreign, independent, classic, and second run films, can check with the following.

ALTERNATIVE AND ART FILM HOUSES

- **Belmont Studio Cinema**, 376 Trapelo Road, Belmont, 617-484-1706, www.studiocinema.com
- **Brattle Theatre**, 40 Brattle Street (Harvard Square), Cambridge, 617-876-6837, www.brattlefilm.org
- **Coolidge Corner Theatre**, 290 Harvard Street, Brookline, 617-734-2500, www.coolidge.org
- **Harvard Film Archive**, 24 Quincy Street (Harvard Square), Cambridge, 617-495-4700, www.harvardfilmarchive.org
- **Kendall Square Landmark Theaters**, 1 Kendall Square, Cambridge, 617-494-9800, www.landmarktheatres.com
- **Landmark Embassy Cinema**, 16 Pine Street, Waltham, 781-893-2500, www.landmarktheaters.com
- **Loews Cineplex Copley Place**, 100 Huntington Avenue, Boston, 617-266-1300
- **Loews Cineplex Harvard Square**, 10 Church Street, Cambridge, 617-864-4580
- **MIT Film Series**, 77 Mass Ave., Cambridge, 617-258-8881
- **Museum of Fine Arts**, 465 Huntington Avenue, Boston, 617-369-3300, www.mfa.org/film

- **Somerville Theater**, 55 Davis Square, Somerville, 617-625-5700, www.somervilletheatreonline.com
- **West Newton Cinema**, 1296 Washington Street, West Newton, 617-964-6060, www.westnewtoncinema.com

Boston also has two venues for the popular **IMAX films**, arrive early as many showings sell out.
- **Mugar Omni Theater**, Museum of Science, Science Park, Boston, 617-723-2500, www.mos.org.
- **Simons IMAX Theater**, New England Aquarium, Central Wharf, Boston, 800-296-7600, www.neaq.org/visit/imax

FILM FESTIVALS

- **Boston Film Festival**, www.bostonfilmfestival.org; 10-day festival every fall that serves as the US or world premiere festival for many major films.
- **Boston Gay & Lesbian Film/Video Festival**, www.mfa.org/film
- **Boston Jewish Film Festival**, 617-244-9899, www.bjff.org; takes place every November with the support of the MFA.
- **Boston Festival of Films from Iran**, www.mfa.org/film
- **Boston Asian American Film & Video Festival**, www.mfa.org/film
- **Boston French Film Festival**, www.mfa.org/film
- **Boston Irish Film Festival** celebrates Ireland and the Irish on screen every April, www.irishfilmfestival.com.
- **New England Film & Video Festival**, 617-783-9241, www.bfvf.org/festival; the biggie, sponsored by the Boston Film and Video Foundation. Takes place in March.

MUSEUMS

Boston is blessed with world-class museums, and US history buffs will be thrilled to call this area home. Indeed, Boston's history is that of our nation, and virtually nowhere else in the country offers such a vivid portal to our nation's past. Many of the historical sites are right in the thick of downtown Boston, and are connected along the not-quite-three-mile **Freedom Trail**. Taking a few hours to walk it is a great way to gain an appreciation of the rich local history and to familiarize yourself with the city. (See below for more information.)

ART AND CULTURE MUSEUMS

In addition to all the museums in and around Boston, patrons of the arts will enjoy taking advantage of the multitude of small galleries dedicated to fine art and photography. Many galleries are concentrated along Newbury Street and in Fort Point Channel, but others can be found throughout the metro area, in Cambridge, Brookline, Somerville, and elsewhere. Take a stroll in one of the hotspots, or look in the *Improper Bostonian* or one of the weekly papers for listings if you have something more specific in mind.

In the meantime, here is a listing of the **major art museums** for the greater Boston area:

- **Davis Museum and Cultural Center**, Wellesley College, 106 Central Street, Wellesley, 781-283-2501, www.wellesley.edu/DavisMuseum
- **DeCordova Museum and Sculpture Park**, Sandy Pond Road, Lincoln, 781-259-8355, www.decordova.org; the museum is a castle-style building on 35 acres of parkland with an 1,800 seat amphitheatre.
- **Harvard University Art Museums**, 617-495-9400, www.artmuseums.harvard.edu; open seven days a week, Monday-Saturday, 10 a.m. to 5 p.m., Sundays, 1 p.m. to 5 p.m. $6.50 regular admission, $5 seniors and students. The following museums, all of which are in Harvard Square, Cambridge, hold Harvard's art collections: **Arthur M. Sackler Museum**, 485 Broadway, offers fine arts and sculpture in the Indian, Asian, Islamic and Ancient traditions; **Busch-Reisinger Museum**, 32 Quincy Street, for German Expressionists; and **Fogg Art Museum**, Werner Otto Hall on Prescott Street, for European and American masters in all media.
- **Institute of Contemporary Art (ICA)**, 955 Boylston Street, Boston, 617-266-5152, www.icaboston.org; contemporary art, including painting, sculpture, photography, film, video, and live performances. Admission is $7 regular, $5 for students and seniors. Free admission Thursdays after 5 p.m.
- **Isabella Stewart Gardner Museum**, 280 The Fenway, 617-566-1401 (617-734-1359 for concert information), www.gardnermuseum.org; the eccentric Mrs. Gardner built this Venetian-style palazzo at the turn of the century to house the results of a lifetime spent collecting European art. A concert series runs from September through June. Free to all students on Wednesdays.
- **Mass MoCA**, 87 Marshall Street, North Adams, 413-664-4481, www.massmoca.org; Massachusetts does have a museum of modern art, it just so happens to be way out in the western part of the state. If you've got a car and a penchant for progressive art, you'll find it well worth the trip. Open 11 a.m. to 5 p.m., except Tuesdays.
- **McMullen Museum of Art**, Boston College, 140 Comm Ave., Devlin Hall 108, Chestnut Hill, www.bc.edu/bc_org/avp/cas/artmuseum; open weekdays, 11 a.m. to 4 p.m., weekends noon to 5 p.m. Free admission and parking.

- **MIT List Visual Arts Center**, 20 Ames Street, Building E15/Wiesner Building, Atrium Level, Cambridge, 617-253-4680, web.mit.edu/lvac; contemporary art. Admission is free and open to the public.
- **Museum of Fine Arts Boston**, 465 Huntington Avenue, Boston, 617-267-9300, www.mfa.org; extensive collections of Asian, Egyptian, Classical Greek, and Roman art; and European and American sculpture, textiles, furniture and paintings. Excellent traveling exhibits. Classes, concerts, singles events, lectures, films, etc. Open seven days, starting at 10 a.m.
- **Museum of the National Center of African-American Artists**, 300 Walnut Avenue, Roxbury, 617-442-8014, www.ncaaa.org; changing exhibitions of contemporary and historical African, African-American, and Caribbean art.
- **New England Quilt Museum**, 18 Shattuck Street, Lowell, 978-452-4207, www.nequiltmuseum.org; $4 adults, $3 for seniors and students.
- **Peabody Essex Museum**, East India Square, Salem, 978-745-9500, www.pem.org; redone in 2003.
- **Rose Art Museum**, Brandeis University, 415 South Street, Waltham, 781-736-3434, www.brandeis.edu/rose; "largest" and "finest" collection of modern and contemporary 20th-century art in New England, the museum just got a big boost in the form of a $3.5 million gift from arts patrons Henry and Louis Foster. Admission $3. Closed Mondays.
- **Semitic Museum at Harvard University**, 6 Divinity Avenue, Cambridge, 617-495-4631, www.fasharvard.edu/~semitic; features Near Eastern archeological and artistic exhibits. The museum was founded in 1889. Admission is free.

HISTORY

FREEDOM TRAIL

The Freedom Trail is a walking tour of Boston covering 300 years of history by linking 16 of the city's most significant historical sites and museums on one relatively easy to follow, two-and-a-half mile path. The National Park Service offers guided tours, but you can walk the Freedom Trail on your own if you prefer. For detailed information about the Freedom Trail go to www.cityofboston.gov/freedomtrail.

The trail begins at the information kiosk on Boston Common. Following the painted red line along the sidewalk (sometimes the line is brick) will take you to the **Statehouse**, recognizable by its imposing size, classic architecture and regal gold dome. Head back out to Park Street to see the **Park Street Church** and then the **Granary Burying Ground**, which serves as the final resting place for such patriots as John Hancock, Samuel Adams,

Paul Revere, Mary Goose (better known as Mother Goose), and the parents of native son Benjamin Franklin. A statue of Franklin stands further down the trail at 45 School Street, by the site of the **first public school**, which you'll get to after you pass the **King's Chapel** and accompanying **Burying Ground**. Other downtown sites include the **Old South Meeting House** on Washington at Milk Street, the site of the **Boston Massacre**, and the **Old Corner Bookstore**, which now houses the Boston Globe Bookstore. After you finish with this downtown section, the Freedom Trail heads toward the North End, but not without making a run through **Faneuil Hall**. The trail then heads past the **Holocaust Memorial**, through **Haymarket** (which will be chaos if you're visiting on a Friday or Saturday), and then into the North End. A tour through the **North End** brings you past the **Old North Church**, where the famous signal was sent out to warn of the British invasion: "One if by land, two if by sea." You'll also see **Paul Revere's house**, which happens to be the oldest standing home in Boston, and the **Copp's Hill Burying Ground**. Finally, the Freedom Trail heads over the Charlestown Bridge to the **Charlestown Navy Yard**, not far from the **Bunker Hill Monument**. The nation's oldest commissioned war ship, **the USS Constitution**, a.k.a. "Old Ironsides," is anchored in the Navy Yard, and it was at Bunker Hill that General Israel Putnam urged his troops not to fire on the British soldiers until they saw "the whites of their eyes."

HISTORIC SITES, TRAILS, AND CULTURAL CENTERS

While, for obvious reasons, the Freedom Trail is the first stop for many tourists and those exploring their new city, there is so much else to visit in Boston that isn't directly accessible from the trail's path. A lesser-known trail, the **Black Heritage Trail**, details the rich history of Boston's African-American community. It's located on the north slope of Beacon Hill, once known as the West End. The attractions include a memorial to a white aristocrat, **Robert Gould Shaw**, who led the all-black 54th Regiment during the Civil War, and the **African Meeting House**, 617-725-0022.

Don't forget to head out of Boston to see what other historical sites the area has to offer. Many famous New England authors lived right around here, so you can visit places like **Longfellow's house** in Cambridge, **Emerson's house** in Concord, Thoreau's **Walden Pond**, Hawthorne's **House of Seven Gables**, and Salem's **Custom House**. In Brookline is the **Olmstead Museum** in the house where Frederick Law Olmstead, father of modern landscape architecture and designer of the Emerald Necklace, lived, as well as **JFK's birthplace**. If you head south to Plymouth you can see historical pilgrim sites, like **Plymouth Rock**, re-creations of the Mayflower and pilgrim life at the village, and a living history museum village called **Plimouth Plantation**.

It's also possible to dine at historically significant sites. **The Union Oyster House**, established in 1826, at 40 Union Street near Faneuil Hall, is America's oldest restaurant. It is also located near a series of back streets that offer a glimpse of what colonial Boston looked like. Along this cobblestone nook you can also visit the **Green Dragon Tavern**, 11 Marshall Street, where patriots drank ale and plotted the uprising that became the Revolutionary War, and in Charlestown, the **Warren Tavern** at 2 Pleasant Street, which dates back to 1780, was one of the favorite watering holes of General Washington and Paul Revere.

For more about area history contact the **Greater Boston Convention & Visitors Bureau**, 888-SEE-BOSTON, www.bostonusa.com, and **Cambridge Discovery**, 617-497-1630.

Following is a list of some of the many **historical museums and sites** in the greater Boston area:

- **Adams National Historic Site**, 135 Adams Street, Quincy, 617-770-1175, www.nps.gov/adam; the birthplaces and homes of presidents John Adams and John Quincy Adams.
- **Boston Historical Society & Museum/Old State House**, 206 Washington Street, Boston, 617-720-1713, www.bostonhistory.org; open daily, 9 a.m. to 5 p.m.
- **Boston Tea Party Ship and Museum**, Congress Street Bridge, Boston, 617-338-1773, www.bostonteapartyship.com
- **Concord Museum**, 200 Lexington Road, Concord, 978-369-9763, www.concordmuseum.org; dedicated to Concord's history, including Revolutionary War, Thoreau, and Emerson exhibits. Open daily year round.
- **Dreams of Freedom**, 1 Milk Street, Boston, 617-338-6022, www.dreamsoffreedom.org; the Boston immigration museum. Open daily from April to December, closed Mondays during the winter.
- **Essex Shipbuilding Museum**, 66 & 28 Main Street, Essex, 978-768-7541, www.essexshipbuildingmuseum.org; local shipbuilding artifacts from a proud and significant local industry. Tours available May-October.
- **Frederick Law Olmstead National Historic Site**, 99 Warren Street, Brookline, 617-566-1689, www.nps.gov/frla; visit the home and office of the founder of American landscape architecture. Open for full tours on Fridays, Saturdays, and Sundays. Limited visitor services on weekdays.
- **Gibson House Museum**, 137 Beacon Street, Boston, 617-267-6338, www.thegibsonhouse.org
- **House of Seven Gables**, 54 Turner Street, Salem, 978-744-0991, www.7gables.org; oldest surviving 17th century wooden mansion in New England, which inspired the Hawthorne book. Includes Hawthorne's birthplace, gardens, and tour guides dressed in period

garb on the property. Open daily year round, except during the first three weeks of January when it is closed.

- **The John F. Kennedy Library and Museum**, Columbia Point off Morrissey Boulevard, UMASS-Boston campus, Dorchester, 617-514-1600, www.cs.umb.edu/jfklibrary; exhibits that'll take you back in time, dedicated to perhaps the most beloved president of the 20th century.
- **Longfellow National Historic Site**, 105 Brattle Street, Cambridge, 617-876-4491, www.nps.gov/long; Longfellow's home for more than 50 years.
- **Lowell National Historical Park**, 67 Kirk Street, Lowell, 978-970-5000, www.nps.gov/lowe; textile mills, canals, worker housing, Suffolk Mill Turbine, and Boot Cotton Mills Museum.
- **Mary Baker Eddy Library for the Betterment of Humanity—Mapparium**, 200 Mass Ave., Boston, 617-450-7000 or 888-222-3711, www.marybakereddylibrary.org; the Christian Science complex in the Fenway section of Boston is imposing, remarkable, regal, and gorgeous. You'll be impressed by the outside of the buildings—the grand dome and reflecting pool. Inside the library is the Mapparium—a three-story, stained-glass globe from the 1930s. Closed Mondays.
- **Minute Man National Historical Park**, 174 Liberty Street, Concord, 978-369-6993, www.nps.gov/mima; American Revolution sites like Concord Green, as well as homes of Alcott and Hawthorne.
- **Mt. Auburn Cemetery**, 580 Mt. Auburn Street, Cambridge, 617-547-7105; one of the nation's most famous cemeteries and the resting grounds for Charles Bullfinch, Oliver Wendell Holmes, Dorathea Dix, B.F. Skinner, Mary Baker Eddy, Winslow Homer, and many others. Peaceful and beautiful place to go for a walk. Visits are free, but if you'd like to take a map, a donation is requested. Great place to bird watch.
- **Museum of Afro-American History**, 46 Joy Street on Beacon Hill, Boston, 617-725-0022, www.afroammuseum.org; for the preservation and exhibition of contributions by African-Americans during the colonial period in New England, includes the African-American Meeting House and Abiel Smith School. Open seven days, 10 a.m. to 4 p.m. during the summer; Monday-Saturday the rest of the year.
- **New Bedford Whaling Museum**, 18 Johnny Cake Hill, New Bedford, 508-997-0046, www.whalingmuseum.org; offers a visual history of whaling.
- **Old South Meeting House**, 310 Washington Street, Boston, 617-482-6439, www.oldsouthmeetinghouse.org; open daily.
- **Old State House**, 206 Washington Street, Boston, 617-720-1713, www.bostonhistory.org
- **Orchard House**, 399 Lexington Road, Concord; home to the Alcott family.

- **Paul Revere House**, 19 North Square (North End), Boston, www.paulreverehouse.org; open daily except from January-March when it is closed on Mondays.
- **Peabody Museum of Archaeology and Ethnology**, Harvard University, 11 Divinity Avenue, Cambridge, 617-495-7535, www.peabody.harvard.edu; open daily, 9 a.m. to 5 p.m. Free with Harvard ID.
- **Sleepy Hollow Cemetery**, Bedford Street and Court Lane near Concord center; where Thoreau, Emerson, Alcott, and Hawthorne are buried, on "Author's Ridge."
- **Spellman Museum of Stamps & Postal History**, Regis College, 235 Wellesley Street, Weston, 781-768-8367, www.spellman.org; open Thursday-Sunday, noon to 5 p.m.
- **The USS Constitution Museum**, Charlestown Navy Yard, 617-426-1812, www.ussconstitutionmuseum.org; interesting, lengthy tour given by well-informed naval officers who can tell you exactly how miserable life was on Old Ironsides and all about her history.
- **Walden Pond/Thoreau Exhibit**, 915 Walden Street, Concord, 978-369-3254, www.state.ma.us/dem/parks/wldn; use the pond and walk the woods for free. Has a nice summer swimming hole and gorgeous fall foliage.

SCIENCE MUSEUMS

- **Harvard Collection of Historical Scientific Instruments**, 1 Oxford Street, Cambridge, 617-495-2779, www.peabody.harvard.edu/museum_scientific
- **Harvard University Museum of Natural History**, 26 Oxford Street, Cambridge, 617-495-3045, www.hmnh.harvard.edu, including the following collections: **Mineralogical and Geological Museum**, 24 Oxford Street, worldwide collection of rocks and ores, www.peabody.harvard.edu/museum_mineral; **Harvard University Botanical Museum** houses the **Garden in Glass** (affectionately known as the "Glass Flowers"), 26 Oxford Street, www.peabody.harvard.edu/museum_botanical; and the **Museum of Comparative Zoology**, 26 Oxford Street, www.mcz.harvard.edu, 150-year-old museum covering the departments of biological oceanography, entomology, herpetology, ichthyology, paleontology, invertebrate zoology, mammalogy, marine biology, mollusks, ornithology, and population genetics.
- **MIT Museum**, 617-253-4444, http://web.edu/museum; has collections in science, technology, architecture, nautical history, and holography. **Main Gallery**, 265 Mass Ave., Building N52, Cambridge; **Compton Gallery**, 77 Mass Ave., Building 10/MIT campus, Cambridge; **Hart Nautical Gallery**, 55 Mass Ave., Building 5/MIT campus, Cambridge.

- **Museum of Science**, Science Park, Boston, 617-723-2500, www.mos.org; in addition to the permanent and traveling exhibits that make this 170-year-old museum a local favorite, the Museum of Science also features changing IMAX shows in its **Mugar Omni Theater**, and laser shows and planetarium shows in the **Charles Hayden Planetarium**. Open daily. Easy access to the Green Line on the T and parking, although the garage fills up on holidays and weekends.
- **New England Aquarium**, Central Wharf (off Atlantic Avenue), Boston, 617-973-5200, www.neaq.org; beautiful central tank for viewing sea life, captivating penguin pool, special shows (sea lions, etc.), and Simons IMAX Theatre. Open daily. Nearby parking or take the Blue Line T to the Aquarium stop.

LITERARY LIFE

In addition to Boston's extensive network of public and academic libraries, there are several special interest private libraries, including the Boston Athenaeum and the Mary Baker Eddy Library where researchers can find scores of rare and exceptional books on their particular subject matter.

Boston is a hotbed of well-attended lecture tours, book signings, and poetry readings. Despite the popularity of online booksellers, Boston has plenty of old-fashioned independent bookstores, particularly in Cambridge. And, while internet shopping has a lot going for it in terms of convenience, for those newcomers wanting to browse a cozy specialty bookshop or even a large chain, your options are varied. Check with the bookstores listed below to find a first-edition Robert Louis Stevensons, to pre-order your copy of Harry Potter, or to find out when your favorite author is coming to town. For more about past and present local writers, see the **Boston Reading List** chapter.

BOOKSTORES

Especially in the suburbs, the national book retailers predominate. However, there are still plenty of smaller, specialty stores, a significant number of which are in Cambridge. Harvard Square, in particular, is known for its high concentration of bookstores. You'll also want to check for stores affiliated with local universities. Here are a few area booksellers to get you started:
- **Avenue Victor Hugo Bookshop**, 353 Newbury Street, Boston, 617-266-7746, www.avenuevictorhugobooks.com; general used bookseller, focusing on classics, popular fiction, science fiction, Westerns, art topics, and history.
- **Barnes & Noble Booksellers**, 395 Washington Street (Downtown Crossing), Boston, 617-426-5184; 325 Harvard Street, Brookline, 617-

232-0594; and 170 Boylston Street, Chestnut Hill, 617-965-7621; there is another Barnes & Noble store that doubles as a university bookstore at BU, 660 Beacon Street, Kenmore Square, 617-267-8484. www.barnes andnoble.com
- **Borders Books & Music**, 10-24 School Street (Downtown Crossing), Boston, 617-557-7188, is a three-level book emporium, with the Irish Potato Famine memorial in front of it. Also at 100 Cambridgeside Place in the Cambridgeside Galleria, Cambridge, 617-679-0887, www.borders.com.
- **Braziian Bookstore**, 137 Broadway, Somerville, 617-623-4460
- **Brookline Booksmith**, 279 Harvard Street (Coolidge Corner), Brookline, 617-566-6660, www.brooklinebooksmith.com; popular little bookseller with a wide selection of titles. Hosts a great many popular authors doing readings and signings.
- **Cathedral Bookstore**, 28 Temple Place (downtown), Boston, 617-423-4719; Anglican and Episcopal bookstore
- **Comicopia**, 464 Comm Ave. #3, Boston, 617-266-4266, www.comicopia.com; comic-book store providing "highbrow, lowbrow … and everything in between."
- **The Coop**, MIT: 3 Cambridge Center (Central Square), Cambridge, 617-499-3200; Harvard, 1400 Mass Ave. (Harvard Square), Cambridge, 617-499-2000, www.thecoop.com
- **Grolier Poetry Bookshop**, 6 Plympton Street (Harvard Square), Cambridge, 617-547-4648, www.grolierpoetrybookshop.com; stocks over 15,000 volumes of trade, small press, and university poetry.
- **Harvard Bookstore**, 1256 Mass Ave. (Harvard Square), Cambridge, 617-661-1515, www.harvard.com; big selection, not just Harvard authors.
- **Israel Bookshop**, 410 Harvard Street, Brookline, 617-566-7113, www.israelbookshop.com
- **MIT Press Bookstore**, 292 Main Street (Kendall Square), Cambridge, 617-253-5479, http://mitpress.mit.edu/bookstore
- **Petropol**, 1428 Beacon Street (Coolidge Corner), Brookline, 617-232-8820, http://petropol.com; Russian language bookstore.
- **Quantum Books**, 4 Cambridge Center (Kendall Square), Cambridge, 617-494-5042, www.quantumbooks.com; 20,000 technical titles for the science fiends.
- **Rand McNally Map & Travel Store**, 84 State Street, Boston, 617-720-1125 www.randmcnally.com
- **Sasuga Japanese Bookstore**, 7 Upland Road (Porter Square), Cambridge, 617-497-5460, www.sasugabooks.com

- **Schoenhof's Foreign Books**, 76 Mt. Auburn Street #A (Harvard Square), Cambridge, 617-547-8855, www.schoenhofs.com; the place for books printed in whatever language you desire.
- **Seven Stars**, 731 Mass Ave., Cambridge, 617-547-1317
- **Trident Booksellers & Café**, 338 Newbury Street, Boston, 617-267-6888; uber-hip, fun bookstore with a coffee shop built in. In addition to the standard best sellers, you can find a great concentration of magazines.
- **Waldenbooks**, go to www.waldenbooks.com to check for the nearest location.
- **We Think the World of You**, 540 Tremont Street (South End), Boston, 617-574-5000, www.wethinktheworldofyou.com; dubbed the city's best gay bookstore by *Boston* magazine.
- **Wordsworth**, 30 Brattle Street (Harvard Square), Cambridge, 617-354-5201, www.wordsworth.com; local favorite, and sponsors sell-out readings by authors like Dave Eggers and Ethan Hawke.

Poetry Readings are plentiful in Boston. Some are hosted by area bookstores, others by small coffee houses. Check the *Globe* on Thursdays and the *Herald* on Fridays for listings, as well as the *Improper Bostonian* and the *Harvard Gazette*.

LIBRARIES

There are public and private libraries galore in Boston. For listings of public library branches, check the resources following the **Neighborhood Profiles**, and for information on obtaining a library card, check the **Getting Settled** chapter. Many popular **private libraries** are open to the public, others are by membership only.

- **Arnold Arboretum Library**, 125 Arborway, Jamaica Plain, 617-524-1718, www.arboretum.harvard.edu/library; horticultural information on the arboretum's woody plant holdings, free use. Visitors must check in at the front desk.
- **Boston Athenaeum**, 10 Beacon Street, Boston, 617-227-0270, www.bostonathenaeum.org, is a nearly 200-year-old private library. First floor is open to the public; membership allows you full use of (sometimes very old) reference materials, special collections, events, and more.
- **Boston Globe Library**, P.O. Box 2378, Boston 02107, http://bostonglobe.com/newsroom/News/OtherServices/library; the library services of the *Globe* are not open to the public, but you can contact them with written requests about information that has appeared in the paper. Requests take a minimum of 10 days to fulfill.

- **Boston Historical Society Library**, 15 State Street, 3rd floor, Boston; 617-720-1713 ext. 12, www.bostonhistory.org; artifacts, books, photographs, and documents relating to the history of Boston, for use during weekdays by appointment. $10 fee for adults, $5 for students; membership costs $35 for individuals, $20 for students, and $25 for seniors.
- **Boston Psychoanalytic Society and Institute's (BPSI's) Hanns Sachs Library**, 15 Comm Ave., Boston; 617-266-0950 ext. 210; historical and contemporary psychoanalytic literature and journals, for use by BPSI members as well as unaffiliated scholars and students—free onsite use, borrowing privileges for an annual subscription fee.
- **Boston Public Library**, 700 Boylston Street, 617-536-5400, www.bpl.org
- **Brookline Public Library**, 361 Washington Street, Brookline, 617-730-2360, www.town.brookline.ma.us/library
- **Congregational Library and Archives**, 14 Beacon Street, Boston, 617-523-0470, www.14beacon.org; contemporary and classical religious studies material open to all researchers free of charge.
- **Federal Reserve Bank of Boston's Research Library**, 600 Atlantic Avenue, Boston; 617-973-3397; www.bos.frb.org/economic/resource/library.htm; economics and monetary policy holdings. ID required for admission.
- **The French Library and Cultural Center/The Alliance Française of Boston and Cambridge**, 53 Marlborough Street, Boston, 617-912-0400, www.frenchlib.org; the second largest French library in the US, which includes books, audiotapes, videos, CDs, courses, and cultural activities.
- **Goethe Institute Library**, 170 Beacon Street, Boston, 617-262-6050; new German books, videos, audiocassettes, journals, magazines, etc.; free use, but no borrowing privileges.
- **JFK Library and Museum**, Columbia Point (on the UMASS-Boston campus), South Boston, 617-514-1600, www.cs.umb.edu/jfklibrary; one of ten presidential libraries administered by the National Archives and Records Administration, this is a library devoted to all things Kennedy. Admission charged.
- **Mary Baker Eddy Library for the Betterment of Humanity** (see above, under **History Museums**).
- **Massachusetts Historical Society Library**: 1154 Boylston Street, Boston; 617-536-1608, www.masshist.org/library; a collection of personal papers for the families and individuals who have lived in the commonwealth, free to the public.
- **Museum of Fine Arts Libraries (William Morris Hunt Memorial Library and W. Van Alan Clark, Jr. Library)**, MFA, 465 Huntington

Avenue, Boston, www.mfa.org/library; Hunt Memorial, 617-369-3385; Clark Library, 617-369-3650; holdings of art and art history literature corresponding to the museum's collections and the museum school, respectively; free admission to the public, but the holdings are non-circulating.
- **New England Historic Genealogical Society (NEHGS)** Libraries, Manuscript Collection, Circulating Library, and Research Library, NEGHS, 101 Newbury Street, Boston, 617-536-5740, www.newenglandancestors.org/libraries
- **Newton Free Library**, 330 Homer Street, Newton, 617-796-1360, www.ci.newton.ma.us/Library
- **West End Branch Library**, 151 Cambridge Street, Boston, 617-523-3957, www.bpl.org/branches/westend

As far as **college** and **university libraries** go, unless you're a student of the school or in an affiliated library network, at best you may be able to go into the library and look at books, but generally you will not be allowed to check out materials. Check with the individual college or university about its library's policy. If you are a student, your school library may be part of a network. For example, Emerson College, Emmanuel College, Lesley University, Wheelock College, Mass College of Art, Mass College of Pharmacy, the MFA, the New England Conservatory, and Wentworth Institute of Technology are all linked through the **Fenway Libraries Online** system, which allows students to borrow from any of the member libraries: http://flo.org, 617-442-2384.

COLLEGES AND UNIVERSITIES

Metropolitan Boston is a student's dream. Within Boston and its environs are some of the world's top colleges and universities, including Harvard, MIT, Brandeis, Boston College, Boston University, and Tufts, in addition to the scores of other educational institutions.

If your move to Boston was prompted by attendance at a college or university, you are in good company. From September through June, Boston is packed to the hilt with the 18- to 22-year old set, on top of the year round presence of graduate students. It is only during the summer when the city returns to the hands of the older folks for a few, albeit fleeting, months.

If you are interested in Boston's many higher education options, check first with the **Massachusetts Board of Higher Education**, www.mass.edu, and the directory of Massachusetts colleges and universities posted by the **Massachusetts Library Information Network**, www.mlin.lib.ma.us/inet. Also check the Yellow Pages under "Schools" for a complete list of colleges and universities in and around Boston.

Following is a sampling of area colleges and universities:
- **Babson College**, Babson Park, Wellesley, 781-235-1200, www.babson.edu; independent school of business and management education.
- **Bentley College**, 175 Forest Street, Waltham, 781-891-2000, www.bentley.edu; co-ed, four-year college offers business and arts and sciences degrees, emphasizing careers in business.
- **Berklee College of Music**, 1140 Boylston Street, Boston, 617-266-1400, www.berklee.edu; one of the best music schools in the country; offers degrees and diplomas. Alumni include Quincy Jones, Melissa Etheridge, Branford Marsalis, and Paula Cole.
- **Boston Architectural Center**, 320 Newbury Street, Boston, 617-262-5000, www.the-bac.edu; private school, BA and MA programs.
- **Boston Center for Adult Education**, 5 Comm Ave., Boston, 617-267-4430, www.bcae.org.
- **Boston College (BC)**, 140 Comm Ave., Chestnut Hill, 617-552-8000, www.bc.edu; co-ed, Jesuit-affiliated university located six miles from downtown Boston. Home to 8,500 undergraduates and 4,000 graduate students. Adult education offered.
- **Boston Conservatory**, 8 The Fenway, Boston, 617-536-6340, www.bostonconservatory.edu; private college offering undergraduate and graduate programs in music, dance, and musical theater.
- **Boston University (BU)**, 121 Bay State Road, Boston, 617-353-2000, www.bu.edu; independent, nonsectarian, co-ed university located on banks of the Charles River in Boston's Back Bay section. BU has 15 schools and colleges, and 30,000 students, many of whom are international. BU also has its Metropolitan College branch, which offers continuing-education on three campuses.
- **Brandeis University**, 415 South Street, Waltham, 781-736-2000, www.brandeis.edu; the only nonsectarian Jewish university in the country.
- **Bunker Hill Community College**, 250 New Rutherford Avenue, Boston, 617-228-BHCC, www.bhcc.mass.edu; two-year community college on Boston's northern edge.
- **Cambridge Center for Adult Education**, 42 Brattle Street, Cambridge, 617-547-6789, www.ccae.org; offers a range of popular, noncredit classes in Harvard Square.
- **Cambridge College**, 1000 Mass. Ave., 800-877-4723, www.cambridgecollege.edu; caters mainly to students of color, offering Masters degrees in education and management.
- **Eliot School of Fine and Applied Arts**, 24 Eliot Street, JP, 617-524-3313, www.eliotschool.org; one of the oldest continually run educational institutions in the country. Open since 1676.
- **Emerson College**, 120 Boylston Street, Boston, 617-824-8500, www.emerson.edu; a four-year school of communications and per-

forming arts overlooking Boston Common; graduate programs and continuing education as well.

- **Emmanuel College**, 400 The Fenway, Boston, 617-735-9715, www.emmanuel.edu; Catholic liberal arts college, offers undergraduate, graduate, and professional programs.
- **Harvard University**, Cambridge, 617-495-1000, www.harvard.edu; America's first and most prestigious university. Offers summer programs, Radcliffe programs, and continuing-ed through the Harvard Extension.
- **Lesley University**, 29 Everett Street, Cambridge, 800-999-1959, www.lesley.edu; located between Harvard and Porter squares, Lesley offers degrees in education and a wide range of human services, management, and the arts, combining internships with classroom work.
- **Longy School of Music**, 1 Follen Street, Cambridge, 617-876-0956, www.longy.edu; small, classical music conservatory in Harvard Square.
- **Massachusetts College of Art**, 621 Huntington Avenue, Boston, 617-879-7000, www.massart.edu; four-year fine arts college, in the Fenway.
- **Massachusetts Institute of Technology (MIT)**, 77 Mass Ave., Cambridge, 617-253-1000, www.mit.edu; premier science university, draws top graduate and undergraduate students from around the world. Also offers degrees in the arts, humanities, and social sciences.
- **New England Conservatory of Music**, 290 Huntington Avenue, Boston, 617-585-1100, www.newenglandconservatory.edu; graduate, undergraduate, preparatory, and continuing education divisions offering instruction in classical music, jazz, and contemporary improvisation.
- **Northeastern University**, 360 Huntington Avenue, Boston, 617-373-2000, www.northeastern.edu; located near the Museum of Fine Arts in the Fenway, Northeastern offers a unique co-op internship program in field study for undergrads. Has graduate programs, including a law school, and continuing education courses.
- **Regis College**, 235 Wellesley Street, Weston, 781-768-7000, www.regiscollege.edu; a Catholic, liberal arts and sciences college for women.
- **Simmons College**, 300 The Fenway, 617-521-2000, www.simmons.edu; four-year women's college focusing on liberal arts and sciences and professional education, also offers co-ed graduate programs.
- **Suffolk University**, 8 Ashburton Place, Boston, 617-573-8000, www.suffolk.edu; located on Beacon Hill in the heart of the city's business, technology, law, medical, and government centers. Suffolk offers undergraduate and graduate degrees in liberal arts and sciences, as well as business and law.

- **Tufts University**, Medford, 02155, 617-627-3170, www.tufts.edu; well-regarded liberal arts programs for graduates and undergraduates. Their dental school campus is in downtown Boston.
- **University of Massachusetts—Boston**, 100 Morrissey Boulevard, Dorchester, 617-287-5000, www.umb.edu; Boston branch of the state's university system, including liberal arts undergraduate and graduate programs, as well as continuing-ed.
- **Wellesley College**, 106 Central Street, Wellesley, 781-283-1000, www.wellesley.edu; elite four-year women's college.
- **Wentworth Institute of Technology**, 552 Huntington Avenue, Boston, 617-989-4590, www.wit.edu; located on a 30-acre campus across from Boston Museum of Fine Arts in the Fenway, offering bachelor's degrees in architecture, design, engineering, technology, and management of technology.

CULTURE FOR KIDS

Boston has a great many attractions that are educational as well as fun. Area museums, theaters, zoos, historical sites, and others are good for the whole family. Before you go anywhere, look into getting a **citypass**, www.citypass.com, 888-330-5008. If you're planning to go to many museums and attractions within a short time period (nine days), you can save up to 50% on admission into the Museum of Science, Aquarium, MFA, Harvard Museum of Natural History, JFK Library & Museum, and the Skywalk Observatory at the Pru.

MUSEUMS

- **The Children's Museum**, 300 Congress Street, Boston, 617-426-8855, www.bostonkids.org
- **Pirate Museum**, 274 Derby Street, Salem, 978-741-2800, www.piratemuseum.com; relive the adventures of famous pirates. Open from May through October, and some nights in November.
- **Salem Witch Museum**, 19 1/2 Washington Square, Salem, 978-744-1692, www.salemwitchmuseum.com; dramatic and presentation on the Salem Witch Trials, with lights, narration, and life-sized figures; open daily.

ZOOS/AQUARIUMS

- **Franklin Park Zoo**, 1 Franklin Park Road, Dorchester, 617-541-LION, www.zoonewengland.com; nice variety of animals and a very friendly

staff. Don't forget to ask about the exotic bird they call "Hannibal." Open daily.
- **New England Aquarium**, Central Wharf (off Atlantic Avenue), Boston, 617-973-5200, www.neaq.org; beautiful central tank for viewing sea life, captivating penguin pool, special shows, and the Simons IMAX Theatre. Open daily. Nearby parking or take the Blue Line T to the Aquarium stop.
- **Stone Zoo**, 149 Pond Street, Stoneham, 781-438-5100, www.zoonewengland.com; open daily.

SPORTS

See **Sports for Kids** in the **Sports and Recreation** chapter.

THEATER

- **Boston Baked Theatre**, 255 Elm Street, Somerville, 617-628-9575, www.basictheatre.org
- **North Shore Music Theatre**, 62 Dunham Road, Beverly, 978-232-7200, www.nsmt.org; musicals, celebrity concerts, and shows for children.
- **Puppet Showplace Theatre**, 32 Station Street (Brookline Village), Brookline, 617-731-6400, www.puppetshowplace.org; the first puppetry center in New England, this theater puts on different shows every weekend year round, and daily during school vacations, and on some weekdays during the summers. Shows are appropriate for children five and up.
- **Underground Railway Theater**, 41 Foster Street, Arlington, 781-643-6916, www.undergroundrailwaytheater.org; national touring and local performing company presenting a synthesis of theater, puppetry, and music ranging from adult cabarets to full-length plays.

SPORTS AND RECREATION

FIVE PROFESSIONAL TEAMS CALL THE BOSTON AREA HOME, AND there are numerous college teams, a wide array of participant sports, abundant hiking and green space, and several mountain ranges within in driving distance. During any given season, viewing or participating in area sports and activities should be a cinch.

Sports fans may also be interested in **The Sports Museum of New England** (a library and archive) at the Fleet Center. Call 617-624-1234 or go to www.sportsmuseum.org for more information.

PROFESSIONAL SPORTS

The Boston area is home to the **Boston Red Sox**, the **Boston Celtics**, the **New England Patriots**, the **Bruins**, and Major League Soccer's **New England Revolution**. Residents of Vermont, New Hampshire, Maine, Rhode Island, Connecticut, and western Massachusetts have to make quite a trek to root for the home team, but they do it, and in droves. To better acquaint yourself with the ins and outs of area sports teams, simply check the sports section in the *Globe* or the *Herald* for the latest.

BASEBALL

- American League East team Boston **Red Sox** play at **Fenway Park**, located right in Kenmore Square (4 Yawkey Way). It is a small park (capacity 34,000), but very dear to local hearts. Built in 1912, Fenway is one of the oldest stadiums in the country. In recent years, there have been various proposals to build a bigger, modern park, which would bring in more revenue for the team and the city, and provide a more comfortable arena. At press time, no official decision had been made to tear down Fenway and rebuild, and in the winter of 2002-3, seats were added to the Green Monster (Fenway's famous green back wall) to expand the capacity. For more information on this issue, go to www.savefenwaypark.org. Baseball season runs from April to October. Even though most games do sell out, it is not terribly difficult to come by tickets. Ticket prices for the 2004 season ranged from $12 for upper bleachers to $300 for premium seating. Season tickets are available on a limited basis. Call 877-REDSOX9 or go online to www.redsox.com for specifics. Get to Fenway by taking any Green Line train (except the E Line Heath train) to Kenmore Square, or the D Line to the Fenway stop. Then just follow the crowd.

- For **minor league baseball** action, locals cheer for the **Portland Sea Dogs**, the AA affiliate of the Red Sox, they play a couple of hours north at Hadlock Field (271 Park Avenue) in Portland, Maine. The Sea Dogs are popular, so if you want to catch a game, get your tickets early. For more information, call 800-936-3647 or visit www.seadogs.com. And then there are the **Lowell Spinners**, the Red Sox's class A affiliate. They play a shorter season at LaLacheur Park (450 Aiken Street, Lowell). To find out more, call 978-459-2255 or visit www.lowellspinners.com.

BASKETBALL

- The **Fleet Center**, which replaced the venerable Boston Garden in 1995, is home to both the Bruins and the Celtics. Professional wrestling, ice skating, gymnastics, the annual college hockey Beanpot tournament, Disney shows, concerts, and the Ringling Bros. and Barnum & Bailey Circus are also staged here. Eastern Conference **Boston Celtics** play November through April, when the playoffs begin. Seating capacity is 19,600. Individual tickets are available at the box office in the Fleet Center and through TicketMaster. For more information, call 617-523-3030 or visit www.nba.com/celtics. Note: the Fleet Center has a T station (North Station) and a few eating places and bars on the premises. Take the Green Line (D and E train) or commuter rail to North Station. Or you can drive if you're willing to tackle the parking nightmare.
- For general information about tickets to **Fleet Center events** and box office hours, call the center at 617-624-1000. You cannot call the box office to order tickets—you must purchase them in person or through TicketMaster, 617-931-2000, www.ticketmaster.com. The box office is open daily from 11 a.m. to 7 p.m., and accepts MasterCard, VISA, American Express, cash and personal checks (drawn on a Massachusetts bank and written at least 24 hours before the event).

FOOTBALL

- The AFC-East's **New England Patriots** play at the new **Gillette Stadium** (1 Patriot Place) in Foxboro (capacity 68,000)—about a half-hour south of Boston. The NFL season runs from September to January with a few pre-season games in August. The playing schedule is released in early May. No longer underdogs, the Patriots won the Superbowl in 2002 and again in 2004. Season tickets may be available but you can expect to be put on a waiting list. For more information, call the Patriots at 800-543-1776 or go to www.patriots.com. Individual game tickets are available through Ticketmaster. Transportation to Foxboro via commuter rail is available during games, but parking at Gillette Stadium is decent with 14,000 parking spaces. Additional stadium amenities include 350 concession stands, 60 bathrooms, and 2,000 luxury suite seats. If you're interested in taking public transportation, call 508-543-0350 or visit www.mbta.com for event-specific information.

HOCKEY

- The **Boston Bruins** are in the Eastern Conference of the NHL. The Bruins share the Fleet Center with the Celtics. Hockey season begins in October and ends in April. Even during down years the Bruins have a mighty and loyal following, making tickets hard to come by. To order season tickets or to put your name on a waiting list, call 617-624-BEAR. For individual tickets, stop by the box office at the Fleet Center (see above) or order them over the phone or online through TicketMaster (again see above). During evening games only, you can buy tickets from the Advance Ticket Sales Booth located on level 4 (southwest corner). For more information on the Bruins, visit www.bostonbruins.com.
- Local **minor league hockey** games offer exciting and less expensive nights out. The **Worcester Ice Cats**, 105 Commercial Street, Worcester, 800-830-CATS, www.worcestericecats.com, and the **Lowell Lock Monsters**, 300 Arcand Drive, Lowell, 978-458-7825, www.lockmonsters.com, play for the American Hockey League. The Ice Cats play their home games at the Worcester Centrum; tickets cost $15 for adults and $10 for children and seniors. The Lock Monsters play at the Tsongas Arena; tickets go for $14 to $17, and $8 for children and seniors. Season passes are available for both teams.

HORSE/DOG RACING

Newcomers who like to spend a day at the track—for horses or greyhounds—will not be disappointed here. Attempts to ban greyhound racing in Massachusetts have not been successful. Both parks are T accessible.
- **Horse racing**: **Suffolk Downs**, 111 Waldemar Avenue, Route 1A, East Boston, 617-567-3900, www.suffolkdowns.com; admission is $2 for grandstands and $4 for the clubhouse. There's parking, or you can take the Blue Line to the Suffolk Downs stop, just a mile past Logan Airport.
- **Dog racing**: **Wonderland Greyhound Park**, 190 VFW Parkway, Revere, 781-284-1300, www.wonderlandgreyhound.com; races six nights a week. Lots of parking, or take the Blue Line to the Wonderland (last) stop.

SOCCER

- The **New England Revolution**, Boston's Major League Soccer team, shares Gillette Stadium with the Patriots, and were winners of the 2002 Eastern Conference. Soccer season runs from April to October. Seating capacity is reduced during soccer season, but you can still get in to see a match. For information about season tickets call 877-GET-REVS or go to www.nerevolution.com.
- **Professional women's soccer**, the **Boston Renegades**, won the national championship in 2001 and 2002. The Renegades play at Bowditch Stadium, 475 Union Avenue in Framingham. Individual tickets cost $8 for adults and $5 for children, and can be purchased at the field on game nights. For more information or to get season passes, call 781-891-6900 or visit www.bostonrenegades.com.
- The **Boston Breakers**, www.bostonbreakers.com, is another local professional women's team that is part of the WUSA. Home games are at BU's Nickerson Field. Individual tickets range from $12 to $26, game packs and season tickets are also available.

COLLEGE SPORTS

If college sports are more your style, you will find plenty of school teams. Harvard University alone has 40 varsity teams. Tickets for some annual college events can be as hard to come by as tickets to professional games. As a matter of fact, tickets for the final match of the **Beanpot** (a series of varsity hockey matches between Harvard, Northeastern, BU, and BC) are virtually impossible to get. The annual **Harvard** vs. **Yale football game** is another big attraction.

Obviously there are too many Boston colleges and universities to list them all. Here are just some of the local schools with popular athletic programs:

- **BC Eagles**: football, hockey, and basketball always offer exciting games. They also have competitive cross-country, fencing, softball, field hockey, golf, lacrosse, rowing, sailing, skiing, soccer, swimming, tennis, track, and volleyball. For tickets or information, call 617-552-GOBC, or visit http://bceagles.ocsn.com.
- **BU Terriers**: men's and women's basketball, cross-country, golf, ice and field hockey, rowing, soccer, swimming, tennis, and indoor/outdoor track. Also, men's wrestling and women's lacrosse and softball. The Nickerson Field arena is a sight to behold. For tickets or information, call 617-353-GOBU, or visit www.bu.edu/athletics.
- **Harvard Crimson**: Harvard claims the nation's largest Division I athletic program. Football tickets are still relatively inexpensive, and you also have your choice of (men's and women's) basketball, crew, cross country, fencing, golf, ice hockey, lacrosse, sailing, soccer, squash, and swimming, as well as baseball, field hockey, skiing, and softball. For information and for tickets, call 877-GO-HARVARD or web.mit.edu.
- **MIT Engineers**: teams (also sometimes called the Beavers) at the varsity level include baseball, basketball, crew, cross country, fencing, field hockey, football, golf, gymnastics, ice hockey, lacrosse, pistol, rifle, sailing, skiing, soccer, squash, swimming, tennis, track and field, volleyball, water polo, and wrestling, as well as a bunch of club sports. For more information, call 617-253-1000, or visit http://web.mit.edu/athletics/www.
- **Northeastern Huskies**: varsity teams in men's and women's basketball, crew, cross-country, ice hockey, soccer, and track, as well as men's baseball and football, and women's field hockey. For tickets and information, call 617-373-GONU or visit www.gonu.com.
- **Tufts Jumbos**: varsity teams in baseball, basketball, crew, cross-country, football, ice and field hockey, lacrosse, soccer, squash, swimming and diving, tennis, track and field, volleyball, fencing, sailing, softball, golf, and cheerleading. For information, call 617-628-5000, or visit http://ase.tufts.edu/athletics.
- **UMASS-Boston Beacons**: Division III basketball, played at Clark Athletic Center at the Columbia Point campus, is probably the best deal in town. Also baseball, cross-country, soccer, ice hockey, tennis, volleyball, and lacrosse games and meets. Call 617-287-7800 or visit www.athletics.umb.edu.

OTHER SPECTATOR SPORTING EVENTS

- The world-famous **Boston Marathon** goes from Hopkinton to Copley Square on Patriot's Day (a state holiday, it commemorates the April 19, 1775 "shot heard around the world," held the third Monday in April). Not only is the Boston Marathon the oldest annual marathon in the world, it is also one of the most prestigious. Because of this you must either qualify by completing another marathon under a certain time, or you can "pay" to run by getting sponsorship. Every winter and early spring, there are lots of fundraisers for locals who run on teams sponsored by charities such as the American Cancer Society or American Liver Foundation. But even those spots are difficult to come by. The **Boston Athletic Association**, 40 Trinity Place, 4th Floor, Boston, 617-236-1652, www.baa.org, has been in charge of the marathon since it was first run in 1897. To watch the fun all you have to do is bring a blanket and a portable radio and locate a suitable spot along the route. Note: as you might expect, this event is popular and traffic in the city during the marathon is terrible. There are also a number of other events staged around the big day, including the Sports and Fitness Expo, the Carbo-Loading Party the night before, as well as the Awards Ceremony—which is usually over before the majority of participants cross the finish line.
- In June of each year you can watch the annual **John F. Kennedy Regatta** in Boston Harbor. For information call 617-847-1800.
- And don't miss the **Head of the Charles Regatta**, usually held during the third weekend in October. College crews from all over the nation compete in this event, which runs from the Boston University Boathouse to the Christian Herter Center in Allston. Find a spot along the Charles to enjoy the show. Call 617-868-6200 or visit www.hocr.org for information.

PARTICIPANT SPORTS AND ACTIVITIES

One of the easiest ways to meet people in your new town is by joining an intramural-type sports league—and it has the added benefit of helping you get fit.

Check newspapers or ask friends, neighbors, and coworkers for recommendations of sports clubs, or check with www.active.com to find out about local leagues and events. You can also see if a **Boston Community Center** near you (617-635-4920, www.cityofboston.gov/bcyf) has facilities or leagues for adults or children. These community centers, called Boston Centers for Youth and Families, are located throughout the city and are open to everyone—not just those with a Boston address.

PARKS AND RECREATION DEPARTMENTS

The **Department of Conservation and Recreation** (**DCR**), with its several divisions, including what is often called "MassParks," the Division of State Parks & Recreation (formerly the Department of Environmental Management), and the Division of Urban Parks & Recreation (formerly the Metropolitan District Commission or MDC) serves Massachusetts in matters of recreation and individual sports, and takes care of rinks, playgrounds, beaches, pools, golf courses, parks, watersheds, reservations, and general nature space.

The DCR has several **Urban Parks and Recreation district offices**. If you need additional information on any event or facility in your neighborhood, call 617-727-5114 or go to www.mass.gov/dcr.

- **Charles District** covers Arlington, East Boston, Brighton, Cambridge, Charlestown, North End, JP, Somerville, Waltham, Watertown, Wellesley, and Weston.
- **Mystic District** covers Chelsea, East Boston, Everett, Malden, Melrose, Nahant, Revere, Saugus, Stoneham, Winthrop, Winchester, and Wakefield.
- **Harbor District** covers South Boston, Dorchester, Quincy, Weymouth, Hingham, Hull, and Cohasset.
- **Neponset District** covers Canton, Dedham, Hyde Park, Mattapan, Roslindale, Braintree, Dover, Weston, Milton, Randolph, and West Roxbury.

Although Massachusetts is one of the smaller states, it has one of the largest state park systems, offering plenty of places to go for camping, hiking, swimming, and other outdoor recreation. The most popular state park closest to Boston is the **Walden Pond State Reservation**. The small freshwater pond is a 103-foot deep glacial kettle that sees lots of swimmers during the summer months, despite its pebbly shores. A welcoming green forest surrounds the pond and displays a gorgeous show of color each fall. For state parks, reservations, forests, and watersheds, contact **MassParks**: 251 Causeway Street, Suite 600, Boston, 617-626-1250, www.state.ma.us/dcr.

In terms of the city of Boston proper, the **Boston Parks and Recreation Department** oversees over 2,000 acres of green space, including 215 parks and playgrounds, the Emerald Necklace, and two golf courses. For more information on the parks that fall under this jurisdiction contact the Boston Parks and Recreation Department, 1010 Mass Ave., 3rd Floor, Boston, 617-635-PARK, www.cityofboston.gov/parks.

What follows are leagues and individual sports and recreational activities that can be found throughout the greater Boston area. For children, see **Sports for Kids** at the end of this chapter.

BASKETBALL

For when a game of horse just isn't enough:
- **Boston Gay Basketball League**, P.O. Box 1159, Boston, www.bgbl.com; GLBT basketball league. Tournaments and a winter season. Games at the South Block Gym at Boston City Hospital.
- **BSSC Basketball**, 617-789-4070 ext. 238, www.bssc.com; Boston Ski & Sports Club runs coed and men's year-round leagues in Watertown, Brookline, and Dedham for all ability levels.
- **Never Too Late Basketball**, 781-488-3333, www.nevertoolate.com; year-round, open for adults of all ages and abilities throughout Boston.

BASEBALL, SOFTBALL, CRICKET

To join a baseball or softball league, call the recreation department of your town. Some municipalities are strict about requiring proof of residence to play on a town league. You can also ask around in neighborhood bars or sporting goods stores to find out who sponsors teams. Or try one of the following:
- **Beantown Softball League**, P.O. Box 15428, Boston 02215, 617-937-5858, www.beantownsoftball.com, is a GLBT softball league that's been running for over 25 years.
- **Boston Men's Baseball League**, 9 Blossom Lane, Wayland, 508-358-4550, www.bostonbaseball.com, is New England's largest amateur baseball league, ages 18 and up.
- **Boston Park League Baseball**, P.O. Box 555, Back Bay Annex, Boston, www.bostonparkleague.org; America's oldest amateur baseball league, games in Eastie, Hyde Park, Brighton, Rozzie, and Dorchester.
- **Boston West Coed Softball**, www.bostonwestcoedsoftball.com; adult co-ed league with games throughout the greater Boston area.
- **Brookline Adult Softball League**, www.brooklinesoftball.com
- **BSSC Softball**, 617-789-4070, www.bssc.com; co-ed, indoor and outdoor games throughout the greater Boston area.
- **FSSC Softball League**, 617-789-5747
- **M Street Softball League**, www.sbsports.com; softball league based in South Boston.
- **Massachusetts State Cricket League**, P.O. Box 190237, Boston, www.mscl.org; games in the greater Boston area from May to September.

BICYCLING

There are a number of bicycle paths in the Boston area as well as bicycling organizations that organize trips around New England. For those newcomers who are interested in mountain or road biking, the hills, mountains, woods, and waterfront areas of New England provide gorgeous views that many feel are best enjoyed when you're pedaling around. Because Boston and its environs are hilly, biking even on paved paths is more challenging and strenuous than in many other US cities. However, unless you're biking along the water, it isn't particularly windy, which is good.

Boston cyclists are subject to the same rules of the road as drivers are, with one exception: bicycles are not allowed on the major highways through the city: I-93, I-90 (the Mass Pike), and Route 1A.

Boston is reviewing ways to make the city more bike-friendly; one idea is the Boston Bicycle Plan, which has a goal of making the city easier for bikers to get around by 2010. To see what's in store, check www.cityofboston.gov/accessboston/pdfs/bicycle_plan.pdf. And Cambridge already is bike-friendly. There are even bike lanes down Mass Ave—the main drag in Cambridge.

As a bicyclist in the Boston area, be *very* careful. Even though only children under 12 are legally required to wear helmets when biking, you shouldn't even think about riding around this city without one.

In terms of parking, riders will find provisions like bike racks and bike-friendly parking structures throughout the metro area. The city of Boston provides a list of some of them on its web site: www.cityofboston.gov/transportation/bike_parking.asp. And for those newcomers who favor intermodal transportation, bikes are allowed on most T trains, with the exception of the Green Line and the Ashmont-Mattapan Line. Contact the **Boston Bicycle Advisory Committee** at 617-635-4680 with questions, concerns, or complaints regarding bicycling in Boston.

Finally, if you are concerned about your bike being stolen, you can register it with the **National Bike Registry**. If police find a bike, they check with the registry to match it to its proper owner. Ten dollars will get your bike registered for the next 10 years. Call 800-848-BIKE or visit www.nationalbikeregistry.com for more information.

The Charles River has an 18-mile multi-use paved path between Science Park and Watertown Square known officially as the **Dr. Paul Dudley White Charles River Bike Path** (www.mass.gov/dcr), but is typically referred to as the Charles River Bike Path. This path is probably the most highly used recreation space in the city. It's filled with runners, cyclists, in-line skaters, and people just out for a stroll. The path is separate from the city, but connects at several points by ramped pedestrian bridges so there's plenty of access.

There are other, slightly less obvious bike paths in the metro area. For example, many parks in the Emerald Necklace provide green and peaceful places to ride: the **Arnold Arboretum** (www.arboretum.harvard.edu) is now open to cyclists, as are some non-zoo areas of **Franklin Park**. There is a mini-trail called the **Jamaicaway Bikepath** running from Jamaica Pond through Olmstead Park and along the Riverway/Route 9 to Leverett Pond; as well as the nearby **Muddy River Bikepath**, which begins near the Fens, from the north shore of the Muddy River along Park Drive almost to Brookline Avenue in Brookline. And finally, there is the **Stony Brook Reservation Bike Path** (www.mass.gov/dcr), which includes some wilder terrain as it runs for four miles along Turtle Pond Parkway, starting at Hyde Park's River Street and ending at Washington Street in West Roxbury.

Aside from the Emerald Necklace, another of Boston's most popular bike paths is the Pierre Lallement Southwest Corridor Bikepath, a.k.a. the **Southwest Corridor**. Here you can ride for four miles parallel to the Orange Line as it goes between the South End, Roxbury, and Jamaica Plain. Originally, planners proposed putting a high-speed roadway here, but instead it became a closed-in park with separate bike and pedestrian paths, community gardens, playgrounds, and more. Where the Southwest Corridor intersects with the Ruggles T stop in Roxbury, you can split off onto the **Melnea Cass Bikepath** and head toward South Boston. Be forewarned: while the signs on this last path are easy to follow, the roads aren't so great. Some local cyclists enjoy riding around the historic and unquestionably beautiful **Forest Hills Cemetery**, www.foresthilltrust.org, in Cambridge. (No bikes in Mt. Auburn Cemetery however.) "America's most celebrated bike path," the **Minuteman Bikeway**, www.minutemanbikeway.org, is a 12-mile path from the Alewife T Station in Cambridge to Bedford, MA. Residents of Somerville, Arlington, Cambridge, Lexington, Concord, and Bedford all have easy access to this rail-trail, which takes cyclists back in history through sites from the start of the American Revolution. There are many places along the way to catch the trail, which is also popular with in-line skaters. **Millennium Park**, in West Roxbury, is a newly opened 250-acre green space that was once a landfill, and features miles of paved pedestrian and bicycle paths.

For **mountain biking**, many locals like to take a short ride north of the city to the **Middlesex** and **Lynn Fells**, www.fellsbiker.com. Between the Wellington Bridge in Everett and Somerville, the **Mystic River Reservation Bike Path** runs for approximately three and a half miles. The **Lower Neponset River Trail**, operated by the DCR like the previous two parks, provides over two miles of bike paths on a former railroad bed along the Neponset River. It runs from Port Norfolk in Dorchester all the way over to Milton. It is popular with cyclists, runners, and walkers, and future extensions are planned. Cyclists in Quincy like to take advantage of the DCR's **Squantum Point Park**. You can find information online on all of these mountain biking paths through the DCR's web site: www.mass.gov/dcr

Wompatuck State Park has 12 miles of bike trails; the park is in Hingham off Route 228. There is another bicycle trail system in Lincoln and Concord, but you could also just head west and bike along the tree-lined back roads. The **Mass Central Rail Trail**, www.masscentralrailtrail.org, comprises about 15 miles of the previously 104-mile-long railway, open for cycling between Boston and parts west.

Local **bike committees and organizations** include:

- **Arlington Bicycle Advisory Committee**, Planning & Community Development Department, Arlington City Hall, Arlington, 781-316-3090, www.abac.arlington.ma.us
- **Boston Bicycle Advisory Committee**, Transportation Department, Room 721, 1 City Hall Plaza, Boston, 617-635-2756 or 617-635-4BTD, www.cityofboston.gov; contact them with questions, requests for bike racks, and complaints about roads, potholes, taxis, bus drivers, lights, etc.
- **Brookline Bicycle Committee**, 617-264-6480
- **Cambridge Bicycle Committee**, Community Development Department, City Hall Annex, 57 Inman Street, Cambridge, 617-349-0604, www.ci.cambridge.ma.us/~CDD/envirotrans
- **Massachusetts Bicycle Coalition (MassBike)**, 59 Temple Place #669, Boston, 617-542-2453, www.massbike.org; great place for information on all things in the Massachusetts bicycling world, including maps of current trails and updates on future projects.
- **New England Mountain Bike Association**, P.O. Box 2221, Acton, MA 01720; 800-57-NEMBA, www.nemba.org
- **Newton Pedestrian/Bicycle Task Force**, 617-552-7135 ext. 111
- **Quincy Bicycle Committee**, www.bikequincy.org
- **Rails-to-Trails Conservancy**, 2 Washington Square, Suite 200, Union Station, Worcester, 508-755-3300, www.railtrails.org/field/new_england
- **Somerville Bicycle Committee**, 617-625-6600 ext. 2503 or 2520, www.ci.somerville.ma.us
- **Waltham Bicycle Committee**, 781-893-4040
- **Watertown Bicycle Committee**, 617-972-6465

If you're interested in bicycling with a group or participating in local biking events, you'll probably get your best tips from the folks at your local bike shop. In the meantime, you could start with one of these **bike clubs**:
- **Boston Bicycle Club**, 67 Jar Brook Road, Holliston, www.bostonbicycleclub.org; riding, racing, and discounts on bike gear.

- **Boston Brevets**, www.gis.net/~ingle/bbs, a series of long distance training and fun rides, for a small fee.
- **BSSC Biking**, 617-789-4070, www.bssc.com/bike.html
- **Charles River Wheelmen**, www.crw.org; over 1200 members of all skill levels get together for weekly rides and social events.
- **Rage On Boston Mountain Biking Club**, www.ragemtb.com; laid-back, loosely-structured, off-road riding club for people of all skill levels. No membership fee.

BOATING, SAILING, WINDSURFING

With the harbor, and the Mystic and Charles rivers at their disposal, area residents spend a lot of time on or near the water. Plus there are the miles of beaches and coastline to the north and south of the city that certainly contribute to Boston's desirability. If boating is your pleasure, perhaps the best place to dip your toes is at **Bostonboating.com**, a site devoted to water sports, including sailing and power boating in New England. Marinas and other water related resources within the greater Boston area and onto the capes are also listed at the site.

The **Charles River** is over 80 miles long and many of the communities and neighborhoods mentioned in this guide sit alongside it. It is Boston's backyard waterway. If you run, walk, bike, skate or go to concerts, you will certainly be spending some time along the Charles. And if you sail or row you'll be on it, although you should probably try to avoid spending too much time immersed in it. Pollution in the Charles reached legendary levels during the latter part of the 20th century due to sewage and waste being dumped into it between 1930 to 1970. In the 1990s a plan to clean up the river was set into place and water quality is better. Fish and other wildlife are returning, good indicators of its improving health. Boats of any type (except inflatables), canoes, kayaks, rowboats, and powerboats, are allowed on the Charles and in Boston Harbor. During the appropriate seasons, you can see the Harvard, MIT, and BU sailing and crew teams practicing and racing along the river. And on good weather days, it's littered with pleasure boaters. The Charles is also particularly popular with boaters on the Fourth of July, as this is where the city holds its annual Independence Day celebration. It's an exciting night—the Boston Pops plays at the Hatch Shell to the throngs along the Esplanade (music is pumped through speakers on both sides of the water), and the firework barge anchors right in the middle of the river.

Obviously, **Boston Harbor**, being part of the Atlantic Ocean, is a much rougher body of water than the Charles. Except during the coldest weather (when chunks of ice in the harbor can bar the passage of even large boats), recreational crafts mix right in here with commercial water vehicles, including fishing boats, whale watching ships, water taxis, and ferries.

Motorized boating is allowed in some of the **state parks and reservations** throughout Massachusetts. If you're interested in doing this, visit www.state.ma.us/dcr or call **Massachusetts State Parks and Recreation** at 617-626-1250, for more information.

Before you head out on the water at all, it's probably a good idea to take a boating safety course. The **Massachusetts Environmental Police** runs a Boating Education Program, where you can take courses in boating basics. For information call 617-727-8760. They also recommend the following **boating safety course providers**:

- **Coast Guard Auxiliary**, 800-848-3942 ext. 8309, www.uscgaux.org
- **US Power Squadrons**, 800-336-2628, www.usps.org
- **New England Maritime**, 508-790-3400, www.nemaritime.com
- **Boatwise**, www.boatwiseclasses.com

The DCR and the City of Boston run boating and sailing programs and lessons for both children and adults. Depending on the sailing club's affiliation, children's lessons can be inexpensive or even free, thanks to government subsidies. Perhaps most popular is the **Community Boating School**, which offers sailing lessons and organizes boating programs. The boathouse was built in 1940 with money from Helen Osborn Storrow, and is located on the Charles River Esplanade between the Longfellow Bridge and the Hatch Shell. Call 617-523-1038 for details. For more options, check the Yellow pages under "Boating Instruction."

To find sailing centers outside the metro area, we recommend checking with BostonBoating.com. If boat ownership is where you are headed, you'll need to get the proper **licenses** and **registration**, as dictated by the Massachusetts Environmental Police and the Department of Fisheries, Wildlife, and Environmental Law Enforcement, www.state.ma.us/dfwele/dle/dle_toc.htm. The commonwealth of Massachusetts requires that all boats with motors (this includes jet-skis, and sailboats with motors in them—even electric) be registered, no matter how infrequently you may use the motor. It also requires that all boats longer than 14 feet with a motor have a certificate of title. Titles cost $25. Registrations vary from $40 to $100, depending on the size of your boat. Once you get your paperwork, the state requires that you paint your boat's registration number on the forward half of the hull in block letters at least 3 inches high. The registration decal goes on the port side of the boat, lined up with and three inches sternward of the registration number. For more information and to download forms, visit www.state.ma.us/dfwele/dle/sptapps.htm, or contact the **Division of Law Enforcement**, Registration and Titling Bureau,

Boston Licensing Office, 251 Causeway Street, 1st Floor, 617-626-1610. You can renew your motorboat license through the department's online licensing site, MassOutdoors, www.sport.state.ma.us.

Although there are marinas galore within Boston proper, many boat owners tie up at marinas outside the city, along the north and south shores, up to Cape Ann, and down to Cape Cod, or even on the islands. There are plenty of places for boat storage in towns like Gloucester, Marblehead, Salem, Newburyport, Beverly, Rockport, Scituate, Hingham, Weymouth, Falmouth, Hyannis, Provincetown, and others. Check www.bostonboating.com or www.marinas.com for a list of public launch ramps and marinas that will be most accessible for you if you are looking outside the city. The DCR also runs a number of **small boat launches** in Boston, Medford and Nahant. Call the Boston Harbor Master, 34 Drydock Avenue, Boston, 617-343-4721, or the DCR for details and locations.

If **rowing** or **crewing** is more your thing, start with **Community Rowing** at Daly Rink on the Charles in Newton. You can contact them at www.communityrowing.org, or 617-964-3455, from April to October, and 617-782-9091 from November to March. (The facility is open from April through October.) **Boston Bay Blades**, www.bayblades.org, is a non-profit rowing and sculling organization for Boston's GLBT community.

Finally, if you're into **rafting**, you'll probably need to get a ways outside the city, if not the state, to find suitable rapids. Check with **BSSC Whitewater Rafting**, 627-789-4070, ext. 229, www.bssc.com/whitewater.html. They offer summer weekend trips up to western Massachusetts, Maine, and Canada for anyone who is interested, regardless of experience levels.

BOWLING

Well, the first thing you should know about bowling in Boston is that most bowling around here is of the candlepin variety, which is more like a combination between bocce and the traditional ten pin, or as Bostonians call it "big-ball" bowling, with which you're likely most familiar. With candlepin bowling there are still ten pins, but the balls are much smaller—bocce ball sized—and they don't have any finger holes, you just palm them in your hand. You get three chances to knock all ten pins down. If you just can't warm up to the notion of candlepin bowling, there are some of the other variety around, but much harder to find. Here are a few of the local bowling alleys. Unless otherwise noted, you can presume they are candlepin:

- **Ball Square Bowling Alley**, 662 Boston Avenue, Medford, 781-306-0716
- **Big League Bowling Center**, 1834 Centre Street, West Roxbury, 617-323-7291

- **Boston Bowl Family Fun Center**, 820 Morrissey Boulevard, Dorchester, 617-825-3800; offers ten pin, candlepin, pool tables, and "cosmic bowling."
- **Central Park Lanes**, 10 Saratoga Street, East Boston, 617-567-7073
- **Lanes and Games**, 195 Concord Turnpike, Cambridge, 617-876-5533, www.lanesgames.com
- **Lucky Strike Lanes**, 289 Adams Street, Dorchester, 617-436-2660
- **Milky Way Lounge & Lanes**, 405 Centre Street, JP, 617-524-3740, www.milkywayjp.com; just a couple of candlepin lanes, but mixed in with a dance floor, bar, and more.
- **Monday Night Bowling League**, www.mnbl.net; candlepin bowling for the GLBT community at the Ryan Family Amusement Center. The league has been around for 30 years.
- **Needham Bowl-A-Way**, 16 Chestnut Street, Needham, 781-444-9614, www.needhambowlaway.com
- **Olindy's Quincy Avenue Lanes**, 170 Quincy Avenue, Quincy, 617-472-3579
- **Ryan Family Amusement Center**, 82 Lansdowne Street, Boston, 617-267-8495, no bar; 466 Main Street, Malden, 781-321-1166
- **Sacco's Bowl Haven**, 45 Day Street, Somerville, 617-776-0552, http://saccosbowlhaven.com
- **South Boston Candlepins**, 543 East Broadway, South Boston, 617-464-4858; no concessions.
- **Town Line Ten Pin**, 665 Broadway, Malden, 781-324-7120
- **Twentieth Century Bowling Lane**, 1231 Hyde Park Avenue, Hyde Park, 617-364-5274

If you're interested in joining a bowling league, check with your local alley, or try one of these:
- **Beantown Bowling**, www.beantownbowling.com; 10-pin GLBT bowling league in Cambridge and Dorchester.
- **Massachusetts Bowling Association**, www.masscandlepin.com
- **International Candlepin Bowling Association**, 3 Arrowhead Drive, Bow, NH, 603-230-9665, www.bowlcandlepin.com

BOXING

The **Boston Sport Boxing Club**, 125 Walnut Street, Watertown, 617-972-1711, www.bostonboxing.com, hosts amateur to Olympic-style boxing lessons for all ability levels, and is open Monday-Saturday, 2 p.m. to 10 p.m.

CHESS

There is definitely a solid chess scene in Boston, or rather, Cambridge (maybe having something to do with all the Harvard and MIT students). If you want to play a competitive game of pick-up chess, the "trendiest" place is at Harvard Square, in the courtyard by Au Bon Pain.

College and graduate students can take advantage of their school's chess clubs. The rest might want to join one of these:
- **Boylston Chess Club**, 140 Clarendon Street, Boston, 617-351-7668, http://world.std.com/~boylston
- **Massachusetts Chess Association**, www.masschess.org
- **MetroWest Chess Club**, P.O. Box 1182, Framingham, 508-788-3641, www.metrowestchess.org, "the largest weeknight chess club in New England," meets in Natick.
- **United States Chess Federation**, 845-562-8350, www.uschess.org

CURLING

Evidently cold air masses are not the only thing we get from Canada. If you'd like to capture the spirit of the great white north with a game of curling, try one of these:
- **Broomstones Curling Club**, 138 Rice Road, Wayland, 508-352-2412, www.broomstones.com; 250 members of all ages play on their four sheets of ice.
- **Canadian Club of Boston**, The Country Club, Brookline, http://ourworld.compuserve.com/homepages/rppurdy/1stpage.htm; supporting all things Canadian, especially curling. Games in Brookline.

DANCE

Depending on your groove, dance classes and dance parties are a fun way to stay fit and meet friends. Clubs, groups, and dance studios offer everything ranging from classes to private lessons to dance nights in salsa, swing, African, etc.
- **Boston Dance Alliance**, 617-482-4588, www.bostondancealliance.org
- **Boston Swing Dance Network**, 617-924-6603, www.bostonswingdance.com; different bands play a variety of swing music, from big band to jump blues, one Saturday per month from September to June.
- **Cambridge Tango Central**, www.cambridgetangocentral.coml; Wednesday night tangos

- **Dance Complex**, 536 Mass Ave., Cambridge, 617-547-9363, www.dance complex.org; a popular place for workshops, classes, and programs in the metro area. Ballet, African, jazz, salsa, hip-hop, modern, flamenco, belly dancing, and more.
- **DanceNet**, www.havetodance.com; swing dance in Boston and New England, detailing lessons, dance nights, calendar, etc.
- **Dance New England**, www.dne.org; a consortium of barefoot freestyle dancing.
- **Folk Arts Center of New England**, 42 West Foster Street, Melrose, 781-662-7475, www.facone.org; teaches traditional ethnic dances, publishes bi-monthly calendar of local dance events.
- **Impulse Dance Company**, 181 Mass Ave., 3rd Floor, Boston, 617-536-6989, www.impulsedance.com; ongoing classes in ballet, hip hop, jazz, modern, social dances, stretch/toning, movement, and choreography.
- **MamBostOn2.com** is a good portal for those interested in mambo; includes a listing of dance events and classes.
- **Massachusetts Amateur Ballroom Dance Association**, www.massabda.org; calendar of monthly dance events, ballroom dance, etc.
- **Maxwell Ho's West Coast Swing Party**, www.havetodance.com/maxwell; regular classes and dances at the St. John's Methodist Church, 80 Mt. Auburn Street, Watertown and Belmont Methodist Church, 421 Common Street, Belmont
- **New England Folk Festival Association**, www.neffa.org
- **SalsaBoston**, www.salsaboston.com; portal for Boston's salsa scene
- **Swing City Dance Club**, 688 Huron Avenue, Cambridge, 617-254-8700, www.wannadance.com; large, air conditioned, smoke-free dance hall for lindy hop and East Coast swing music.
- **Swingtime Boston**, 617-364-7207, www.djdee.com/swingtime; monthly swing, Latin, and ballroom dance for Boston's GLBT community at Ballet Etc., 185 Corey Street, Brookline.
- **Tango Society of Boston**, 617-669-OCHO, www.bostontango.org; instruction and dance nights.
- **Tap Boston**, www.havetodance.com/tapboston; portal for links to tap classes and dance nights around the city.
- **Tempo Dance Center**, 380 Washington Street, Brighton, 617-783-5467, www.havetodance.com/tempodancecenter; weekly lessons and classes in swing, Latin, hustle, etc., and bimonthly Friday dance parties.
- **Topf Center for Dance Education**, 551 Tremont Street, Boston, 617-482-0531, www.topfcenter.org/new; community outreach, interracial understanding, and dance instruction.

FENCING

For when you want to get a touché from an epee:
- **Boston Fencing Club**, 110-2 Clematis Avenue, Waltham, 781-891-0119, www.bostonfencingclub.org
- **Metro Boston Fencing**, http://users.primushost.com/~sky/fencing
- **New England Division of the USFA**, www.neusfa.org, includes a list of greater Boston fencing clubs.

FISHING

The state's fishing and wildlife agency, **MassWildlife** www.state.ma.us/dfwele/dfw_toc.htm, is a subsection of the **Massachusetts Department of Fisheries, Wildlife, and Environmental Law Enforcement**. MassWildlife was founded in 1866 as the state fisheries commission, and has expanded its reach over the past 150 years to cover all of the flora and fauna of the state. This office should be the first government agency to contact with questions regarding where you can fish and what the requirements are. They can give you details about seasons, limits, regulations, and stocking schedules, and where to get maps. MassWildlife's Boston office is at 251 Causeway Street, Suite 400, 617-626-1590.

Saltwater fishing is free, and freshwater fishing licenses in Massachusetts range from about $11 to $38; no charge for seniors (age 70 or over) and some people with disabilities. You can pick up your fishing license throughout the state, including town and city clerks, sporting goods stores, and bait and tackle shops; check with MassWildlife. Or, for maximum ease, you can get them online from **MassOutdoors** (www.sport.state.ma.us, 617-626-1600). Note: if you want to trap lobsters, you'll need a special permit, also available through this web site.

Fishermen and women who want to bring their catch home to their families should note that the EPA, FDA, and Massachusetts Department of Public Health advise young children and pregnant or breastfeeding women against eating shark, swordfish, king mackerel, tuna steak, and tilefish, as well as any Massachusetts freshwater fish, due to mercury pollution. Furthermore, be careful fishing in the Charles River or in Boston Harbor (despite its reputation for good bluefish and striper). The state cautions children and childbearing women against eating flounder and shellfish from Boston Harbor, and moving further south doesn't remedy the problem either: fish and shellfish from New Bedford Harbor have an elevated level of polychlorinated biphenyl compounds (PCBs) that they pick up from toxic substances in the water. Despite the precautions, there are many places in and around Boston where you can catch some tasty and safe freshwater or saltwater fish. Freshwater fish found in area lakes that are stocked by the Massachusetts Department of Fisheries and Wildlife such as trout, broodstock salmon, northern pike, and tiger muskie are fine. DCR- and MassWildlife-run fishing areas close to Boston can be found at www.mass.gov/dcr.

Those interested in a fishing club can check with the **Massachusetts Striped Bass Association**, Viking Club, Route 53, Quincy, 617-984-0530, www.msba.net. If you're an ice fisherman (or fisherwoman), you are one of the few. For obvious reasons, **ice fishing** is not as popular here as it is in a place like Minnesota. However, the DCR allows ice fishing in some areas of the Charles. Call them at 617-727-7090 or Bear's Bait Shop in Waltham at 781-647-040 for information on permits.

FOOTBALL, RUGBY

For those newcomers who like the rough stuff:
- **BSSC Coed Indoor Flag or Touch Football**, 617-789-4070 ext. 242, www.bssc.com; individuals and groups may sign up for games played in Brighton.
- **Boston Irish Wolfhounds**, 617-254-9732, www.bostonirish wolfhounds.com; all abilities welcome, training in JP, games in Canton.
- **Boston Ironsides Rugby Football Club**, http://bostonironsides rfc.org; rugby league for gay men.
- **Boston Rugby Club**, 617-566-2732, www.brfc.org; national-level team
- **Boston Women's Rugby Football Club**, 781-340-2192, www.bwrfc.org; games in Brookline and Cambridge.
- **Charles River Rugby Football Club**, crrfc-recruiting@egroups.com, www.crrfc.com; weekly practices at Daly Field in Brighton.
- **FLAG Flag Football**, http://flagflagfootball.tripod.com; GLBT flag football league, games on weekends, all skill levels welcome.
- **Mystic River Rugby Club**, P.O. Box 477, Malden, 781-322-0898, www.mysticrugby.com; Division I competitive men's rugby.
- **Old Gold Rugby Club**, 617-742-9648, www.oldgoldrugby.com; all levels, games on Saturdays.

FRISBEE

Frisbee isn't just a game you play with your dog. Ultimate Frisbee turns freestyle disc throwing into a structured team sport, and is popular and fun, especially with the twenty- to thirty-something set.
- **BSSC Ultimate Frisbee**, 617-789-4070, www.bssc.com; coed weekly games in Charlestown from May to August.
- **Boston Ultimate Disc Alliance** (**BUDA**), P.O. Box 79242, Waverly, 617-484-1539, www.buda.org; several Ultimate Frisbee leagues in the

Boston area—spring, summer, fall, open/corporate—most are coed. Many games are held JP English High School field in JP.

GOLF

The Boston area features a number of public 18-hole golf courses and a 36-hole course at the **Blue Hills Reservation**. Most courses are open from dawn to dusk and require reservations on weekends and holidays. It's always best to call ahead. For listings and reviews of all public and private courses in Boston go to www.golfboston.com or check with the Massachusetts Golf Association, www.mgalinks.org. Information about public courses will also be available through your city's parks and recreation department and through the **DCR**, www.mass.gov/dcr. There is no shortage of private courses in the Boston metro area. If you're interested in applying for membership to a private golf club, check the Yellow Pages under "Golf Courses-Private." If you're interested in joining a different kind of club, **BSSC Golf**, 617-789-4070, www.bssc.com; offers scrambles, weekend outings, and lessons during the spring, summer, and fall.

HIKING, ROCK CLIMBING, AND MOUNTAINEERING

Great hiking can be found throughout New England, particularly as you head north into the less populated and wilder areas of Vermont, New Hampshire, and Maine. Mountain climbers find life here very satisfactory as well. For example, New Hampshire's Mount Monadnock claims it is the second most climbed mountain in the world. When climbing, use common sense and be extremely cautious during the winter season; reports of people freezing to death on the icy peak of Mount Washington in New Hampshire are, sadly, not uncommon.

On a more local scale, the DCR maintains hiking trails at several area reservations. Go to www.mass.gov/dcr for details.
- **Blue Hills Reservation**, Milton and Canton, 617-698-1802; hiking, rock climbing and bouldering at the Quincy Quarries in Quincy.
- **Beaverbrook Reservation**, Mill Street, Belmont and Waltham, 617-484-6357; open fields, wetlands, and woodlands.
- **Belle Isle Reservation**, Bennington Street, East Boston, 617-727-5350; Boston's last remaining salt marsh.
- **Boston Harbor Islands**, www.bostonislands.com; there are many islands in the harbor, each of which offers a slightly different experience, and many offer hiking and camping. Three of them—George's, Peddock's, and Lovell's—are run by the DCR (see **Greenspace and Beaches** for more information).

- **Breakheart Reservation**, Forest Street, Saugus, 781-233-0834; 640-acre hardwood forest with rocky hills, two lakes, and one river.
- **Hammond Pond Reservation**, Hammond Pond Parkway, Newton/Brookline, 617-698-1802; open year-round, dawn to dusk, rock climbing and bouldering.
- **Hemlock Gorge/Cutler Park**, Needham and Newton, 617-698-1802
- **Middlesex Fells Reservation** runs through Medford, Malden, Melrose, Stoneham, Winchester: 781-322-3851 or 781-662-5230
- **Neponset River Reservation**, Dorchester and Milton, 617-727-5290; one large park and a main trail.
- **Stony Brook Reservation**, Turtle Pond Parkway, West Roxbury and Hyde Park, 617-361-6161; hills, valleys, rocky outcroppings, and wetlands.

For more ideas on where to go hiking anywhere in New England, you can always pick up a guidebook on hiking in New England. Two are *Hiking Southern New England* and *National Geographic's Guide to America's Outdoors: New England*. Investigate the numerous **state parks** through the MassParks web site, www.massparks.org.

If you are interested in **rock climbing**, you should try the **Quincy Quarries** near the Blue Hills Reservation and **Menotomy Rocks Park** in Arlington. You can keep your rock climbing skills honed year-round by joining the **Boston Rock Gym**, an indoor facility with climbing walls, located at 78 Olympia in Woburn. Call 781-935-7325 or visit www.bostonrockgym.com for information.

Area **hiking and climbing organizations** include:
- **Appalachian Mountain Club**, 5 Joy Street in Boston, 617-523-0655, www.amcboston.org; conducts hiking and skiing tours and trips and maintains a cabin system in the White Mountains.
- **Boston Hiking Guide**, www.geocities.com/Yosemite/Trails/1171; provides links to the best hiking areas and walking paths in the greater Boston area.
- **New England Bouldering**, www.newenglandbouldering.com
- **BSSC Hiking**, 617-789-4070, www.bssc.com; guided day and weekend trips during the spring, summer, and fall.
- **BSSC Rock Climbing**, 617-789-4070, www.bssc.com; indoor course

HOCKEY—FLOOR, FIELD, ROLLER

There are a number of intramural **hockey leagues** and teams around, but it can be hard to break in as a newcomer. If you're interested in playing hockey with a team there are a number of ways to go about it: area bars sponsor teams, so you could visit local pubs in your neighborhood and ask

around, visit the ice rinks, or check the sports pages for ads—sometimes organizations will advertise for players in the *Globe*. You can also check with the **Boston Ski & Sports Club**, 617-789-4979, www.bssc.com, or one of the following:
- **Boston Pride Hockey**, www.bostonpridehockey.org; GLBT ice hockey league, games at rinks throughout the greater Boston area.
- **BSSC Coed Floor Hockey**, 617-789-4070 ext. 238, www.bssc.com; all levels, individuals and teams, in Newton and Brighton.
- **New England In-Line Hockey League**, Boston, 617-269-0087
- **Newton Indoor Sports Center Roller Hockey League**, Newton, 617-964-0040

HORSEBACK RIDING

A number of area stables offer both lessons and rentals, but you're definitely going to have to break away from the city. If you're interested in taking a lesson or renting a horse, try www.horserentals.com, www.northhorse.com, www.justhorses.com, or www.horsemensguide.com. Or check the Yellow Pages under "Horse Riding Stables."

Horseback riding is allowed on some **DCR reservation trails**:
- **Blue Hills Reservation**, Milton/Canton/Quincy/Braintree/Randolph/Dedham/Boston; horses from a number of private stables, 617-698-1802, www.mass.gov/dcr
- **Middlesex Fells Reservation**, Malden/Medford/Winchester/Stoneham/Melrose, 781-322-2851 or 781-662-5320, www.mass.gov/dcr

There are also trails at state parks where horseback riding is permissible. For more information, check with MassParks at 617-626-1250, or visit www.massgov/dcr for a full list of all the parks where you can ride. Parks with **riding trails** in the greater Boston area include:
- **Ames Nowell State Park**, Linwood Street, Abington, 781-857-1336
- **Borderland State Park**, 259 Massapoag Avenue, Easton/Sharon, 508-238-6566
- **Bradley Palmer State Park**, Asbury Street, Topsfield, 978-887-5931
- **Callahan State Park**, Millwood Street, Framingham, 508-653-9641
- **F. Gilbert Hills State Forest**, Mill Street, Foxboro, 508-543-5850
- **Georgetown Rowley State Forest**, Route 97, Georgetown, 508-887-5931
- **Great Brook Farm State Park**, 984 Lowell Road, Carlisle, 978-369-6312
- **Harold Parker State Forest**, 1951 Turnpike Street, Route 114, North Andover, 978-686-3391

- **Lowell-Dracut-Tyngsboro State Forest**, Trotting Park Road, Lowell, 978-453-0592
- **Maudslay State Park**, Curzon Mill Street, Newburyport, 978-465-7223
- **Willowdale State Forest**, Linebrook Road, Ipswich, 978-887-5931
- **Wompatuck State Park**, Union Street, Hingham, 781-747-7160

ICE SKATING

The DCR maintains a number of ice rinks in the area, open from mid-November to mid-March. If you're interested in ice rentals, we recommend you call 617-727-4708. Information about the more than 20 **Metro Boston DCR rinks** can be accessed at www.mass.gov/dcr. **Larz Andersen Park**, 617-730-2069, www.town.brookline.ma.us/recreation/LarzAnderson.html, in Brookline offers an outdoor rink during winter months, and the Town of Watertown runs a private rink: **Ryan Skating Arena**, 1 Paramount Place, Watertown, 781-972-6468 (rentals available). But perhaps the quintessential Boston experience is skating on **Frog Pond** in the **Boston Public Garden**. There may be nothing quite as charming and romantic as skating in the middle of the common on a crisp winter night with the statehouse and Beacon Hill's bowfront homes rising around you. For more information, call 617-635-4504 or visit www.ci.boston.ma.us/parks/sports.asp.

Skating clubs include:
- **New England Figure Skating Club**, 121 Donald Lynch Boulevard, Marlborough, 508-229-2700 ext. 212, www.newenglandfsc.com
- **Skating Club of Boston**, 1240 Soldiers Field Road, Boston, 617-782-5900, www.scboston.org; general public skating on Tuesdays and Saturdays.
- **North Shore Skating Club**, 953 Broadway, Saugus, 781-233-3706

IN-LINE/ROLLER SKATING

In-line skating is popular in Boston, and there are many paths where you can use your blades. For fun hills, try the Arnold Arboretum. For distance try the Charles River Bicycle Trail, the Minute Man Bicycle Trail, and Marine Park in Southie. Skateboards.org is a great web site where you can find skate shops and parks in Massachusetts and elsewhere.

Some community and adult-education schools offer lessons and classes, including **Beacon Hill Skate In-Line**, 135 Charles Street, Boston, 617-482-7400 and **Boston In-Line Skate School**, 51 Philips, Boston, area code 617-248-3838.

In-line skating clubs include:
- **Inline Club of Boston**, P.O. Box 426185, Cambridge, 781-932-5457, www.sk8net.com; paid membership gets you weekly group skate nights, skate parties, skate tours, etc.
- **New England In-Line Hockey League**, Boston, 617-269-0087
- **Newton Indoor Sports Center Roller Hockey League**, Newton, 617-964-0040

Skate parks and rinks include:
- **Chez Vous Disco Rink**, 11 Rhoades Street, Dorchester, 617-825-6877
- **Hanger 18**, 1108 Boylston Street, Boston, 617-236-6944
- **Roller World**, 425 Broadway, Saugus, 781-231-1111
- **Z.T. Maximus Skate Park**, 324 Rindge Avenue, Cambridge, 617-576-4723, Bowl, Indoor, Mini Ramp, Pro Shop, Street Course, Vert Ramp. Pads are required and you must pay to play.

KICKBALL

- **BSSC Kickball**, 617-789-4070, www.bssc.com; individuals and teams welcome, weekly games in Charlestown and Newton.

RACQUET SPORTS—TENNIS AND SQUASH

A number of area health clubs offer racquetball, squash, handball, and tennis courts that you can use if you have a membership. However, the DCR does maintain public tennis courts where you can play for free. (See the **Parks and Recreation Departments** section above for contact information.) The unlit courts are open until dusk; lighted courts are open until 10 p.m.

Additionally, the City of Boston operates tennis courts at some of its community centers. For example, the **Stillman Tennis Center**, part of the Charlestown Community Center, 255 Medford Street, Boston, 617-635-5364, offers three indoor and seasonally-open air courts. The **Paris Street Community Center**, 112 Paris Street, East Boston, 617-735-5125, **Harborside Community Center**, 312 Border Street, East Boston, 617-635-5114, and **Curley Community Center**, 1663 Columbia Road, South Boston, 617-635-5304, all offer racquetball courts. **Boston Common** and the **Esplanade** also have tennis courts. Check the Yellow Pages for a list of private tennis courts.

Bostonians also like to play **squash**. Many clubs have squash courts and so do the colleges. Probably the most famous place for squash is the private **Harvard Club**, 374 Comm Ave., Boston, 617-536-1260, www.harvardclub.com. The **Allston-Brighton Squash & Fitness Club**, 15 Gorham Street, Allston, 617-731-4177, is a public squash court. You may also contact the **Massachusetts Squash Racquets Association**, www.ma-squash.org, if you're interested in playing with the state's competitive league. Check the Yellow Pages for a list of private squash courts.

If you're interested in joining a **racquet sport league**, here are a few:
- **New England Badminton**, www.geocities.com/Colosseum/Loge/7554
- **Boston Boasts Squash Club**, www.bostonboasts.com; the nation's oldest and largest GLBT squash league.
- **BSSC Tennis**, 617-789-4070, www.bssc.com; indoor and outdoor clinics, mixed double tennis parties, and more.

RUNNING

In Boston there are many beautiful areas in which to run. For interesting paths or trails, see above under **Hiking**, **In-line Skating**, and **Biking** for various types of terrain. The most popular places to run within Boston proper are the paths around the Charles River; go to www.mass.gov/dcr for details.

If running competitively is your thing, there are many annual races, including the mother of them all—the Boston Marathon. For the complete skinny on running in the region including a calendar of races and track and field events, go to **New England Runner**, www.nerunner.com, or contact the **Boston Athletic Association**, 617-236-1652, www.baa.org, or the **Bill Rogers Running Center**, 617-723-5612, www.billrodgers.com, at Faneuil Hall Marketplace. The calendar sections of the weekly papers and the *Improper Bostonian* list race details.

If you'd like to join a **running club** for some company, consider one of the following:
- **Back Bay Road Runners**, http://members.tripod.com/~backbayrr; informal running club that runs around the Charles on Tuesday nights.
- **Boston Athletic Association Running Club**, 617-236-1652, www.baa.org; competitive weekly workouts with the best of the best.
- **Boston Hash House Harriers**, 617-499-4835, www.bostonhash.com; "serious drinkers with a running problem." Year-round weekly runs on Wednesday or Sundays.
- **Cambridge Running Club**, www.cambridgerunning.org; weekly runs in tracks in Cambridge and Allston.
- **Cambridge Sports Union**, www.csurun.org/csu.htm; join 200 men and women for coaching, races, and weekly workouts at the Harvard race track and around Fresh Pond.
- **Community Running**, 617-542-2RUN, www.communityrunning.org; three coached workouts weekly, year-round, for all ages and abilities.

- **Frontrunners Boston**, www.frontrunnersboston.org; 25-year-old GLBT running club, for runners, walkers, and joggers of all levels. Includes both shorter and longer runs/walks on weekdays and weekends.
- **Greater Boston Track Club**, P. O. Box 183, Back Bay Annex, Boston, 781-543-3710, www.gbtc.org; "friendly, competitive, team-oriented environment" for runners "who compete at the local, regional, and national levels." They also post a great list of local running clubs on their web site, check it for clubs you don't see listed here.
- **Heartbreak Hill Striders**, www.heartbreakhill.org; short and long runs west of the city, in Wellesley and in Chestnut Hill by Heartbreak Hill.
- **Irish American Track Club**, www.iatc-boston.org; competitive and social runs and workouts, long and short, tracks and all terrain, Malden, Medford, JP. Not just for the Irish.
- **Khoury's 4-Mile Free Fun Run**, 118 Broadway, East Somerville, 781-275-1584, www.srr.org; weekly runs on Thursday nights.
- **L Street Running Club**, www.lstreet.org; for the recreational runner to the serious competitor, South Boston.
- **North Medford Club**, www.northmedfordclub.org; oldest running club in the US—no frills, low cost, winter and summer races.
- **Parkway Running Club**, www.parkwayrunning.org, West Roxbury.
- **Somerville Road Runners**, www.srr.org; fun group based in Somerville, $20 annual fee.
- **Stellar Running Club**, www.stellarrunning.org; distance training, Belmont.
- **West Roxbury Running Club**, 617-327-2989; less formal gathering of 60 runners who do short weekday and long weekend runs starting from the Y in West Roxbury.

SKIING—CROSS COUNTRY

The snowfall in the Boston area varies from year to year. Some winters you'll be shoveling out once a week; others, there isn't even enough snow to ski in the mountains. If the winter is a good one (that is if you like snow), you can cross country ski in the city, especially along the **Emerald Necklace** (see the **Greenspace** chapter). The Arnold Arboretum offers both flat stretches and hills.

Cross country skiing is permitted in all DCR reservations, but the Middlesex Fells, Blue Hills Reservation, and Charles River Reservation are the most popular places. Check the section on **Hiking** for a complete listing. It is also permitted in many of the state parks throughout Massachusetts. Visit www.mass.gov/dcr for a complete listing. For more information on the greater Boston cross-country scene, check the web site of the New England

Nordic Skiing Association, http://nensa.northcottweb.com, or www.crosscountryski.com.

Here are a few favored **cross-country venues**:
- **Charles River Recreation Ski Touring and Cross-Country**, at the Martin Golf Course, Weston, 781-891-6575; lighted groomed trails, rentals, snowmaking, refreshments, showers, lockers, equipment repairs/maintenance, and lessons. Open daily.
- **Middlesex Fells Ski Touring and Cross-Country**, at the Middlesex Fells Reservation, www.mass.gov/dcr, 617-662-5230; six-mile trail with two loops, for a variety of skill levels. Free and open to the public during daylight hours.
- **Blue Hills Reservation**, Milton/Canton, 617-698-1802, www.mass.gov/dcr; open to the public during daylight hours.
- **Great Brook Farm State Park** in Carlisle, 978-369-6312, www.state.ma.us/dcr
- **Walden Pond State Reservation**, Concord, 978-369-3254, www.state.ma.us/dcr
- **Boston Harbor Islands—World's End**, www.bostonislands.com/frmset_isle.html

If you're interested in joining a cross country skiing or ski racing club, try the **Cambridge Sports Union Ski Club**, www.csuski.org or the Boston branch of the **Appalachian Mountain Club**, www.amcboston.org.

SKIING—DOWNHILL AND SNOWBOARDING

If you want a quick alpine ski fix, head to Blue Hills Reservation where you'll find the **Blue Hills Ski Area**, Milton/Canton, www.mass.gov/dcr. It sports seven slopes (three of which are lit), snowmaking, a ski school, ski patrol, rentals, night skiing, ski shop, restaurant, and a double chair lift. There are also several other small mountains in Massachusetts.

If you're looking for more serious skiing, you'll have to travel a bit. The Green Mountains, White Mountains, and Berkshires stand between 1,000 and 3,000 feet above sea level, and since snow conditions in this part of the country are not reliable—some winters it never stops coming and in others it barely snows at all—many local ski areas compensate by making their own. That said, New England skiing and snowboarding is popular and accessible. Many locals go in together on condos and houses for fun winter weekends at ski areas in New Hampshire, Vermont or Maine, available within two to four hours drive of Boston. To find a complete listing of all New England's ski mountains and their offerings, visit www.newenglandski.com.

Joining a **ski club** can be a great way to meet friends. If this appeals to you, consider investigating:

- **BSSC Skiing**, 617-789-4070, www.bssc.com; day trips, weekends, full-on vacations, and racing.
- **Outryders**, 113 Sheridan Street #2, JP, www.outryders.org; GLBT skiing and snowboarding club.
- **Boston Ski Party**, www.bostonskiparty.org; African-American skiing and snowboarding club.
- **Appalachian Mountain Club Boston Chapter Ski Committee**, www.amcboston.org

SOCCER

Area **soccer leagues** include:

- **BSSC Indoor and Outdoor Soccer**, 617-789-4070, www.bssc.com; individuals and teams are welcome to sign up for games in Charlestown, Cambridge, Brighton, Reading, and Canton.
- **Los Guapos Football Club**, www.guapos.org; coed soccer club based in Boston.
- **Boston Strikers**, www.bostonstrikers.com; GLBT soccer club, with indoor and outdoor games.
- **Fun Sport & Social Group**, www.fssgboston.com; coed, six on six, indoor recreational soccer league. Games in Revere.

SWIMMING

Boston has many beaches within the city limits, and there are plenty on the north and south shores, reachable by car, T, and commuter rail. And for serious beach enthusiasts, you can take day trips to or rent summer houses on Cape Cod, Martha's Vineyard, or Nantucket. See the **Greenspace and Beaches** chapter for more details.

For those who are afraid of fish nibbling your toes, there are many **public pools** throughout the Boston area. For example, the DCR maintains a number of swimming pools and spray pools (see below under **Sports for Kids**) open from the end of June to Labor Day. Call the DCR office that covers your neighborhood for rates and hours of operation:

Charles and Mystic districts: 617-727-4708

- **Allied Veterans Memorial Pool**, Elm Street, Everett
- **Brighton/Allston Pool**, North Beacon Street, Brighton
- **Connors Memorial Pool**, River Street, Waltham
- **Dealtry Memorial Pool**, Pleasant Street, Watertown
- **Dilboy Field Memorial Pool**, Alewife Brook Parkway, Somerville

- **Hall Memorial Pool**, North Border Road, Stoneham
- **Holland Memorial Pool**, Mountain Avenue, Malden
- **Latta Brothers Memorial Pool**, McGrath Highway, Somerville
- **Lee Memorial Pool**, Charles Street (West End), Boston
- **McCrehan Memorial Pool**, Rindge Avenue, Cambridge
- **Veterans Memorial Pool**, Memorial Drive, Cambridge
- **Vietnam Veterans Memorial Pool**, Carter Street, Chelsea

Harbor and Neponset districts: 617-727-8865
- **Cass Memorial Pool**, Washington Street, Roxbury
- **Connell Memorial Pool**, Broad Street, Weymouth
- **Olsen Memorial Pool**, Turtle Pond Parkway, Hyde Park; has a spray pool.
- **Phelan Memorial Pool**, VFW Parkway, West Roxbury
- **Reilly Memorial Pool**, Cleveland Circle, Brighton

In addition to the DCR pools, the City of Boston operates a number of indoor pools year round and two outdoor pools seasonally. These pools are maintained by the **Boston Centers for Youth and Families**. You do not need to be a Boston resident to use Boston's community centers, although entrance rates may be a little higher. For general information, including rates and hours of operation, call 617-635-4920 or visit www.cityofboston.gov/bcyf/. For pools in neighboring communities call your town or city hall or check with your town or city recreation department.

If you'd like to find out more about group and **competitive swimming** in Massachusetts, you might want to check out www.neswim.com and www.planetswim.com. To swim competitively or just get a weekly workout by doing laps with a team, give one of the following groups a shot:
- **LANES** (Liquid Assets New England Swim Team), www.swim-lanes.org; is a team for the local GLBT community and friends, open to swimmers of all ability levels.
- **Bernal's Gator Swim Club**, 8 Woodchester Circle, Waltham, www.xmission.com/~arts/swim/gator/; for swimmers ranging in age and ability from elementary school children to former Olympians. Participates in US swimming-sponsored meets throughout the country.
- **Cambridge Masters Swim Club**, 617-484-0550, www.cambridgemasters.com; for all levels of dedicated masters level swimmers and triathletes. Swims at pools in Cambridge and Belmont.
- **New England Masters Swim Club**, 888-SWIMNEM, www.swimnem.org; not as intimidating as it sounds, for swimmers over 19 of all abilities.

VOLLEYBALL

Here are a few local leagues with enough options to keep you rotating year round:
- **Asgard Volleyball League**, University Park, Cambridge, 617-577-9100; weekly league for Cambridge businesses. Games on Wednesday nights.
- **BSSC Volleyball League**, Boston Ski & Sports Club, 617-789-4070 ext. 222, www.bssc.com; coed teams and individuals of all abilities welcome to play in Cambridge, Watertown, Brookline, and Newton.
- **Boston Volleyball Association**, www.bostonvolleyball.com; indoor and outdoor coed volleyball league for players of all abilities. Games in Allston, Brighton, and Newton.
- **Yankee Volleyball Association**, 617-491-7102, www.yankee.org/menu.html; indoor men's, women's, and coed tournaments from September to May.
- **Cambridge-Boston Volleyball Association**, www.gayvolleyball.net; twenty-year-old volleyball league for Boston's GLBT community, part of the National Gay Volleyball Association. Games on Sundays at King School in Cambridge, for all abilities. Annual fee.

YOGA

If yoga is your thing, you can probably find classes at your local gym (see below) or one of the many yoga studios. A comprehensive listing of greater Boston area yoga studios is available at the DigitalCity Boston (www.digitalcity.com/boston) site. Here are a few:
- **The Arlington Center**, 369 Mass Ave., Arlington, 781-316-0282, www.arlingtoncenter.org
- **Back Bay Yoga Studio**, 1112 Boylston Street #3, Boston, 617-375-0785, www.backbayyoga.com
- **Baptiste Power Vinasa Yoga**, www.baronbaptiste.com; many consider him to be *the* local yoga guru: Boston Studio, 139 Columbus Avenue (South End), Boston, 617-441-2144; Cambridge Studio, 2000 Mass Ave. (Porter Square), Cambridge, 617-661-YOGA.
- **Bikram Yoga**, 108 Lincoln Street, Boston, 617-742-6334, www.bikramyogaboston.com
- **BKS Iyengar Yoga Center**, 781-648-3455, www.yoganow.net
- **Center of Light Yoga Studio**, 663 Centre Street, JP, 617-522-4411, www.centeroflightyoga.com
- **Integral Yoga**, 613 Mount Auburn Street, Watertown, 781-924-6085, www.integralyogaofma.com

- **Lauren Fawcett's Bikram Yoga/Yogaduzit**, www.yogaduzit.com, 32 Cottage Park Avenue, Cambridge, 617-868-6006; 1065 Comm Ave., Allston, 617-789-3733
- **Mystic River Yoga**, 196 Boston Avenue, Suite 3900, Medford, 781-396-0808, www.mysticriveryoga.com
- **O2 Yoga Studio**, 288 Highland Avenue (Davis Square), Somerville, 617-625-0267, www.o2yoga.com
- **Yoga for You**, 1854 Centre Street, West Roxbury, 617-325-3244, www.yogaforyou.net
- **Yoga in Harvard Square**, 1151 Mass Ave., Cambridge, 617-864-9642, www.yogainharvardsquare.com
- **The Yoga Studio**, 74 Joy Street (Beacon Hill), Boston, 617-523-7138, www.theyogastudio.org
- **Yoga Studio & Namaste Café**, 340 River Street, West Newton, 617-480-3864, www.yoga-cafe.com

HEALTH CLUBS AND GYMS

There are hundreds of health clubs in the metro Boston area. Get a tour, and if possible a free pass or two, before signing on the dotted line—you may decide that the reality of exercising to skull-pounding music is not so healthful after all. When you're told that the club you're visiting is having a "sale," take it with several grains of salt; with few fixed prices, words like "special," and "discount" are next to meaningless in the fitness business. The person on the treadmill next to you may have paid double or half what you paid. Ask at your place of work if they offer an employer-sponsored program. Finally, don't let yourself be pressured into signing up for a long-term commitment—unless you're *really* sure you want that multi-year membership.

A few area clubs include:
- **Bally Total Fitness**, www.ballyfitness.com, 25 Guest Street, Brighton (Landing), 617-779-7200; 1815 Mass Ave. (Porter Square), Cambridge, 617-868-5100; 200 Boston Avenue, (West) Medford, 781-393-3500; 561 Squire Road, Revere, 781-286-5400
- **Beacon Hill Athletic Club**, www.beaconhillathleticclubs.com, 3 Hancock Street, Boston, 617-367-2422
- **Boston Athletic Club**: 653 Summer Street (Government Center), Boston, www.bostonathleticclub.com
- **Boston Sports Club**, www.nysc.com, numerous locations
- **Cambridge Racquet and Fitness Club**, 215 First Street, Cambridge, 617-491-8989, www.cambridgefitness.com
- **Crunch**, 17 Winter Street (Downtown Crossing), Boston, 617-338-9001, www.crunch.com

- **Fitcorp**, www.fitcorp.com, numerous locations
- **Healthworks Fitness Center for Women**, www.healthworksfitness.com: 441 Stuart Street, Boston (Back Bay), 617-859-7700; 920 Comm Ave., Brookline, 617-731-3030; St. Mary's WIC, 90 Cushing Avenue, Dorchester, 617-825-1600; Porter Square, Cambridge, 617-4979-4454
- **The Sports Club/LA**, 4 Avery Street at Tremont (downtown), 617-375-8200, www.thesportsclubla.com
- **Waverly Oaks Athletic Club**, 411 Waverly Oaks Road, Waltham, 781-894-7010, www.waverlyoaks.com
- **Wellbridge Athletic Club**, www.wellbridge.com: 695 Atlantic Avenue, Boston, 617-439-9600; 1079 Commonwealth Avenue, Boston, 617-254-1711; 135 Wells Avenue, Newton, 617-928-2000; 5 Bennett Street, Cambridge, 617-441-0800

For one of the best fitness deals in town, try the **YMCA**. (Check the White Pages under "YMCA" for a complete list of greater Boston area YMCAs):
- **Boston**, www.ymcaboston.org
- **Cambridge**, www.cambridgeymca.org
- **Malden**, www.maldenymca.org
- **South Shore**, www.ssymca.org
- **West Suburban**, www.ymcainnewton.org

SPORTS FOR KIDS

For many, the first choice for children's sports programs are the **Boston Centers for Youth and Families** (community centers) located throughout the city. Programming and facilities vary from center to center, and you're likely to find a diverse group of kids who go there. For more information, call 617-635-4920 or go to www.cityofboston.gov/bcyf. Another resource is **GoCityKids**, www.gocitykids.com, an activities-based city guide for parents. They profile several cities across the country, of which Boston is one, and offer information on outdoor adventures, camps, parks and playgrounds, and sports. Then there are the **Boys & Girls Clubs of Boston**, 50 Congress Street, Suite 730, Boston, 617-994-4700, www.bgcb.org, and your local **YMCA**.

If your little tyke wants to cool off on a hot summer day, you can take him to one of the **spray pools** operated by the DCR (go to www.mass.gov/dcr for a complete list):
- **Allied Veterans Memorial Pool**, Elm Street, Everett
- **Beaver Brook Reservation**, Trapelo Road, Belmont
- **Lee Memorial Pool**, Charles Street (West End), Boston, at the Artesani playground
- **McCrehan Memorial Pool**, Rindge Avenue, Cambridge

GREENSPACE AND BEACHES

BOSTON IS TRULY BLESSED WITH AN ABUNDANCE OF GREEN SPACE. The city and surrounding communities are replete with parks, waterways, forests, reservoirs, reservations, beaches, and arboreta. In fact, Boston was the final home to Frederick Law Olmstead, the father of American landscape architecture who was responsible for many of the nation's foremost parks and park systems, including New York's Central and Prospect parks. To Boston he contributed the Emerald Necklace, an interlaced system of several parks equivalent to six miles of connected linear green space. Even the area cemeteries are spectacular.

The following is an overview of greater Boston's larger green areas and beaches. Of course, there are many smaller neighborhood parks and pocket parks, which you are sure to stumble across as you explore your new environs.

Contact information for **local parks and nature areas** includes:

- **City of Boston Parks and Recreation Department**, 1010 Mass Ave., 3rd Floor, 617-635-PARK, www.cityofboston.gov/parks
- **Emerald Necklace Conservancy**, www.emeraldnecklace.org
- **Island Preserves**, 617-233-8666, www.bostonislands.com
- **Massachusetts Audubon Society**, 800-AUDUBON, www.massaudubon.org
- **Massachusetts Division of State Parks & Recreation (MassParks)**, 251 Causeway Street, Suite 600, Boston, 617-626-1250, www.mass.gov/dcr; runs public forests and some area parks.
- **Massachusetts Division of Urban Parks & Recreation** (formerly the **MDC**), 617-727-5114, www.mass.gov/dcr. (For a list district offices, which run the parks programs in communities around Boston, see **Participant Sports and Activities** in the **Sports and Recreation** chapter.)
- **National Park Service**, www.nps.gov
- **Trustees of Reservations**, 978-921-1944, www.thetrustees.org

BOSTON COMMON, BOSTON PUBLIC GARDEN, COMMONWEALTH AVENUE MALL

The heart of Boston is **Boston Common**, established in 1634. Originally, the common was functional open pasture for grazing livestock. There was a military component to the common as well: the colonial militia trained for the Revolutionary War here, and the Redcoats occupied the common for eight years beginning in 1768. Anti-slavery meetings were also held here before and during the Civil War.

Today, people come to the common with their dogs and children instead of their pigs and cows, and it is smaller (its original four hills have been leveled), but it is still Boston's most popular outdoor space. The common's location in the heart of downtown makes it a neighborhood park for those who live on Beacon Hill, Back Bay, and Chinatown. There is also a baseball field for use in the summer, and the ever-popular Frog Pond for ice skating in the winter. An annual Christmas tree lighting takes place on the common every holiday season. Two T stops serve Boston Common—Park Street (Red and Green lines), and Boylston (Green Line).

Next to Boston Common is **Boston Public Garden**, or the "Gardens" for short, established in 1837. The 24-acre Victorian-style park, designed by George V. Meacham, is reminiscent of those found in London (think Kensington Gardens) and was created as a public botanical garden. In the summer, many stop in for a ride on one of the Swan Boats (call 617-591-1150 or visit www.swanboats.com for information). Bicycling and in-line skating are not permitted in the Gardens. The Arlington T stop (Green Line) is just across the street from the southwest corner of the Gardens, but you can also get off at the Boylston T stop and walk.

The **Commonwealth Avenue Mall** is a formal avenue with 35 acres of green space running the length of the Back Bay. Until the mid-1800s, the Back Bay really was a bay—or rather, tidal flats—of the Charles River. Starting in 1857, gravel from quarries in West Needham was shipped in trains and dumped into the flats to create a landfill that eventually became a neighborhood. The Back Bay's unique layout—French-influenced Victorian—still survives. Streets were laid out in a grid around a central promenade, the Comm Ave. Mall, which was created by Arthur Gilman. Today, the mall is lined with sweet gum, green ash, maple, linden, zilkova, Japanese pagoda, and elm trees, which in the winter twinkle with holiday lights. Local residents come here to relax or walk their dogs. The Comm Ave. Mall links Boston Public Garden to the **Back Bay Fens** at Charlesgate, commencing the Olmstead-designed portion of Boston's six-mile park system known as the Emerald Necklace.

EMERALD NECKLACE

The **Emerald Necklace** is managed by the Emerald Necklace Conservancy. It ends roughly by Brookline Avenue, where the Muddy River and the Riverway begin. Boston Common, the Gardens, and the Comm Ave. Mall are the only parks in the necklace's string that Frederick Law Olmstead did not create for Boston. Including these three there are nine parks in all, making it possible to walk nearly seven miles across Boston—stem to stern—without leaving the parks.

Olmstead created the **Fens** section of the necklace in response to problems that arose from damming the Charles River (necessary in order to make the Back Bay). To be blunt, it stank. The area that is now called the Fens was a saltwater marsh, which, because it didn't have tidal flushing after the damning of the Charles, became stagnant—and a public health issue. Olmstead flushed out the waterways by building water gates to regulate the tidal flow and tried to create a semblance of the original tidal marsh ecosystem. It didn't work—the damming of the Charles a mile downstream from the Fens changed the water from brackish to fresh, and all the saltwater vegetation there died. Today the Fens is a mixture of green space surrounding a decidedly pleasant marsh area. While the greenery in the Fens is different from Olmstead's original vision, the park is still much used and appreciated. In it are the **WWII Victory Gardens** (community gardens for which you can apply for a plot of your own to grow flowers and vegetables), the **James P. Kelleher Rose Garden**, and **Roberto Clemente Field**, which has two baseball diamonds and basketball courts. Note: while the Fens are generally deemed perfectly safe during the day, they are not the safest place to be after dark. Tall reeds make good cover for illicit activities and the occasional spot of violence after hours. To get to the Fens, you'll have to walk a bit from any of the following Green Line T stops: Hynes/ICA (B, C, and D trains), Symphony, Northeastern, or Museum on the E train.

The Riverway is the result of Olmstead's rerouting of the man-made Muddy River that coincided with flushing of the Fens. With its steep, tree-filled banks and gently flowing water, this park gives you the sense that you really are in the woods. The carriage roads and bridle paths are now used as bike paths. What may be most interesting about this park is that on one side the trees are native to the area, and on the other Olmstead selected trees from Europe and Asia. The Riverway (the road) bisects the park system just northeast of where the Muddy River starts. This portion of the park runs south to the border of Brookline until the Muddy River joins up with Leverett Pond in Olmstead Park. You can access the Riverway best from the Longwood and Fenway stops on the Green Line D train.

Olmstead Park is sort of an informal boundary between Boston and Brookline. Olmstead's original vision was to have the park serve as an educational display with small pools used as natural history exhibits. Today, however, the pools are filled in, and the park's 180 acres are popular for walks and bike rides. Olmstead Park does feature the man-made Wards Pond and Leverett Pond, and Daisy Field, a community softball diamond. All are peaceful retreats from the busy medical area nearby. The park begins where Route 9 bisects the parks, and continues south to JP (between Pond Avenue and the Jamaicaway) where it is cut off by Perkins Street. Your best bet for getting to Olmstead Park is at any of the four final stops on the Green Line E train: Mission Park, Riverway, Back of the Hill, and Heath Street.

From Perkins Street to the southern border with the Jamaicaway is **Jamaica Park**, important because it houses Jamaica Pond. The "pond," a 120-acre glacial kettle, is the largest body of water in Boston. Once upon a time, JP was a summer retreat for Boston's wealthiest citizens and Jamaica Pond was the site of their summer homes. In the 1890s, the city bought the land and removed the houses (save for a few stunning mansions that still survive) and used the area for the ice-cutting industry. Olmstead restored it to what he called "a natural sheet of water with quiet graceful shores." Today Jamaica Pond is a vibrant part of Jamaica Plain's community life. Locals come for free concerts, children's programs, and other community events at the boathouse. Runners, skaters, dog walkers, fishers, and strollers enjoy looping the pond's one-mile circumference. Jamaica Pond is also Boston's back up reservoir, so no swimming allowed. At present, to get to Jamaica Pond, take the Orange Line to either Stony Brook or Green Street and head west into JP, and then it's about a 10-minute walk. If and when streetcar service is extended to Centre Street, getting to the park will be much easier.

South and west of Jamaica Pond, connected by the Arborway, is the 265-acre **Arnold Arboretum**. It is bound by Center and Washington streets and the Jamaicaway, and is shared by the communities of JP and Roslindale. For this "jewel" in the Emerald Necklace, Olmstead collaborated with Charles Sprague Sargent, a scientist who collected thousands of specimens of trees, flowers, and shrubs. The Arboretum features a remarkable collection of maples, laurels, azaleas, crabapples, lilacs, and rhododendrons, and has over 15,000 vines, trees, and shrubs documented and identified. Also here: the largest collection of Asian trees and shrubs outside of Asia. In a unique agreement, Harvard University has leased the Arboretum from the city at the cost of $1 for 1,000 years. Harvard maintains the greenery and the city maintains the roads and walls. Take the Orange Line to the Forest Hills stop and you will be within close walking distance.

And finally, the last link in the chain, also accessible by the Forest Hills T stop, is **Franklin Park and Zoo**. It lies south and slightly east of the

GREENSPACE AND BEACHES

Arboretum, connected by the Arborway, and bound by Seaver and Morton streets, the American Legion Highway, and Blue Hill Avenue. Franklin Park consists of 527 acres, making it the largest park in the necklace. It is accessible to Roxbury, Dorchester, JP, and Roslindale. Olmstead created it as a "country park." It includes a woodland preserve, a zoo, and a golf course. For information about the zoo, call 617-541-LION or visit www.zoo newengland.com.

CITY/NEIGHBORHOOD PARKS

The Emerald Necklace is by no means the only green space around. There are many smaller parks throughout the city, many with playground structures. The **City of Boston Parks and Recreation Department** oversees 215 parks and playgrounds, 65 squares, urban woodlands, burying grounds, and golf courses, and the aforementioned parts of the Emerald Necklace. The **Charles River Reservation** (617-722-5436, www.mass. gov/dcr), run by the DCR, provides 17 miles of riverfront green space accessible to many communities. Boston's Beacon Hill, the Back Bay, Allston-Brighton, and the communities of Cambridge, Watertown, Newton, and Waltham all border the river. There are bike and pedestrian trails for walking, running, biking, and inline skating, a number of playgrounds, outdoor theaters, boathouses, and ice rinks along the Charles. Residents also use the river itself for sailing, canoeing, kayaking, and rowing. The part of the Charles parallel to the Back Bay and Beacon Hill, bound by Storrow Drive, is called the **Esplanade** and is where you'll find the Hatch Memorial Shell. On the Cambridge side, bound by Memorial Drive, is the five-mile-long **JFK Park**. Further west, on the north side of the river in Waltham, is **Landry Park** and the **Lakes District**. The riverbanks west of downtown are part of the Upper Charles River, and is where you will find Newton and Needham's **Hemlock Gorge**, a 23-acre wild area along the banks of the river. Also here is **Brook Farm**, 179 acres of rolling fields and wetland in West Roxbury; **Cutler Park**, a large freshwater marsh in the middle of the Charles in Dedham and Needham; and **Village Falls Park** in Needham.

Waterfront Park (also known as **Christopher Columbus Park**) is located right at the edge of Boston Harbor, between the Waterfront and the North End. As if its incredible view of the harbor weren't enough, it just received a facelift and has new landscaping, pathways, and sod. It's close to the Haymarket (Orange and Green lines), Government Center (Green and Blue lines), and Aquarium (Blue Line) T stops.

Boston's Charlestown has several smaller parks: the Navy Yard, Monument Square, Berry Playground, City Square, John Harvard Mall, and the Training Field. Part of the Boston National Historic Park, the **Navy Yard**, www.nps.gov/bost/Navy_Yard.htm, 617-242-5601, constitutes 17 acres of Charlestown's waterfront between Chelsea Street (near Route 1) and Boston Harbor where it meets up with the Mystic River. Truth be told, it's a bit of a concrete jungle, but the views are gorgeous and many people come here to visit the USS Constitution. **Monument Square** is a small green park surrounding the unmistakable Bunker Hill Monument, bound by Tremont, High, Lexington, and Pleasant streets. The **Training Field**, a.k.a. Charlestown Common, is bound by Adams, Winthrop, and Park streets. And further south, in the shadow of the remaining artery and Charlestown Bridge on the shore of the Harbor is another wee green patch called **City Square**. The closest T stop is Community College on the Orange Line, but it's a bit of a walk.

Boston residents of West Roxbury, Rozzie, and Hyde Park, and neighboring Dedham have immediate access to the 475-acre **Stony Brook Reservation**, bound primarily by East and West Boundary streets and bisected by the Turtle Pond and West Roxbury parkways and Washington Street. The reservation offers hiking, biking, baseball fields, tennis courts, a swimming pool, tot lot, and skating rink. You can fish in Turtle Pond or climb 325 feet to the top of Bellevue Hill, the tallest remaining hill within Boston's city limits. It's accessible by the Orange Line Forest Hills stop.

At the southernmost part of Dorchester and running over into Mattapan, Hyde Park, and neighboring Milton is the **Neponset River Reservation**, which offers 750 acres long the Neponset River and includes marsh and wetlands. Inside the reservation are playgrounds, community gardens, a concert venue (the Martini Shell), and several separate parks, including the Lower Neponset River Trail, and Squantum Point Park.

An old drive-in theater and landfill was converted into **Pope John Paul II Park**, which connects Dorchester with the Neponset River estuary, and now boasts a restored saltwater marsh and replanted native flora. Locals come here to enjoy the picnic and playground facilities, soccer fields, and walking and jogging paths. It is also a good location for bird watching, particularly black ducks, mergansers, snowy egrets, and great blue herons. Future restoration projects may bring fishing areas and bike paths. To get here, take the Red Line Ashmont train to Fields Corner and then take the #20 bus to either the Neponset Circle or Hallet Street entrance.

The **Lower Neponset River Trail** is a 2.4-mile trail for bikes and pedestrians along the Neponset River. At present it runs from Port Norfolk in Dorchester, through Pope John Paul II Park, across Granite Avenue, through the Neponset Marshes and Lower Mills, ending up on Central Avenue in Milton. The DCR hopes to extend it to Mattapan and Castle Island. You can pick up the trail at any of the following Red Line (Ashmont) stops: Butler, Milton Village, or Central Avenue.

You can also pay a visit to **Squantum Point Park**, on the site of a former Navy airfield. People come for bird watching, picnicking, fishing, canoeing, inline skating, running or walking. To get there, take the Red Line Braintree train to North Quincy Station and pick up the #211 bus.

The **Belle Isle Marsh Reservation**, in East Boston, is the city's only remaining saltwater marsh left after all the landfill projects of the 1800s. There are pathways, benches, an observation tower, and guided walks provided by the DCR. You can get here by taking the Blue Line to Suffolk downs and entering off Bennington Street.

For more specifics about these or other parks scattered throughout the greater Boston area or the State of Massachusetts, contact your local parks district (city web sites are listed with the community profiles); DCR's **MassParks**, 617-626-1250, www.mass.gov/dcr; or DCR's **Division of Urban Parks & Recreation**, 617-727-5114, www.mass.gov/dcr.

CEMETERIES

Some take advantage of the lovely and historic **Forest Hills Cemetery**, www.foresthillstrust.org, which forms the boundary with JP, Roslindale, Roxbury, and Dorchester. This 275-acre garden burial ground was founded in 1848 by Henry Dearborn, then governor of Roxbury and the first president of the Massachusetts Horticultural Society. Visitors come to see the final resting places of such famous figures as poets Anne Sexton and e.e. cummings, and playwright Eugene O'Neill. Locals come here for walks, picnics, and jogs, and dogs and bikes are welcome. In the summer, Forest Hills holds the annual Buddhist-inspired Lantern Festival, a lovely tribute by those who want to remember lost ones by releasing lit lanterns with personal messages onto Lake Hibiscus at sundown. As with the Stony Brook Reservation, get off the Orange Line at the Forest Hills stop.

The **Mt. Auburn Cemetery**, an arboretum in its own right with over 4,000 species of trees and 130 species of shrubs, is located on Mt. Auburn Street between Watertown and Cambridge. It is the smaller, but slightly older cousin of the above mentioned Forest Hills Cemetery, and was founded in 1831 by the Massachusetts Horticultural Society. Today, this gorgeous 174-acre site draws people for many reasons, including hiking and tours. 87,000 people are buried here, including many famous Bostonians, such as Mary Baker Eddy, Oliver Wendell Holmes, Charles Bullfinch, Henry Wadsworth Longfellow, Fannie Farmer, Isabella Stewart Gardner, and B.F. Skinner. Bird watching is popular; during peak migration periods you may see up to 100 different species in a day and the cemetery posts a daily list of sightings at their entrance gate. Note: pets, horseback riding, picnicking, and biking are strictly forbidden. Gates close at 5 p.m. Buses #71, 72, and 73 stop there.

NATURE PRESERVES

STATE PRESERVES

Travel a little outside of Boston for more natural preserves. **Walden Pond** and **Walden Woods** in Concord, 978-369-3254, are part of the state park system and are only about 20 minutes away. You can learn about Henry David Thoreau, visit a re-creation of his cabin, go on a walking tour with the Thoreau Society or hike, swim, skate, or ski—depending on the season. In addition to its connection with Thoreau, Walden Pond is special because its origin as a glacial kettle gives it excellent drainage. The water remains clean and clear throughout the summer and the thin, pebbled shores are crowded with sunbathers and swimmers.

The Middlesex Fells Reservation (in Medford, Melrose, Malden, Stoneham, and Winchester) and Blue Hills Reservation (in Milton, Canton, Quincy, Braintree, Randolph, and Boston) have miles and miles of trails for hiking and mountain biking. Bikes are not allowed on the foot trails, which are designed to give challenging climbs, but cyclists can ride the fire roads and specially designated trails. It's possible to complete simple loops or to hike from end to end along the sky line trails. Blue Hills Reservation features a wheel-chair accessible boardwalk through a bog.

Following are more **area reservations**:

- **Blue Hills Reservation**, Milton, Canton, Quincy, Braintree, Randolph, and Boston, 617-698-1802, www.mass.gov/dcr; the mother of all local wild areas, it offers more than 7,000 acres of terrain. The hills and surrounding area have been managed for public use for over 100 years. In addition to forests, marshes, swamps, bogs, ponds, rivers, hills, and even some species of endangered wildlife, there are 16 historic sites on the land. Come here for camping, hiking, biking, fishing, swimming, horseback riding, golfing, rock climbing, skiing (cross-country and downhill), softball, and ice-skating. Open during daylight hours. Pets must be leashed. Some areas accessible via the Red Line (Ashmont and Mattapan stations).
- **Breakheart Reservation**, Saugus, 781-233-0834, www.mass.gov/dcr; 640 acres of hardwood forest with two freshwater lakes (Silver and Pearce), ponds, and seven rocky hills over 200 feet high. No public transit available.
- **Elm Bank Reservation**, Wellesley, www.mass.gov/dcr; 182 acres of woods, fields, and old estate property surrounded by the Charles River. Bird watching, fishing, boating, hiking. No public T access.
- **Middlesex Fells Reservation**, 781-322-2851, www.mass.gov/dcr; over 2,500 acres of rocky hills, runs through Medford, Malden, Melrose, Stoneham, and Winchester. Popular for hiking, horseback riding, rock

climbing, mountain biking, cross-country skiing, fishing, skating, swimming, picnics, and kites. Big enough not to feel crowded. Dogs allowed. Maps not sold at the reservation; you can buy one or order from the Friends of the Middlesex Fells, www.fells.org. Take the Orange Line to Wellington Station and then the #100 bus to the Roosevelt Circle Rotary.
- **Lynn Woods Reservation**, Lynn, www.lynndpw.com; the second largest municipal park in the country, Lynn Woods offers 2,200 acres of wilderness, with 30 miles of trails for hiking, biking, running, horseback riding, and cross-country skiing and three ponds for fishing, boating, and swimming. Dog-friendly, but they must be leashed.
- **Saugus River Rumney Marsh Reservation**, Saugus, Revere, and Lynn, 617-727-5350, www.mass.gov/dcr; over 600 acres of salt marshes within the Saugus River and Pine River estuary. Natural and cultural history walks, fishing, hiking, boating, bird watching. Take the Lynn/Salem bus to Route 107.
- **Weymouth Back River Reservation**, Hingham and Weymouth, 617-727-5290, www.mass.gov/dcr; walking trails and green space along the water at Stoddard's Neck and Abigail Adams Park. Take bus #220.
- **Wilson Mountain Reservation**, Dedham, 617-698-1802, www.mass.gov/dcr; is the largest remaining piece of open space in Dedham. It offers 213 acres for hiking and bird watching. No access via public transit.

For more nature preserves throughout the state, contact the **Trustees of Reservations**, www.thetrustees.org, 978-921-1944, an organization devoted to conserving historic and environmentally significant spaces in Massachusetts. They own and run property, waterfront, and open spaces throughout the state.

ISLAND PRESERVES

Some of Boston's most underutilized natural resources are the **Harbor Islands**. Visitors enjoy fishing, sea kayaking, guided walks, historic forts and ruins, and picnic areas on most of the islands. (Biking and inline skating are not allowed.) Thirty-four islands, of which 11 are accessible by public transportation, are managed by a partnership of 13 different organizations. Those 11 include Bumpkin Island, Deer Island, Gallop's Island, George's Island, Grape Island, Great Brewster Island, Little Brewster Island, Lovell's Island, Peddock's Island, Thompson Island, and World's End, which are serviced via ferry from Boston. A few others are open to visitors who reach them with their own boats. The islands are open from spring to fall, although their peak visiting time (and when you'll find the most transportation options) is on weekends from Memorial Day to Labor Day. Some special excursions and boat trips take place during the winter months, particularly those run by the **Friends of the Boston Harbor Islands**, 781-740-4290, www.fbhi.org, and the DCR. Each island offers something entirely different. If you do plan on visiting any of them, bring fresh water and food because only one island (George's) offers concessions. For more information, visit www.bostonislands.com.

Getting to the islands requires some effort. Going to George's means just a 45-minute ferry ride from Long Wharf in Boston (daily), or from the Hingham Shipyard at Hewitt's Cove in Hingham (weekends), Pemberton Point in Hull, Squantum Point in Quincy (weekends), or Salem Ferry Landing in Salem (weekends). **Boston Harbor Cruises** (617-227-4321, www.bostonboats.com), provides the ferry service, which runs several times daily during the summer months. To get to any of the other islands from George's (with the exception of Little Brewster and Thompson) you must pick up a (free) inter-island water taxi. To get to Little Brewster Island, take the M/V Hurricane from Old Northern Avenue at Fan Pier, South Boston or Columbia Point at the JFK Library and Museum in Dorchester. These ferries depart twice daily (10 a.m. and 2 p.m.) on weekends from May to October. And finally, to get to Thompson Island, the Outward Bound ferry runs on Saturdays from June through August, departing at 11:30 a.m. from Northern Avenue at Fan Pier and at noon from EDIC Pier #10 off of Drydock Avenue in the Marine Industrial Park, both in South Boston. You can also take your own boat to George's, Bumpkin, Grape, Little Brewster, Lovell's, and Peddock's islands, but you can only dock at George's; at the others only pick up and drop off are allowed.

Check with the following agencies for information about camping permits and reservations on the islands: the **DCR** manages Bumpkin, Gallop's, Grape, Great Brewster, Lovell's, Peddock's and George's islands. **Thompson Island Outward Bound Education Center**, 617-328-3900, www.thompsonisland.org, runs Thompson Island. The **Massachusetts Water Resources Authority**, 617-788-1170, www.mwra.com, has responsibility for Deer Island. World's End is run by the **Trustees of Reservations**, 978-921-1944, www.thetrustees.org. The **Coast Guard**, www.uscg.mil/USCG.shtm, takes care of Little Brewster Island.

STATE PARKS AND FORESTS

STATE PARKS

MassParks, part of the Massachusetts Department of Environmental Management, runs state parks, popular for hiking, horseback riding, and fishing. The western portion of the state is the most rural and is where most can be found. That said, there are still quite a few state parks within easy driving distance (about an hour or so) from Boston. For information on all of the parks, including directions, locations, and what each offers, call 617-626-1250 or go to www.mass.gov/dcr.

STATE FORESTS

Many of the city and state parks and reservations are forested; in addition, the following state parks are designated specifically as forests. Go to www.mass.gov/dcr or call one of the following for more information:
- **Boxford State Forest**, Boxford, 978-686-3391
- **F. Gilbert Hills State Forest**, Foxboro, 508-543-5850
- **Georgetown-Rowley State Forest**, Georgetown, 978-887-5931
- **Harold Parker State Forest**, North Andover, 978-686-3391
- **Lowell-Dracut-Tyngsboro State Forest**, Lowell, 978-453-0592
- **Willowdale State Forest**, Ipswich, 978-887-5931

NATIONAL PARKS

National parks in the Boston area, overseen by the **National Park Service**, www.nps.gov, are mostly historic rather than natural sites, with the possible exception of the Harbor Islands. Two of particular interest that also have some acreage are the **Frederick Law Olmstead National Historic Site**, www.nps.gov/frla, 617-566-1689, which includes his house and grounds in Brookline, or the **Minute Man National Park**, www.nps.gov/mima, comprising 900 acres of Revolutionary War history in Lexington, Concord, and Lincoln.

A two-hour drive from Boston, one of the most famous parks in the National Park System, the **Appalachian Trail**, bisects the westernmost portion of Massachusetts on its way from Maine to Georgia. To learn more about the trail, or get information on the parts of it within the state, visit www.nps.gov/appa.

WILDLIFE SANCTUARIES

Massachusetts is home to a bevy of wildlife refuges, many run by the **Massachusetts Audubon Society**, www.massaudubon.org, 800-AUDUBON. Opened in 1896, it is the largest conservation group in all of New England, protecting over 29,000 acres of land with 41 wildlife conservancies open to the public. Area Audubon lands range from beaches and marshes to forests and mountains, and present an array of green environs for hiking and learning about wildlife. The society also offers educational programming. On conservancy lands visitors may not bike, hunt, fish, trap, jog, bring pets, vehicles, firearms or alcohol, or remove specimens.

Listed here are a few sanctuaries close to Boston:
- **Blue Hills Trailside Museum**, 1904 Canton Avenue, Milton, 617-333-0690; the DCR runs the Blue Hills Reservation, but Mass Audubon runs the museum.
- **Boston Nature Center and Wildlife Sanctuary**, 500 Walk Hill Street, Mattapan, 617-983-8500; two miles of trails and boardwalks past wetlands, woods, and fields in the middle of the city.
- **Broadmoor Wildlife Sanctuary**, 208 Eliot Street, Natick, 508-655-2296; nine miles of trails through woodlands and wetlands, including Indian Brook and marsh.
- **Daniel Webster Wildlife Sanctuary**, off of Winslow Cemetery Road in Marshfield; 481 acres of grass, woods, and wetlands. Excellent for bird watching.
- **Eastern Point Wildlife Sanctuary**, off Eastern Point Boulevard in Gloucester; coastal beach vistas, sea birds, and butterflies.
- **Habitat Education Center and Wildlife Sanctuary**, 10 Juniper Road, Belmont, 617-489-5050; gardens, fields, woods, and a pond on a former estate. Lots of wildflowers.
- **Ipswich River Wildlife Sanctuary**, 87 Perkins Row, Topsfield, 978-887-9264; the largest sanctuary, 10 miles of trails, canoeing, camping, glacial formations, river wildlife.
- **Joppa Flats Wildlife Sanctuary**, Newburyport, 978-462-9998; migratory birds and marine mammals.
- **Marblehead Neck Wildlife Sanctuary**, off Risley Road in Marblehead; swamp, thickets, and woodlands on the coast. Birds are plentiful, especially warblers.
- **Moose Hill Wildlife Sanctuary**, 293 Moose Hill Street, Sharon, 781-784-5691; the oldest sanctuary, 2,000 acres of forest, grasslands, swamp, and bogs.
- **Nahant Thicket Wildlife Sanctuary**, off Wharf Street in Nahant; butterflies and birds (warblers, scarlet tanagers, hummingbirds, sea birds). No trails.

The **Crane Wildlife Refuge**, operated by the Trustees of Reservations (978-356-4351, www.thetrustees.org) for the past 30 years, is nearly 700 acres of protected area on the North Shore, near Ipswich's Crane Beach. The reservation includes a portion of Castle Neck River and the Essex River Estuary, the Great Marsh (salt), and several islands, including Long, Dilly, Pine, Patterson, Round, and finally, Hog (a.k.a. Choate), the largest island. The reservation is open daily, year-round for exploration. Deer hunting is permissible during hunting season. Dock a boat on Long Island for 3.5 miles of hiking and walking trails.

Further up the North Shore is the **Parker River National Wildlife Refuge** (www.parkerriver.org, 978-465-5753), located on Plum Island in Newburyport. This property far outstrips the Crane Refuge in size—over 4,600 acres of dunes, tidal pools, salt marsh, beach, and one drumlin—and is also one of the last remaining barrier beach-salt marshes in this portion of the country. You will find over 300 species of birds throughout the year, making it one of most popular birding sites in America. Additionally, you can come here to hike, canoe, kayak, fish, clam, and hunt waterfowl during appropriate seasons.

Another popular reserve for birders is the **Great Meadows National Wildlife Refuge**, just west of Boston along the Sudbury and Concord rivers. It encompasses the towns of Sudbury, Lincoln, Concord, Wayland, Bedford, Carlisle, and Billerica. The 3,000 acres of freshwater wetlands attract mostly migratory birds—over 220 species have been spotted there over the past decade.

BEACHES

Bostonians do love to go to the beach. After long cold winters, the welcoming miles of sun, sand, and surf on the New England coastline are especially pleasing. There are a few beaches in the city, but traditionally area residents head to picturesque stretches along the north and south shores of Massachusetts. Weekends are often spent at B&Bs or rental houses on Cape Cod, Nantucket, or Martha's Vineyard. Those who like to get even further away will head up to coastal New Hampshire, Maine, Rhode Island, and Connecticut.

Resist the temptation to swim in the Charles as it is recovering from years of pollution. As it improves you can expect the Magazine Beach in the Cambridgeport area of Cambridge to become popular once again.

The DCR maintains 16 miles of regularly cleaned ocean beaches, most of which are accessible by public transportation. DCR beaches have lifeguard services from the end of June to Labor Day, but many are open (albeit not guarded) year round. Call 617-727-5114 or visit www.mass.gov/dcr for details.

Easily accessible Boston beaches include:
- **Carson Beach, Castle Island Beach, City Point Beach, Pleasure Bay Beach, and M Street Beach**, Day Boulevard in South Boston; take the Red Line to Broadway or the City Point bus to the end of the line.
- **Constitution Beach** in East Boston; take the Blue Line to Orient Heights. The DCR is rehabbing this beach to include parking, a bathhouse, and recreational facilities.
- **Lovells Island** (Boston Harbor Island) in Boston Harbor; take the Blue Line to Aquarium, then take the ferry to George's Island and catch a free water taxi to Lovells Island.

- **Malibu Beach** and **Savin Hill Beach**, in Dorchester off Morrissey Boulevard; take the Red Line to Savin Hill.
- **Tenean Beach** in Dorchester on Tenean Street off Morrissey Boulevard; take the Red Line to Savin Hill, then the #20 bus to the beach.

Call the DCR for additional freshwater and saltwater swimming spots outside of Boston. There are many **private** and **state-run beaches** in the greater Boston area, reachable by car and public transport. In fact, over 70% of Massachusetts coastline is privately-owned. Of the beaches open to the public, some require payment for use. Here are a few to consider:
- **Marshfield**: Humarock Beach, Rexhame Beach, Breakwater Beach, Brant Rock Beach, and Green Harbor Beach
- **Manchester-by-the-Sea**: Singing Beach
- **Gloucester**: Wingaersheek Beach, Good Harbor Beach, and Long Beach
- **Rockport**: Front Beach and Back Beach
- **Ipswich**: Crane Beach (beware of nasty biting flies in late summer).
- **Marblehead**: Gashouse Beach and Devereux Beach, Marblehead
- **Newburyport**: Plum Island, 6.5 miles of sandy beach run by Parker Wildlife Refuge, 978-465-5753, www.parkerriver.org

GREATER BOSTON AREA BEACHES

If you make a run for the border to New Hampshire, you can go to Salisbury Beach and Hampton Beach. **Salisbury Beach** (technically in Massachusetts, although you have to cross over into New Hampshire for a minute to get there), is popular. Go in the fall and winter for the chance to spy harbor seals hanging out in the sun on the jetty. **Hampton Beach**, www.hamptonbeach.org, over the border in New Hampshire, is a scene that should definitely be experienced by everyone at least once. Whereas most beaches in the area are relatively serene, with a hot dog stand at best, Hampton Beach is more like the region's answer to Coney Island, complete with a boardwalk and loads of cars cruising the strip. To get there, just take Route 1 North until you see the signs.

The famous **Cape Cod** is too vast to profile here. Suffice it to say that the arm of Massachusetts that stretches 40 miles out into the ocean has about 100 beaches. The best thing to do would be to pick a town—say Falmouth, Hyannis, or Provincetown—and then pick a beach. Most people don't go to the Cape for just the day. For more information go to www.capecodonline.com.

If you want to head to **Martha's Vineyard** for a few days, you will have a plentiful choice of beaches. You can make it down as a day trip, just be prepared for a three-hour commute (car, T, bus, and ferry) each way. To get to the Vineyard, you can take a ferry from Woods Hole (either to Oak Bluffs or Vineyard Haven), New Bedford (to Oak Bluffs), Hyannis (to Oak Bluffs), or Falmouth (to Oak Bluffs or Edgartown). When you get there, you can rent a bike or a Jeep and head to your choice of over 30 beaches. There are wildlife preserves and state parks here, too. Of all the beaches, South Beach might be the most popular, but be careful, as the undertow is fierce.

In terms of commute and atmosphere, **Nantucket** is similar Martha's Vineyard. It's further out than the Vineyard and a little smaller, so there are only about a dozen beaches. All Massachusetts ferries to Nantucket leave from Hyannis.

STATE PARKS
The following state parks in the greater Boston area have saltwater beaches or lakes. Go to www.mass.gov/dcr for more:
- **Boston Harbor Islands**, 781-749-7160; reachable by ferry.
- **Ellsville Harbor State Park**, Route 3A, Plymouth, 508-866-2580
- **Cochituate State Park**, Route 30, Natick, 508-653-9641
- **Harold Parker State Forest**, Route 114, North Andover, 978-686-3391
- **Walden Pond**, 915 Walden Street, Concord, 978-369-3254
- **Demarest Lloyd State Park**, Barney's Joy Road, Dartmouth, 508-636-8816

ADDITIONAL RESOURCES

The tourism industry in Massachusetts—what with the coast, the seasons, the culture, the history—is too broad to give a listing of tour agencies. For starters, contact the **Massachusetts Office of Travel and Tourism**, www.massvacation.com, 617-973-8500, for all the information you could want on exploring your new state.

WEATHER AND CLIMATE

BOSTON IS A FOUR-SEASON TOWN. WINTERS ARE COLD AND OFTEN snowy, springs are mild and rainy, summers are hot and sunny, and autumns are crisp and colorful. This means, depending on where you are coming from, you may need to add to your wardrobe to cope with the seasons. And, although Boston is sometimes subject to the occasional blizzard or hurricane, it's not prone to the more destructive and severe weather/environmental disturbances like tornadoes, floods, or earthquakes.

One major moderating factor in the weather throughout the region is the Atlantic Ocean. In general, the closer you are to the ocean, the milder the weather. This rule applies for both summer and winter. In the summer, the ocean breezes offer a cooling effect, making life less steamy by the water. And in colder weather, it will be slightly warmer. On the downside, offshore storms sometimes create ravaging waves that punish sea walls, erode beaches, and sometimes flood nearby homes. The Atlantic also contributes to Boston's summer humidity.

Springtime in Boston is lovely but fleeting. Comfortably warm and breezy days are usually squeezed in between the last bitter cold days of winter, which often linger through March, and the sticky hot days of summer. March is a fickle month, sometimes offering a few warm days only to be followed by a sudden and fierce spring snowstorm. But, as April and May roll in, the mercury rises more predictably into the 40s, 50s, and 60s, with the last frost occurring before mid-May. Of course, there is the requisite amount of spring showers.

In the **summer**, get ready for the three "H's"—hazy, hot, and humid. Although the National Oceanic Atmospheric Administration (NOAA) data places average temps in the 60s, 70s, and lower 80s, those averages seem to belie the truth, which is that it gets hot in these parts. Although May and early June are not always miserable, by July and August daily temperatures are generally in the 80s and 90s, often with oppressive humidity. During this time of year, it is not uncommon for Boston to experience droughts and heat waves. The heat waves bring temperatures in the upper 90s for days on end, the only reprieve being an occasional afternoon thunderstorm. Temperatures don't cool down much at night, which is something to consider when looking for a place to live. If it doesn't have air conditioning, be sure it has some kind of cross ventilation. Summer brings people to the city *en masse*, be they locals or tourists. Bars, restaurants, parks, stadiums, and T trains are packed to the gills with people enjoying the warm weather. Many restaurants extend their dining areas to patios, which fill up quickly, and outdoor bars along the waterfront are positively hopping, even on the first warm night of the season. As is typical in most parts of the country, **allergy sufferers** will have problems in the spring and summer here, particularly in the greener suburbs. But even on tree-lined city streets, you will often find your car coated in green pollen during the spring when the trees are budding.

Boston experiences the quintessential New England **autumn**, with crisp days, gorgeous fall foliage, and the arrival of lots of college students. Temperatures drop dramatically between September and November, falling from the 70s to the 40s and tending to the colder side of that range. By the end of September/early October a hard frost will settle in overnight. It's not unheard of for Boston to experience an odd hurricane during the late summer and early fall. They tend to hit once every few years but rarely are very destructive. October is when incoming flights are packed with visitors coming for foliage tours. Locals have the benefit of touring right around home or perhaps swinging up to Vermont, New Hampshire, or Maine for the weekend. As with the spring, fall weather can vary, bringing a few surprisingly warm days. Eighty degrees on Halloween is possible (so is a white Thanksgiving). Such unseasonably warm weather in the late fall after the first killing frost is called **Indian summer**, and locals love it.

Come mid- to late-November it's pretty much **winter**, which stays sometimes through March. The coldest months are December, January, and February, with average temperatures in the 20s and 30s. Recently, El Niño, and its counterpart La Niña, have been regularly affecting Boston's winter weather, giving the area either exceptionally warm (El Niño) or cold and snowy (La Niña) winters. Some winters, temperatures barely dip below the freezing mark; others bring seemingly endless weeks of single digit temperatures. Having a white Christmas in Boston is possible but never predictable; the average annual **snowfall** is 41 inches and some of that can certainly hit in December. Unlike other residents of some eastern seaboard cities, Bostonians are not afraid to drive in the snow, and unless the storm is a doozy, school and work probably won't be cancelled during a snow event. The most fearsome winter storms in these parts are called Nor'Easters, which bring lots of snow or even blizzards. Technically, a Nor'Easter is a strong area of low pressure that moves in off the Atlantic and brings heavy snow or rain (if it picks up enough moisture on its way in), oversized waves, and gusty northeasterly winds. Outside of these events, the good news is that temperatures rarely drop below zero here (although on windy days, the wind chill makes it feel much colder than thermometer readings), and there is a good bit of winter sunshine.

During winter it is wise to take some precautions. Proper outer gear is essential: warm coat, hat, scarf, and mittens or gloves. Snow boots are also a good idea. In your car you should keep a small shovel and a bag of sand or kitty litter in case you get stuck. A car mat placed under the tire has been known to work as well. Car owners will also want decent all-season tires or snow tires, windshield wiper fluid with antifreeze, and an ice scraper. Also, those needing to park on the street should pay attention to street crews. If you don't move your car, you may find that the snowplow has buried it while clearing the street, or worse, on main arteries, the city will tow during "snow emergencies" (look for postings on the street).

METRO BOSTON WEATHER STATISTICAL INFORMATION

Below are the average Boston temperatures, snowfalls, rainfalls, etc., according to the NOAA (www.noaa.gov):

MONTH	DEGREES FARENHEIT
January	22° to 36°
February	23° to 38°
March	31° to 46°
April	40° to 56°
May	50° to 67°
June	59° to 76°
July	65° to 82°
August	64° to 80°
September	57° to 73°
October	47° to 63°
November	38° to 52°
December	27° to 40°

- Prevailing wind: from the west
- Average wind velocity: between 10 and 13 mph.
- Lowest recorded temperature: -18.4°F (February 1934)
- Highest recorded temperature: 104°F (July 1911)
- Average number of days per year over 90°F: 12
- Average number of days per year below freezing: 62.2
- Average number of days per year below 0°F: 1
- Normal annual precipitation: 41.5 inches

On average, Boston experiences clear skies 27% of the time, partly cloudy skies 28% of the time, and cloud cover 45% of the time. The clearest months are August through October. The cloudiest months are January and March. Boston isn't terribly foggy; on average, Boston gets about 23 days per year when visibility is less than a quarter mile. It usually only rains about three or four inches at a time here, but the largest significant rainfall ever recorded in one day was 8.4," back in 1955.

AIR POLLUTION

Boston is not known for its poor air quality. Even in downtown Boston on a hot, humid summer day, you'll probably be just fine. That said, you will hear television meteorologists discussing "bad air days" (ratings range from good to moderate to unhealthy to very unhealthy) throughout the summer, especially on the really hot and muggy days. This is because strong sunshine and high temperatures are key factors in the generation of ozone, the predominant ingredient in smog, which is a powerful lung irritant. Days coined "unhealthy for sensitive groups" may be noticeable to the old, the young, and people with respiratory problems like asthma, emphysema, or bronchitis. On days where conditions are rated "very unhealthy," even those without respiratory problems might be affected. Symptoms include cough, runny/stuffy nose or sneezing, sore throat, chest pain, asthma, shortness of breath, and susceptibility to respiratory infection.

The **"ozone season"** generally lasts from May to/through September, depending on the weather. The peak hours for ozone problems are in the afternoons and evenings, so if you're concerned, those are the times to stay in. Boston's worst ozone episodes occur as a result of large, high-pressure weather systems over the mid- and southern Atlantic that expand westward across the US called "Bermuda" highs. When these weather systems hit the area, they scoop up the air pollution along the eastern seaboard (Washington D.C., Baltimore, Philadelphia, New York) and then sweep it in, along with loads of high humidity.

During the ozone season, you can get the **daily ozone forecast** through the state web site, www.mass.gov, by clicking on "Home & Health," then "Environment," then "Air Quality." The EPA provides a chart to help you understand air quality ratings and what they mean for you—the higher the number of the Air Quality Index (AQI) the worse the air is. To learn more about ozone, visit the Massachusetts Department of Environmental Protection's Ozone FAQ page on their web site: www.state.ma.us/dep/bwp/daqc.

Other air quality related groups and resources include:
- **Project Clean Air**, www.projectcleanair.org, 661-833-5740
- **EPA's AirNow**, www.epa.gov/airnow

- **Massachusetts Department of Environmental Protection**, www.state.ma.us/dep, 617-292-5500

INSECTS

If you live in the city, be prepared for the occasional visit by your friendly neighborhood cockroaches. This is part of urban living and nothing an exterminator can't handle, even for those living near restaurants.

In the summer the significant concerns are mosquitoes and ticks. Aside from being plain pesky, mosquitoes are an issue because of **West Nile virus**, which causes an infection similar to encephalitis. Although the virus most commonly plagues birds and horses, it is possible for a person bitten by a mosquito carrying West Nile to become infected. According to the Massachusetts Department of Health (DPH), about 20% of those bitten by an infected mosquito will exhibit symptoms such as fever, headache, muscle weakness, body aches, swollen lymph glands, and rashes. Those suffering a more severe case may also have a high fever, neck stiffness, stupor, disorientation, coma, tremors, convulsions, paralysis, and encephalitis. Between 3% and 15% of those with visible infection may die, particularly the elderly. The best prevention is to avoid going out for prolonged periods at night, particularly to woodsy or swampy areas, and to wear bug spray, and make sure you have screens on your windows. Each spring and summer the state evaluates the mosquito population and sprays where necessary. For more information on this issue, the DPH has a web page and phone line devoted to the West Nile virus: www.state.ma.us/dph, 866-MASS-WNV.

Also in New England are deer ticks, which are known to carry **lyme disease**, a big concern because, unlike West Nile virus, it is somewhat common. In 2001, the rate of disease in Massachusetts was 18.3 cases of lyme disease per 100,000—three times the national average and the seventh highest infection rate in the country. Although it likely won't kill you, its symptoms can be painful and lifelong. Lyme disease is an infection caused by a corkscrew-shaped bacteria that is passed through the bite. In the early stages, you'll just feel like you have a bad case of the flu; in later stages, it can severely affect your joints, nervous system, and heart. The good news is that tick bites are easily avoided and if you have been bitten there is treatment. The first sign that you might have lyme disease is, of course, finding a small tick in your skin. Second, you may develop a classic target-like rash around the bite—usually occurring within three and thirty days. If you have found a tick or if you develop this classic rash, get yourself to the doctor quickly. Your physician will probably give you a blood test and then put you on antibiotics, which, if administered soon enough can be an effective treatment. To prevent being bitten there are precautions you should take. Ticks tend to be found in the tall grasses and plants near dunes, woods, and ponds. Should you need to visit such an area, wear a long sleeved shirt and long pants that are tucked into your socks. Light colors are preferable so that you can readily spot a tick. Also, spray yourself with insect repellent containing DEET (check the label for use on young children). Before heading home, be sure to check everyone, dogs too, for ticks. They sometimes burrow into your scalp so look and feel closely. If you do find a tick, don't panic, but do pull it straight out (slowly and steadily) with a pair of thin-lipped tweezers. For more information on lyme disease, check with the Massachusetts DPH at www.state.ma.us/dph or call them at 617-983-6800.

PLACES OF WORSHIP

ALTHOUGH BOSTON WAS FOUNDED BY PURITANS AND THEN "run" by wealthy Protestants, Boston's religious landscape underwent a transaction in the 19th and 20th centuries when the Irish Catholic population boomed and political leadership of the city and the state changed as a result. In this part of New England Catholicism is still dominant, tying into the Italian, Irish, and Latino populations so prevalent here. Other religions, including Judaism, Islam, Hinduism, and many other branches of Christianity are well represented, with numerous churches, temples, and mosques catering to a variety of religions throughout the metro region. But to put it in perspective, as one lifelong Bostonian stated: "It wasn't until I was in college in the Midwest that I realized the entire country, let alone world, wasn't Catholic!"

Finding a suitable church or synagogue may be as simple as getting a suggestion from an acquaintance, or it may be as intensely personal and complex as choosing a spouse. Most places of worship are listed by denomination in the Yellow Pages. Those listed below are included for a variety of reasons, maybe because it is a historic structure or congregation, or has a strong outreach program, or a popular music program. Certainly it is not a comprehensive list. You can contact the **National Council of Churches**, 212-870-2227, www.ncccusa.org, which publishes the *Yearbook of American & Canadian Churches*, a directory listing thousands of Christian churches. Order one for $35 at 888-870-3325 or browse the directory links at www.electronicchurch.org. Other online directories of churches—generally limited to Christian denominations—include http://netministries.org, http://churches.net, and www.forministry.com. Synagogues serving all branches of Judaism are listed at www.jewish.com. If you are intersted in becoming involved in interfaith projects, try visiting the **Greater Boston Interfaith Organization** at www.gbio.org.

BAHÁ'Í

Although Bahá'í houses of worship may differ from one another in architectural styles, they are often stunning, and are recognizable by their nine sides and central dome, which symbolize "the diversity of the human race and its essential oneness." To read up on the Bahá'í religion, visit its main web site, www.bahai.org. To find out about the local Bahá'í community, go to www.bostonbahai.org.
- **Boston Bahá'í Center**, 595 Albany Street, Boston, 617-695-3500
- **Bahá'í Faith**, 68 High Street, Malden, 781-322-2662

BUDDHIST

Buddhism dates back over two millennia, and today over 350 million people across the globe consider themselves Buddhists. There are many different sub-traditions, including **Zen**, **Tibetan**, **Tantric** (**Vajrayana**), and **Mahayana**.

An informative resource for Buddhism is www.buddhanet.net; for the Zen community of Boston go to www.zcboston.net.

CHRISTIAN

AMERICAN METHODIST EPISCOPAL (AME)/EPISCOPAL ZION

If you'd like to find an AME or Episcopal Zion church in your neighborhood, you can consult AME's New England conference on the web at www.1stdistrict-ame.org/newe.htm. Not only does it provide a church locator for the region, there are also contact numbers for church officers, if you'd prefer speak to a real person. Or, you can investigate one of the following churches:
- **Bethel African Methodist Episcopal Church**, 215 Forest Hills Street, Jamaica Plain, 617-524-7900, www.bethelame.org
- **Columbus Avenue AME Zion Church**, 600 Columbus Avenue, Boston, 617-266-2758
- **St. Paul AME Church**, 37 & 85 Bishop Richard Allen Drive, Cambridge, 617-661-1110, www.st-paul-ame.org

ANGLICAN/EPISCOPAL

The Episcopal and Anglican churches are both descended from the Church of England. The Episcopal Church took root in America as early as 1607, with the first permanent English settlement in Jamestown, Virginia. There are plenty of Episcopal and Anglican churches in Boston, and a couple of them are even quite famous. There is the **Old North Church** (a.k.a. Christ Church, 193 Salem Street, Boston, 617-523-6576, www.oldnorth.com), that is to say, *the* Old North Church where the lanterns were hung on the night of Paul Revere's famous ride in 1775. This beautiful historic building, which was built in the style of Christopher Wren in 1723, is smack dab in the middle of the North End and remains an active church. Also famous, the **Trinity Church** (206 Clarendon Street, Boston, 617-536-0944, www.trinityboston.org) is one of Boston's most prominent landmarks. Built in the 1870s in the "Richardsonian Romanesque" style, Trinity Church is a hallmark of American architecture. It commands a prominent position in the middle of Copley Square, and attracts many visitors.

For general information about the **Episcopal Church of the US**, visit www.episcopalchurch.org; for the **Anglican Church** worldwide, go to http://anglicansonline.org. At the local level, you can access information on the Anglican and Episcopal Diocese of Massachusetts at www.diomass.org, which offers a great deal of information on local spiritual life, including a detailed listing of churches in the region.

ASSEMBLY OF GOD

Assemblies of God are the largest Pentecostal denomination of the Protestant church in the US. Their homepage, http://ag.org/top, is informative and provides a complete directory of its churches nationwide.

BAPTIST

American, **Free Will**, and **Southern Baptists** are all found in Boston. To find out more about Southern Baptists go to www.sbc.net; for more on Free Will Baptists, go to www.nafwb.org; and for American Baptists, go to http://abc-usa.org, locally at www.tabcom.org.

Some Baptist churches in the Boston area include:
- **United Parish**, 210 Harvard Street, Brookline, 617-277-6860
- **Immanuel Deaf Church**, 30 Gordon Street, Allston, 617-254-3323
- **Community Baptist Church**, 31 College Avenue, Somerville, 617-625-6523
- **Concord Baptist Church**, 190 Warren Avenue, Boston, 617-266-8062, www.cbcboston.org
- **First Baptist Church of Arlington**, 819 Mass Ave., Arlington, 781-643-3024, www.fbcarlington.org
- **First Baptist Church of Jamaica Plain**, 633 Centre Street, Jamaica Plain, 617-524-2420
- **First Baptist Church of Boston**, 110 Comm Ave., Boston, 617-267-3148, www.firstbaptistchurchofboston.org

- **Old Cambridge Baptist Church**, 1151 Mass Ave., Cambridge, 617-864-9275, www.oldcambridgebaptist.org
- **Hill Memorial Baptist Church**, 279 North Harvard Street, Brighton, 617-782-4524
- **Roslindale Baptist Church**, 52 Cummins Highway, Roslindale, 617-327-5262
- **South End Neighborhood Church of Emmanuel**, 2 San Juan Street, Boston (South End), 617-262-0900
- **Twelfth Baptist Church**, 150-160 Warren Street, Roxbury, 617-442-7855, www.tbcboston.org
- **Mt. Calvary Baptist Church**, 541 Mass Ave., Boston, 617-247-8614

CHRISTIAN SCIENCE

The Church of Christian Science, started by Mary Baker Eddy, has its world headquarters in Boston; the **Mother Church**, as the complex is called, is nothing less than magnificent. Located in the middle of the Fenway, the Christian Science campus covers 14 acres of land, which is comprised of the church building, a reflecting pool, a reading room, the Mary Baker Eddy Library for the Betterment of Humanity (a museum including the Hall of Ideas, the colorful and stunning Mapparium, and Quest Gallery), and the offices of the *Christian Science Monitor* (www.christianscience monitor.com). While the entire complex is a draw for tourists, the church itself is a magnificent Romanesque building with a bell tower, stained glass windows, and a 13,290-pipe organ. To learn more about the library and visiting the sites, go to www.marybakereddylibrary.org. To learn more about the Mother Church and Christian Science in general, visit www.tfccs.com.

Area churches include:
- **First Church of Christ, Scientist**, The Mother Church Headquarters and General Offices, 175 Huntington Avenue, Boston (the Fenway), 617-450-2000, www.tfccs.com
- **Second Boston Church of Christ, Scientist**, 33 Elm Hill Avenue, Roxbury, 617-442-8448
- **Third Boston Church of Christ, Scientist**, 126 Arlington Street, Hyde Park, 617-361-5923
- **Cambridge First Church of Christ, Scientist**, 13 Waterhouse Street (at Mass Ave.), 617-354-2866
- **Belmont First Church of Christ, Scientist**, 199 Common Street, 617-484-3963
- **Needham First Church of Christ, Scientist**, 879 Great Plain Avenue, 781-444-2877
- **Newton First Church of Christ, Scientist**, 391 Walnut Street, 617-332-6376

- **Quincy Church of Christ Scientist**, 20 Greenleaf Street, 617-472-0055

CHURCH OF CHRIST

Area Churches of Christ include the following (check the Yellow Pages for suburban locations):
- **Brookline Church of Christ**, 416 Washington Street, Brookline, 617-277-2452
- **Mattapan Church of Christ**, 574 River Street, Mattapan, 617-298-0151
- **Blue Hills Church of Christ**, 1505 Blue Hill Avenue, Mattapan, 617-296-5882
- **Church of Christ in Roxbury**, 81 Walnut Avenue, Roxbury, 617-442-5826

CHURCH OF GOD

Area Churches of God include:
- **Church of God of Prophecy**, 270-72 Warren Street, Roxbury, 617-427-7766
- **Shawmut Community Church of God**, 600 Shawmut Avenue, Boston, 617-445-3263
- **Church of God of Prophecy**, 179 Glenway Street, Dorchester, 617-282-0142
- **Church of God of Prophecy of Mattapan**, 118 Hollingsworth Road, Milton, 617-698-6457

CHURCH OF THE NAZARENE

For information about the Church of the Nazarene and a church locator service, try the main web site for the Church of the Nazarene, www.nazarene.org. Area churches include:
- **Cambridge Church of the Nazarene**, 234 Franklin Street (Central Square), Cambridge, 617-354-5065
- **Church of the Nazarene of Somerville**, 52 Russell Road, Somerville, 617-628-1898
- **Church of the Nazarene of West Somerville**, 82 Chandler Street, Somerville, 617-776-4212
- **Church of the Nazarene of the First**, 529 Eastern Avenue, Malden, 781-321-4230
- **Church of the Nazarene**, 1450 Trapelo Road, Waltham, 781-890-7629

- **Eben-Ezer Church of Nazarene**, 207 Delhi Street, Mattapan, 617-696-3605
- **Immanuel Church of the Nazarene**, 806 Blue Hill Avenue, Boston, 617-825-1766
- **Second Church in Dorchester, Church of the Nazarene**, 600 Washington Street, Dorchester, 617-825-2797

CONGREGATIONAL/UNITED CHURCH OF CHRIST

The Congregational Church, also known since the 1950s as the **United Church of Christ (UCC)**, is a Protestant denomination loosely connected to the Puritans who settled Massachusetts. As a result of this tie to early American heritage, many of the Congregational churches around Boston are not only quite old, but look the part of a New England church: picturesque white steeples with front doors opening directly onto the sanctuary, and rows of wooden pews. Historically significant Boston UCC churches include **Park Street Church** (One Park Street, 617-523-3383, www.parkstreet.org) and **Old South Church UCC** (645 Boylston Street, 617-536-1970, www.oldsouth.org). Located atop Beacon Hill across from the State House, the Wren-inspired red-brick Park Street Church was founded in 1809 and is one of the more commanding architectural sites in the city, particularly when it casts its soft lights over the common at night. The Old South Church, built in 1875 of Roxbury puddingstone (the state rock), has a congregation that dates back to 1699, with famous parishioners including Samuel Adams, William Dawes, Benjamin Franklin, Elizabeth Vergoose (Mother Goose), and Phyllis Wheatley. Parishioners met at two other sites, including the Old South Meetinghouse of Downtown Crossing, before building the Old South Church. In Harvard Square, the **First Church of Cambridge** (11 Garden Street, 617-547-2724, www.firstchurchcambridge.org), has been standing since 1872.

For more information on the local Congregational community, try the **Massachusetts Conference of the UCC**, www.macucc.org, or check with the **Congregational Library and Archives** at 14 Beacon Street (Back Bay), Boston, 617-523-0470, www.14beacon.org.

FRIENDS (QUAKER)

Members of the **Society of Friends**, a.k.a. **Quakers**, can trace their church's roots back to some of the first European settlers. Persecuted in England for their beliefs and then again in Massachusetts by their fellow Puritans, some did manage to remain in Boston, but more fled to New Jersey, North Carolina, Virginia, Maryland, New York, Rhode Island, and Pennsylvania—the latter two of which were their strongest and best-known colonies. For a time, they comprised the majority of persons in Rhode Island, and Pennsylvania was founded in 1681 by a Quaker named William Penn.

To learn more about the Friends church, visit www.quaker.org. Local Friends Houses include:
- **Beacon Hill Friends House**, 6 Chestnut Street, Boston, 617-227-9118, www.bhfh.org
- **Friends Meeting At Cambridge**, 5 Longfellow Park (Harvard Square), Cambridge, 617-876-6883, www.brightworks.com/quaker

INTERDENOMINATIONAL/INDEPENDENT/NONDENOMINATIONAL

The following churches are a few that identify themselves as independent or inter-/non-denomimational:
- **Boston Chinese Bible Study Group**, www.bcbsg.org
- **Chinese Christian Church of New England**, 1835 Beacon Street, Brookline, 617-232-8652, www.cccne.org
- **Community of Faith Christian Fellowship**, 410 Washington Street, Brighton, 617-783-2833, www.cfcfboston.org
- **Covenant Church**, 9 Westminster Avenue, Arlington, 781-646-9027
- **Emmanuel Gospel Center**, 2 San Juan, Boston, 617-262-4567, www.egc.org
- **Grace Christian Fellowship Church**, 858 Hyde Park Avenue, Hyde Park, 617-364-3344
- **Metropolitan Community Church (MCC)**, office at 4258 Washington Street #9 in Roslindale, 617-973-0404, www.mccboston.org; services are held in the Old West Church at 131 Cambridge Street on Sunday evenings at 6 p.m.
- **Mt. Olive Temple of Christ**, 234 Norfolk Street, Dorchester, 617-288-8830
- **Mt. Auburn Gospel Hall**, 226 Mt. Auburn Street, Watertown, 617-924-7696
- **United Parish in Brookline**, 210 Harvard Street, Brookline, 617-277-6860, www.unitedparishbrookline.org

JEHOVAH'S WITNESS

For information about Jehovah's Witness or to find a kingdom hall, visit www.watchtower.org or www.jw-media.org.

LUTHERAN

Lutheranism came to the New World with the immigrants of the northern Europeans countries, including Norway, Sweden, Denmark, Finland, and

Germany. Today, about two thirds of American Lutherans belong to the Evangelical Lutheran Church in America (www.elca.org), the largest conference of Lutherans in the country. Missouri Synod is the more conservative branch of the Lutheran church.

Area ELCA churches include:
- **Bethlehem Evangelical Lutheran Church**, Cliftondale and Kittredge streets, Roslindale, 617-325-4559
- **Christ Lutheran Church**, 597 Belmont Street, Belmont, 617-484-4352
- **Faith Lutheran Church**, 201 Granite Street, Quincy, 617-472-1247, http://home.attbi.com/~faithlutheran
- **Faith Lutheran Church**, 311 Broadway Street, Cambridge, 617-354-0414, www.faithchurchcambridge.org
- **First Lutheran Church**, 62 Church Street, Malden, 781-324-7133, www.firstlutheranmalden.org
- **First Lutheran Church of Boston**, 299 Berkeley Street, Boston, 617-536-8851, http://world.std.com/~flc
- **First Lutheran Church of Waltham**, 6 Eddy Street, Waltham, 781-893-6563, www.luther95.com/FELC-WMA
- **Lutheran Church of the Newtons**, 1310 Centre Street, Newton, 617-332-3893, http://home.earthlink.net/~newtonslutheran
- **Our Savior's Lutheran Church**, 500 Talbot Avenue, Dorchester, 617-265-5670
- **Resurrection Lutheran Church**, 94 Warren Street, Roxbury, 617-427-2066
- **St. Paul Evangelical Lutheran Church**, 929 Concord Turnpike, Arlington, 781-646-7773, www.stpaularlington.org
- **University Lutheran Church**, 66 Winthrop Street, Cambridge, 617-876-3256, www.unilu.org

MENNONITE

Until the 19th century, most Mennonites were concentrated in rural farming communities, speaking German, and spurning much of the secular world. Since the 1800s, there have been divisions in the church, yielding the Old Mennonite Church, General Conference Mennonite Church, Mennonite Brethren, and Old Order Amish. For more information about the Mennonite Church of the USA, try http://mcusa.mennonite.net or www.mennoniteusa.org. The **Mennonite Congregation of Boston** meets at 1555 Mass Ave. in Cambridge. Call 617-868-7784 for worship times.

METHODIST (UNITED)

On the local level, Methodists are organized by the New England Conference of the Methodist Church, www.neumc.org. You can search their web site for a church near you or try one of the following:
- **College Avenue Methodist Church**, 14 Chapel Street (Davis Square), Somerville, 617-776-4172,
- **Community United Methodist Church**, 519 Washington Street, Brighton, 617-787-1868, www.gbgm-umc.org/Community-BrightMA
- **Grace United Methodist Church**, 56 Magazine Street, Cambridge, 617-864-1123, www.gbgm-umc.org/cambridgegrace
- **Greenwood Memorial United Methodist Church**, 378A Washington Street, Dorchester, 617-288-8410, www.gbgm-umc.org/greenwoodmemorial
- **Harvard Epworth United Methodist Church**, 1555 Mass Ave., Cambridge, 617-354-0837, www.gbgm-umc.org/harepumc; open and affirming, GLBT-friendly.
- **Immanuel United Methodist Church**, 545 Moody Street, Waltham, 781-893-7250, www.gbgm-umc.org/immanuel-waltham
- **Old West Church**, 131 Cambridge Street (Government Center), Boston, 617-227-5088, www.oldwestchurch.org
- **St. Andrew's United Methodist Church**, 171 Amory Street, JP, 617-522-1535
- **United Methodist Church of Newton**, 430 Walnut Street, Street, 617-244-0275, www.gbgm-umc.org/newtnumc

CHURCH OF JESUS CHRIST OF LATTER-DAY SAINTS (MORMON)

Boston's Mormon population is particularly active in Belmont where the local temple is. And in 2002, Massachusetts elected a Mormon governor, Mitt Romney. For more information on the Church of Jesus Christ of Latter-day Saints, visit www.lds.org; for more about Boston's Mormon community, visit the Massachusetts Boston Mission sites at www.mbmission.com and www.ldsboston.org.

ORTHODOX (COPTIC, EASTERN, GREEK, ALBANIAN, RUSSIAN)

For more information on the Orthodox Church in America, visit www.oca.org or try the **Greek Orthodox Archdiocese of America** at www.goarch.org/en/archdiocese.

PENTECOSTAL/CHARISMATIC

For more information about the **Pentecostal/Charismatic Churches of North America** and to find a local church, go to www.pccna.org. For more about the **International Communion of the Charismatic Episcopal Church**, go to www.iccec.org. Or try the **Pentecostal-Charismatic Theology Inquiry** International at www.pctii.org.

PRESBYTERIAN (USA)

A Protestant Church with its roots in 17th century England, it was the Scottish and Irish who brought Presbyterianism to the US in the late 1600s. The largest Presbyterian branch in the US is the **Presbyterian Church (USA)**; find them on the web at www.pcusa.org.

Area Presbyterian churches include:

- **Church of the Covenant**, 67 Newbury Street, Boston, 617-266-7480, www.churchofthecovenant.org; also has membership with United Church of Christ. GLBT-friendly.
- **Clarendon Hill Presbyterian Church**, 155 Powderhouse Boulevard, Somerville, 617-625-4823, http://home.tiac.net/~chpc
- **First Presbyterian Church in Brookline**, 32 Harvard Street (Coolidge Corner), Brookline, 617-232-7962, www.fpcbrookline.org
- **First United Presbyterian Church of Cambridge**, 1418 Cambridge Street, Cambridge, 617-354-3151
- **First Presbyterian Church of Quincy**, 270 Franklin Street, Quincy, 617-773-5575, www.firstpresbyquincy.org
- **First Presbyterian Church of Waltham**, 34 Adler Street, Waltham, 781-893-3087, http://fpcwaltham.org
- **First Reformed Presbyterian Church**, 53 Antrim Street, Cambridge, 617-864-3185, www.reformedprescambridge.com
- **Fort Square Presbyterian Church**, 22 Pleasant Street, Quincy, 617-471-6806, http://fortsquarepresbyterian.freeservers.com
- **Fourth Presbyterian Church**, 340 Dorchester Street, South Boston, 617-268-1281
- **New Covenant Presbyterian Church**, 1310 Centre Street, Newton, 617-558-3223, www.ncpcboston.org
- **Newton Presbyterian Church**, 75 Vernon Street, Newton, 617-332-9255, www.newtonpres.org

ROMAN CATHOLIC

Roman Catholicism is the predominant religion in Boston. Although the recent Catholic clergy sexual abuse scandal probably hit hardest in Massachusetts, the state is still home to a population of firm believers. According to the Roman Catholic Archdiocese of Boston, there are more than two million Catholics in the greater Boston area, and seven affiliated colleges and universities, 11 hospitals and medical centers, and 191 Catholic elementary, middle, and high schools.

Start your search with the **Roman Catholic Archdiocese of Boston**, 2121 Comm Ave., Boston, 617-254-0100, www.rcab.org, who can connect you with the Vatican, Catholic charities, marriage preparation, Catholic Social Services, job opportunities, and a list of churches for each town. For Catholic media outlets, there is **Boston Catholic Television** (**BCTV**), www.catholictv.org; *The Pilot*, America's oldest Roman Catholic newspaper (comes out every Friday); and **Boston Catholic Radio**, www1.shore.net/~rreed. To subscribe to *The Pilot*, call 617-746-5889 or visit www.rcab.org/pilot.

The greater Boston area has too many Roman Catholic churches to list here. Suffice it to say the town or neighborhood without a Catholic Church is the exception; many churches conduct masses in other languages, including Italian, Spanish, German, and ASL. To find the closest parish, you can call the Archdiocese or go to the web site and use the "parish finder" option.

SEVENTH DAY ADVENTIST

Area Seventh Day Adventist churches include:
- **Berea Seventh Day Adventist Church**, 108 Seaver Street, Boston, 617-427-8885, www.tagnet.org/bereasda
- **Bethel Church of God Seventh Day**, 1026 Blue Hill Avenue, Boston, 617-288-2045
- **Boston Temple Seventh Day Adventist Church**, 105 Jersey Street (Fenway), Boston, 617-424-8933, www.tagnet.org/bostontemple
- **Cambridge Seventh Day Adventist Church**, 62 Dexter Street, Medford, 781-391-8839
- **Ephese Seventh Day Adventist Church**, 366 Washington Street, Boston, 617-288-7700
- **JP Spanish Seventh Day Adventist Church**, 40 Elm Street, JP, 617-983-1076
- **Spanish Boston Temple Seventh Day Adventist Church**, 50 Stoughton Street, Boston, 617-436-6802

- **Temple Salem of the Seventh Day Adventists**, 222 Woodrow Avenue, Boston, 617-288-8845

UNITARIAN UNIVERSALIST ASSOCIATION (UUA)

The Unitarian Universalist Association (UUA) dates back to 1961, when the Universalism and Unitarianism movements officially merged. The **UUA's Headquarters** are at 25 Beacon Street. To contact the UUA, go to http://uua.org. Visit the **Mass Bay District of UU Churches** at http://www.mbd.uua.org.

UNITY CHURCHES

For information about local Unity Churches, visit the Association of Unity Churches' web site: www.unity.org.

ETHICAL SOCIETIES

Ethical Society of Boston, P.O. Box 38-1934, Cambridge, MA 02238, 617-739-9050, www.bostonethical.org; not a conventional religious organization, ethical societies offer a meeting place and fellowship to members and visitors. Their "focus is on core ethical values that people have in common." Acknowledging that humans are both individualistic and social in nature, the society explores what it means to understand the inner workings of self and how to relate to each other in a respectful/ethical/moralistic way. For more information go to www.ethicalsociety.org.

HINDU

Hinduism is as complex and multifaceted as the many gods it incorporates. Nearly 13% of the world's population is Hindu. Although most still live in India, there are roughly one million Hindus in the United States. Two Boston area temples include:
- **New England Hindu Temple**, 117 Waverly Street, Ashland, 508-881-5775
- **Swaminarayan Temple**, 405 Andover Street, Lowell, 978-934-9390

ISLAM

To tap into the local Islamic community try: **MA Islamic News & Events**, http://welcome.to/isnews; the **Islamic Council of New England**, http://salam.muslimsonline.com/~icne/index.html; the **Islamic Society of Boston**, 204 Prospect Street, Cambridge, 617-876-6268, www.isboston.org; or the **Islamic Center of New England**, 407 South Street, Quincy, 617-479-8341.

Area Islamic centers and mosques include:
- **Boston Islamic Center**, 3381 Washington Street, JP, 617-522-1881
- **Islamic Center of Boston**, 126 Boston Post Road, Wayland, 508-358-5885, www.icbwayland.org
- **Islamic Center of New England**, 470 South Street, Quincy, 617-479-8341, www.iane.org/icne.html
- **Islamic Society of Boston**, 204 Prospect Avenue, Cambridge, 617-876-3546
- **Masjid Al-Quran**, 35 Intervale Street, Dorchester, 617-445-8070
- **Mosque for the Praising of Allah**, 724 Shawmut Avenue, Roxbury, 617-442-2805

JEWISH

Unlike most of the country, Boston has a sizable Jewish population, with the heaviest concentrations in Newton and Brookline where they make up at least one third of the total population. Other areas include Marblehead, Swampscott, Peabody, Framingham, Needham, and Sharon. The local media outlet is the *Jewish Advocate*, which you can subscribe to online at www.thejewishadvocate.com or by calling 617-367-9100. For socializing, try the **Jewish Community Centers of Greater Boston**, 333 Nahanton Street, Newton Centre, 617-558-6500, www.jccgb.org. And finally, for information on everything and anything Jewish in the Boston area, go to www.shalomboston.com. To learn more about Judaism in general, try Judaism 101, www.jewfaq.org. If you are a student, professor, or otherwise affiliated with one of Boston's many colleges and universities, you can likely attend one of your school's Hillels or Chabad houses. Here are a few congregations.

CONSERVATIVE

- **Congregation Kehillath Israel**, 384 Harvard Street (Coolidge Corner), Brookline, 617-277-9155, www.congki.org
- **Congregation Mishkan Tefila**, 300 Hammond Pond Parkway, Chestnut Hill, 617-332-7770, www.mishkantefila.org

- **Temple Beth Israel**, 25 Harvard Street, Waltham, 781-894-5146
- **Temple Beth Shalom of Cambridge**, 8 Tremont Street, Cambridge, 617-864-6388, www.tremontstreetshul.org
- **Temple Beth Zion**, 1566 Beacon Street, Brookline, 617-566-8171, www.templebethzion.org
- **Temple B'nai Brith**, 201 Central Street, Somerville, 617-625-0333, www.templebnaibrith.org
- **Temple B'nai Moshe**, 1845 Comm Ave., Brighton, 617-254-3620, www.bnaimoshe.net
- **Temple Emmeth**, South and Grove streets, Chestnut Hill, 617-469-9400, www.uscj.org/neweng
- **Temple Reyim**, 1860 Washington Street, Newton, 617-527-2410, www.reyim.org

HASIDIC

- **Congregation B'nai Jacob of Boston and Newton**, 15 School Street, Boston, 617-227-8200; 955 Beacon Street, Newton, 617-965-0066, www.rebbe.org
- **Congregation Lubavitch**, 100 Woodcliff Road, Chestnut Hill, 617-469-4000
- **Lubavitcher Shul of Brighton**, 239 Chestnut Hill Avenue, Brighton, 617-782-8340
- **Congregation Beth Pinchas/New England Chasidic Center**, 1710 Beacon Street, Brookline, 617-734-5100

ORTHODOX

- **Adams Street Shul**, 168 Adams Street, Newton, 617-630-0226, www.adamsstreet.org
- **Congregation Beth-El Atereth Israel**, 561 Ward Street, Newton Centre, 617-244-7233, www.geocities.com/congbethel
- **Congregation Kadimah-Toras Moshe**, 113 Washington Street, Brighton, 617-254-1333
- **Congregation Shaarei Tefillah**, 35 Morseland Avenue, Newton Centre, 617-527-7637, www.shaarei.org
- **Sephardic Community of Greater Boston**, 74 Corey Road, Brookline, 617-232-7979, www.rluipa.com/cases/Sephardic.html
- **Young Israel of Brookline**, 62 Green Street, Brookline, 617-734-0276, http://world.std.com/~yi/brookline

RECONSTRUCTIONIST

- **Shir Hadash Reconstructionist Havurah**, 1310 Centre Street, Newton, 617-965-6862, www.jrf.org/shirhadash/
- **Congregation Dorshei Tzedek**, 60 Highland Street, Newton, 617-965-0330, www.dorsheitzedek.org

REFORM

- **Beth-El Temple Center**, 2 Concord Avenue, Belmont, 617-484-6668, www.uahc.org/congs/ma/ma002
- **Temple Israel**, 477 Longwood Avenue, Boston, 617-566-3960, www.tisrael.org
- **Temple Beth Avodah**, 45 Puddingstone Lane, Newton Centre, 617-527-0045, www.bethavodah.org
- **Temple Ohabei Shalom**, 1187 Beacon Street, Brookline, 617-277-6610, www.ohabei.org
- **Temple Shalom of Newton**, 175 Temple Street, Newton, 617-332-9550, www.templeshalom.org/~shalom
- **Temple Sinai of Brookline**, 50 Sewell Avenue (Coolidge Corner), Brookline, 617-277-5888, www.uahc.org/ma/sinai-brookline
- **Temple Tifereth Israel**, 539 Salem Street, Malden, 781-322-2794, www.uahcweb.org/congs/ma/ma003

NON-MOVEMENT AFFILIATED

- **Progressive Chavurah**, www.chav.net
- **Boston Synagogue**, 55 Martha Road, Boston, 617-523-0453, www.bostonsynagogue.org
- **Congregation Eitz Chayim**, 134-6 Magazine Street, Cambridge, 617-497-7626, www.eitz.org

NEW AGE

Information about the local Subud community can be found at **Subud Boston**, www.subudboston.org. To learn more about Subud in general, visit the official site of their world association at www.subud.org.

The other major New Age religion in these parts is **Wicca**. Although Wiccans do call themselves witches, this name is often misinterpreted—they do not engage in Satanism or devil worship, as many mistakenly believe, but rather focus on revering nature. Perhaps because of Salem's history, many Wiccans live in and around Boston, and Salem itself has quite a healthy population of Wiccans, sustained no doubt by the crossover with the tourism industry. There is even a self-appointed, official Witch of Salem—a woman named **Laurie Cabot**, who runs a shop called The Cat, the Crow, and the Crown (www.lauriecabot.com). For information on the local Wiccan scene, check out some of the New Age shops in Salem or try one of the following:

- **Boston Pagan**, www.bostonpagan.com
- **Church of Magick**, www.churchofmagick.com, with links for Boston, Brookline, Dedham, Malden, Salem, and many other Massachusetts communities.
- **Goddess Womyn**, www.geocities.com/goddesswomyn13/
- **Society of Elder Faiths**, www.elderfaiths.org

SIKH

Although there are over 20 million Sikhs throughout the world, only 220,000 live in America. There is enough of a Sikh population in Boston for a gurdwara—**Gurdwara Guru Nanak Darbar**, 226 Mystic Avenue, Medford, www.gurunanakdarbar.net. For more information on Sikhism, go to www.sikhs.org.

VOLUNTEERING

SERVING AS A VOLUNTEER IN A NEW CITY CAN BE BENEFICIAL FOR both you and your new community. Human services, charitable organizations, and even area museums are often under-funded, and many rely heavily on volunteer labor. As a volunteer you will be providing your community with a valuable service—as well as tapping into a social circle with those who share your concerns.

You will find volunteer opportunities listed in the newspapers or see below for a list of places that you can contact directly.

VOLUNTEER PLACEMENT SERVICES

If you'd like to donate your time but you don't know where to start, try one of the following volunteer placement services:

- **Boston Cares**, PMB 200, 167 Milk Street, Boston, 617-263-CARE, www.bostoncares.org
- **Boston Jaycees**, 1 Beacon Street, Boston, 617-367-5710, www.bostonjaycees.org
- **Chelsea Community Volunteer Center**, 300 Broadway, Chelsea, 617-889-6080, www.chelseacollab.org/CommunityVolunteerCenter
- **Harvard Public Service Network**, www.fas.harvard.edu/~pbh/psn
- **Leonard Carmichael Society**, 17 Chetwynd Avenue, 2nd Floor, Medford, 617-627-3643, http://ase.tufts.edu/lcs
- **Oxfam America, Inc.**, World Headquarters, 26 West Street, Boston, 800-77-OXFAMUSA, www.oxfamamerica.org
- **People Making a Difference**, P.O. Box 120189, Boston, 617-282-7177, www.pmd.org
- **Somerville Volunteer Service Corps**, 50 Evergreen Avenue, Somerville, 617-625-6000

- **St. Vincent Pallotti Center**, 159 Washington Street, Brighton, 617-783-3924, www.pallotticenter.org
- **The United Way of Massachusetts Bay**, 245 Summer Street, Suite 1401, Boston, 617-624-8000, www.uwmb.org
- **Volunteer Solutions**, www.volunteersolutions.org; lists a great number of local organizations that are currently looking for volunteers.

AREA CAUSES

- **Boston By Foot**, 77 North Washington Street, Boston, 617-367-2345, www.bostonbyfoot.com
- **The Boston Foundation**, 75 Arlington Street, 10th Floor, Boston, 617-338-1700, www.tbf.org
- **Museum of Science**, Science Park, Boston, 617-589-0380 (volunteer opportunity line), www.mos.org/info/vol

AIDS

- **AIDS Action Committee**, 294 Washington Street, Boston, 617-437-5200, www.aac.org
- **AIDS Housing Corporation**, 29 Stanhope Street, Boston, 617-927-0088, www.ahc.org
- **Boston Living Center**, 29 Stanhope Street, Boston, 617-236-1012, www.bostonlivingcenter.org
- **Cambridge Cares About AIDS**, 7 Temple Street, Cambridge, 617-661-3040, www.ccaa.org
- **Community Servings**, 125 Magazine Street, Roxbury, 617-445-7777, www.servings.org/home
- **Haitian Center for Community, Health, Education, Research** (formerly Haitian Community AIDS Outreach Project), 420 Washington Street, Dorchester, 617-265-0628, www.ccher.org
- **Women of Color AIDS Council**, 409 Blue Hill Avenue, Dorchester, 617-541-1050

ALCOHOL AND DRUG DEPENDENCY

- **Bay Cove Human Services**, 66 Canal Street, Boston, 617-371-3000, www.baycove.org
- **Habit Management Institute**, 99 Topeka Street, Boston, 617-442-1499, www.habitmanagement.com
- **Massachusetts Substance Abuse Information and Education Helpline**, c/o The Medical Foundation, 95 Berkley Street, Boston, 617-536-0501, ext. 201, www.helpline-online.com

ANIMALS

- **City of Boston Animal Shelter**, 26 Mahler Road, Roslindale, 617-635-1800, www.cityofboston.gov/animalcontrol/
- **MSPCA**, 350 South Huntington Avenue, Boston, 617-522-7400, www.mspca.org

CHILDREN

- **Cambridge Family & Child Services**, 929 Mass. Ave., Suite 1, Cambridge, 617-876-4210, www.helpfamilies.org
- **The Children's Room—Center for Grieving Children and Teenagers**, 819 Mass Ave., Arlington, 781-641-4741, www.childrensroom.org
- **Horizons Initiative**, 90 Cushing Avenue, Dorchester, 617-287-1900, www.horizonsinitiative.org
- **Massachusetts Society for the Prevention of Cruelty to Children**, Central Support: 399 Boylston Street, Boston, 617-587-1500, www.mspcc.org; Boston Region: 555 Amory Street, JP, 617-983-5800
- **The Home for Little Wanderers**, 271 Huntington Avenue, Boston, 888-HOME-321 or 617-267-3700, www.thehome.org
- **Starlight Children's Foundation**, 529 Main Street, Suite 608, Charlestown, 617-241-9911, www.nestarlight.org

CRIME PREVENTION

- **Peace Games**, 285 Dorchester Avenue, Dorchester, 617-464-2600, www.peacegames.org

CULTURE AND THE ARTS

- **Boston Institute for Arts Therapy**, 90 Cushing Avenue, Dorchester, 617-288-5858, www.biat.org

DISABLED ASSISTANCE

- **Boston Center for Independent Living**, 95 Berkeley Street, Suite 206, Boston, 617-338-6665, www.bostoncil.org
- **Boston Self Help Center**, 18 Williston Road, Brookline, 617-277-0080
- **Cambridge Law Center for Disability Rights, Inc.**, 2067 Mass. Ave., 4th floor, Cambridge, 617-492-6789

- **D.E.A.F., Inc.** (Developmental Evaluation and Adjustment Facilities, Inc.), 215 Brighton Avenue, Allston, 617-254-4041
- **Easter Seals Massachusetts**, 1 Lincoln Plaza, 89 South Street, 1st floor, Boston, 800-922-8290, www.eastersealsma.org
- **Greater Boston Aid to the Blind**, 1980 Centre Street, West Roxbury, 617-323-5111, www.gbab.org
- **Helping Hands—Monkey Helpers for the Disabled**, 541 Cambridge Street, Boston, 617-787-4419, www.helpinghands monkeys.org
- **Massachusetts Association for the Blind**, 200 Ivy Street, Brookline, 800-682-9200 or 617-738-5110, www.mablind.org
- **Recording for the Blind and Dyslexic**, 58 Charles Street, Cambridge, 617-577-1111, www.rftb.org/Units/Boston

ENVIRONMENT

- **Boston GreenSpace Alliance**, 36 Bromfield Street, #201, Boston, 617-426-7980, www.greenspacealliance.org
- **Conservation Law Foundation**, 62 Summer Street, Boston, 617-350-0990, www.clf.org
- **Environmental League of Massachusetts**, 14 Beacon Street, Suite 14, Boston, 617-742-2553, www.environmentalleague.org
- **Massachusetts Audubon Society**, 208 South Great Road, Lincoln, 781-259-9500 or 800-AUDOBON, www.massaudubon.org
- **Save the Harbor/Save the Bay**, 59 Temple Place, Suite 304, Boston, 617-451-2860, www.savetheharbor.org
- **Sierra Club**, 100 Boylston Street, Boston, 617-423-5775, www.sierra clubmass.org
- **Somerville Environmental & Recycling Volunteers** (**SERV**), 617-628-8850

GAY AND LESBIAN

- **Boston Alliance of Gay Lesbian Bisexual Transgender Questioning Youth**, 14 Beacon Street, #506, Boston, 617-227-4313, www.bagly.org
- **Gay & Lesbian Advocates & Defenders**, 294 Washington Street, Suite 301, Boston, 617-426-1350, www.glad.org
- **Gay Men's Domestic Violence Project**, PMB 131, 955 Mass Ave., Cambridge, 617-354-6072, www.gmdvp.org
- **SpeakOut**, 29 Stanhope Street, Boston, 617-450-9776, www.speak outboston.org

HEALTH AND HOSPITALS

- **American Cancer Society**, Massachusetts Bay Region, 4th floor, 25 Stuart Street, Boston, 617-559-7400, www.cancer.org
- **American Lung Association of Massachusetts**, 1 Abbey Lane, Middleboro, 508-947-7204, www.lungsusa.org/massachusetts
- **Beth Israel Deaconess Medical Center**, 330 Brookline Avenue, Boston, 617-667-3026, www.bidmc.harvard.edu/volunteers
- **Dana Farber Cancer Institute**, 44 Binney Street, Boston, 617-632-3307, www.dana-farber.org/how/volunteer
- **Hospice & Palliative Care Federation of Massachusetts**, 1420 Providence Highway, Suite 277, Norwood, 781-255-7077, www.hospicefed.org
- **Jimmy Fund**, 10 Brookline Place West, 6th floor, Brookline, 800-52-JIMMY, www.jimmyfund.org
- **Joslin Diabetes Center**, 1 Joslin Place, Boston, 617-732-2400, www.joslin.harvard.edu
- **Legacy of Hope Foundation**, P.O. Box 66, Boston, 617-323-0939, www.thelegacyofhope.com
- **Mass General Hospital**, 55 Fruit Street, Boston, 617-726-8540, www.mgh.harvard.edu/depts/vol
- **New England Baptist Hospital**, 125 Parker Hill Avenue, Boston, 617-754-5173, www.nebh.caregroup.org
- **Project HEALTH**, Dowling 3 South, Room 3505, 1 Boston Medical Center, Boston, www.projecthealth.org
- **Samaritans of Boston**, 654 Beacon Street, 6th Floor, Boston, 617-536-2460, www.samaritansofboston.org
- **VNA Care Network**, 800-728-1862 or 508-751-6860, www.vnacarenetwork.org

HISTORICAL RESTORATION

- **Historic Boston Incorporated**, 3 School Street, Boston, 617-227-4679, www.historicboston.org

HOMELESS

- **Christmas in the City**, P.O. Box 24, Charlestown, 617-242-3534, http://isers.rcn.com/citc
- **Habitat for Humanity**, 455 Arborway, Boston, 617-524-8891, www.habitatboston.org

- **Homeless Empowerment**, 1151 Mass Ave., Cambridge, 617-497-1595, www.homelessempowerment.org
- **Massachusetts Housing and Shelter Alliance**, 5 Park Street, Boston, 617-367-6447
- **Pine Street Inn**, 444 Harrison Avenue, Boston, 617-482-4944, www.pinestreetinn.org
- **Shelter, Inc.**, 109 School Street, Cambridge, 617-547-1885
- **Somerville Homeless Coalition**, 1 Davis Square, Somerville, 617-623-6111, http://somervillehomelesscoalition.org

HUMAN SERVICES

- **Action for Boston Community Development (ABCD)**, 178 Tremont Street, Boston, 617-357-6000, www.bostonabcd.org
- **American Red Cross of Massachusetts Bay**, 285 Columbus Avenue, Boston, 617-375-0700, www.bostonredcross.org
- **Bay Cove Human Services**, 66 Canal Street, Boston, 617-371-3000, www.baycove.org
- **Boston Centers for Youth and Families**, 1433 Tremont Street, Boston, 617-635-4920, www.cityofboston.gov/bcyf
- **Boston Rescue Mission**, 39 Kingston Street, Boston, 617-482-8819, www.brm.org
- **Catholic Charitable Bureau of the Archdiocese of Boston**, 75 Kneeland Street, Boston, 617-482-5440, www.ccab.org
- **Combined Jewish Philanthropies of Greater Boston, Inc.**, 126 High Street, Boston, 617-457-8500, www.cjp.org
- **Executive Service Corps of New England**, 87 Summer Street, 3rd Floor, Boston, 617-357-5550, www.escne.org
- **Freedom House**, 14 Crawford Street, Roxbury, 617-445-2802, www.freedomhouse.com
- **Generations Incorporated**, 59 Temple Street, Suite 200, Boston, 617-423-6633, www.generationsinc.org
- **Massachusetts Service Alliance**, 100 North Washington Street, 3rd Floor, Boston, 617-542-2544, www.msalliance.org
- **Parental Stress Line**, 142 Berkley Street, Boston, 617-528-5800, www.pcsonline.org/about/programs/helplines
- **Salvation Army**, 147 Berkley Street, Boston, 617-338-4155 ext. 172, www.salvationarmy-ma.org/help/volunteering
- **Urban League of Eastern Massachusetts**, 88 Warren, Roxbury, 617-442-4519, www.ulem.org
- **University Lutheran Church**, 66 Winthrop Street, Cambridge, 617-876-3256, www.unilu.org/programs/current_volunteer

- **Volunteers of America**, 441 Centre Street, Jamaica Plain, 617-522-8086, www.voamass.org

HUNGER

- **The Food Project**, 555 Dudley Street, Dorchester, www.thefoodproject.org
- **Greater Boston Food Bank**, 99 Atkinson Street, Boston, 617-427-5200, www.gbfb.org
- **Project Bread—The Walk for Hunger**, 160 North Washington Street, Boston, 617-723-5000, www.projectbread.org

INTERNATIONAL

- **Afrihope International**, P.O. Box 190706, Boston, 617-957-1613, www.afrihopeinc.org
- **Amnesty International Northeast Regional Office**, 58 Day Street, Somerville, 617-623-0202, www.amnestyusa.org.
- **Boston Area Returned Peace Corps Volunteers**, P.O. Box 391618, Cambridge, 781-646-6376, www.barpcv.org
- **Tecschange—Technology for Social Change**, 83 Highland Street, Roxbury, 617-442-4456, www.tecschange.org

LEGAL

- **American Civil Liberties Union of Massachusetts**, 99 Chauncy Street, Suite 310, Boston, 617-482-3170, www.aclu-mass.org
- **Greater Boston Legal Services**, 197 Friend Street, Boston, 617-371-1234 or 800-323-3205, www.gbls.org

LITERACY

- **Greater Boston Jewish Coalition for Literacy**, 617-457-8661, www.jcrcboston.org/bjclcoal
- **Literacy Volunteers of Massachusetts**, 15 Court Square, Room 540, Boston, 617-367-1313, http://members.tripod.com/lvmass

MEN'S SERVICES

- **Boston Men's Center**, P.O. Box 138, Boston, 617-825-3918

POLITICS—ELECTORAL

- **League of Women Voters of Massachusetts**, 133 Portland Street—lower level, Boston, 617-523-2999, www.lwv.org

POLITICS—SOCIAL

- **Bikes Not Bombs**, 59 Amory Street, #103, Roxbury, 617-442-0004, www.bikesnotbombs.org

SENIOR SERVICES

- **Ethos**, 555 Amory Street, JP, 617-522-6700 ext. 323, www.ethoscare.org
- **Match-up Interfaith Volunteers**, 140 Clarendon Street, Boston, 617-536-3557, www.matchelder.org
- **Mass Senior Action Council**, 186 Lincoln Street, Suite 901, Boston, 617-350-6722
- **American Association of Retired Persons**, 1 Boston Place, Suite 1900, Boston, 617-720-5600, www.aarp.org/statepages/ma
- **Operation A.B.L.E. of Greater Boston**, 186 South Street, Boston, 617-542-4180, www.operationable.net

WOMEN'S SERVICES

- **Battered Women Support Committee**, 905 Main Street, Waltham, 781-891-0724
- **Junior League of Boston**, 117 Newbury Street, Boston, 617-536-9640, www.jlboston.org
- **Mass NARAL**, 41 Winter Street, Suite 65, Boston, 617-556-8800, www.massnaral.org
- **National Organization For Women**, 214 Harvard Avenue, Allston, 617-232-1017, http://bostonnow.site.yahoo.net
- **RESPOND, Inc.**, P.O. Box 555, Somerville, 617-625-5996, www2.primushost.com/~respond
- **Rosie's Place**, 889 Harrison Avenue, Boston, 617-442-9322, www.rosies.org
- **Women in Community Service**, 125 Kingston Street, 6th floor, 617-423-6445 or 800-666-WICS, www.charityadvantage.com/wics
- **Women's Institute for Housing and Economical Development**, 14 Beacon Street, Boston, 617-367-0520, www.wihed.org

YOUTH SERVICES

- **Big Brothers of Massachusetts Bay**, 55 Summer Street, 8th floor, Boston, 617-542-9090, www.bbmb.org
- **Big Sister Association of Greater Boston**, 161 Mass Ave., 2nd floor, Boston, 617-236-8060, www.bigsister.org
- **Boston Partners in Education**, 44 Farnsworth Street, Boston, 617-451-6145, www.bostonpartners.org
- **Boys and Girls Clubs Boston**, 50 Congress Street, Suite 730, Boston, 617-994-9700, www.bgcb.org
- **Citizen Schools**, 308 Congress Street, 5th Floor, Boston, 617-695-2300, www.citizenschools.org
- **City Year**, 285 Columbus Avenue, Boston, 617-927-2600, www.cityyear.org/boston
- **Jewish Big Brother & Big Sister Association of Greater Boston**, 333 Nahanton, Newton Centre, 617-965-7055, www.jbbbs.org
- **Massachusetts Service Alliance**, 100 North Washington Street, 3rd floor, Boston, 617-542-2544, www.msalliance.org

YOUTH—TUTORING

Many schools welcome volunteers. Check the **Childcare and Education** chapter for a list of area schools to call to offer your services.

TRANSPORTATION

GETTING AROUND

UNLIKE RESIDENTS OF MANY OTHER LARGE CITIES, BOSTONIANS have a rather undefined relationship with the automobile. In contrast to New York and London, with their high-density living conditions and extensive public transit systems that make car ownership optional and the other extremes of LA and Atlanta, where cars are a necessity, Boston falls somewhere in the middle. Indeed, it seems that in this facet Bostonians are distinctly average—we neither love our cars, nor hate them. Some of us have them, many of us do not. Like all large metropolitan areas, however, driving in the city is not for the meek. Many drivers are aggressive, and navigating the convoluted, centuries-old streets can be a lesson in humility, not to mention the maddening challenge of trying to find parking once you reach your destination. Many Bostonians are able to live well here without a car. MBTA T and bus service is more than adequate for getting around to most parts of the city. For those that don't want to deal with the fuss and muss of owning a car, but still want to have one readily available, you can join **Zipcar** (www.zipcar.com, 866-4ZIPCAR), which is an hourly car rental subscription service. If you do plan to live in Boston without a car, you should purchase a copy of *Car-Free Boston*, a publication produced by the Association for Public Transportation, 617-482-0282, www.car-free.com; available at most bookstores.

BY CAR

Traveling in Boston by car is confusing at best, especially in recent years with the monumental multi-billion dollar construction project known as the "**Big Dig**" (www.bigdig.com). While this conversion of the Central

Artery (Interstate 93) from an elevated freeway running through the city's Financial District along Boston Harbor to an underground roadway is in its completion stages, traffic detours, newly added on-ramps to the tunnel, demolition of the Central Artery, and landscaping continues.

The Big Dig aside, finding your way around Boston's old, narrow and confusingly laid out streets is no picnic. Footpaths laid the first lines for the early roads here, and the area's hilly topography discouraged the development of a grid system for city streets. The best advice: buy a good map of the entire metro area (not just Boston) and be patient. It might seem daunting at first, but since the city is so small, you'll soon come to recognize the winding, one way streets that only days ago were your arch enemy. Area expressways and major highways can save you some time depending on the hour of the day. However, during rush hours you'll more than likely return to the city streets, no matter how narrow or crooked, looking for ways to avoid being caught in gridlock on the major arteries.

For the uninitiated, the most intimidating New England traffic institution is known as the "rotary," elsewhere called a "roundabout" or "traffic circle." These are often used instead of traffic lights, especially when more than two streets intersect. Traffic already in the circle has the legal right of way, but the real rule of the road is a combination of "no guts no glory" and "go with the flow." Get in there and circle around to your exit.

A final caution: Boston drivers are impatient, assertive, and expressive (read: honking, swearing, yelling, cutting you off, many times simultaneously).

Some of the **major highways and byways** are as follows:

- **I-93** links up with **Route 3** in Quincy heading north through downtown Boston into Charlestown. (Route 3, also known as Memorial Drive, heads west to Cambridge over the Longfellow Bridge.)
- **Route 1** goes all the way up and down the East Coast from Maine to Florida In Boston and south of the city, it follows along with I-93, splitting off in Westwood/Dedham, where it picks up with "Old Route 1 (which, farther north, becomes the Arborway, the Jamaicaway, the Riverway, and the Fenway and then disappears). North of the city, Route 1 is an active three-lane highway lined with stores, restaurants, and malls.
- **Route 2** is simply **Comm Ave**. until it crosses the Charles at the Boston University Bridge. On the other side of the river, Route 2 joins Route 3, both of which run along Memorial Drive. Memorial Drive then veers into the Fresh Pond Parkway and Alewife Brook Parkway, where routes 2 and 3 are then briefly joined by Route 16. At the intersection with the Concord Turnpike; routes 3 and 16 head northeast, continuing the Alewife Brook Parkway, and Route 2 joins up with the Concord Turnpike, heading northwest. Route 2 offers a scenic drive to Western Massachusetts.

- **I-90**, the Massachusetts Turnpike, known as "the Pike," heads west from Boston to Seattle. Thanks to the Big Dig, you can now take it all the way to Logan Airport. Outside of rush hours, the Pike is a good way to get quickly from Boston to the western suburbs (Waltham, Newton, etc.), since the only alternative is by slower city streets. And try to resist the temptation to speed, it's well patrolled. Note: I-90 is a toll road. You can use a Fast Lane Pass to save time (see below for details).
- **I-95** and **Route 128** are highways combined in a semi-circular loop that skirts Boston and the suburbs along the western edge, I-95 then heads north to New Hampshire along the coast.
- **Route 9** is also Huntington Avenue in Boston, and Boylston Street in Brookline and Newton. It heads west and south through Boston to Brookline and Newton, where it links with Route 128 and I-95.
- **The Fenway** begins where Boylston veers around the Fens. The Fenway heads south along the Fens and the Emerald Necklace. It becomes the Riverway which becomes the Jamaica Way which becomes the Arborway. The Arborway is also Route 203. Be careful on this road—it is narrow and winding and at night it isn't well lit.

Are you confused yet? Don't despair. Learning your way around metro Boston by car is a challenge that can be mastered only by trial and error. You'll know you are fully assimilated once you've discovered how to get across town during rush hour without getting trapped in traffic. Ex-Bostonians report boredom with cities that are laid out on a grid. After all, where's the challenge if a street doesn't double back on itself and its name doesn't change two or three times along the way?

A final note for those regularly using the toll roads. **Fast Lane**, www.mtafastlane.com, 877-627-7745, sponsored by the Massachusetts Turnpike Authority, is an electronic toll collection program that allows you to electronically pay your toll—i.e., no scrounging for change, and no waiting for the car ahead of you. There are electronic booths at many tolls, including those for the Sumner/Callahan tunnels, the Ted Williams Tunnel, the Tobin Bridge, and parts of the Mass Pike. A transponder costs $27.50, including a refundable deposit, and you can transfer it from car to car.

CARPOOLING

Aside from cutting down on traffic, saving you money on gas, and saving the environment, car pooling (also known as "ride matching") can save you time on your daily commute because some routes have carpool only lanes, which are open during rush hour. If you'd like to start or join a carpool call **Caravan for Commuters, Inc**., a private non-profit organization, 888-4-COMMUTE, or go to www.commute.com.

PARK & RIDES

MassHighway, the MassPike, and the MBTA run Park & Rides, places for suburban commuters to park their cars and then use public transportation for the rest of the trip. For a map of all the Park & Ride commuter lots, visit www.ctps.org/bostonmpo/info/pnr/pr.htm. Here are a few:
- **Newton**: Route 30 West, near Pike exit 14/15, Auburn Street; Route 16 East, near Pike exit 16; Route 16, near Pike exit 16, Webster Street
- **Weston**: off Route 30, near Pike exit 14/15, and St. Demetrious Church on Brown Street
- **Milton**: Granite Avenue at Thistle Avenue just off I-93 South exit 11
- **Canton**: Route 138, north of Blue Hill River Road, near Route 128 exit 2
- **Braintree**: Route 128 exit 6, on Forbes Road
- **Scituate**: Plymouth Brockton Greenbush Terminal, Old Driftway, Route 3A
- **Hull**: Main Street, Point Pemberton
- **Hingham**: Shipyard Drive off Route 3A
- **Quincy**: Fore River Shipyard off Route 3A
- **Framingham**: Shopper's World at Flutie Pass, near routes 9 and 30; Route 9 eastbound, near Pike exit 12
- **Woburn**: I-93 exit 37C on Atlantic Avenue
- **Peabody**: 164 Newbury Street (Route 1)

CAR RENTAL

If you have decided to live car-free in Boston, but need to get your hands on a car for a weekend away, the following car rental agencies serve the greater Boston area. Obviously, the most popular place to pick up/drop off a car is at the airport, but there are other locations around. Also check ZipCar (see the introduction) for a more long-term solution to renting a car in Boston.
- **Alamo**, 800-327-9329, www.alamo.com
- **Avis**, 800-331-1212, www.avis.com
- **Budget**, 800-527-0700, www.budget.com
- **Dollar**, 800-800-4000, www.dollar.com
- **Enterprise**, 800-325-8007, www.enterprise.com
- **Hertz**, 800-654-3131, www.hertz.com
- **National**, 800-227-7368, www.nationalcar.com
- **Thrifty**, 800-367-2277, www.thrifty.com

TAXIS

You'll find taxi stands all over the city, particularly near the major tourist centers, or you can call and schedule a pick-up. Some popular cab stands are those in front of Faneuil Hall by the greenhouse, in Cambridge's Harvard Square in front of the Coop, and in Brookline on Harvard Street right in Coolidge Corner. There isn't a stand in the North End, but tourists go there so often that you can count on finding a cab there easily, day or night. The same goes for Newbury Street and Boylston Street in the Back Bay. However, other areas that are a little further out of the way, like Charlestown, do not have many roving taxis, so call for a pick-up.

As far as hailing cabs goes, paying attention to the "for hire" light on the tops of the taxis is pointless. Whether they're lit up or not seems irrelevant. And unless you have eagle eyes, you won't be able to see if they've got a passenger until they're too close and you miss them. So your basic strategy should be to hail away.

If you've got a problem with your cab or your cab driver, Boston taxicabs are regulated through the **Hackney Carriage Office, Boston Police Department**, 154 Berkeley Street, Boston, 617-343-4475. For towns outside of Boston, check with your town or city hall for regulations.

Here are a few of the local cab companies if you need to call. Check the Yellow Pages for a company that services your neighborhood.
- **Bay State Taxi and Red Cab**, 617-730-8424
- **Boston Cab**, 617-536-5010
- **City Cab of Boston**, 617-536-5100
- **Independent Taxi Operators Association**, 617-282-4000
- **Metro Cab**, 617-242-8000

BY BIKE

It is not unusual to see people biking to work in and around Boston, and it is a particularly popular means of transit among the huge student population. The most popular locale for bicycle commuting—students and worker bees alike—is in socially conscious, eco-friendly Cambridge, which even has bike lanes on portions of Mass Ave.

For those who want to bike and ride, bikes are allowed on the Red, Orange, and Blue lines of the T during off-peak hours—weekdays from 10 a.m. to 2 p.m. and then after 7:30 p.m.; and all day on weekends. Bikes are not permitted on any Green line trains, the Mattapan trolley, or at the Park Street and Government Center stations. They are only allowed at Downtown Crossing station if you are transferring. As for the commuter rail, you may bring your bike on any train any time outside of rush hour.

Bikes are allowed on all MBTA boats and ferries at all times. And the crosstown buses have bike racks on their front available for use at all times, but ask the driver for help.

When you're biking, safety should be a concern, particularly in brazen Boston. Be a defensive rider and wear protective gear, especially a helmet.

The local group, **Caravan for Commuters**, offers good information and specifics on why and how you should bike to work and it has a list of places where you can park your bike in downtown Boston. Go to www.commute.com/bicycle_walk.html for details. For more information on biking to work or biking for leisure, check the **Sports and Recreation** chapter, or try one of the following:

- **Massachusetts Bicycle Coalition**, www.massbike.org, 617-542-2543
- **MassHighway**, www.state.ma.us/mhd, 617-973-7329 for information on bicycle programs or 617-973-7512 for information on roadway and bridge design to accommodate cyclists.
- **Cambridge Bicycle-Pedestrian Program**, www.ci.cambridge.ma.us
- **League of American Bicyclists**, www.bikeleague.org
- **FHA Bicycle and Pedestrian Program**, www.fhwa.dot.gov/environment/bikeped/index.htm

BY PUBLIC TRANSPORTATION
MBTA

The **Massachusetts Bay Transit Authority** (**MBTA**) is Boston's public transportation system, and the first subway system in North America. Construction on the subway line began on March 28, 1895 and three years later, on September 1, 1897, the first train carried passengers three-fifths of a mile from Tremont to Boylston streets. The subway is called the "T"—never the subway—and it has four train lines. The MBTA (which is also frequently referred to as the T), also operates the bus system, commuter trains, and some commuter boats.

When you first begin riding the T you have to remember just two things: inbound and outbound. Inbound always means going toward downtown Boston (no matter which direction that might be) and outbound always means going away from downtown Boston. What constitutes "downtown Boston" varies, so pay attention to the signs at any given station. One of the first things you should do is familiarize yourself with an MBTA map that shows all the T routes. Most of the large stations have free bus schedules as well as T maps for sale. Contact the MBTA with questions and clarifications about schedules, fares, passes, etc.: www.mbta.com, 617-222-3200.

TRANSPORTATION

The **four rapid transit train lines** that service the Boston area all intersect downtown and you can transfer between them where they intersect at no extra charge. The lines are known by their colors: blue, orange, red, and green. Each of the lines is above ground for part of its route, but the Green Line is above ground for most of its route. There are even parts where it is elevated above the street. The Green Line trains are much different than the others—they look like streetcars, whereas the Blue, Red, and Orange lines look like subway trains. You'll probably also hear tell about the new Silver Line, but don't be confused. At least as yet, the **Silver Line** is just a bus system that the MBTA is trying to convince Bostonians is part of the subway. It costs 90 cents to ride and you can use a bus pass on it. If it looks like a bus and runs like a bus…

- The **Blue Line**, so named because it goes under the ocean, serves mainly the outlying areas in Revere and East Boston. Most importantly, the Blue Line goes to Logan Airport.
- The **Orange Line** got its name because when it was opened it served Orange Way (now named Washington Street). It begins at the Malden/Melrose border and has stops in Everett, Somerville, and Charlestown before it hits central Boston, where it serves the following neighborhoods: Downtown Crossing, South End, Chinatown/Theater District, Roxbury, JP and the border of Roslindale.
- Named after the crimson of Harvard University where it has a stop, the **Red Line** is the main source of public transit for Cambridge, with a stop on the border of Arlington and one in Davis Square, Somerville. It crosses over the Charles River to stop at Beacon Hill, South Station, and South Boston. There are actually two separate Red Line routes that diverge after the JFK/UMASS stop: Ashmont and Braintree. Ashmont trains continue on through Dorchester and connect up to the Mattapan line that includes Milton. Braintree trains go through Quincy.
- The **Green Line**, which got its name for connecting points along the Emerald Necklace, actually has four different routes that split off at Copley: the "E" trains run through Boston down Huntington Avenue to Heath Street; the "B" trains run down Comm Ave. through Allston-Brighton to Boston College; the "C" trains run along Beacon Street through Brookline to Cleveland Circle; and the "D" trains run through Brookline and Newton to Riverside.

The **cost** of riding the T is very reasonable. A ride on nearly all T trains is $1.25, or one T token, although, depending on the line and where you are boarding, rates can go as high as $3 a ride, or sometimes the ride is free. If you get to a station with a turnstile, you must use a token to get in. Some underground (Green Line) stations don't have turnstiles, as is the case with Green Line surface (street level) stops. In this case, you pay on the train, with *exact change* and *not* paper money, or you can use a token or a pass. You will likely see people folding up dollar bills and stuffing them into a hole in the driver's token box, but it is up to the individual driver's discretion whether to permit it—officially it is not allowed. The T offers special **discounts** for seniors, youths, and passengers with disabilities. Contact the MBTA by phone or online for fare specifics: www.mbta.com, 617-222-3200. Special needs passengers, refer to the **Getting Around** section of the **Helpful Services** chapter.

Monthly passes are available for purchase at a few of the stations, such as Back Bay, South Station, and Government Center during the first and last five days of the month. You can also get them at North Station throughout the month. Stations that sell passes are listed on the MBTA's web site. A basic subway pass is $44, a combo (subway + bus) is $71, or a combo-plus (subway, bus, and ferry) is $79. Passes are available for other zones and for ferry service as well. Check with the MBTA for specifics. Weekly passes, visitor passes, and student passes also are available.

Bikes and pets are permitted on the T, although there are some restrictions. Of course, service animals are allowed on all trains at all times. Non-service dogs are allowed on all trains during non-rush hour periods, although technically this is at the driver's discretion. Your dog must be leashed, and it may not annoy other passengers or take up a seat. Bikes are allowed on Red, Orange, and Blue line trains during non-peak hours (10 a.m. to 2 p.m. and after 7:30 p.m. on weekdays and at any time on the weekends). They are never allowed, however, on the Green Line, nor may you bring them to the Park Street or Government Center stations. They are allowed at Downtown Crossing only if you are changing trains.

T trains run from 5 a.m. to 1 a.m. **Night Owl** bus service fills the gap, somewhat. It operates on Fridays and Saturdays until 2:30 a.m. along bus routes 1N, 28N, 57N, 66N, and 111N, and on bus routes that run along the T routes. Night Owl bus fare ranges from $1.50 to $4 (no paper money please), and passes are not valid on Night Owl buses.

For questions about the T, visit www.mbta.com, or call:
- **MBTA Main Switchboard**, 617-222-5000
- **Travel Information Line**, 617-222-3200 or 800-392-6100; TTY 617-222-5146
- **Customer Relations**, 617-222-5215
- **Monthly Pass Program**, 617-222-5218
- **Lost & Found**, 617-222-5000
- **Senior Citizens/Transportation Access Passes**, 617-222-5976, TTY 617-222-5854
- **The Ride**, 617-222-5123
- **Lift Bus Info & Reservations**, 800-LIFT-BUS; TTY 617-222-5854
- **MBTA Police**, 617-222-1212 (emergency), 617-222-1000 (business)

BY BUS

The MBTA runs over 170 bus routes, including three cross town buses, and several express buses. Most of them are "feeder service" routes that link neighborhoods and suburbs to train stations, but there are a few routes that service the city. Bus stops are marked by signs with the "T" logo. (Although the city buses are run by the T, riding the T specifically means the Red, Orange, Blue and Green Line trains.) Most buses, with the exception of a few express ones and those "zoned local" cost 90 cents/ride and you can get transfers valid for two hours from the time of issue. In some situations you can even get bus to T transfers. Check with MBTA (see above) for more information.

Monthly bus passes are available for $31. The same sales information as for regular T passes applies. A combination subway bus pass costs $71.

BY COMMUTER RAIL

The commuter rail, shown in purple on MBTA maps, runs from downtown Boston to the suburbs of Eastern Massachusetts—in some cases as far as 60 miles away, going west to Worcester, north to Newburyport, and south all the way into Providence, Rhode Island. All commuter rail stations have parking, except for the following: Ayer, Belmont, Endicott, Foxboro, Greenwood, Hastings, Mishawum, Morton Street, Natick, Newtonville, Plimptonville, Prides Crossing, Porter, Silver Hill, Uphams Corner, Waverly, West Newton, Wilmington, Windsor Gardens, and Yawkey. Its 13 lines are run by the T, and all trains leave out of either North or South Station in Boston, although there are sometimes stops at Back Bay or Porter Square. Fares are slightly more expensive than the T with a maximum fare of $5.75. The last ride usually leaves the station around midnight. Note: the Foxboro station is only open during events (concerts and Patriots games) at Gillette Stadium. Contact the MBTA, 617-222-3200, for additional commuter rail information.

BY FERRY

Because of the coastline and heavy traffic, depending on where you live, transportation via water may be a quicker and more efficient way to travel. The MBTA runs commuter ferries to downtown Boston (by the Aquarium at Longwharf and by North Station at Lovejoy Wharf) from South Boston, Chelsea, Charlestown, Hingham, Hull and Quincy. And the Airport Water Shuttle sure beats the Callahan/Sumner tunnels as a way to get to Logan Airport when the weather's good and the traffic's not. The only time commuting by sea around Boston Harbor isn't so great is during the cold snaps in the winter when service is sometimes not possible due to ice in the harbor. Fortunately, it doesn't get that cold here all that often.

The following are the commuter **ferry routes run by the MBTA**. With the exception of the Long Wharf-Quincy-Hull ride, you can bring your bike on at no charge. Monthly passes are available. They all have ample weekday service; ferries out of Long Wharf run on weekends and holidays as well. For more information, contact the MBTA at 617-222-3200, or www.mbta.com and click on "boats."

- **Long Wharf (by the Aquarium)-Charlestown Navy Yard**
- **Long Wharf-Fore River Shipyard, Quincy-Pemberton Point, Hull**
- **Lovejoy Wharf (at North Station)-Charlestown Navy Yard**
- **Lovejoy Wharf-US Federal Courthouse (Fan Pier)-World Trade Center**
- **Rowes Wharf (downtown waterfront)-Hewitt's Cove, Hingham Shipyard**

To **commute via water from Logan Airport**, you have two options: Massport and Harbor Express. **Harbor Express**, www.harborexpress.com, 617-222-6999, runs a ferry route between Logan, Long Wharf, and Quincy Shipyard. It costs $12 one way. **Massport**, 617-428-2800, www.massport.com, runs its **Airport Water Shuttle** between Logan and Rowes Wharf and the US Federal Courthouse on weekdays between 7 a.m. and 6 p.m. It costs $10 one way, $17 round trip. Children under 12 ride for free.

If you're in a hurry, you can take a water taxi that services Boston Harbor. **City Water Taxi**, www.citywatertaxi.com, 617-422-0392, runs daily, from 7 a.m. to 10 p.m., Monday-Saturday, and until 8 p.m. on Sundays. The taxi costs $10 per person and will make the following stops at your request: Logan Airport (Harborside Hyatt), Long Wharf Marriott at Christopher Columbus Park, FleetBoston Pavilion, World Trade Center/Seaport Hotel, Anthony's Pier 4, Museum Wharf/Congress Street, USS Constitution Fan Pier/US Federal Courthouse, Barking Crab Restaurant, Marriott Residence Inn, Sargent's Wharf, Burrough's Wharf, and North Station/Fleet Center. Limited stops in the winter.

In the summer there are boats to the Boston Harbor Islands, Provincetown, Martha's Vineyard, and Nantucket that leave from Boston or Cape Cod, depending.

- **Bay State Cruise Company**, 617-748-1428, www.baystatecruises.com; runs ferries to Provincetown from the World Trade Center in Boston. Regular ferry, $29 round trip; Express ferry, $55 round trip.

TRANSPORTATION

- **Boston Harbor Cruises**, 617-227-4321, www.bostonharbor cruises.com, runs ferries to Provincetown (MacMillan Wharf) and the Boston Harbor Islands from Long Wharf in Boston, and between the Harbor Islands and Hingham. $8 adults, $7 seniors, $6 kids
- **Capt. John Boats**, 508-747-2400 or 800-242-2469, www.province-townferry.com; express ferry between Plymouth and Provincetown. $30 round trip for adults.
- **Hy-Line Cruises**, 508-778-2600 or 800-492-8082, www.hylinecruises.com, runs ferries to Nantucket and Martha's Vineyard from Hyannis, and between Nantucket and Martha's Vineyard. $27 round trip, bikes $10 extra.
- **Island Queen**, 508-548-4800, www.islandqueen.com, runs the ferry between Falmouth (Inner Harbor) and Martha's Vineyard (Oak Bluffs). No vehicles allowed on this one, but pets and bikes okay. $10 round trip; bikes $6 extra.
- **Steamship Authority**, 508-477-8600, runs ferries from Woods Hole to both Oak Bluffs and Vineyard Haven in Martha's Vineyard, from New Bedford to Martha's Vineyard, and Hyannis to Nantucket. Fares vary.

AMTRAK

Trains are a favored mode of travel for Bostonians heading to New York City and sometimes Washington, D.C. With stations right in downtown Boston and no need to drive to the airport or check in an hour and a half before a flight, it can be faster to go by train to New York or D.C. than by plane. Amtrak is also convenient for trips to Connecticut, Rhode Island, Philadelphia, Maryland, Maine, or Canada. In addition, Amtrak's **Acela** is a luxury high-speed train that runs along the Northeast corridor route, between Boston, New York City, and Washington D.C. Acela Express trains travel at speeds up to 150 m.p.h., getting you to New York City in under four hours, and to D.C. in seven. Not only are the trains faster, but they're nicer too—you can plug in your lap top, spread out at a conference table, or retreat to the quiet car. Of course, you pay for the faster service, but if you've got to make the trip and prefer not to fly, it's a comfortable way to go.

You can board **Amtrak** trains at four metro Boston stations: **Back Bay**, 145 Dartmouth Street, **South Station**, Atlantic Avenue and Summer Street, **North Station**, 135 Causeway Street at Canal Street, or **Route 128**, 50 University Avenue in Westwood. South Station is the big central terminus. Contact Amtrak, 800-USA-RAIL, www.amtrak.com, for more information.

NATIONAL/REGIONAL BUS SERVICE

The national bus line **Greyhound**, 800-231-2222 or 617-526-1800, www.greyhound.com, provides service in and around Boston, but is by no means the only option. In Boston, the South Station, 700 Atlantic Avenue, is where you board Greyhound buses as well as regional lines, including **Peter Pan Bus Lines**. Contact Peter Pan at 800-343-9999 or 413-781-3320, www.peterpanbus.com, for service to Framingham, Lowell, Newton, Palmer, Worcester, Springfield, Sturbridge, Western Massachusetts (Amherst, Lee, Lenox, Northampton, Pittsfield), Connecticut, Delaware, Maryland, New York, New Hampshire, New Jersey, and Pennsylvania. More **Regional bus lines** can be found in the Yellow Pages under "Bus." For lists and contact information of bus companies that serve the suburbs outside Boston, try the **Caravan for Commuters** web site at www.commute.com/buses.html#AmEaglebus.

Greyhound and Peter Pan bus lines run each hour from South Station to the Port Authority in **New York City**, and they are popular—not only because they are much cheaper than the train or plane, but because they are fast, often getting to New York in less time than the train. Note: some Greyhound and Peter Pan buses leave earlier than their scheduled times—yes earlier—seemingly without regard for whether or not they are full or if there are passengers that might arrive at the last minute.

If you'd like to save money and don't mind budget travel, try the **Fung Wah** or "Chinatown" bus, that runs from Chinatown in Boston to Chinatown in New York. The operation is very low-frills (you buy your ticket from someone at a table at 68 Beach Street in Chinatown), but by all accounts they get rave reviews. It's cheap—only $20 round trip—and runs hourly. For more information, visit www.fungwahbus.com or call 617-338-1163.

BY AIR

As the fish swims, **Boston Logan International Airport** is only two miles from downtown Boston. However, during those times that you're stuck in the Callahan Tunnel it might as well be 200. Alternatively, the Ted Williams Tunnel was recently opened to private vehicles (it used to be just commercial), and its traffic isn't as bad as the Sumner or Callahan tunnels. Although during rush hour, Sunday afternoons, or holidays any route will be congested.

If you want to investigate alternate means of getting to Logan, there are plenty of other options. The Blue Line goes to Airport Station. Although, unlike at other airports, such as O'Hare or Heathrow, where the El and Tube go right to the actual terminals, once you get to Logan on the Blue Line you'll have to pick up a (free) Massport shuttle-bus to the terminals. It will add a few minutes to your trip, more during times of heavy traffic, so plan accordingly. For persons with disabilities, Logan offers an inter-terminal accessible van. Call 617-561-1769 with questions. Buses and shuttle vans to and from Logan are also an option (see below). The Airport Water Shuttle, 617-428-2800, www.massport.com, leaves from Rowes Wharf and lands at the airport ferry dock where you can catch a different free Massport shuttle bus. The water shuttle runs every fifteen minutes on weekdays and every half-hour on weekends and holidays. Additional information about Logan International Airport, including tips on getting to and from the airport, can be found at www.massport.com/logan or call 800-23-LOGAN.

The following list details major airlines with service to/from Logan Airport. They're listed by terminal, although that is subject to change pending the completion of construction projects at the airport.

TERMINAL B
- **Alaska Airlines**, 800-252-7522, www.alaskaair.com
- **America West**, 800-235-9292, www.americawest.com
- **American** (except int'l arrivals) and **American Eagle**, 800-433-7300, www.aa.com
- **ATA: American Trans Air**, 800-225-2995, www.ata.com
- **Delta Shuttle**, 800-221-1212 , www.delta.com
- **Qantas**, 800-227-4500, www.qantas.com.au
- **US Airways**, **US Air Shuttle**, **US Air Express**, 800-428-4322, www.usairways.com

TERMINAL C
- **Air Canada** (Except Halifax arrivals), 888-247-2262, www.air canada.ca
- **Air France** (departures only), 800-237-2747, www.airfrance.com
- **Air Jamaica** (departures only), 800-523-3515, www.airjamaica.com
- **Cape Air**, 800-352-0714, www.flycapeair.com
- **Continental**, 800-525-0280, www.continental.com
- **Delta Air Lines**, 800-221-1212, www.delta.com
- **Delta Express**, 800-325-5205, www.delta.com
- **Midwest**, 800-452-2022, www.midwestexpress.com
- **Song**, 800-221-1212, www.flysong.com
- **Swiss** (departures only), 877-359-7947, www.swiss.com
- **United**, 800-241-6522, www.ual.com

TERMINAL D
- **Air Tran**, 800-247-8726, www.airtran.com

- **Alitalia** (departures only), 800-223-5730, www.alitalia.it
- **Charters** (may use other terminals)

TERMINAL E (INTERNATIONAL TERMINAL)
- **Aer Lingus**, 800-474-7424, www.aerlingus.ie
- **Air Canada** (Halifax arrivals only), 888-247-2262, www.aircanada.ca
- **Air France**, 800-237-2747, www.airfrance.com
- **Air Jamaica**, 800-523-3515, www.airjamaica.com
- **Alitalia**, 800-223-5730, www.alitalia.it
- **American**, 800-433-7300, www.aa.com
- **British Airways**, 800-247-9297, www.british-airways.com
- **Delta Air Lines** 800-221-1212, www.delta.com
- **Icelandair**, 800-223-5500, www.icelandair.com
- **KLM**, 800-374-7747, www.klm.com
- **Lufthansa**, 800-645-3880, www.lufthansa.com
- **Northwest**, 800-225-2525, www.nwa.com
- **Swiss**, 877-359-7947, www.swiss.com
- **TACA**, 800-535-8780, www.taca.com
- **Virgin Atlantic**, 800-862-8621, www.fly.virgin.com

One major airline that does not fly into Logan is **Southwest Airlines**, www.southwest.com, 800-I-FLY-SWA, which goes instead to nearby Manchester, NH, and to Providence, RI, both about an hour away, north and south respectively. **Manchester Airport**, 603-624-6539, www.fly-manchester.com, and **T.F. Green Airport** in Providence, 888-268-7222 or 401-737-8222, www.tfgreen.com, are popular alternatives to Logan and worth investigating for cheaper fares. You can even get a bus to them. A slightly closer alternative to Logan is **Hanscom Field**, 781-869-8000, www.massport.com in Bedford, which hosts US Airways flights.

PARKING AT LOGAN
Since 9/11, parking in front of airport terminals is prohibited. You may quickly drop off a passenger, but otherwise you'll need to put your car in a lot. **Short-** and **long-term parking** for terminals B, C, D, and E is available in the Central Parking Lot, with access to all the terminals via a pedestrian bridge on level four. Parking rates are as follows: 0 to 30 minutes, $2; 31 minutes to one hour, $5; one to one-and-a-half hours, $8; one-and-a-half hours to two hours, $11; two to three hours, $14; three to four hours, $17; four to seven hours, $20; seven to 24 hours, $22. There is no weekly rate. Also, if you're going to Terminal B, their lot is open, but your car is subject to a security search. The rates are about the same for Central Parking. For **long term parking** only, try the Economy Lot: $16/day,

weekly rate of $80. A shuttle will bring you from this lot to any of the terminals. Credit cards are accepted at all parking facilities.

AIRPORT BUS SERVICE
The MBTA runs three routes, #448, #459, and CT3, to Logan. Private bus companies, including Bonanza, Plymouth & Brockton Bus Lines, Concord Trailways, C&J Trailways, and Vermont Transit, also provide service to Logan (see the Yellow Pages under "Bus"). In addition, there are **shared shuttle vans**:
- **Boston Beats Limo**, 617-267-5856, service to Boston hotels.
- **Knights Airport Limousine Service**, 800-822-5456, www.knights airportlimo.com, service to metro-west (Ashland, Auburn, Framingham, Granton, Holden, Hopkinton, Hudson, Leicester, Marlboro, Milford, Milbury, Natick, Northboro, Northbridge, Paxton, Shrewsbury, Southboro, Sutton, West Boylston, Westboro, Worcester).
- **Logan Express**, 800-23-LOGAN, www.massport.com, for park-and-ride type service between Logan and Braintree, Framingham, Peabody, and Woburn.
- **Logan/Boston Hotel Shuttle**, 617-561-9500, www.loganhotel shuttle.com, service to Boston hotels.

FLIGHT DELAYS
Information about flight delays can be checked online on your airline's web site, or at www.fly.faa.gov. Similarly, the site www.flightarrivals.com offers real-time arrival, departure, and delay details for commercial flights.

CONSUMER COMPLAINTS—AIRLINES
To register a complaint against an airline, the Department of Transportation is the place to call or write: 202-366-2220, Aviation Consumer Protection Division, C-75 Room 4107, 400 7th Street SW, Washington, D.C. 20590.

TEMPORARY LODGINGS

Boston, a major tourist destination for people from around the globe, a financial center, and host to dozens of colleges and universities has an array of temporary lodgings. Options run the gamut from hostels to motels to classic, ornate New England hotels.

For newcomers who need a temporary place to stay while looking for a permanent home, you may be able to take advantage of the transience of the area's student population. Although there is a glut of colleges and universities, most do not offer housing to non-students during the summer, however, many students live off campus and, as such, need to sublet their year-long leases during the summer months.

If you are going to stay at a hotel (as opposed to taking a short-term rental), keep in mind that room rates vary by the season. In summer, prices rise along with the temperatures, but there is also a rate hike in the fall during leaf-peeping time. Local conventions will also affect room availability and pricing.

The following list of places to stay is just a glimpse of the full bevy of lodgings available in Boston and its environs. For a more complete listing, look in the Yellow Pages, pick up an AAA travel guide (free to members), or check with the **Massachusetts Lodging Association**, www.masslodging.com, 617-720-1776.

Once you've found the hotel, motel, inn, or other option that suits your fancy, you've got to decide how you want to reserve your room. Do you want to call and reserve directly or go through a reservation service? If you contact the hotel directly, don't forget to ask about packages and weekend specials. Here are a few reservation services and online travel agents that can assist you with finding a place to stay:

- **BizTravel**, www.biztravel.com
- **Central Reservation Services**, www.reservation-services.com, 800-548-3311
- **Expedia**, www.expedia.com, 800-397-3342

- **Hotels.com**, www.hotels.com, 800-364-0501
- **Hotwire.com**, www.hotwire.com, 888-362-1234
- **Orbitz**, www.orbitz.com
- **Priceline.com**, www.priceline.com
- **Quickbook**, www.quickbook.com, 800-789-9887

A word of advice: when making reservations through any discount site it is always wise to ask about their cancellation policy and if the rate quoted includes the hotel tax, which in Boston is 12.5% per day. Also, some services require a full payment when making the reservation.

LUXURY HOTELS

The following luxury accommodations begin at $250 and go up from there. Rates vary greatly based on availability and season.

- **Boston Harbor Hotel**, 70 Rowes Wharf, Boston, 800-752-7077, www.bhh.com; spa resort with gorgeous views of the harbor and the city.
- **Boston Park Plaza Hotel & Towers**, 64 Arlington Street, Boston, 617-426-2000, www.bostonparkplaza.com
- **Charles Hotel**, 1 Bennett Street (Harvard Square), Cambridge, 617-864-1200 or 800-882-1818, www.charleshotel.com
- **Fairmont Copley Plaza**, 138 St. James Avenue, Boston, 888-880-8801, www.fairmont.com
- **Fifteen Beacon**, 15 Beacon Street, Boston, 617-670-1500
- **Four Seasons Hotel**, 200 Boylston Street, 617-338-4400, www.fourseasons.com/boston; prices range from $425 to $815 depending on the suite and view. Ask about weekend specials.
- **The Lenox Hotel**, 710 Boylston Street, Boston, 888-767-9901, www.lenoxhotel.com
- **Nine Zero Hotel**, 90 Tremont Street, Boston, 888-462-7296, www.ninezerohotel.com
- **Omni Parker House**, 60 School Street, Boston, 617-227-8600, www.omnihotels.com
- **Ritz-Carlton**, 15 Arlington Street, Boston, 617-536-5700, www.ritzcarlton.com/hotels/boston/; **Ritz Carlton Boston Common**, 10 Avery Street, 617-574-7100, www.ritzcarlton.com/hotels/boston_common

MIDDLE-RANGE HOTELS

The following hotels range between about $100 and $200 nightly. Many are national chains.

- **Best Western**, 800-780-7234, www.bestwestern.com; three in Boston, one in Cambridge, and 12 in the greater Boston area.

- **Doubletree Hotels & Guest Suites**, 800-222-TREE; three in Boston, three in Cambridge (the Hotel @ MIT, the Inn at Harvard, and the Harvard Square Hotel), and one in Waltham.
- **Embassy Suites Hotel Boston at Logan Airport**, 207 Porter Street, Boston, 617-567-5000, www.embassysuites.com
- **Hilton**, 800-774-1500, www.hilton.com; one in the Back Bay, one at Logan Airport, and one in Dedham.
- **Holiday Inn Government Center**, 5 Blossom Street, 617-742-7630
- **Hyatt Hotels & Resorts**, www.hyatt.com: Hyatt Harborside at Logan Airport, 617-568-1234, and Hyatt Regency in Cambridge, 617-492-1234
- **Marriott Hotels/Residence Inns**, 888-236-2427, www.marriott.com; four in Boston (Long Wharf, Copley, Custom House, and Tudor Wharf), two in Cambridge, one in Brookline, and over 30 in the surrounding suburbs.
- **Radisson Hotels & Resorts**, www.radisson.com: Radisson Hotel Boston, 617-482-1800, Radisson Hotel Cambridge, 617-492-7777; six in the greater Boston area.
- **Royal Sonesta Hotel**, 5 Cambridge Parkway, Cambridge, 617-806-4200, www.sonesta.com
- **Seaport Hotel & World Trade Center**, 1 Seaport Lane, South Boston, 877-SEAPORT, www.seaporthotel.com
- **Sheraton Hotels & Resorts**, 888-625-5144, www.starwood.com/sheraton; one in Boston (Sheraton Boston), one in Cambridge (Sheraton Commander), and seven in the suburbs.
- **Westin Hotels**, www.starwood.com/westin: **Westin Copley Place**, 10 Huntington Avenue, 617-262-9600; **Westin Waltham-Boston**, 70 Third Avenue, Waltham, 781-290-5600
- **Wyndham Hotels & Resorts**, 800-WYNDHAM, www.wyndham.com; two in Boston (including The Tremont Boston, a historic hotel), and six in the greater Boston area.

INEXPENSIVE HOTELS

If budget matters more than ambiance, check one of the following; prices range between $60 to $150 per night:

- **Home Suites Inn**, 455 Totten Pond Road, Waltham, 800-424-4021
- **Best Western Terrace Motor Lodge**, 1650 Comm Ave., Brighton, 617-566-6260
- **Choice Hotels**: Sleep Inn, Comfort Inn, Quality Inn, Clarion, Rodeway, MainStay, and Econo Lodge, 800-424-6423, www.choicehotels.com
- **Constitution Inn**, 150 Second Avenue, Charlestown Navy Yard, 617-241-8400, www.constitutioninn.com; reduced rates for military personnel and AAA members.

- **Days Inn**, 800-329-7466, www.daysinn.com; two in Allston/Brighton and one near Logan International.
- **Hampton Inn**, 800-HAMPTON, www.hamptoninn.com; one in Cambridge and seven more throughout the metro area.
- **Red Roof Inn**, 800-RED-ROOF, www.redroof.com; five in the greater Boston area.

EXTENDED STAY HOTELS

If your stay will be longer than a week, you may prefer an extended stay option, where the rooms are more like small furnished apartments than traditional hotels—with kitchenettes, refrigerators, and onsite laundry. You can expect to pay between $80 and $170 per night. Note: you're most likely to find these in the suburbs, rather than the city.

- **Extended Stay America**, 800-EXT-STAY, www.exstay.com; locations in Braintree, and Danvers.
- **Homewood Suites**, 800-CALL-HOME, www.homewoodsuites.com; locations in Peabody and Billerica.
- **Residence Inn by Marriott**, 800-331-3131, www.residenceinn.com; locations in Boston, Cambridge, and throughout the greater Boston area.

SHORT-TERM LEASES/CORPORATE HOUSING

A short-term lease or corporate apartment might be a good option, depending on what your situation is. Accommodations are studios, one-bedrooms, and two-bedrooms. Depending on the establishment, rates range from about $300 per week for a studio to $1,400 per week for a two-bedroom. There may be a discount if you commit to a month's stay.

- **AAA Corporate Rentals**, 120 Milk Street, Boston, 617-357-6900, www.furnishedapt.com; studios available. Throughout Boston, including Back Bay, Beacon Hill, North End, Financial District, and Waterfront; outside of Boston in Charlestown and South End.
- **Agency Suites**, 617-536-1302, www.463beacon.com
- **Apartment Resources**, 94 Adams Street, Waltham, 781-893-1130; studios available.
- **Baron Associates**, 229 Berkeley Street, Boston, 617-437-0337, www.gis.net/~baron studios available.
- **Boston Realty Associates**, 1102 Comm Ave., 617-277-5100; upscale apartment buildings in some of Boston's best neighborhoods. Studios available. Three- to four-month "leases."
- **J. E. Furnished Apartments**, 617-479-4110, http://jefurnished apartments.com

- **Oakwood Corporate Housing** also has options for Boston, 800-888-0808, www.oakwood.com.
- **Short-Term Solutions**, 247 Newbury Street, Boston, 617-247-1199, www.short-term.com; luxury short-term furnished apartments.

BED & BREAKFASTS

B&Bs are charming and homey. Of course, they're more popular in the country, but there are some in the city too. And in Boston they can have a colonial or Victorian feel. Here are a few:
- **Bed & Breakfast Agency of Boston**, 617-720-3540 and 800-248-9262, www.boston-bnbagency.com; furnished apartment suites with locations throughout the city.
- **Bed & Breakfast Inns Online**, http://bbonline.com/ma/boston.html; lists B&Bs throughout the Boston area. Includes pictures and descriptions.
- **Bed & Breakfast International**, www.ibbp.com; brief descriptions, pictures, and reservation information on their web site, each inspected by a B&B International representative for quality assurance.

HOSTELS/YMCAS

Hostels are *the* low-budget travel lodging of choice among students. They offer no frills—with communal bunk rooms, mandatory out-of-room times, and curfews—but you can't beat the price; ditto for residence YMCAs and YWCAs. Here are a few resources in the Boston area. For more options, go to www.hostels.com, www.ymca.com and www.ywca.org.
- **Beantown Hostel**, 222 Friend Street, Boston, 617-723-0800; in the North Station area.
- **Hostelling International Boston**, 12 Hemenway Street, Boston, 617-536-9455, www.bostonhostel.org; if you are a member of Hostelling International, you can stay here for $32 to $25 a night for a bed in a dorm room or between $69 and $89 nightly for a private room. Without a membership card, your price goes up by $3. (See below for their summer only accommodations.)
- **Irish Embassy International Tourist Backpackers Hostel**, 232 Friend Street, Boston, 617-973-4841; in the North Station area; recently renovated.
- **YMCA of Greater Boston**, 316 Huntington Avenue, 617-536-7800; a single costs $45 per night without a bath. Men only from September to June.

- **YWCA Boston/Berkeley Residence**, 40 Berkeley Street, Boston, 617-375-2524, www.ywcaboston.org; $56 per night for a single; $86 per night for a double; $99 per night for a triple. Breakfast is included.

SUMMER ONLY

In Boston, it is not common practice for the colleges and universities to rent out dorm rooms and student housing during the off season. But, since many students live in off-campus housing, you can likely find a summer sublet. Also, there is one summer-only youth hostel: **Hostelling International Boston at Fenway**, 575 Comm Ave., Boston, 617-267-8599, www.bostonhostel.org/fenway; open from June to August.

ACCESSIBLE ACCOMMODATIONS

Perhaps because of its compact size and good public transit system, Boston is a very disabled-friendly city. Hotels are required to provide handicap-accessible rooms, the sidewalks have ramps, and handicap parking spaces are found even in the tightest parts of town, kept open by parking meter attendants armed with high ticket fines.

A number of hotel chains in Boston have a particular reputation for offering services for people with disabilities: **Hilton Hotels** (800-774-1500, TTY 800-368-1133, www.hilton.com), **Hyatt Hotels** (800-532-1496, TTY 800-228-9548, www.hyatt.com), **Sheraton Hotels** (800-325-3535, TTY 800-325-1717, www.starwood.com/sheraton), and **Marriott Hotels** (800-228-92920, TTY 800-228-7014, www.marriott.com). Because accommodations can vary from community to community, and from hotel to hotel, you should call ahead and check with the particular hotel you're planning your stay with to discuss your specific needs and their provisions. Federal law requires a hotel to guarantee reservations for handicapped-accessible rooms, but only if it does so for regular rooms.

Other good resources with information about accessible accommodations include the **Massachusetts Office on Disability**, 617-727-7440, TTY 800-322-2020, www.state.ma.us/mod; **Access Tours**, www.accesstours.org, 800-929-4811, which puts together tour packages; and **Society for Accessible Travel & Hospitality**, 212-447-7284, www.sath.org, offers advice and publishes a magazine for disabled travelers called *Open World*. For more information on services for people with disabilities, check the **Helpful Services** chapter of this book.

QUICK GETAWAYS

HAVING THE COUNTRYSIDE OF NEW ENGLAND RIGHT AT YOUR doorstep is one of the best perks of living in Boston. Whether it's heading off in the summer for family camping or an oceanside hamlet, in the fall for a countryside color tour, a wintertime ski trip, or a spring maple fest, Bostonians are set for quick getaways. Within Massachusetts, historical tours and sites abound, and day trips to Salem and Cape Ann on the north shore or perhaps Plymouth and New Bedford to the south are easy. The Berkshires, Cape Cod, Nantucket, and Martha's Vineyard are popular as well.

MASSACHUSETTS

- **Salem** is chock full of sights commemorating the Puritans who settled there and, of course, the infamous witch trials of 1692. It's about 45 minutes north of the city by car and the commuter rail can take you there as well. Sites and museums include the Witch History Museum, the Salem Maritime National Historic Site (includes Custom and Derby houses), the House of Seven Gables (as in Nathaniel Hawthorne), the New England Pirate Museum, Pioneer Village, and Pickering Wharf. For more information and links to many of the sites, visit Salem's online city guide: www.salemweb.com.
- Also on the north shore is **Cape Ann**, which includes the communities of Gloucester, Rockport, Essex, and Manchester-by-the-Sea. Whereas a trip to Salem is all about history, a trip to Cape Ann is all about the Atlantic. You can easily drive and be there in less than an hour, or take the commuter rail, with stops in Manchester and Rockport, and two in Gloucester. Things to see include the Cape Ann Historical Museum and Hammond Castle (a stone replica of a medieval castle). Many go to Woodman's for famous fried clams. Popular beaches in Gloucester

include Wingaersheek, Good Harbor, Niles, and Half Moon; in Manchester there is Singing Beach (named for the sand's sound) and White Beach; and in Rockport, Front, Back, Long, Old Garden, Cape Hedge, and Pebble beaches. Whale watches are also a big draw. For theater, head to the Gloucester Stage Company (run by playwright-in-residence Israel Horovitz), and for local art, check the artists' colony in Rockport or the Rocky Neck colony in Gloucester. For more information, visit www.cape-ann.com.

- American history buffs can head northwest of the city to visit **Lexington**, http://ci.lexington.ma.us, and **Concord**, www.concordnet.org or www.concordma.com. The first battles of the American Revolution were fought in these two towns, and later some of the great New England writers and Transcendentalists made their homes here. Things to see: Lexington Green, Minuteman Statue, Buckman Tavern, Hancock-Clarke House, Munroe Tavern, Museum of our National Heritage, George Abbott Smith Museum, Minute Man National Historic Park, Old North Bridge, Ralph Waldo Emerson House, Walden Pond, Old Manse, Orchard House, Wayside, Thoreau Lyceum, Concord Museum, Fiske House, Hartwell Tavern, Paul Revere Capture Site, and Sleepy Hollow Cemetery.
- **Plymouth** is an easy 40-mile drive south of Boston, down I-93 to Route 3, or by commuter rail. Some things to see and do include visiting Plymouth Rock, the Mayflower II (recreation of the original), and Plimoth Plantation (living history village recreating the original 1627 pilgrim settlement). Also popular are the Plymouth National Wax Museum and the Mayflower Society Museum. Historic houses include the Spooner House, Hedge House, Sparrow House, and Howland House. More contemporary sites are Cranberry World (Ocean Spray bog) and the Children's Museum of Plymouth. Visit http://pilgrims.net/plymouth for further details.
- Curled like a muscle man's flexing arm, **Cape Cod** ("the Cape") draws many lucky souls out of Boston each summer, some for a long weekend, others for the entire season. Cape Cod consists of 65 miles of mostly sandy dunes and beaches, and has always been popular with anyone who has the time and money. Many head to a B&B for a weekend or rent a house for a week or two. Nearest points on the Cape take at least an hour-and-a-half to get to from Boston by car. Heavy traffic will add to your time—which backs up interminably over the bridges (Sagamore and Bourne) on virtually every summer weekend. There are 15 official towns dotting the arm: Barnstable, Bourne, Chatham, Brewster, Dennis, Eastham, Falmouth, Harwich, Mashpee, Orleans, Provincetown, Sandwich, Truro, Wellfleet, and Yarmouth, all of which prove suitable launching points for fun in the sun. Folks come for swim-

ming, sailing, tennis, lighthouse tours, and seafood. Of all the towns, Provincetown, or P-town, at the very tip, is the most distinctive. While it was the first stopping point for the Pilgrims on their way to Plymouth in 1620, today it is the local gay Mecca. Take the ferry from Boston to get there in about two hours. For more information on Cape Cod, go to http://allcapecod.com.

- Usually mentioned in the same breath as Cape Cod are "the islands"—**Martha's Vineyard**, www.mvol.com, and **Nantucket**, www.nantucket.net or www.nantucketonline.com. Both are reached by ferries from Cape Cod. Of the two, the Vineyard is closer, larger, and more relaxed, although that might not be the right word, as both are somewhat exclusive. Martha's Vineyard, you may remember, was a favorite vacation place for President Clinton and his family. Nantucket is about a third the size of the Vineyard and is a little less glam, a little more blue-blood, and not a hair out of place. Both of them have picturesque seaside New England down to an art, with beaches and boats aplenty, and shingled saltbox houses covered with gray, sea-weathered wood. To get to the Vineyard, you can pick up one of several ferries leaving daily from Woods Hole, New Bedford, Hyannis, or Falmouth. To get to Nantucket, the only point of departure in Massachusetts is Hyannis. Depending on which ferry and when you're going, you might want to book ahead—especially if you're thinking of bringing a car. (Or bring your bike and rent a Jeep once you get to the island.) If boats aren't your thing, you can actually fly via Island Airlines, 800-248-779, www.nantucket.net/trans/islandair, or Cape Air/Nantucket Airlines, 800-635-8787, www.flycapeair.com.

- Finally, if you're looking for a more rural, woodsy, quiet place to get away, think about the **Berkshires**. About two hours by car (via the Mass Pike, or a little longer but a lot more scenic via Route 2) west of Boston, the Berkshires are a gentle range of low mountains through the western part of the state, near the border with New York. Amid the hills and forests that dominate the region lie some of the state's proudest colleges—Williams, Smith, Amherst, the University of Massachusetts, and Mt. Holyoke. And although this part of Massachusetts is distinctly un-touristy, Berkshire activities center on the arts and the outdoors—skiing, hiking, boating, fishing, and camping. Other hot spots are the Clark Art Institute (modern art), Williamstown Theatre Festival, Hancock Shaker Village, Berkshire Museum, Tanglewood (summer home of the BSO), Shakespeare & Co. (summer Shakespeare theater), Jacob's Pillow Dance Festival, Berkshire Theater Festival, Norman Rockwell Museum, the Appalachian Trail, the Mohawk Trail, Mount Greylock, Williams College Museum of Art, Arrowhead (Herman Melville's home), Berkshire Botanical Garden, and Bash Bish Falls.

For more information on what to do close to home, try the **Greenspace and Beaches** chapter, as well as the **Massachusetts Office of Travel and Tourism**, 617-973-8500 or 800-227-MASS, www.massvacation.com.

NEW HAMPSHIRE

Anyway you slice it—up Route 95, Route 93, or Route 1—southern New Hampshire is but an hour away from Boston. Yet, while New Hampshire is geographically close, it feels very different. By and large, where Massachusetts is densely settled and urban, New Hampshire is sparse and rural; where Massachusetts is firmly liberal and Democratic, New Hampshire is resolutely conservative and Republican; where Massachusetts has been called "Taxachusetts," New Hampshire is virtually tax-free ... you get the idea. Whether you want to go skiing for the weekend, antiquing, or to spend the summer on a lake, New Hampshire is worth exploring. Its mountain range, the **White Mountains**, provides great opportunities for outdoor adventure—hiking, skiing, camping—and is more rugged than what you'll find in Massachusetts. Mounts Monadnock and Washington are local favorites, despite Mt. Washington's proclivity for harsh weather during the off-season.

- At the southeast tip of the state is **Hampton Beach**, www.hamptonbeach.org, with its loud strip of stores and boardwalk amusements, the antithesis of much of the rest of New Hampshire. However, if you want that crazy Coney Island feel, it is only about an hour by car from Boston.
- Further up, toward the middle of the state, is the more subdued **Lake Winnipesaukee**, www.winnipesaukee.com, the largest body of water in New Hampshire—180 miles around—and surrounded by a jagged and heavily-forested shore. Not a few Bostonians take advantage of its proximity (roughly two and a half hours by car up I-93); many opting to buy a summer cottage in this more affordable environ—not so on the Cape. Each June, Motorcycle Week brings a deluge of enthusiasts here for an annual festival.
- Elsewhere in New Hampshire are the storybook New England towns, the biggest of which are Concord, Portsmouth, and Hanover. **Portsmouth**, www.portsmouthnh.com, is just up the coast off routes 1 and 93, sandwiched in the small wedge of New Hampshire between Maine and Massachusetts that borders the Atlantic. Along with neighboring Exeter, Portsmouth is a quaint and cute relic of colonial New England. Further inland lies the state capital **Concord**, www.ci.concord.nh.us, which is at the junction of routes 93 and 81. Here you can find New Hampshire's historical and political sites: the State House, Museum of New Hampshire History, New Hampshire Historical Society, and the Christa McAuliffe Planetarium. Further northwest, about two-and-a-half hours

from Boston off of I-81 at the border of Vermont, is **Hanover**, www.hanovernh.org, better known as the home of Dartmouth College.

For more, contact the **New Hampshire Division of Travel and Tourism Development**, 800-FUN-IN-NH, www.visitnh.gov.

VERMONT

Vermont, which lies north of the western portion of Massachusetts, is rural, a lovely composite of rolling hills and mountains, dairy farms, white clapboard inns and country stores. With few exceptions, big industry seems to have bypassed this state. Unlike the rest of New England, Vermont seems to do the bulk of its business in the fall, when people come to poke around its backwoods towns, stay at B&B's, and enjoy the fall colors. Winter is also popular, with many coming in to ski in the **Green Mountains**. Summer offerings include alpine slides, horseback riding, and hiking.

To get to Vermont from Boston is at least a two-hour drive, and some parts are more like three or four hours away. **Burlington**, www.discoverburlington.com, is Vermont's biggest city. It's a delightful small city about three-and-a-half hours north of Boston, on the state's western border and situated on Lake Champlain. You will find a small conglomeration of colleges—the University of Vermont, St. Michael's College, Trinity College, and Champlain College.

A few other places to visit in Vermont include: **Bennington**, **Barre** (pronounced "Barry"), **Manchester** (big with shoppers and the après ski crowd), **Middlebury**, **Montpelier** (Vermont's capital, for the State House and Vermont Museum), **Waterbury** (for Ben & Jerry's Ice Cream Factory), **Plymouth Notch**, **St. Johnsbury**, and **Woodstock** (for the Vermont Raptor Center and a 165-foot chasm four miles east of town called Queechee Gorge), and the **Northeast Kingdom** (the northernmost part of the state). If skiing interests you, see the **Sports and Recreation** chapter for contact information. For particulars on visiting Vermont go to www.travel-vermont.com or http://vermont.gov.

MAINE

Once upon a time, Maine, the land of moose and lobster, was actually part of Massachusetts—the "main" part. Not until 1820 did it become a state in its own right. Maine wins the contest for the largest New England state by far; it's bigger than all the rest combined, yet it has the smallest population—many attribute this to the inclement winter weather and rain.

The northern parts of Maine are sparsely populated, and are quite a drive for Bostonians. The desirable vacation spots for many Bostonians are

in the southern, coastal portion of the state, between two to four hours away by car. And unlike Vermont, Maine is mostly a summer destination.
- Maine's capital is **Augusta**, but there is much more to see and do in the far bigger **Portland**, www.portlandmaine.com, population of 65,000, about one hour away. Portland is a laid-back coastal town, with circa-1860 red brick streets and salty sea-air; reminiscent of a (very) wee Seattle. It's a little more than two hours from Boston via Route 1 or I-95.
- About 30 minutes north of Portland is **Freeport**, www.freeport usa.com, an aesthetically-pleasing center of commercial chain store outlets, including the L.L. Bean store, which is open 24/7. Many families make an annual pilgrimage to Freeport to outfit everyone for the year. There are also factory outlets in **Kittery**, www.thekitteryoutlets.com, which is considerably closer to Boston, at Maine's southernmost tip.
- Elsewhere in Maine: **Waterville**, **Brunswick**, **Kennebunkport** (Bush family summer compound), **Old Orchard Beach** (Coney Island, Maine-style), **York**, **Bar Harbor**, **Acadia National Park** (good for camping), **Bangor**, and **Bath**, to name just a few. For more, try the **Maine Office of Tourism**, 207-287-5711, www.visitmaine.com.

RHODE ISLAND

Rhode Island's claim to fame is that it is the smallest of all the states. With a total area of only 1,214 square miles, the whole state feels like a giant extended suburb of its capital, Providence.
- **Providence**, www.providenceri.com, is about an hour to the south of Boston down I-95. It's a small city with two prominent institutions of higher education: Brown University and Rhode Island School of Design. Attractions include RISD Museum of Art, Benefit Street, Providence Preservation Society, Federal Hill, Brown University, State House, Old State House, Athenaeum, First Baptist Church, John Brown House, Haffenreffer Museum of Anthropology, Heritage Harbor Museum, Roger Williams Park, and WaterFire.
- In the days of the Rockefellers and Vanderbilts, **Newport**, www.go newport.com, was the summer playground for the rich and richer. No expense was spared for the building of palatial summer homes. Today, summertime finds a lot of Bostonians coming here to take advantage of the beach (summer shares of rental houses are big with the post-college crowd). Others come for the historic sites, and still others for the annual Newport Folk Festival, where singers of no small mien set up camp for a few days. Newport is about 30 miles south of Providence by car. Things to see and do include tours of Trinity Church, Touro Park, Touro Synagogue, Hunter House, Wanton-Lyman-Hazard House, the Museum of Newport History, the Doll Museum, the Tennis Hall of Fame, and the

mansions: Hammersmith Farm (Jackie O's childhood summer home), Kingscote, the Elms, Chateau-sur-Mer, the Breakers, Rosecliff, Beechwood Mansion, Marble House, and Belcourt Castle.
- Finally, **Block Island** is like Nantucket's subtler, smaller, quieter little sister. It's a good place to go to catch some sun and sand along with peace and quiet. Ferry service will take you there in the summer from Point Judith, RI.

For tips on visiting Rhode Island, try the official **Rhode Island tourism** site, http://visitrhodeisland.com.

CONNECTICUT

Because Connecticut has a good run of coastline, some Bostonians are willing to drive a little further and come here instead of going to New Hampshire, Maine, or Rhode Island. Summer houses and cottages are popular in many of the small towns along the Atlantic. If you head west out the Mass Pike and then south down I-91, you can be at the northern part of Connecticut's shores in about two hours.
- These days, the biggest tourist draws are the casinos: **Foxwoods**, www.foxwoods.com, is run by Native Americans from the Mashantucket Pequot tribe, and **Mohegan Sun**, www.mohegansun.com, is run by Mohegans.
- Other places to visit in Connecticut include: **New Haven** (for Yale University and its museums and theaters), **New London**, **Norwalk**, **Mystic** (seaport, aquarium, etc.), and **Hartford** (Harriet Beecher Stowe House, Mark Twain House, Wadsworth Athenaeum, and Old State House).

For information on Connecticut tourism, contact **Connecticut Bound**, www.tourism.state.ct.us, 800-CTBOUND.

NATIONAL PARKS

In Massachusetts alone, there are 17 parks, sites, and trails run by the National Park Service, including the Appalachian Trail, which runs through part of every New England state except Rhode Island. Some national park areas, such as the Cape Cod National Seashore and the Boston Harbor Islands, are preserved natural environs. Others, like the Adams National Historic Park and the JFK National Historic Site, are historic in nature. National parks in Maine include St. Croix Island on the northern coast, 207-288-3338, Roosevelt Campobello International Park in Lubec, 506-752-2922, and the biggie, Acadia National Park in Bar Harbor on the coast, 207-288-3338. New Hampshire has the Saint Gaudens National Historic Site in Cornish along the border with Vermont, 603-675-2175, and in

Vermont it is the Marsh-Billings-Rockefeller National Historic Park in Woodstock, 802-457-3368. Connecticut offers the Quinebaug and Shetucket Rivers Valley in Putnam, 860-963-7226, and Weir Farm in the southwest corner of the state, 203-834-1896. And in Rhode Island, the National Park Service runs three sites: Blackstone River Valley in northern Rhode Island, 401-762-0250, Roger Williams National Memorial in Providence, 401-521-7266, and Touro Synagogue in Newport, 401-847-4794.

If you would like more information or would like to make camping reservations, contact the **National Park Service** at 800-365-2267, www.nps.gov.

NATIONAL FORESTS

If you like to camp in a National Forest, you've got plenty of options. In the White Mountains of Maine, you can camp at the Basin Campground and Cold River, both 15 miles north of Fryeburg, or Hastings Campground off Route 113 just south of Gilead. Offerings in the White Mountains of New Hampshire include Barnes Field Campground and Dolly Copp Big Meadow, both just miles south of Gorham. Other options include the Campton Campground (exit 28 of I-93); Covered Bridge is six miles west of Conway; Osceola Vista Campground and Waterville Campground are both near Waterville Valley; Sugarloaf Campground is just east of Twin Mountain in the central part of the state; and White Ledge Campground is in Albany near Conway. In Vermont there is Winhall Brook at Ball Mountain Lake in Jamaica, 802-824-4570, or Hapgood Pond just east of Manchester in the Green Mountains, 802-824-6456. Indian Hollow at Knightville Dam in the Berkshires, 413-667-3430, is the only National Forest in Massachusetts, and Connecticut's only is West Thompson Lake in North Grosvenordale, 860-923-2982. There are none in Rhode Island.

If a phone number was not listed above for a campgrounds or to do a little more research on your own, contact the **National Forest Service** at 877-444-6777, www.reserveusa.com.

A BOSTON YEAR

TO GET A HANDLE ON ALL THE GOINGS ON IN AND AROUND Boston, you'll want to check the *Boston Globe's* "Calendar" section or *Boston Magazine*, the *Improper Bostonian*, or *The Phoenix*. Also contact the Greater Boston Convention and Visitors Bureau at 888-SEE-BOSTON, www.bostonusa.com or the Mayor's Office of Special Events, Tourism and Film, 617-635-3911, on the web at www.cityofboston.gov/spevents. In the meantime, here are a few annual events:

JANUARY

- **Chinese New Year**; festivities take place for three weeks (can go into February), held in Chinatown. Includes dragon dancing and fireworks. Call 888-733-2678 for information.
- **Martin Luther King Jr. Birthday Celebration**; various events held on the third Monday in January.

FEBRUARY

- **Beanpot Hockey Tournament**, 617-624-1000, www.fleet.com; varsity hockey teams from Harvard, Northeastern, BU, and BC face off. This is a big deal and sells out early! Held at the Fleet Center.
- **Black History Month**; events and lectures around town, as well as special tours and programs on the Black Heritage Trail.
- **Boston Wine Expo**, 877-946-3976, www.wine-expos.com/boston/; largest consumer wine event in the country, held at the World Trade Center.
- **New England Boat Show**, www.naexpo.com/boatshow/; largest boat show in the Northeast, with over 600 sail and motorboats. Held at the Bayside Expo Center.

MARCH

- **Evacuation Day**; celebrated only in Suffolk County, commemorating the day in 1776 when the British redcoats ended their occupation of Boston.
- **New England Spring Flower Show**; five acres of landscaped gardens, flower arrangements, and horticultural displays at the Bayside Expo Center. Hosted by the Massachusetts Horticultural Society. For more information, visit www.masshort.org.
- **Reenactment of the Boston Massacre**; historical re-enactors haul out their muskets and colonial garb and gather at the Old State House to act out the Boston Massacre. Run by the Bostonian Society, www.bostonmassacre.org, 617-720-1713.
- **St. Patrick's Day Parade**; one of the largest parades in the country takes place in South Boston on the weekend of St. Patty's Day. No dyeing the river green here, but you will see floats, bands, veterans, and of course very packed bars and pubs. For more information, visit www.saintpatricksdayparade.com/boston/boston.htm.

APRIL

- **Boston Marathon**; one of the biggest running events in the country. Held on the third Monday in April. Much of the Back Bay is blocked off and ends in front of the main branch of the Boston Public Library. Visit www.bostonmarathon.org or call 617-236-1652 for more information.
- **Lantern Hanging**; on the Sunday before the nineteenth of April, two lanterns are hung in the steeple of the Old North Church to commemorate Paul Revere's ride. Call 617-523-6676 for more information.
- **Patriots' Day Parade/Reenactment**; public holiday on the third Monday in April, Paul Revere rides again, and a full-scale reenactment takes place on Lexington Green.
- **Swan Boats** come out of winter storage; Boston Public Garden, www.swanboats.com.

MAY

- **Albanian Festival**; celebrating Albanian food, film, fine art, music, clothing, dance, etc. Held in Worcester. Call 508-756-1690 for information.
- **Armenian Fair**; cultural foods and wares, held annually in Watertown. Call 617-923-0498.
- **Boston Kite Festival**; held in Franklin Park during the middle of the month.

- **Figawi Race**, www.figawi.net; sailboat race between Cape Cod and Nantucket over Memorial Day weekend.
- **Harpoon Brewstock**, 617-574-9551; indoor/outdoor festival at the Harpoon Brewery in South Boston.
- **Lilac Sunday**; the third Sunday in May, visit the 400+ varieties of lilacs in bloom at the Arnold Arboretum in JP. For more information, visit www.arboretum.harvard.edu.
- **Make Way for Ducklings Parade**; on Mother's Day parents and kids dress up like the book characters and parade around Beacon Hill.
- **Spring Planting Moon**; three-day Native American pow-wow in Topsfield, marking the beginning of the planting season, thrown by the Massachusetts Center for Native American Awareness, 617-884-4227.
- **Street Performers Festival** in Faneuil Hall Marketplace.

JUNE

- **African Festival**; food, music, and wares of cultures from the African continent. Held in Lowell. Call 978-453-6677 for more information.
- **AIDS Walk/Run**; on the Esplanade, first part of June. Call 617-424-WALK for more details.
- **Annual American Indian Pow-wow**; held in Canton, sponsored by the Order for the Preservation of Indian Culture: music, drumming, food.
- **Bloomsday Celebration**; local James Joyce enthusiasts meet under the Old Elm Tree in the public gardens to read from *Ulysses*. Call 617-635-4505.
- **Boston Celebrates Israel**; held in the World Trade Center, celebrations of Israeli music, dancing, jewelry, and food. Call 617-558-6506 for details.
- **Boston Dairy Festival/Scooper Bowl**; eat ice cream for charity—your entrance fee gets you all the ice cream you can eat and the proceeds go to the Jimmy Fund. Held at the Government Center. Call 800-52JIMMY for more info.
- *Boston Globe* **Jazz & Blues Festival**; go to www.boston.com/jazzfestival/ for information.
- **Boston Harbor Seaport Festival**, 888-767-7223, www.bostonseaportfestival.com
- **Bunker Hill Day**; third weekend in June, a reenactment of the Battle of Bunker Hill and a parade in Charlestown.
- **Grecian Festival** at: St. Athanasius Church in Arlington, 781-646-0705, Annunciation of the Virgin Mary Greek Orthodox Church in Woburn, 781-935-2424, and at Archangels Greek Orthodox Church in Watertown, 617-924-8182.

- **Irish Festival**, 888-GO-IRISH, www.irishculture.org; one of the largest Irish cultural gatherings in New England, organized by the Irish Cultural Center. Includes Irish bands, step dancing, meat pies, Guinness beer.
- **Jacob's Pillow Dance Festival**, www.jacobspillow.org; summer-long dance festival held in western Massachusetts.
- **Lesbian & Gay Pride Festival**, 617-262-9405, www.bostonpride.org; usually coincides with the AIDS walk, during the first week of June, ends with a parade in the South End and a carnival.
- **Massachusetts Special Olympics**; hosted by BU and MIT, for physically and mentally challenged athletes. Takes place during the third week of June. Go to www.specialolympicsma.org for more information.
- **Nantucket Film Festival**, 212-708-1278, www.nantucketfilmfestival.org; one of the bigger local entertainment industry events.
- **Polish Festival**; traditional music, food, and mass, held in New Bedford. Call 508-992-9378 for information.
- **Saint Peter's Festa**, 978-283-1601, www.stpetersfesta.org; parades, prayers, midnight procession, fireworks, food, rowing races, and so on. In Gloucester. Annual attendance: over 100,000.
- **Scandinavian Midsummer Festival**; summer solstice celebration with traditional music, dance, and food in Rockport.
- **Tanglewood Opens**; summer home of the BSO in Lenox, MA; 888-266-1200, www.bso.org.
- **Two Sisters Pow-wow**; in Lowell; drummers, singers, dancing, storytelling, crafts, and food. Call 978-459-7214 for information.
- **Williamstown Theatre Festival**, 413-597-3400, www.wtfestival.org
- **Woods People Monadnock Valley Pow-wow**; storytelling, music, dancing, campfire, buffalo, wares, etc., to celebrate the Summer Solstice in Winchendon. Call 978-297-1228 for information.

JULY

- **Bastille Day**; hosted by the Boston French Center in the Back Bay, celebrated with French food, wine, music and a boat on the Harbor. For more information, call 617-914-0400 or visit www.frenchlib.org.
- **Boston Pops Concert & Fireworks**; the city celebrates the Fourth of July on the Esplanade with a concert in the Hatch Shell by the Boston Pops, ending in a fireworks display over the Charles River.
- **Cambridge Summer Music Festival**, www.cambridgesummermusic.com; city's largest annual classical music festival.
- **Cape Verdean Independence Day Festival**; put on by the Cape Verdean Task Force, 617-442-6644.
- **Festival Betances** is a Puerto Rican celebration, includes a parade, music, dance, and food. In the South End.

- **Glasgow Lands Scottish Festival**, www.glasgowlands.org; clan dinner, bagpipes, haggis, wool spinning, pony rides, duck herding, etc. held in Westfield.
- **Harborfest**, 617-227-1528, www.bostonharborfest.com; six-day long Fourth of July festival, including concerts and the **Chowderfest** at City Hall Plaza.
- **Italia Unita Festival**, www.italiaunita.org; Italian food, music, dancing, carnival in East Boston.
- **Lantern Floating Festival**, www.foresthillstrust.org; Buddhist festival.
- **Lowell Folk Festival**; celebrates the music, dance, storytelling, food, and crafts of the ethnic immigrants who came to Lowell to work in the factories. Held the fourth weekend of the month. Visit www.lowellfolkfestival.org for more info.
- **North End Festivals**, www.northendweb.com; Catholic saints' feast days are celebrated in the North End with parades, food, etc. on many weekends in July and August.
- **Puerto Rican Festival**; held in Franklin Park, with a parade, bands, dancing and carnival rides.
- **Sommerfest**, 508-660-2018, www.germanclub.org; the Schul-Verein throws a German summer festival in the woods of Walpole. Beer, music, and wurst Bavarian style.
- **Turning of the Constitution**; USS Constitution takes an annual spin around Boston Harbor on the Fourth of July: 617-426-1812, www.ussconstitutionmuseum.org.

AUGUST

- **African Gastro**; celebrates the food, clothing, and music from African and Caribbean cultures and nations. Held in Dorchester or Roxbury.
- **August Moon Festival**, held in Chinatown. Traditional Asian food, as well as special moon cakes.
- **Boston Antique and Classic Boat Festival**; show of vintage vessels and a blessing of the fleet. Held at Hawthorne Cove Marina in Salem Harbor, 617-666-8530, www.by-the-sea.com/bacbfestival/.
- **Boston Chinatown Festival**; food, wares, and entertainment.
- **Caribbean Carnival**, www.bostoncarnival.com; held the weekend before Labor Day in Franklin Park. Celebrates Caribbean culture with traditional food, arts, crafts, and dance.
- **Dominican Independence Celebration**; in Franklin Park and JP, with food, parades, floats, and dancing.
- **Feast of the Three Saints**; Italian *festa* celebrating saints Alfo, Filadelfo, and Cirino in Lawrence. Call 978-681-0944.

- **Gloucester Waterfront Festival**; lobster bake, whale watches, music, nautical crafts, etc. during mid-August in Gloucester.
- **India Day**; traditional dancing, music, food, etc., at the Esplanade by the Hatch Shell. Call 978-667-1695 for more information.
- **Latin American Festival**; 35,000 come to enjoy food, drink, dancing, music, and goods from all over South America, held on Worcester Common in Worcester. Call 508-798-1900.
- **Provincetown Carnival Week**; Mardi Gras style GLBT event. Third week of August.
- **Rhythm & Roots Festival**, 888-855-6940, www.rhythmandroots.com; Cajun/Creole three-day festival held annually in Charlestown.
- **Southeast Asian Water Festival**; mid-August at the Lowell Heritage State Park. Celebrates Cambodian, Laotian, and Vietnamese cultural events with foods and painted boat races.
- **US Pro Tennis Championship**; held the fourth week of the month at the Longwood Cricket Club in Brookline.

SEPTEMBER

- **Art Newbury Street**; sidewalk art, food, and music with exhibitions by the local galleries. Held during the end of September.
- **Boston Film Festival**, 617-331-9460, www.bostonfilmfestival.org; the big local independent film event, held the second week in September.
- **Brazil Independence Festival**; over 3,000 people turn out for the food-filled salsa party on Magazine Beach in Cambridge.
- **Cambridge River Festival**; international festival with music, dance, bazaar, arts and crafts, and children's events. Held on the Sunday after Labor Day along the Charles.
- **Eastern European Festival**; polka, eat pirogi, and listen to accordion music with Latvians, Poles, Czechs, and Lithuanians; in Deerfield. Call 413-774-7476 for more information.
- **Harwich Cranberry Festival**, 508-430-2811, www.harwichcranberryfestival.com; kid-friendly festival with fireworks, family picnic on the beach, parade, county jamboree, and a cranberry bog in full bloom. Held in mid-September.
- **Italian Festival of Saints Cosmas and Damian**; night carnival, healing service, and mass in East Cambridge. Call 617-661-1164.
- **King Richard's Faire**, 508-866-5391, www.kingrichardsfaire.net; the local Renaissance Festival opens each Labor Day and goes through October. Held in Carver, MA.

OCTOBER

- **Boston Fashion Week**, www.bostonfashion.com; area fashion designers put on fashion shows, parties, and panel discussions during the second week of the month.
- **Columbus Day**; parade and the day off, the second Monday in October.
- **Harvard Square Oktoberfest**, www.harvardsquare.com/events/oktoberfest/; traditional Bavarian Oktoberfest with food, music, art, and beer in Harvard Square.
- **Head of the Charles Regatta**, www.hocr.org; annual rowing race takes place on the Charles River during the 2nd weekend in October.
- **Salem's Haunted Happenings**, www.hauntedhappenings.org; two weeks of Halloween celebration in Salem, including parade, haunted house tours, magic shows, psychics' fair.
- **Spooky World**, 978-838-0200, www.spookyworld.com; Halloween theme park at Gillette Stadium.
- **Tufts 10K Race for Women**, 888-767-RACE, www.tufts-health.com/tufts10k/; popular annual charity running event.

NOVEMBER

- **Thanksgiving at Old Sturbridge Village**, www.osv.org; recreation of early Thanksgivings in this colonial living history village.
- **Veteran's Day parades and memorial services**—throughout Boston

DECEMBER

- **Christmas Tree Lightings**; at the Prudential Center and at Boston Common on the first weekend in December.
- **First Night**, www.firstnight.org; Boston's New Year's Eve celebration on December 31, includes performances, ice sculptures, and a fireworks show.
- **Reenactment of the Boston Tea Party**; on December 13th or the nearest Sunday, actors reenact the Boston Tea Party, beginning at the Old South Meeting House and then parading down to the waterfront.

A BOSTON READING LIST

From Emerson to Plath to Dubus, Massachusetts has been home to more famous writers than you can shake a stick at, and a fair share of books have been written about this historical commonwealth too. Below is an abbreviated list of the writings by native sons and daughters, books about Massachusetts history, as well as architectural books, local guides, and children's titles. If you'd like to learn a little more about Massachusetts' more famous writers, try looking them up on www.bartleby.com.

You should be able to find most of these books in your local library or bookstore (see **Literary Life** in the **Cultural Life** chapter for a list of libraries and bookstores):

BOSTON—ARTS AND ARCHITECTURE

- *AIA Guide to Boston* by Susan and Michael Southworth (Globe Pequot Press)
- *Boston Boy* by Nathaniel Hentoff (Alfred A. Knopf); about Boston's jazz scene.
- *A Guide to Public Art in Greater Boston, from Newburyport to Plymouth* by Marty Carlock (Harvard Common Press)
- *The Life of Emily Dickinson* by Richard B. Sewall (Harvard University Press)
- *Literary New England: A History and Guide* by William Corbett (Faber and Faber)
- *The Literary Trail of Greater Boston* by Susan Wilson and the Boston History Collaborative (Houghton Mifflin)

FICTION

- *A Man with a Squirrel* by Nicholas Kilmer (Henry Holt and Company); murder mystery that takes place in Beacon Hill.
- *Asa, As I Knew Him* and *Far Afield* by Susanna Kaysen (Vintage Books)
- *The Bell Jar* by Sylvia Plath (Perennial)
- *Blunt Darts* by J.F. Healy (Walker and Co.); detective novel set in the area.
- *The Collected Works of Edgar Allan Poe—Volumes II and III: Tales and Sketches* by Edgar Allan Poe (Belknap Press of Harvard University Press); master of the macabre, Poe was born in Bay Village in 1806.
- *Hateship, Friendship, Courtship, Loveship, Marriage: Stories* by Alice Munroe (Vintage)
- *Heartbreak Hill: The Boston Marathon Thriller* by Tom Lonergan (Writers Club Press)
- *Johnny Tremain: A Novel for Old and Young* by Esther Forbes (Dell); about a young silversmith's growing up in Revolutionary War era Boston.
- *Little Women, Jo's Boys, Little Men,* and many others, including some lesser-known books for adults by Louisa May Alcott (Price Stern Sloan)
- *Make Way for Ducklings* by Robert McCloskey (Viking Press); this children's classic takes place in Boston. Fans will be excited to see the duckling statues in the Public Gardens and attend the parade on Mother's Day in Beacon Hill.
- *Niebla* by Andre Dubus III (Vintage)
- *The Lieutenant, Separate Flights, Adultery and Other Choices, Finding a Girl in America,* and other works by Andre Dubus (Vintage Books); this beloved writer lived on the North Shore until his passing in 1999.
- *Mortal Friends* by James Carroll (Little Brown & Company)
- *On the Road, The Dharma Bums, The Subterraneans, Big Sur, Desolation Angels, Tristessa, Visions of Cod, Maggie Cassidy* and more by Jack Kerouac (Penguin USA)
- *Ragged Dick,* by Horatio Alger (Viking Press).
- *The Scarlet Letter* and other works by Nathaniel Hawthorne (Library of America); born in Salem in 1800, most famous for bringing the story of Hester Prynne to life.
- *While I Was Gone* and *The Good Mother* are just two of the novels by local author Sue Miller (Harper & Row).
- *Zodiac* by Neal Stephenson (Bantam Spectra); eco-thriller set in and around Boston.

NONFICTION—BIOGRAPHY AND AUTOBIOGRAPHY

- *A Clearing in the Distance: Frederick Law Olmsted and America in the Nineteenth Century* by Witold Rybczynski (Touchstone Books)
- *All Souls: A Family Story from Southie* by Michael Patrick MacDonald (Ballantine Books)
- *The Autobiography of Malcolm X* by Malcolm X (Ballantine Books)
- *Benjamin Franklin, His Autobiography* by Benjamin Franklin (Dover)
- *Eminent Bostonians* by Thomas H. O'Connor (Harvard University Press)
- *The Fitzgeralds and the Kennedys: An American Saga* by Doris Kearns Goodwin (Simon & Schuster)
- *John Adams* by David McCullough (Simon & Schuster)
- *Mrs. Jack* by Louise Hall Tharp (Little Brown & Company); biography of Isabella Stewart Gardner.
- *The Proper Bostonians* by Cleveland Amory (E.P. Dutton)
- *The Rascal King: The Life and Times of James Michael Curley, 1874-1958* by Jack Beatty (Addison-Wesley)
- *Saints and Stranger* by George S. Willison (Parnassus Imprints); about the first settlers from the Mayflower.
- *The Secret Six: The True Tale of the Men Who Conspired with John Brown* by Edward J. Renehan (University of South Caroline Press)
- *We Can't Eat Prestige: The Women Who Organized Harvard* by John P. Hoerr (Temple University Press)

NONFICTION—REGIONAL POLITICS AND HISTORY

- *All on Fire: William Lloyd Garrison and the Abolition of Slavery* by Henry Mayer (St. Martin's)
- *The Big Dig* by Dan McNichol, Andy Ryan, and the Massachusetts DPW (Silver Lining Books)
- *Black Mass: The True Story of the Unholy Alliance Between the FBI and the Irish Mob* by Dick Lehr and Gerard O'Neill (Perennial)
- *Blizzard of '78* by Michael Tougias (On Cape Publications).
- *Boston A to Z* by Thomas H. O'Connor (Harvard University Press)
- *The Boston Irish: A Political History* by Thomas H. O'Connor (Little Brown & Co.)
- *Boston: A Topographical History* by Walter Muir Whitehill and Lawrence Kennedy (Harvard University Press)
- *The Boston Massacre* by Hiller B. Zobel (W.W. Norton)
- *Boston (Photographic Tour)* by Ted Landphair and Carol M. Highsmith (Random House)
- *Boston Rediscovered* by Urilke Welsch and William O. Taylor (Commonwealth Editions)

- *The Boston Tea Party* by Benjamin Woods Labree (Northeastern University)
- *Boston Then and Now* by Elizabeth McNulty (Thunder Bay Press)
- *Cityscapes of Boston: An American City Through Time* by Robert Campbell (Houghton Mifflin)
- *Common Ground* by Anthony J. Lukas (Alfred A. Knopf). History of the 1960s busing crisis.
- *The Curse of the Bambino* by Dan Shaughnessy (Penguin USA); history of the Red Sox losing streak.
- *The Great Boston Trivia & Fact Book* by Merrill Kaitz (Cumberland House)
- *Historic Walks in Old Boston* by John Harris (Globe Pequot Press)
- *The Hub: Boston Past and Present* by Thomas H. O'Connor (Northeastern University Press)
- *Indian New England Before the Mayflower* by Howard S. Russell (University Press of New England)
- *Inventing the Charles River* by Karl T. Haglund and Renata Von Tscharner (MIT Press)
- *The Last Hurrah* by Edwin O'Connor (Little Brown & Co.) about the Irish political machine.
- *Lexington and Concord: The Beginning of the War of the American Revolution* by Arthur B. Tourtellot (W.W. Norton)
- *Lost Boston* by Jane Holtz Kay (Mariner Books)
- *Mapping Boston* by Alex Krieger, David Cobb, and Amy Turner (MIT Press)
- *The Other Bostonians: Poverty and Progress in the American Metropolis, 1880-1970* by Stephan Thernstrom (iUniverse.com)
- *The Oxford W.E.B. DuBois Reader* by W.E.B. DuBois (Oxford University Press); civil rights advocate and cofounder of the NAACP.
- *Paul Revere's Ride* by David Hackett Fischer (Oxford University Press)
- *Petticoat Whalers: Whaling Wives at Sea, 1820-1920* by Joan Druett (Haper Collins)
- *Planning the City Upon a Hill: Boston Since 1630* by Lawrence W. Kennedy (University of Massachusetts Press)

FOOD

- *Boston Neighborhoods: A Food Lover's Walking, Eating, and Shopping Guide to Ethnic Enclaves in and Around Boston* by Lynda Morgenroth and Carleen Moira Powell (Globe Pequot Press)
- *The Cook's Guide to Boston Restaurants* by Rebecca Hayes (Boston Common Press)
- *Secret Boston: The Unique Guidebook to Boston's Hidden Sites, Sounds & Tastes* by Laura Purdom and Linda Rutenberg (ECW Press)
- *Zagat Survey: Boston Restaurants* (Zagat Survey, LLC)

QUICK GETAWAYS

- *Fun With the Family in Massachusetts: Hundreds of Ideas for Day Trips With the Kids* by Marcia Glassman-Jaffe (Globe Pequot Press)
- *Moon Handbooks: Massachusetts* by Jeff Perk (Avalon Travel Publishing)
- *New England Camping: The Complete Guide to More Than 82,000 Campsites for Tenters, Rovers, and Car Campers* by Carol Connare and Stephen Gorman (Foghorn Press)
- *Quick Escapes Boston: 25 Weekend Getaways from the Hub* by Sandy MacDonald (Globe Pequot Press)

SPORTS AND RECREATION

- *25 Mountain Bike Tours in Massachusetts; from Cape Cod to the Connecticut River* by Robert Morse, David DeVore, and Jane DeVore (Backcountry Press)
- *26 Miles to Boston: The Boston Marathon Experience from Hopkinton to Copley Square* by Michael Connelly (Parnassus Imprints)
- *Country Walks Near Boston* by Alan Fisher (Rambler Books)
- *The Deerfield River Guidebook: Whitewater, Fishing, Recreation* by Bruce Lessels and Norman Sims (New England Cartographics)
- *Exploring In and Around Boston on Bike and Foot* by Lee Sinai and Joyce S. Sherr (Appalachian Mountain Club Books)
- *Fly-Fishing Boston: A Complete Saltwater Guide from Rhode Island to Maine* by Terry C. Tessein (Countryman Press)
- *Mountain Bike America: Greater Boston* by Jeff Cutler and Beachway Press (Globe Pequot Press)

USEFUL PHONE NUMBERS & WEB SITES

For the most part, information here is included for the City of Boston only. If you live in one of the surrounding communities, contact your town or city hall or visit your town or city web site (listed under your community's description in the **Neighborhoods** chapter) to look up the appropriate information.

ANIMALS

- **Angell Memorial Animal Hospital**, 617-522-7282, www.angell.org
- **Animal Bites**, 911
- **Animal Rescue League of Boston**, 617-426-9170, www.arl-boston.org
- **Boston Animal Control** (including for dog licenses), 617-635-5348, www.cityofboston.gov/animalcontrol/
- **City of Boston Animal Shelter and Adoption Center**, 617-635-1800
- **MSPCA**, 617-522-7400, www.mspca.org/boston

Note: Dog licenses can be obtained through your city or town clerk's office.

AUTOMOBILES

- **AAA Southern New England**, 800-JOIN-AAA (membership), 800-AAA-HELP (roadside service), www.aaa.com
- **Abandoned Vehicle Removal** (through BTD), 617-635-4500, www.cityofboston.gov/transportation/abandoned.asp
- **Boston Transportation Department (BTD)**, 617-635-4680, www.ci.boston.ma.us/transportation/; contact for all tickets, towing, boot removal, etc.

- **BTD Tow Lot**, 617-635-3900
- **Massachusetts Consumer Affairs & Business Regulation, Auto**, 617-973-8787 (consumer hotline), www.mass.gov/consumer
- **Massachusetts Registry of Motor Vehicles**, 617-351-4500, 800-858-3926, www.mass.gov/rmv
- **NHTSC Auto Safety Hotline**, 888-DASH-DOT, www.nhtsa.dot.gov

BIRTH AND DEATH RECORDS

- **City of Boston, Registry Division**, 617-635-4175, www.cityofboston.gov/registry/
- **City of Cambridge, City Clerk**, 617-349-4260, www.ci.cambridge.ma.us/~CityClrk/
- **Massachusetts State Registry of Vital Records**, 617-740-2600, www.vitalrec.com/ma.html

CHAMBERS OF COMMERCE

- **Arlington Chamber of Commerce**, 781-643-4600
- **Brookline Chamber of Commerce**, 617-739-1330, www.brooklinechamber.com
- **Chamber of Commerce of East Boston**, 617-569-1945, www.eastbostonchamber.com
- **Cambridge Chamber of Commerce**, 617-876-4100, www.cambridgechamber.org
- **Greater Boston Chamber of Commerce**, 617-227-4500, www.bostonchamber.com
- **Malden Chamber of Commerce**, 781-322-4500
- **Medford Chamber of Commerce**, 781-396-1277
- **Newton/Needham Chamber of Commerce**, 617-244-5300, www.nnchamber.com
- **South Shore Chamber of Commerce**, 617-479-1111, www.southshorechamber.org
- **Somerville Chamber of Commerce**, 617-776-4100, www.somervillema.org
- **Waltham-West Suburban Chamber of Commerce**, 781-894-4700, www.walthamchamber.com
- **Watertown-Belmont Chamber of Commerce**, 617-926-1017, www.wbcc.org

For additional towns and cities, search on www.chamberofcommerce.com.

CONSUMER COMPLAINTS AND SERVICES

- **AARP**, 800-424-3410, www.aarp.org
- **Better Business Bureau**, 508-652-4800, www.bosbbb.org
- **Boston Bar Association**, 617-742-0615, www.bostonbar.org
- **Consumer Product Safety Commission**, 800-638-2772, www.cpsc.gov
- **Division of Professional Licensure**, 617-727-3074, TTY 617-727-2099, www.state.ma.us/reg/home.htm
- **Federal Trade Commission (FTC)**, 877-FTC-HELP, www.ftc.gov/ro/northeast.htm
- **Federal Citizen Information Center**, 800-FED-INFO, www.firstgov.gov
- **Help Me Hank** (WHDH-TV), www.whdh.com/features/main/helpmehank, e-mail helpmehank@whdh.com
- **Attorney General's Insurance Consumer Helpline**, 888-830-6277, www.ago.state.ma.us
- **Massachusetts Bar Association**, 617-338-0500, http://massbar.org/
- **Massachusetts Board of Bar Overseers/Office of the Bar Counsel**, Attorney and Consumer Assistance Program, 617-728-8750, www.mass.gov/obcbbo
- **Massachusetts Division of Insurance**, 617-521-7777, TTY 617-521-7490, www.state.ma.us/doi/
- **Massachusetts Office of Consumer Affairs & Business Regulation**, 617-973-8787or 888-823-3757, www.mass.gov/consumer
- **MassPIRG (Massachusetts Public Interest Research Group)**, 617-292-4800, www.masspirg.org
- **Mayor's Office of Consumer Affairs and Licensing**, 617-635-4165, www.cityofboston.gov/consumeraffairs/
- **National Consumers League**, 202-835-3323, www.natlconsumersleague.org
- **WBZ Call for Action**, 617-787-7070, www.wbz1030.com

CRIME

- **Crime in Progress**, 911
- **Governor's Auto Theft Strike Force**, 800-HOT-AUTO
- **Attorney General's Insurance Fraud Tipline**, 617-727-2200 ext. 3256
- **Massachusetts Office for Victim Assistance**, 617-727-5200, www.mass.gov/mova

- **Massachusetts Most Wanted**, 800-KAPTURE
- **Massachusetts Neighborhood Crime Watch Commission**, 888-80-WATCH
- **Massachusetts State Police Terrorism Tip Line**, 888-USA-5458
- **SafeFutures** (Boston), 617-635-4920, www.cityofboston.gov/bcyf/safefutures.asp
- **Safe Neighborhood Initiative**, 617-727-2200

CRISIS HOTLINES

ADDICTIONS
- **Alcoholics Anonymous**, 617-426-9444, www.alcoholics-anonymous.org
- **Alcohol & Drug Referral Hotline**, 800-327-5050
- **Alcohol Drug Rehab Referral**, 800-375-4577, www.nationalhotline.org
- **Alcohol Information Center**, 781-321-2600
- **Alcoholism Hotline**, 800-252-6465
- **Coalition on Addiction, Pregnancy, and Parenting**, 617-661-3991
- **Cocaine Abuse Helpline and Treatment**, 800-374-2800
- **Gamblers Anonymous**, 617-338-6020, www.gamblersanonymous.org
- **MA Substance Abuse Hotline**, 800-327-5050 or 617-338-6020
- **National Drug and Treatment Referral Routing Service**, 800-662-HELP
- **Smoker's Quitline**, 800-TRY-TO-STOP
- **Statewide Substance Abuse Information Line**, 800-ALCOHOL and 800-COCAINE

CHILD ABUSE & FAMILY VIOLENCE
- **Battered Women's Hotline**, 800-992-2600
- **Girls and Boys Town National Hotline**, 800-448-3000, TTY 800-448-1833, www.girlsandboystown.org
- **Child Abuse Reporting Hotline**, 800-792-5200
- **Childhelp USA**, 800-422-4453, www.childhelpusa.org
- **Common Purpose** (batterers' group), 617-522-6500, www.commonpurpose.com
- **DSS Child at Risk Hotline**, 800-792-5200, www.jbcc.harvard.edu/programs/hotline.htm
- **Elder Abuse Hotline**, 800-922-2275, www.elderabusecenter.org/report/
- **Emerge** (batterers' group), 617-547-9879, www.emergedv.com

USEFUL PHONE NUMBERS AND WEB SITES

- **Massachusetts Society for the Prevention of Cruelty to Children**, 617-587-1500 (after hours, 508-767-3005), www.mspcc.org
- **National Domestic Violence Hotline**, 800-799-SAFE, www.ndvh.org
- **Parental Stress Line**, 800-632-8188, www.pcsonline.org/about/programs/helplines.htm
- **Parents Helping Parents**, 800-882-1250, www.php.com
- **Safelink**, 877-785-2020, TTY 877-521-2601, www.casamyrna.org/programs/safelink.html

RAPE
- **Boston Area Rape Crisis Center**, 617-492-RAPE or 800-580-5908 (non-crisis line, 617-492-8306), www.barcc.org
- **Rape Crisis Hotline (Spanish)**, 800-870-5905

SUICIDE
- **National Suicide Hotline**, 800-SUICIDE, http://hopeline.com/
- **Samaritans (Suicide Prevention)**, 617-247-0220, www.samaritansofboston.org

DISCRIMINATION

- **Boston Commission for Persons with Disabilities**, 617-635-2500, www.cityofboston.gov/civilrights/disability.asp
- **Boston Human Rights Commission**, 617-635-2500, www.cityofboston.gov/civilrights/rights.asp
- **Boston Human Services Cabinet**, 617-635-3446, www.cityofboston.gov/humanservices/
- **Department of Labor and Workforce Development**, 617-727-6573, www.state.ma.us/dlwd/
- **Disabled Persons Protection Commission**, 800-426-9009 (voice and TTY), www.state.ma.us/dppc/
- **Disabilities Information Hotline**, 800-692-0249
- **Attorney General's Elder Hotline**, 888-AG-ELDER
- **Attorney General's Fair Labor Hotline**, 617-727-3465
- **Governor's Task Force on Hate Crimes**, www.state.ma.us/stophate/core.htm
- **MA Tenant Organization and Resource Center**, 617-367-6260
- **Massachusetts Commission Against Discrimination**, 617-727-3990, TTY 617-727-3990, www.state.ma.us/mcad/
- **Massachusetts Department of Housing and Community Development**, 617-727-7147, www.state.ma.us/dhcd/

- **Massachusetts Office of Affirmative Action**, 617-727-7441, www.state.ma.us/hrd/
- **Office of the Massachusetts Attorney General**, 617-727-8400, TTY 617-727-4765, www.ago.state.ma.us
- **US Department of Fair Housing & Discrimination Hotline**, 800-424-8590
- **Women's Commission**, 617-635-4427, www.cityofboston.gov/women/

ELECTED OFFICIALS

BOSTON
- **Boston Assessor**, 617-635-4264, www.cityofboston.gov/assessing/
- **Boston City Clerk**, 617-635-4600, www.cityofboston.gov/cityclerk/
- **Boston City Council**, 617-635-3040, www.cityofboston.gov/citycouncil/
- **Boston City Hall**, 617-263-3000, www.cityofboston.gov
- **Boston Election Department**, 617-635-4635, www.cityofboston.gov/elections/
- **Boston Mayor's Office**, 617-635-4450, www.cityofboston.gov/mayor/

COUNTY
- **Middlesex County District Attorney's Office**, 781-322-2020, www.middlesexda.com
- **Norfolk County District Attorney's Office**, 781-830-4800, www.state.ma.us/da/norfolk/
- **Suffolk County District Attorney's Office**, 617-619-4000, www.state.ma.us/da/suffolk/

STATE
- **Attorney General's Office**, 617-727-2200, www.ago.state.ma.us
- **Governor's Council**, 617-725-4015
- **Governor's** (and Lieutenant Governor's) Office, 617-725-4005, TTY 617-727-3666, www.mass.gov
- **President of the Senate**, 617-722-1500, www.state.ma.us/legis/member/ret0.htm
- **Secretary of the Commonwealth's Office**, 617-727-7030 or 800-392-6090, www.state.ma.us/sec/index.htm
- **Speaker of the House of Representative's Office**, 617-722-2500, www.state.ma.us/legis/member/tmf1.htm
- **State Auditor's Office**, 617-727-2075, www.state.ma.us/sao/
- **Treasurer and Receiver General's Office**, 617-367-6900, www.state.ma.us/treasury/

USEFUL PHONE NUMBERS AND WEB SITES

- **US House of Representatives**, 202-224-3121, TTY 202-225-1904, www.house.gov
- **US Senate**, 202-224-1388, www.senate.gov

For all information on wards and precincts in Massachusetts, and the elected officials in them, your source is the **Elections Division of the Secretary of the Commonwealth**, www.state.ma.us/sec/ele/eleidx.htm.

EMERGENCY

- **Fire, Police, Medical**, 911
- **Boston Fire Department**, 617-343-3550, www.cityofboston.gov/bfd/index.html
- **Boston Police Department**, 617-343-4200, www.cityofboston.gov/police/
- **Boston EMS**: www.cityofboston.gov/ems/
- **Boston Emergency Storm Center**, 617-635-3050, www.cityofboston.gov/storm/
- **FEMA Disaster Assistance Information**, 800-525-0321, www.fema.gov
- **MEMA Info Line**, 508-820-2000
- **Poison Control Hotline**, 617-284-8400

ENTERTAINMENT

- **ArtsBoston** (includes **Bostix**), 617-262-8632, www.artsboston.org
- *Boston Globe* (Arts Section), www.boston.com
- *Boston Herald* (Arts Section), www.bostonherald.com
- *Boston Phoenix* (Arts & Entertainment paper), www.bostonphoenix.com
- **Citysearch**, www.boston.citysearch.com
- **DigitalCity**, www.digitalcity.com/boston
- **Mayor's Office of Cultural Affairs** (Boston), 617-635-3245, www.cityofboston.gov/arts/
- **Mayor's Office of Special Events, Tourism, and Film** (Boston), 617-635-3911, www.cityofboston.gov/spevents/
- **New England Theater 411**, www.netheater411.com
- **Next Ticketing**, 617-423-6000, www.nextticketing.com
- **StageSource**, 617-720-6066, www.stagesource.org
- **TheaterMirror**, www.theatermirror.com
- **TicketMaster**, 617-931-2000, www.ticketmaster.com

FEDERAL OFFICES/CENTERS

- **Federal Consumer Information Center**, 888-PUEBLO, www.pueblo.gsa.gov
- **Federal Government Information Center**, 800-688-9889, TTY 800-326-2996
- **SSA**, 800-772-1213, TTY 800-325-0778 (both 7 a.m. to 7 p.m., Monday-Friday), www.ssa.gov; click "contact us" to locate the nearest office.

HEALTH AND MEDICAL CARE

- **AIDS Action Hotline**, 800-255-2331
- **Childhood Lead Poisoning Prevention Program & Lead Paint Hotline**, 800-532-9571 or 617-284-8400, www.state.ma.us/dph/clppp
- **Children's Medical Security Plan**, 800-909-2677
- **Health Care for All**, helpline, 617-350-7279 or 800-272-4232, www.hcfama.org
- **HIV/AIDS Bureau**, 617-624-5300, TTY 617-624-5387, www.state.ma.us/dph/aids/hivaids.htm
- **Hospice Care**, 800-962-2973 or 781-255-7077, www.hospicefed.org
- **Massachusetts Bureau of Family and Community Health**, 617-624-6060, www.state.ma.us/dph
- **Massachusetts Commission for the Blind**, 617-727-5550, www.state.ma.us/dph/
- **Massachusetts Dental Society** (dental referrals), 508-480-9797 or 800-342-8747, www.massdental.org/public/findadentist.cfm
- **Massachusetts Department of Health**, 617-624-6000, TTY 617-624-6001, www.state.ma.us/dph
- **Massachusetts Department of Mental Health**, 617-626-8000, TTY 617-727-9842, www.state.ma.us/dmh
- **Massachusetts HIV/AIDS Hotline**, 800-235-2331, TTY 617-437-1672
- **Massachusetts League of Community Health Centers**, 617-426-2225, massleague.org
- **Mayor's Health Line**, 800-847-0710
- **National Alliance for the Mentally Ill (NAMI)**, 800-370-9085, www.pplm.org
- **Poison Control Hotline**, 617-284-8400
- **US Department of Health and Human Services**, 800-336-4797

USEFUL PHONE NUMBERS AND WEB SITES

HOUSING

- **Building Problems**—Boston, 617-635-5300
- **Boston Department of Neighborhood Development**, 617-635-3880, www.cityofboston.gov/dnd/
- **Boston Fair Housing Commission**, 617-635-2500, www.cityofboston.gov/civilrights/housing.asp
- **Boston Housing Authority**, 617-988-4230, TTY 800-545-1833, www.bostonhousing.org
- **Boston Redevelopment Authority (BRA)**, 617-722-4300, www.cityofboston.gov/bra/
- **Boston Rental Housing Resource Center**, 617-635-4200, www.cityofboston.gov/rentalhousing/
- **Citizens' Housing and Planning Association**, 617-742-0820 (voice and TTY), www.chapa.org
- **Discrimination Complaints**, 617-565-5308
- **Fair Housing Information Clearinghouse**, 800-343-3442
- **Housing Consumer Information Centers**, 617-800-224-5124, www.masshousinginfo.org
- **Massachusetts Commission Against Discrimination**, 617-994-6000, TTY 617-994-6196, www.state.ma.us/mcad
- **Massachusetts Department of Housing and Community Development (DHCD)**, 617-727-7765, www.state.ma.us/dhcd/
- **Massachusetts Housing Partnership Fund**, 617-338-7868 or 877-MHP-FUND, www.mhp.net
- **Office of Consumer Affairs and Business Regulation**, 617-973-8787 or 888-283-3757, www.state.ma.us/consumer/
- **State Board of Building Regulations and Standards**, 617-727-7532 or 800-223-0933, www.state.ma.us/bbrs
- **US Department of Fair Housing and Discrimination**, 800-477-5977, www.fairhousing.com/fhsc

LEGAL REFERRAL

- **Boston Bar Association**, 617-742-0615, www.bostonbar.org
- **Boston Public Defender's Office**, 617-482-6212, www.state.ma.us/cpcs/pdpage.htm
- **Cambridge Public Defender's Office**, 617-868-3300, www.state.ma.us/cpcs/pdpage.htm
- **Dedham Public Defender's Office**, 781-326-0632, www.state.ma.us/cpcs/pdpage.htm

- **Massachusetts ACLU**, 617-542-2235, www.aclu-mass.org
- **Massachusetts Board of Bar Overseers**, 617-728-8200, www.state.ma.us/obcbbo/
- **Massachusetts Bar Association**, 617-338-0500, www.massbar.org. Tel-Law line: 617-542-9069, 24-hour information tape on legal issues.
- **National Consumer Law Center**, 617-542-8010; www.consumerlaw.org
- **Roxbury Public Defender's Office**, 617-445-5640, www.state.ma.us/cpcs/pdpage.htm

LIBRARIES (MAIN PUBLIC)

- **Arlington**, 781-316-3200, www.robbinslibrary.org
- **Belmont**, 617-489-2000, www.belmont.lib.ma.us
- **Boston**, 617-536-5400, www.bpl.org
- **Brookline**, 617-730-2375, www.town.brookline.ma.us/Library/
- **Cambridge**, 617-349-4040, www.cambridgema.gov/~CPL
- **Dedham**, 781-751-9280, www.dedhamlibrary.org
- **Malden**, 781-324-0218, http://mbln.lib.ma.us/malden/index.htm
- **Medford**, 781-395-7950, www.medfordlibrary.org
- **Milton**, 617-698-5757, www.miltonlibrary.org
- **Needham**, 781-455-7559, www.town.needham.ma.us/Library/
- **Newton**, 617-796-1360, www.ci.newton.ma.us/Library
- **Quincy**, 617-376-1301, http://ci.quincy.ma.us/tcpl/
- **Somerville**, 617-623-5000, www.somervillepubliclibrary.org
- **Waltham**, 781-314-3425, www.waltham.lib.ma.us
- **Watertown**, 617-972-6431, www.watertownlib.org

Consult the resources following the **Neighborhood Profiles** for the locations and contact information to branch libraries. Also see **Literary Life** in the **Cultural Life** chapter for more on area libraries.

MARRIAGE LICENSES

City and town clerks issue marriage licenses in Massachusetts. Look for your city web site, mentioned in the resources following each neighborhood or city profile.
- **City of Boston**, Registry Division, 617-635-4175, www.cityofboston.gov/registry/

PARKING

- **Boston Office of the Parking Clerk—Resident Parking Stickers**, 617-635-4682, www.cityofboston.gov/transportation/parkprogr.asp
- **Boston Transportation Department (BTD)**, 617-635-4680, www.ci.boston.ma.us/transportation/. Contact for all tickets, towing, boot removal, etc.
- **BTD Tow Line**, 617-635-3900—the most likely place your car will be if it was towed by the City of Boston

For information on parking rules, tickets, towing, and snow emergencies, see the **Getting Settled** chapter or visit your community's web site.

PARKS AND RECREATION DEPARTMENTS

You can find information on the municipal and statewide parks and recreation departments in the **Sports and Recreation** chapter. Contact information for the **Boston Parks Department** is 617-635-PARK, www.cityofboston.gov/parks.

POLICE

Check your neighborhood or city profile for the address and phone number of your local police department or go to www.state.ma.us/CCJ/locals.htm.

- **Police Emergencies**, dial 911
- **Boston Police Commissioner**, 617-961-3046
- **Boston Police** (business), 617-343-4200, www.cityofboston.gov/police/
- **Governor's Highway Safety Bureau**, 617-973-8900, www.massghsb.com
- **Harvard University Police**, 617-495-1212, www.hupd.harvard.edu;
- **Massachusetts Executive Office of Public Safety**, 617-727-7775, www.state.ma.us/eops/
- **MBTA Police** (emergency) 617-222-1212; (business) 617-222-1000, www.mbtapolice.com
- **MIT** Police, 617-253-1212, http://web.mit.edu/cp/www/
- **State Police**, 617-523-1212, www.state.ma.us/msp/
- **US Coast Guard**, 617-565-9200, www.uscg.mil/USCG.shtm
- **US Marshall**, 617-748-2500, www.usdoj.gov/marshals/

POST OFFICES (MAIN)

- **US Postal Service**, 800-275-8777, www.usps.com
- **Boston: Fort Point Station**, 25 Dorchester Avenue near South Station, 617-654-5302
- **Arlington Post Office**, 781-648-5376
- **Belmont Post Office**, 617-484-4201
- **Brookline Post Office**, 617-738-1649
- **Cambridge Post Office**, 617-876-0550
- **Dedham Post Office**, 781-326-4768
- **Malden Post Office**, 781-322-4685
- **Medford Post Office**, 781-396-2444
- **Milton Post Office**, 617-698-8139
- **Needham Post Office**, 781-449-0707
- **Newton (Centre) Post Office**, 617-558-1399
- **Quincy Post Office**, 617-773-6641
- **Somerville Post Office**, 617-666-2332
- **Watertown Post Office**, 617-924-1215
- **Waltham Post Office**, 781-893-9752

For branch post offices, check the resources following the **Neighborhood Profiles** or go to the USPS locator at www.usps.com.

ROAD CONDITIONS/TRAFFIC INFORMATION

- **MBTA**, 617-222-3200 or 800-392-6100, www.mbta.com
- **SmarTraveler**, 617-374-1234, www.smartraveler.com
- **State Police Road Conditions**, 800-828-9104

SANITATION AND GARBAGE

- **Arlington DPW**, 781-316-3108, www.town.arlington.ma.us/townhall.htm
- **Belmont Highway Department**, 617-489-7171, http://town.belmont.ma.us/highway/trash.htm
- **Boston DPW**, 617-635-4900, www.cityofboston.gov/publicworks/Sanitation.asp; recycling, 617-635-4959
- **Bottle Law**, 617-556-1054
- **Brookline DPW**, Sanitation Division, 617-730-2156, www.townofbrooklinemass.com/Dpw/
- **Cambridge DPW**, 617-349-4800, www.cambridge.ma.gov

- **Dedham DPW**, Solid Waste Services, 781-326-5770, www.town.dedham.ma.us/recycle/
- **Hazardous Waste Management Hotline**, 617-292-5898
- **Malden DPW**, 781-397-7160, www.ci.malden.ma.us/government/
- **Massachusetts Bureau of Waste Prevention**, Department of Environmental Protection, 617-292-5500, www.state.ma.us/dep/bwp/
- **Medford DPW**, www.medford.org/fGoverment.htm, Highway Division—781-393-2417, Recycling—781-393-2419
- **Milton DPW**, 617-696-5732, www.townofmilton.org
- **Needham DPW**, RTS, 781-455-7568, www.town.needham.ma.us/DPW/RTSHours.htm
- **Newton DPW**, 617-796-2000, www.ci.newton.ma.us/DPW; Recycling, 781-796-1000
- **Quincy DPW**, 617-770-BINS
- **Somerville DPW**, 617-625-6600, ext. 5100, www.ci.somerville.ma.us
- **Used Motor Oil Return Law**, 617-556-1049
- **Waltham DPW**, Street and Forestry Division, 781-314-3855 or 781-314-3850, www.city.waltham.ma.us/pubworks/street.html
- **Watertown DPW**, 617-972-6420 or Watertown Recycling, 617-972-6413

SCHOOLS

- **Boston Public Schools**, 617-635-9000, www.bostonpublicschools.org
- **BPS Superintendent's Office**, 617-635-9050, www.bostonpublicschools.org
- **Massachusetts Department of Education**, 781-338-3000, TTY 781-439-0183, www.doe.mass.edu
- **Massachusetts ED Parent Information Center**, 800-297-0002
- **MCAS Parent Information Hotline**, 866-MCAS220

For additional information, check the resources following the **Neighborhood Profiles** as well as the **Childcare and Education** chapter.

SENIORS

- **AARP**, 800-424-3410, www.aarp.org
- **Alzheimer's Information Hotline**, 800-351-2299
- **American Bar Association Commission on Law and Aging**, 202-662-2000, www.abanet.org/aging/
- **Elder Abuse Hotline**, 800-922-2275

- **Elderly Commission** (Boston), 617-635-4362, www.cityofboston.gov/elderly/
- **Information and Referral Line**: 800-882-2003, TTY 800-872-0166
- **Massachusetts Attorney General's Elder Hotline**, 888-AG-ELDER, www.ago.state.ma.us
- **Massachusetts Executive Office on Elder Affairs**, 617-727-7750 or 800-AGE-INFO, www.ageinfo.com
- **National Academy of Elder Law Attorneys**, 520-881-4005, www.naela.org
- **National Council on the Aging**, 202-479-1200, TTY 202-479-6674, www.ncoa.org
- **National Senior Citizens Law Center**, 202-289-6976; www.nsclc.org
- **Social Security and Medicare Eligibility Information**, 800-772-1213, www.ssa.gov
- **Senior Law**, www.seniorlaw.com

SHIPPING SERVICES

- **Boston Craters & Freighters**, 800-866-278-3787, www.cratersandfreighters.com; for especially heavy or bulky items: 254 Bodwell Street, Unit B, Avon
- **DHL Airborne Express**, 800-AIRBORNE (800-247-2676), www.airborne.com
- **DHL Worldwide Express**, 800-CALL-DHL (800-225-5345), www.dhl-usa.com
- **FedEx**, 800-GO-FEDEX (800-463-3339), www.fedex.com/us/
- **UPS**, 800-PICK-UPS (800-742-5877), www.ups.com, www.theupsstore.com
- **US Postal Service** Express Mail, 800-ASK-USPS (800-275-8777), www.usps.com

SPORTS

- **Boston Bruins**, 617-624-BEAR, www.bostonbruins.com
- **Boston Celtics**, 617-523-3030, www.nba.com/celtics
- **Boston College Eagles**, 617-552-GOBC, http://bceagles.ocsn.com/.
- **Boston Red Sox**, 877-REDSOX9, www.redsox.com
- **Boston University Terriers**, 617-353-GOBU, www.bu.edu/athletics
- **Harvard University Crimson**, 877-GOHARVARD, www.athletics.harvard.edu

- **MIT Engineers**, 617-253-1000, http://web.mit.edu/athletics/www/
- **New England Patriots**, 800-543-1776, www.patriots.com
- **Northeastern University Huskies**, 617-373-GONU, www.gonu.com
- **Tufts University Jumbos**, 617-628-5000, http://ase.tufts.edu/athletics/.
- **UMass/Boston Beacons**, 617-287-7800, www.athletics.umb.edu

STREET MAINTENANCE

- **Boston DPW**, 617-635-4900, www.cityofboston.gov/publicworks/
- **Boston Highway Reconstruction**, 617-635-4950, www.cityofboston.gov/publicworks/hwy4.asp
- **Boston Highway Maintenance**, 617-635-7560, www.cityofboston.gov/publicworks/hwy4.asp
- **Central Artery/Third Harbor Tunnel Project** (Big Dig), 617-951-6400, www.bigdig.com
- **Governor's Highway Safety Bureau**, 617-973-8900, www.massghsb.com
- **Massachusetts Highway Department**, 617-973-7800, www.state.ma.us/mhd/
- **Massachusetts Turnpike Authority**, 617-248-2800 or 877-MASSPIKE (toll fastline), TTY 800-831-1206, www.massturnpike.com
- **National Highway Traffic Safety Commission**, www.nhtsa.dot.gov

TAXES

FEDERAL
- **Internal Revenue Service Teletax Information Line**, 800-829-4477, www.irs.gov

STATE
- **Massachusetts Department of Revenue**, 617-887-MDOR or 800-392-6089, TTY 617-887-6140, www.dor.state.ma.us
- **Telefile**, 617-660-2001
- **Property Tax Bureau**, 617-626-2400, www.dls.state.ma.us/ptb.htm

BOSTON
- **Assessing**, 617-635-4264, www.cityofboston.gov/assessing/
- **Excise Tax Information**, www.cityofboston.gov/excise/
- **Taxpayer Referral and Assistance Center**, 617-635-4287, www.cityofboston.gov/trac/

TAXIS

- **Bay State Taxi and Red Cab**, 617-730-8424
- **Boston Cab**, 617-536-5010
- **City Cab of Boston**, 617-536-5100
- **Independent Taxi Operators Association**, 617-282-4000
- **Metro Cab**, 617-242-8000

TELEPHONE

- **AT&T**, 800-222-0300, www.att.com
- **GTC Telecom**, 800-486-4030, www.gtctelecom.com
- **IDT**, 800-CALL-IDT, www.idt.com
- **MCI**, 800-444-3333, www.mci.com
- **Qwest Communications**, 800-899-7780, www.qwest.com
- **SmartPrice**, 877-550-5317, www.smartprice.com
- **Sprint**, 800-877-7746, www.sprint.com
- **Telecommunications Research and Action Center**, (**TRAC**), 202-263-2950, www.trac.org
- **Verizon**, 800-870-9999, www.verizon.com
- **Working Assets**, 877-255-9253, www.workingforchange.com

For **directory assistance**, dial 411.

TIME

- **Time**, 617-637-1234

TOURISM AND TRAVEL

- **Greater Boston Convention and Visitors' Bureau**, 888-SEE-BOSTON or 617-536-4100, www.bostonusa.com
- **National Park Service**, www.nps.gov
- **Massachusetts Office of Travel and Tourism**, 617-973-8500 or 800-227-MASS, www.massvacation.com
- **Secretary of State's, Citizens Information Service**, 617-727-7030, www.state.ma.us/sec/cis
- **International Association for Medical Assistance to Travelers**, 716-754-4883

USEFUL PHONE NUMBERS AND WEB SITES

TRANSPORTATION

AIRPORTS
- **Logan Airport**, 617-567-5400 or 800-23-LOGAN, www.massport.com
- **Hanscom Field**, 781-869-8000, www.massport.com
- **Worcester Regional Airport**, 888-FLY-WORC, www.massport.com/worce/
- **Manchester Airport** (NH), 603-624-6539, www.flymanchester.com
- **T.F. Green Airport** (Providence), 888-268-7222 or 401-737-8222, www.tfgreen.com

BUS SERVICE
Regional bus lines can be found in the Yellow Pages under "Buses."
- **Greyhound**, 800-231-2222 or 617-526-1800, www.greyhound.com
- **Peter Pan Bus Lines**, 800-343-9999 or 413-781-3320, www.peterpanbus.com

FERRIES
- **MBTA** (route and schedule info), 617-722-3200, www.mbta.com
- **Bay State Cruise Company**, 617-748-1428, http://boston-ptown.com/
- **Boston Harbor Cruises**, 617-227-4321, www.bostonharborcruises.com
- **Capt. John Boats**, 508-747-2400 or 800242-2469, www.provincetownferry.com
- **City Water Taxi**, 617-422-0392, www.citywatertaxi.com
- **Harbor Express**, 617-222-6999, www.harborexpress.com
- **Hy-Line Cruises**, 508-778-2600 or 800-492-8082, www.hylinecruises.com
- **Island Queen**, 508-548-4800, www.islandqueen.com
- **Massport Airport Water Shuttle**, 617-428-2800, www.massport.com
- **Steamship Authority**, 508-477-8600

SUBWAY
- **MBTA** (route and schedule info), 617-222-3200, www.mbta.com

TRAINS
- **Amtrak**, 800-872-7245, www.amtrak.com
- **Cape Cod Central Railroad**, 888-797-RAIL or 508-771-3800, www.capetrain.com
- **Commuter Rail** (route and schedule information), 617-222-3200, www.mbta.com

UTILITY EMERGENCIES

- **Attorney General's Utilities Hotline**, 888-514-6277, www.ago.state.ma.us
- **Boston Water and Sewer Commission**, 617-989-7000, www.bwsc.org
- **Keyspan Energy Delivery**, 800-732-3400, www.keyspan.com
- **Massachusetts Department of Telecommunications and Energy, Consumer Division**, 800-392-6066 or 617-305-3531, TTY 800-323-3298, www.state.ma.us/dpu/consumer/index.htm
- **Massachusetts Water Resources Authority**, 617-242-6000, www.mwra.com
- **No Heat Complaints** (Boston), 617-635-5332
- **NSTAR**, 800-592-2000, www.nstaronline.com
- **NSTAR Gas**, 800-592-2000, www.nstaronline.com
- **Verizon**, 617-555-1611, www.verizon.com

WEATHER

- **Local Weather Service**, 617-936-1234
- **National Weather Service**, 508-828-2672, www.nws.noaa.gov
- **Boston Emergency Storm Center**, 617-635-3050, www.cityofboston.gov/storm/
- **The Weather Channel**, www.weather.com

ZIP CODE INFORMATION

- **USPS Zip Codes Request**, 800-275-8877, www.usps.com

INDEX

AAA Southern New England 241, 447
AIDS 394, 435-436, 454
AME 378
Abandoned Vehicle Removal 447
Aberdeen 27, 29, 94
Abiel Smith School 8, 311
Access Pass 245
Accessible Accommodations 424
Acton 142, 233, 264, 333
Adams Shore 133-136
Adams Village 42, 44
Adams, John Quincy 133, 310
Adams, John 133, 310, 443
Addictions 450
Address Locator 15, 17, 19
Affordable Housing 51-52, 108, 147, 155, 175, 178
African Meeting House 8, 38, 309
Agassiz 60, 85, 87, 92, 94
Agawams 4
Airlines 415-416, 427
Airport Bus Service 417
Airports 50, 414, 463
Alcohol & Drug Dependency 394
Alcott, Louisa May 8, 35, 442
Alewife Brook Reservation 82, 95, 111
Allergy Sufferers 372
Allston Village 27, 29-30
Allston-Brighton 17-18, 27-28, 30, 33, 53-54, 118, 150, 153, 157-158, 167, 211, 213, 262, 346, 359, 409
Alternative and Art Film Houses 305
Alternative, Rock, Punk, Hip-hop 297
American Methodist Episcopal 378
American Repertory Theatre 304
American Society of Home Inspectors 177
Amtrak 413, 463
Andover Newton Theological Seminary 103, 106
Andover 103, 106, 139, 229, 264, 266, 273, 344, 365, 369, 388
Anglican/Episcopal 378
Animal Control 231-232, 447
Animal Hospital 232-233, 447
Animal Rescue League 231-232, 447
Animal Shelter 231-232, 395, 447
Animals 395, 447

Anne Sexton 58, 147, 361
Antique Shops and Districts 269, 279
Apartment Hunting 150
Apartment Rental Costs 1, 149
Appalachian Trail 365, 427, 431
Appliances 162, 178, 196, 273, 275-276
Area 4 85, 89
Area Causes 394
Area Codes 202
Area Codes Map 488
Arlington Center 78-79, 82, 352
Arlington Heights 78-79, 82
Arlington Reservoir 79, 82
Arlington 78-82
Arnold Arboretum 57-58, 60, 64-66, 233, 315, 332, 345, 348, 358, 435
Arsenal Mall 79, 116, 118, 271, 274-276
Arsenal 116-118
Art and Culture Museums 306-307
Arts and Architecture 441
Arts Boston 290, 308, 395
Ashcroft 125-126
Ashmont 42-43, 45, 129, 360, 362, 409
Aspinwall Hill 118-119
Assemblies of God 379
Association of Independent Schools in New England 266
Athens of America 1, 289
Atlantic Neighborhood, Quincy 133
Atrium 271
Attleborough 137
Attorney General 164-165, 183, 186-187, 200, 207, 235, 242, 246, 258, 449, 451-452, 460, 464
Au Pairs 257
Auburndale 101, 104-108, 113
Audubon Circle 51-54
Augusta 430
Auto Safety Hotline 448
Auto Safety 448
Auto Theft 234, 236, 449
Automobile Insurance and Accidents 218
Automobile Registration 216
Automobile Repair 241
Automobile Safety 219
Automobiles 195-196, 214, 220, 223-224, 241, 243, 447

BC 12, 17, 27, 29, 31, 103, 106-107, 212, 267, 307, 318, 326-327, 433
BC Eagles 327
BJ's Wholesale Club 282
BOSTIX 34, 290, 453
BSO Tickets 293
BU 11, 13, 17-18, 27-30, 34, 51-54, 56-57, 74-75, 89, 229, 291, 303, 305, 314, 318, 326-327, 334, 433, 436, 460
BU Terriers 327
BU Theatre 52, 56
Baby-sitting 257
Back Bay Fens 52, 55, 233, 356
Back Bay Landfill 103
Back Bay 0-1, 8, 10, 15-18, 28, 31-36, 52, 55, 61-62, 70-71, 73-75, 78, 88, 103, 131, 150-151, 154, 156-158, 167, 318, 330, 347-348, 352, 354, 356-357, 359, 382, 407, 434, 436
Bahá'í 378
Baldwin, Maria 92
Ball Square 108, 110, 336
Ballet 96, 295, 339
Banking 160, 192-193, 243
Banks 191-194
Banned in Boston 10
Baptist 5, 379
Baron Haussmann 31
Baseball 52-53, 63, 323-324, 327, 330, 356-357, 360
Basketball 52, 73, 324, 327, 330, 357
Bay Village 3, 70, 73-75, 442
Beaches 50, 67-68, 77, 133, 137, 139, 141, 148, 287, 329, 334, 342, 350, 355, 357, 359, 361, 363, 365, 367-369, 371, 425-428
Beacon Hill 0-2, 5, 7-9, 13, 15, 18, 21, 33, 35-38, 40, 52, 61-62, 71, 73, 87, 150-151, 154, 156-158, 167, 213, 221, 319, 345, 353, 356, 359, 382-383, 435, 442
Beanpot 324, 326, 433
Beaver Brook Reservation 84, 114-115, 354
Bed & Breakfast Inns 423
Bedford 137, 142, 209, 234, 257, 264, 311-312, 332, 340, 367, 369, 413, 416, 425, 427, 436
Beds, Bedding, and Bath 276
Belle Isle Marsh 50, 361
Belmont Center 82-84, 272, 279
Belmont 83-85, 339, 342, 348, 351, 354, 366, 380, 384, 391, 456, 458
Bentley College 112, 114-115, 318
Berklee College of Music 52, 56, 290, 299, 318

Berklee Performance Center 33, 290, 299, 302
Berkshires 210, 293, 349, 425, 427, 432
Better Business Bureau 183, 186, 219, 241-242, 449
Beverly 139, 228, 249, 264, 296, 321, 336
Bicycling 331, 333, 356
Big Dig 2-3, 13, 18, 63, 135, 403-405, 443, 461
Bike Clubs 333
Bike Committees and Organizations 333
Bike Registry 331
Birth and Death Records 448
Block Island 431
Blue Hills Reservation 126, 128-129, 133, 145, 233, 342-344, 348-349, 362, 366
Blue Hills Ski Area 349
Blue Laws 2, 13, 287
Board of Health 164
Board of Registration of Real Estate 171
Boat Launches 336
Boating Safety 335
Boating, Sailing, Windsurfing 334
Bookstores 15, 85, 90, 122, 269, 313, 315, 403, 441
Boot Removal 223
Boston Animal Control 231-232, 447
Boston Archdiocese 267
Boston Area Codes Map 488
Boston Area Rape Crisis Center 235, 451
Boston Arts Academy 261
Boston Assessor 452
Boston Athenaeum 315
Boston Athletic Association 328
Boston Ballet 295
Boston Bar Association 197-198, 449, 455
Boston Baroque 291, 294
Boston Bicycle Advisory Committee 331
Boston Brahmins 6
Boston Breakers 326
Boston Bruins 323-325, 460
Boston Calendar of Events 433
Boston Camerata 291
Boston Celtics 323-325, 460
Boston Center for the Arts 71, 73-74, 302
Boston Chamber Music Society 291
Boston City Clerk 452
Boston City Council 31, 452
Boston City Hall 164, 222, 452
Boston College 12, 17, 28, 103, 106-107, 163, 307, 317-318, 409, 460
Boston Common 7, 15, 18, 33-34, 36-38,

INDEX

47, 233, 302, 308, 319, 346, 356-357, 420, 439, 444
Boston Community Center 50, 328
Boston Community Development 163
Boston Conservatory of Music 52
Boston Convention & Visitors Bureau 310, 462
Boston Election Department 452
Boston Fair Housing Commission 163, 455
Boston Film Festival 306, 438
Boston Gay Men's Chorus 291, 294
Boston Globe Library 315
Boston Harbor Cruises 364, 413, 463
Boston Harbor Islands 342, 349, 364, 369, 412-413, 431
Boston Historical Society 310, 316
Boston Historical Society Library 316
Boston Housing Authority 455
Boston Latin Academy 261
Boston Logan International Airport 414
Boston Lyric Opera 292
Boston Marathon 328, 347, 434, 442, 445
Boston Massacre 6, 309, 434, 443
Boston Mayor's Office 163, 452-453
Boston Modern Orchestra Project 292
Boston Natural Areas Fund 50
Boston Neighborhoods 21-76
Boston Neighborhoods Map 24
Boston Parent's Paper 254
Boston Parks and Recreation 329, 355, 359, 457
Boston Philharmonic 291-292, 294
Boston Police Commissioner 457
Boston Police 235, 407, 453, 457
Boston Pops 1, 289, 292-293, 334, 436
Boston Psychoanalytic Society and Institute's Hanns Sachs Library 316
Boston Public Garden 356
Boston Public Library 32, 47, 197, 228, 316, 434
Boston Public Schools Health Service 263
Boston Public Schools 261-263
Boston Reading List, A 441-445
Boston Redevelopment Authority 10, 72, 175, 455
Boston Renegades 326
Boston RMV 215
Boston Rock Opera 303
Boston Symphony Orchestra 33, 289-290, 292
Boston Tea Party 4, 6, 67, 69, 310, 439, 444
Boston Transportation Department 187, 222, 447, 457

Boston University 13, 27-28, 30, 34, 53, 58, 72, 317-318, 320, 328, 384, 404, 460
Boston Water and Sewer Commission 206, 464
Boston Year, A 433-439
Boston Zip Codes Map 488
Bowling 59, 97, 242, 336-337
Boxing 337
Boylston, Zabdiel 119
Bradford 72
Brahmins 6, 36
Braintree 133-134, 145, 194, 265, 272-279, 329, 344, 361-362, 406, 409, 417, 422
Brandeis University 112-113, 115, 308, 318
Bread & Circus 282
Breakers 326, 431
Breakheart Reservation 234, 343, 362
Breed's Hill 7, 39
Bright Horizons Family Solutions 254
Brighton Center 27, 29
Brighton 17, 19, 27-30, 101, 103, 107, 119, 122, 124, 152, 188, 238, 244, 272, 275-276, 280-282, 296-301, 303, 329-330, 339, 341, 344, 350-353, 380, 383, 385, 390, 394, 396, 421-422
Bristol County 137
British Empire 6
Broadcast and Print Media 209
Brockton 147, 234, 266, 406, 417
Brook Farm 75, 234, 344, 349, 359
Brookline Community Partnership for Children 254
Brookline Hills 19, 118-119, 122, 125
Brookline Public Library 316
Brookline Reservoir 19, 124
Brookline Village 19, 118-119, 122-125, 280, 285, 321
Brookline 8-9, 16-17, 19, 21, 26-27, 29, 31, 33-34, 42, 52-57, 59-60, 72, 74, 76, 78, 86, 101, 103, 106-107, 118-119, 122-125, 150, 294, 298, 301, 305, 307, 309-310, 313-314, 316, 321, 330, 332-333, 338-339, 341, 343, 345, 352, 354, 357-358, 365, 421, 438, 448, 456, 458
Brophy Park 48-49
Buddhist 378
Bundled Telecommunications 204, 210
Bunker Hill Community College 40, 42, 318
Bunker Hill Day 7, 39, 435
Bunker Hill Monument 7, 39-40, 42, 309, 360
Bunker Hill 7, 39-40, 42, 303, 309, 318, 360, 435
Burlington Mall 142, 271, 273, 277-279

Burlington 142, 144-145, 210, 229, 264, 271, 273, 276-279, 429
Bus Service 245, 411, 414, 463
Bussey, Benjamin 58
Buyer's Agent 170-171
Buying a Home 166-167, 170, 179
Buying a Used Car 217
Buying Process 172, 176, 195
By Air 414
By Bike 407
By Bus 411
By Car 403
By Commuter Rail 411

Cable Television 210
Cabot, John 4
Call for Action 243
Callahan Tunnel 414
Cambridge Cemetery 93, 95
Cambridge College 95, 318
Cambridge Common 87, 92, 95
Cambridge Highlands 85, 87, 94
Cambridge Public Library 90
Cambridge Water Department 205
Cambridge 85-96, 291, 294-301, 304-305, 307-315, 317-319, 329, 331-333, 337-339, 341, 346-347, 349-354, 359, 361, 367, 436, 438, 448, 455-456, 458
Cambridgeport 85, 87, 89-91, 301, 367
Cambridgeside Galleria 87-88, 96, 215, 271, 273-274, 276, 314
Candlepin Bowling 336
Cape Ann 13, 141, 210, 336, 425
Cape Cod 11, 13-14, 134, 137, 141, 143, 145, 147-148, 154, 191, 202, 210, 231-232, 249, 280, 336, 350, 367-368, 412, 425-427, 431, 435, 445, 463
Car Rental 403, 406
Car Talk 241
Caravan for Commuters 405
Carpooling 405
Castle Square 72
Cellular Phones 202-203
Celtics 323-325, 460
Cemeteries 361
Central Square 18-19, 58, 75, 85, 89-91, 94, 96, 270, 276, 286, 295-296, 298-301, 314, 381
Centre Street 64-65
Chambers of Commerce 448
Charles District 329, 350
Charles Hayden Planetarium 313
Charles Playhouse 303

Charles Regatta 328, 439
Charles River Bike Path 331
Charles River Reservation 359
Charles River Village 130, 132
Charles River 1, 4, 8, 12-13, 17-19, 27, 30-31, 33-39, 51, 55, 77, 85-89, 95, 101-105, 107, 112-113, 115-117, 125-127, 130, 132, 289, 303, 318, 331, 334-335, 340-341, 345, 347-349, 356-357, 359, 362, 409, 436, 439, 444
Charles Street 36-37, 45, 70, 74, 115, 269, 280, 345, 351, 354, 396
Charles Tufts 99
Charlestown Navy Yard 39-40, 42, 206, 309, 312, 421
Charlestown 4-5, 7, 9, 21, 39-42, 62-63, 76, 86-87, 108, 150, 154, 157-158, 206, 329, 341, 346, 350, 359-360, 435, 438
Charter Schools 259, 262, 266
Checking and Savings Accounts 193
Checking it Out 158
Chelsea 26, 41, 48, 77, 202, 228, 244, 254, 266, 304, 329, 351, 360, 393, 411
Chess 338
Chester Square 72
Chestnut Hill Reservoir 17, 29-30, 107, 124
Chestnut Hill 17, 29-30, 101, 103, 106-108, 118-119, 122-125, 307, 314, 318, 348, 390
Child Abuse & Family Violence 450
Child Care Choices of Boston 254
Child Care Resource Center 254
Child Safety 220, 258
Childcare and Education 254-268
Childcare and Family Support Division 254
Children's Museum 320
Children—Moving 188
Chinatown 8, 13, 18, 36, 45-48, 70, 72, 74, 356, 433, 437
Choosing a School 260
Christian Science 52-53, 141, 214, 311, 380
Christmas Tree Lightings 439
Christopher Columbus Park 63-64, 359, 412
Church of Christ 381
Church of God of Prophecy 381
Church of God 381, 387
Church of Jesus Christ of Latter Day Saints 385
Church of the Nazarene 381
Churches 65, 106, 109, 119, 146, 192, 377-384, 386-388
Citizens Housing and Planning Association 175, 246, 455

INDEX

City Hall Plaza 10, 36, 38, 163-164, 166, 208, 225, 232, 333, 437
City Point 67-69, 367
City Square 39-41, 244, 359-360
City/Neighborhood Parks 359
Civil War 9, 49, 104, 147, 271, 309, 356
Claremont 71
Classical Music 291, 319, 436
Cleveland Circle 17, 19, 27, 29, 31, 119, 124-125, 351, 409
Coast Guard 335, 364, 457
Codman Square 42-44
Coffeehouses 290, 298
Cohasset 145-148, 229, 265, 329
College Sports 326
Colleges and Universities 1, 21, 305, 317-318, 327, 387, 389, 419, 424
Combat Zone 13, 46
Comedy 110, 289
Commonwealth Avenue Mall 356
Commonwealth of Massachusetts 2, 176, 179, 192, 196, 198-199, 335
Communication, Disabled 246
Community Boating School 335
Community Boating School 335
Community Care for Kids 254
Community Gardens 58, 281, 283, 332, 357, 360
Community Theater 58, 127, 142, 302
Commuter Ferries 411
Commuter Parking 223
Commuter Rail 411
Commuter Rail Map 487
Competitive Power Suppliers 199
Competitive Swimming 351
Computers and Software 275
Concert Facilities 296
Concord Museum 310
Concord 7, 13, 72, 84, 92, 95, 142-143, 225, 228, 264, 273, 277, 279, 291, 309-312, 332-333, 337, 349, 362, 365, 367, 369, 379, 384, 391, 404, 417, 426, 428, 444
Condominiums 58, 123, 168
Congregational Library and Archives 316
Congregational/United Church of Christ 382
Connecticut 227, 280, 323, 367, 413-414, 431-432, 445
Conservative—Jewish 389-390
Constitution Beach 50, 367
Consumer Affairs and Business Regulation 165, 187, 198, 219, 221, 240, 455
Consumer Complaints 186, 193, 239, 242, 417, 449

Consumer Complaints—Airlines 417
Consumer Complaints—Banking 193
Consumer Complaints—Movers 186-187
Consumer Product Safety Commission 242, 449
Consumer Protection 164, 183, 207, 220, 241, 417
Consumer Protection—Automobiles 220
Consumer Protection—Rip-off Recourse 241
Consumer Protection—Utility and Oil Complaints 207
Contemporary Music 296
Contingencies 176
Coolidge Corner 19, 118-119, 122-125, 270, 285, 305, 314, 386, 390-391, 407
Coolidge Square 116
Cooperatives 168, 201
Copley Place 34, 56, 60, 74, 270-273, 279, 305, 421
Copley Plaza 32, 420
Copp's Hill Burying Ground 7, 61, 309
Copp's Hill 7, 61, 64, 309
Cosmopolitan 71
Costco 282
Country/Bluegrass Music 300
Countryside of New England 425
Craddock, Matthew 99
Credit Bureaus 173, 195, 240
Credit Cards 172, 194, 227, 417
Credit Reports 195
Credit Unions 192, 194
Crewing 336
Cricket 330
Crime Prevention 395
Crime Watch Commission 235, 450
Crime 21, 26, 55, 76, 94, 114, 152, 167, 234-236, 395, 449-450
Crisis Hotlines 450
Cultural Centers 308
Cultural Life 289-321
Culture for Kids 320
Cummings, e.e. 58, 361
Curley, James 9
Curling 338
Curry College 129-130
Cushing Square 83
Cutler Park 127, 343, 359

DCR 329, 355-369
DEP 206-207, 374-375, 459
DJs/Spinning, Lounges, Piano Bars 301

Dance Clubs 301
Dance Troupes 295
Daniel Webster 35, 366
Davis Museum and Cultural Center 307
Davis Square 19, 92-93, 108-112, 297, 299-300, 306, 353, 385, 398, 409
Dawes, William 6, 382
Daycare 253-256
Deciding Whether, What, and Where to Buy 167
DeCordova Museum and Sculpture Park 307
Dedham Mall 77, 126-127, 274
Dedham 3, 13, 26, 74, 77, 105, 107, 125-128, 130-131, 329-330, 344, 359-360, 363, 392, 404, 421, 455-456, 458-459
Department of Conservation and Recreation 329
Department of Education 259-260, 262, 267, 459
Department of Energy Resources 200
Department of Housing and Urban Development 175
Department of Neighborhood Development 455
Department of Public Works 205-206
Department of Telecommunications and Energy 186-187, 199, 207, 210, 464
Department Stores 47, 269-270, 272, 274
Diaper Services 237
Dickinson, Emily 8, 441
Directory Assistance 204, 462
Disability Plates 246
Disabled Assistance 245, 395
Discount Department Stores 274
Discrimination 164, 193, 242, 451-452, 455
Division of Law Enforcement 335
Division of Professional Licensure 177, 230, 233, 449
Dog Licenses 232, 447
Dog Racing 326
Dog-friendly Parks 233
Domestic Services 237
Dorchester 9, 13, 18, 42-45, 47, 62, 67, 69, 128-129, 133, 214, 329-330, 332, 337, 343, 346, 354, 359-361, 364, 368, 437, 458
Douglass, Frederick 8
Dover 146
Down Payment 174
Downtown Boston 45-47
Downtown Crossing 18, 38, 45-48, 62, 269, 273-275, 313-314, 353, 382, 407, 409-410

Downtown Waterfront 61-63
DPW 206, 208-209, 224, 443, 458-459, 461
Dreams of Freedom 310
Driver's Licenses and State IDs 214
Driving Under the Influence 219
Dry Cleaning 237-238
Dudley 42-43, 55, 75, 331, 399

Eagle Hill 48-49
East Arlington 31, 78-79
East Boston 13, 15, 17-18, 39, 48-51, 61, 67-68, 77, 85, 191, 326, 329, 337, 342, 346, 361, 367, 437, 448
East Cambridge 18, 78, 83, 85, 87-88, 95, 116, 286, 438
East Dedham 125-127
East Fenway 27, 51-52
East Indian Tea Company 6
East Milton 128-129
Ecological Innovations Oil Buying Network 201
Eddy, Mary Baker 141, 311, 313, 316, 361, 380
Edward Everett Square 42-43
Eight Streets 72
Elder Hotline 242, 451, 460
Elderly 97, 163-164, 242-243, 375, 460
Elected Officials 452-453
Electricity 199-200
Electronic Income Tax Filing 197
Electronics 275
Eliot Square 57, 59
Ellis 71
Elm Bank Reservation 362
Emerald Necklace Conservancy 60, 355, 357
Emerald Necklace 8, 43, 60, 309, 329, 332, 348, 355-359, 405, 409
Emergency 453
Emerson College 48, 317, 319, 481
Emerson, Ralph Waldo 8, 261, 426
Emissions 218
Emmanuel College 53, 56, 317, 319
Endicott 125-127, 139, 411
Entertainment 453
Environment 396
Environmental Inspection 177
Esplanade 33-34, 36, 38, 289, 293, 303, 334-335, 346, 359, 435-436, 438
Essex County 139
Essex Shipbuilding Museum 308
Ethical Societies 388
Ethnic Foods 284

INDEX

Eviction 163-165
Excise Tax 196, 461
Extended Stay Hotels 422

FMCSA 183-184, 186
FTC 207, 242, 449
Fair Housing Information 455
Fairbanks House 126-127
Family Resource Center 261-262
Faneuil Hall 7, 62, 64, 269-270, 277, 287, 290, 296-298, 300-301, 309-310, 347, 407, 435
Farmers' Markets 281, 283
Farrakhan, Louis 11
Fast Lane 405
Federal Income Tax 196
Federal Motor Carrier Safety Administration 183
Federal Offices 454
Federal Reserve Bank of Boston's Research Library 316
Federal Trade Commission 207, 242, 449
Fencing 327, 340
Fenway Libraries Online 317
Fenway Park 53-54, 56, 323
Fenway/Mission Hill 51-56
Ferries 51, 335, 364, 369, 408, 411-413, 427, 463
Fiction 442
Fields Corner 42-45, 360
Filene's 47, 269, 271-274
Film Festivals 306
Film 305
Financial District 15, 45-47, 63, 404, 422
Financial Institutions 191
Finding a Health Care Provider 229
Finding a Physician 199
Finding a Place to Buy 169
Finding a Place to Live 149-179
First Night 439
Fisher Hill 118
Fishing 129, 135, 139, 335, 340-341, 360, 362-364, 427, 445
Fixed-term 152, 160, 165, 181
Flat of the Hill 35-36
Fleet Boston Pavilion 296
Fleet Center 62, 64, 296, 323-325, 412, 433
Flight Delays 417
Flood Insurance 177-178
Folk/Coffeehouses 298
Fontbonne Academy 129-130, 267
Food 281-287, 444

FoodMaster 41, 62, 281
Football 101, 146, 325-327, 341, 350
For Sale by Owner 172
Fore River 135, 406
Forest Hills Cemetery 58, 60, 64, 332, 361
Forest Hills 57-60, 64, 332, 358, 360-361, 378
Forests 100, 105, 329, 355, 362, 364-365, 427, 432
Fort Point Channel 18, 67-68, 239-240, 300, 307
Four Corners 42-43, 101, 104
Fowl Meadow Reservation 126-127
Foxboro 146, 325
Foxwoods 431
Framingham 13, 143-144, 210, 234, 237-238, 264, 273-274, 276-277, 326, 338, 344, 389, 406, 414, 417
Franklin Park Zoo 43-44, 60, 66, 320, 358
Franklin Park 17, 42-44, 57-58, 60, 66, 320, 332, 358-359, 434, 437
Franklin-Blackstone 72
Frederick Law Olmstead National Historic Site 310, 365
Free Concerts 89, 293-294, 303, 358
Freedom Trail 7, 40, 47, 61, 269, 306, 308-309
Freeport 272, 430
French Library 317
Fresh Pond Mall 79, 95, 271
Fresh Pond 18, 79, 83, 85, 87, 93-95, 205, 233, 271, 347, 404
Friends 382
Frisbee 341
Fugitive Slave Act 8
Fuller, Margaret 89
Fulton Heights 98-99
Fung Wah 414
Furniture 28, 87, 196, 274, 277-278, 308

GLAD 396
GLBT Newspapers 250
GYBSO 291
Garbage and Recycling 208
Garden Centers 279
Garden in Glass 312
Gardner, Isabella Stewart 54, 307
Garrison, William Henry 89
Gas Company 200-201
Gay, Lesbian, Bisexual, and Transgender (GLBT) Life 249
George Washington 7, 16, 39, 68, 86, 89
Germantown 133-135
Getting Around, Disabled 245

Getting Settled 199-236
Gibson House Museum 310
Gillette Stadium 296, 325-326, 411, 439
Gloucester 13, 17, 139-141, 228, 264, 289, 304, 336, 366, 368, 425-426, 436, 438
Goethe Institute Library 316
Golf 342, 349, 359
Good Will Hunting 68
Government Center 62
Governor's Auto Theft Strike Force 449
Granary Burying Ground 38, 48, 308
Great Bridge 86
Greater Boston Area 137-148
Greater Boston Area Map 138
Greater Boston Area Public Schools 263
Greater Boston Convention & Visitors Bureau 310, 433, 462
Greater Boston Interfaith Organization 377
Greater Boston Real Estate Board 171
Green Mountains 349, 429, 432
Green Street Studios 295
Greenspace and Beaches 354-369
Greyhound 414
Groceries 281, 284-285

HUD 175
Hackney Carriage Office 407
Hamilton, Alexander 32
Hammond Pond 19, 103, 107, 123, 343, 390
Hampton Beach 368, 428
Hancock, John 32, 35, 133, 261, 308
Handel & Haydn Society 294
Handicapped/Disabled Services 245
Hanns Sachs Library 316
Hanover 62-64, 273, 276-277, 428-429
Hanscom Field 416
Harbor District 329, 351
Harbor Islands 342, 349, 363-365, 369, 412-413, 431
Harborfest 437
Hardware and Garden Centers 279
Harvard Bridge 88
Harvard Crimson 327
Harvard Square 1, 18, 27, 85, 87-88, 90-93, 95-96, 270, 273, 277, 286, 297-298, 300, 305, 307, 313-315, 318-319, 338, 353, 382-383, 407, 420-421, 439
Harvard University 30, 85, 95, 230, 304, 307-308, 312, 319, 326, 358, 409, 441-443, 457, 460
Harvard University Art Museum 307
Harvard University Botanical Museum 312

Harvard, John 39, 41, 85, 359
Harvest Co-op Markets 282
Hasidic 390
Hatch Memorial Shell 1, 34, 38, 303, 359
Hatch Shell 289, 293, 334-335, 436, 438
Haymarket 62, 64, 283, 287, 309, 359
Head of the Charles Regatta 328, 439
Health & Medical Care 243, 454
Health and Hospitals 397
Health Care Providers 229
Health Clubs and Gyms 353
Health Food Stores 87
Help Me Hank 243, 449
Helpful Services 237-251
Hemlock Gorge 107, 343, 359
Higher Education 317, 430
Hiking 129, 145, 323, 329, 342-343, 347-348, 360-366, 427-429
Hiking, Rock Climbing, and Mountaineering 342
Hindu 377, 388
Hingham 64, 147-148, 229, 234, 266, 272-273, 329, 333, 336, 345, 363-364, 406, 411-413
Historic Sites, Trails, and Cultural Centers 309-310
Historical Restoration 397
History 4
Hockey 324-327, 343-344, 346, 433
Holmes, Oliver Wendell 1, 6, 36
Holocaust Memorial 64, 309
Home Delivery 281
Home Warranties 178
Homeless 397
Homeschooling 266, 268
Horse Racing 134, 326
Horseback Riding 129, 145, 344, 361-364, 429
Horticultural Hall 52, 56, 294
Hostels 419, 423
Hotels 63, 89, 142, 148, 417, 419-422, 424
Hough's Neck 133-135
House Cleaning Services 238
House Hunting 36, 171, 175, 485
House of Seven Gables 310
House/Condo Hunting 166
Household Goods Consumer Complaint 183, 186
Household Shopping 275
Housewares 270, 274-275, 278-279
Housing Styles 99, 148, 166
Housing 455

INDEX

Housing, Disabled 246
Hub of the Universe 1, 4
Hull 64, 148, 229, 266, 329, 335, 364, 406, 411-412
Human Services 398
Humane Society 231
Hunger 399
Hurley Block 72
Hyde Park 18, 59, 128-129, 192, 228, 244, 262, 329-330, 332, 337, 343, 351, 360, 380, 383
Hyde Square 57, 59
Hynes, John B. 10, 37

IMAX 306, 313, 321
Ice Skating 117, 324, 345, 356
Immunizations 263
Inexpensive Hotels 421
In-Line/Roller Skating 345
Inman Square 18, 85, 88, 90, 95, 110, 272, 285-286, 297, 299-300
Inquilinos Boricuas En Accion/Villa Victoria 72
Inspections 176
Institute of Contemporary Art 33-34, 307
Insurance Fraud 242, 449
Insurance, Auto 218-219
Insurance, Homeowner's and Renter's 165-166
Interdenominational/Independent/Nondenominational Churches 383
Internet Service Providers 204
Interstate Movers 183
Intrastate Movers 186
Introduction 1-14
Irish and Celtic Music 300
Isabella Stewart Gardner Museum 307
Islam 11, 377, 389
Island Preserves 355, 363

JFK Crossing 118, 122
JFK Library 44, 316, 320, 364
JFK Park 359
Jacob's Pillow 295, 427, 436
Jamaica Park 60, 358
Jamaica Plain 13, 52, 54, 57-60, 65, 75-76, 118-119, 126, 315, 332, 358, 378-379, 399
Jamaica Pond 57-58, 60, 332, 358
Jamaicaway 16, 51, 59-60, 118, 124, 332, 358, 404
James, Henry 35
Jazz, Blues, R&B, Cabaret 299
Jeffries Point 48-49, 51

Jehovah's Witness 383
Jewish 389-391
John D. O'Bryant School of Mathematics and Science 261
John Hancock Tower 32
Jordan Hall 291-292, 294
Judaism 377, 389
Junior Operator License Law 215
Junk Mail 240, 243

Karaoke 298, 301
Kendall Square 19, 85, 87-88, 95, 273, 298, 305, 314
Kenmore Square 17, 19, 34, 38, 51-53, 55, 57, 233, 296, 314, 323-324
KeySpan 201
Kickball 112, 346
King's Chapel & Burying Ground 7, 38, 48, 309
Kitchen Appliances 162
Kite Festival 434
Kittery 272, 430

Lacrosse 327
Lake Winnipesaukee 11, 428
Lakes District 359
Lakeview 112, 114
Landfill Projects 8, 15, 70, 361
Landlord Problems 164
Landlord/Tenant Rights and Responsibilities 162
Landlords and Tenants 160
Landry Park 359
Latin School 75, 90, 95, 261
Law Enforcement 235, 242, 335, 340
Lawrence Estates 98-99
Lawrence 46, 97-100, 140, 229, 264, 437, 443-444
Lead Law 258
Lead Poisoning 258-259
Leather District 45-46, 68
Lechmere 85-88, 96
Lectures 91, 289, 308, 433
Legal Access 162
Legal Aid 164
Legal Mediation/Referral Programs 243
Legal Protection for Tenants 163
Legal Referral 455
Legal Services 163
Lemon Law 220
Lesbian & Gay Pride Festival 436
Lesley College 92

Lexington 7, 18, 41, 51, 78-79, 82-83, 104, 112, 114-115, 143, 210, 238, 257, 265, 275, 278, 310-311, 332, 360, 365, 426, 434, 444
Liberty Tree Mall 271, 276
Libraries 228-229, 315-317, 441, 456
Library Cards 199, 228-229, 315
Liquor ID Cards 216
Liquor Stores 287
Literacy 399
Literary Life 229, 313, 441, 456
Little Armenia 116
Lobster 11, 141, 286-287, 429, 438
Local Lingo 12
Local Movers 186
Local Phone Service 202
Lodgings 156, 419, 421, 423, 485
Logan International Airport 49-50, 414-415
Long Distance Service Providers 203
Longfellow National Historic Site 311
Longfellow, Henry Wadsworth 6, 8, 86, 361
Longwood Medical Area 53, 55, 57, 75
Longwood 51-57, 60, 75, 118-119, 122-125, 192, 229, 357, 391, 438
Lost in Boston 15
Louisburg Square 35-36
Low Emission Vehicle Program 217
Lowell Lock Monsters 325
Lowell National Historic Park 311
Lowell Spinners 324
Lowell 13, 82, 140, 143, 265, 297, 308, 311, 324-325, 344-345, 365, 388, 414, 435-438
Lower Neponset River Trail 332, 360
Lower South Boston 67
Lower Southie 68
Lutheran 384
Luxury Hotels 420
Lyman Estate 112, 115
Lyman Pond 112, 114-115
Lyme Disease 375-376
Lynn Woods Reservation 140, 363
Lynn 140, 210, 234, 259, 264, 275, 332, 363

MBTA 406, 408-412, 417, 457-458, 463
MBTA Elevator Update Line 245
MBTA T Map 486
MCAS 142, 259-260, 268, 459
MCAS Parent Information Hotline 260
MDC 329, 355
MIT 18, 85, 87-89, 95-96, 155, 212, 273, 292, 305, 308, 312, 314, 317, 319, 327, 334, 338, 421, 436, 444, 457, 460

MIT Engineers 327, 460
MIT List Visual Arts Center 308
MIT Museum 312
MSPCA 231-233, 395, 447
MWRA 205-206, 364, 464
Macy's 32, 47, 269, 271-274
Magoun Square 108, 110
Mail Delivery and Shipping 239
Mail Receiving Services 240
Main Thoroughfares 17-19
Maine Office of Tourism 430
Maine 11, 154, 202, 272, 323-324, 336, 342, 349, 365, 367, 372, 404, 413, 428-432, 445
Major Highways and Byways 404
Make Way for Ducklings 37, 435, 442
Malcolm X 11, 262, 443
Malden 96-99, 125-126, 268, 277, 284, 329, 337, 341, 343-344, 348, 351, 354, 362, 448, 456, 458-459
Mall at Chestnut Hill 108, 271, 277
Malls 32, 79, 106, 137, 140, 143-144, 215, 270-272, 295, 404
Manchester Airport 416
Manchester-by-the-Sea 368, 425
Mansfield 137, 264, 267, 297
Maps 22, 24, 80, 118, 138, 486-488
Mapparium 311, 380
Marblehead 140, 228, 264, 267, 336, 366, 368, 389
Marina Bay 133-136
Marriage Licenses 456
Martha's Vineyard 202, 210, 231, 350, 367, 369, 412-413, 425, 427
Mary Baker Eddy Library 311
Mass Central Rail Trail 333
Mass Energy Consumers Alliance 201
Mass Eye & Ear Infirmary 37
Mass General Hospital 10, 18, 34, 38, 41, 47, 63, 69, 397
Mass MoCA 307
Massachusetts Association of Realtors 171
Massachusetts Attorney General's Office 164, 165, 207, 242
Massachusetts Audubon Society 355, 365, 396
Massachusetts Bar Association 164, 198, 243, 449, 456
Massachusetts Bay Colony 83, 85, 103, 109
Massachusetts Bay Transit Authority 408-413
Massachusetts Board of Higher Education 317
Massachusetts Board of Registration in Medicine 230

INDEX

Massachusetts Child Care Resources and Referral Agency 254
Massachusetts College of Art 292, 319
Massachusetts College of Pharmacy 273
Massachusetts Comprehensive Assessment System 259
Massachusetts Consumer Affairs & Business Regulation 448
Massachusetts Consumers' Coalition 242
Massachusetts Dental Society 230
Massachusetts Department of Education 259-260, 262, 459
Massachusetts Department of Environmental Management 364
Massachusetts Department of Environmental Protection 207, 374-375
Massachusetts Department of Housing and Community Development 175, 247, 451, 455
Massachusetts Department of Mental Health 230
Massachusetts Department of Public Health 230
Massachusetts Department of Revenue 196-198, 461
Massachusetts Department of Telecommunications and Energy 186-187, 199, 207, 464
Massachusetts Division of Insurance 166, 219, 449
Massachusetts Division of State Parks & Recreation 355
Massachusetts Division of Urban Parks & Recreation 355
Massachusetts Electric 200
Massachusetts General Hospital 13, 37
Massachusetts Historical Society Library 316
Massachusetts Historical Society 52, 56, 316
Massachusetts Housing Consumer Education Centers 149
Massachusetts Institute of Technology 87, 319
Massachusetts Library Information Network 229, 316
Massachusetts Lodging Association 419
Massachusetts Neighborhood Crime Watch Commission 235, 450
Massachusetts Office for Victim Assistance 234
Massachusetts Office of Child Care Services 253
Massachusetts Office of Consumer Affairs and Business Regulation 165, 187, 219, 448
Massachusetts Public Interest Research Group 243, 449

Massachusetts Registry of Motor Vehicles 214, 219, 448
Massachusetts State Parks and Recreation 335
Massachusetts State Registry of Vital Records 448
Massachusetts Tenants' Organization 164
Massachusetts Water Resources Authority 205, 364, 464
MassHousing 175
MassParks 329, 343-344, 355, 361, 364
MassPIRG 243, 449
Mattapan 129-130, 228, 244, 262, 299, 329, 360, 362, 366, 381-382, 407, 409
Maverick Square 48-49
Mayflower 5
Maynard 143-144, 265
McMullen Museum of Art 307
Meadow Glen Mall 100, 271
Medford Hillside 98-99
Medford Square 98, 100
Medford 26, 41-42, 78-79, 82, 96-101, 108, 110-111, 320, 336, 343-344, 346, 348, 353, 362, 387, 392-393, 448, 456, 458-459
Media Sponsored Call for Action Programs 243
Meeting House Hill 42-43, 45
Melnea Cass Bikepath 332
Melrose 96-98, 108, 144, 210, 231, 234, 244, 265, 304, 329, 339, 343-344, 362, 409
Melville, Herman 8, 137, 427
Memorial Drive 18, 88-89, 91, 93-95, 117, 282, 351, 359, 404
Men's Services 399
Mennonite 384
Menotomy Rocks Park 79, 82, 343
Merrimack Valley Library Consortium 228
Merrymount 133, 135-136
Methodist 385
Metro Boston Library Network 228
Michael Dukakis 119
Mid-Cambridge 85, 87, 90, 95
Middle-Range Hotels 420
Middlesex County 78-118, 142-145
Middlesex County Map 80
Middlesex Fells Reservation 98, 100-101, 144, 234, 343-344, 349, 362
Millennium Park 332
Milton Academy 129-130, 266
Milton Center 128-129
Milton Hospital 127, 129

Milton Village 128-129, 360
Milton 3, 26, 127-130, 133, 329, 333, 342-344, 349, 360, 362, 366, 456, 458-459
Minor League Baseball 324
Minor League Hockey 325
Minute Man National Historical Park 311, 365
Minuteman Bikeway 79, 82, 332
Minutemen Library Network 228
Mission Hill 3, 51, 54-57, 208, 262, 297, 299
Mohegan Sun 431
Money Matters 191-198
Montclair 133
Montessori Schools 267
Monthly Pass 410
Monument Square 39-42, 359-360
Mormon 385
Mortgages 155, 173, 174, 178
Motels 419
Mother Brook 126
Motor Vehicle Tax 195-196
Motorcycle 216
Mt. Auburn Cemetery 93, 95, 117, 311, 332, 361
Mt. Auburn Street 84, 95, 116-117, 157, 277, 311, 314-315, 339, 361, 383
Mountain Biking 332
Movers 182-183, 185-187
Movie Theaters 126
Moving and Storage 181-190
Moving Book, The 189
Moving, Children 188
Moving, Taxes 189
Museum of Afro-American History 311
Museum of Comparative Zoology 313
Museum of Fine Arts Boston 308
Museum of Fine Arts Libraries 316
Museum of Natural History 312
Museum of Science 313
Museum of the National Center of African-American Artists 308
Museums 306-313
Music—Contemporary 296
Music—Symphonic, Choral, Opera, Chamber 291-294
Mystic District 329, 350
Mystic Lake 82, 98
Mystic River Reservation Bike Path 332
Mystic River Reserve 100
Mystic Side 96

NSTAR Electric 200
NSTAR Gas 201

Nannies 256-257
Nanny Taxes 257
Nantucket Film Festival 436
Nantucket 136, 202, 231, 350, 367, 369, 412-413, 425, 427, 431, 435-436
Narragansetts 4
Natick Mall 271, 273, 279
Natick 14, 144, 210, 242, 265, 271, 273, 276-279, 338, 366, 369, 411, 417
National Council of Churches 377
National Credit Union Administration 192, 194
National Forests 432
National Oceanic Atmospheric Administration 371, 373
National Park Service 308, 355, 365, 431-432, 462
National Parks 365, 431
National/Regional Bus Service 414
Nature Preserves 362
Nausets 4
Navy Yard 39-42, 206, 309, 312, 359, 412, 421
Needham Center 130-132
Needham Heights 130-132
Needham 3, 14, 26, 31, 66, 77, 102, 125, 127, 130-132, 337, 343, 356, 359, 448, 456, 458-459
Neighborhood 10 85, 93
Neighborhood 9 85, 90, 92-93
Neponset District 329, 351
Neponset River Reservation 44, 129-130, 343, 360
Neponset 42, 44, 126, 128, 133, 329, 332, 351, 360
New Bedford Whaling Museum 311
New Bedford 137, 209, 264, 311, 340, 369, 413, 425, 427, 436
New England Aquarium 313, 321
New England Conservatory of Music 52, 56, 291, 293, 319
New England Historic Genealogical Society 317
New England Patriots 323-325, 460
New England Quilt Museum 308
New England Revolution 323, 326
New Hampshire Division of Travel and Tourism Development 429
New Hampshire 13, 171, 195, 204, 209-210, 229, 287, 323, 342, 349, 367-368, 372, 405, 414, 428-429, 431-432
Newburyport 140-141, 229, 234, 264, 336, 345, 366-368, 411, 441

INDEX

Newport 11, 430, 432
Newspaper Classifieds 151, 153, 169, 256
Newspapers and Magazines 212
Newton Centre 101-103, 106-108, 157, 279, 389-391, 401, 458
Newton Corner 101-103, 105-107
Newton Free Library 317
Newton Highlands 101, 103-104, 106-108, 278, 304
Newton Lower Falls 101-102, 104, 106-107
Newton Upper Falls 101-102, 106-107, 275
Newton 17, 19, 26-27, 29, 34, 71-72, 74, 76, 101-108, 112-113, 116, 118-119, 123-124, 130, 132, 294, 304, 306, 317, 333, 336, 343-344, 346, 352-354, 359, 448, 456, 458-459
Newtonville 101-102, 104-108, 132, 158, 239, 256, 282, 411
Next Ticketing 290, 453
Night Owl 410
Nightclubs 91, 297
Nonantum 101-102, 106-107
Nonfiction 443
Norfolk County 118-136, 145-147
Norfolk County Map 120
North Beacon/Market 27-29
North Cambridge 35, 85, 87, 92-93, 95
North End/Waterfront 61-63
North of Boston Library Exchange 228
North of Tremont 71
North Quincy 133-134, 136, 361
North Shore Mall 271, 273-274, 278-279
North Slope 9, 35-37, 309
North Station 35-36, 39, 64, 87, 226-227, 296-297, 301, 324, 410-413, 423
North Waltham 112, 114-115
Northeastern Huskies 327
Northeastern University 52, 56, 58, 319, 444, 461
Norwood 146, 238, 266, 277, 397

O'Neill, Eugene 58, 361
Oak Hill 101, 105-107
Oak Square 27, 29
Oakdale 125-126
Oakley Country Club 116-117
Office of Cable Communications 210
Office of Child Care Services 253
Office of Consumer Affairs and Business Regulation 187
Office of Consumer Affairs and Licensing 163
Off-Leash Areas 233
Oil 46, 152, 177, 199, 201, 207, 459

Oktoberfest 439
Old Bemis Mills 116
Old Colony Library Network 229
Old Dover 72
Old North Church 6-7, 61, 64, 309, 379, 434
Old South Meeting House 7, 47-48, 309, 311, 439
Olmstead Park 17, 57-58, 60, 124, 332, 357-358
Olmstead, Frederick Law 8, 17, 43, 52, 57-58, 60, 68, 119, 124-125, 309-310, 332, 355, 357-359, 365
Online Banking 193
Online Resources 151, 154, 171, 178, 256
Online Resources—Daycare 256
Online Resources—House Hunting 171
Online Resources—Mortgages 178
Online Resources—Renting 154
Online Travel Agents 419
Open Rehearsals 293
Opera 289, 291-292, 294, 303
Operation Ceasefire 43
Orchard House 311
Orient Heights 48-51, 367
Orpheum Theater 146, 296
Orthodox (Coptic, Eastern, Greek, Russian) 386
Orthodox—Jewish 390
Outlet Malls 272
Ozone Forecast 374

PITI 174
Packard's Corner 27-28
Pamets 4
Parents in a Pinch 254, 258
Park & Rides 406
Park Street Church 38, 48, 308, 382
Parking Clerk 222-224, 457
Parking Permits 26, 37, 222, 457
Parking Tickets 222-223
Parking 221, 457
Parking—Beyond Boston Proper 223
Parks and Recreation Departments 329, 346, 457
Parochial Schools 266-267
Participant Sports and Activities 328, 355
Passports 226, 228
Patriots' Day Parade 434
Paul Revere House 312
Pavillion 67
Pawtuckets 4
Payson Hill 83

Peabody Essex Museum 308
Peabody Museum 312
Peabody/Neighborhood 9, 85
Peapod 281
Pennacooks 4
Pentecostal/Charismatic 386
Pest Control 237, 239
Pet Laws and Services 232
Peter Pan Bus 414
Pets 231
Phillips Academy 266
Phone Numbers and Web Sites 447-464
Phone Service 202-203
Photo ID 229
Piers Park 49-51
Pilgrims 4, 148, 285, 426-427
Pilot Block 71
Places of Worship 377-392
Playwrights' Platform 303
Plimouth Plantation 4, 309
Plymouth 4, 27, 147-148, 210, 229, 266, 309, 369, 406, 413, 417, 425-427, 429, 441
Poe, Edgar Allan 8, 68, 73, 441, 442
Poetry Readings 91, 313, 315
Pokanokets 4
Police 457
Political Parties 226
Politics—Electoral 400
Politics—Social 400
Pope John Paul II Park 360
Pops Tickets 293
Porter Exchange Mall 93, 272
Porter Square 18, 85, 92-96, 110, 276-278, 285, 297-298, 314, 352-354, 411
Portland Sea Dogs 324
Portland 164-165, 207, 242, 248, 324, 400, 430, 483, 485
Portsmouth 428
Post Office 41, 47, 59, 63, 66, 74, 76, 90, 95, 131, 228, 240, 458
Powderhouse Circle 108, 110
Pre-approval 172-173, 175
Pre-qualification 172
Presbyterian 5, 386
Presidential 83
Presidents Hill 133
Private Schools 259-260, 266
Private/Parochial/Religious Schools 266
Professional Sports 323
Professional Theater 302-303
Property Tax 169, 196, 461

Prospect Hill Park 109, 113-115
Prospect Hill 108-109, 113-115
Providence 126-127, 137, 139, 157, 209, 274-275, 277, 397, 411, 416, 430, 432, 463
Pru 14, 32-33, 71, 270-271, 320
Prudential Center 10, 32-34, 74, 270, 272-274, 439
Prudential 10, 14, 32-35, 57, 74, 270, 272-274, 439
Public Defender's Office 455-456
Public Pools 350
Public Schools 11, 30, 34, 38, 41, 44, 47, 50, 56, 60, 64, 66, 69, 74, 76, 82, 84, 95, 98, 101, 105, 107, 111, 115, 117, 125, 127, 130, 132, 136, 143, 145, 196, 260-266, 459
Public Transportation 408-413
Purchase and Sale (P&S) Agreement 176
Puritans 4-5, 39, 42, 85, 381-382, 425
Putterham Circle 118, 124

Quabbin Reservoir 205
Quakers 5, 10, 382
Quick Getaways 452-432, 445
Quincy Center 133-136, 280
Quincy Point 133-134
Quincy 14, 26, 44, 48, 95-96, 128-129, 133-136, 304-305, 307, 310, 318, 329, 333, 337, 341-344, 361-362, 364, 456, 458-459
Quincy, John 133, 310

Racquet Sports—Tennis and Squash 346
Radio Stations 210, 243
Rafting 336
Rail Trail 333
Rape 235, 451
Reading List 441
Real Estate Broker 170
Reconstructionist 391
Recycling Hotline 208
Recycling 208-209, 396, 458-459
Red Sox 32, 53, 323-324, 444, 460
Reform—Jewish 391
Reggae, Funk, World Beat, Gospel, Brazilian and Spanish 298
Register a New Vehicle 217
Registry of Motor Vehicles 195-196, 214, 246, 448
Relocation and Moving Information 190
Renegades 326
Rent and Eviction Control 164

INDEX

Rent Control 150, 164
Rent Stabilization 150
Rental Agents 152-154, 156
Rental Housing Resource Center 164, 455
Rental Publications 154
Renter's/Homeowner's Insurance 165-166
Resident Parking Stickers 222, 457
Restaurants 283-287
Revere 77
Revere, Paul 1, 6-7, 39, 61, 64, 116, 308-310, 312, 379, 426, 434, 444
Revolutionary War 6, 13, 39, 54, 86, 89, 93, 109, 116, 142-143, 310, 356, 365, 442
Rhode Island 5, 10, 137, 209-210, 323, 367, 383, 411, 413, 430-432, 445
Rinks 329, 344-346, 359
Riverside 85, 87, 90-91, 93, 99-101, 104, 108, 409
Riverway 16, 51, 55-57, 60, 118, 123-124, 304, 332, 357-358, 404-405
Road Conditions 458
Road Restrictions, Moving 187
Roberto Clemente Field 52, 357
Roche Bros. 76, 132, 282
Rock Climbing 342-343, 362
Rockport 141, 270, 336, 368, 425-426, 436
Roller Skating 345
Roman Catholic 387
Rose Art Museum 308
Roslindale Square/Roslindale Village 64-65
Roslindale 64-66
Rotaries 15-16
Rowing 30, 327, 336, 359, 436, 439
Roxbury Latin School 75
Roxbury 11, 17-18, 43, 54, 56-57, 60, 64-66, 70-77, 86, 101, 105, 118, 124-126, 130, 150, 153, 157, 167, 214, 336, 343, 348, 351, 353, 359-361, 394, 396, 398-400, 409, 437, 456
Rugby 341
Running 347
Runzheimer International 1, 149, 216, 253
Rush Tickets 293
Rutland Square 71
Rutland Street 72

Safe Neighborhood Initiative 235, 450
Safety and Crime 234
Safety and Emissions Inspections 218
Sagamore John 98
St. Botolph's 71
St. Mary/Lower Beacon Street 118
St. Patrick's Day Parade 68-69, 434

Salem Witch Trials 4, 320
Salem 4-5, 62, 64, 97-98, 100, 135, 140-141, 148, 157, 210, 228, 237, 264, 275, 280, 308-310, 320, 336, 363-364, 379, 388, 391-392, 425, 437, 439, 442
Sales and Use Tax 195
Sanitation and Garbage 458
Sanitation Division of the DPW 208
Saugus River Rumney Marsh Reservation 363
Savin Hill 42-45, 368
Savings Accounts 193
School Application 262
School Report 261
School Resources 260
School Wise Press 261
Schools 459
Schrafft's Tower 39-40
Science Museums 312
Science Park 38-39, 85-87, 96, 306, 313, 331, 394
Scituate 147-148, 231, 266, 336, 406
Seafood 140, 281, 284, 286-287, 427
Seaport District 67-68
Seaport Festival 435
Second-hand Shopping 279
Security Deposits 161
Seller's Agent 170
Semitic Museum 308
Senior Pass Program 245
Senior Services 400
Seniors 243, 307-308, 316, 325, 340, 410, 413, 459
Service Animals 245
Services for People with Disabilities 3, 237, 245, 424
Seventh Day Adventists 387
Sharon 146, 229, 266-267, 344, 366, 389
Shaw, Robert Gould 9, 309
Shaw's 281-282
Shawmut Peninsula 5, 7, 15
Shawmut 5, 7, 15, 42-43, 45, 72, 74, 250, 381, 389
Shipping Services 240, 460
Shopping Districts 100, 106, 269
Shopping for the Home 269-287
Shopping Malls 271
Shops at the Prudential Center 270, 272
Short Term/Sublets 155, 422
Shubert Theatre 292, 303
Shuttle Vans 417
Sikh 392
Simmons College 53, 56, 319

Skate Parks 346
Skating Clubs 345-346
Skiing—Cross Country 348
Skiing—Downhill and Snowboarding 349
Slang 12
Small Claims Courts 243-244
SmartPrice 203, 462
Smith, John 4
Snow Emergency 222-223
Snow Removal 221
Snowfall 348, 372
Soccer 323, 326-327, 350, 360
Social Security 226, 454
Softball 327, 330, 358, 362
Somerville Open Studios 110
Somerville Theatre 110-111, 297
Somerville 19, 21, 26, 78, 82, 85, 87-90, 92-93, 98-99, 108-111, 117, 134, 297-301, 304, 306-307, 314, 321, 329, 332-333, 337, 348, 350-351, 353, 448, 456, 458-459
South Boston Waterfront 67-69
South Boston 3, 9, 14-15, 17-18, 21, 26, 39, 48, 50, 67-70, 296, 316, 329-330, 332, 337, 346, 348, 364, 367, 434-435
South End/Bay Village 70-75
South Medford 98-99
South of Tremont 71-72
South Quincy 133-134
South Shore Plaza 145, 272-274, 278-279
South Slope 35-36
South Waltham 115
Southeast Waltham 112-113
Southie 14, 17-18, 62, 67-70, 76, 233, 239, 244, 345, 443
Southwest Corridor 56, 60, 70, 73-74, 283, 332
Specialty Grocers 281-282
Spellman Museum 312
Sporting Goods 28, 275, 330, 340
Sports and Recreation 323-354, 445, 460
Sports Museum of New England 323
Spray Pools 354
Spring Hill 108-110
Spy Pond 79, 82
Squantum Point Park 333, 360
Squantum 133-134, 136, 333, 360, 364
Square One Mall 272, 274
Staking a Claim 159
Star Market 33, 123, 281-282
Starting or Moving a Business 197
State Forests 365

State IDs 214, 216
State Income Tax 197
State Parks 329, 335, 343-344, 348, 355, 364-365, 368-369
State Police 450, 457-458
State Preserves 362
Stolen Automobiles 224
Stone Zoo 321
Stony Brook Reservation 64-66, 76, 126-127, 332, 343, 360-361
Stop & Shop 36, 59, 62, 88, 98, 137, 280-281, 285
Storage 187-188
Storrow Drive 18, 33-38, 51, 54-55, 88, 233, 359
Strawberry Hill 85, 87, 94
Street Address Locator 15-19
Street Maintenance 461
Street Occupancy Permit 187
Street Patterns 1, 12, 15
Sublets 153, 155
Subud 391
Suffolk County 27-77
Suffolk County Map 22
Suffolk Downs 48, 50-51, 77, 326, 361
Suffolk University 38, 48, 319
Suicide 451
Sullivan Square 39-42
Sumner Hill 57, 59
Sumner, William H. 49
Supermarkets 281
Support and Activist Groups 250
Surrounding Communities 78
Swampscott 140-142, 210, 228, 264, 389
Swan Boats 356, 434
Swimming 350-351, 367-369
Symphony Hall 53, 56, 291-294
Synagogues 106, 118, 377

T.F. Green Airport 416
TRAC 179, 203-204, 461-462
Tanglewood 293, 427, 436
Taunton 137, 139, 249, 264
Taxes 189, 195-197, 461
Taxes—Moving 189
Taxis 11, 63-64, 246, 333, 335, 407, 462
Technology Highway 112, 114
Ted Williams Tunnel 405, 414
Teele Square 108, 110
Telecommunications Research and Action Center 203, 462
Telephone Numbers 485

INDEX

Telephone 202, 462
Television Stations 209
Temporary Housing 156
Temporary Lodgings 419-424
Ten Hills 108-109
Tenant Advocacy 164
Tenant Rights and Responsibilities 162
Tenant-at-will 160, 165
Terrorism Tip Line 450
The Fenway 3, 8, 16, 18-19, 26, 51-56, 70, 119, 122-123, 154, 233, 239, 307, 311, 317-320, 324, 380, 404-405, 481
The Riverway 51, 55-56, 118, 123, 304, 332, 357, 404-405
Theater District 36, 46, 70, 73-74, 285, 289, 292, 302-303, 409
Theater 1 302-305, 321
Thompson Square 39-40
Thompsonville 101, 103
Thoreau, Henry David 8, 362
Thrift and Vintage Shops 280
Ticketmaster 290, 293, 295-296, 324-325, 453
Tickets 290-293, 295, 296, 302, 324-327, 447, 457, 462
Time 462
Title Insurance 176-177
Title Law 216
Title Search 175-176
Titles 216
Totten Pond Road 114-115, 421
Tourism and Travel 462
Tow Lot 223, 448
Trader Joe's 33, 282
Traffic Circles 15
Traffic Information 458
Traffic 2-3, 11, 13-17, 31-32, 40, 49-50, 63, 65, 90, 114, 123, 129, 134-135, 146, 167-168, 219-221, 223-224, 328, 404-405, 411, 414-415, 426, 458, 461
Training Field 39-41, 359-360
Transportation Division of the Massachusetts Department of Telecommunications and Energy 186-187
Transportation 403-417, 463
Travel and Tourism 4, 369, 428-429, 462
Triangle Trade Route 5
Trimountaine 5
Trinity Church 32, 379, 430
Truck Rentals 181
Trust for Public Land 50
Trustees of Reservations 355, 363-364, 366
Tsongas Arena 297, 325

Tufts Jumbos 327
Tufts University 19, 98-101, 108, 110-111, 320, 461
Tweeter Center 137, 297

UMASS-Boston 42, 44, 311, 316, 327
US Coast Guard 457
US Department of Transportation 183
US Marshall 457
USS Constitution 7, 40, 42, 63, 116, 309, 312, 360, 412, 437
Union Park 72, 74
Union Square 89, 108-111, 163, 301
Unitarian Universalist Association 388
Unitarian 99, 388
Unity Churches 388
Urban Parks and Recreation 329
Use Tax 195
Used Vehicle Warranty Law 220-221
Useful Phone Numbers and Web Sites 447-464
Utilities 170, 172, 176, 195, 199-202, 206-207, 242, 464
Utility Complaints 203
Utility Emergencies 464

Vale 112
Verizon 203, 204
Vermin 162, 239
Vermont 11, 77, 204, 323, 342, 349, 372, 417, 429-432
Veteran's Day 439
Veterinarians 232
Victory Gardens 52, 56, 283, 357
Villa Victoria 72
Village Falls Park 359
Vital Records 448
Volleyball 327, 352
Volunteer Placement Services 393
Volunteering 393-401
Voter Registration 225

WBZ Call for Action 243, 449
Waban 101, 103-104, 106-108
Wakefield 144, 210, 239, 244, 265, 329
Walden Pond State Reservation 329, 349
Walden Pond 142, 309, 312, 329, 349, 362, 369, 426
Walden Woods 362
Waldorf Schools 267
Walpole Mall 272
Waltham Center 112-113

Waltham Watch Company 112
Waltham 14, 26, 72, 78, 83-84, 105, 107, 112-117, 131, 303, 305, 308, 318, 329, 333, 340-342, 350-351, 354, 359, 381, 456, 458-459
Wampanoags 4
Wang Center for the Performing Arts 295
Warehouse Shopping 281-282
Warren Tavern 39, 310
Washington Square 19, 118, 122-123, 125, 194, 285, 320, 333
Washington Street Corridor 43, 72
Water Quality 206-207, 334
Waterfront Park 235, 359
Waterfront 61-63
Watertown Mall 271
Watertown Square 116-117, 331
Watertown 17, 26, 78-79, 83, 85, 94-95, 107, 112-113, 116-117, 153, 157, 285, 329-331, 333, 337, 339, 345, 350, 352, 359, 361, 383, 434-435, 456, 458-459
Waverly 83-84, 86, 107, 115, 341, 354, 388, 411
Weather and Climate 371-376, 464
Web Sites 447-464
Wellesley College 307, 320
Wellesley 104, 130, 146-147, 210, 212, 228, 238, 265-266, 279, 307, 312, 318-320, 329, 348, 362
Wellington 98-101, 111, 332, 363
Wellington-Harrington 85, 87-88
Wentworth Institute 54, 56, 317, 320
West Cambridge 78, 85, 87, 90-91, 93
West Concord Street 72
West End 8, 10, 35, 37-39, 112-113, 309, 317, 351, 354
West End Branch Library 317
West Fenway 51-53
West Medford 82, 96, 98-101, 353
West Newton 71-72, 74, 101, 103, 105-108, 224, 244, 306, 353, 411
West Nile Virus 375
West Quincy 133-134

West Roxbury 18, 57, 64-66, 70, 75-77, 101, 105, 118, 124-126, 329, 332, 336, 343, 348, 351, 353, 359-360, 396
West Somerville 108, 110-111, 381
Westbrook Village 118, 124
Weston 104, 112-116, 144-146, 228, 238, 244, 265, 312, 319, 329, 349, 406
Weymouth Back River Reservation 363
Weymouth 147-148, 233, 266, 275, 277, 329, 336, 351, 363
Whale Watches 63-64, 426, 438
What to Bring 11
What to Look for in Daycare 255
Wheelock College 53, 56, 317
White Mountains 11, 343, 349, 428, 432
Whole Foods Market 282
Wicca 391
Wildlife Sanctuaries 141, 365
Wilson Mountain Reservation 363
Winter Hill 108, 110-111
Winthrop 77
Winthrop, John 4, 7, 85, 109
Winthrop Square/Training Field 39
Woburn 14, 145, 210, 238, 265, 272-273, 275-277, 343, 406, 417, 435
Wollaston Hill 133-134
Wollaston 129, 133-134, 136
Women's Services 400
Wompatuck State Park 333
Wonderland Greyhound Park 326
Worcester Centrum 297, 325
Worcester Ice Cats 325
Worcester Square 72

YMCAS 354, 423
YWCAS 423
Yoga 352
Youth Services 401

Zip Code Information 464
Zipcar 3, 403, 406
Zoos/Aquariums 320

ABOUT THE AUTHOR

HEATHER GORDON is a lifelong Bostonian, having grown up on the North Shore. Although she fled to the Midwest for college (BA, University of Michigan) and graduate school (MAPH, University of Chicago), she moved back to Boston to study creative writing at Emerson College and to work as an editor. She wishes to thank Nicholas Mistry, Tracie Santiago, Jason Korb of the Fenway CDC, David Refsland, and most of all, Joshua Huntington, for all their help on this book. She lives in the North End and loves it.

READER RESPONSE FORM

We would appreciate your comments regarding this fourth edition of the *Newcomer's Handbook® for Moving to and Living in Boston*. If you've found any mistakes or omissions or if you would just like to express your opinion about the guide, please let us know. We will consider any suggestions for possible inclusion in our next edition, and if we use your comments, we'll send you a *free* copy of our next edition. Please send this response form to:

Reader Response Department
First Books
6750 SW Franklin, Suite A
Portland, OR 97223 USA

Comments:

_____
_____
_____
_____
_____
_____
_____

Name: _____
Address _____
_____
Telephone (   ) _____
E-mail _____

FIRST BOOKS®
6750 SW Franklin, Suite A
Portland, OR 97223
503-968-6777
www.firstbooks.com

NEWCOMER'S HANDBOOK
ORDER FORM

THE ORIGINAL, ALWAYS UPDATED, ABSOLUTELY INVALUABLE GUIDES FOR PEOPLE MOVING TO A CITY!

Find out about neigborhoods, apartment and house hunting, money matters, deposits/leases, getting settled, helpful services, shopping for the home, places of worship, cultural life, sports/recreation, volunteering, green space, schools and education, transportation, temporary lodgings and useful telephone numbers!

	# COPIES	TOTAL
Newcomer's Handbook® for Atlanta	_____ x $17.95	$_____
Newcomer's Handbook® for Boston	_____ x $23.95	$_____
Newcomer's Handbook® for Chicago	_____ x $21.95	$_____
Newcomer's Handbook® for London	_____ x $20.95	$_____
Newcomer's Handbook® for Los Angeles	_____ x $17.95	$_____
Newcomer's Handbook® for Minneapolis-St. Paul	_____ x $20.95	$_____
Newcomer's Handbook® for New York City	_____ x $20.95	$_____
Newcomer's Handbook® for San Francisco	_____ x $20.95	$_____
Newcomer's Handbook® for Seattle	_____ x $21.95	$_____
Newcomer's Handbook® for Washington D.C.	_____ x $21.95	$_____
	SUBTOTAL	$_____
U.S. POSTAGE & HANDLING (*$7.00 first book, $1.00 each add'l.*)		$_____
	TOTAL	$_____

SHIP TO:

Name _____

Title _____

Company _____

Address _____

City _____ State _____ Zip _____

Phone Number (_____) _____

E-mail _____

Send this order form and a check or money order payable to:
First Books

First Books, Mail Order Department
6750 SW Franklin, Suite A, Portland, OR 97223
Allow 1-2 weeks for delivery

T MAP

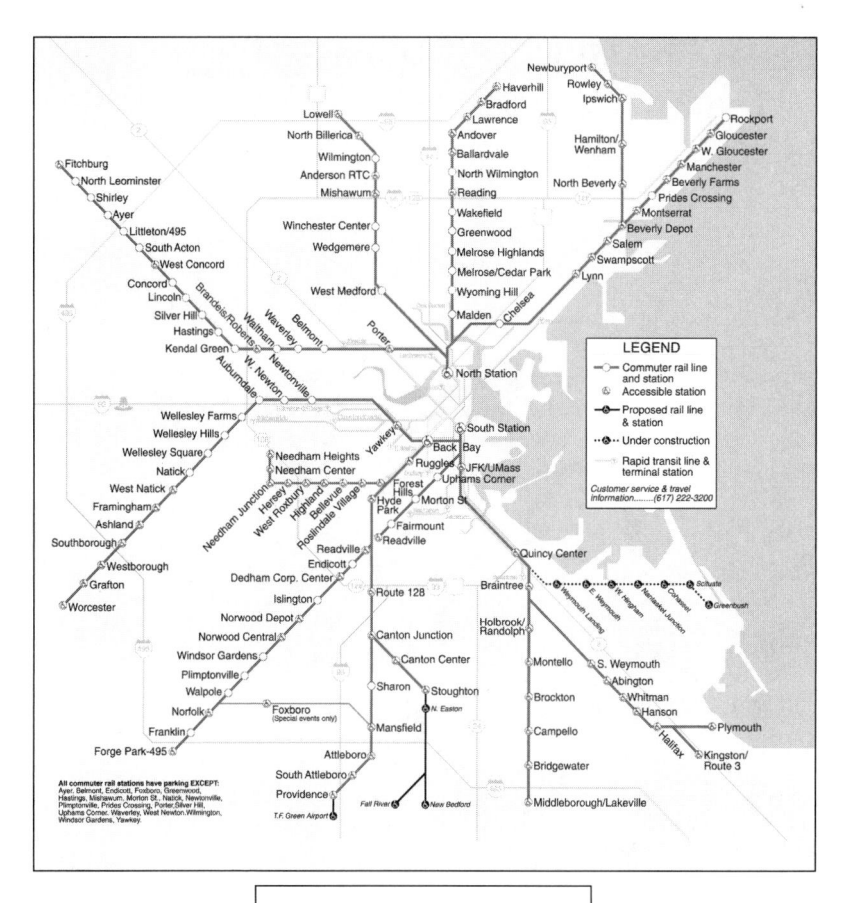

COMMUTER RAIL MAP

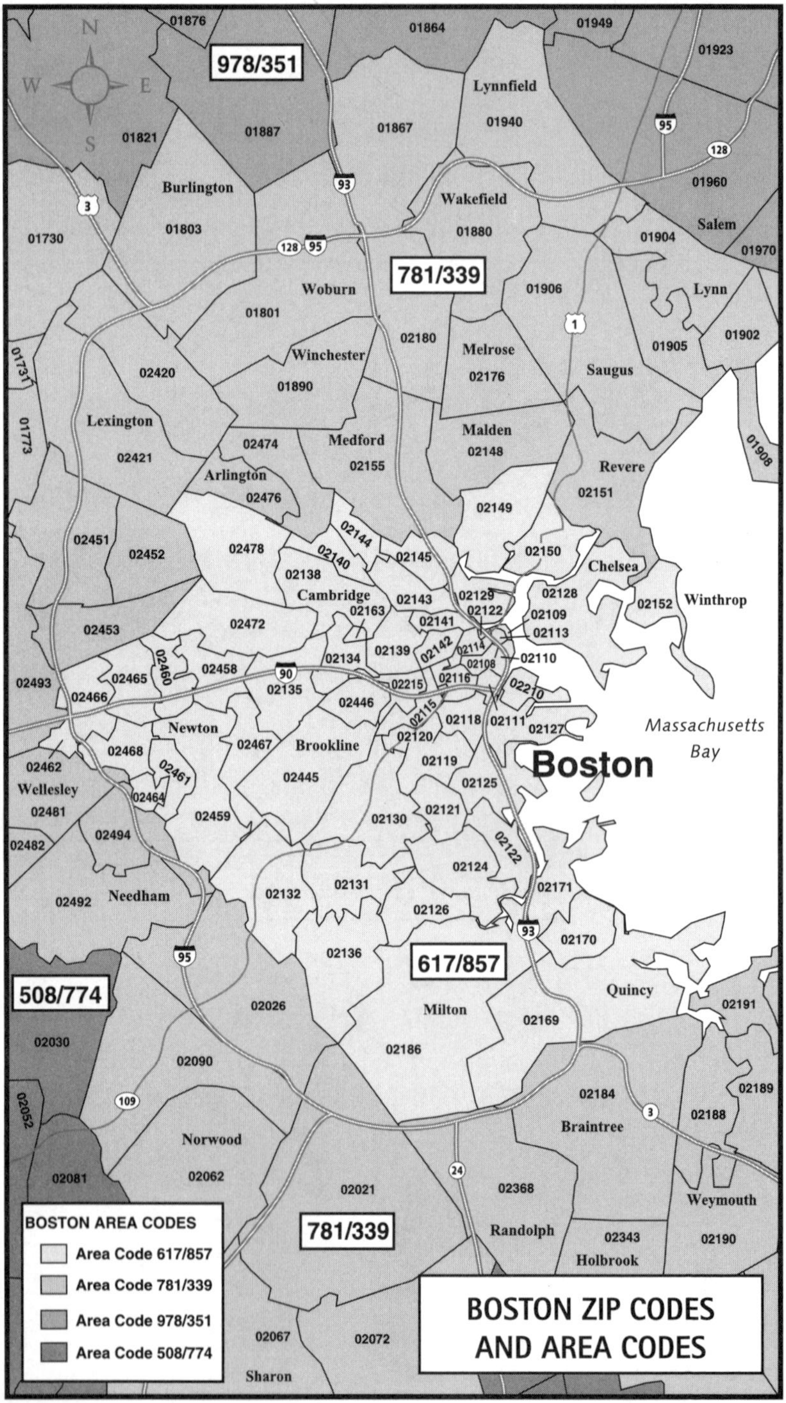
BOSTON ZIP CODES AND AREA CODES
BOSTON AREA CODES
Area Code 617/857
Area Code 781/339
Area Code 978/351
Area Code 508/774
978/351
781/339
617/857
508/774
781/339
N
S
E
W
01876
01864
01949
01923
Lynnfield
01940
01821
01887
01867
95
128
93
3
01960
Salem
01970
Burlington
01803
Wakefield
01880
01730
01904
128
95
01906
Lynn
Woburn
01801
02180
Melrose
02176
1
01905
01902
Saugus
Winchester
01890
01731
02420
Lexington
02421
01773
02474
Medford
02155
Malden
02148
Revere
02151
01908
Arlington
02476
02149
02144
02145
02150
Chelsea
02451
02452
02478
02140
02138
Cambridge
02163
02143
02129
02122
02128
02152
Winthrop
02109
02113
02453
02472
02141
02142
02114
02110
02108
02460
02139
02134
02116
02210
02493
02465
02458
90
02135
02215
02466
02446
02115
02118
02111
02127
Massachusetts
Bay
Newton
02467
Brookline
02120
02468
02119
02462
02461
02445
Boston
02125
Wellesley
02481
02464
02459
02130
02121
02482
02494
02122
02124
02492
Needham
02132
02131
02171
02126
93
02170
95
02136
Quincy
02026
Milton
02191
02030
02169
02186
02090
02184
02189
02052
109
3
02188
Braintree
Norwood
02081
02062
24
02021
02368
Weymouth
Randolph
02343
02190
Holbrook
02067
02072
Sharon